Women, Men, and News

This volume focuses on the news consumption gap between the sexes from the perspective of media consumers—newspaper and magazine readers, television and cable news viewers, and radio news listeners. It helps readers understand the issues, including the complexities, subtleties, and assumptions in today's news media landscape. Experts on the complex issues in the present news media landscape contribute their voices, exploring the news consumption sex divide from diverse perspectives, including young adults, feminists, women of color, and women around the globe.

Women, Men, and News has many insights to offer scholars, researchers, and graduate students in journalism and communication; media literacy; women's and gender studies; and related areas. Professionals in the news industry will also find this volume to be enlightening reading.

Paula Poindexter, a journalism professor at the University of Texas at Austin, has worked on the editorial and business sides of the news media. Formerly a manager and executive at the *Los Angeles Times*, Poindexter also worked as a reporter and producer at the NBC-affiliate TV station in Houston. Her primary research focus is the audience for news.

Sharon Meraz, who has worked in information technology for seven years, joined the faculty of the University of Illinois, Chicago's Department of Communication, in January 2008, where she teaches new media classes. Her research interests include blogging, mobile technologies, social media applications, and citizen political engagement.

Amy Schmitz Weiss, a doctoral candidate in journalism at the University of Texas at Austin who co-founded her college's online newspaper, previously worked at Chicago Tribune Online, Indianapolis Star News Online, and several Chicago Internet firms. Multimedia journalism is her research interest.

LEA'S COMMUNICATION SERIES
Jennings Bryant/Dolf Zillmann, General Editors

Selected titles in Journalism (Maxwell McCombs, Advisory Editor) include:

Conrad
The Business of Sports: A Primer for Journalists

Friedman/Dunwoody/Rogers
Communicating Uncertainty: Media Coverage
of News and Controversial Science

Garrison
Professional Feature Writing, Fourth Edition

Iorio
Taking It to the Streets: Qualitative Research
in Journalism

Li
Internet Newspapers: The Making of a
Mainstream Medium

Merrill/Gade/Blevens
Twilight of Press Freedom: The Rise of
People's Journalism

Merritt/McCombs
The Two W's of Journalism: The Why and
What of Public Affairs Reporting

Roush
Show Me the Money: Writing Business and
Economics Stories for Mass Communication

Salwen/Garrison/Driscoll
Online News and the Public

Titchener
Reviewing the Arts, Third Edition

Women, Men, and News

Divided and Disconnected in the News Media Landscape

Edited by
Paula Poindexter,
Sharon Meraz, and
Amy Schmitz Weiss

Routledge
Taylor & Francis Group

NEW YORK AND LONDON

Contents

Illustrations

Figures

Tables

women of color, and women around the globe. In the three chapters that explore women worldwide, including Europe, the Middle East, Africa, India, Asia, Latin America, and the Caribbean, we find that although the geography, history, culture, and language vary, the gap between women and men in society and in news remains intact.

We conclude *Women, Men, and News* by looking to the future. We unveil a blueprint for the news media landscape of tomorrow that includes recommendations for the Fourth Estate, schools of journalism, and the relevant stakeholders in society at large for closing the news consumption divide between women and men, engaging the next generation in news, and reinforcing the ideal that in a democratic society an informed citizen is vital.

Part I

Women, Men, and News Consumption

Chapter 1

Trouble in the News Media Landscape

Paula Poindexter

When *The Feminine Mystique* was published in 1963, the media landscape was comprised primarily of radio, three television networks and their local affiliates, morning and afternoon newspapers that published women's pages devoted to homemaking and family, and national publications such as *Time*, a newsweekly, *Life*, a weekly picture magazine, and magazines such as *Ladies' Home Journal* and *Good Housekeeping* that catered to women.

The News Media Landscape Transformed

By the early 1970s, when African Americans and women were beginning to reap the benefits of the Civil Rights and Women's Movements, and baby boomers were experiencing their first independent steps as adults, a shift was taking place in the news media landscape. In time, this change would shut down afternoon newspapers and national weekly picture magazines, establish television as the dominant source of news, launch the first 24-hour cable news channel CNN, debut *USA Today*, a feisty national newspaper bursting with color that would be greeted with adoration by consumers and derision by media critics, and introduce a fourth television network FOX. By the last decade of the twentieth century, when executive suites, boardrooms, and mastheads were finally starting to include women, the transformation of the news media landscape would continue with the unveiling of two more 24-hour cable news channels and consumer acceptance of the Internet that would lead to the proliferation of news websites produced by traditional news companies as well as individuals and organizations with no previous news experience.

As the news media landscape was transformed and more news outlets were available than at any other time in history, a new media trend would emerge. Attention to newspapers, network and local news, and news on the cable channels would decline and consumption of news would differ for women and men.

Sex Differences Woven into American Society

Although the disparity in women's and men's news consumption became apparent more than a decade before the twenty-first century dawned, sex differences in legal, political, economic, educational, social, and personal arenas have been a factor in American society from the moment the first colonists disembarked in a new land.[1] During colonial times, women were treated differently in the areas of property rights, educational opportunities, and voting rights. Initially continuing the English common law tradition in the colonies, the legal existence and property rights of women disappeared

But a movement had been launched, which they could either join or ignore, that would leave its imprint on the lives of their daughters and of women throughout the world.

(Flexner and Fitzpatrick, 1996, p. 72)

The Declaration of Sentiments, which was adopted at the convention, included facts to support women's fight for their rights:

Women could not vote, were subject to laws made without their representation, were considered civilly dead once married, and could not own property or earn wages independently of their husbands. They also could not attend college or become teachers of law or medicine [plus] they were excluded from the ministry and from most church participation.

(Mills, 1995, p. 48)

Six decades after the ratification of the Nineteenth Amendment that gave women the right to vote, the news media began reporting that women and men differed in their presidential candidate preferences, presidential approval ratings, political party attachments, and political attitudes. For example, during the 1980 presidential race between Ronald Reagan and Jimmy Carter, women were significantly more likely to vote for Jimmy Carter, the Democratic candidate, and men were significantly more likely to vote for Ronald Reagan, the Republican candidate (Sussman, 1988). The media dubbed this difference in voting and political attitudes a "gender gap."

According to Frank Newport of the Gallup Poll, the gender gap, "wherein men are more positive about Republican presidential candidates and Republican presidents, and women are more positive about Democrats," is a fact of political life (Newport, 2006). An analysis of 124 Gallup polls on President Bush's approval ratings found the president consistently received higher approval ratings among men and in only three polls was the approval among men lower than approval among women (ibid).

The approval differential grows with education. According to an analysis of 40,000 interviews for the *USA Today*/CNN/Gallup Poll conducted from January through November 2003, among high school graduates, the presidential approval difference between women and men was ten percentage points but among college graduates, the difference was 20 percentage points (Page, 2003, p. 1A). For those who had taken postgraduate courses, women and men differed 28 percentage points in their approval of the president (ibid.).

Although in the 2004 presidential election, men were more likely to vote for the Republican candidate, President George W. Bush, and women were more likely to support the Democratic candidate, Senator John Kerry of Massachusetts, the difference between women and men decreased from past elections. Even so, according to *The New York Times*, an analysis of interviews with 13,600 voters after the 2004 presidential election showed: "A gender gap is seen in all age groups, ranging from 4 points among voters under 30 to 11 points among those over 60" (Connelly, 2004, p. 4).

Differences between women and men have also been identified in attitudes toward spending cuts, pornography, gun control, e-mail monitoring by the government, and environmental policies. For example, an analysis of national polls conducted by *The Washington Post* and *ABC News* after the 1980 presidential election found, regardless of political party, women were significantly more likely than men to feel that cuts in social programs hurt people (Sussman, 1988).

A 1986 *Washington Post/ABC News* Poll found that an overwhelming 72 percent of women felt laws on pornography were not strict enough, while only 41 percent of men thought laws on pornography were not strict enough (Sussman, 1988). When asked which was more important, gun control or protecting owners' rights, 73 percent of women said gun control, compared to 59 percent of men (Pew Research, 2000). Differences between women and men were also apparent in a *Los Angeles Times* Poll on civil liberties. When surveyed about government monitoring of e-mail to hunt for terrorists, 54 percent of women approved but only 48 percent of men approved (Richardson, 2001). Women have also been found to be more concerned than men about the administration's environmental policies (Bruni, 2001).

Comparing News Use by Women and Men

The differences in attitudes as well as the political, economic, legal, educational, and social barriers that have constrained women throughout America's history may be connected to women's and men's news consumption displayed in Table 1.1. Differences between the sexes can be found in reading newspapers, watching television news, and reading news on the Internet.

While women are less likely than men to read newspapers, they are more likely than men to watch television news. With the development of a new medium for news, a difference between women and men surfaced in news on the Internet, that is, women are less likely than men to read news online.

The newspaper industry first began to fret about the loss of readership among women almost two decades ago (Stein, 1990). Appearing on a "News for Women" panel at the Associated Press Managing Editors convention, the *Des Moines Register* features editor attributed much of the loss of newspaper readership to the loss of women readers. Citing Newspaper Advertising Bureau statistics, *Register* features editor Bob Shaw said between 1982 and 1987, "there was a drop of 26% in women who were frequent

Table 1.1 A comparison of media use by sex (%)

Media Activity	2006		1998	
	Female	Male	Female	Male
Online news yesterday	19	28	15*	25*
Newspaper yesterday	38	44	46	50
Nightly network TV news regularly	31	25	40	34
Local TV news regularly	55	53	66	61
Cable news regularly	33	35	20	25
Morning news regularly	28	17	27	17
Radio news yesterday	31	42	46	52
National public radio regularly	16	18	15	15
Political talk radio shows regularly	17	23	11	16
Newsmagazines regularly	13	16	13	18
Newsmagazine shows regularly	25	21	42	30

Note. * Numbers reflect getting news online at least once a week. Used with permission from The Pew Research Center for the People and the Press.

Sources: "Online Papers Modestly Boost Newspaper Readership," 2006; "Internet News Takes Off," 1998.

readers of newspapers" (ibid., p. 18). The features editor asserted that when newspapers killed their women's pages 20 years before, they were saying farewell to their women readers. According to Shaw, newspapers abandoned traditional women's pages in response to the Women's Movement, but "they failed to replace them with anything of substance"(ibid., p. 18). Shaw added that editors were wrong in their "assumptions that women were shedding family life for careers." In reality, he said, women were "adding careers to family responsibilities" (ibid., p. 18).

Although the sex differential in news use may be related to political, social, economic, and educational disparities woven into American society or even the demise of traditional women's pages, the differences between women and men and their attention to news may also be a function of intervening forces that range from socialization to a decision-making process about paying attention to news. Societal expectations, uses and gratifications, attitudes, and constraints can also be influential in the sex—news use relationship and have some bearing on whether or not women and men read or watch the news, or ultimately turn away.

The differences between women and men displayed in Table 1.1 suggest a simple dichotomy of paying attention or not paying attention to the news, but the reality of reading, watching, or listening to news is more complex. To fully understand this reality, first the meaning of news must be clarified.

Defining News and News Values

Generations of journalists, sociologists, journalism scholars, and journalism textbook authors have dissected the nature of news, its properties and values. Sociologist Robert Park distinguished news from history and emphasized news is a perishable commodity, remaining news only until "it has reached the persons for who it has 'news interest'" (1940, p. 676).

Mitchell Stephens, the author of *A History of News*, also emphasized the newness of news in his definition of news: "new information about a subject of some public interest that is shared with some portion of the public" (1997, p. 4).

Sociologist Denis McQuail, who stressed the uniqueness of news in media content that includes opinion, analysis, advertising, entertainment, and information, said "news provides the component which elevates or distinguishes something called a newspaper from other kinds of media, earns it the protection of free press theory or the sanctions of authoritarian theory, and by convention allows it to express opinion in the name of the public" (1983, p. 138). News-making, according to McQuail (1983), unlike almost all other types of authorship or cultural creation, cannot be done privately or even individually.

Richard Campbell underscored that an understanding of culture is required to grasp the meaning of news:

> As culture, news is both a product and a process. It is both the morning paper or evening newscast and a set of subtle values and rituals that have been adapted to historical and social circumstances ... As culture, then, news in the twentieth century has become the process of gathering information and making narrative reports—edited by individuals in a news organization—which create selected frames of reference; within those frames, news helps the public make sense of prominent people, important events, and unusual happenings in everyday life.
>
> (Campbell, 1998, p. 388)

Whether hard news or soft news, new information about an event, issue, person, place, thing, or trend is published or broadcast as news because it meets at least one of the traditional criteria for judging news value: audience, impact, proximity, timeliness, prominence, unusualness, and conflict. For broadcast news, visual or audio impact is added to the criteria. Although the twenty-first-century news media landscape has expanded to include new online news venues that are available through the Internet, the First Amendment-protected gathering, editing, and reporting of new information, using established criteria for judging news value, remain unchanged.

Taxonomy of News Users

Because the relationship of women and men to news is both varied and multi-dimensional, we have identified seven types of consumers in the news media landscape: news enthusiasts, news monitors, news betweeners, news eclectics, news accidentals, news intenders, and news avoiders. (See Table 1.2.)

Strongly connected to the news, news enthusiasts represent the segment of the public most passionate about and most devoted to news, whether print, broadcast, or online. News avoiders are the opposite of news enthusiasts; disconnected, they intentionally avoid the news. News monitors, on the other hand, are connected because they regularly track news that is personally relevant to them, while news intenders have good intentions about keeping informed, but some barrier, perhaps lack of time, always prevents them from reading the newspaper or catching the evening news. The good intentions make intenders marginally connected to the news and prevent them from being categorized as news avoiders. While news betweeners seek news one to six days a week, news accidentals generally do not look for news but manage to read or watch the news while doing something else. Perhaps, an intriguing headline on the newsstand catches their attention or while surfing the Internet, they notice a news story and take a few moments to scan it. Finally, news eclectics, on any given day, can be any of the news consumer types—devoted to the news one day, ignoring the news the next.

Each news user type is also linked to at least three dimensions that further elaborate their connection to the news: news medium used, number of days per week paying attention to news, minutes per day reading, watching, or listening to news. For example, news enthusiasts can be loyal to newspapers and local television news but disregard network television news. News accidentals may inadvertently get news while on the

Table 1.2 Taxonomy of news user types

1. **News enthusiasts**—news consumers who are *strongly* connected to the news because they are passionate about keeping abreast of the news.
2. **News monitors**—news consumers who are *connected* to the news in order to keep an eye on news of personal importance.
3. **News betweeners**—news consumers who are connected to the news one to six days weekly.
4. **News eclectics**—news consumers who are *more or less moderately connected* to the news; they lack a pattern to keeping informed and lack allegiance to a specific news medium or type of news.
5. **News accidentals**—news consumers who have a weak connection to the news; their exposure to news, which is non-purposeful, usually happens while not looking for news.
6. **News intenders**—news consumers who plan to read or watch the news but something always prevents them from doing so; they are *marginally connected* to the news.
7. **News avoiders**—because these consumers deliberately shun the news, they are *disconnected*.

> . . . for democracy to succeed and prosper (and not incidentally, continue to tolerate and nurture journalistic freedom), people must be broadly and deeply engaged in it. And to be engaged, people need shared, relevant information. That is, they need agreed-on facts on which to base a conversation aimed at answering the fundamental question of democracy: "What shall we do?" Without a body of shared, relevant facts, that conversation cannot have coherence and accomplish its goal.
>
> (Merritt and McCombs, 2004, p. xiv)

If women have a lesser amount of shared, relevant information because they are less informed about the news, they will not be an equal shareholder in discussing, interpreting, and prioritizing issues that may be relevant to the goals of their community or country. Furthermore, if women know less about what is reported in the news, they will be less capable of making sound recommendations about how best to respond to events and issues in the news.

Impact on Future Generations

Relinquishing power and equal participation that result from not being informed of the news may also affect future generations of women, who, while growing up as girls, were not exposed to powerful images of female role models becoming informed of the relevant issues of the day by reading newspapers or news online. Without exposure to the women in their lives reading newspapers, young girls may grow up to become aliterates, that is, they can read the news but choose not to.

Future generations might also be affected by culture transmission breakdowns. Just as transmission of culture is an activity of the press, transmission of culture is an activity of the family that affects future generations. Although family history, traditions, and folklore are the mainstay of transmitted family culture, some transmitted culture, because it was first reported in the news, is both part of a national news conscience and part of the national culture: the assassination of President Kennedy, the Civil Rights Movement, the Women's Movement, Roe v. Wade, the assassination of Dr. Martin Luther King, Jr., the Vietnam War, Watergate and the resignation of President Richard Nixon, the Gay Rights Movement, the explosion of the Challenger, 9/11, the Iraq War, and Hurricane Katrina. If women are less informed about the news, they will not be a part of the national news conscience, which will hamper their role as authentic transmitter of news as culture to their offspring (Lasswell, 1974; Wright, 1975).

Impact on News Organizations

A difference in news consumption by women and men can also have an impact on the industry that produces the news. As consumers, women and men have been turning away from news for years, causing circulation and ratings declines, and eroding the news media's power. If the news media continue to lose power through dwindling circulation and ratings, can it continue to be regarded as the Fourth Estate or will it simply become the watchdog that is no longer feared because it has more bark than bite?

Declining circulation and ratings also affect the news industry's financial health. If advertisers feel newspapers and broadcast news programs are inadequate for reaching their target markets, they will reject the news media and turn to non-news vehicles, which will cause declines in revenue and profit, ultimately shrinking a news organization's resources for covering the news, eroding its power as a watchdog, and minimizing its role as a major player in a democracy.

Concerned about its loss of readers and circulation for more than three decades, the newspaper industry has developed and implemented a variety of initiatives to cultivate new readers and recapture lost readers. From Newspapers in Education (NIE) that focuses on newspapers in schools to public journalism that relies on community forums to connect to readers, to re-inventing women's pages after abandoning them following the Women's Movement (Harp, 2002) and starting up free weekly tabloids that target young adults, the solutions that have been identified and tried by an industry that has its own gender gap in leadership, bylines, content, perspectives, and news sources have failed to halt circulation declines or the growing divide between women and men among its present readers.

It is hoped that by shining a spotlight on women's continued rejection of newspapers and failure to embrace news online, *Women, Men, and News* will attract the attention of those who are in a position to thoughtfully and creatively tackle a problem that won't go away. If the newspaper and online news industries' tenuous relationship with women is not addressed, the disparity between female and male readers may grow, which will likely make it difficult to reverse declines in total newspaper readership and circulation or increase traffic to online news sites.

Statistics show that although women lag behind men in getting news from newspapers and the Internet, the reverse is true for news from morning and network television. Similarly, non-traditional sources of news and information have captured women's attention. Perhaps, understanding why broadcast news and alternative news and information sources appeal to women can provide additional insight that will contribute to erasing the division between women and men that troubles the twenty-first-century news media landscape.

Note

1   Women and men of color have faced discrimination throughout America's history. Blacks fought for their rights during the Civil Rights Movement in the 1950s and early 1960s, but it was not until the passage of the Civil Rights Act (1964) and the Voting Rights Act (1965) did racial discrimination become illegal.

References

Bruni, F. (2001, August 1). G.O.P. is trying to counter erosion of women's support. *The New York Times,* pp. A1, A12.

Campbell, R. (1998). *Media and Culture: An introduction to mass communication.* New York: St. Martin's Press.

Comstock, G., Chaffee, S., Katzman, N., McCombs M., & Roberts D. (1978). *Television and Human Behavior.* New York: Columbia University Press.

Connelly, M. (2004, November 7). How Americans voted: A political portrait. *The New York Times,* p. 4, Section 4.

Evans, B. (2003, November 21). Study: Women still make 20% less than men. *Austin American-Statesman,* pp. C1, C3.

Flexner, E. (1975). *Century of Struggle: The women's rights movement in the United States* (revised edition). Cambridge: Belknap Press.

Flexner, E. & Fitzpatrick, E. (1996). *Century of Struggle: The women's rights movement in the United States* (revised edition). Cambridge: Belknap Press.

Friedan, B. (2001). *The Feminine Mystique.* New York: W.W. Norton & Company.

Goldin, C. (1990). *Understanding the Gender Gap: An economic history of American women.* New York: Oxford University Press.

Harp, D. (2002). Desperately Seeking Readers: US newspapers and the creation, termination, and reintroduction of women's pages. Unpublished doctoral dissertation, University of Wisconsin-Madison.

Introduction and summary: A year after Columbine public looks to parents more than schools. (2000, April 19). *The Pew Research Center for the People and the Press*. Retrieved September 2006 from http://people-press.org/reports/display.php3?ReportID=40.

Introduction and summary: Internet news takes off. (1998, June 8). *The Pew Research Center for the People and the Press*. Retrieved September 2006 from http://people-press.org/reports/display.php3?ReportID=88.

Jayson, S. (2003, November 28). Engineering: It's not just for the men. *Austin American-Statesman*, pp. B1, B3.

Lasswell, H.D. (1974). The structure and function of communication in society. In W. Schramm & D.F. Roberts (Eds.) *The Process and Effects of Mass Communication* (revised edition), pp. 84–99. Urbana: University of Illinois Press.

Madrick, J. (2004, June 10). Economic scene. The earning power of women has really increased, right? Take a closer look. *The New York Times*, p. C2.

McCombs, M. & Poindexter, P. (1983). The duty to keep informed: news exposure and civic obligation. *Journal of Communication*, 33(2), 88–96.

McQuail, D. (1983). *Mass Communication Theory: An introduction*. London: Sage.

Merritt, D. & McCombs, M. (2004). *The Two W's of Journalism: The why and what of public affairs reporting*. Mahwah: Lawrence Erlbaum Associates.

Mills, K. (1995). *From Pocahontas to Power Suits: Everything you need to know about women's history in America*. New York: Plume.

Naisbitt, J. (1982). *Megatrends: Ten directions transforming our lives*. New York: Warner Books.

Newport, F. (2006). Gender gap alive and well: Bush has higher job approval rating among men than women. In A.M. Gallup & F. Newport (Eds.) *The Gallup Poll: Public Opinion 2004* (pp. 95–7), Lanham: Rowman & Littlefield.

Overview: News audiences increasingly politicized. (2004, June 8). *The Pew Research Center for the People and the Press*. Retrieved August 2006 from http://people-press.org/reports/display.php3?ReportID=215.

Overview: Online papers modestly boost newspaper readership. (2006, July 30). *The Pew Research Center for the People and the Press*. Retrieved August 2006 from http://people-press.org/reports/display.php3?ReportID=282.

Page, S. (2003, December 18). Till politics do us part: Gender gap widens. *USA Today*, p. 1A.

Park, R.E. (1940). News as a form of knowledge: a chapter in the sociology of knowledge. *The American Journal of Sociology*, 45(5), 669–86.

Poindexter, P.M. & McCombs, M.E. (2001). Revisiting the civic duty to keep informed in the new media environment. *Journalism & Mass Communication Quarterly*, 78 (1), 113–26.

Richardson, J.D. (2001, December 21). Poll analysis: Concern growing over loss of civil liberties. *Los Angeles Times*. Retrieved August 2006 from www.latimes.com/news/nationworld/times poll/la-463pa3an,1,457920.story?coll=la-news-times_poll-nation&ctrack=1&cset=true.

Ripley, A. (2005, March 7). Who says a Woman can't be Einstein? *Time*, pp. 50–60. In *Time* magazine cover story, The math myth: The real truth about women's brains and the gender gap in science.

Stein, M.L. (1990, November 17). Reaching women readers. *Editor & Publisher*, p. 18.

Stephens, M. (1997). *A History of News*. Fort Worth: Harcourt Brace College.

Sussman, B. (1988). *What Americans Really Think, and Why our Politicians Pay No Attention*. New York: Pantheon Books.

Wright, C.R. (1975). *Mass Communication: A sociological perspective* (2nd edition). New York: Random House.

Chapter 2

Factors Contributing to the Sex Divide in Newspapers and Television News

Paula Poindexter

Around the time that Betty Friedan, the author of the groundbreaking book *The Feminine Mystique*, criticized American society for preventing women from developing their full potential and confining them to the role of housewife, journalism scholars were asking questions about the presence of nonreaders in the news media landscape. In the first published study that focused exclusively on daily newspaper nonreaders, Westley & Severin (1964) identified numerous variables that distinguished nonreaders from readers, but sex was not one of them. The results of that 1964 state-wide study of nonreaders revealed that 13.3 percent of women and 13.9 percent of men could be classified as nonreaders of newspapers (ibid., p. 45). With 86 percent of the survey respondents reading newspapers every day, 37 percent reading more than one newspaper, and 8 percent reading three or more newspapers, the authors called reading the daily newspaper "one of the most thoroughly institutionalized behaviors of Americans" (ibid., p. 45).

Today, neither reading a daily newspaper nor consuming news in general would be described as "one of the most thoroughly institutionalized behaviors of Americans" (Westley & Severin, 1964, p. 45). More than 40 years ago, when reading a daily newspaper was almost universal, the news media landscape appeared to be inhabited primarily by news enthusiasts, news monitors, and news betweeners. But today, new breeds of consumers such as news eclectics, news accidentals, news intenders, and news avoiders share the news media terrain. If changes in society, changes in the news media landscape, and changes in the roles of women are linked to the decline in newspaper reading as a thoroughly institutionalized behavior, do these changes also explain the news consumption divide between women and men?

If women and men were equally as likely to be nonreaders of newspapers in 1964, why are women more likely than men to be nonreaders today? And, why are women more likely than men to get their news from television? To fully understand the factors that contribute to this sex divide, it is first necessary to examine the concepts and variables that have been identified as directly and indirectly related to news media use.

The published research on news media use has devoted more attention to reading newspapers than consumption of any other news medium. This focus on newspaper reading is a reflection of newspapers' dominance in the news media landscape, from the publication of what is regarded as the first American newspaper, *Publick Occurrences, Both Forreign and Domestick* in 1690, through the first half of the twentieth century (Stephens, 1997).

The second half of the twentieth century witnessed declines in newspaper reading and the takeover of television as the dominant source of news. By the last decade of the twentieth century, in which cable news and information channels multiplied and news websites on the Internet proliferated, newspaper reading continued to drop. As the dawn of the twenty-first century became yesterday's news, the downward slide in consumption of newspapers appeared to have also infected television news, prompting news executives, journalism scholars, and popular culture critics to ask why.

Although early in the twentieth century, newspaper columnist and social critic Walter Lippmann (1922) theorized about the meaning of the relationship between newspaper readers and their newspapers, it was not until two decades later that empirical links between newspapers and readers appeared in the published literature. Dozens of social, economic, cultural, political, and psychological variables representing individual differences were investigated in order to answer the fundamental question: Who is the newspaper reader?

Individual Differences

Even though the portrait of the newspaper reader could have been that of a woman or a man, since women were equally as likely as men to read newspapers, research investigators were able to identify specific variables that distinguished newspaper readers from nonreaders. Study after study showed newspaper readers were more likely than nonreaders to be middle aged, educated, affluent, and white (Schramm & White, 1949; Westley & Severin, 1964; Greenberg & Dervin, 1970; Sharon, 1973/1974; Penrose *et al.*, 1974; Stevenson, 1977; Jackson, 1978; McCleod & Choe, 1978; Shaw, 1978; Stephens, 1978; Burgoon & Burgoon, 1980; Bogart, 1981).

Individual Differences and Television News

As newspaper reading declined, scholars conducted studies on television news audiences to determine the role of television news in the decline. Results of studies showed that age and education were significant variables in television news consumption. Younger adults were much less likely than older adults to watch television news; adults with some high school education were less likely than college-educated adults to watch news on television. Television news viewing for women and men was similar, and unlike the race gap that had been identified in newspaper reading, whites and blacks watched television news about equally (Robinson & Jeffres, 1979).

Socialization

Although the literature on socialization and news consumption is sparse, and in some cases, contradictory, we believe children are socialized in ways that can influence whether they grow up to become a news enthusiast or news avoider. What children learn through the socialization process is a product of a variety of factors, including what they are exposed to at home, at school, in the park, in the mall, in a religious or cultural setting, or through the media. In any one of these environments, parents, siblings, teachers, peers, religious leaders, politicians, celebrities, athletes, or textbooks, to give a few examples of socialization agents, can directly or indirectly influence exposure to news as adults.

For instance, a child growing up in a home in which both parents read a daily newspaper and watch network TV news may grow up to become a news enthusiast. Similarly, a child growing up in a home that does not read a newspaper and rarely turns on the local news may grow up to become a news avoider. To a great extent, the presence or absence of newspapers in the home is dependent on the parents' education and income.

Leo Bogart, the executive vice president and general manager of the Newspaper Advertising Bureau and author of the 1981 book, *Press and Public: Who Reads What, When, Where, and Why in American Newspapers*, proclaimed childhood exposure is linked to adult newspaper reading habits (p. 100). However, evidence from an earlier 1971 study of 1,300 families contradicted that proclamation when it found: "little support to the notion that parental example in media use provides an important model for the adolescent, except perhaps in a negative fashion" (Chaffee *et al.*, 1971, p. 329). Even though contradictions appeared to surround the socializing influence of parents on children's news use, there was a consensus that the newspaper is the last medium introduced to children, and that introduction usually takes place through the comic strips (Schramm *et al.*, 1960, p. 35). If children, in some cases as young as four years old, first become acquainted with newspapers through the comics and later move on to the "serious parts of the paper" (Schramm *et al.*, 1960, pp. 39–40), the question becomes: who first introduced children to newspapers and which of the primary socialization agents—family, schools, television, peers—were directly or indirectly instrumental in producing future news enthusiasts or news avoiders?

As some scholars explored social, economic, and cultural backgrounds of parents as well as parental values, family communication patterns, parental interaction with children and their activities, and parental interest in public affairs to pinpoint exactly how parents directly or indirectly influenced their children's news consumption (Chaffee *et al.*, 1971; Clarke, 1965), the newspaper industry counted on the schools to act as a socialization agent that could help children "grow" into news enthusiasts who would regularly read newspapers as adults (Bogart, 1981, p. 100). In addition to NIE programs that encouraged schools to make the newspaper a part of the curriculum, independently, thousands of teachers used newspapers to get children interested in reading and shine a light on the subjects they taught.

Evidence showed growing up with newspapers in the home and newspapers in the school made a difference in readership of newspapers as adults. According to data analyzed in *People and the Press* (Bogart, 1981), of children who grew up with newspapers at home, 70 percent were frequent readers as adults; of children who did not grow up with newspapers at home, 56 percent were regular newspaper readers as adults (ibid., p. 100). Since the data found little difference between children who had newspapers in school versus those who did not, it was concluded: "Children who had the newspaper at home as a daily presence would probably be more likely to grow up to be newspaper readers, whether or not they had the paper in school" (ibid., p. 101).

But what does growing up in a home with a newspaper really mean and why can it have an impact on reading the newspaper as an adult? Does it simply mean newspapers are physically present in the home even if they are not being read? Does it mean mothers and fathers are reading newspapers in the presence of their children so that children will model the behavior as they grow into adults? Does it mean that parents verbally express what they are reading in the newspaper and they engage in conversations about events in the news? Does it mean the act of reading a newspaper is an integral and enjoyable part of family life? Or does it mean parents communicate through actions and words that keeping up with the news is important and good citizens have a responsibility to keep up with the news? Except for the role that discussing news can play in later newspaper reading, little empirical research is available to help us understand what growing up in a home with newspapers really means.

What happens when a newspaper is not present in the home and children are only exposed to newspapers at school? Evidence suggests that children with newspapers at school only are more likely to grow up to become newspaper readers than children growing up without newspapers at home or school (Bogart, 1981, p. 101; Grusin & Stone, 1993).

With more and more children growing up without newspapers in the home, teachers play an even greater role as a socialization influence. "The teachers' ability to influence students' attitudes toward newspapers should not be underestimated, especially in the absence of parental influence" (Grusin & Stone, 1993, p. 16). After a survey of adults ages 18 to 34 in the Memphis, Tennessee area, researchers made the point that memories of the experience with the newspaper in the classroom may have consequences for adult newspaper consumption. For example, if using the newspaper in the classroom is remembered as an enjoyable and rewarding activity, that positive memory could contribute to a young person growing into a news enthusiast. But if use of the newspaper in the classroom is remembered as a dreadful activity, that memory could lead to an adult developing into a news avoider. Whether the newspaper experience is enjoyable or dreadful is, of course, related to teachers, "who may be the people with whom students associate their first and most extensive experience with newspapers" (ibid.).

Since many of the benchmark studies that focused on the socialization influences on children's news consumption were conducted from the early 1960s through the early 1990s, in later chapters, we'll revisit the role of socialization in news consumption, especially for teens and young adults in today's twenty-first-century news media landscape. Plus, we'll ponder the weight of sex-based socialization influences in the news consumption equation. In other words, what does it mean for news consumption if a society has differential expectations for girls and boys?

Variations in the socialization of girls and boys may lead to differential gender expectations that contribute to differences in what girls and boys read in the newspaper. In fact, at a time when reading the daily newspaper was called "one of the most thoroughly institutionalized behaviors of Americans" (Westley & Severin, 1964, p. 45), a journalism scholar investigating the socialization values of parents and the relationship to their children's newspaper reading, noted: "it usually is expected in our society that boys will become concerned about public affairs ... Girls usually are not expected to become absorbed with political developments" (Clarke, 1965, p. 545). Later in this chapter, we'll examine the news content of interest to women and men and ask why, when women and men read the newspaper at the same rate, was there a sex difference in the type of news content read?

Normative Beliefs

Although journalism scholars have paid little attention to the role of normative beliefs in explaining news consumption, that does not diminish the importance of this concept in illuminating why some individuals faithfully consume the news and others ignore it. Normative beliefs, which represent what we stand for, what we believe to be true, the values we hold, the principles we live by, can influence countless behaviors ranging from what we eat, to how we spend our leisure time, to the roles we take on in our homes or in the workplace, to whether or not we participate in civic activities or inform ourselves of the news.

If, in a democratic society, it is believed that a good citizen is an informed citizen, might that lead to a societal norm that a good citizen has a duty to keep informed?

Inspired by democratic and political theories that asserted keeping up with the news was part of a citizen's civic obligation (Renshon, 1974), researchers used data from newspaper markets in the Northeast and Midwest to explore the role of a civic norm in news media consumption (McCombs & Poindexter, 1983). It was believed that a civic duty norm to keep informed might provide insight into why the majority of the public paid attention to the news just as a civic norm helped explain why the majority of voting-age citizens exercised their right to vote.

Where do civic norms come from? Just as a civic norm that makes an individual feel a duty to vote is learned, a sense of duty to keep informed is learned through the socialization process (Milbrath & Goel, 1977):

> Why is it that some persons so define themselves and their role that it includes the responsibility to be interested in, informed about, and actively participate in political affairs? These beliefs are learned in the formative years and come about partly as a function of the milieu in which a person grows up and partly as a function of the basic personality of the individual. The impact of social status on participation is mediated almost totally through the socialization process; persons from a higher status have been taught to be interested in politics, to keep informed, and to shoulder a responsibility to participate. The role training coming from the environmental milieu interacts with basic personality factors which operate differently to produce different role conceptions for different individuals.
>
> (Ibid., p. 53)

A product of the socialization process, this sense of duty to keep informed is one of several factors that may motivate an individual to consume news. In 1945, although newspapers readers in New York City were not asked about a duty to keep informed, they were asked "Do you think it's very important that people read the papers or not?" (Berelson, 1949, p. 312). When the researchers reported "Almost everyone answered with a strong 'yes'," they seemed to imply that reading the newspaper was motivated by a higher purpose, like a civic responsibility (ibid., p. 114).

Using the University of Michigan Survey Research Center civic obligation to vote measurements as a model and data collected from surveys of newspaper markets in the Northeast and Midwest, researchers analyzed the responses of more than 2,500 randomly selected individuals who were asked to agree or disagree with four statements that when analyzed as a whole would epitomize the civic responsibility of keeping informed of the news:

1. We all have a duty to keep ourselves informed about news and current events.
2. It is important to be informed about news and current events.
3. So many other people follow the news and keep informed about it that it doesn't matter much whether I do or not.
4. A good deal of news about current events isn't important enough to keep informed about.

(McCombs & Poindexter, 1983, p. 90)

Analysis of the responses produced a civic duty to keep informed that ranged from weak to strong. Furthermore, the researchers determined there was a definite relationship between a strong sense of duty to keep informed and frequent news consumption, especially reading newspapers and watching network television news. In other words, individuals that strongly felt a duty to keep informed were more likely to read newspapers and watch national television news than were individuals with a weak sense of duty to keep informed.

Although the researchers did not address the origins of the duty to keep informed, they did answer the question: which individuals feel a duty to keep informed? The answer to that question was virtually the same as the answer to the question: who is the newspaper reader? Individuals who feel a duty to keep informed were "highly educated, upper-income, middle-aged" (McCombs & Poindexter, 1983, p. 94). Just as newspaper readers during the middle of the twentieth century were equally as likely to be a woman or a man, individuals who believed they had a duty to keep informed were just as likely to be a woman or a man (ibid.).

The civic duty to keep informed was explored further in a special issue of the *Newspaper Research Journal*, the journal published by the Newspaper Division of the Association for Education in Journalism and Mass Communication (AEJMC). Particularly relevant to understanding the role of the norm in news consumption was the study that sought to determine if the duty to keep informed norm differed conceptually from gratifications sought from the news. By factor analyzing the four statements that comprised the civic duty norm to keep informed and five separate statements that measured gratifications, the authors were able to determine that there was a distinct difference between the norm and gratifications sought from the news (Blood *et al.*, 1983). The statements measuring gratifications were:

1. Reading the newspaper gives people an understanding of what's going on.
2. Reading the newspaper helps people keep up with the latest events.
3. Much of the information I use in daily living, I get in the newspaper.
4. It's fun to read the newspapers.
5. Reading the newspaper provides people with a way to relax and pass the time.
(Ibid., pp. 45–6)

In recognition of the vastly changed news media landscape since the original 1983 study, the study's authors revisited the civic duty to keep informed norm in 2001:

The sweeping changes in the media landscape suggest that there could be changes in the civic duty to keep informed. Since the original 1983 study, there has been a decline in traditional news media use and an explosion of new media. When the data were collected for the 1983 study, there was no cable news. Today, there are five twenty-four-hour cable news channels. When the original data were collected, there were only dreams of computers in every home and preliminary discussions about experiments in which news could be delivered to consumers through home computers. Today, there are computers in more than half of all households; 42 percent of households have access to the Internet and 44 percent of Americans go online. In addition, newspapers, television networks, local TV stations, news magazines, and cable news channels are delivering news on the Internet.
(Poindexter & McCombs, 2001, p. 116)

Replicating the original study among 606 randomly selected adults in a southwestern metropolitan area, the authors found empirical support for a civic duty to keep informed. Equally as important, it was determined that in the twenty-first century, just like the twentieth century, the civic duty to keep informed mattered in news consumption. Significant correlations between a strong civic duty to keep informed and frequent news consumption were found for newspapers reading, network and local TV news viewing; cable news viewing, and reading national and presidential election news on the Internet.

Once again, the authors asked: Which individuals feel a duty to keep informed? And the answer remained unchanged. "Consistent with the 1983 study, income, education, and age are significantly related to the civic duty to keep informed and gender is not" (Poindexter & McCombs, 2001, p. 121).

Although in 1983, the researchers did not explore the origins of this civic duty to keep informed, in the 2001 replication, the authors sought "to determine if the civic duty to keep informed was more than an independent variable in a two-variable relationship; the civic duty to keep informed might actually be an intervening variable serving in the role that Rosenberg called '. . . a *landmark* on the intellectual journey from cause to effect'" (Poindexter & McCombs, 2001, pp. 115–16; Rosenberg, 1968, p. 65).

The authors found the civic duty to keep informed served as an intervening variable between education and watching cable news, and education and reading national news on the Internet. For newspaper reading and network TV news viewing, there was partial support for the assertion that the duty to keep informed intervened between education and newspaper reading, and education and watching network TV news. In other words, the authors found evidence that the civic norm to keep informed was a *consequence* of an individual's level of education and a *determinant* of some news consumption (Poindexter & McCombs, 2001, p. 122).

What does it really mean that the duty to keep informed is a consequence of education? A glance back at Figure 1.2 in Chapter 1 is a reminder that socialization has a crucial role in the news consumption model. Since schools and families are important agents of socialization, they can cultivate and reinforce the normative belief that in a democratic society good citizens have a duty to keep informed. If a strong belief is cultivated and reinforced, individuals may mature into news enthusiasts or news monitors. But if individuals are not socialized to believe in a duty to keep informed, they may grow up to become news avoiders.

Does the normative belief that there is a duty to keep informed play an intervening role in the news consumption divide between women and men? Since there was no difference between women and men, on the duty to keep informed, the duty to keep informed norm is disqualified as a possible explanation for the news consumption divide between women and men. Perhaps motivations and attitudes may provide more insight into the sex divide in news consumption.

Motivations

In the hunt for explanations as to what motivates an individual to consume news, the uses and gratifications perspective stands out as the most researched area of scholarship. Dating back to the "beginning of empirical mass communication research" (Katz, Blumler & Gurevitch, 1973–4, p. 509) researchers in the early 1940s explored audience gratifications in relation to content such as quiz programs, serious music, soap operas, and media such as radio, comic books, magazines, and newspapers (Katz, Blumler & Gurevitch, 1973–4).

The first published study to empirically chart the uses and gratifications of newspapers was conducted during the second week of a 1945 newspaper strike in New York City. When the delivery men of eight New York City newspapers stopped delivering newspapers, commercial and academic researchers set out to learn what the public missed about newspapers. One study, sponsored by Columbia University's Bureau of Applied

Social Research, used the results of 60 intensive interviews to construct a typology that represented the roles and functions of a newspaper. In addressing "What Missing the Newspaper" means, the researchers acknowledged the roles and functions included in the typology were not mutually exclusive and "different people read different parts of the newspaper for different reasons at different times" (Berelson, 1949, p. 117).

The researchers found that some readers viewed the newspaper as "indispensable as a source of information about and interpretation of the 'serious' world of public affairs" (Berelson, 1949, p. 117). This perception of the newspaper as an indispensable source for public affairs information was not limited to the availability of news articles; readers also valued editorials and columns, which provided material to aid the formation of opinions about public affairs (ibid., p. 118).

The newspaper was also viewed as an important "tool for daily living," with readers saying they relied on the newspaper to find out what programs were on the radio, what movies were showing, who died, how a stock performed, or what shopping information was published in the advertisements (Berelson, 1949, p. 118).

The "respite" value of newspapers was also pointed out by readers. For many readers, the newspaper served as an escape, providing psychological relaxation and "relief from the boredom and dullness of everyday life" (Berelson, 1949, p. 119). Newspapers also provided "social prestige" for some readers (ibid.). One reader noted: "You have to read in order to keep up a conversation with other people. It is embarrassing not to know if you are in company who discuss the news" (ibid., p. 120). Instead of prestige, for some, newspapers satisfied a need for "social contact," especially human interest stories and advice and gossip columns (ibid.).

The authors also found that newspapers enabled some readers to satisfy their need to read, regardless of the content they read in the newspapers. For other readers, the newspaper helped overcome insecurity, that is, a feeling one might have when you didn't know what was going on. Finally, for many readers, the newspaper was simply a "ceremonial or ritualistic or near-compulsive act" (Berelson, 1949, p. 129). The author of this first uses and gratifications study concluded that gratifications related to news and information were rational but gratifications unrelated to news were irrational. Examples of irrational gratifications included social contacts, social prestige, security, ceremonial, ritualistic, or near-compulsive acts.

In 1958, some 13 years after the 1945 newspaper strike, New York City was hit again, and once again, intensive interviews were conducted with newspaper readers. But this time the goal was to replicate the original 1945 study on the meaning of missing the newspaper. After conducting interviews with 164 regular newspaper readers around the New York City area, the author found support for the gratifications that had been identified in the study from the 1945 newspaper strike. But, in addition to reading the newspaper for respite, social prestige, social contact, security, reading for its own sake, and ritual, the new study identified two additional gratifications: stimulation and occupation. One newspaper reader, who depended on the newspaper for stimulation, confessed: "I miss the murders, robberies, and killings. I've been reading the good stories in old copies of the *Daily News* all over again"(Kimball, 1959, p. 396). Readers who relied on the newspaper to occupy time divulged:

> I'm reading Dr. Zhivago now. I've been meaning to for a long time. It would sit there on the living room table, but by the time I finished with the papers I didn't feel like starting a book.

> I made myself a suit last Sunday for the first time in my life.

I finally got around to fixing up a few things around the house that have been piling up for a long time.

(Kimball, 1959, p. 396)

Although pioneers in uses and gratifications research sought to "treat audience requirements as intervening variables in the study of traditional communication effects," (Katz et al., 1973–4, p. 518) we view uses and gratifications as one of several types of motivations intervening in the decision to consume or ignore news. Scholars who assemble the pieces for a uses and gratifications approach to audience study theorized that these motivations were the end result of individual differences and the environment: "the combined product of psychological dispositions, sociological factors, and environmental conditions that determines the specific uses of the media by members of the audience" (Katz et al., 1974, p. 27).

Understanding uses and gratifications in the news consumption model also requires recognizing differences in types of exposure. In fact, in a review of the psychology behind audience gratifications, noted psychologist William McGuire distinguished between initial exposure and continued exposure:

> While personal needs may have some impact on search and initial exposure to the media, it must be granted that external circumstances and chance are compelling in most instances. One has little opportunity to watch television or read a newspaper, as compared with listening to one's car radio as one drives home from work. The discovery of a favored book or television program often depends on accidental exposure or a casual remark. Where the uses-and-gratifications approach seems more powerful is when we turn to the question of maintaining continued exposure once one has found appropriate material. While the initial tuning in to a television program (or newspaper column or magazine feature or whatever) may have been largely haphazard and unmotivated, behavioral theory's "law of effect" reminds us that such exposure would soon extinguish in the absence of reinforcement to maintain the habit.

(McGuire, 1974, p. 170)

The significance of uses and gratifications as a motivation in habitual news consumption is apparent in some investigations. Furthermore, when gratifications sought (motivations) are distinguished from gratifications obtained (rewards) as some scholars have recommended, the role of uses and gratifications in reinforcing habitual news consumption behavior is clarified (Swanson, 1979, p. 33). The gratifications sought (motivations) are related to expectations (beliefs), which influence media consumption:

> Such consumption results in the perception of certain gratifications obtained, which then feed back to reinforce or alter an individual's perceptions of the gratification-related attributes of a particular newspaper, program, program genre, or whatever.

(Ibid., p. 37)

For example, a study conducted by Indiana University scholars considered both gratifications sought (motivations) and gratifications obtained (rewards) when 786 adolescents, young adults, middle-aged adults, and older adults were surveyed by telephone. The most important motivations, which the researchers called personal needs, were the need to keep tabs on what's going on and the need to relax and release tension; the least important needs were the need to kill time and the need for companionship. Newspapers were rated most satisfying for helping people keep tabs and least satisfying for the need to be entertained, kill time, avoid feeling lonely, and know oneself better. The researchers concluded: "personal needs are much more important than traditional demographic factors, *except* age, in predicting and explaining newspaper and television use in Indianapolis" (Weaver *et al.*, 1979, p. 7).

Since research has identified an array of distinctive gratifications, it is important to ask: Are gratifications sought (motivations) and obtained (rewards) the same for women and men? Are women and men equally as likely to view the newspaper as an indispensable source for news and opinion on public affairs? Or are women more likely to view the newspaper as a respite "from the boredom and dullness of everyday life" while men view the newspaper as providing social prestige (Berelson, 1949, p. 119)? If women and men differ in the gratifications sought and obtained, these differences could help explain the sex divide in news consumption that emerged as the twentieth century began to wane.

Similarities and differences between women and men were identified during the 1958 newspaper strike in New York City when New Yorkers were asked what they missed about not having a paper (Kimball, 1959). Women and men were similar when it came to the intensity of missing the paper and missing the general news in the paper. But women were more likely than men to greatly miss advertising and the gossip columns, while men were more likely than women to miss headline news, world news, front-page news, and the sports pages.

Women were also more likely than men to articulate gratifications that the first uses and gratifications study labeled non-rational, that is, social contact, social prestige, security, ceremonial, ritualistic, or near-compulsive acts. Differences between women and men in "non-rational" gratifications were attributed to women's work inside the home and man's work outside the home:

> The male orbit outside the home and on the job, especially for those in a professional or executive status, provided compensations for the newspaper . . . Housewives, in addition to "shopping in the dark," spoke feelingly of the hole left in their day. And college-educated women ordinarily spent more time with their papers than the less-educated women interviewed in this survey. Thus, the adjustment to a household routine without the papers was probably more noticeable to them as well as more difficult.
>
> (Kimball, 1959, p. 398)

Almost two decades after it was determined that women and men differed on some gratifications, data from newspaper markets in the Northeast found similar gratifications differences (Becker, 1976). Sex comparisons were made on 17 reasons for reading a newspaper, representing six distinct types of gratification: surveillance of the environment, decisional guidance, reinforcement, entertainment, communicatory utility, and participation. Although the majority of the motivations were similar for women and men, women were more likely than men to read newspapers to: "obtain useful information for daily life"; "just to pass time"; "for information in advertisements"; "to show or read items to other people so that they can enjoy them" (ibid., p. 8).

Indiana University researchers also found that women and men differed on some gratifications and their perceptions of media as they relate to the gratifications. For example, adult males favored newspapers for keeping tabs but middle-aged and older females favored television for keeping tabs on what's going on around them. Women did favor newspapers for having influence on things around them while men favored newspapers for "finding out what other people are saying about important things" (Weaver *et al.*, 1979, p. 4).

Motivations and TV News

Are uses and gratifications the same for newspapers and TV news? Results from four separate surveys that compared gratifications sought from political content in newspapers and TV news led one scholar to conclude:

> The data are quite clear on one point: the gratifications do not seem to be media specific. The evidence suggests that people seeking a specific gratification from one medium seek that gratification from another as well.
>
> (Becker, 1979, p. 72)

A separate investigation, which focused exclusively on the audience experience with television news, identified four dimensions of uses and gratifications: surveillance-reassurance, which included freedom from worry that the world was safe and secure; cognitive orientation, that is, acquiring information for opinion formation; dissatisfactions, which included negative evaluations about the form and importance of TV news; diversion, that is escape from boredom and routine.

Although the uses and gratifications that were identified in the study were not analyzed by sex, the study's author did compare other aspects of the TV news experience and found differences between women and men in several areas. Men were more likely to be "appointment" viewers (Levy, 1978, p. 5) but women were more likely than men to select a specific channel to watch the 6 p.m. newscast based on active criteria such as news quality, program format, and newscasters (ibid., p. 8). Finally, women and men differed in their assessment of the importance of news; women were more likely to rate the news as moderately important or important (ibid., p. 10).

Since most uses and gratifications studies have been conducted during times of normality, the question becomes, in times of crisis, are uses and gratifications the same? The 1973 Yom Kippur War in Israel provided an opportunity to investigate uses and gratifications during a national crisis. When respondents were asked to assess the importance of radio, television, newspapers, and conversations for: "(1) obtaining information about the situation, (2) understanding the significance of what was happening, and (3) relieving tension," results showed radio was judged as best for getting news and television was considered best for tension release (Peled & Katz, 1974, p. 54). No sex differences were found in the expectation for television to provide information and relieve tension (ibid., p. 56).

Five months after terrorists flew airplanes into the twin towers of the World Trade Center, researchers asked respondents why they sought more news after 9/11. Results revealed that in addition to four categories of uses and gratifications, including surveillance, other, curiosity, fear and anxiety during the national crisis, respondents described five distinct types of surveillance that satisfied five distinct needs:

> Although keeping up with the latest developments (45%) far exceeded other types of surveillance, keeping up because of personal impact (8%), looking to the news

to learn about new threats (6%), trying to ascertain the world's reaction (5%) and gathering information about new regulations (3%) were also examples of surveillance.

(Poindexter & Conway, 2003, p. 121)

Avoidances

It was not until after newspaper reading declined as a thoroughly institutionalized behavior that scholars began to ask *why* some individuals ignore newspapers (Poindexter, 1979; Burgoon & Burgoon, 1980; Lipschultz, 1987).

Just as uses and gratifications encouraged news consumption, avoidances, motivations that are theoretically and empirically distinct from gratifications, motivated some to shun the news. Although the first avoidance studies focused on political content and voters, subsequent studies tried to identify reasons for avoiding news media, specifically newspapers (McLeod & Becker, 1974; Becker, 1979).

Since the publication of the first studies that looked at the reasons for ignoring newspapers, news avoiders have multiplied in the news media landscape. Chapter 3 will examine the published research on news avoiders, including reasons they turn their backs on news, and explore what happens when women ignore the news.

Need for Orientation

Although need for orientation evolved as a theoretical component of agenda setting, need for orientation is also an example of a motivation that can contribute to news consumption (Weaver, 1977). Need for orientation, which offers a psychological explanation for seeking out news and acquiring the media's agenda, was first proposed and documented years before the computer, Internet, and media visionaries such as Ted Turner, founder of CNN, and Al Neuharth, founder of *USA Today*, changed the news media landscape forever.

After the seminal agenda-setting study was conducted during the 1968 US presidential election, the scholars who led the way in agenda-setting research sought to determine why agenda-setting effects occurred (McCombs & Shaw, 1972).

In a follow-up study with a panel of Charlotte, North Carolina voters during the 1972 presidential election, empirical support for a psychological explanation for agenda-setting effects, called need for orientation, was found. Conceptually, an individual's need for orientation is defined by relevance and uncertainty, and the level of relevance and uncertainty can produce different levels of need for orientation, which can lead to different levels of news consumption. In the 1972 study that investigated need for orientation, four-fifths of voters with a high need for orientation frequently used mass media for political information but fewer than half of voters with a low need for orientation frequently used mass media for this type of information (Weaver, 1977).

At the start of the twenty-first century with a transformed news media landscape, the relationship between frequent attention to news and a need for orientation was revisited as the 2000 presidential primary kicked off. Although the measurements differed from the original 1972 investigation and the study was conducted among the general population, after determining relevance and uncertainty, correlations were still found between level of need for orientation and frequent use of news media (Poindexter *et al.*, 2003).

To determine relevance, survey participants were asked if they had an issue of personal importance; uncertainty was determined by asking survey participants how much information they needed about the issue. Survey participants who had an issue of personal importance and needed a great deal more information about the issue were considered to have a high need for orientation, but survey participants who had an issue that mattered but knew enough about the issue were considered to have a low need for orientation. Survey participants without an issue of importance were considered to have no need for orientation.

As a psychological explanation for agenda-setting effects, need for orientation also sheds light on news consumption motivations that may produce news consumers such as news monitors or news avoiders. News monitors may have an issue of importance in which they need more information, motivating them to monitor the news. News avoiders may not have an issue that matters so they are not motivated to follow the news. It is also possible, though, that news avoiders do have an issue of personal importance, but because they have "personal encounters" with the issue, they feel a high level of certainty about the issue, making it unnecessary to read newspapers or watch news on television to fill in the gaps in their knowledge about the issue (McCombs, 2004).

Although the psychological concept of need for orientation helps us understand news consumption in the context of agenda setting, it tells us little about the sex divide in news consumption since previous studies have failed to find evidence of a sex difference with need for orientation (Poindexter et al., 2003).

Attitudes

Attitudes which are learned stand for a favorable or unfavorable evaluation of a news-centered object. For example, the motivation to read newspapers by a 30-something attorney who works a 12-hour day may be overshadowed by an unfavorable evaluation that is developing toward reading newspapers. Early Monday, Wednesday, and Friday mornings, the attorney works out at the gym and watches the morning news while running four miles on the treadmill. On Tuesday and Thursday mornings, immediately after arriving at her office, the attorney clicks on Google News, scanning the most recently posted stories. Although the attorney subscribes to the Sunday paper, she only has time to read it once a month. On Mondays, when she recycles the unread Sunday paper, she feels guilty and vows to cancel her subscription. Recently, she has admitted to herself that it is not just that she feels guilty; she no longer enjoys sitting down reading the paper. Perhaps she thinks it is time to have the news e-mailed like her colleagues who also are on the fast track. She could check the e-mailed news on her PDA while waiting around the courtroom for the judge to call her case. Her wireless hand-held connection to the Internet would also be perfect for checking news while waiting in the check-out line at the grocery store. This news eclectic is motivated to keep up with the news, but because her experience in reading newspapers has turned negative, even though her motivation to keep up with the news remains strong, she will likely abandon newspapers in the near future.

This example provides insight into the components of attitude and the dimensions of the object evaluated. Although favorable and unfavorable components of attitudes are universally accepted concepts in attitude research, journalism scholars have not previously explored the idea of a multi-dimensional, news-centered object that will be evaluated. But to fully understand the dynamics of news consumption, it is necessary to understand that the news-centered object that is evaluated by the attitude is not

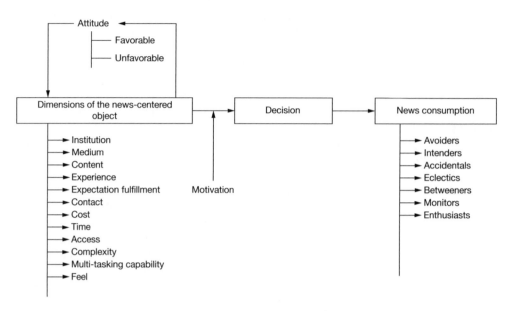

Figure 2.1 Attitudes and dimensions of the news-centered object[1]

monolithic. In fact, as Figure 2.1 illustrates, there are at least 12 dimensions of the news-centered object that could be assessed: institution, medium, content, experience, expectation fulfillment, contact, cost, time, access, complexity, multi-tasking capability, and feel. The salience of any one dimension at any time can vary. Dimensions of high importance dominate dimensions of lesser importance, making the high-importance dimension of the news-centered object the focal point of the attitude's favorable or unfavorable judgment.

What determines which dimension of the news-centered object is most important to the individual? Salience of a dimension, which can vary over time, especially during different life stages, can be a function of individual differences, socialization, normative beliefs, motivations, and even attitudes. For the fast-track attorney described earlier, the salient dimension of the news-centered object was experience. Because the newspaper reading experience received a negative evaluation, the attorney was on the path to removing the newspaper from her life.

Attitudes, Dimensions, and Decisions

News consumption for a news enthusiast or news monitor is routine, a daily habit. But a habit can be broken when circumstances change. If, for example, time becomes a salient dimension and a newspaper is evaluated unfavorably because it is perceived as taking too much time to read, news enthusiasts and news monitors may decide to stop reading it. Attitudes toward a salient dimension of the news-centered object can also play a role in a news accidental's decision to consume news or not. For example, if content is the salient dimension of the news-centered object and a news accidental evaluates the content as fair and balanced, this favorable evaluation will likely lead to a decision to read the news when it is accidentally encountered. But if a news accidental gives the newspaper a failing grade in fair and balanced coverage, next time the news accidental notices an intriguing headline, he or she may decide to ignore the story. Similarly, if medium is the salient dimension for a 20-something and newspapers as a medium for news are perceived as old-fashioned and mind-numbing, the 20-something will likely ignore newspapers and turn to another medium for news.

The expectation fulfillment dimension of the news-centered object seemed to be the focus of a study of more than 4,000 respondents in four different regions of the country when researchers asked respondents to rate their satisfaction with the paper, specifically on how well the paper did in keeping them well informed and helping them make day-to-day decisions. Researchers determined that there was a consistent correlation with being satisfied on this dimension and reading the newspaper frequently (Burgoon & Burgoon, 1980).

The expectation fulfillment dimension was also relevant in a survey in which the public was asked about its expectations of local news. A factor analysis revealed the public had distinct expectations of local news and the dominant expectation was that of being a good neighbor:

> Although the segment of the public that had a strong good neighbor expectation did not differ from the segment with a weak good neighbor expectation in terms of news media use, there was a difference in how these two segments of the public evaluated the news media's ability to address their concerns. Almost three-fifths (59 percent) said television was the best news medium to address local concerns but only 27 percent gave their endorsement to newspapers.
>
> (Poindexter *et al.*, 2006, p. 84)

Furthermore, the good neighbor expectation was related to individual differences. "Being a good neighbor was more strongly valued by women, African Americans, Hispanics, segments of the public with less income and education, and long-time and newer residents" (ibid., p. 85).

The fact that women are more likely than men to watch television news may be due in part to their attitude toward television news. In addition to perceiving television as best able to address their concerns, women were more likely than men to consider TV coverage as sufficiently detailed (Bogart, 1981).

Although attitudes can be potent factors in the decision to consume news, published empirical research provides little insight into how attitudes toward the different dimensions of the news-centered object interact with socialization, normative beliefs, motivations, and individual differences to influence news consumption. When we think of individual differences, demographic variables such as age, income, education, race and ethnicity, and sex primarily come to mind. But individual differences can also include religion, culture, marital status, personality, sexual orientation, family background, political party, political ideology, lifestyle, and stage in the life cycle.

Individual differences can be fixed (e.g., biological sex); they can increase over a lifetime (e.g., age); they can influence other individual differences (e.g., income and political party). Individual differences also play a vital role in the socialization process. How individuals are socialized and what they learn are functions of the individual differences that define the environment they grow up in and the external forces such as media and peers they are exposed to. Individual differences can also be influential in the salience of the dimensions in the news-centered object that will be evaluated.

Age, education, and income have been the dominant individual difference variables studied in news consumption. Although sex has been linked to some motivations and specific types of news content, sex has consistently been overshadowed by variables that have offered more promise in understanding news consumption. No doubt, the failure of the sex variable to distinguish newspaper readers from nonreaders for almost three decades led researchers to dismiss it as a crucial individual difference variable in news consumption.

Sex Has Always Mattered for Certain Types of Content

Although the sex divide in news consumption did not surface until the late 1980s, women and men have always differed in content interests. When women and men were given a list of non-news subjects and asked to tailor a paper to their own interests, double-digit gaps between the subject interests of women and men were readily apparent. Women were more likely than men to want to give the following subjects more space: recipes (52 percent vs. 22 percent); women's fashions (50 percent vs. 24 percent); beauty tips (39 percent vs. 16 percent); personal advice (44 percent vs. 27 percent); obituaries (50 percent vs. 34 percent); home furnishings (56 percent vs. 41 percent); health, nutrition, medical advice (82 percent vs. 68 percent); weddings and engagements (37 percent vs. 23 percent); religion (56 percent vs. 43 percent); book reviews (50 percent vs. 37 percent); best food buys (84 percent vs. 72 percent). The biggest differential in which more men than women wanted more space devoted to the subject included, not surprisingly, sports (72 percent vs. 47 percent), and hunting and fishing (52 percent vs. 26 percent) (Bogart, 1981, p. 214).

Sex has always mattered for specific content, and in today's news media landscape, sex matters for newspapers, television news, and news on the Internet. Forty years ago, newspaper reading was a thoroughly institutionalized behavior for women and men but that's not the case today. Although newspaper reading has declined for both sexes, there has been a steeper decline for women. Why are women less likely than men to read newspapers but more likely to watch news on television? By focusing on sex, exploring the interaction of sex with other individual difference variables, and analyzing the relationship between sex and socialization, normative beliefs, motivations, and attitudes, especially the dimensions of the news-centered object, subsequent chapters in *Women, Men, and News* will identify the factors, large and small, that directly and indirectly play a role in news consumption and answer the question, why is there a sex divide in paying attention to news?

Notes

1   **Explanation of Dimensions**
    Institution refers to the press, the Fourth Estate, the news media, or journalists. **Medium**, which can be general such as newspapers or specific such as *The New York Times*, has an image such as trustworthy, accurate, biased, old-fashioned, cool, etc. **Content** can be specific types of stories or the way stories are framed. **Experience** can be direct or observed; it refers to the process of reading or watching news in general or interaction with a specific news medium. **Expectation Fulfillment** is a function of the uses and gratifications that played a role in seeking news initially and a perception of how well the news medium delivered. **Contact** ranges from delivery of the newspaper to writing a letter to the editor or phone call to the local TV station to picking up a newspaper at the newsstand. **Cost** means the price of a newspaper or magazine subscription or single copy. **Time** is a reference to the amount of time required to read a newspaper or newsmagazine, watch network, local or cable news, or read news on the Internet. **Access** describes abailability of a news medium, such as access to newspapers or the Internet. **Complexity** is the perceived level of difficulty using the medium or how a news story is written. **Multi-tasking Capability** is the ability to participate in at least two activities

simultaneously, such as watching TV news while exercising. **Feel** is the physical response to interacting with the newsprint that a newspaper is published on, the touching of glossy pages of a magazine or tapping a keyboard.

References

Becker, L.B. (1976, May). Reasons Given for Newspaper Reading. Northeastern Newspaper Audience Survey Report #2. Unpublished report, Syracuse University Communication Research Center.

Becker, L.B. (1979, January). Measurement of gratifications. *Communication Research* 6(1), 54–73.

Berelson, B. (1949). What 'missing the newspaper' means. In P.F. Lazarsfeld & F.N. Stanton (Eds.) *Communications Research 1948–1949*, pp. 111–29. New York: Harper & Brothers.

Blood, W.R., Keir, G.J., & Kang, N. (1983). Newspaper use and gratification in Hawaii. *Newspaper Research Journal*, Special Issue, 4(4), 43–52.

Bogart, L. (1981). *Press and Public: Who reads what, when, where, and why in American newspapers*. Hillsdale: Lawrence Erlbaum Associates.

Burgoon, J.K. & Burgoon, M. (1980). Predictors of newspaper readership. *Journalism Quarterly*, 57, 589–96.

Chaffee, S., McLeod, J.M., & Atkin, C. (1971). Parental influences on adolescent media use. *American Behavioral Scientist*, 14(3), 323–40.

Clarke, P. (1965). Parental socialization values and children's newspaper reading. *Journalism Quarterly*, 42, 539–46.

Greenberg, B. & Dervin, B. (1970). Mass communication among the urban poor. *Public Opinion Quarterly*, 34, 224–35.

Grusin, E.K. & Stone, G.C. (1993, October). The newspaper in education and new readers: Hooking kids on newspapers through classroom experiences. *Journalism Monographs*, 141, 1–39.

Jackson, M.M. (1978, May 24). A comparison of newspaper use by lower-income and middle- and upper-income blacks. *ANPA News Research Report*, 11, 1–6.

Katz, E., Blumler, J.G., & Gurevitch, M. (1973–4). Uses and gratifications research. *Public Opinion Quarterly*, 37(4), 509–23.

Katz, E., Blumler, J.G., & Gurevitch, M. (1974). Utilization of mass communication by the individual. In J.G. Blumler & E. Katz (Eds.) *The Uses of Mass Communication: Current perspectives on gratifications research*, pp. 19–34. Sage Annual Reviews of Communication Research, Vol. III, Beverly Hills: Sage.

Kimball, P. (1959). People without papers. *Public Opinion Quarterly*, 23, 389–98.

Levy, M.R. (1978). The audience experience with television news. *Journalism Monographs*, 55, 1–29.

Lippmann, W. (1922). *Public Opinion*. New York: Simon & Schuster.

Lipschultz, J.H. (1987, Summer). The nonreader problem: A closer look at avoiding the newspaper. *Newspaper Research Journal*, 8(4), 59–69.

McLeod, J.M. & Becker, L.B. (1974). Testing the validity of gratification measures through political effects analysis. In J.G. Blumler & E. Katz (Eds.) *The Uses of Mass Communications: Current perspectives on gratifications research* (pp. 137–64). Sage Annual Reviews of Communication Research, Vol. III, Beverly Hills: Sage.

McCleod, J.M. & Choe, S.Y. (1978, March 14). An analysis of five factors affecting newspaper circulation. *ANPA News Research Report*, 10, 1–6.

McCombs, M. (2004). *Setting the Agenda: The mass media and public opinion*. Cambridge: Polity Press.

McCombs, M. & Poindexter, P. (1983). The duty to keep informed: News exposure and civic obligation. *Journal of Communication*, 33(2), 88–96.

McCombs, M.E. & Shaw, D. (1972). The agenda-setting function of mass media. *Public Opinion Quarterly*, 36(2), 176–87.

McGuire, W.J. (1974). Psychological motives and communication gratification. In J.G. Blumler & E. Katz (Eds.) *The Uses of Mass Communications: Current perspectives on gratifications research*, pp. 167–96. Sage Annual Reviews of Communication Research, Vol. III, Beverly Hills: Sage.

Milbrath, L. & Goel, M.L. (1977). *Political Participation: How and why do people get involved in politics?* Chicago: Rand McNally College Publishing Company.

Peled, T. & Katz, E. (1974). Media functions in wartime: The Israel home front in October 1973. In J.G. Blumler & E. Katz (Eds.) *The Uses of Mass Communications: Current perspectives on gratifications research*, pp. 49–69. Sage Annual Reviews of Communication Research, Vol. III, Beverly Hills: Sage.

Penrose, J., Weaver, D., Cole, R., & Shaw, D. (1974). The newspaper non-reader 10 years later: A partial replication of Westley-Severin. *Journalism Quarterly*, 51, 631–8.

Poindexter, P. (1979). Daily newspaper non-readers: Why they don't read? *Journalism Quarterly*, 56(4), 764–70.

Poindexter, P.M. & Conway, M. (2003). Local, network TV news shows significant gains. *Newspaper Research Journal*, 24(1), 114–27.

Poindexter, P.M., Heider, D., & McCombs, M. (2006). Watchdog or good neighbor? The public's expectations of local news. *The Harvard International Journal of Press/Politics*, 11(1), 77–88.

Poindexter, P.M. & McCombs, M.E. (2001). Revisiting the civic duty to keep informed in the new media environment. *Journalism & Mass Communication Quarterly*, 78(1), 113–26.

Poindexter, P., McCombs, M., & Smith, L. (2003). La necesidad de orientacion: una explicacion psicologica de los efectos del agenda-setting [Need for orientation: A psychological explication of agenda-setting effects]. In M. McCombs & I. Luna Pla (Eds.) *Agenda-setting de los medios de communicacion*, pp. 107–19. Mexico City: Universidad Ibero Americana and Univesidad de Occidente.

Renshon, S.A. (1974). *Psychological Needs and Political Behavior: A theory of personality and political efficacy.* New York: Free Press.

Robinson, J.P. & Jeffres, L.W. (1979, September). The changing role of newspapers in the age of television. *Journalism Monographs*, 63, 1–31.

Rosenberg, M. (1968). *The Logic of Survey Analysis.* New York: Basic Books.

Schramm, W., Lyle J., & Parker, E. (1960). Patterns in children's reading of newspapers. *Journalism Quarterly*, 37, 35–40.

Schramm, W. & White, D.M. (1949). Age, education, economic status: factors in newspaper reading. *Journalism Quarterly*, 26, 149–59.

Sharon, A. (1973/1974). Racial differences in newspaper readership. *Public Opinion Quarterly*, 37(4), 611–17.

Shaw, E.F. (1978, June 9). *ANPA News Research Report*, 12, 1–8.

Stephens, L.F. (1978, December 20). *ANPA News Research Report*, 17, 1–7.

Stephens, M. (1997). *A History of News.* Fort Worth: Harcourt Brace College.

Stevenson, R. (1977, October 21). The frequency of newspaper readership. *ANPA News Research Report*, 7, 1–8.

Swanson, D. (1979). Political communication research and the uses and gratifications model: A critique. *Communication Research*, 6(1) 37–53.

Weaver, D.H. (1977). Political issues and voter need for orientation. In D.L. Shaw & M.E. McCombs (Eds.) *The Emergence of American Political Issues: The agenda setting function of the press*, pp. 107–20. St. Paul: West Publishing.

Weaver, D.H., Wilhoit, G.C., & Reide, P. (1979, July 20). *ANPA News Research Report*, 21, 1–7.

Westley, B.H. & Severin, W.J. (1964). A profile of the daily newspaper non-reader. *Journalism Quarterly*, 41, 45–50.

Chapter 3

When Women Ignore the News

Paula Poindexter

With activity on the Internet accelerating at an ever-increasing pace and newspaper circulation on a downward slide, the newspaper's place in today's world is being debated offline and online. The headline "Women Using Newspapers to Line Canary Cage," which was posted in the blogosphere, attracted the attention of women who agreed that newspapers were not relevant to their lives. One female blogger, who noted that newspapers were not even around to line the bird cage, elaborated: "some of us just opted to unsubscribe to local newspapers and prefer to go to online papers" ("Women Using Newspapers," 2005). A First Wave baby boomer blogger concurred: "I'm a sixty-year-old woman with a Master's degree and I haven't subscribed to a newspaper in about 10 to 15 years. The reason? I felt invisible! I didn't like that my interests were delegated to the 'Women's Section'" (ibid.).

These women have not turned away from news as a whole; they have simply dropped out of reading newspapers. These newspaper dropouts remind us that news avoiders are more complex than their name suggests. Some news avoiders avoid all news all the time while others avoid a specific news medium such as newspapers, TV, cable news, newsmagazines or online news. Furthermore, this avoidance of news or a specific news medium can be deliberate or unintentional. Even so, regardless of intent, the consequence is the same: more and more consumers are ignoring news and news avoiders are growing and upsetting the equilibrium of the news media landscape.

A glance at Table 3.1 shows how news avoiders have increased in the news media landscape over a 12-year period. In 1994, news avoiders were 10 percent of adults and by 2006, they represented 19 percent. Scanning the various sources of news listed in Table 3.1 reveals which news medium has the most news avoiders, which has the least, and how the number of news avoiders has changed during the 12 years.

Although slightly more than three-quarters of adults avoid news online, that percentage increases significantly when the focus is on online newspapers only. In 2006, a whopping 90 percent did not read a newspaper online. Perhaps, the most important numbers to monitor are the years 2000, when consumers really began to embrace the Internet, and 2006, when the Internet had become an integral part of our daily lives. In 2000, 70 percent did not go online but by 2006 only 47 percent did not go online. The question becomes if the number of people avoiding the Internet is decreasing why are so many people avoiding newspapers online?

The First News Avoiders Profiled

Who are these news avoiders and why have they turned away from news? The first study to concentrate exclusively on news avoiders focused on adults who did not read

Table 3.1 Daily life without news

Activity	1994	1998	2000	2002	2004	2006
Did not get any news yesterday	10	15	17	20	15	19
Did not watch TV news	28	41	44	46	40	43
Did not go online	96	75	70	57	53	47
Did not read a newspaper	51	52	53	59	58	60
Did not listen to radio news	53	51	57	59	60	64
Did not watch cable news	—	—	—	67	62	66
Did not read any news online	—	—	88	84	76	77
Did not read a newspaper online	—	—	—	—	—	90

Note: Compiled from the tables "News and Daily Life" (p. 8), newspapers online (p. 56), and cable news channels (p. 60) in "Online Papers Modestly Boost Newspaper Readership," 2006. One percentage point differences from the actual report reflect The Pew Research Center for the People and the Press adjustments in order to be consistent with results from the question itself in the topline. Did not get any news yesterday computed by subtracting percentages from 100% or compiling "never" responses. Used with permission from The Pew Research Center for the People and the Press.

newspapers. Conducted four and a half decades ago, when newspaper reading was considered a thoroughly institutionalized behavior, this benchmark study sketched the first profile of newspaper nonreaders (Westley & Severin, 1964). Although younger and older adults were more likely than middle-aged adults to be newspaper nonreaders, there was no evidence in 1964 that women were more likely than men to ignore newspapers. The link between age and avoiding newspapers has continued into the twenty-first century, that is young adults are significantly less likely to read newspapers ("Biennial news consumption," 2006).

Age has not only been linked to ignoring newspapers; it has also been associated with avoiding TV news and news online. In the first study to focus exclusively on non-viewers of TV news, it was determined that young adults were less likely than older adults to watch either local or national TV news (Poindexter, 1980). A similar pattern was found for news avoiders of online news at the end of the twentieth century but that pattern was short-lived. Although in 1999, as the Internet was set to experience an explosion in growth and newspaper websites were coming of age, news avoiders on the Internet were more likely to be younger and older with 63 percent of 18- to 22-year-olds and 82 percent of 65 plus Internet users saying they never or seldom read online news (Poindexter & Heider, 2001). That same age link is no longer true today. When it comes to the relationship with age, Internet news avoiders are more likely to be older and less likely to be younger adults. Although the first newspaper nonreader study did not find a sex divide in reading newspapers, a different scenario emerged with reading online news. Women were more likely than men to be online news avoiders; 55 percent of avoiders of Internet news were female but only 31 percent were male (Poindexter & Heider, 2001).

Age and sex are not the only variables that have been linked to avoiding news. Over the years, a variety of socio-psychological variables have been tied to turning away from newspapers. Results of a variety of studies have shown newspaper nonreaders are poorer with less education and they are less likely to interact socially, participate politically, live in an urban area, live a long time in the same residence, identify with the community, feel a civic duty to keep informed, and understand what's going on (Westley & Severin, 1964; Penrose *et al.*, 1974; Schweitzer, 1974; Burgoon & Burgoon, 1980; McCombs & Poindexter, 1983; Lipschultz, 1987; Wanta, Hu, & Wu, 1993).

Avoidances Have a Long History

A review of studies in the public domain reveals that news avoidances have been studied during every decade since the 1970s. Over the years, adults have been asked why they avoid newspapers, shun network and local TV news, ignore online news, and disregard the Internet. Just as uses and gratifications explained why individuals consumed news, avoidances, motivations that are theoretically and empirically distinct from gratifications, explained why some rejected the news. Although the first avoidance studies focused on political content and voters, subsequent studies tried to identify reasons for avoiding news media, specifically newspapers (McLeod & Becker, 1974; Becker, 1979).

Reasons for Avoiding Newspapers

Newspaper reading had already declined as a thoroughly institutionalized behavior before researchers began to ask *why* some individuals ignored newspapers (Poindexter, 1979; Burgoon & Burgoon, 1980; Lipschultz, 1987). The first published study to explore why nonreaders did not read newspapers surveyed adults using a two-step process. In the first step, nonreaders were asked to explain their reasons for not reading newspapers in their own words (Poindexter, 1979). Although according to the open-ended responses the most popular reasons for ignoring newspapers included lack of time (20 percent); preference for another medium (18 percent); cost (16 percent); and lack of interest (15 percent), other reasons included health problems such as poor eyesight (9 percent); circulation problems (8 percent); language problems (6 percent); newspaper content (4 percent); miscellaneous (4 percent); don't like to read (3 percent) (Poindexter, 1979).

The second step of the nonreader study involved sorting the verbatim words of nonreaders into categories, which were organized into a checklist of reasons for not reading newspapers. The checklist, which was used in subsequent surveys, asked nonreaders how much each reason explained why they did not read newspapers. The responses to the checklist were then factor analyzed, producing five distinct categories of reasons for avoiding newspapers: newspaper content, use of other media, poor eyesight, newspaper bias, and lack of time (Poindexter, 1979).

Atypical Nonreaders Have Different Avoidances

As the categories of reasons for avoiding newspapers were dissected, an unexpected and troubling element in the news media landscape came into view: atypical nonreaders, that is, consumers who are expected to read but don't . . . they are middle-age, middle and upper income, and well educated (Poindexter, 1979). When the reasons atypical and typical nonreaders rejected newspapers were compared, two reasons stood out. Atypical nonreaders were more likely than typical nonreaders to avoid newspapers because of lack of time and dissatisfaction with newspaper content (ibid.).

Subsequent studies that looked at why nonreaders ignored newspapers found newspaper avoidances that matched Poindexter's earlier study. Plus, previously unidentified news avoidances were discovered: lack of usefulness, lack of trust, lack of attractiveness, and the amount of detail (Burgoon & Burgoon, 1980; Lipschultz, 1987; Huntress, 1994).

A Generational Shift in Newspaper Avoidances

By the start of the twenty-first century, the benchmark study on why nonreaders avoided newspapers was revisited to determine if reasons for steering clear of newspapers had changed or remained the same (Poindexter, 2000). With the availability of multiple cable news outlets and news websites on the Internet causing dramatic shifts in the news media landscape, the author sought to determine the impact, if any, on reasons for ignoring newspapers (see Table 3.2). As a reason for avoiding newspapers, lack of time increased from 20 percent to 35 percent, and although at first glance, preference for another medium appeared to show little change from 18 percent to 22 percent, a closer look revealed there was a change indeed. Other medium preferred in 1979 meant television, radio, or magazines but at the start of the twenty-first century, preferred other medium now included news on the Internet, which was the explanation given by 10 percent of nonreaders. A preference for TV news was given by 11 percent and 1 percent said they preferred magazines (ibid.).

Follow-up analysis of the newspaper avoidances found no significant sex differences. Women and men were equally as likely to give the same reasons for not reading newspapers. Approximately one-third of women and one-third of men said lack of time was a reason for not reading newspapers.

Reasons for Avoiding TV News

One of the first studies to compare reasons for ignoring local and network TV news found two different types of time were related to avoiding TV news: time conflicts (26 percent for local TV news and 35 percent for network TV news) and lack of time (20 percent for local TV news and 21 percent for network TV news) (Huntress, 1994). Nonviewers also expressed dissatisfaction with content or presentation (22 percent for local TV news and 13 percent for network TV news); and preference for another medium (4 percent for local TV news and 7 percent for network TV news) (ibid.).

Reasons for Avoiding News on the Internet

With the rapid expansion of the Internet as a consumer medium and the proliferation of news websites, researchers wondered why some consumers did not embrace news online. Results of a survey that explored reasons for avoiding news on the Internet identified lack of interest (26 percent) as the primary reason for ignoring news on the

Table 3.2 Reasons for not reading newspapers: comparing twentieth- and twenty-first-century avoidances (%)

Reasons	Twentieth century	Twenty-first century
Lack of time	20	35
Preference for other medium	18	22
Cost	16	5
Lack of interest	15	9
Health problems	8	0
Circulation problems	8	11
Language	6	7
Newspaper content	4	3
Miscellaneous	4	9
Don't like to read	3	1
	100	100
(Base)	(281)	(112)

Note: Twentieth century, Poindexter (1979); twenty-first century, Poindexter (2000).

Internet (Poindexter & Heider, 2001). Other reasons for avoiding news on the Internet included already read newspapers (19 percent); lack of time (18 percent); other/no reason (10 percent); do not use Internet (9 percent); too time consuming (7 percent); prefer TV news (4 percent); dislike format (4 percent); not proficient surfing (3 percent) (ibid.).

Comparing Reasons Women and Men Avoid News on the Internet

Because being online is a prerequisite to reading news on the Internet, news avoiders of Internet news are of two types: non-Internet users who do not have access to online news or even if they have access, they do not use the Internet and consumers who are on the Internet but ignore news. In fact, in a survey that asked the reasons for not reading news on the Internet, 9 percent of the respondents said they did not read news on the Internet because they did not use the Internet (Poindexter & Heider, 2001).

If 73 percent of adults are on the Internet, that means 27 percent are not on the Internet. These non-internet users would also not be able to read news online ("Internet Penetration and Impact," 2006). What are some of the reasons adults are not on the Internet and how are reasons different for women and men? Although a Pew Internet & American Life Project (2005) survey found women were as likely as men to say they were not on the Internet because they did not have time, women were significantly more likely than men to say they were not online because: "they didn't need it; didn't want it; were worried about online porn, credit card theft, and fraud; it was too expensive; and too complicated and hard to understand" ("How women and men use the Internet," 2005, p. 39).

Even though women and men differed in their reasons for not being online, according to Table 3.3, overall, there were no significant sex differences in the reasons for avoiding news on the Internet. Even so, women were almost three times more likely than men to say they avoided news on the Internet because they lacked time.

A News Avoidance Typology

Since 1979, a variety of research studies in the public domain have reported reasons adults give for avoiding different news media but no study has synthesized the diverse

Table 3.3 A comparison of reasons women and men avoid reading news on the Internet (%)

Reasons	Women	Men
Lack of time	22	8
Not interested	22	28
Already read paper	18	25
Other	14	5
Do not use Internet	10	8
Too time consuming	7	8
Do not like format	4	5
Not proficient surfing net	2	5
Prefer TV	1	10
(Base)	(91)	(40)

Note: X^2=13.249, p =.104; Poindexter (2000).

news avoidances into a single rational explanation that can be applied to all media, including newspapers, local TV news, network TV news, cable news, radio news, the Internet, newsmagazines, and online news. The news avoidance typology in Table 3.4 is an attempt to synthesize the news avoidances identified in studies over the past quarter century in order to produce a theoretical and pragmatic framework that accurately reflects the reasons for avoiding news, regardless of medium, and serves as a springboard for addressing the growing news avoider problem in the news media landscape.

The news avoidance typology suggests that, although from the perspective of consumers, there may be many reasons for rejecting the news or a specific news medium, in reality, there are four primary explanations for avoiding news: other medium preferred or used; perceived constraints; real constraints; rejection of medium or news. Preference for a medium is the polar opposite of rejection of a medium. Up until the emergence of the Internet as a major medium for news, television was most preferred as the alternative medium for news avoiders. More recently the Internet is as likely as television to be the preferred alternative medium. In some cases, consumers say they prefer the other medium; in other cases consumers report they have already gotten their news from the alternative.

The Time Conundrum

The presence of time among perceived and real constraints in the news avoidance typology displayed in Table 3.4 and the percentage increase of news avoiders saying they ignore news because they lack time, provide support for the argument that over the past quarter century, time has been a contributing factor to the increasing numbers of news avoiders in the news media landscape. But time's persistent presence in the news media landscape only underscores the fact that little is understood about how to get to the bottom of the time conundrum. Is time a perceived constraint, a real constraint, or both? Is lack of time just a socially acceptable excuse that news avoiders give to pollsters when asked why they do not read newspapers? Or does the phrase lack of time represent a legitimate time deficit or scarcity with no available hours in the day to read newspapers?

In an effort to gain greater insight into the meaning of lack of time, a question in The Pew Research Center Biennial News Consumption Survey (2004) connecting avoiding news with a shortage of time was analyzed by sex, newspaper readers and nonreaders, and news avoiders of online news. Survey participants had been asked if they completely or mostly agreed or if they completely or mostly disagreed with the statement: "I am often too busy to keep up with the news." Although women (37 percent) were more likely than men (32 percent) to completely or mostly agree that they were often too busy to keep up with the news, an analysis of the statement by

Table 3.4 A typology of news avoidances

Other medium preferred or used—TV, Internet, magazines, radio

Perceived constraints—lack of time, time consuming, lack of usefulness

Real constraints—time deficit, time conflict, health problems, language barriers, cost, circulation problems, not proficient using Internet, do not use Internet

Rejection of medium or news—dislike content, format, structure, presentation, unattractiveness, purposelessness, and amount of detail; dislike bias; distrust; disinterested; dislike reading

news consumers and news avoiders revealed that lack of time does not necessarily mean a scarcity of time.

First, the statement, "I am often too busy to keep up with the news" suggests that consumers who agree or mostly agree with the statement would not be among newspaper readers but would primarily be among news avoiders but Table 3.5 points out that is not the case: 27 percent of women who completely agree and 47 percent who mostly agree are newspaper readers. Among men who completely agree, the percentage of newspaper readers is even higher: 34 percent who completely agree that they are "often too busy to keep up with the news" are regular newspaper readers. This analysis hints at other factors keeping these consumers connected to newspapers, because in spite of often being too busy to keep up with the news, these busy women and men have not turned away from newspapers.

One would also expect that if being too busy meant a scarcity of time or a time deficit, a larger percentage of news avoiders who completely or mostly agreed that they were too busy to keep up with the news would be among newspaper avoiders and Table 3.5 shows that is indeed the case. Among women, 25 percent who completely agree and 13 percent who mostly agree never read newspapers. The percentage of men is slightly lower: 21 percent who completely agree and 12 percent who mostly agree never read newspapers.

If time scarcity is legitimate and not a socially acceptable excuse, there would be no women or men among the news avoiders who disagreed that they were often too busy to keep up with the news. Because 22 percent of women and 16 percent of men who completely or mostly disagreed with the statement are still among the news avoiders, this implies that other factors beyond time may be responsible for avoiding newspapers.

When a similar analysis of The Pew Research Center Biennial News Consumption Survey (2004) data was done for online news avoiders, a wider gap was found between women and men avoiders of online news. Women (35 percent) were more likely than men (24 percent) to completely or mostly agree with the statement, "I am often too busy to keep up with the news" ("Biennial news consumption," 2004).

Women Lack Time Because They Are Busy With Household Chores

Support for the argument that women are busier than men can be found in Bureau of Labor Statistics: "On an average day in 2005, 84% of women and 65% of men spent

Table 3.5 What newspaper readers and news avoiders say about the statement: "I am often too busy to keep up with the news" (%)

	Completely agree	Mostly agree	Mostly disagree	Completely disagree
Regular newspaper readers				
Women	27	47	62	68
Men	34	48	63	71
News avoiders of newspapers				
Women	25	13	11	11
Men	21	12	8	8

Source: Analysis of The Pew Research Center for the People & the Press 2004 Biennial News Consumption Survey data.

some time doing household activities, such as housework, cooking, lawn care, or financial and other household management" ("American time use," 2006, pp. 2–3). In addition to a larger percentage of women involved in household activities, women spent more time in household activities. An analysis of diaries found women spent 2.7 hours on household activities while men spent 2.1 hours ("American time use," 2006). More women (53 percent) than men (19 percent) did housework such as cleaning or laundry. Similarly, women (66 percent) were more likely than men (35 percent) to prepare food and clean up afterwards ("American time use," 2006).

In households with the youngest child under age six, women provided 2.5 hours of primary childcare while men provided 1.3 hours ("American time use," 2006). Women spent more time than men bathing, dressing, or feeding a child. Women provided 1.1 hours while men provided 0.5 hours, which represented about 30 minutes (ibid.).

Finding time to follow the news was particularly difficult for mothers, according to a survey conducted by The Pew Research Center for the People and the Press (2002). "Fully six-in-ten (62%) say they wish they had more time for the news, more than fathers (52%) and women who do not have children at home (48%)" ("Introduction and summary," 2002, p. 3).

But men did surpass women in leisure activities. On an average day, men spent 5.7 hours while women spent 5.0 hours involved in a leisure activity such as watching TV, socializing, or exercising ("American time use," 2006).

When Time is a Conflict

As an explanation for avoiding news, time does not always mean that it is in short supply—it sometimes means a conflict. This is especially true when it comes to network news, which is broadcast at a specific time. If for example, the network evening news is broadcast at 5:30 p.m. but a consumer does not arrive home from work until 6:10 p.m., a time conflict, as an explanation for avoiding network news, is a real constraint.

Avoidances Beyond Time Constraints

Time-related constraints are not the only obstacles standing between news avoiders and consuming news. Health problems, language barriers, cost, non-use of the Internet or lack of Internet proficiency are constraints that are intractable and real and they stand in the way of consuming news.

Perhaps the most entrenched news avoidance displayed in the typology is rejection of medium or news. News avoiders reject a news medium or news for a range of reasons. They dislike the content, format, structure, or amount of detail. News avoiders also reject a news medium because they evaluate it as biased and untrustworthy. Finally, it is not unusual for a news avoider to turn away from a news medium because of disinterest in the news medium or news or in the case of newspapers, because they dislike reading.

While the typology represents news avoidances from studies conducted over three and a half decades of asking news avoiders their reasons for turning away from news media, Table 3.6 compares news perceptions, interests, and expectations of women and men who avoid reading newspapers. Further analysis of The Pew Research Center Biennial News Consumption Survey (2004) data found the difference between women and men in their perceptions, interests, and expectations of news ranged from ten to thirteen percentage points. Over half (52 percent) of women newspaper avoiders compared to 39 percent of men want news to contain information that is helpful in their daily lives. Enjoyment plays a more significant role for women than men when it comes to reading and news. Women newspaper avoiders (49 percent) were more likely than men (36 percent) to say they enjoy reading a lot and women newspaper avoiders (47 percent) were more likely than men (36 percent) to like it "when a news source makes the news enjoyable and entertaining."

Not only do women news avoiders enjoy reading more than men news avoiders, studies have found "women of every age group, regardless of time constraints, spend more time reading each week than men of their age do. The difference? Women spend the bulk of their time with magazines and books, men with newspapers" (Miller, 1998, p. 41).

As displayed in Table 3.6, women newspaper avoiders were also more likely than men newspaper avoiders to regularly follow morning news shows such as *The Today Show* (25 percent vs. 14 percent) or network newsmagazine shows such as *20/20* (23 percent vs. 13 percent). Women news avoiders were also much more likely than men news avoiders to have a penchant for following health news (23 percent vs. 13 percent).

Even though it was not a sentiment held by a majority of women, it was a concern expressed more by women than men. Women newspaper avoiders (28 percent) were more likely than men newspaper avoiders (16 percent) to agree with the statement "watching and reading the news often depresses me" ("Biennial news consumption," 2004).

Unlike Table 3.6, which displayed differences between women and men news avoiders, Table 3.7, which displays the results of additional analyses of The Pew Research Center Biennial News Consumption Survey (2004) data, compared women who are regular newspaper readers with women who avoid newspapers. One big difference between these two groups of women is that women who are regular newspaper readers (74 percent) are much more likely than women who are newspaper avoiders (49 percent) to enjoy reading a lot. Enjoyment is not limited to reading. Regular newspaper readers

Table 3.6 News perceptions, interests, and expectations: a comparison of women and men newspaper avoiders

Attitudes	Women (%)	Men (%)	Difference*
Completely agree: I want the news to contain information that is helpful in my daily life	52	39	13
Enjoy reading a lot	49	36	13
Like it when a news source makes the news enjoyable and entertaining	47	36	11
Completely agree: watching and reading the news often depresses me	28	16	12
Regularly watch *The Today Show*, *Good Morning America*, or the *Early Show*	25	14	11
Regularly watch newsmagazine shows such as *60 Minutes*, *20/20*, or *Dateline*	25	12	13
Very closely follow health news either in the newspaper, on television, or on radio	23	13	10

Note: *Absolute difference.

Source: Analysis of The Pew Research Center for the People & the Press 2004 Biennial News Consumption Survey data.

Table 3.7 A comparison of news perceptions, interests, and expectations of women who regularly read and avoid newspapers

News attitudes	Readers (%)	Avoiders (%)	Difference*
Enjoy reading a lot	74	49	25
Enjoy keeping up with the news a lot	67	39	28
Like it when a news source has reporters and anchors with pleasant personalities	63	54	9
Like it when news sources include ordinary Americans	52	49	3
Completely agree: I want the news to contain information that is helpful in my daily life	51	52	1
Like it when a news source is sometimes funny	50	42	8
Like it when a news source makes the news enjoyable and entertaining	49	47	2
Very closely follow health news either in the newspaper, on television, or on radio	40	23	17
Regularly watch *The Today Show*, *Good Morning America*, or the *Early Show*	33	25	8
Regularly watch newsmagazine shows such as *60 Minutes*, *20/20*, or *Dateline*	33	25	8
Completely agree: watching and reading the news often depresses me	16	28	12

Note: *Absolute difference.

Source: Analysis of The Pew Research Center for the People & the Press 2004 Biennial News Consumption Survey data.

(67 percent) are also much more likely than newspaper avoiders (39 percent) to enjoy keeping up with the news a lot. In fact, these regular newspaper readers are examples of news enthusiasts and news monitors.

The only assertion in Table 3.7, which a significantly larger percentage of news avoiders than newspaper readers agreed with, was the depressing effect of news. When women newspaper readers were compared with women news avoiders, newspaper avoiders (28 percent) were more likely than regular newspaper readers (16 percent) to completely agree that watching and reading the news is often depressing. It is possible that this feeling that news is depressing plays a role in why women newspaper avoiders have turned away.

Big News Stories Can Attract News Avoiders to the News

Although on an average day, news avoiders ignore news, when a big story hits, news avoiders will tune in. 9/11, one of the biggest and most shocking news stories on American soil, can be viewed as a case study for understanding the impact of big news stories on news avoiders. Using trend and cross-sectional analyses, researchers tried to determine if and how 9/11 affected the news consumption of news avoiders. News avoiders of newspapers (47 percent) were significantly more likely than regular newspaper readers (30 percent) to say they paid attention to the news after 9/11 (Poindexter & Conway, 2003, p. 121). A uses and gratifications analysis produced four categories of gratifications for paying attention to the news: surveillance (67 percent), other (16 percent), curiosity (9 percent), fear and anxiety (8 percent) (ibid.). Dissecting surveillance revealed this motivation for keeping up with 9/11 news was comprised of five dimensions. Although keeping up with latest developments was reported by 45 percent of the survey respondents, for others, surveillance meant keeping up because of personal impact (8 percent), finding out about new threats (6 percent), finding out about the world's reaction (5 percent), and finding out about new regulations (3 percent) (ibid.).

When news avoiders of newspapers were compared with newspaper readers, non-readers (58 percent) were less likely than readers (82 percent) to identify a surveillance reason for keeping up with news about 9/11 but more likely to identify non-surveillance reasons. Nonreaders (42 percent) were more than twice as likely as readers (18 percent) to pay attention to 9/11 news because of curiosity and fear and anxiety (Poindexter & Conway, 2003, p. 121).

Have Atypical News Avoiders Stopped Hiding in the Closet?

Once upon a time when newspaper reading was considered a thoroughly institutionalized behavior and being informed was the hallmark of a good citizen, it was considered socially undesirable to admit to being a news avoider, especially if you were middle-age, middle or upper income, and well educated, traditional characteristics of newspaper readers. But when the President of the United States, whose socio-economic profile, prominent status, and job responsibilities would lead one to believe that he would be a newspaper enthusiast rather than a newspaper avoider, admitted on national television that he did not read newspapers, one can only wonder how much President George W. Bush's confession to Diane Sawyer on *20/20* influenced others who heretofore believed it was socially undesirable to ignore newspapers. One also wonders if atypical nonreaders felt they were free to emerge from the closet when the "Atypical Nonreader in Chief" appeared to show pride in his decision to shun newspapers (Johnson, 2003).

Historically, atypical nonreaders have functioned in a world of newspaper reading adults, which is why more than a decade before the end of the twentieth century, atypical nonreaders were described as "newspapers' greatest threat—and greatest promise. Atypical non-readers are exposed to newspaper readers in their offices, on the tennis court, the golf course and in their middle- and upper-class neighborhoods" (Poindexter-Wilson, 1989, p. 28). Like newspaper readers, atypical nonreaders are also "more likely to participate in civic and social activities in their respective communities" (ibid.).

In 1989, the author of the first study to identify atypical nonreaders argued in *Presstime*, the trade magazine for newspaper publishers, that "Either directly or indirectly, atypical non-readers have the potential to influence newspaper readers to join their more exclusive 'atypical non-reader club'" (Poindexter-Wilson, 1989, p. 28).

National survey data provide evidence that over the years more and more people have signed up for membership in the news avoider club and unless newspapers develop and implement effective strategies, the "atypical non-reader club" may become the norm, that is, typical news avoiders may have the same characteristics of individuals who once were expected to read newspapers: middle age, middle and upper income, and well educated.

But just because a newspaper reader drops out of reading newspapers does not mean that individual has turned away from all news or all sources of news produced by newspapers. For example, Second Wave baby boomer, Barb, who is an artist and a manager, no longer reads the newspaper but she still consumes news. In fact, according to a questionnaire that she completed for *Women, Men, and News*, what caused Barb to stop reading newspapers regularly was unrelated to a scarcity of time, preference for another news medium, or even the newspaper's content. What initially caused Barb to stop reading newspapers was that the paper was delivered after she had already left for work and she was too tired to read the newspaper at the end of the day. Today Barb says she does not read the newspaper because it is not convenient and there was too much to recycle. According to her questionnaire, she would not miss newspapers at all if they were not available but she would miss the Internet and TV "a lot" because they have become her primary sources of news. Because she believes it is very important to keep up with the news, Barb regularly gets news from TV and the Internet. But even though she reads news online almost every day, she doesn't go to the newspaper's website. Instead, she visits the websites of CNN and the local *ABC*-affiliate TV station as well as blogs.

Former newspaper readers such as Barb represent the latest quandary in the newspaper's long circulation and readership decline: twice-lost readers. The first loss is when newspaper readers stop reading the paper and the newspaper fails to lure them back. The second loss is the failure to convert the lost newspaper readers to the newspaper's website. Once news avoiders decide to turn their backs on a news medium, whether a newspaper, a news website, magazine, or TV station, winning them back is not easy. Although it is not impossible to win back lost news consumers, it is a difficult, time-consuming, and expensive undertaking. It is far more effective to make use of ongoing strategies that nurture current and future news consumers with the goal of achieving life-long loyalty, regardless of whether news is read online or off.

References

American time use survey—2005 results announced by BLS. (2006, July 27). *Bureau of Labor Statistics*. United States Department of Labor, Washington D.C. Retrieved August 15, 2006 from www.bls.gov/news.release/atus.nr.htm.

Becker, L.B. (1979). Measurement of gratifications. *Communication Research, 6*(1), 54–73.

Biennial news consumption survey: Online newspapers modestly boost newspaper readership. (2006, July 30). *The Pew Research Center for the People and the Press*. Retrieved November 1, 2006 from http://people-press.org/reports/display.php3?PageID=1068.

Biennial news consumption survey: News audiences increasingly politicized. (2004, June 8). *The Pew Research Center for the People and the Press*. Retrieved April 14, 2006 from http://people-press.org/reports/display.php3?PageID=837.

Burgoon, J.K. & Burgoon, M. (1980). Predictors of newspaper readership. *Journalism Quarterly, 57*(4), 589–96.

How women and men use the Internet. (2005, December 28). *The Pew Internet and American Life Project*. Retrieved September 9, 2006 from www.pewinternet.org/pdfs/PIP_Women_and_Men_online.pdf.

Huntress, B.B. (1994). A Comprehensive Portrait of the News Non-User. Unpublished Master's thesis, The University of Texas at Austin.

Internet penetration and impact. (2006, April 26). *The Pew Internet and American Life Project*. Retrieved September 9, 2006 from www.pewinternet.org/PPF/r/182/report_display.asp.

Introduction and summary: Public's news habits little changed by September 11. (2002, June 9). *The Pew Research Center for the People and the Press*. Retrieved March 25, 2006 from http://people-press.org/reports/display.php3?PageID=612.

Johnson, P. (2003, December 21). Bush's disdain for the news media puzzles, angers many journalists. *USA Today*. Retrieved September 9, 2006 from www.usatoday.com/advertising/orbitz/orbitz-window-unldPop.htm.

Lipschultz, J.H. (1987). Nonreader problem: A closer look at avoiding the newspaper. *Newspaper Research Journal*, 8(4), 59–69.

McCombs, M. & Poindexter, P.M. (1983). The duty to keep informed: News exposure and civic obligation. *Journal of Communication*, 33(2), 88–96.

McLeod, J.M. & Becker, L.B. (1974). Testing the validity of gratification measures through political effects analysis. In J.G. Blumler & E. Katz (Eds.) *The Uses of Mass Communications: Current perspectives on gratifications research*. Sage Annual Reviews of Communication Research, Vol. III, Beverly Hills: Sage.

Miller, S.H. (1998, April). Women and content. *Presstime*, 41. Retrieved from LexisNexis database.

Overview: Online papers modestly boost newspaper readership. (2006, July 30). *The Pew Research Center for the People and the Press*. Retrieved August 2006 from http://people-press.org/reports/display.php3?ReportID=282.

Penrose J., Weaver, D., Cole, R., & Shaw, D. (1974). The newspaper non-reader 10 years later: A partial replication of Westley-Severin. *Journalism Quarterly*, 51, 631–8.

Poindexter, P.M. (1979). Daily newspaper non-readers: Why they don't read? *Journalism Quarterly*, 54(4), 764–70.

Poindexter, P.M. (1980). Non-news viewers. *Journal of Communication*, 30(4), 58–65.

Poindexter, P.M. (2000). Daily Newspaper Nonreaders: Why they don't read; a partial replication, a generation later. Unpublished manuscript.

Poindexter, P.M. & Conway, M. (2003). Local, network TV news show significant gains. *Newspaper Research Journal*, Special Issue on Media Studies of September 11, 24(1), 114–27.

Poindexter, P.M. & Heider, D. (2001). Non-Users of Internet News: Who are they and why do they avoid TV news and newspaper websites? Paper presented at the Annual Association for Education in Journalism and Mass Communications Conference, Radio-Television Journalism Division, Washington D.C.

Poindexter-Wilson, P. (1989, March). Atypical non-readers are good targets in efforts to boost daily circulation. *Presstime*, 28. Retrieved from LexisNexis database.

Schweitzer, J.C. (1974). The newspaper and its community: An analysis of nonreadership. Unpublished doctoral dissertation, University of North Carolina at Chapel Hill.

Wanta, W., Hu, Y., & Wu, Y. (1993). Nonreaders, single readers and multiple newspaper readers: A discriminant analysis. Paper presented at the Annual Association for Education in Journalism and Mass Communications Conference, Newspaper Division, Kansas City.

Westley, B.H. & Werner, J.S. (1964). A profile of the daily newspaper non-reader. *Journalism Quarterly*, 41, 45–50, 156.

Women Using Newspapers to Line Canary Cage. (2005, May 9). *WonderBranding: Marketing to Women*. Retrieved March 24, 2006 from http://michelemiller.blogs.com/marketing_to_women/2005/05/colleague_jan_h.html.

Chapter 4

IM, Downloading, *Facebook*, and Teen Magazines

Gateways or Barriers to News?

Paula Poindexter

When the first baby boomers were born in 1946, one year after the end of World War II, it is doubtful that anyone could have predicted this generation's impact with any degree of accuracy. Baby boomers, the first generation to grow up with television, surpassed previous generations in size, education, wealth, and power. As they came of age during the 1960s and 1970s, baby boomers took the Civil Rights and Women's movements to new levels. As James Brown's "Say It Loud—I'm Black and I'm Proud" (Wikipedia, 2006a) and the "feminist anthem" Helen Reddy's "I Am Woman," (Wikipedia, 2006b) played on different AM radio stations, baby boomer African Americans and women, although navigating different paths, broke through barriers in education, law, medicine, business, politics, media, and sports. During the next decade and a half, baby boomers also experimented with and invested in new computers, communications, and information technologies, transforming every aspect of society, from education and the economy, to science and medicine, to media and leisure time. The first wave of boomers who started turning 60 during the middle of the first decade of the twenty-first century gave birth to Generation X, the generation first associated with MTV; the second wave of boomers gave birth to the generation that started using computers during elementary school and the Internet during middle school. Called Millennials, Generation Y, the Digital Generation, and even the Instant Message Generation, this generation has surpassed baby boomers in size and diversity; only time will tell if this generation will surpass boomers in impact.

As Millennials navigated the teenage years and began maturing into adults, the newspaper industry should have been experiencing déjà vu. Reminiscent of an earlier era when Second Wave boomers found their way through the teenage years and into adulthood and First Wave boomers started turning 30, the newspaper industry had a readership problem that, if ignored, could have spiraled into a crisis. Boomers were not picking up the newspaper reading habit as their parents had. The readership problem persisted as Generation X, the children of First Wave boomers that MTV targeted when it was launched in 1981, also did not pick up the newspaper habit (BBC News, 2001). As Millennials, the children of Second Wave boomers, also grow into adulthood, the question becomes will IM, downloading, social networking sites such as *Facebook* and *MySpace*, and teen magazines such as *Cosmogirl!* serve as gateways or barriers to news?

Lessons from Past Generations

When baby boomers were teenagers, the media landscape paled in comparison to the media landscape today. As boomers grew up, their media world consisted primarily of three fledgling television networks that produced programming for network-owned or affiliated TV stations in markets around the country, plus morning and afternoon newspapers, radio, magazines, comic books, books, and movies that could be watched at movie theaters. Baby boomers would have to wait until they started turning 30 before VCRs and the video rental industry would make watching rented movies at home a weekend pastime (Wikipedia, 2006c).

What happens to established media when a new medium is introduced? What, for example, happened to comic books, radio, and movies as television began to dominate in the homes of baby boomer teens? How were newspapers affected as MTV and other cable channels captured the attention of Generation X teens? Likewise, what happened to television as the Internet began to dominate the homes of Millennial teens? By extrapolating media consumption data from two benchmark twentieth-century media studies and various media studies conducted during the twenty-first century, an impressionistic snapshot of the media activity of teenagers representing three generations can be discerned. The value of examining media consumption activity of baby boomers (First Wave and Second Wave), Generation X, and Millennials during their teenage years is not limited to analyzing the past, the data displayed in Table 4.1 will also provide insight into the future. A careful inspection of Table 4.1 brings into focus the route that Millennials will likely take to get news once they complete their teenage years and mature into adults, that is, unless the print and broadcast news industries give Millennials a compelling reason to travel a different path.

Although demographers traditionally define baby boomers as the generation born during an 18-year period between 1946 and 1964, notice in Table 4.1 that we distinguished between baby boomers born between 1946 and 1956, which we designated First Wave, and boomers born between 1957 and 1964, which we called Second Wave. In 1946, when the first baby boomers were born, only 8,000 black and white television sets, representing 2 percent of households were in use (DeFleur & Ball-Rokeach, 1982, p. 96). After a sluggish start, caused by the interruption of the production and distribution of television sets during World War II, television penetration jumped to 24 percent in 1950 and by 1955, television penetration soared to 78 percent (ibid.). As First Wave baby boomers began experiencing their teenage years around the early 1960s, at least one television set was in every household (ibid., pp. 96, 97).

The rapid diffusion of television was responsible for a flurry of studies on television's impact, which were compiled in the book *Television in the Lives of Our Children* (Schramm *et al.*, 1961). Published in 1961, this seminal book addressed society's anxieties about this new entertainment medium that became the focal point of living rooms everywhere.

Second Wave boomers, unlike First Wave boomers, literally grew up with television. The children of First Wave boomers, who became known as Generation X, also grew up on television. In fact, when the children of First Wave boomers were born between 1965 and the early 1980s, television was not only a dominant presence in living rooms, it was the dominant communication medium in society. Except for, perhaps, the introduction of MTV in 1981, when Generation Xers began turning 16 years of age, the media environment that Generation X grew up in was similar to the media environment that Second Wave boomers experienced growing up. Although similarities existed in the media environments of Second Wave boomer teens and Generation X teens, the media environment of Millennial teens, born between 1983 and the end of the 1990s, could not have been more different than the two generations that came before them.

Table 4.1 shows that some media, such as radio, movies, magazines, books, comic books, and newspapers, have been present in the media landscape since the birth of each generation, and some media emerged as the generation matured. A glance across each generation of teens also reveals the changing role of traditional media. Movies and comic books, for example, were big for First Wave boomer teens but not very important for Second Wave boomer, Generation X, and Millennial teenagers. Although magazines were not as popular for Second Wave boomers, Generation X, and Millennial teens as they were for First Wave boomer teens, this print medium has always been a significant part of the media mix for teenagers. In fact, after a drop in popularity for Second Wave boomer teens and Generation X teens, magazines rebounded in popularity for Millennials. This rebound may be due to the launching of adult magazines' younger siblings such as *Cosmogirl!*, *Teen People*, and *Teen Vogue*. Of all the media available, radio is the only medium that has been popular for each generation of teens, regardless of growing up in the 1950s or the 1990s.

It is also clear from Table 4.1 that each generation experienced a sex gap in media consumption. A larger percentage of First Wave boomer girls than boys listened to radio and read books, and among Second Wave boomer, Generation X, and Millennial teens, a larger percentage of girls than boys read magazines. A divide between the sexes in newspaper reading, though, has not been consistent across generations. First Wave boomer and Generation X teenage girls were less likely than boys to read newspapers but for Second Wave boomer and Millennial teens, about the same percentage of girls and boys read newspapers. Even so, First Wave boomer boys surpassed girls with a different print medium, that is, comic books. Three-quarters of teenage boys read comic books while only three-fifths of girls read comic books.

How girls and boys rated the prestige of the different media may have been related to the medium's popularity, and in some cases the sex divide. Both girls and boys rated books most prestigious of all media, but more boys than girls rated newspapers as prestigious. Prestige ratings changed as First Wave boomer children matured. In the eighth grade, books were considered the most prestigious medium, followed by TV, radio, magazines, movies, and newspapers. In the twelfth grade, books were still considered most prestigious, but newspapers had moved up in prestige as the standing of radio and TV declined (Schramm *et al.*, 1961, pp. 52–3).

Although First Wave baby boomer teens rated magazines lower in prestige than newspapers, it is likely that girls and boys were rating different magazines because the type of magazine read appeared to be related to sex role socialization:

> As they grow older and learn their sex roles, boys tend to read more hobby, sports, and news magazines. Girls read more screen and confession magazines. A little later, when they become devotees of *Glamour*, *Mademoiselle*, and similar publications, they tend to read less in the pulps.
>
> (Schramm *et al.*, 1961, p. 247)

When comparing traditional media as a whole across generations, it is obvious from Table 4.1 that a smaller percentage of Millennial teenagers than First Wave boomer teens consumed traditional media but when compared to Second Wave boomer and Generation X teens, Millennial teen consumption of traditional media appeared to be on the upswing, especially for movie going and reading magazines and books.

It is interesting that when baby boomers are not viewed as a homogenous group and a differentiation is made between First Wave and Second Wave boomers, unexpected

Table 4.1 Media activities for three generations of teenagers: baby boomers (First Wave and Second Wave), Generation X, and Millennials (%)

Activities	First Wave baby boomer teens		Second Wave baby boomer teens		Generation X teens		Millennial teens	
	Girls	Boys	Girls	Boys	Girls	Boys	Girls	Boys
Traditional								
Radio	91	81	92	87	82	70	80	69
Movies	87	89	20	14	13	6	50	51
Magazines	86	88	46	32	39	32	73	58
Books	75	59	26	11	31	19	67	44
Comic books	61	75	4	3	8	18	—	—
Newspapers	48	62	60	61	40	47	53	54
New								
E-mail							93	84
Go to websites about movies, TV shows, music groups, or sports stars							88	81
Instant messaging							77	74
Get information about a school you might attend							61	53
Research for school							58	48
Look for news or information about politics and the presidential campaign							57	53
Play games online							50	64
Download music							45	57
Sample music clips							42	38
Access daily information (weather, horoscope)							41	22
Surf for hobbies or interests							38	43
Look for stuff on-line to buy							37	37
Health, dieting, fitness information							37	26
Look for information about a job							28	32
Look for information about a health topic that's hard to talk about							27	18
Read a blog							26	14
Visit online news site							21	20

Note: Although the ages and grades are not perfect matches with the birth years of each generation, they are close enough to provide an overall impression of the media consumption similarities for each generation. In 1960, First Wave baby boomers were in the tenth grade. In 1978, Second Wave baby boomers were aged 15 to 17, which would make them born between 1961 and 1963. Generation X was aged 12 to 14 in 1978, which would make them born between 1964 and 1966; Millennials were aged 15 to 17 in 2004–5.

The following media use operationalizations were extrapolated for First Wave baby boomers:

(1) Every day newspaper readership by tenth grade girls and boys (Schramm et al., 1961, p. 262).
(2) Median number of magazines read per month by tenth grade girls was 3.1; median number of magazines read per month by tenth grade boys was 4.7 (Schramm et al., 1961, p. 259).
(3) Listen to popular music on the radio (Schramm et al., 1961, p. 250).
(4) Attend movie with someone own age (Schramm et al., 1961, p. 255).
(5) Calculated percentage of children who read a book in past month from those that did not read a book; 25 percent of tenth grade girls read no book; 41 percent of tenth grade boys read no book (Schramm et al., 1961 p. 257).
(6) Comic book reading calculated using percentage not reading comics: 38.8 percent of girls read no comics; 24.7 percent of boys read no comics; 29.4 percent of boys read 9 or more comics per month; 17.2 percent of girls read 9 or more comics (Schramm et al., 1961, p. 262).

For Second Wave boomers and Generation X, every day or most day media use was compiled from Bogart (1981, p. 87). Radio listening for Millennials was extrapolated using proportion who listened to at least five minutes of radio the previous day (Roberts et al., 2005). For magazine use, teens were asked if they subscribed to a magazine (Roberts & Foehr, 2004, p. 101). The following data sources were used for Millennials: Lenhart et al. (2005); Consumer Insight: Shedding Light on Key Prospects: Targeting Teens (2005); Teen Content Creators and Consumers (2005).

similarities between Second Wave boomer teens and Generation X teens emerge. Unlike First Wave boomer teens, both Second Wave boomer teens and Generation X teens grew up on television, which may help explain why going to movies and reading magazines and books dropped for both girls and boys.

Although Generation X is associated with MTV, the cable music channel launched in 1981, it is unlikely that MTV had a large following of Generation X during their teenage years. By the time cable channels such as MTV, HBO, CNN, and ESPN, which offered entertainment, news, and sports programming, became popular reasons to subscribe to cable, Generation Xers had just about finished their teenage years and the oldest Xers were about to turn 30 years of age.

What happens when a fresh medium appears on the scene of a new generation? Although Table 4.1 should be interpreted cautiously because it displays statistics from different studies using different methodologies at different time periods, the data suggest that as new media are introduced, they may displace old media that had been favorites for previous generations, especially if new media are perceived as superior in prestige, convenience, accessibility, cost, gratification satisfaction, multi-tasking capability, and likeability. A glance down the far right column of Table 4.1 also suggests that when it comes to media, not only do Millennial teens differ substantially from past generations of teenagers, the future news consumption of this generation will likely be unlike anything we have observed in the past.

Even though network and cable television are not displayed in Table 4.1, it should be remembered that some network and cable channels target teenagers and teens respond. So in addition to the traditional media that First Wave boomer teens, Second Wave boomer teens, and Generation X teens experienced, Millennial teens have been courted by network television and cable channels such as FOX, MTV, BET, Nickelodeon, Comedy Central, and UPN and WB, which in 2006 merged to become the new cable channel CW.

Millennial teens have also been wooed by teen-targeted magazines such as *Seventeen*, which has been there for every generation of teens since it was first published in the 1940s, as well as a new breed of sassy magazines with familiar names (The Henry J. Kaiser Family Foundation, 2006, p. 1). *Teen People*, which debuted in 1998, was one of the first younger sibling magazines created exclusively for this new generation of teens. Although others followed, *Cosmogirl!* and *Teen Vogue* were among the few younger sibling magazine survivors in this crowded field. Although *Teen People* did not survive in its print form, it was given a reprieve in cyberspace when it switched to an online-only edition fourth quarter, 2006 (Seelye, 2006, p. C5). In addition to being targeted by TV networks, cable channels, and teen magazines, Millennial teens have had access to an astounding array of content and time-consuming activities on the Internet, making this on-demand, interactive medium a gargantuan force in their young lives.

Because Millennials are the only generation to experience the Internet as teenagers, a generational comparison cannot be made, but it is possible to compare the most popular medium for each generation of teens in order to put the popularity of Internet-driven activities in perspective. For example, according to Table 4.1, when compared to other Internet activities and traditional media, for Millennial teenagers, e-mail ranks first in popularity. Comparing across generations of teens, it can be seen that the only medium to rank close to the popularity of e-mail in the lives of Millennials was movies for First Wave boomers when almost nine out of ten girls and boys went to the movies. Going to websites about movies, TV shows, music groups, or sports stars, which ranks behind e-mail, is as popular for Millennials as magazines were for First Wave baby boomers when they were teens.

Although approximately three-quarters of Millennials "IM" or Instant Message, this real-time interactive Internet activity does not surpass the popularity that radio, movies, or magazines had for First Wave boomer teens. Furthermore, while Instant Messaging is wildly popular for Millennials, its popularity does not equal or surpass the popularity of radio for Second Wave boomer teens.

If the Internet activities listed down the far right column in Table 4.1 are sorted according to larger functions, it can be seen in Table 4.2 that teenagers are basically engaged in five categories of activities: communicating and networking, pursuing pastimes and hobbies, researching rites of passage information, doing school or job-related work, and getting informed. A larger percentage of Millennial teens, both girls and boys, use the Internet for communicating and networking than for any other activity. E-mail and IM are the cyberspace equivalents of talking on the phone and hanging out with friends, activities that occupied the time of previous generations of teens. *Facebook* and MySpace.com are examples of communicating and social networking innovations that inhabit the news media landscape and occupy the time and attention of Millennials (Arnold, 2006, pp. 1D, 4D).

The Internet is a popular place to pursue pastimes and hobbies. In three of the pastimes and hobbies, including playing games and downloading music, pursued online, boys were more likely than girls to use the Internet for this purpose. About the same percentage of girls and boys looked for stuff to buy on the Internet and girls were more likely than boys to pursue information about celebrities from the entertainment and sports worlds, and health, dieting, and fitness information. Using the Internet to do research for school is more popular for girls than boys and getting informed is the least popular of all Internet activities. Although almost twice as many girls than boys access weather and horoscopes, about the same percentage of Millennial girls and boys visited news websites.

Rites of passage, including a first kiss, passing a driver's license test, getting a first speeding ticket, taking the SAT, registering to vote, voting for the first time, applying for a first job, going to a first prom, applying to and selecting a college, are experienced by every generation of teenagers. In many cases, Millennial teens turned to the Internet to search for information that would make their passage flow smoothly. Generation X and First Wave and Second Wave boomer teens also experienced these rites of passage but they would have had to acquire information to help them through the passage in a different way. For three of the four rites of passage listed in Table 4.2, a larger percentage of girls than boys turned to the Internet. Looking for job information was the only rite of passage in which more boys than girls searched online.

Compared to newspapers, news websites have much less of a presence in the lives of Millennial teens. Furthermore, when the presence of newspapers in the lives of First Wave, Second Wave, and Generation X teenagers is compared to news websites for Millennial teens, news websites still fall short. Is this disparity good for the future of newspapers? Or does it simply mean that teens' greater involvement with newspapers is more a reflection of use of newspapers in the classroom while visiting news websites is something that a teen would likely do at home? Should producers of news websites take comfort in the statistic that one-fifth of teens online visited news websites or is that statistic worrisome knowing that with all of the activity on the Internet, visiting news websites is the least popular activity for teenagers? Although a case study cannot provide definitive answers to these important questions, taking a close-up look at media and the

Table 4.2 How Millennial teens are really spending their time on the Internet (%)

Activity	Girls	Boys
Communicating and networking		
E-mail	93	84
IM (Instant messaging)	77	74
Facebook*		
MySpace*		
Pursuing pastimes and hobbies		
Go to websites about movies, TV shows, music groups, or sports stars	88	81
Played games online	50	64
Download music	45	57
Sampled music clips	42	38
Surfed for hobbies or interests	38	43
Looked for stuff on-line to buy	37	37
Dieting, health, fitness information	37	26
Researching rites of passage information		
Get information about a school you might attend	61	53
Look for news or information about politics and the presidential campaign	57	53
Look for information about a job	28	32
Look for information about a health topic that's hard to talk about	27	18
Doing school or job related work		
Research for school	58	48
Getting informed		
Accessed daily information (weather, horoscope)	41	22
Read a blog	26	14
Visited online news site	21	20

Note: See Table 4.1 notes. *Although not asked about in this survey, social networking sites are popular among Millennials.

Internet in the lives of a Millennial teenage girl and boy may provide some insight into the factors that influence their present news consumption and factors that may determine whether as adults they will become news enthusiasts, news avoiders, or a news consumer that is some where in between.

A Case Study: Media and the Internet in the Life of a Millennial Girl and Boy

As the child of news enthusiasts who read two newspapers daily, a newsmagazine weekly, watch network, local, and cable news every day, listen to NPR's *All Things Considered* regularly, and even occasionally catch PBS's *Washington Week*, past research would predict that Alex,[1] a Millennial teenage girl, would grow up to become a news enthusiast like her parents. But do assumptions from an earlier period hold true in a media environment that is unlike anything from the past? By examining Internet activity logs and self-administered questionnaires of Alex and John, a Millennial teenage boy, it is possible to find some clues that may provide insight into the future news consumption of a generation that has unlimited online and offline media choices to pick from.

Although one is a girl and the other a boy, Alex and John were similar in many ways when they agreed to keep a log of their Internet activity. Both were seniors at one of the largest suburban high schools in the area. Both played on the high school tennis team and had USTA tennis rankings in the state. Both enrolled in Advanced Placement courses to receive college credit and both had summer jobs after graduation. In addition to providing childcare for a family with three young children and at one of the most family-friendly gyms in the area, Alex worked for a trendy girls' clothing store in the mall and John taught tennis to kids at one of many popular public tennis centers in the metropolitan area. Both attended large state universities, although Alex, recipient of a Millennium Scholarship, chose to go out of state to a university in the Midwest where she would major in psychology while John, a National Merit Scholar, chose the honors liberal arts major of an in-state university closer to home.

Table 4.3 displays Internet activity which Alex and John made note of in their logs. During the week that Alex and John kept logs, the primary activity for both teenagers was Instant Messaging or IM. In her log, Alex emphasized her multi-tasking tendencies; it was not unusual for her to IM, watch TV, study, and conduct research simultaneously. In his log, John emphasized reading online music reviews and downloading music.

Table 4.3 Log of Internet activity of a girl and boy

Days	Time logged on Internet	Time logged off Internet	Activities online	Read news online?
Day 1				
Alex	10:03 p.m.	11:43 p.m.	IM, Multi-tasking	No
John	4:32 p.m.	12:56 a.m.	IM, Downloading Check e-mail	Yes
Day 2				
Alex	8:30 p.m.	9:21 p.m.	IM, Research, Multi-tasking*	No
	10:04 p.m.	12:55 a.m.	Check e-mail	No
John	4:26 p.m.	1:10 a.m.	IM, Read reviews	Yes
Day 3				
Alex	11:38 p.m.	12:28 a.m.	IM, Study	No
John	11:23 a.m.	12:27 p.m.	IM, Read reviews	No
	7:01 p.m.	1:47 a.m.	IM, Read reviews	No
Day 4				
Alex	10:22 p.m.	1:07 a.m.	IM, Check e-mail	No
John	6:59 p.m.	2:01 a.m.	IM	No
Day 5				
Alex	10:13 p.m.	12:25 a.m.	IM	No
John	6:14 p.m.	12:04 a.m.	IM	Yes
Day 6				
Alex	9:47 p.m.	11:57 p.m.	IM, Multi-tasking**	No
John	4:11 pm.	10:17 p.m.	IM, Download	No
Day 7				
Alex	9:32 p.m.	11:02 a.m.	IM, Multi-tasking***	No
John	5:01 p.m.	1:37 a.m.	IM, Read reviews	Yes

Note: *Watch *Friends, Simpsons, King of the Hill*; **Watch *Simpsons, Seinfeld, King of the Hill*; ***Watch *Dateline, Fox News, Simpsons, Seinfeld*

News was notable by its presence in John's log and its absence in Alex's log. According to his log, John read news online four of the seven days that he kept the log. A look through Alex's log found no evidence of reading news online at any time during the seven-day period.

Influences on News Consumption

In addition to keeping a log for a week, Alex and John completed questionnaires that asked about their history with computers and the Internet, their interests, and their attitudes toward media. The first questionnaire was completed just before graduation; they completed the second questionnaire after the first year of college. According to their questionnaires, Alex and John started using the computer while in elementary school. John was 8 years old and Alex was 10. Both said they played games as their first activity on the computer. John was also introduced to the Internet by way of playing games while Alex's introduction to the Internet came by way of "looking up things for school." Both Alex and John were 11 years old when they first used the Internet.

Alex noted in her questionnaire that she spent three to five hours on the Internet daily; John said he spent four hours every day. When comparing their estimates of time spent on the Internet as indicated on the questionnaire with the actual log, it appears that Alex overestimated and John underestimated time spent on the Internet. Being logged on, though, does not necessarily mean active on the computer. Just as one can have the television on but not watch it, one can be logged on to the Internet but not be actively engaged.

According to their questionnaires for Year 1, both Alex and John were exposed to news at home and news at school. Alex said most teachers from elementary through high school regularly included news in her school work. John said on his questionnaire that some teachers regularly included news. Teachers who used news in school work, generally used newspapers, according to the questionnaires of both Alex and John. Table 4.4, which summarizes the news consumption of Alex and John for Year 1 and Year 2 shows similarities, differences, and even some changes for the Millennial teenagers.

Although IM was a popular Internet activity for both Alex and John, the Year 1 questionnaire that both teens filled out revealed how different they were when it came to news consumption. If it were not for the three or four days a week that she watched news on television during Year 1, Alex would be classified as a news avoider. John, on the other hand, would be classified as a news enthusiast. As Table 4.4 shows, during Year 1, John regularly read newspapers, watched news on television one or two days, and read news online even more often.

Table 4.4 Alex's and John's news media consumption

	Newspaper	TV news (local)	Cable news	Online news
Alex's use of news media				
Year 1	Never	3 or 4 days	Never	Never
Year 2	1 or 2 days	Never	Never	3 or 4 days
John's use of news media				
Year 1	Nearly daily	1 or 2 days	Never	3 or 4 days
Year 2	Nearly daily	1 or 2 days	3 or 4 days	Nearly daily

Even though Alex recalled observing both her mother and father regularly reading newspapers and watching news on television, her negative attitude toward newspapers played a role in her avoiding newspapers. When asked why she did not read newspapers in the Year 1 questionnaire, she responded "do not like the feel; boring."

A glance at Year 2 in Table 4.4 shows growth and change in news consumption for both teenagers. The Year 2 questionnaire, in which John revealed that he increased his sources of news, provides more evidence that John is a news enthusiast. He read the newspaper and news online almost daily. He read news on the Internet in his dorm room, the library, and cybercafés. In addition to continuing to watch television news one or two days a week, John added cable news to his news consumption menu. Although Alex revealed in her Year 2 questionnaire that she no longer watched news on television, she did indicate that she had adopted two new sources of news that were not mentioned in the Year 1 questionnaire. In her Year 2 questionnaire, Alex said she read newspapers one or two days a week and she read news online even more frequently.

Millennial Girl Adopts Online News

In one year, Alex evolved from being a borderline news avoider to a newspaper and Internet news adopter with a positive attitude toward news on the Internet. To grasp this conversion, it is first necessary to understand Alex's experiences with news as described in the Year 2 questionnaire.

Although news accidentals are more likely to be female than male, Alex made it clear that she was not a news accidental. Given a choice between searching for news while on the Internet or reading news while doing something else, Alex, who reported that she read online news in her dorm room and in the library, said she purposely searched for news. When asked why she read news on the Internet, Alex emphasized the multi-tasking capability of reading news online rather than the content of news: "Reading news on the Internet is convenient because you can do other activities on the computer as well."

Asked to indicate which type of news and information she read on the Internet, Alex said she often read national news and sometimes read international news and news from her hometown. It is likely that Alex's frequent reading of national news on the Internet was related to the upcoming presidential election. In her Year 1 questionnaire, she said: "I'm excited about voting in my first election." Other types of news that Alex often read on the Internet included: weather, sports, entertainment, fashion, and health and fitness. Alex said she sometimes read science and medicine but never read local, technology, or business news.

Not only had Alex evolved into more of a news consumer, but for the first time, the Internet had been transformed into a news medium for her. When asked what she most used the Internet for during her first year of college, Alex said: "keeping in touch with friends, research for class and or papers, reading about news and current events." Alex said that she now had a greater interest in news, which is why for her, the Internet had evolved from a medium for communicating and networking and researching for school to a medium that she could turn to in order to get informed of the latest news.

While Alex was adopting newspapers and the Internet as sources of news, John expanded his sources to include the cable news channel MSNBC, which he used to keep up with the presidential election because he said: "they covered many possible angles to every story." But John did not limit himself to traditional news, he also

readers' lives more directly, or incorporating that aspect into more stories in general" would make a difference. "I think a lot of young adults are primarily concerned with themselves, and understandably since it is a critical point in our lives, so in many ways news that doesn't hit too close to home is seen as irrelevant."

Testing the Case Study against the News Consumption Model

The News Consumption model, displayed in Chapter 1's Figure 1.2, described the factors and forces that contribute to the ultimate news consumption decision. Individual differences, socialization, normative beliefs, motivations, and attitudes play critical roles in the decision to consume news or not. When these factors and forces are examined in the teenage lives of Alex and John, one would expect that both Alex and John would be news enthusiasts. Both have educated parents who are professionals; both teens grew up with newspapers at home and at school; and both teens observed their parents consuming news. So why is only one of the Millennial teens—the boy—a news enthusiast? Why has the teenage girl who discussed news a lot with her family during the summer after her first year of college embraced the Internet, magazines, and books but not newspapers? Is Alex just a late bloomer or is this lack of enthusiasm for newspapers permanent? The answer, which has implications for the news consumption divide between women and men, can likely be found in the attitude component of the news consumption model introduced earlier.

As discussed in detail in Chapter 2, attitudes are learned and stand for a favorable or unfavorable judgment of a news-centered object, which is comprised of at least 12 dimensions that can be evaluated. The dimensions that are most important to consumers are the focus of the favorable and unfavorable evaluations. The words Alex used to describe news and different news media reflect her evaluation of dimensions most important to her. Alex used the word "biased" to describe news in general and television news in particular. She described newspapers in terms of their texture and size, explicitly stating that newspapers were "too large and bulky." "Easy" and "fast" were used to describe news on the Internet.

Alex's evaluations suggest that some dimensions are more salient for certain media. Newspapers were evaluated on the dimensions of content and feel; Internet news was evaluated on the dimensions of access and multi-tasking capability. News as a whole and television news in particular were also evaluated on the content dimension.

Regardless of medium, content was the most important dimension evaluated by John. News in general was important and vital, newspapers were concise and unbiased, television news was loud and polarizing, and Internet news was expansive. Although one certainly cannot draw conclusions from a case study with a teenage girl and boy, the difference in dimensions evaluated by Alex and John cannot be ignored. The consistency of content as a salient dimension for John, compared to the range of dimensions that varied by medium for Alex, suggests that if newspapers are to understand and close the sex divide in news consumption, attention has to be given to more dimensions than content.

By all accounts, Alex, who grew up with news all around her, should be a news enthusiast like her parents and John, but she is not. Is Alex an anomaly or is she typical of Millennial teenage girls? When the Internet transformed the media landscape, it not only made the media and technology experience for Millennial teens unlike the media experience of previous generations of teenagers, it also made past assumptions about news consumption by teenagers obsolete. Never before have teenagers had such an array of choices and never before have media been evaluated by their multi-tasking capability. Only by fully understanding Millennial teenage girls and boys in the context of the factors and forces that influence news consumption, as well as the unprecedented role of the Internet in their lives, will it be possible to identify fresh assumptions that can be used for developing effective offensive and defensive strategies, that if properly executed, will both cultivate future news enthusiasts and narrow the sex divide in news consumption as Millennial teens grow into adulthood.

Note

1   Alex, a teenage girl, was selected to keep a log on her Internet activities and answer questions about her news media use because she is a member of the Millennial Generation who grew up in a home in which both parents read two newspapers every day. Alex was also selected because, as the daughter of the first editor, her Internet activities and news media use could be observed daily. The observation served as a validity check on the log and questionnaire that Alex completed. Both Alex and John, the Millennial Generation teenage boy whose activities on the Internet and news media use and attitudes were compared with Alex's, received modest cash incentives for keeping the Internet activity logs and completing the self-administered questionnaires. Before the teenagers filled out the first questionnaire, written permission was obtained from John's mother. For a postscript on their news consumption in their senior year in college, see Chapter 18, notes.

References

Arnold, T.K. (2006, August 1). Niche competitors crowd into MySpace: Teens grow into other social sites. *USA Today*, pp. 1D, 4D.

BBC News. (2001, July 31). MTV's irresistible rise. Retrieved August 26, 2006 from http://news.bbc.co.uk/1/hi/entertainment/music/1456093.stm.

Bogart, L. (1981). *Press and Public: Who reads what, when, where, and why in American newspapers*. Hillsdale: Lawrence Erlbaum Associates.

Consumer Insight: Shedding light on key prospects: Targeting teens. (2005, October). NAA Business Analysis & Research Department. *Newspaper Association of America*. Retrieved February 25, 2006 from www.naa.org/marketscope/TargetingTeensBrief.pdf.

DeFleur, M.L. & Ball-Rokeach, S.J. (1982). *Theories of Mass Communication*. New York: Longman.

The Henry J. Kaiser Family Foundation. (2004). Tweens, teens, and magazines. Retrieved February 22, 2006 from www.kff.org/entmedia/upload/Tweens-Teens-and-Magazines-Fact-Sheet.pdf.

Lenhart, A.L., Madden, M., & Hitlin, P. (2005, July 27). Teens and technology: Youth are leading to a fully wired and mobile nation. *The Pew Internet and American Life Project*. Retrieved February 24, 2006 from www.pewinternet.org/pdfs/PIP_Teens_Tech_July2005web.pdf.

Roberts, D.F. & Foehr, U.G. (2004). *Kids and Media in America*. Cambridge: Cambridge University Press. Retrieved February 26, 2006 from www.netlibrary.com.content.lib.utexas.edu:2048/Reader/.

Roberts, D.F., Foehr, U.G., & Rideout, V. (2005, March). *Generation M: Media in the lives of 8–18 year olds*. Retrieved February 26, 2006 from www.kff.org/entmedia/upload/Generation-M-Media-in-the-Lives-of-8–18-Year-olds-Report.pdf#search=%22Generation%20M%3A%20Media%20in%20the%20Lives%20of%208–18%20Year%20Olds%2C%20Kaiser%20Family%20Foundation%20p.%2028%20www.kff.org%22.

Schramm, W., Lyle, J., & Parker, E.B. (1961). *Television in the Lives of our Children*. Stanford: Stanford University Press.

Seeyle, K. (2006, July 26). People magazine closes, but website will continue. *The New York Times*, p. C5.

Teen Content Creators and Consumers. (2005, November 2). *The Pew Internet and American Life Project*. Retrieved February 26, 2006 from www.pewinternet.org/pdfs/PIP_Teens_Content_Creation.pdf.

Wikipedia. (2006a). Say it loud—I'm black and I'm proud. Retrieved August 26, 2006 from http://en.wikipedia.org/wiki/Say_It_Loud_-_I'm_Black_and_I'm_Proud.

Wikipedia. (2006b). I am woman. Retrieved August 26, 2006 from http://en.wikipedia.org/wiki/Helen_Reddy.

Wikipedia. (2006c). Video cassette recorder. Retrieved August 26, 2006 from http://en.wikipedia.org/wiki/Videocassette_recorder.

Part II

Women in the News;
Women in the Newsroom

Chapter 5

Finding Women in the Newsroom and in the News

Paula Poindexter

Savvy people in the news business know that the masthead—not the front page—is the most influential section of a newspaper. Usually displayed on the editorial page, the masthead lists the names and positions of the powerful people who run a newspaper. Historically, women have been excluded from these power positions and that exclusion, according to one woman who dared publicly admonish her newspaper's most senior executives, stood in the way of greatness.

The respectful but firm rebuke happened in 1990 at the *Los Angeles Times* during the quarterly meeting of *Los Angeles Times* executives and middle managers. It was two years after *A Place in the News: From the Women's Pages to the Front Page* chronicled the slow-moving progress of women in newspapers. Narda Zacchino, then editor of the Orange County Edition of the *Los Angeles Times*, stood up in the elegant Harry Chandler Auditorium and proclaimed that the *Los Angeles Times*, which was widely considered one of the three best papers in the country, could never be a truly great paper until women and minorities were appointed to positions at the very highest levels.[1]

Although her title sounded impressive, the editor of *The Times*' Orange County edition was not listed on the masthead with other senior executives who established the editorial direction of the newspaper, influenced marketing, promotion, and circulation strategies, decided who got hired and promoted, and most importantly, signed off on the budget and allocated resources. In fact, on the day that Narda Zacchino's statement startled some and inspired others, only one woman and no minorities were listed on the masthead of the *Los Angeles Times*. The woman's name was Jean Sharley Taylor and, as associate editor, she reigned over "View," the lifestyle section, the Sunday magazine, which had been transformed from *Home* to a more gender neutral *Los Angeles Times Sunday Magazine*, *Calendar*, which covered arts and entertainment, the book review section, and the food, travel, and real estate sections. The associate editor's domain included the feature sections of the newspaper. Commonly called soft news, some journalists considered soft news less serious, less important, second tier, and, for some, even second rate.

In 1988, a quarter century after Betty Friedan's *The Feminine Mystique* inspired a new generation of women to demand equal opportunities in professional schools, the workplace, sports, law, and in every aspect of American society, the author of *A Place in the News* explained why it was important that the best newspapers appointed women to the highest levels of management: "The dearth of women in top jobs is an industry-wide condition. It is especially damaging at the nation's biggest papers, the ones that could provide leadership because they are on virtually everyone's list of the tops in the business" (Mills, 1988, p. 275).

How well are women doing today at the top of the news business? A newspaper's masthead, which includes positions at the most senior levels of the newspaper, and the organizational chart, which also includes mid-level editorial and management positions, can offer clues. Other hints as to how well women are doing can be found in what stories get published on the front page, the bylines or names of authors, front page and lead stories, topics covered, how stories are framed, official and expert sources consulted to report stories, who gets picked for prestige assignments, whether or not initiatives are implemented to address issues of concern to women within the newsroom, and the development and implementation of strategies for closing the newspaper readership divide that has emerged between women and men.

Deciding what news gets published or broadcast is one of the most important and powerful positions in a news organization. In 1950, "Mr."—not "Ms."—"Gates" came to symbolize who determines what gets published in a newspaper. "Mr. Gates" was the name given to the news wire editor, who was studied in depth to understand the reasons for selecting and rejecting news stories. This famous case study was the first systematic attempt to observe the decision-making process of an editor or gatekeeper in the real world of a newsroom (White, 1950). Although the subject of the study was one wire service editor, the reality of a newsroom is that there are many gatekeepers, beginning with the reporter, followed by section editors, the managing editor, and leading to the top editor, the ultimate decision-maker who determines if a story will get published and how prominently it will be displayed. Similarly, photographers and photo editors serve as gatekeepers, deciding pictures that are taken and published.

By 1991, when women held more editorial positions, the 1950 gatekeeping case study was replicated with one primary difference. "Mr. Gates" was replaced by "Ms. Gates." The wire editor was a woman. A comparison of wire service stories selected by Mr. Gates in the 1950 study and Ms. Gates 41 years later revealed similar news judgments in the selection of news (Bleske, 1991). In both cases, the top wire stories selected were human interest. In 1950, the next most selected stories were national politics and international politics, while in 1991, not too long after the start of the Persian Gulf War, stories about international politics were selected most followed by national politics (ibid.).

When Ms. Gates was asked specifically: "Do you believe that your gender plays any role in your selection of news stories," Ms. Gates responded "not usually"(Bleske, 1991, p. 95). However, Ms. Gates acknowledged "she is more likely to run a story about women instead of men when last-minute extra space opens in the newspaper" (ibid.). The author of the study concluded that "the male domination of the content selected by Ms. Gates suggests that prejudice against women cannot be overcome just by assuring that women assume leadership roles in newsrooms" (ibid., p. 96). That may be the case because the keepers of the gates are not influenced by one single factor, such as one's sex; countless interlocking forces have some bearing on which stories get reported, who reports them, the sources and framing of the story, and ultimately the story's prominence when it is published. Journalism training, supervisors, professional norms and routines, newsroom culture, and unconscious gender assumptions are some of the most influential factors and forces pressuring the keepers of the gate.

Influence of Journalism Training

Journalism training, according to "The American journalist in the twenty-first century" study is the "greatest influence" on what journalists consider newsworthy (Weaver *et al.*, 2003). In fact, almost four-fifths (79 percent) of the journalists who participated in the national survey conducted by Indiana University journalism professors said journalism training is one of the most influential factors in their news judgment (ibid., p. 11).

Even though journalism training is often thought of as formal education in a classroom, the opportunities for journalism training are wide-ranging. Journalism training takes place during internships, while working on college newspapers, while talking to a journalism professor after class or during office hours, on the job, and through training seminars offered by individual newspapers and TV stations, professional and journalism education associations, and training institutes such as Poynter. "Nearly two-thirds of the journalists surveyed in 'The American journalist in the twenty-first century' study said they have had additional training since becoming a journalist" (ibid., p. 11).

Influence of Supervisors

After journalism training, supervisors had the biggest influence on news judgment, according to the national survey of journalists. When asked to name influences on perceptions of newsworthiness, 56 percent of the journalists participating in "The American journalist in the twenty-first century" study said supervisors. According to a 1955 benchmark study in which 72 newsroom staffers were interviewed, supervisors played an important role in socializing newcomers to the newsroom to ensure that policy is followed (Breed, 1955). Much of the socialization that takes place is indirect because of the potential conflict between newspaper policies and journalistic norms. Reporters, therefore, often learn newspaper polices by reading the newspaper they work for and observing their superiors. If, for example, breakthrough health stories that primarily concern men are prominently displayed on the front page but groundbreaking health stories that primarily involve women are buried inside, reporters quickly learn the preferences of their superiors. This method of socialization becomes "a process of social control, in which deviations are punished (usually gently) by reprimand, cutting one's story, the withholding of friendly comment by an executive, etc" (ibid., p. 332).

Outfoxing Newsroom Policy

Every reporter on staff does not obey newspaper policy that dictates what is newsworthy; reporters with "star" status can ignore newsroom policy and their stories will pass through the gate, receiving star treatment, prominently displayed on the front page (Breed, 1955). According to one star reporter who worked for a major newspaper before starting graduate studies in journalism, star status has certain privileges and one of those privileges is to report stories about previously ignored topics.

One measure of star status of reporters, according to a sociologist who studied newsroom dynamics, is the "star" status of sources: "The higher the status of sources and the greater the scope of their positions, the higher the status of the reporters" (Tuchman, 1978, p. 69). According to her newsroom observations: "'Big stories' go to the high-status reporters, even if that means breaching current specialties" (ibid., p. 70).

Another measure of star status is the beat or assignment. Foreign correspondents, White House correspondents, Washington bureau chiefs, to name a few, have star status. For example, when one Washington bureau chief visited the home office, he was treated like a rock star. Even the advertising executives would invite him to share behind-the-news information that only a bureau chief would be privy to about the Washington elite. The Washington bureau chief also had the opportunity to lunch in the Picasso Room, the Steinberg Room, or the Tamayo Room, one of three private dining rooms named after the original artwork that hung on the walls.

Professional Values, Norms, and Routines

First and foremost, the foundation of professional journalism values in the United States is rooted in the First Amendment, the first of ten amendments to the US Constitution. Known as the Bill of Rights, the first ten amendments "went into effect on December. 15, 1791, when the state of Virginia ratified it" ("First Amendment Center," 2006):

> Congress shall make no law respecting an establishment of religion, or prohibiting the free exercise thereof; or abridging the freedom of speech, or of the press; or the right of the people peaceably to assemble, and to petition the Government for a redress of grievances.
>
> (The First Amendment to the US Constitution, 1791)

In addition to The First Amendment, "objectivity became codified as the great law of journalism," according to journalism historian and author of *Just the Facts*, David Mindich (Mindich, 1998, p. 114):

> The "objective" ethic that emerged in the last part of the nineteenth century paralleled a rising sense of journalism as a profession. Before the Civil War there were no professional societies, college programs, or textbooks for journalists in the United States. [. . .] American journalists thought of themselves as professionals as early as 1876, when the Missouri Press Association was formed, complete with its own code of ethics.
>
> (Ibid., p. 115)

More than 50 years later, in 1922, the first meeting of the American Society of Newspaper Editors (ASNE) was held and a code of ethics called "Canons of Journalism" was adopted (Branson, 2004). The code emphasized responsibility; freedom of the press; independence; sincerity; truthfulness; accuracy; impartiality; fair play; and decency. In 1975, the Canons were replaced with ASNE's "Statement of Principles" (ASNE, 2002). Ethics codes with similar sentiments have also been adopted by the Society of Professional Journalists and other professional journalism groups.

Journalistic routines have also influenced gatekeepers. Routines involved in publishing a new newspaper every day, producing a fresh newscast, or updating cable news or a news website are "ongoing activities" designed to ensure there will be a continuous supply of new news since "news is a depleteable consumer product that must be made fresh daily" (Tuchman, 1978, p. 31). Routines, which make it possible to both plan for scheduled newsworthy events and manage the flow of news about unexpected events, also put pressure on the keepers of the gate. Although routines have been found to be more influential than individual factors in what became news, the film *All the President's Men*, which depicted how *Washington Post* reporters Bob Woodward and Carl Bernstein investigated the Watergate scandal that led to President Richard Nixon's resignation in 1974, suggests that it is the editors sitting in the daily editorial news conference—not the routines—that have the most influence on what passes through the gate. As the ultimate gatekeepers, these editors determine both what is newsworthy and what is worthy of being on the front page. Influences on what becomes news are not limited to routines, individuals, or editors (Shoemaker & Reese, 1996). Furthermore, some influences in the newsroom are so entrenched, that gatekeepers are oblivious to their impact on what is reported as news.

Newsroom Culture

If culture is defined as values, assumptions, understandings, and norms of an organization that members share and pass on to new members (Daft, 2005, p. 557), newsroom culture would be the values, assumptions, understandings, and norms shared by journalists and passed on to new journalists. Experts on organizations stress there are three levels of culture: visible, invisible, and embedded (ibid.). The visible level of culture includes observable things such as "manner of dress, patterns of behavior, physical symbols, organizational ceremonies, and office layout" (ibid., pp. 557–8); the invisible level, which is not observable, includes "expressed values and beliefs" (ibid., p. 558); the embedded level includes values, beliefs, and assumptions that are so entrenched that "organization members take them for granted and often are not even aware of the assumptions that guide their behavior, language, and patterns of social interaction" (ibid.). In fact, because assumptions about gender are often unconscious and entrenched, gatekeepers are unaware how much their decisions may be influenced by them.

If women hold the top positions on the newsroom's organizational chart, the visible level of newsroom culture can be transformed, at least according to the results of one ethnographic study. In interviews conducted with journalists at the *Sarasota Herald Tribune* in Florida, this study found the following attributes associated with the female-led newsroom: "family-friendly policies, an atmosphere of openness and transparency in decision making, a consensus-building managerial style, and clear communication between management and employees" (Everbach, 2006, p. 483). Although gender discrimination in beat assignments was eliminated in this female-led newsroom, new gender, race, and ethnicity issues emerged. A former managing editor, who was a woman, observed that "the female-led newsroom discouraged traditional, tough male journalists from applying for jobs," (ibid., p. 486) and although the circulation area had become more diverse, racial and ethnic diversity declined in the newsroom (Everbach, 2006).

Employment of Women in Newspapers

In addition to a newspaper's masthead and organizational chart, evidence of how well women are doing in the newsroom can be found in ASNE employment statistics. By 2006 women represented 37.7 percent of newsroom personnel, barely a change from the 2005 percentage of 37.5 percent. Similarly, the percentage of minority women in the newsroom scarcely increased: 17.55 percent vs. 17.2 percent (ASNE, 2006).

When analyzed by job category, women were more likely to be copy/layout editors than supervisors. According to 2006 ASNE statistics, women represented 35.5 percent of supervisors, 41.5 percent of copy/layout editors, 39.7 percent reporters, and 27.4 percent of photographers (ASNE, 2006b). A closer look at the statistics suggests women may have stalled in their effort to penetrate the glass ceiling. In 1999, 33.8 percent of women were supervisors but seven years later, the percent of women holding supervisory positions had increased a miniscule 1.7 percent (ibid.).

Because newspapers fill out the annual employment census questionnaire, the positions that get counted in the supervisor category can vary somewhat across newspapers. Even so, supervisor is a broad category that can include editor, managing editor, assistant managing editor, assistant city editor, or even copy desk supervisor. Plus the broad category of supervisor conceals the fact that women hold only 26 percent of the top editorial positions (editor/executive editor/sr vp/vp news) in newspapers, according to statistics compiled by Northwestern University's Media Management Center (Arnold & Nesbitt, 2006, p. 28). (See Table 5.1.)

Women Working in Television News

The announcement that long-time *Today Show* co-host Katie Couric would become the first woman ever to be the sole anchor of a network television news program once again focused attention on the advancement of women in broadcast news. Historically, the most prestigious position in broadcast journalism, the network news anchor chair, has always been occupied by men. Although there have been three ultimately unsuccessful efforts to pair a woman with a man, a woman had never been the sole occupant of an anchor chair until Katie Couric anchored the CBS Evening News on Tuesday, September 5, 2006. Not only is Couric anchoring the network news, she is also managing editor, a position also never before held by a woman.

Since local television news started pairing women with men in the 1970s, the local television news scene has been perceived as woman friendly. But does equality on the local TV news screen translate into equality behind the screen? At 40 percent of the television news workforce, women may have reached a plateau. According to Bob Papper, who conducts the RTNDA/Ball State University Annual Survey which tracks employment statistics in the broadcast news industry: "Overall, there has been relatively little change in the percentage of women in TV news in quite a few years" (B. Papper, personal communication, July 21, 2006).

Table 5.1 Percentage by title in executive tally in 2003, 2006 (%)

Job titles	2003		2006	
	Female	Male	Female	Male
President/Publisher/CEO	18	82	18	82
Asst/Assoc Pub	83	17	80	20
Executive VP/GM	16	84	10	90
CFO/Controller/VP Finance	20	80	23	77
Personnel/Sr VP/VP/Dir HR	63	37	67	33
Sr VP/VP/Dir Legal Counsel	43	57	38	63
Sr VP/VP/Dir Comm Affairs	73	27	78	22
Sr VP/VP/Dir Advertising	31	69	34	66
Sr VP/VP/Dir Marketing	47	53	54	46
Sr VP/VP/Dir Circ	12	88	8	92
Editor/Exec Editor/Sr VP/VP News	22	78	26	74
CIO/Sr VP/VP/Dir IT	18	82	23	77
Sr VP/VP/Dir Prod	7	93	14	86
Managing Editors	40	60	39	61
Totals	100	100	100	100
Female and male	27	73	29	71

Note: Arnold & Nesbitt (2006, p. 28). Used with permission from Mary Arnold, Ph.D. and Mary Nesbitt, Media Management Center, Northwestern University.

Table 5.2 shows in some ways women are still "window dressing on the set." The final gatekeeper, that is, the news director, is almost four times more likely to be a man than a woman.

The next most prestigious position in broadcast news after the network news anchor is the network correspondent. An analysis of 20 years of Vanderbilt Television News Index and Abstracts from 1983 to 2002 found that although over the 20-year period, the gap between the number of female and male correspondents narrowed, "the gap between the long-term tenure of men and women never narrowed" (Foote & Price, 2005, p. 8). An examination of 20 years of network news programs found "men averaged 8.09 years reporting for the evening news while women averaged 5.21" (ibid.). Furthermore, of the 80 correspondents who averaged ꞏꞏꞏꞏ the air at least once a week, 71 percent were male (ibid.).

Finding Women in Online Journalism

Did the promise of opportunities for women at the helm of online news websites turn out to be wishful thinking? As the "American journalist in the twenty-first century" study, "the percentage of online women journalists is almost equal to the percentage working for ... ...)" (Weaver et al., 2007, p. 214). Furthermore, after a deca... ... ...men are few at the most senior editorial levels at the news websites ... receive the highest traffic:

> Although the new media promised to revolutionize both the news industry and in many ways, the newsroom itself, fewer women than ever before appear to serve as executive editors or editors-in-chief of the top online news sites, and only a handful of women comprise their top-level editorial teams as senior projects editors or managing editors.
>
> (Thiel, 2005, p. 1)

Table 5.2 2005 TV positions by gender (%)

Title	Male	Female
News Director	78.7	21.3
Assistant News Director	68.3	31.7
Managing Editor	72.5	27.5
Executive Producer	45.1	54.9
News Anchor	42.8	57.2
Weathercaster	79.0	21.0
Sports Anchor	92.8	7.2
News Reporter	42.2	57.8
Sports Reporter	89.5	10.5
Assignment Editor	53.6	46.4
News Producer	34.1	65.9
News Writer	44.4	55.6
News Assistant	33.7	66.3
Photographer	93.4	6.6
Tape Editor	68.0	32.0
Graphics Specialist	58.4	41.6
Internet Specialist	61.1	38.9

Used with permission from RTNDA/Ball State University Annual Survey.

For the top news websites, USAToday.com, NYTimes.com, MSNBC, and CNN.com, "none of the executive editors or editors-in-chief of these news sites are women, and only a handful of women comprise their top-level editorial teams as senior projects editors or managing editors" (Thiel, 2005, p. 2).

"Gendering" of News Topics

After a journalism professor was invited by the local newspaper to give a brown bag talk about women and news, she decided to content analyze the front page of the newspaper and compare it with the front page of *The New York Times* to have some recent data on the presence of women on the newspaper's front page. Although the journalism professor only analyzed the most recent week of front pages, she thought the analysis would be a good place to start the brown bag conversation about news coverage of women. This was not the first time the journalism professor had done this exercise so she was not surprised at the results, which found women were mostly absent from front-page stories and bylines in both the local newspaper and *The New York Times*. What did surprise the journalism professor was the fact that the senior female editor in the room disputed the journalism professor's definition of women's news as well as the results of her week-long content analysis. Because the editor's definition of women's news included stories about education and the economy, she disagreed that the front page was devoid of women's news.

What is women's news? Is it news about women or is it news of interest to women? If it is news of interest to women, what makes a story appealing to women? Is it the topic or are there other dimensions that make a story engaging to women? Although historically, women are more likely than men to read local news and fashion and men are more likely to read sports and business, these topics and most topics covered in the news are not inherently female or male. Even so, the principal subject of the story, the section of the newspaper in which the story runs, the type and sex of sources used to report the story, the framing of the story, the newsroom traditions associated with the story topic, and even the labeling of the story as hard or soft can assign a gender to the story, which may impact the story's newsworthiness. In fact, one study of female and male gatekeepers found a story's newsworthiness diminishes when the principal news subject is a woman (Whitlow, 1977).

Is second-tier newsworthiness the reason women were barely represented in network evening news coverage? According to a year-long analysis of all three network news programs—NBC, *ABC*, *CBS*—female protagonists in the news averaged 14 percent compared to males who averaged 86 percent (Media Tenor, 2003, p. 29). Of the top ten females included in network news, one was an adviser to the President (Condoleeza Rice), four were senators (Hillary Clinton, Dianne Feinstein, Barbara Boxer, Susan Collins), one was the First Lady (Laura Bush), one was a queen (Queen Elizabeth), two were cabinet heads (Gale Norton and Christine Whitman), and one was a talk show host (Oprah Winfrey). Secretary of State Condoleeza Rice, who was National Security Adviser when the study was conducted, appeared on the news the most at 45 times. Senator Hillary Rodham Clinton had 27 appearances and First Lady Laura Bush followed with 20. The picture was worse when female protagonists were analyzed in connection with issues. "In the context of the top issues, foreign affairs, out of 4,234 appearances of individuals, only 208 were women. Similarly, out of 1,845 individual appearances in the context of political issues, women appeared only 115 times" (ibid., pp. 29–30).

Overall the analysis of network news from January to December 2002, found that in the "context of the 'big issues,'" "women were generally not a factor" but women could be found in network news stories about crime, health, society, general interest, and the environment (Media Tenor, 2003, p. 30). And when women were included in network news coverage, they were "more likely to be a victim of crime, an educator, a health care professional, or a mother" (ibid.).

Women as Sources for News

Who gets cited more often as a news source—women or men? Studies that have addressed this topic have usually focused on one medium at a time and found that women are less likely to be used as a source for a news story (Zoch & Turk, 1998). Does that finding hold across news medium and news story type? The most comprehensive look to date at the sex of sources of news stories found women lagged behind men as sources of news across every news medium—newspapers, television, cable news, online news—and every type of news story except lifestyle. Defining a source as "anyone providing information to the report, be it through a direct quotation, indirect quotation, or as the person to whom data or other information is attributed," the Project for Excellence in Journalism study found only 33 percent of news stories contained one female source but 76 percent of the same stories contained one male source ("Project for Excellence in Journalism," 2005). When stories were analyzed for two or more sources, it was harder to find women sources. Only 14 percent of news stories cited two or more female sources but 55 percent of the stories included two or more male sources (ibid.).

Although newspaper stories contained a higher percentage of female sources than online news, network evening and morning news, the *NewsHour* on PBS and cable news, when all news outlets were compared, men still dominated as sources. (See Table 5.3.)

Whether a story published in the newspaper was staff written or wire copy also mattered when analyzing news sources. "Staff-written stories were about twice as likely as wire service stories to contain a female source (47% vs. 25%)," according to the analysis of stories published in the newspaper (Project for Excellence in Journalism, 2005, p. 6). An overall comparison found 47 percent of staff-written stories had one or more female sources compared to 91 percent of staff-written stories that had at least one male source. For wire stories, 25 percent cited at least one female source compared to 87 percent that contained at least one male source (ibid.).

Inclusion of women as sources was also related to the size of the newspaper and the section of the newspaper. Forty-six percent of stories published in large newspapers contained at least one female source but only 33 percent of stories published in small newspapers contained at least one female source ("Project for Excellence," 2005,

Table 5.3 Female versus male sources, percent of all stories (%)

	Newspapers	Online	Network Evening	PBS NewsHour	Network Morning	Cable
Female: 1+	41	36	27	17	34	19
Male: 1+	88	89	63	59	55	53

Note. Source: *The Gender Gap: Women are Still Missing as Sources for Journalists.* Project for Excellence in Journalism, 2005. Used with permission from Project for Excellence in Journalism.

pp. 6–7). Small newspapers are more likely than large papers to use wire stories while large newspapers are more likely to publish staff-written stories.

Half of the stories published on the front page, the most prominent section of the newspaper, contained at least one female source. The front page of the metro section saw an increase of female sources with almost three-fifths of stories containing a female source. The front page of the sports section was least likely to contain a female source. While 86 percent of the stories on the front page of the sports section cited a male source, only 14 percent cited a female source ("Project for Excellence," 2005, p. 3).

The cable news networks—CNN, FOX, and MSNBC—did not fare much better than the front page of the sports section when it came to including women as sources. An analysis of 6,550 cable stories on the 24-hour cable news networks found that fewer than one-fifth (19 percent) cited a female source ("Project for Excellence," 2005, p. 7).

When experts are quoted, women are much less likely than men to be the source of the quote. When 1,102 expert sources used in stories published in 30 different newspapers were analyzed, 18.9 percent of the expert sources were women and 62.4 percent were men (Craft *et al.*, 2003, p. 9). A study of 27 weeks of *60 Minutes* found 23 percent of the sources were female compared to 78 percent male and women represented 15 percent of the experts (Grabe *et al.*, 1999). Males were also more prevalent as sources and newsmakers in the network evening news (Ziegler & White, 1990; Liebler & Smith, 1997).

In an effort to determine if the predominant sex of the newspaper's management had an effect on the sex of sources reporters used, researchers determined that in newsrooms with a high percentage of women managers "male and female reporters did not differ in their use of sources" (Craft *et al.*, p. 10), however, in male-dominated newsrooms reporters were more likely to use non-expert sources of the same sex. Plus both female and male reporters were more likely to use male experts as sources.

Scholars have also examined gender of reporter and genre of source to better understand the role of gender in selecting sources for news stories. Although studies have found a relationship between reporter's gender and gender of sources used in reporting a story, that is, female reporters are more likely to use female sources while male reporters are more likely to use male sources (Armstrong, 2004; Freedman & Fico, 2005; Zeldes & Fico, 2005), the same gender relationship does not hold for story genre (Armstrong, 2006.) A content analysis of 31 newspapers found "when both men and women are in the same profession or position, men are still more likely to be chosen as sources" (Armstrong, 2006, p. 77). Further, it must be kept in mind that although female reporters may be more likely than male reporters to use female sources, that does not change the overall finding that women are less likely than men to be used as sources in news stories.

Finding Women in Local TV News

Because of local TV's domination as a source of news, researchers analyzed the presence of women anchors and reporters as well as the types of stories and the use of women experts as sources in the news stories broadcast. A total of 596 news stories from noon, early evening and late evening local newscasts broadcast by 26 different stations in 12 cities representing different geographic regions and market sizes over an 11-year period from the late 1980s to the late 1990s were content analyzed. In addition to coding gender of reporter, anchor, and source; race and ethnicity of reporter and source, topic of story, six different types of sources were coded. Sex differences were found in anchors, reporters, topics reported, and use of expert sources (Poindexter *et al.*, 2003).[2]

Although both women and men anchored the news, male anchors were more likely than female anchors to speak first. "Over three-fifths (62%) of the first anchors to speak were male" (Poindexter *et al.*, 2003). Plus, over three-fifths of the reporters were male. Of the female reporters, 73 percent were white, 17 percent were African American, 7 percent were some other race or ethnicity, 3 percent were Latino, and 0 percent were Asian-American (ibid.).

Men were almost four times as likely as women (27 percent vs. 7 percent) to cover non-crime spot news, such as fires, floods, and accidents, while women were twice as likely as men (16 percent vs. 8 percent) to report stories on consumer, business, and economic issues, and sixteen times more likely than men to report health-related topics (16 percent vs. 1 percent) (Poindexter *et al.*, 2003).

Little difference between the sexes was found in reporting crime-courts, sports, social issues, politics and government, or other topics.

Whether first source or fourth source in a story, males were significantly more likely than females to be used as a source in a local television news story, and they were three times more likely than females to be the first source (75 percent vs. 25 percent). To more fully understand the relationship between the sex of the source and their use, six types of sources were coded for analysis: "1) private which included witnesses, neighbors, consumers, students, voters, etc.; 2) politicians and candidates; 3) political activists; 4) expert, authority, spokesperson for a company or organization; 5) celebrity; 6) unable to determine or other" (Poindexter *et al.*, 2003, p. 6).

This distinction among source types revealed a sex-based divide in local television news sources: men were presented in the news as authorities and experts while women were used to comment on the private arena. This sex divide in sources held true regardless of whether the source was the first or the fourth (see Table 5.4).

Are local TV news reporters more likely to select sources of the same sex? Although both female and male reporters were more likely to select the same sex for their first source, a much larger percentage of male than female local TV news reporters followed this pattern in reporting the news story. Slightly more than three-fifths (61 percent) of female local TV news reporters selected female sources but more than four-fifths (82 percent) of male reporters selected male sources (Poindexter *et al.*, 2003).

Racial and ethnic diversity of female sources emerged when at least three female sources were used. Among first sources that were female, 79 percent were white,

Table 5.4 Gender of private citizen and spokesperson-expert sources (%)

		Female	Male
1st source:	Spokesperson-expert	19	54
	Private citizen	68	34
2nd source:	Spokesperson-expert	22	55
	Private citizen	70	37
3rd source:	Spokesperson-expert	15	40
	Private citizen	85	45
4th source:	Spokesperson-expert	0	36
	Private citizen	82	45

Note: Adapted from Poindexter, Flores, & Smith (2003). Used with permission from Paula Poindexter.

16 percent were African American, and no Latino or Asian-American female sources were used. When three female sources were used, 55 percent were white, 30 percent were African American, and 10 percent were Latino. Female Asian-American sources were never used in the local television news stories analyzed (Poindexter, Flores, & Smith, 2003).

"First Woman" Stories Still Treated as First-Tier News

Just as the announcement that *Today Show* co-host Katie Couric would become the first woman ever to solo in the network news anchor chair was a major news story around the country, the election of "the first woman to lead a church in the worldwide Anglican Communion" was treated as front-page news by *The New York Times* when the Episcopal Church "elected Bishop Katharine Jefferts Schori of Nevada as its presiding bishop" (Banerjee, 2006, pp. A1, A15).

Even when the first woman ever qualified for a "season-long exemption on the P.B.A. Tour" by "bowling, nine games a day for five days in a row," *The New York Times* announced this achievement on the front page: "Woman Breaks the Pin Barrier In Making the Pro Bowlers Tour" (Macur, 2006, pp. A1, C20). "First Woman" stories are still treated as front-page news while important news directly affecting women receives second-tier treatment.

Women's Issues Treated as Second-Tier News

Although topics are not inherently female or male, topics that directly affect women, such as sexual harassment, would be classified as a woman's issue while topics such as erectile dysfunction would be categorized as a man's issue. But women's issues are not necessarily synonymous with topics of interest to women although they could be the same.

One of the biggest issues to directly affect women over the past four decades was not a single issue but a movement. The "unofficial inception" of the women's movement, according to sociologist Gaye Tuchman, was the 1965 White House Conference on Equal Opportunity followed by the official birth in 1966 of the National Organization for Women (NOW) (Tuchman, 1978, p. 136). The sociologist who studied newsrooms and newsworkers for 10 years noted in her groundbreaking book *Making News: A Study in the Construction of Reality* (1978) that early news coverage of the women's movement, which male editors slighted by using the nickname "women's lib," both ridiculed and ostracized women's demands for equality. For example, when Betty Friedan held a news conference to announce the founding of NOW in 1966, *The New York Times* published a brief story in the women's pages "between a recipe for turkey stuffing and an article announcing that hairstylist Pierre Henri was returning to his job at Saks Fifth Avenue" (ibid., p. 147).

Although the formation of NOW was concrete evidence of the beginning of a movement that could radically change women's status and opportunities in society, *The New York Times* treated the announcement as a second-tier event. But what happens to the coverage of women's issues in the context of a major news story such as a presidential election and does it make a difference when the network correspondents are women? Defining women's issues as topics directly affecting women, a researcher looked at how female and male network news correspondents covered the following topics: "reproductive health, family planning, abortion, childcare, sexual harassment, rape, sexual discrimination, domestic violence, feminism" during the 1996 presidential election (Piper-Aiken, 2003, p. 14).

Even though the list of women's issues was not exhaustive, of the women's issues coded for, four-fifths of the news packages or stories reported on the presidential election by network correspondents did not reference any women's issue. In other words, in 80 percent of the stories, women's issues were ignored. In election stories that did include a reference to a woman's issue, stories reported by female network correspondents (38 percent) were almost three times more likely than stories reported by male network correspondents (13 percent) to include a reference to a woman's issue (Piper-Aiken, 2003).

Hairstyles and Attire of Female Candidates are Treated as "Newsworthy"

Women are not only ignored as sources for front-page presidential election news stories (Lueck, 2005), but female candidates and office holders are not always treated as serious news subjects; sometimes their hairstyles, attire, family life, and access to bathrooms are treated as newsworthy (Carroll & Schreiber, 1997). From Geraldine Ferraro, the first woman ever to be nominated on the ticket of a major political party, when she was the vice presidential candidate in 1984 on the Democratic ticket headed by former vice president Walter Mondale, to Elizabeth Dole who ran for the Republican Party's nomination for president in 2000, to the fictional female president in the critically acclaimed, but short-lived, 2005–6 ABC prime-time drama *Commander-in-Chief*, a different set of standards seemed to apply.

For example, when Elizabeth Dole, former president of the American Red Cross and former Labor Secretary in the cabinet of George H.W. Bush, 41st President of the United States, ran for the Republican Party's nomination for president in 2000, news coverage focused more on the personal than on her stand on issues (Aday & Devitt, 2000). Furthermore, the news media were more likely to paraphrase Dole's quotes, while quoting her male competitors directly. It will be interesting to observe what standards the news media use in the reporting of Senator Hillary Rodham Clinton's 2008 presidential candidacy.

Health News Affecting Females Given Second-Tier Treatment

Health news directly affecting women would certainly qualify as a woman's issue so how are the results of an important study published in a prestigious medical journal treated by *The New York Times*? Called definitive, the study's results, which were published in *The New England Journal of Medicine*, received a headline in *The New York Times* that made it clear the news was important but the placement on page 18 suggested the level of importance was second-tier. The headline "Condoms Found to Block a Virus Harmful to Women" left no doubt that this news directly affected women. Specifically, the researchers at the University of Washington in Seattle who conducted the five-year study among female college students found: "The consistent use of condoms protects against human papillomavirus, a cause of warts and cervical and other female cancers" (Altman, 2006, p. A18).

On the same day *The New York Times* published a story directly affecting women's health on page 18, a story about four diabetes drugs was published on the front page despite the fact that one of the drugs had already been on the market, two of the drugs were awaiting Food and Drug Administration approval and one drug would not be available at pharmacies until the next month. Although once all four diabetes drugs are on the market, they are expected to have a *future* impact on the treatment of diabetes, that news received front-page exposure, but news that condoms prevent infection by a female cancer causing-virus, which can have an *immediate* impact on women's health, was buried inside the newspaper.

Eight days later *The New York Times* treated another health news story that directly affected women as second-tier. When "a federal vaccine advisory panel voted unanimously yesterday to recommend that all girls and women ages 11 to 26 receive a new vaccine that prevents most cases of cervical cancer," *The New York Times* published the news about the Merck-produced vaccine Gardasil on page 12, in spite of the fact that the head of the recommending federal panel, "the Advisory Committee on Immunization Practices, Dr. Anne Schuchat, director of the immunization program at the Centers for Disease Control and Prevention, called the panel's approval of Gardasil historic and 'a breakthrough for women's health'" (Harris, 2006, p. A12). According to *The New York Times*, worldwide, every year cervical cancer kills 233,000 women (ibid.). In the United States, every year millions of women have Pap smears to test for cervical cancer, "9,710 women contract cervical cancer, and 3,700 die" from the deadly disease (ibid.).

Supreme Court Ruling Affecting Women Has Second-Tier Status

When the Supreme Court unanimously ruled in support of a woman's complaint of sexual harassment, should that have qualified as front-page news? Not according to *The New York Times*, which placed the story on page 24 with the headline: "Supreme Court Gives Employees Broader Protection Against Retaliation in Workplace" (Greenhouse, 2006b, p. A24). Even though the lead said the unanimous Supreme Court decision "substantially enhanced legal protection against retaliation for employees who complain about discrimination or harassment on the job" and attorneys for both the plaintiff and the defense "agreed about the decision's significance," (Greenhouse, 2006b, p. A24) this story, according to *The New York Times*, was not so significant that it warranted front-page placement. A further signal that this story was second-tier could be found on the editorial page (*The New York Times*, 2006, p. A26). No editorial commented on the significance of the Supreme Court's 9–0 decision that "adopted a broadly worded and employee-friendly definition of the type of retaliation that is prohibited by the basic federal law against discrimination in employment" (Greenhouse, 2006b, p. A24). Approximately "20,000 retaliation cases were filed with the Equal Employment Opportunity Commission in 2004, a number that has doubled since 1992" (Greenhouse, 2006b, p. A24).

Four days after *The New York Times* snubbed this unanimous Supreme Court ruling that directly affected women, *The New York Times* reported a 6–3 Supreme Court decision that ruled "Vermont's limits on campaign contributions and on campaign spending by candidates are unconstitutional," on the front page above the fold (Greenhouse, 2006c, p. A1). To emphasize the significance of this Supreme Court decision, *The New York Times* followed up its front-page coverage with an editorial ("Campaign Finance Reform Survives," 2006, A18).

Publishing an editorial to accompany news of a Supreme Court ruling is not unusual. An examination of *The New York Times* news coverage of five Supreme Court decisions during a ten-day period from June 20 to June 30, found four of the five rulings (wetlands, campaign limits, re-districting in Texas, and trying detainees) received front-page coverage above the fold plus an editorial. But the unanimous Supreme Court decision on retaliation received neither front-page coverage nor an accompanying editorial (Greenhouse, 2006a, 2006c, 2006d, 2006e).

Focusing on Women in News Photographs

Because women are less likely to be the subject of front-page news stories, they are also less likely to be the subject of photographs published on the front page. Women are also rare in election photographs unless they are relatives of candidates, children, or anonymous faces at campaign stops and rallies (Lueck, 2005).

Frames that Empower, Restrict, and Fault Women

In addition to treating news that affects women as second tier, displaying "First-Woman" stories on the front page, and making the hairstyles and attire of female candidates newsworthy, the news media have long employed frames that occasionally empower and often undermine women. For example, during the 1984 US presidential election, the news media framed women as a potentially powerful voting bloc that could determine the outcome of a presidential election. The phrase gender gap became the frame for the potential power of the women's vote. It was said that whichever candidate attracted the women's vote would become the next President of the United States.

Three presidential elections later, the gender gap frame, which represented the power of the female vote, was replaced by a new frame—soccer mom. Superficial and stereotypical, this frame no longer said women could elect the next president of the United States. This frame restricted women to the domestic domain, transporting their kids to and from soccer practice.

When the 2004 presidential election began and 9/11 was still very much on the minds of voters, soccer moms morphed into security moms who were anxious and fearful of another attack. By framing women as moms, whether soccer or security, the news media and candidates ignored women's diverse roles and professional and educational achievements, instead settling for a stereotype that uniformly limited women's role to mother and her place in the home (Vavrus, 2000; Piper-Aiken, 2003; Lueck, 2005).

In addition to restricting women's roles by including "mom" and not "woman" in the frame, the news media framed women's support for increased national security spending as due to some sort of post-9/11 syndrome:

> Polls in the weeks after 9/11 found far more women than men reporting that they were depressed, losing sleep and fearful from the news coverage they had watched. "All the polls showed women feeling much more personally vulnerable, much more personally threatened," says Andrew Kohut, director of the Pew Research Center for the People and the Press. "I don't want to play to some stereotypes, but it just comes screaming out of all of the data."
>
> (Tumulty & Novak, 2003)

Even when women are covered in the domestic domain, the news media can weave in a negative frame that turns women into old maid spinsters, desperate singles, and bad mothers. Perhaps *Newsweek* (1986) created one of the most memorable and egregious frames when it reported in a cover story two decades ago that a 40-year-old single woman had a greater chance of being killed by a terrorist than getting married. It took *Newsweek* 20 years to admit in a follow-up cover story that it was wrong and irresponsible (McGinn, 2006, pp. 40–8). Ironically, as a result of linking a single woman's chances of getting married to the probability of being a victim of a terrorist act, the original 1986 *Newsweek* cover story terrorized a generation of single women. "For a lot of women, the retraction doesn't matter. The article seems to have lodged itself permanently in the national psyche," said a *New York Times* article that reported on *Newsweek*'s retraction of the 20-year-old story (Yellin, 2006, pp. 1, 3). But by publishing the follow-up story under the headline, "Single, Female and Desperate No More," *The New York Times* seemed to say that for the past 20 years, single women had been desperate, sort of like the troubled women who live on Wisteria Lane in the highly rated *ABC* TV show *Desperate Housewives* (Yellin, 2006, pp. 1, 3).

Will *The New York Times* headline "Breast-Feed or Else" terrorize the next generation of new mothers just like the 1986 *Newsweek* article terrorized single women for two decades? (Rabin, 2006, p. F1). By writing a lead that suggested a hypothetical situation in which cans of infant formula would be stamped: "Warning: Public health officials have determined that not breast-feeding may be hazardous to your baby's health" and displaying an oversized baby bottle crossed out in pink, did the "Science Times" front-page story frame new mothers who do not breast-feed as potential child abusers, endangering the lives of their newborns? (ibid.).

Attracting or Offending Women?

Just as it is often a challenge to find women on the front page of a newspaper, it is equally hard to find women in a newspaper's business pages, a prestigious section of the newspaper that is read by more men than women. But when *The New York Times* detected a "boomlet" in the intimate apparel business, women prominently graced the front page of "Business Day" in *The New York Times* (Barbaro, 2006, p. B1). Written by Michael Barbaro and illustrated with photographs of scantily clad mannequins, the article on the $10 billion underwear business purported to solve the mystery of "What Women Want" (ibid.). Although the headline was engaging, it was also misleading. The article was less a story about the needs of women and more about how Bloomingdale's, The Gap, Chico's and other retailers plan to compete with Victoria's Secret, the specialty retailer that boosts its intimate apparel sales with "ubiquitous, sexually charged come-hither marketing" (ibid., p. B4).

The high school art teacher was not scantily clad in the photos she posted online—she was nude, and when the teacher's "art" photographs were discovered, the school district fired her. While the newsworthiness of the story which ran in the second section, was not in question, the front-page placement of one nondescript photograph *sans* story of the art teacher raises questions about what women have to do to become front-page news (Anonymous, 2006, p. A1). If nude photos posted on the Web had not been part of the story, would the bland photo of the art teacher sitting in her car chatting with students who demonstrated in support of her keeping her job, been displayed above the fold on the front page of the *Austin American-Statesman*? If the story had been about a male art teacher who had posted his nude "art" photos online, would a bland photo of him sitting in a car chatting with students been published so prominently?

Despite the fact that females are more often the victims of sex crimes and not the perpetrators, the *Associated Press* made one female sex offender who had been convicted of "statutory rape for having sex with a 15-year-old when she was 39" the face of registered sex offenders when it distributed a story through its wire service on a new law in the state of Georgia that would bar registered sex offenders from living near school bus stops (Bluestein, 2006, p. A1). By publishing the wire story along with a photo of the woman above the fold on its front page, the *Austin American-Statesman* seemed to agree with the wire service's representation of women as the face of sex offenders. Since the female sex offender was a party to a lawsuit that challenged the new sex offender law, her inclusion in the story is not in question. What is in question is the news judgment that represented the woman as the face of registered sex offenders and the prominent placement the story received. If a man had been the focus of the story, would the *AP* story about a lawsuit in Georgia still have been published on the front page of a newspaper in Austin, Texas?

In addition to the news media's use of a woman to represent the face of registered sex offenders, a woman was used to represent the face of illegal immigration on the cover of *The New York Times Magazine*, when it published a story that sorted out economists' differing views on the impact of illegal immigration on the US economy (Lowenstein, 2006). Although the cover of *The New York Times Magazine* hid the face of the woman in shadows, her work clothes, apron, and yellow rubber gloves were visible. Also noticeable on the cover was the question that framed the woman as a menace to the economy: "What is she really doing to American jobs and wages?" (ibid.).

Window on the World?

Three decades ago, sociologist Gaye Tuchman, author of one of the most significant books published on the production of news said: "News is a window on the world. Through its frame, Americans learn of themselves and others, of their own institutions, leaders, and life styles, and those of other nations and their peoples" (Tuchman, 1978, p. 1).

But do women learn of themselves through the news? Do women learn they are important members of society and the issues that are important to them are significant? And what do women learn from the news about the value of women's expertise? After reading or watching the news, do women feel valued? A review of studies on news coverage of women as well as an examination of numerous stories published by the top newspaper in the United States that proclaims every day on the front page, "All the News That's Fit to Print" suggests more likely than not, women as well as news and issues of importance to women are treated as second best, unless some novelty pushes them to front-page news.

The reason women are treated as second best is a consequence of a variety of factors, including the importance gatekeepers assign to news of interest to women and unconscious assumptions about gender. So while mastheads, organizational charts, and industry statistics confirm more women are in newsrooms and at the highest levels of the news media, analyses of news coverage provide evidence that increased numbers of women in newsrooms, on mastheads, and in top positions in broadcast news is insufficient to push news of interest to women to first-tier status. And until there is a commitment to cover women by design and not just coincidence, the news will continue to fail as a window on the world for women, and women will likely continue to abandon newspapers and other news media that treat them as second class.

Notes

1   I was Special Projects Manager and a member of the executive incentive group at the *Los Angeles Times* when editor of the Orange County edition of *The Times*, Narda Zacchino, also a member of the executive incentive group, publicly expressed her concern to senior executives about the lack of women and minorities at the highest levels of the newspaper. Following her brief speech, Narda and I, as well as other women committed to increasing women at the highest levels of the newspaper, organized the Times Women in Management group. As an editor, Narda was highly respected by the publisher and she became our spokesperson. In addition to scheduling the first meetings, I conducted a survey to identify concerns and priorities of women managers at the *Los Angeles Times*.

   Although in 1991 I left the *Los Angeles Times* and joined the journalism faculty at the University of Texas at Austin, the Times Women in Management group continued and became very effective in increasing women at the highest levels of the newspaper. In fact, not too long after I left, the first woman vice president was appointed. "Zacchino" (2001) gives Narda's perspective on the formation of Times Women in Management. In 2001, Narda became the highest-ranking woman at the *San Francisco Chronicle* when she was appointed deputy editor. Her name was listed fourth on the masthead, after the names of the publisher and president, executive vice president and editor, and vice president and managing editor until she left in 2007.

2   To understand the impact of gender on sources in local TV news, content analysis data from Poindexter, Smith & Heider (2003) was re-analyzed with a focus on women.

References

Aday, S. & Devitt, J. (2000, September 28). Style over substance: Newspaper coverage of female candidates: Spotlight on Elizabeth Dole. Paper presented at the National Press Club. Washington, D.C. Retrieved June 22, 2006 from www.thewhitehouseproject.org/research/Style-substance_Dole_report.pdf.

Altman, L.K. (2006, June 22). Condoms found to block a virus harmful to women. *The New York Times*, p. A18.

Anonymous. (2006, June 22). Drawing attention to art teacher. *Austin American-Statesman*, p. A1.

Armstrong, C.L. (2006). Story genre influences whether women are sources. *Newspaper Research Journal*, 27(3), 66–81.

Armstrong, C.L. (2004). The influence of reporter gender on source selection in newspaper stories. *Journalism & Mass Communication Quarterly*, 81(1), 139–54.

Arnold, M. & Nesbitt, M. (2006). *Women in Media 2006: Finding the leader in you*. Media Management Center at Northwestern University: McCormick Tribune Foundation. Retrieved July 19, 2006 from www.mediamanagementcenter.org/publications/data/wim2006.pdf.

ASNE census shows newsroom diversity grows slightly. (2006, April 25). *American Society of Newspaper Editors (ASNE)*. Retrieved June 16, 2006 from www.asne.org/index.cfm?id=6264.

ASNE newsroom employment census, Table M—numbers and percentage of men and women by job category. (2006b, April 25). *American Society of Newspaper Editors (ASNE)*. Retrieved June 16, 2006 from www.asne.org/index.cfm?id=5660.

ASNE statement of principles. (2002, August 28). *American Society of Newspaper Editors (ASNE)*. Retrieved September 5, 2006 from www.asne.org/kiosk/archive/principl.htm.

Banerjee, N. (2006, June 19). Woman is named Episcopal leader: Historic choice as church faces threat of schism. *The New York Times*, pp. A1, A15.

Barbaro, M. (2006, July 15). What women want: A boomlet in the underwear-as-apparel market. *The New York Times*, pp. B1, B4.

Bleske, G.L. (1991). Ms. Gates takes over: An updated version of a 1949 case study. *Newspaper Research Journal*, 12(4), 88–97.

Bluestein, G. (2006, June 24). Can laws on sex offenders be too tough? Strict Georgia statute will make living there impossible, suit says. *Austin American-Statesman*, pp. A1, A11.

Branson, C. (2004, June 21). A look at the formation of ASNE. Retrieved 5, September 2006 from www.asne.org/index.cfm?ID=3460.

Breed, W. (1955). Social control in the newsroom: A functional analysis. *Social Forces*, 33(4), 326–35.

Campaign finance reform survives. (2006, June 27). *The New York Times*, p. A18.

Carroll, S.J. & Schreiber, R. (1997). Media coverage of women in the 103rd Congress. In P. Norris, (Ed.) *Women, Media, and Politics*, pp. 131–49. New York: Oxford University Press.

Craft, S., Wanta, W., & Lee, C. (2003). A comparative analysis of source and reporter gender in newsrooms managed by men versus women. Paper presented at the Association of Education in Journalism and Mass Communication Conference, the Newspaper Division, Kansas City.

Daft, R.L. (2005). *The Leadership Experience* (3rd edition). Mason: South-Western.

Editorials/Letters. (2006, June 23). *The New York Times*, p. A26.

Everbach, T. (2006). The culture of a woman-led newspaper: An ethnographic study of the Sarasota Herald Tribune. *Journalism & Mass Communication Quarterly*, 83(3), 477–93.

First Amendment Center. (2005). About the First Amendment. Retrieved September 5, 2006 from www.firstamendmentcenter.org/about.aspx?item=about_firstamd.

Foote, J. & Price, C. (2005). Women correspondent visibility on network television news— A twenty-year longitudinal study. Paper presented at the Association of Education in Journalism and Mass Communication Conference, Commission on the Status of Women, San Antonio.

Freedman, F. & Fico, F. (2005). Male and female sources in newspaper coverage of male and female candidates in open races for governor in 2002. *Mass Communication & Society*, 8(3), 257–72.

The gender gap: Women are still missing as sources for journalists. (2005, May 23). *Project for Excellence in Journalism*. Retrieved July 14, 2006 from www.journalism.org/resources/research/reports/gender/default.asp.

Grabe, M.E., Zhou, S., & Barnett, B. (1999). Sourcing and reporting in news magazine programs: 60 minutes versus hard copy. *Journalism & Mass Communication Quarterly*, 76(2), 293–311.

Greenhouse, L. (2006a, June 20). Justices divided on protections over wetlands. *The New York Times*, pp. A1, A14.

Greenhouse, L. (2006b, June 23). Supreme Court gives employees broader protection against retaliation in workplace. *The New York Times*, p. A24.

Greenhouse, L. (2006c, June 27). Justices reject campaign limits in Vermont case: Money ceiling too low. *The New York Times*, pp. A1, A14.

Greenhouse, L. (2006d, June 29). Justices uphold most remapping in Texas by G.O.P. *The New York Times*, pp. A1, A15.

Greenhouse, L. (2006e, June 30). Guantanamo case: Military panels found to lack authority— new law possible. *The New York Times*, pp. A1, A18.

Harris, G. (2006, June 30). Panel unanimously recommends cervical cancer vaccine for girls 11 and up. *The New York Times*, p. A12.

Liebler, C.M. & Smith, S.J. (1997). Tracking gender differences: A comparative analysis of network correspondents and their sources. *Journal of Broadcasting & Electronic Media*, 41(1), 58–68.

Lowenstein, R. (2006, July 9). The immigration equation. *The New York Times Magazine*, pp. 36–43.

Lueck, T.L. (2005). A woman's place in 2004 election coverage: Stereotypes and feminist inroads. Paper presented at the Association of Education in Journalism and Mass Communication Conference, Commission on the Status of Women, San Antonio.

Macur, J. (2006, June 15). Woman breaks the pin barrier in making the pro bowlers tour. *The New York Times*, pp. A1, C20.

McGinn, D. (2006, June 5). Marriage by the numbers. *Newsweek*, pp. 40–8.

Media Tenor. (2003). US television news ignore women. 2, 29–30.

Mills, K. (1988). *A Place in the News: From the women's pages to the front page*. New York: Columbia University Press.

Mindich, D. (1998). *Just the Facts: How "objectivity" came to define American journalism*. New York: New York University Press.

The marriage crunch. (1986, June 2). *Newsweek*. Retrieved September 6, 2006 from www.msnbc.msn.com/id/12940202/site/newsweek/.

Piper-Aiken, K.S. (2003). It's in the visuals! Journalists and gender issues in television network news coverage of the 1996 US Presidential election. Paper presented at the Association of Education in Journalism and Mass Communication Conference. Radio-Television Journalism Division, Kansas City.

Poindexter, P.M., Flores, M., & Smith, L. (2003). Gender and local television news: The framing of women on the set and in the news. Unpublished manuscript, University of Texas at Austin, School of Journalism.

Poindexter, P., Smith, L., & Heider, D. (2003). Race and ethnicity in local television news: Framing, story assignments, and source selections. *Journal of Broadcasting & Electronic Media*, 47(4), 524–36.

Rabin, R. (2006, June 13). Breast-feed or else: Is choosing bottle over breast like smoking during pregnancy? A controversial new public effort suggests it is. *The New York Times*, p. F1.

Rethinking "the marriage crunch". (2006, June 5). *Newsweek*, pp. 40–8.

Shoemaker, P.J. & Reese, S.D. (1996). *Mediating the Message: Theories of influences on mass media content* (2nd edition). New York: Longman.

Thiel, S. (2005, April 9). Increased legitimacy, fewer women? Analyzing editorial leadership and gender in online journalism. Paper presented at International Symposium on Online Journalism, Austin.

Tuchman, G. (1978). *Making News: A study in the construction of reality*. New York: Free Press.

Tumulty, K. & Novak, V. (2003, June 2). Goodbye, soccer mom. Hello, security mom. *Time*. Retrieved August 31, 2006 from www.time.com/time/magazine/printout/0,8816,1004926,00.html.

Vavrus, M.D. (2000). From women of the year to 'soccer moms': The case of the incredible shrinking women. *Political Communication*, 17(2), 193–213.

Weaver, D., Beam, R., Brownlee, B., Voakes, P.S., & Wilhoit, G.C. (2003). The American journalist in the twenty-first century: Key findings. Paper presented at the Association of Education in Journalism and Mass Communication Conference, Kansas City.

Weaver, D., Beam, R., Brownlee, B., Voakes, P.S., & Wilhoit, G.C. (2007). *The American Journalist in the Twenty-First Century: US news people at the dawn of a new millennium*. Mahwah: Lawrence Erlbaum Associates.

White, D.M. (1950). The "gate keeper": A case study in the selection of news. *Journalism Quarterly*, 27, 383–96.

Whitlow, S.S. (1977). How male and female gatekeepers respond to news stories of women. *Journalism Quarterly*, 54(3), 573–9, 609.

Yellin, J. (2006, June 4). Single, female and desperate no more. *The New York Times*, pp. 1, 3, Section 4.

Zacchino takes her heart to San Francisco. (2001, August 20). *Women's eNews*. Retrieved September 6, 2006 from www.womensenews.org/article.cfm/dyn/aid/623/context/jounalistof themonth.

Zeldes, G.A. & Fico, F. (2005). Race and gender: An analysis of sources and reporters in the networks' coverage of the 2000 presidential campaign. *Mass Communication & Society*, 8(4), 373–85.

Ziegler, D. & White, A. (1990). Women and minorities on network television news: An examination of correspondents and newsmakers. *Journal of Broadcasting & Electronic Media*, 34(2), 215–23.

Zoch, L.M. & Turk, J.V. (1998). Women making news: Gender as a variable use. *Journalism & Mass Communication Quarterly*, 75(4), 762–75.

Chapter 6

The Softer Side of News

Paula Poindexter and Dustin Harp

Traditionally, the distinction between hard and soft news in the newsroom has symbolized a news hierarchy: hard news, at the top of the newsroom ladder, has been viewed as important news that men do; soft news, several rungs below hard news, has been perceived as less important news that women do. But do women news consumers feel soft news is less important? Or do they feel soft news is the only thing keeping them connected to the newspaper?

Although the terms hard news and soft news are used often, a look at the definitions of these terms by a historian, journalism professors, political scientists, and the author of the first significant book to chronicle women's progress from the women's pages to the newspaper's front page suggests little agreement about what distinguishes hard news from soft. Over 50 years ago, news historian Frank Luther Mott said hard news and soft news represented "the double standard of news evaluation with which editors must cope" (Mott, 1952, p. 32). He defined hard news as "the less exciting and more analytical stories of public affairs, economics, social problems, science, etc." while soft news was viewed as "that which any editor immediately recognizes as interesting to his readers and therefore 'important' for his paper" (ibid.).

Although Mott was vague in what constituted soft news, journalism professors at the University of Missouri were more specific in their textbook definitions. Hard news was defined as "coverage of the actions of government or business; or the reporting of an event, such as a crime, an accident, or a speech" while soft news was defined as stories about trends, personalities, or lifestyles (Brooks *et al.*, 1985, p. 529).

Stories that emphasize events vs. people have also been used to distinguish hard from soft news. Hard news was defined as "events involving top leaders, major issues, or significant disruptions to daily routines," while soft news included "celebrity profiles, lifestyle scenes, hard-luck tales, good-luck tales, and other human-interest stories" (Patterson & Seib, 2005, p. 192).

Author of *A Place in the News: From the Women's Pages to the Front Page* Kay Mills noted both the gender implications and the Four F's when she distinguished hard from soft news:

> Hard news? Soft news? Where did these terms come from? Their sexual implications fairly leap from the page. Hard news is news about foreign policy, the federal deficit, bank robberies. Historically, men's stuff. The right stuff. Soft news is news about the Four F's—family, food, fashion, and furnishings. Women's stuff. Back of the book. Plays, movies, books. Lifestyle.
>
> (Mills, 1988, p. 110)

But what do news consumers think about hard and soft news? Since the lifestyle or feature sections are considered soft news, we asked a non-random sample of women, including news enthusiasts and news betweeners, what they liked most about these sections. Although many of the likes fit into the "Four F's" of family, food, fashion, and furnishing, readers of lifestyle sections were also fond of stories about people and community as well as the newspaper's role as a gateway to relaxation, entertainment, and leisure activities.

How news betweeners feel about the newspaper's lifestyle section is especially important because even though this group of news consumers is not as committed as news enthusiasts, they haven't yet turned away like news avoiders. Newspaper betweeners who read the newspaper between one and six days per week are critical to the newspaper's future. If betweeners were to read more frequently, they would be classified as news enthusiasts or monitors, but if they began paying less attention to newspapers, they could become news avoiders.

What Women Like About the Lifestyle Section

When we asked a Generation Xer and a pre-baby boomer: "What do you like most about the lifestyle or features section of the newspaper?" we received similar responses. In spite of the fact that the two women represented different generations, they both said they liked the interesting people stories.

Overall, the women who responded to our questionnaire, regardless of generation, liked different aspects of the lifestyle section. For Jessica and Samantha, the food section, recipes, and restaurant reviews were most appealing while Lourdes liked health and diets most. The guide to weekend activities and movies was popular with Denise but Gail liked crossword puzzles best.

For some of the women who completed our questionnaires, the lifestyle section was an integral part of their routine. For Cassandra, reading the features section was a pleasurable part of her lifestyle: "I read two comic strips during the week, the food/taste section on Wednesdays, and if I'm able to, I'll skim the rest of the lifestyle sections over breakfast/lunch. I like the low stress of the lifestyle sections as the rest of the news usually makes me cranky."

And for Jennifer, Sunday morning would not be the same without the lifestyle section: "I read the Style and Travel sections on Sunday (usually online) as sort of a lazy morning routine, where I take more time with the paper and read the magazine articles, the travel and other fantasy-related sections of the paper."

If in some cases the lifestyle section is the only thing still connecting women to the newspaper, why is it perceived as less important? According to *San Diego Union*, Senior Editor/Special Sections Chris Lavin, who answered our questions about newspapers and lifestyle sections, women's interests have been a low priority for newspapers for years:

> In general, many of the areas of special interest for women have been driven out of newspapers over the last 50 years. Newspapers today are edited largely for a male audience and newspaper resources are directed heavily at a male audience—dominated by coverage of sports and public government issues which have themselves been male dominated as well.
>
> (C. Lavin, personal communication, July 2006)

A 25-year veteran who has held a variety of editorial positions at various newspapers, including assistant managing editor, executive city editor, and general assignment reporter, Lavin is well aware of women's interests because he relies on research to find out what women want.

"I have made readership surveys available to my editors to help guide them in making the feature sections more accessible to women readers. Our research shows that these sections are read more heavily by women." And being aware that women are more interested in these stories provides guidance for areas to increase coverage:

> We've increased fashion, health and consumer coverage and boosted home and décor coverage that had waned over the years as these were judged, I believe, to be stereotypical female issues and were thus to be avoided. We have also endeavored to revivify our coverage of family and child-rearing issues which also ranked well in research gauging female reader interests.
>
> (C. Lavin, personal communication, July 2006)

Research provides insight into the needs, interests, and concerns of women while framing speaks to how a story is reported and edited. And if research is consistently ignored and the framing of a story regularly excludes women's interests, the end-result is that women's concerns are not addressed, which can lead to women turning away from newspapers:

> Frankly I think newspaper editors simply need to start believing their own research. The boom in recent decades of special interest magazines suggests women will read if they are supplied with stories that interest them or help them handle the challenges of their varied, busy lives. However, newspapers continue to be edited for a metropolitan male audience. Editors may identify education coverage and issues like Medicare and Medicaid as "of importance" to female readers, but much of that coverage is actually tax and politics coverage, not a useful, practical engagement in care and education that women readers might actually engage with in greater numbers.
>
> (C. Lavin, personal communication, July 2006)

Editors call it editing and journalism scholars call it framing. Regardless of what it is called, if the story is edited or framed where it excludes or puts women off, women will turn to other sources that better address their interests and needs. A news story's frame is important because it organizes the story, supplies the context, and "suggests what the issue is through the use of selection, emphasis, exclusion, and elaboration" (Tankard *et al.*, 1991).

"Much of the power of framing", according to James Tankard, Jr. who applied framing to journalism research in the early 1990s, "comes from its ability to define the terms of a debate without the audience realizing it is taking place. Media framing can be likened to the magician's sleight of hand—attention is directed to one point so that people do not notice the manipulation that is going on at another point" (Tankard, 2001, p. 97).

Women, though, do notice that their interests have been edited out of the newspaper. The *San Diego Union*, Senior Editor/Special Sections emphasized:

> the major news of the day is as appealing to women as men but then women get more selective with more limited time, searching through sections to find stories

that deal more directly with their lives—with a heavier dose of attention to family issues, food, health and the guilty pleasures of fashion and shopping.

Although he is not advocating for a women's page, the *San Diego Union*, Senior Editor/Special Sections does recognize the mistake newspapers made:

> I'm not a fan of the "women's page" as an institution, but I do think newspapers made a big mistake when, in the name of equality, it drove from its pages the type of material traditionally found on the "women's page." If we edited our newspapers to fully represent the complete range of readers' interests, we'd do a better job for women than we do.

The Appeal of Morning News Shows and Women's Magazines

Perhaps that's why women watch morning network news shows such as *Today*, *Good Morning America*, and *CBS Morning News* and read women's magazines—because by fully representing the complete range of readers' interests, they do a better job for women.

Even though they may not use the terms or definitions, women do understand the hard news–soft news distinction and they appreciate the respect that the softer side of news shows them. When, for example, we asked a non-random sample of women representing different generations to describe the words they associated with the newspaper's front page, the lifestyle section, morning network news shows such as *Today*, and women's magazines, it was clear they understood the differences.

Gracie, a Generation Xer, associated community, people, and interesting places with the lifestyle pages of the newspaper, and she thought women's magazines were silly and morning news shows such as *Today* and *Good Morning America* were light-hearted. But when asked about the front page, she responded "lead story" and "important."

Married with two small children and living in Kentucky, Jessica described the lifestyle section, which she reads three or four days a week, with words such as "fun, soft, family oriented." Her words for the front page included "main news, most important stories." While Jessica used positive and negative words such as "shallow, single-focused, repetitive, fun, fashion, outward focused," to describe women's magazines, she reserved words such as "soft, feel good, not news" to describe *Today* and *Good Morning America*.

Although her primary source of news is TV, Lourdes reads the lifestyle section of the newspaper at least twice a week. Married with two grown children, she said about the lifestyle section: "It is good overall." Her words describing the front page of the newspaper suggest she doesn't consider it fresh: "That is usually the same news, a trend such as another death or murder or weather or food, but generally nothing new." She had positive words to describe women's magazines: "It is nice advice and pretty dresses and trendy clothes. Nice health advice." And for morning news shows such as *Today* and *Good Morning America*, she said: "That it is a good way to start the day."

Lourdes is not alone in her opinion about the morning news shows. When we analyzed Pew data, we found evidence of the popularity of morning news shows such as *Today*, *Good Morning America*, and *The Early Show*. In fact, 51 percent of women compared to 35 percent of men said they watched the morning news shows regularly or sometimes ("Online Papers Modestly Boost Newspaper Readership," 2006).

A qualitative analysis of the first hour of the morning news shows during the week of May 22, 2006 provided insight into their appeal. After reporting headlines, hard news, and weather during the first 20 minutes of Monday's *Today Show*, the focus switched to the softer side of news. During the next 40 minutes, a succession of filmed and in-studio live interviews explored the opening weekend of the release of the Ron Howard-directed film based on the blockbuster best-selling book *The Da Vinci Code*, the Royal Family's three princes, a hunt for an alligator in South Florida, and the pros and cons of 50-year mortgages.

Good Morning America used a similar formula in its Tuesday edition. Headlines, hard news, and weather were followed by stories about *An Inconvenient Truth*, former vice president and presidential candidate Al Gore's documentary about global warming. Other stories focused on *American Idol* runner-ups, a 7 year old who swam from Alcatraz to shore in 47 minutes, and the country music group the Dixie Chicks. Local news, weather, and traffic cut-ins at 25 minutes after the hour provided helpful local information.

What is it about shows such as *Today* and *Good Morning America*, women's magazines, and lifestyle sections that appeal to women? It is not just about including stories of special interest for women; it is also about respect. And part of that respect is recognizing what women want and need and providing information that is helpful in the daily lives of women. In fact, when we analyzed data from The Pew Research Center Biennial News Consumption Survey (2004), we found women (50 percent) were more likely than men (43 percent) to agree with the statement: I want the news to contain information that is helpful in my daily life.

The Paradox and History of Soft News

Traditionally, for newspapers, providing information helpful to the daily lives of women had been the responsibility of women's pages. However, more than three and a half decades ago those pages were transformed into lifestyle sections, complicating the relationship with women inside the newsroom and news consumers outside. Understanding this history—how the newspaper industry courted women readers throughout the years and constructed content that both satisfied and stereotyped their needs—sheds light on this complex and contradictory relationship. It also offers insight into why women often turn away from newspapers at a higher rate than men do. After all, newspapers have notoriously and most visibly served men through front pages about public life and conflict. In turn, editors regularly placed content meant to attract or interest women, from health news to fashion, inside the newspaper and often behind advertising inserts and even the classifieds. In other words, what news executives understood to be "women's content" most often was relegated to the inside and back of the newspaper. Not only does this placement send a message to women readers about the importance of the content they find interesting and useful, newsroom attitudes and economics reinforced this message. It is not surprising then that so many women passed on newspapers and turned toward magazines and morning news programs where content and a sense of respect for readers and viewers was offered.

The Emergence of Women's Pages

Newspaper publishers and editors overtly began courting women readers during the latter part of the nineteenth century when they started identifying certain topics under women's headings. Joseph Pulitzer is typically credited with creating the first women's pages during the 1890s though some accounts point to women's pages in the decade before (Jordan, 1938; Marzolf, 1977). Prior to the creation of women's pages newspapers had offered some content for women, typically in the form of columns written by women, but during the 1890s editors devoted entire pages. For example, by 1894 Pulitzer's *New York Daily World* published at least one page daily "For and About Women" (Marzolf, 1977). By 1896 William Randolph Hearst's *New York Evening Journal* had developed pages of women's content (Jackson, 1993). The stories and columns on these pages covered what has become known as the four Fs—food, fashion, furnishings, and family. Women's magazines had become quite popular by this time and newspaper editors followed these periodicals in developing content topics for their female readers (Harp, 2007).

But this plan to offer women content specifically developed for them had less to do with the needs of female readers and much more to do with the business of newspapers and wishes of advertisers (Yang, 1996; Harp, 2007). This was a time when industrialization and urbanization resulted in families moving from the country to the city and leaving farms for factories. It meant that rather than producing food and home goods themselves, a growing number of families were buying more of what they needed. More specifically, women were buying the necessities to take care of their families, as they became the primary household shoppers. They made buying decisions about everything from which brand of food, to which clothing and furniture to purchase. With these changes department stores flourished along with national advertisers, and naturally more than anyone else, these advertisers wanted to reach women because they were choosing what to buy (Mott, 1962; Zuckerman, 1998). Savvy publishers, such as Pulitzer and Hearst, took this opportunity to appeal to advertisers by creating and popularizing women's pages. But in doing so, these men and their contemporaries made a long-lasting mark on how the newspaper industry thinks about women readers—one that too often shows little respect for women beyond their market value and their limited role as homemaker and mother.

Women's sections remained standard fare for nearly a century, most often titled or subtitled to indicate the sex-specific audience that editors had in mind. But along with articles and columns that have long been described as "fluff," these women's pages carried important news either about or deemed of importance to women. So while women's pages offered relationship advice, recipes for the perfect meatloaf, and the latest fashion trends, news about child abuse, rape laws, and women's rights also found a home on these inside pages constructed for women only (Marzolf, 1977; Beasley & Gibbons, 2003). Women working on these pages often felt insulted by their male editors' lack of attention to serious topics related to women—topics thought of as "women's issues." This inattentiveness meant women journalists most often covered stories about women and these "women's issues." And because women typically edited and wrote for the women's pages, these stories ended up there rather than on the front pages where serious news belongs. This has meant that some of the most important stories of interest to women throughout the last century—the suffragist movement, birth control, and the pending nomination of the first female vice president—first appeared on the women's pages rather than front pages of US newspapers (Marzolf, 1977; Mills, 1988). Throughout the last century news about children's issues, health, rape law changes, domestic violence, and women's wages has also been published in these sex-specific sections (Lont, 1995).

This placement of serious news related to women on the same inside pages as the more frivolous fashion news was then (and still is today) insulting for both women journalists and readers. Not only does this placement indicate that the stories and topics of importance to women are less significant than the news content found on the front pages, but it relays the message to men that these stories are of interest only to women and that they need not concern themselves with them. This positioning of stories then reinforces stereotypical notions of women and men, while indicating that such social issues as childcare, rape laws, and domestic abuse are problems for women to work out.

Many women editing these sections have felt like second-class citizens in the newsroom, because they were paid less than reporters of other sections and expected to succumb to the wishes of advertisers, unlike reporters working on any other section of the paper. Further, they had little respect from other reporters. Women editors and reporters of these women's sections were caught in a sort of double-bind—appreciative of the opportunities they had to define news but frustrated by their inability to move news of importance to women and their bylines onto the front pages (Mills, 1988; Chambers et al., 2004). With all of these problems in mind, women journalists and readers pushed for changes. They argued that women's pages "ghettoized" news of importance to women and served as a "dumping ground" for anything related to women (Lont, 1995). Toward the end of the 1960s newspaper executives started paying attention to the complaints (Mills, 1988). It is not a coincidence that these changes in the newspaper industry occurred during the United States' second wave feminist movement when women were asking for respect, equality, and rights in all areas of their lives (Harp, 2007).

Ridding Newspapers of Women's Pages

In January 1969, *The Washington Post* led the movement to rid newspapers of the traditional and explicitly named women's pages when they published "Style" instead of their women's section (Yang 1996). The *Los Angeles Times* planned a similar transition away from its women's pages in the late 1960s, first publishing "View" in July of 1970 (Mills, 1988). *The New York Times* simply changed the page one index to read "family/style" instead of "women's news" in September of 1971, and altered the logo on the women's section to read "Family, Food, Fashions, Furnishings" rather than "Food, Fashion, Family, Furnishings" (Greenwald, 1999). Clearly some changes were of a grander scale than others, but the point to alter how newspapers attended to women readers was on the minds of newspaper publishers and editors. Newspaper editors across the country followed suit throughout the decade, ridding their newspaper of explicitly named women's pages and offering newly developed lifestyle sections. The time is touted in the industry as the birth of the modern day feature section (Harp, 2007). However, what few studies exist that have analyzed and compared the content of the women's and style sections indicate that not a lot other than the name actually changed with this industry-wide move (Guenin, 1975; Miller, 1976). *The New York Times*' subtle alteration seems to be an indication of the manner of change at many papers. Further, the changes that did occur were not necessarily for the better. For example, rather than finding more stories by and about women and "women's issues" throughout the paper, much of this content just disappeared while the new sections focused more on movies, books, theater, and the arts. Also, more men began editing and writing for lifestyle sections, which meant fewer women had the power to define news.

This all may seem like ancient history in the newspaper industry and irrelevant to the issues newspapers face today with their women readers. The tale of women's pages, however, sets the stage for what has happened more recently between newspapers and their women readers. And both the recent and past history offer clues in how newspapers might seek out and satisfy contemporary women readers.

The Comeback of Women's Pages

While lifestyle sections have been a mainstay since their development starting in 1969, explicitly named women's pages made a comeback in 1989 and throughout the 1990s. The not so original idea to create pages just for women occurred after much industry talk about the increasing decline of women readers. While newspapers experienced a loss of both male and female readers in the 1980s, the decline of women readers was much steeper, especially at large daily metros. The industry buzzed with statistics on this readership divide. The *Washington Journalism Review* explained that the frequent readership (reading a paper four days out of five) of women declined by 23 percent between 1970 and 1990 for the country's largest newspapers, while for male readers the decline ended at 16 percent (Braden, 1991). What may seem like a relatively minor difference in percentage points translates into millions of readers. One report explained, "Had we maintained our appeal to women equal to what it was in 1970, we would have 17 million more readers" (Knight-Ridder, 1991, p. 8).

Industry leaders came to the conclusion that women were turning away from newspapers at a higher rate than men because they did not see themselves reflected on the pages of newspapers (Harp, 2007). Research from the time backed up this notion —stories by and about women were lacking in our largest newspapers, particularly on the front pages. The Women, Men and Media project, which began tracking newspaper coverage of and by women in 1989, looks at front pages of major-market, general-interest newspapers in diverse geographical areas. The research project found that during January of 1993, front-page stories referred to or solicited men for comment 85 percent of the time; men wrote 66 percent of the front-page stories; and men appeared in 73 percent of the front-page photos (Bridge, 1995). In order to rectify the situation and get women readers back, newspaper publishers and editors considered a number of strategies. These included ensuring more women were hired in decision-making positions in the newsroom; inviting female reporters to budget meetings; restructuring beats to cover issues rather than institutions; and rather than simply reporting facts, explaining what those facts mean to people's lives (Miller, 1989; Hansen, 1992; Kelly, 1993; Schmidt & Collins, 1993; Miller, 1998).

Another idea gained popularity as well: revive explicitly named women's pages. The *Chicago Tribune,* one of the nation's largest metropolitan dailies, was among the papers that chose this route (Harp, 2007). The *Tribune* began publishing a Sunday section called "Woman News," while the *Lexington Herald-Leader* (Kentucky) presented "YOU" with the subtitle "News for Today's Women." The *Arizona Republic*, the Cleveland *Plain Dealer*, the *Virginian-Pilot* (Norfolk, Virginia's), *Ledger-Star*, the *Corpus Christi Caller-Times* (Texas), and the *Portsmouth Herald* (New Hampshire) introduced new women's pages with names such as "Woman Wise," "Women's Weekly," "For Women Only," and "Hampton Roads Woman" (Knight-Ridder, 1991; Pearl, 1992). By 1992 one article estimated about ten newspapers published women's pages (Hansen, 1992) and a 1993 article estimated at least 40 US newspapers had revived explicitly named women's sections (Schmidt & Collins, 1993).

As was the case nearly a century earlier, newspaper executives wanted women readers back because advertisers are particularly interested in access to this demographic.

That fact alone is simply the reality of the industry. But segregating women's content, an idea born in a different time, is an easy, though not the most effective or creative solution to the problem of declining women readers. Gendered segregation of content, which during the turn of the nineteenth century may have made sense as women's primary place was in the home dealing with domestic duties, to many is an archaic and insulting way to view women and newspaper content. After all, women's lives and roles in the community have changed tremendously since the original development of women's sections. Women's pages were created at a time when women were not even allowed to vote. The gendered split between the public and private spheres was firmly in place as women occupied the role of housewife and mother. Unfortunately as women's place in American society has changed, newspapers, too often, have not kept pace with these changes. Even resurrecting women's pages did not solve the readership problem among women. In fact, most of the women's pages that sprung up in the 1990s have since been dissolved, including the *Chicago Tribune's* Women News (Harp, 2007; Voss, 2006).

Insight from the World of Magazines

Newspapers' troubles with appealing to women and maintaining a female readership cannot be explained away by simple conclusions such as women are too busy or just not interested in reading. One need look no further than readership statistics of women's magazines for proof that women will make time to read if their interests are respected.

A woman's magazine is "one that appeals to a woman as a woman, and not alone to her extracurricular interests" (Wolseley, 1972, p. 293). Beyond exclusively women's magazines that appeal to women as women, and not alone to their extracurricular activities, there are magazines that cater to women's service, shelter, and fashion interests such as *Ladies' Home Journal* and *Good Housekeeping*; *Better Homes and Gardens* and *House Beautiful*; and *Harper's Bazaar* and *Vogue*. Women's magazines are also published to appeal to different lifestyles (*Cosmopolitan* and *Women's Health & Fitness Magazine*); life stages (*Brides* and *Working Mother*); or even one's race or ethnicity (*Essence*, a magazine for African-American women, and *Latina* for today's Hispanic woman).

Women's magazines began publishing in the United States more than 178 years ago, with one of the earliest great women's magazines being *Ladies' Magazine* in 1828 (Johnson, 1993). Since their inception, women's magazines have offered women a means of entertainment, information, and resources. Different from newspapers, magazines tend to offer more depth in coverage than most newspaper articles. Yet, these periodicals also deal with less timely issues, often trends and issues of importance to women. Because of the sheer number of magazines and how often new ones come into the marketplace while older ones disappear, it is difficult to say exactly how many women's magazines exist today (Johnson, 1993). In 1999, those agencies counting magazines offered various numbers for different types of periodicals, ranging from 12,000 to 100,000 (Johnson & Prijatel, 2000). What is known though is a large female audience regularly reads women's magazines. And one of the most successful women's magazines with a large female readership is *O, The Oprah Magazine*, founded by Oprah Winfrey, the nationally syndicated billionaire talk show host. Published by Hearst Communications, Inc. in conjunction with Winfrey's company, Harpo, *O, The Oprah Magazine*, respects women in its editorial pages, advertising, and editorial mission statement:

With this magazine we have an opportunity to make a real mark.

To speak and connect to women in a way no other publication ever has.

To help women see every experience and challenge as an opportunity to grow and discover their best self.

To convince women that the real goal is becoming more of who they really are.

To embrace their life.

("Oprah," 2006)

The respect Winfrey shows for women probably explains why her magazine is thick with advertising and on its fifth anniversary claimed to have "13 million readers every month" ("Business Wire," 2005, p. 2).

O, the Oprah Magazine is only one of many magazines that appeal to women. In fact, the answers to our questions about women's magazines produced a mosaic of titles that women read regularly.

A business manager, Gail, reads the newspaper, the lifestyle section, and five or more magazines regularly, including *Marie Claire*. She would miss magazines a lot if they were not available because they help her relax. Betti, a university administrator, reads four newspapers, including *The New York Times* and *Los Angeles Times*, three to four days a week and six different magazines regularly. Although she doesn't read the lifestyle section of the newspaper, she reads two women's magazines, *In Style* and *Lucky*. She says she reads those magazines because: "They are entertaining and a diversion from the stress in my life." If the magazines were not available, Betti says she would also miss the magazines. For her the women's magazines represent "an easy way to fantasize about fashion without spending money shopping."

The relationship that women have with women's magazines is different from the relationship they have with newspapers and the way they think about newspapers and magazines may ultimately determine whether newspapers can hold on to readers who are starting to turn away. In general, when women talked about newspapers in the questionnaires they completed, they used the word "important" but when they described women's magazines, they used the word "interesting." One respondent seemed to sum up the difference between these two reading forms when she said she liked to relax with a glass of wine and her magazine at the end of the day. The question becomes then, can newspapers serve these varied functions for women? Can newspapers be important and interesting; relevant, fun, and relaxing to read?

But just as important, can newspapers, both print and online, connect with women through more than the soft news of the lifestyle section? Can newspapers make women feel connected throughout the newspaper the way women feel connected to the morning news shows and the women's magazines? The advantage that newspapers have over morning network news programs and women's magazines is that newspapers are local. In fact, women (33 percent) were more likely than men (23 percent) to say they very closely follow news either in the newspaper, on television, or on radio about people and events in their own community. If newspapers can provide important and interesting information customized to the local community and be like the good neighbor who respects them and looks out for their interests, they may be able to hold on to their women readers. Until newspapers learn how to serve in the many roles that women expect, women may continue to turn away and look to other sources that respect them and provide news that is helpful in their daily lives.

References

Beasley, M.H. & Gibbons, S.J. (2003). *Taking their Place: A documentary history of women and journalism* (2nd edition). State College: Strata Publishing.

Biennial news consumption survey. (2004, June 8). News audiences increasingly politicized. *The Pew Research Center for the People and the Press*. Retrieved April 14, 2006 from, http://people-press.org/reports/display.php3?PageID=837.

Braden, M. (1991, June 13). Women: special again. *Washington Journalism Review*, pp. 30–2.

Bridge, J. (1995, November/December). Men mostly missing from coverage of parental issues. *Quill*, 18.

Brooks, B.S., Kennedy, G., Moen, D.R., & Ranly, D. (1985). *News Reporting and Writing* (2nd edition). New York: St. Martin's Press.

Business Wire. (2005, April 1). O, the Oprah magazine celebrates five years with gift book of Oprah's wisdom included with every copy of May issue; May breaks record for largest-ever issue with more than 400 pages. Retrieved from LexisNexis Academic database.

Chambers, D., Steiner, L., & Fleming C. (2004). *Women and Journalism*. New York: Routledge.

Greenwald, M.S. (1999). *A Woman of the Times: Journalism, feminism, and the career Charlotte Curtis*. Athens: Ohio University Press.

Guenin, Z.B. (1975). Women's pages in American newspapers: Missing out on contemporary content. *Journalism Quarterly*, 52, 66–75.

Hansen, M. (1992, September). Reconcilable differences? *News Inc.*, 23–8.

Harp, D. (in press). *Desperately Seeking Women Readers: US newspapers and the construction of a female readership*. Lanham: Lexington Books.

Jackson, N.B. (1993, August). 1990s women's news: The roots. Paper presented at the Commission on the Status of Women, Association for Education in Journalism & Mass Communication Conference, Kansas City.

Johnson, S. (1993). Magazines: Women's employment and status in the magazine industry. In P.J. Creedon, (Ed.) *Women in Mass Communication* (2nd edition), pp. 134–53. Newbury Park: Sage.

Johnson, S. & Prijatel, P. (2000). *Magazine Publishing*. Lincoln: NTC/Contemporary Publishing Company.

Jordan, E. (1938). *Three Rousing Cheers*. New York: Appleton-Century.

Kelly, C. (1993, May/June). The great paper chase: Losing women readers, the dailies try to win us back. *Ms.*, 34–5.

Knight-Ridder. (1991, December). How newspapers can gain readership among women . . . and why it's important. A report from the Knight-Ridder Women Readers Task Force.

Lont, C. (1995). *Women and Media: Content/careers/criticism*. Belmont: Wadsworth.

Marzolf, M. (1977). *Up from the Footnote: A history of women journalists*. New York: Hasting House.

Miller, S.H. (1976). Changes in women's/lifestyle sections. *Journalism Quarterly*, 53, 641–7.

Miller, S. (1989, September). The latest editorial challenge is to regain women readers. *ASNE Bulletin*, 8–12.

Miller, S. (1998, April). Women and content. *Presstime*, 41–5.

Mills, K. (1988). *A Place in the News: From the women's pages to the front page*. New York: Dodd, Mead & Co.

Mott, F.L. (1952). *The News in America*. Cambridge: Harvard University Press.

Mott, F. (1962). *American Journalism: A history, 1690–1960* (3rd edition). Macmillan.

Online papers modestly boost newspaper readership. (2006, July 30). *The Pew Research Center for the People and the Press*. Retrieved August 2006 from http://people-press.org/reports/display.php3?ReportID=282.

Oprah. (2006). Editorial Mission Statement, O Media Kit. Retrieved September 2, 2006 from www.omediakit.com/r5/showkiosk.asp?listing_id=385214&category_code=edit.

Patterson, T. & Seib, P. (2005). Informing the Public. In G. Overholser & K.H. Jamieson (Eds.) *The Press*, p. 192. New York: Oxford University Press.

Pearl, D. (1992, May 4). Newspapers strive to win women back. *Wall Street Journal*, p. B1.
Schmidt, K. & Collins, C. (1993, July/August). Showdown at gender gap. *American Journalism Review*, 39–42.
Tankard, J.W. Jr., Hendrickson, L., Silberman, J., Bliss, K., & Ghanem, S. (1991). Media Frames: Approaches to conceptualization and measurement. Paper presented at the Association for Education in Journalism and Mass Communication Conference, Boston.
Tankard, J.W., Jr. (2001). The empirical approach to the study of media framing. In S.D. Reese, O.H. Gandy, Jr., & A.E. Grant (Eds.) *Framing Public Life: Perspectives on media and our understanding of the social world*, pp. 95–106. Mahwah: Lawrence Erlbaum Associates.
Voss, K.W. (2006). The Penney-Missouri Awards. *Journalism History*, 32(1), 43–50.
Wolseley, R.E. (1972). *Understanding Magazines* (second edition). Ames: The Iowa State University Press.
Yang, M. (1996). Women's pages or people's pages: The production of news for women in The Washington Post in the 1950s. *Journalism & Mass Communication Quarterly*, 73(2), 364–78.
Zuckerman, M.E. (1998). *A History of Popular Women's Magazines in the United States, 1792–1995*. Westport: Greenwood Press.

Part III

Women, Technology, and News

Chapter 7

Women and Technology

How Socialization Created a Gender Gap

Sharon Meraz

For a majority of the US population, the Internet has woven itself into the natural rhythms of everyday life. Innovations such as cell phones, wireless Internet hot spots, and portable devices such as Blackberries, Palm Treos, and iPhones, which have extended the Internet's reach outside the confines of a desktop computer or laptop, have facilitated the Internet's seamless integration into daily life. As we progress through the twenty-first century, the Internet will continue to mainstream into an invisible and unobtrusive part of daily life, be it in the workplace, on school campuses, in the home, in the mall, in the park, on the beach, or in our automobiles (Pew Internet & American Life Project, 2005).

It is noteworthy that it took six years after the development of the first World Wide Web browser in 1994 for women to achieve parity with men in terms of access to the Internet. Beginning in 1994, annual surveys conducted by Georgia Institute of Technology (1994, 1995, 1996, 1997, 1998) found an overwhelming male Internet audience; however, by 1998, these surveys revealed that the male Internet audience had declined to 61 percent of total Internet users as more women began to go online. Since 2000, several Internet usage reports have tracked the growth of women as Internet users, first to parity with men and, eventually, to outnumbering men as a percentage of total Internet users (ComScore, 2000). As of 2006, women continue to outnumber men as a larger percentage of total Internet users due to their greater relative raw numbers when compared to males in the US population (Fallows, 2005).

Locating the Technology Gender Gap: A Look at Usage

Although Internet access statistics since the year 2000 suggest gender parity on the Web, the focus on access statistics masks significant differences in how women and men relate to the Internet. Because women show a strong preference for usage of the Internet as a communications medium to connect to family, friends, and social networks, they are commonly perceived as communicators while men are the information seekers on the Internet. For example, women surpass men in their use of e-mail, particularly for the purpose of extending relationships with kin, friends, and family (Rainie *et al.*, 2000; Boneva *et al.*, 2001).

Unlike women, the majority of men use the Internet for reading online, surfing adult websites, and pursuing hobbies (Fallows, 2005). Men are considered to be more avid information searchers and tend to use the Internet to sustain a broader range of activities such as searching for news, accessing do-it-yourself activities from websites, reading sports and financial information, and conducting work/research. Unlike men, most women use the Internet for accessing health and spiritual information (Horrigan & Rainie, 2002; Fallows, 2005).

Men are also more inclined to aggressively pursue content creation in categories other than text blogging. Although there is no gender gap in terms of creating blogs or reading blogs, men are more likely to get involved in the technical aspects of Web content creation such as downloading computer programs, remixing files, using a Webcam, maintaining their own website, owning iPods or Mp3 players, and making Voice Over Internet Protocol calls (Fallows, 2005; Rainie & Madden, 2005). Men are also more intense Internet users than women. Men are more likely to go online more frequently and for a longer time (Fallows, 2005). As it relates to Internet connection speeds, men are more likely to have broadband or high speed connections at home, which empowers men to post user-generated content such as audio and video to the Web (Horrigan, 2006a). Since broadband Internet users are also more prone to read news online, men are also leading the way as online newsreaders (Horrigan, 2006b). Men's greater facility with experimentation is evident in the fact that they are also more likely to download music and practice file swapping; in 2001, 43 percent of males 18 and over engaged in file swapping in comparison to only 26 percent of females in the same age group (ComScore, 2001b).

Men are not only comfortable as power users of technology, but are also actively engaged with the machine as a technical device. Male computer users are more aware of the technical aspects of computing and its associated technologies when compared to women. Unlike women, men are more likely to know the latest technical terms (Rainie, 2005). Men are also more likely to embrace such technical tasks as computer maintenance, installing computer software, changing Web browser homepages, setting up virus protection, and fixing computer hardware and software problems by themselves (Fallows, 2005). The rapid uptake of Internet technologies by men continues when assessing the newer, more emergent technologies. In addition to comprising most of the broadband users, men tend to be the ones who connect to the Internet from wireless devices. Males comprise 72 percent of the Internet users who access the Internet via cell phones or personal device assistants (ComScore, 2002). Men are more prone to use their cell phones to surf the Internet and take pictures (Rainie & Keeter, 2006).

Positioning Socialization Within Theories of Gender and Technology

Why is it that women and men relate differently to technology? Scholars have advanced several theories to explain the relationship between women and information and communications technologies (ICTs). Liberal feminist theory assumes that women can be encouraged to enter the science and technology fields by active campaigns to drive women into technical occupations (Adam, 1997). The weakness of this theory is its emphasis on women as the primary agents of change. This theory does not address the hostility of the technological field to women, nor does it answer the question why men dominate the higher-end jobs in technical fields as opposed to jobs as word processors or data entry personnel.

Other reductive arguments that fail to address the complexity of the relationship between technology and gender are gender essentialist arguments (Gefen & Straub, 1997; Ventakesh & Morris, 2000; Trauth et al., 2004). Gender essentialism ascribes certain traits to males and females based on biological characteristics. These arguments typically suggest that men possess greater analytical, logical, and problem-solving abilities than women and are thus more suited to technical fields than women. Women are ruled by the body instead of the mind, and possess too much emotion to excel at technical fields. The lack of women in math and science fields is offered as evidence to support women's inability to engage in mathematical analysis.

One of the more helpful theories in deconstructing the relationship between gender and technology has been the social construction of technology (SCOT) theory. This theory, which has arisen out of the intersection between feminist studies and science and technology studies (S&TS), examines both the role that technology plays in the shaping and construction of gender, and the role that gender plays in the shaping and construction of technology (Faulkner, 2001). For example, there is a strong association between domestic technologies and femininity; male designers usually picture users of domestic technology as women. Sometimes designers of technologies make assumptions about the target user of a technology in order to design gender into the machine or artifact.

A more recent theory that has been developed to escape the limiting definitions of both gender essentialism theory and social construction theory is the individual differences theory. This theory actively pursues an individualist interpretation of how individuals, located within their specific gender, respond to technology. The individual differences theory uses a socio-cultural interpretation of both information technology work and power relations in an effort to understand how women interact with technology (Morgan et al., 2004; Trauth et al., 2004). In this theory, the focus is within rather than between genders, seeking explanations for gender-technology positioning through both personal characteristics and environmental influences.

Though these theories offer different explanations for how technology is gendered, many of these theories fall into two main theoretical camps: person-centered or dispositional explanations and situation-centered or structural explanations (Ibarra, 1992, 1993, 1997). Dispositional explanations attribute differences between the genders to such characteristics as individual preferences, personality, and behavior patterns. Structural explanations for gender differences locate the reasoning for gender differences outside the individual and within the social environments in which the individuals are embedded.

How socialization, which is a product of social environments, can shape gender's interaction with technology is illustrated in Figure 7.1. Notice both historical invisibility and stereotypes affect socialization, technology adoption, and the relationship between socialization and technology adoption.

As a result of childhood socialization in the home and school environments, the forces of historical invisibility and stereotypes can gain a foothold. Women's relationship toward technology continues to be shaped outside the home and school contexts in the workplace and through media. When combined, these factors can influence women's confidence, comfort, and facility with technology.

The Invisible Force of Stereotypes

In January 2005, then president of Harvard University Larry Summers suggested that an innate difference in aptitude between women and men could be responsible for the low numbers of women enrolling in science, technology, engineering, and math (STEM) fields. Summers' speech drew public rancor, resulting in more than 50 Harvard professors signing a letter protesting the statement, and alumni threatening to withhold donations (Bombardierie, 2005). Summers eventually issued a public apology, remaining as the president of Harvard until he tendered his resignation in February 2006.[1] As unsuitable as Summers' public declarations appeared, his statements exposed a long held explanation for why women are less visible in science and technology fields.

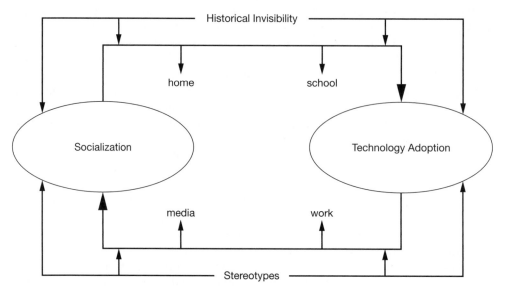

Figure 7.1 Factors impacting socialization and technology adoption

The belief that girls are not as good as boys in math has been a popular dispositional explanation for the gender gap in technology; yet, the evidence for a gender gap remains inconclusive. Math is widely held as a predictor of fluency in computer science and information technology fields, and the search for sex differences in math aptitude has preoccupied scholars for many years in their effort to decipher the reasons for the math and science gender gap (Benbow & Stanley, 1980; Kolata, 1980; Segal, 1987; Shibley Hyde *et al.*, 1990). One meta-analysis of the literature on sex differences in mathematics performance found only small gender differences in overall math ability: girls outperformed boys in computational abilities while boys developed their greater problem solving skills in high school as opposed to elementary or middle school (Shibley Hyde *et al.*, 1990).

While researchers continue to question the role of biological factors in the gendered relationship between sex and math, what often gets ignored is the role that socialization plays in creating these widespread societal stereotypes about differences in sex aptitude toward math. For females to excel in math fields, they must be able to overcome low outward expectations of teachers, family, and society, all social foci that create a strong association between competence in math and masculinity (Steele, 1997). In assessing the difficulty that females and racial minorities face, Steele noted that stereotypes about these groups work to shape social structures, ultimately defining and creating boundaries around academic identities and performance outcomes. Steele argued that the situational effect of a negative stereotype could be internalized either in the individual's acceptance of the stereotype, or in the constant threat faced by those individuals who gain membership into desired communities, but face continuous questions about their competence in the field due to their membership in negatively defined groups.

These internalized stereotypes can aid in explaining how the different genders approach technology. Technology is said to have a very masculine aura and women have been found to have lower self-esteem and confidence in their computing abilities (Turkle, 1986; Compeau *et al.*, 1999; Herring *et al.*, 2006). Although the bulk of evidence supports the existence of these differences in the older generations, more recent studies capture the ambivalence and lower self-confidence of the Millennial Generation of females (Herring *et al.*, 2006).

Self-efficacy is also a major predictor of success in computing, and women generally report lower levels of self-efficacy and confidence with computers (Dambrot *et al.*, 1985). This diminished self-efficacy also manifests itself outside the classroom environment and in the technology work environment. Women tend to feel more job stress in response to changing technology as information technology professionals, a finding that could also be explained by the stereotype that women have lower facility with computers than men (Gardiner & Tiggerman, 1999).

Rather than look to biology and genetics to explain women's lower self-confidence, self-esteem, and comfort with technology, explanations for women's discomfiture with technology can best be explained by gender socialization. In other words, women are socialized to fear technology; men are socialized to feel confident about technology.

Historical Invisibility: Boy's Toy, Women's Tool

It is easy to understand how computer technology became gendered when one examines the larger masculine culture of other established science and technology professional areas that preceded computer science. These earlier technologies set a precedent for the alignment of computer technology with masculine identity. With the advent of the industrial revolution, the domestic/reproductive/private sphere was disconnected from the economically productive work/public sphere. Most middle- and upper-class women retreated into the household, while the poorer women supplemented their husband's income by working in sewing and laundry. This gender stratification lessened when women earned formal rights to education and suffrage. In the decades following World War II, the birth of a technological nation enabled an expansion of opportunities for women to find employment.

Much of the work on women's historical invisibility from technological development has been conducted by a core group of women scholars. As an early pioneer in the study of the patriarchal culture of science and technology, renowned sociologist Sally Hacker (1982) conducted studies of women in such industries as insurance, printing and publishing, agribusiness, and telecommunications. She found pervasive barriers to women's ability to work outside the home due to limited employment options, unresponsiveness of unions, and opposition from husbands and male coworkers. Hacker is best known for her work on women in engineering, observing its culture through classroom seminars, social gatherings, and in-depth interviews with engineering faculty. She found a pervasive masculine culture underlying teachings in the classroom: after conducting an analysis of jokes in a course on telephone technology, she discovered that students were encouraged to laugh at women.

Another prominent researcher who has contributed vital insight into women's invisibility within the technology field is Cynthia Cockburn. Like Hacker, Cockburn (1985) examined several industries such as clothing, mail warehouses, X-ray equipment industries, and engineering firms. Cockburn found that women were stuck in routine occupations, with very few occupying higher-level technical jobs. Though women were found operating the machinery, they had no knowledge of the inner workings of the machine. They were essentially button pushers. Tracing women's relationship to the workplace from the advent of the industrial revolution to before the women's liberation period, Cockburn pointed out that men could not stop capital from engaging women;

thus, they created avenues to segregate women, resulting in sexual divisions of labor. Women were pushed into the less skilled, lower paying jobs, and excluded from unions. Women were not only prevented from entering male domains of technical knowledge, but their work was consistently undervalued, both by pay and perception.

It is within this culture that computer technologies were developed. When typing was introduced in the United States, it immediately became identified as women's work (Davies, 1988). Though this technical innovation assisted in bringing women out from the private sphere of the household and into the public sphere of the workplace, it also assisted in stratifying women into such occupations as bookkeepers, cashiers, accountants, stenographers, and typists. Within the workplace, the computer's association with the typewriter made keyboarding a woman's occupation. For example it has been noted that the design of the word processor was deliberately modeled on the typewriter in an effort to market word processors to the female workforce (Webster, 1993).

The enduring symbolic relationship between the computer and word processing or data entry persists to this day. According to 2004 data from the US Bureau of Labor Statistics (2004), women comprise almost 94 percent of word processors and typists and approximately 80 percent of data entry workers (p. 32). In sharp contrast, women are less represented in the professions that often require a degree in computer science, information technology, science and technology, or certifications in programming languages. In 2004, women comprised fewer than 27 percent of computer scientists and computer analysts, computer programmers, computer software engineers, computer support specialists, and network systems administrators (p. 32). Like earlier technologies, women remain ghettoized in the lower-paying and lower-skilled administrative jobs as it relates to computer technologies. These occupations often place a glass ceiling on the skills that women can develop on the job such that women employed in a clerical position often lack both the access and the autonomy to surf the Internet during the day.

In tracing the brief history of the Internet, it is obvious that the accomplishments of males are often cited at the forefront of its development. The Internet's early development has strong associations with the military and academia, both male-dominated spheres of influence (Edwards, 1990, 1996). An examination of most scientific journals, online encyclopedias, and technology timelines that chart the development of the Internet highlight the Internet's inventors as mostly male engineers, computer scientists, and programmers. Many popular books on the history of the Internet often credit the creative experimentation phase of the Internet's development to the work of male hackers and male professionals. In the popular book, *Where Wizards Stay up Late*, credit for the Internet is given to such male scientists and engineers as Bob Taylor, Larry Roberts, Joseph Licklider, and Paul Baran (Hafner, 1996). In another popular book, *Hackers: Heroes of the Computer Revolution*, male hackers are of three types: orthodox, hardware, and game hackers (Levy, 1984). Although these different categories cover almost three generations of hackers from the late 1950s to the 1980s, only male hackers are profiled. These books suggest that the Internet's development was a central playground for male technology enthusiasts who are given such playful names as "wizards" and "hackers."

Though the numbers by gender breakdown show a preponderance of men in computer development as engineers and computer scientists, women have played an important role in the development of computing and programming as a professional field. Augusta Ada Byron, Countess of Lovelace, was a mathematician who collaborated with Charles

Babbage on the Difference and Analytical Engines, which was regarded as the theoretical foundation for the modern computer (Gurer, 1995). Lovelace, who died at age 38, was strong-willed, creative, and intelligent, and dared to enter the field of science at a time when the presence of women in science was rare (Plant, 1997).

Another noted female developer was Grace Murray Hopper, a mathematician who was credited with developing the first computer compiler, A-0, and its successor, A-2. Hopper was also responsible for developing the only business data processing language in use at that time, FLOW-MATIC. The COBOL community, an industry-wide group, partially supervised by Hopper, used FLOW-MATIC as a model for its data standards, and Hopper is often referred to as the grandmother of the programming language COBOL (Danis, 1997). Women were also arguably the world's first programmers. During World War II, women's technical skills were called upon because of the absence of men due to their involvement in the war. In 1946, the first electronic general purpose computer called the Electronic Numerical Integrator and Computer (ENIAC) was designed and six women programmers, who got the nickname "computers," were selected from a group of 100 to program the machine (Brown, 1997). Sadly, these six women programmers were robbed of recognition in their day by being labeled clerks and sub-professionals (Perry & Greber, 1990).

It is possible that the invisible history of women's involvement in computing technologies has fostered a lack of identification of women with technology. If women are only exposed to male historical role models in computing, it is possible that mental associations have linked women's incompetence in technology with their lack of presence in designing and developing computing technology. The overlooking of women's contributions can also frame expectations on who should be using technology and how each gender should use technology in such contextual environments as home, school, and work.

Socialization in Learning Environments: Home and School

The gender gap in technology adoption can be traced back to early childhood socialization when boys more than girls were actively encouraged to develop an intimate relationship with computers. Boys growing up in the 1980s were at least three times more likely than girls to use a computer at home, participate in computer-related clubs or activities, or attend a computer summer camp (Kramer & Lehman, 1990). This active socialization enabled males to develop greater experience in computing namely in the areas of programming and game playing as opposed to word processing (Chen, 1986; Shashaani, 1997).

The socialization of males toward an intimate relationship with computing technology was, and still is in many cases, solidified in the school environment. By the mid-1970s, many schools within the United States had introduced computers into the classroom. Some studies examining that time period found small gender differences favoring boys' greater access toward computer technologies in schools (Sutton, 1991). Studies also found that young women and girls were underrepresented in elementary, middle, and high school elective programming and game playing before and after school use (Chen, 1986; Becker & Sterling, 1987; Sutton, 1991). Studies conducted on later generations also found a gender gap in access. Boy's confidence in technological pursuits is often affirmed through the school system when curricula and teacher support are geared toward boys as opposed to girls (Margolis & Fisher, 2002). When both genders get to college, girls often lose interest in technology because of the weight of experience that boys have gathered in computing, which gives boys more confidence and technical facility with computing, programming, and technology.

Attention must be directed toward the dynamics of the classroom environment as an added deterrent to girls succeeding in technology environments. It is here that many scholars draw on dispositional differences between the genders by providing evidence that women prefer a more cooperative form of usage of the computer as opposed to competitive computer activities (Hesse-Biber & Gilbert, 1994; Gneezy et al., 2003). The performance of girls has been shown to decrease in competitive environments with men as opposed to same sex environments (Gneezy et al., 2003).

Chilly Social Environments and the Geek Image

Though occupational and contextual factors explain some differences in the gendered adoption of technology, it has been realized that women possess different motivations for adopting technology (Venkatesh & Morris, 2000; Venkatesh et al., 2004). Women also have strong reasons for turning their backs on technology. As opposed to being forced to turn away from computing due to lack of access or encouragement, some women consciously resist computing technology (Turkle, 1986). This resistance is partly based on their negation of the male's intimate relationship with the computer.

Even though significant strides have been made in the information technology workplace, the work environment continues to exude a masculine culture. Women who work for such Silicon valley companies as Sun Microsystems, Apple Computer, Intuit, Electronic Arts, and Netscape Communications confess to feeling entrapped in a "geek atmosphere" of male coworkers who play video games and Lego (Chaudhry, 2000). These women's frustrations with the technology work culture of toys and games can be exacerbated in those work environments where male employees are younger and closer to college age—a trend in the modern-day technology industries.

A pervasive image of computing enthusiasts is the geek image of the hacker (Levy, 1984; Hapnes, 1996). Hackers are generally defined as males with an abiding interest in mechanical and electronic construction, and the Internet has grown in large part due to the influence of hackers. This association of computer enthusiasts with the hacker symbol has become a powerful deterrent to women's entrance into computer technology fields. Hackers have a strong interest in comics, science fiction, and computer games, and the hacker culture is often defined by endurance competitions based on the number of hours spent programming without sleep or food (Hapnes, 1996). The male hacker's joy in experimentation, muddling, and tinkering with computer technology can be a deterring cultural symbol to women, who may prefer a more balanced relationship with computing technology.

But, the question can alternatively be asked, why is the geek image so pervasive in framing descriptions of technology environments? Clearly, not every technology professional is a geek, and it is disconcerting that this image is the most enduring mental picture of a technology enthusiast. Is it possible that the media has played a role in shaping the pictures in our minds of technology professionals? How has socialization cemented these geek images in women's minds? It is apparent that these common stereotypes have had a more dangerous and enduring impact, evidenced by the low representation of women in the technology field.

Hostile Workplace Environments

Do women in professional technology positions face different problems when compared to women in other high-level professional fields? First-hand accounts suggest that women face unique problems as workers in technology environments. These environments have directly contributed to the present-day socialization of many women away from technology fields. Consider the following first-hand evidence:

1. Dr. Ellen Spertus (1991), one of the first women computer scientists, noted the pervasive negative consequences of male-dominated technical environments. Through interviews with graduate students and faculty members, Spertus identified many instances of sexist or sexual humor, sexual displays, and overt sexual discussions as seen in the display of nude pictures as backgrounds on computer terminals. Spertus, who works as an associate professor of computer science at Mills College and as a part-time computer scientist for the search engine giant Google, has had to endure being tagged the Sexist Geek alive in 2001, a title that she seems to embrace with pride (Spertus, n.d.).
2. In citing reasons for women's early absence from the computer science field, Janet Cottrell (2002) noted that women were disadvantaged due to poorly lit passageways from the computer labs to their apartments. Women would often have to stay back late in the labs to run their computer programs, and many did not have the benefit of an escort service.
3. Dr. Francis Grundy, who has worked in computing since the 1960s, found that women who work in the information technology industry are often given the tedious jobs of writing report programs, inputting data, and merging databases. Grundy (1996) noted that in the early 1970s, punched cards were used to input data and programs. As the lone woman programmer in the computer center, she was the only person asked to assist in punching cards when the department was short on punch card operator staff.
4. In an open document suggesting ways to encourage women in Linux development, Hensen (2002) provided some basic advice to men as it related to common industry problems, which included refraining from the following: telling sexist jokes, staring and pointing at women when they come into the room, making sexual advances toward female coworkers, calling women bitches, inviting male-only speakers at conferences and sessions, and underestimating wives and girlfriends.

In addition to these issues, which still exist in the modern-day technology workplace, women employed in the technology industry are faced with problems ranging from lack of recognition to overt sexual discrimination.

Gendered Social Networks

The role of gender as an influencing variable in how individuals form social networks has also proven to be a barrier for women in computing and information technology fields. Social networks can signal what is appropriate as a profession or hobby, and the homophily or "birds of a feather flock together" concept has been used to explain the tendency of individuals to self-select in homogeneous social networks based on such factors as shared socio-economic status, demographic similarities, or shared values (Lazarsfeld & Merton, 1954; McPherson et al., 2001). For example, it has been found that sex homophily precedes sex segregation in the workforce, beginning as early childhood play when boys and girls unconsciously separate into gender homogenous social networks (Ridgeway & Smith-Lovin, 1999).

Among the variety of reasons offered for why women and men tend to form different social networks, evidence suggests that structural or situation-centered factors may be responsible for the breakup of social networks along gender lines. Structural factors such as young mothers' withdrawal from the labor force upon either marriage or child-rearing often results in women having significantly more friendships with kin or neighbors as opposed to workplace contacts (Fisher & Oliker, 1983). Men tend to form social networks with other men as a result of their higher social status, while women tend to mix their networks of women and men for instrumental and emotional support respectively (Ibarra, 1992, 1993, 1997). Women are said to have fewer connections to high power males in their networks and weaker connections to larger voluntary organizations—places where men tend to network with other men (McPherson & Smith-Lovin, 1982, 1986, 1987; Ibarra, 1992). All of these factors negatively impact the ability of women to network in information technology fields.

The lack of women in technology fields coupled with the gendering of social networks within technology fields has contributed to the sense of isolation that women feel when employed in these environments. First discovered during the late 1980s, the phenomenon of women disappearing from the computer science ranks at every stage of the school system and in industry has been dubbed the "shrinking pipeline" (Frenkle, 1990; Cottrell, 2002). For example, degrees awarded to women in computer science declined from a high of approximately 37 percent in 1983–4 to around 28 percent in 1993–4 even though women comprised the greater percentage of all university admissions, irrespective of departmental affiliation (Camp, 1997, p. 2).

Evidence exists that this phenomenon of the shrinking pipeline still persists. In 2004, women in the IT workforce declined by almost 20 percent from a high of 41 percent in 1996 to 32.4 percent in 2004, and this sharp drop occurred while the percentage of women in the overall workforce remained largely unchanged at approximately 46 percent during this 8-year period (ITAA, 2005).

Sexual Discrimination on the Internet

Similar to technology environments, women have always faced a hostile climate on the Internet. This hostile climate is evident in male–female interactions in Internet chat rooms and in the proliferation of pornography online, which tends to show that women are treated as sexual objects through images and language (Harp & Heider, 2002).

Susan Herring, who has conducted much of the groundbreaking work on the rhetorical differences between genders in online communication, found that male participants are more prone to harass female participants on different online forums through verbal speech patterns and sexual intimidation (Herring, 1993, 1994, 1999, 2000, 2001, 2002, 2004). Exposing this culture of male interaction with females online as a "male rhetoric of violence," Herring (2002) noted that cyber violence, which can be both physical as well as emotional/psychological, involves mostly women as victims in online spaces, with men as the perpetrators.

Impact of Household, Children, and Leisure

The core role that women play managing the household and childrearing means they often do not have the luxury to work long hours in the workplace, a requirement of many technology professions. Professional technology jobs can involve frequent travel, late nights, working weekends, and ad hoc meetings (Salveker, 2004). The competitive nature of software development results in a peculiar culture of working through to the morning, living on fast food take out, and sleeping in the office, sacrifices that women cannot make if they are responsible for taking care of children and the household (DeBare, 1996). This culture of 80-hour working weeks has positively biased the industry toward young, unmarried males who see this kind of work ethic as a masculine status symbol.

This second shift that women face in their role as workers in both the private and public sphere has resulted in a gendering of leisure time. Men report more time to pursue hobbies on the Internet (Madden & Rainie, 2003; Fallows, 2005). Because most women have less leisure time than men, women have less time to tinker with technology, often the way that technology workers stay abreast of new computer programming languages and emerging technologies. This lack of time has meant that women have not always had the luxury to pursue additional training outside of their normal work day, thus reducing their chances for career advancement and better job prospects. Since careers in science and technology usually necessitate on-going training to remain on the cutting-edge of new technological developments, women's inability to take advantage of job training avenues has often resulted in lower qualifications and lessened desirability in the eyes of employers who seek out workers with the best experience to fill vacant technology jobs within their organization.

Entertainment Media: Gaming Culture

It is no secret that boys usually develop an interest in computing through their early introduction to computer games (Sutton, 1991; Clegg & Trayhurn, 2000). Though it is popularly believed that women are not avid gamers, a report on gaming from the Consumer Electronics Association found almost 47 percent of the sample were women, with female gamers in the 25–34 age category outnumbering males in the same age group (Woodbury, 2006). Similarly, a 2006 report from the Entertainment Software Association found that 43 percent of gamers are women. Interestingly, the majority of this growth in women's gaming can be attributed to the large numbers of middle-aged women who play casual, online games (BBC News, 2004).

Though there is some level of parity in game playing between the genders, there are sharp differences in how adult women and men game. Adult women are more prone to play online puzzle games such as Tetris and Bejeweled as opposed to gaming through such console devices as Sony PlayStation 2, Microsoft's X-box, or the Nintendo Game Cube ("Business Wire," 2006; Mindlin, 2006). More adult men are players of massively multiplayer online role-playing games (MMORPG) such as World of Warcraft (WoW) and Second Life. Adult women are also said to spend less time playing games, and are considered to gravitate toward games that take less time, are less violent, and are less complicated in terms of game controls (Hermida, 2004; Kohler, 2006). These differences have resulted in adult women being branded casual gamers, in contrast to men who are considered hardcore, serious gamers (Guilded Lilies, 2006; Kohler, 2006). As assumptions continue to be made about women gamers, the preponderance of advertising dollars and production budgets continue to be dedicated to console gaming, where men are considered to outnumber women (Gaudiosi, 2006). Meanwhile, women's affiliation with playing puzzle games online has provided an easy marketing tag for women. Companies such as *LimeLife* are now developing such puzzle games as Solitaire, Freecell, and Wordheaven for women to play on their cell phones.

One has only to examine the representations of women in gaming to understand why women have embraced online puzzle games more readily than console gaming. As it relates to developing games for women and girls, the industry has taken a lazy approach to understanding what women want in a game. Industry has focused on producing special "pink" games for females that are nonviolent and cooperative (Case, 2004). These simpler games, marketed often to young girls, are using television and movie characters that are popular with adolescent and teenage girls. These games also tend to involve less creativity and challenge, while incorporating more flashy graphics, colors, and accessories. Since it is the challenge and uncertainty in computer games that contribute to developing higher order thinking skills in logic, reasoning, and abstract thinking, girls who play these "pink" games are missing out on an opportunity to develop these skills that are considered essential for careers in technology.

Since computer games provide the medium through which children get introduced to computing, it is not surprising that girls become socialized into believing that the computer is a male toy.

Women as the New E-commerce Consumer

Now that women have achieved parity with men on the Internet, women's relationship to Internet technology has been redefined. Marketing and public relations firms have identified women, particularly middle-income and wealthy women, as one of the biggest e-commerce markets (Consalvo & Paasonen, 2002; Shade, 2002). This courtship of the high income female audience as shoppers and consumers has led to a proliferation of online stores selling products related to beauty, fitness, health, cosmetics, apparel, housekeeping, and parenting. Recognizing the profitability of the female online shopper, NBC acquired iVillage in 2006 for $600 million in an effort to expand its offerings in health and women's interests (Red Herring, 2006). A glimpse into iVillage's content offerings shows the topics that are considered to be of interest to women: beauty and style, health and well-being, diet and fitness, love and sex, pregnancy and parenting, home and food, entertainment, and magazines. Markedly absent are topics for interest in news, technical content, or financial analysis.

Women are said to now account for approximately 50 percent of technology purchases, which has not gone unnoticed by leading technology companies. Many technology companies are now including gadget advertising in such women's magazines as Oprah Winfrey's *O at Home*, *Ladies' Home Journal*, and *Cosmogirl!* (Gogoi, 2005). The entrance of women into the technology marketplace as consumers of gadgets has also led to a surge in product designs for the female consumer (Twist, 2004). The preponderance of colorful laptop skins, mirrors, and cosmetic accessories on technology products reveals that marketers continue to frame technology as a product that needs to be disguised or dressed up for women to adopt it. Why do women need to have their cell phone display screen turn into a mirror? Or why do women need calorie counters on their mobile phones?

Socialization, Technology, and the Millennial Generation

If computers have been a part of the lives of Millennials since childhood, would socialization factors that created a gender gap in technology for older generations have the same effect on the Millennial Generation? It is likely that those same socialization factors would not have the same effect because both Millennial girls and boys are immersed in technology. In addition to Millennial teens' online activities displayed earlier in Table 4.1, almost 20 percent of teens have created blogs (Lenhart & Madden, 2005a, p. 2). Teen bloggers share content over the Web by remixing pre-existing content and creating personal Web pages, and they help older adults with their technological needs (Lenhart & Madden, 2005a). But, do Millennial girls show the same level of engagement with technology as Millennial boys? As shown earlier, in Table 4.1, a larger percentage of girls than boys are engaged in a wider array of activities. In addition to communicating, networking, and seeking information, Millennial girls are creating content on the Internet. In fact, Millennial girls lead Millennial boys in the Web activity of blogging, with 25 percent of online girls keeping a blog compared with 15 percent of boys (Lenhart & Madden, 2005a, p. 3). Girls also lead boys in photo blogging: girls in the 12–17 age group are almost three times more likely to visit image hosting sites when compared to average users (Gonsalves, 2005). But, boys appear more fearless and confident in their use of the technology. Older boys are more likely to download multimedia, be it audio or video through all age groups, and boys are more likely to download music or share copyrighted material when compared to girls (Lenhart & Madden, 2005a). Boys also exhibit more confidence in their abilities with computer technologies: boys are more inclined than girls to say they know more about technology than their parents. Furthermore, boys are more likely to say they are self taught while girls are more likely to report they learned computer technologies from their parents (Lenhart & Rainie, 2001).

Although historically, socialization steered girls growing up in older generations away from technology, today's generation of girls has grown up embracing technology. Today Millennial girls are curious about, interested in, and excited about technology, including the opportunities to create content on the Internet. It would be another opportunity lost if girls growing up today lose their avid interest in technology because socialization forces in home, school, workplace, and media environments do not respect and support the curiosity, interest, and excitement that girls express about the technology that has been woven into their daily lives.

Note

1   Ironically, Summers was replaced by a woman. The founding dean of the Radcliffe Institute for Advanced Study and a distinguished historian, Drew Faust is the first woman in Harvard University's 371-year history to become president.

References

Adam, A. (1997). Information technology cultures and women's lives. In *Technology and Society at a Time of Sweeping Change: Proceedings of the 1997 international symposium*, 20–1, 75–81.

BBC News. (2004, June 10). Net games lure "bored" housewives. Retrieved August 19, 2006 from http://news.bbc.co.uk/2/hi/technology/3791983.stm.

Becker, H.J. & Sterling, C.W. (1987). Equity in school computer use: National data and neglected considerations. *Journal of Educational Computing Research*, 3(3), 289–311.

Benbow, C.P. & Stanley, J.C. (1980). Sex differences in mathematical ability: Fact or artifact. *Science*, 210(4475), 1262–4.

Bombardierie, M. (2005, January 17). Summers' remarks on women draw fire. *The Boston Globe*. Retrieved August 19, 2006 from www.boston.com/news/education/higher/articles/2005/01/17/summers_remarks_on_women_draw_fire/.

Boneva, B., Kraut, R., & Frohlich, D. (2001). Using email for personal relationships: The difference gender makes. *American Behavioral Scientist, 45*(3), 530–49.

Brown, J. (1997, May 8). Women proto-programmers get their just reward. *Wired News.* Retrieved August 19, 2006 from www.wired.com/news/culture/0,1284,3711,00.html.

Bureau of Labor Statistics. (2004). Table 11: Employed persons by detailed occupation and sex, 2004 annual averages. Retrieved August 19, 2006 from www.bls.gov/cps/wlf-table11–2005.pdf.

Business Wire. (2006, June 5). Online games making inroads against board games—and now trump packaged software, new vendare media survey finds; nationwide study reveals nearly one in four Americans find online gaming 'most rewarding' way to play. Retrieved August 28, 2006 from www.findarticles.com/p/articles/mi_m0EIN/is_2006_June_5/ai_n16441292.

Camp, T. (1997). The incredible shrinking pipeline. *Communications of the ACM, 40*(10), 103–10.

Case, S. (2004, January 12). Women in gaming. *Microsoft.* Retrieved May 18, 2006 from www.microsoft.com/windowsxp/using/games/learnmore/womeningames.mspx.

Chaudhry, L. (2000, July 5). Sili Valley: Unfriendly to women? *Wired News.* Retrieved August 19, 2006 from www.wired.com/news/culture/0,1284,37047,00.html.

Chen, M. (1986). Gender and computers: The beneficial effects of experience on attitudes. *Journal of Educational Computing Research, 2*(3), 265–82.

Clegg, S. & Trayhurn, D. (2000). Gender and computing: Not the same old problem. *British Educational Research Journal, 26*(1), 75–89.

Cockburn, C. (1985). *Machinery of Dominance: Women, men, and technical know-how.* London: Pluto Press.

Compeau, D., Higgins, C.A., & Huff, S. (1999). Social cognitive theory and individual reactions to computing technology: A longitudinal study. *MIS Quarterly, 23,* 145–58.

ComScore Media Matrix. (2000, August 9). Women outpace men online in number and growth rate according to Media Metrix and Jupiter communications. Retrieved August 19, 2006 from www.comscore.com/press/pr.asp?year=2000.

ComScore Media Matrix. (2001, October 10). Users of file-swapping alternatives increase nearly 500 percent in the US, surpassing Napster, reports Jupiter Media Metrix. Retrieved August 19, 2006 from www.comscore.com/press/pr.asp?year=2001.

ComScore Media Matrix. (2002, August 27). Ten million Internet users go online via a cell phone or a PDA, reports ComScore Media Matrix. Retrieved August 19, 2006 from www.comscore.com/press/release.asp?press=87.

Consalvo, M. & Paasonen, S. (Eds.) (2002). *Women and Everyday Uses of the Internet: Agency and identity.* New York: Peter Lang Publishing.

Cottrell, J. (2002). I'm a stranger here myself: A consideration of women in computing. Retrieved August 19, 2006 from www.eff.org/Net_culture/Gender_issues/cottrell_stranger.article.

Dambrot, F., Watkins-Malek, M., Silling, S., Marshall, R., & Garver, J. (1985). Correlates of sex differences in attitudes toward and involvement with computers. *Journal of Vocational Behavior, 27*(1), 71–86.

Danis, S.A. (1997). Rear Admiral Grace Murray Hopper. Retrieved August 19, 2006 from http://ei.cs.vt.edu/~history/Hopper.Danis.html.

Davies, M.W. (1988). Women clerical workers and the typewriter: The writing machinery. In C. Kramarae (Ed.) *Technology and Women's Voices: Keeping in touch.* New York: Routledge & Kegan Paul.

DeBare, I. (1996). High-tech industry is zipping along but women often are left behind. *The Sacramento Bee.* Retrieved August 19, 2006 from www.sacbee.com/static/archive/news/projects/women/wcmain.html.

Edwards, P. (1990). The army and the microworld: Computers and the politics of gender identity. *Signs: Journal of Women in Culture and Society, 16*(1), 102–27.

Edwards, P. (1996). *The Closed World: Computers and the politics of discourse in Cold War America.* Cambridge: MIT Press.

Entertainment Software Association. (2005). Essential facts about the computer and the video game industry. Retrieved August 19, 2006 from www.theesa.com/files/2005EssentialFacts.pdf.

Fallows, D. (2005). How men and women use the Internet. *The Pew Internet and American Life Project*. Retrieved August 19, 2006 from www.pewInternet.org/PPF/r/171/report_display.asp.

Fisher, C. & Oliker, S. (1983). A research note on friendship, gender, and the life cycle. *Social Forces*, 62(1), 124–33.

Frenkle, K. (1990). Women in computing. *Communications of the ACM*, 33(11), 34–46.

Gardiner, M. & Tiggerman, M. (1999). Gender differences in leadership style, job stress, and mental health in male-and-female dominated industries. *Journal of Occupational and Organizational Psychology*, 72(3), 301–15

Gaudiosi, J. (2006). Product placement to die for. *Wired News*, 14(4). Retrieved August 19, 2006 from www.wired.com/wired/archive/14.04/gads.html.

Gefen, D. & Straub, D.W. (1997). Gender differences in the perception and use of email: An extension to the technology acceptance model. *MIS Quarterly*, 21(4), 389–400.

Georgia Institute of Technology (1994). Graphics, visualization, and usability study. Retrieved August 19, 2006 from www.gvu.gatech.edu/user_surveys/survey-01–1994/.

Georgia Institute of Technology (1995). Graphics, visualization, and usability study. Retrieved August 19, 2006 from www.gvu.gatech.edu/user_surveys/survey-10–1995/.

Georgia Institute of Technology. (1996). Graphics, visualization, and usability study. Retrieved August 19, 2006 from www.gvu.gatech.edu/user_surveys/survey-10–1996/.

Georgia Institute of Technology. (1997). Graphics, visualization, and usability study. Retrieved August 19, 2006 from www.gvu.gatech.edu/user_surveys/survey-1997–10/.

Georgia Institute of Technology. (1998). Graphics, visualization, and usability study. Retrieved August 19, 2006 from www.gvu.gatech.edu/user_surveys/survey-1998–10/.

Gneezy, U. Niederle, M., & Rustichini, A. (2003). Performance in competitive environments: gender differences. *The Quarterly Journal of Economics*, 118(3), 1049–79.

Gogoi, P. (2005, November 28). Meek Jane geek. *BusinessWeek Online*. Retrieved August 19, 2006 from www.businessweek.com/magazine/content/05_48/b3961113.htm?chan=tc.

Gonsalves, A. (2005, September 13). Blogging sparks boom in photo hosting sites. *TechWeb*. Retrieved August 19, 2006 from www.techweb.com/showArticle.jhtml?articleID=170702929&cid=test1_rssfeed.

Grundy, A.F. (1996). *Women and Computers*. Exeter: Intellect Books.

Guilded Lilies. (2006, March 8). Update: Annie get your BFG. *Guilded Lilies*. Blog post posted to http://ninthwavedesigns.typepad.com/guilded_lilies/2006/03/annie_get_your_1.html.

Gurer, D. (1995). Pioneering women in computer science. *Communications of the ACM*, 38(1), 45–54.

Hacker, S. (1982). The culture of engineering: Woman, workplace, and machine. In J. Rothschild (Ed.) *Women, Technology and Innovation*. New York: Pergamon Press.

Hafner, K. (1996). *Where Wizards Stay up Late: The origins of the Internet*. New York: Simon and Schuster.

Hapnes, T. (1996). Not in their machines: How hackers transform computers into subcultural artifacts. In M. Lie & K.H. Sorensen (Eds.) *Making Technology our Own: Domesticating technology into everyday life*. Oslo: Scandinavian University Press.

Harp, D. & Heider, D. (2002). New hope or old power: Democracy, pornography, and the Internet. *Howard Journal of Communication*, 13(4), 285–99.

Hensen, V. (2002, October 29). HOWTO encourage women in linux. Retrieved August 19, 2006 from www.tldp.net/HOWTO/Encourage-Women-Linux-HOWTO/index.html.

Hermida, A. (2004, September 1). Women take a shine to video games. *BBC News*. Retrieved August 19, 2006 from http://news.bbc.co.uk/1/hi/technology/3615278.stm.

Herring, S.C. (2004). Slouching toward the ordinary: Current trends in computer-mediated communication. *New Media & Society*, 6(1), 26–36.

Herring, S.C. (2002). Cyber violence: Recognizing and resisting abuse in online environments. *Asian Women*, 14, 187–212. Retrieved May 24, 2006 from http://ella.slis.indiana.edu/~herring/violence.html.

Herring, S.C. (2001, October). Gender and power in online communication. Retrieved August 19, 2006 from http://rkcsi.indiana.edu/archive/CSI/WP/WP01–05B.html.

Herring, S.C. (2000). Gender differences in CMC: findings and implications. *CPSR Newsletter.* Retrieved August 19, 2006 from www.cpsr.org/issues/womenintech/herring.

Herring, S. (1999). The rhetorical dynamics of gender harassment online. *The Information Society,* 15(3), 151–67.

Herring, S.C. (1994). Politeness in computer culture: Why women thank and men flame. In *Cultural Performances: Proceedings of the Third Berkeley Women and Language Conference,* pp. 278–94. Berkeley Women and Language Group.

Herring, S.C. (1993). Gender and democracy in computer mediated communication. *EJC/REC,* 3(2). Retrieved August 19, 2006 from www.Internetstudies.pe.kr/txt/Herring.txt.

Herring, S.C., Ogan, C., Ahuja, M., & Robinson, J.C. (2006). Gender and the culture of computing in applied IT education (in press). In E. Trauth (Ed.) *Encyclopedia of Gender and Information Technology.* Hershey: Information Science Publishing.

Hesse-Biber, S. & Gilbert, M.K. (1994). Closing the technological gender gap: Feminist pedagogy in the computer-assisted classroom. *Teaching Sociology,* 22(1), 19–31.

Horrigan, J.B. (2006a, May 28). Home broadband and adoption 2006. *The Pew Internet and American Life Project.* Retrieved August 19, 2006 from www.pewInternet.org/pdfs/PIP_ Broadband_trends2006.pdf.

Horrigan, J.B. (2006b, March 22). Online news. *The Pew Internet and American Life Project.* Retrieved August 19, 2006 from www.pewInternet.org/pdfs/PIP_News.and.Broadband.pdf.

Horrigan, J.B. & Rainie, L. (2002, December 29). Counting on the Internet. *The Pew Internet and American Life Project.* Retrieved May 1, 2006 from www.pewInternet.org/pdfs/PIP_ Expectations.pdf.

Ibarra, H. (1992). Homophily and differential returns: Sex differences in network structure and access in an advertising firm. *Administrative Science Quarterly,* 37(3), 422–47.

Ibarra, H. (1993). Personal networks of women and minorities in management: Conceptual framework. *Academy of Management Review,* 18(1), 56–87.

Ibarra, H. (1997). Paving an alternate route: Gender differences in network strategies for career development. *Social Psychology Quarterly,* 60(1), 91–102.

ITAA diversity study: numbers of women, minorities in tech too low. (2005, June 22). *Information Technology Association of America (ITAA).* Retrieved June 1, 2006 from www.itaa. org/newsroom/release.cfm?ID=1952.

Kolata, G.B. (1980). Math and sex: Are girls born with less ability. *Science,* 210(4475), 1234–5.

Kohler, C. (2006, March 6). Women gamers duke it out. *Wired News.* Retrieved May 6, 2006 from www.wired.com/news/technology/0,70313-0.html?tw=rss.index.

Kramer, P.E. & Lehman, S. (1990). Mismeasuring women: A critique of research on computer ability and avoidance. *Signs: Journal of Women in Culture and Society,* 16(1), 158–72.

Lazarsfeld, P. & Merton, R.K. (1954). Friendship as a social process: A substantive and methodological analysis. In M. Berger, T. Abel, & C. Page. (Eds.) *Freedom and Control in Modern Society,* pp. 18–66. New York: Van Norstrand.

Lenhart, A. & Madden, M. (2005, November 2). Teen content creators and consumers. *The Pew Internet and American Life Project.* Retrieved August 19, 2006 from www. pewInternet.org/PPF/r/166/report_display.asp.

Lenhart, A. & Rainie, L. (2001, June 21). Teenage life online. *The Pew Internet and American Life Project.* Retrieved May 31, 2006 from www.pewInternet.org/report_display.asp?r=36.

Levy, S. (1984). *Hackers: Heroes of the computer revolution.* Garden City: Anchor Press/Doubleday.

Madden, M. & Rainie, L. (2003, December 22). America's online pursuits: The changing picture of who's online and what they do. *The Pew Internet and American Life Project.* Retrieved August 19, 2006 at www.pewInternet.org/report_display.asp?r=106.

McPherson, J.M. & Smith-Lovin, L. (1982). Women and weak ties: Differences by sex in the size of voluntary organizations. *American Journal of Sociology* 87, 883–904.

McPherson, J.M. & Smith-Lovin, L. (1986). Sex segregation in voluntary associations. *American Sociological Review, 51,* 61–79.

McPherson, J.M. & Smith-Lovin, L. (1987). Homophily in voluntary organizations: Status distance and the composition of face-to-face groups. *American Sociological Review, 52,* 370–9.

McPherson, J.M., Smith-Lovin, L., & Cook, J.M. (2001). Birds of a feather: Homophily in social networks. *Annual Review of Sociology, 27,* 415–44.

Mindlin, A. (2006, April 17). It seems girls go for computer games too. *The New York Times.* Retrieved August 28, 2006 from www.nytimes.com/2006/04/17/technology/17drill.html? ei=5070&en=2e93cf48566572c1&ex=1156910400&adxnnl=1&adxnnlx=1156789007-3wwev36KqWtyNW2UreLYGA.

Morgan, A.J., Quesenberry, J.L., & Trauth, E.M. (2004). Exploring the importance of social networks in the IT workforce: Experiences with the 'boy's club.' In J. Luftman (Ed.) *Proceedings of the Americas Conference on Information Systems,* pp. 1313–20. New York: USA.

Perry, R. & Greber, L. (1990). Women and computers: An introduction. *SIGNS: Journal of Women in Culture and Society,* 16(1), 74–101.

The Pew Internet and American Life Project. (2005). Internet: The mainstreaming of online life. Retrieved August 19, 2006 from www.pewInternet.org/pdfs/Internet_Status_2005.pdf.

Plant, S. (1997). *Zeroes and Ones: Digital Women and the New Technoculture.* New York: Doubleday.

Rainie, L. (2005, September 20). Public awareness of Internet terms. *The Pew Internet and American Life Project.* Retrieved August 19, 2006 from www.pewInternet.org/PPF/r/161/report_display.asp.

Rainie, L. & Keeter, S. (2006, April 3). How Americans use their cell phones. *The Pew Internet and American Life Project.* Retrieved August 19, 2006 from www.pewInternet.org/PPF/r/179/report_display.asp.

Rainie, L. & Madden, M. (2005, April). Podcasting catches on. *The Pew Internet and American Life Project.* Retrieved August 19, 2006 from www.pewInternet.org/pdfs/PIP_podcasting.pdf.

Rainie, L., Fox, S., Horrigan, J., Lenhart, A., & Spooner, T. (2000). Tracking online life: How women use the Internet to cultivate relationships with family and friends. *The Pew Internet and American Life Project.* Retrieved August 19, 2006 from www.pewInternet.org/pdfs/Report1.pdf.

Red Herring. (2006, March 6). NBC buys iVillage for $600m. Retrieved August 19, 2006 from www.redherring.com/Article.aspx?a=15964&hed=NBC+Buys+iVillage+for+%24600M.

Ridgeway, C.L. & Smith-Lovin, L. (1999). The gender system and interaction. *Annual Review of Sociology, 25,* 191–216.

Salveker, A. (2004, May 12). Technology's too small sisterhood. *BusinessWeek Online.* Retrieved August 19, 2006 from www.businessweek.com/technology/content/may2004/tc20040512_2760_tc147.htm.

Segal, S.L. (1987). Is female math anxiety real? *Science,* 237(4813), 350.

Shade, L.R. (2002). *Gender & Community in the Social Construction of the Internet.* New York: Peter Lang Publishing.

Shashaani, L. (1997). Gender differences in computer attitudes and use among college students. *Journal of Educational Computing Research,* 16(1), 37–51.

Shibley Hyde, J., Fennema, E., & Lamon, S.J. (1990). Gender differences in mathematics performance: A meta-analysis. *Psychological Bulletin,* 107(2), 139–55.

Spertus, E. (1991, August). Why there are so few female computer scientists. Retrieved August 19, 2006 from http://people.mills.edu/spertus/Gender/why.html.

Steele, C.M. (1997). A threat in the air: How stereotypes shape intellectual identity and performance. *American Psychologist,* 52(6), 613–29.

Sutton, R.R. (1991). Equity and computers in the schools: A decade of research. *Review of Educational Research,* 61(4), 475–503.

Trauth, E.M., Quesenberry, J.L, & Morgan, A.J. (2004). *Understanding the Underrepresentation of Women in IT: Toward a theory of individual differences.* Tucsom: SIGMIS.

Twist, J. (2004, October 11). Technology gender balancing act. *BBC News*. Retrieved August 19, 2006 from http://news.bbc.co.uk/1/hi/technology/3680146.stm.

Turkle, S. (1986). Computer reticence: Why women fear the intimate machine. In C. Kramarae (Ed.) *Technology and Women's Voices: Keeping in touch*, pp. 41–61. New York: Routledge & Kegan Paul.

Venkatesh, V. & Morris, M.G. (2000). Why don't men ever stop to ask for directions? Gender, social influence, and their role in technology acceptance and user behavior. *MIS Quarterly*, 24(1), 115–39.

Venkatesh, V., Morris, M.G., Skyes, T.A., & Ackerman, P.L. (2004). Individual reactions to new technologies in the workplace. *Journal of Applied Social Psychology*, 34(3), 445–67.

Webster, J. (1993). From the word processor to the micro: Gender issues in the development of information technology in the office. In E. Green, J. Owen, and D. Pain (Eds.) *Gendered by Design? Information Technology and Office Systems*, p. 115. London: Taylor & Francis.

Woodbury, J. (2006). New study shows thirty-five percent of Americans play video games. *Entertainment Software Association*. Retrieved August 19, 2006 from www.theesa.com/archives/2006/01/new_study_shows.php.

Chapter 8

Online News

Factors Influencing the Divide Between Women and Men

Amy Schmitz Weiss

By the turn of the century, women had reached parity with men on the Internet, but by 2006, women had yet to reach parity with men in online news consumption. Why women have lagged behind men in adopting news on the Internet is connected to the Internet's development as well as factors that have influenced the adoption of computers and Internet access and use.

In 1969, six years after the 1963 publication of *The Feminine Mystique*, Betty Friedan's groundbreaking book that exposed the limitations American society imposed on women, computer scientists at UCLA, Stanford, University of California at Santa Barbara, and the University of Utah linked computers to a network called the Advanced Research Projects Agency Network or ARPANET (Ceruzzi, 2003, pp. 194, 259). This network made it possible for computer scientists to send and receive data across the country.

For more than 20 years, ARPANET was a digital information highway that was available to select academics, computer scientists and government officials. By the 1980s, the technology landscape would change with the development of the Bulletin Board System (BBS), a text-only system on the computer (Ceruzzi, 2003, p. 298). The BBS made the Internet accessible to the public, allowing them to now chat, post discussions, publish articles, and play games from their personal computers.

Tim Berners-Lee's creation of the first website and his online how-to guide for building a website in the 1990s would set into motion a global domino effect (Ceruzzi, 2003, p. 302). By 1994, the Web would be transformed from an exclusive, academic, and scientific community to a consumer-based one in which companies began to see the Web as a viable medium for communication, entertainment, shopping, banking, marketing, and news. Diverse companies including newspapers quickly developed a presence online (Sabo, 1995); by the twenty-first century, 3,300 newspaper, television and cable news websites had been established on the Internet (Yahoo Internet News Directory, 2003).

The speed at which the Internet was adopted by consumers and companies was phenomenal. In fact, the Internet was adopted into society "more rapidly than any other electronic technology, taking only 7 years to reach 30 percent of households, in comparison to 38 years for the telephone and 17 years for television" (Schmitz Weiss *et al.*, 2003, p. 4). Spreading rapidly around the world, this innovation would be adopted differently by women and men. But the gender gap in the adoption of the Internet would not be independent from the gender gap in the adoption of the computer.

Computer Ownership, Usage at Home, and in the Workplace

According to a 1988 US Census report on computer ownership, men were more likely than women to have a personal computer and use it more often from home. Men's personal use of the computer at home would set the stage for their early adoption of later Internet innovations such as participation in BBS activities or surfing the Web.

As for women's use of computers in 1988, the census report showed 29 percent of women used computers at their workplace compared to 21 percent of men (Bureau of the Census, 1988). The type of work that women and men participated in also revealed a gender difference in computer usage. In the technical, sales, and administrative support occupations, 38 percent of women used a computer compared to 36 percent of men (ibid.). These occupations involved usage of the computer primarily for word processing: a fact that explains why women's usage of the computer surpassed that of men's when computers were first introduced into the workplace. These workplace differences in computer use between the sexes would remain constant for almost ten years (Kominski & Newburger, 1999).

During this time period, women had access to computers but were using them for work while men accessed their computers from home for recreational activities. This gender gap in computer use would lay the foundation for the gender divide that later emerged in Internet adoption and online news use.

A Brief History of Content Online

In the late 1970s, long before the Internet became a consumer-oriented interactive communication medium and before personal computers were adopted in great numbers, then-Knight-Ridder Newspapers partnered with AT&T before its court-mandated breakup into regional phone companies in the 1980s, to "develop a videotex service in Coral Gables, Florida, and test consumer reaction to it" (Poindexter & McCombs, 2000, p. 362). A forerunner to the Internet and World Wide Web, videotex:

> was a communication medium for sending and receiving information, including news, entertainment and games, travel, advertising, financial and shopping transactions, and inter-personal communication, over a telephone line or cable between a large central computer and a dedicated terminal hooked up to a television-like monitor or personal computer.
>
> (Ibid.)

Knight-Ridder was not the only newspaper company to experiment with videotex. The then-parent company of the *Los Angeles Times*, Times Mirror, teamed up with Infomart, a Canadian company, to develop a similar videotex service in Orange County, California. After spending millions of dollars in market trials to test consumer interest in electronic newspapers as well as other types of electronic content, Knight-Ridder and Times Mirror discontinued their videotex experiments, concluding the technology was ahead of the market. In contrast to the American videotex experience, which was market-driven, the European experience was government-driven. The British, French, and other European governments implemented videotex systems in their countries that made electronic delivery of information the norm.[1]

By the early 1990s, news organizations were again experimenting with electronic content; however, this time they were constructing websites on the Internet. In 1992, versions of *The Chicago Tribune* went online followed by versions of the *San Jose*

Mercury News in 1993; and by 1994, versions of *The New York Times* went on America Online (Carlson, 2005; Garrison, 2005). By 1994, 20 US newspapers were online, and, by 1995, that number increased ten-fold ("F.Y.I.," 1995). Even though newspapers had a presence on the Internet, the presentation of news content on websites such as *The New York Times* was limited. This limited content delivery was primarily due to slow Internet connection speeds. At most, newspapers offered a photo and/or an image on the online newspaper's homepage with hyperlinks of headlines to stories from that day's print version. Once inside the website, the news pages contained the text of the story, hyperlinks to the main navigation of the website, and a banner advertisement on the page. In addition to being limited by Internet bandwidth, many newspapers were not publishing original work on their websites but moving content from their print editions to their online counterpart. Applications and systems for pushing content to the Web were limited so many online staffers had to learn Hypertext Markup Language (HTML) and other programming languages to post their news stories and photos to the online newspaper's website.

The watershed moment that boosted the potential for offering news online was the 1995 Oklahoma City bombing in which 168 women, men, and children were killed when a truck bomb exploded in front of the Federal Building (Cochran, 1995). This breaking news story made online newspaper staffs across the country scramble to post stories on the Internet from the wire or from their local print staff. "We updated the front [page] with an edited wire story within 10 minutes after the AP story moved," said Lorraine Cichowski, head of the *USA Today* division in a June 1995 quote to a journalism publication (Cochran, 1995, p. 12). This historic moment, which prior to 9/11 was the worst terrorist attack on American soil, demonstrated the power and immediacy of Web publishing, which would set the stage for other critical online news moments.

The 1995 Oklahoma City bombing also defined the activity of getting news online. Although Internet connectivity was limited in its diffusion and reach, traffic to US news sites skyrocketed throughout the day as updates were posted and people checked news websites for breaking news (Cochran, 1995). This defining moment helped news organizations realize the Internet's potential to offer updated news. In addition, online news consumers realized they no longer needed to rely on the production schedules of radio or television newscasts. News consumers could now go online 24 hours a day to get news.

Other historic moments helped shape the Internet as an online news medium. When the Starr Report, Independent Counsel Kenneth Starr's investigation into whether President Bill Clinton committed impeachable offenses, was released online in September 1998, Web traffic data revealed this event to be the busiest day in Internet history. The world flocked onto the Internet on September 11, 2001, when terrorists flew airplanes into the World Trade Center in New York and the Pentagon. In 2003, when President George W. Bush started the war in Iraq as part of the war on terror, the trend in turning to the Internet for news gained momentum.

What would a news consumer find at a newspaper website? A study of 83 US online newspapers of varying circulation sizes found that between the years 1997 and 2000, many of the newspapers offered few features in the areas of presentation of news content, multimedia, interactivity, and revenue-generating features (Greer & Mensing, 2004). Specifically, in 1997, most news websites mainly featured local news with very few multimedia and interactive elements. As for updated content, 71 percent were updating their pages daily in comparison to 90 percent by 2003 (ibid., p. 105). Other content features such as newswires, national news, and archives to past articles were gradually added to the websites over the seven years tracked by the researchers.

Similar results were found in an e-mail survey and content analysis of 135 online newspapers. Almost three-fifths (57 percent) of online staff said they updated their websites every 24 hours in comparison to 41 percent who did this more frequently within the 24-hour timeframe. The content analysis showed that less than 10 percent of the online newspapers offered multimedia features such as audio, video, or animations with news stories (Tankard, 1998). Updates to content on news sites were limited due to constraints in resources, technology, and access.

By 2005, the presentation of content on news websites had changed dramatically when compared to a decade earlier. With the growth in adoption of broadband, more data could be pushed back and forth from the news website to the end user's computer in a shorter amount of time. This speed allowed online news users to get media-rich content such as audio, video, and flash movies from news websites to their computer (or other devices). *The New York Times*, for example, no longer offered just text and a few images on its website; they developed new models of storytelling that included photo slideshows and flash movies, both of which incorporated audio and video. The advancements made in applications, computer systems and network infrastructure helped news organizations offer more content and a richer news experience to their news audience.

The Gender Gap in Online Activity Emerges

In the mid-1990s, males were the early adopters of the Internet; however, a half decade later, there would be a shift in the online population from being heavily dominated by men to almost an equal representation between the sexes ("Women a Formidable Force on the Web," 2001). This shift in the online population would take place across the globe, according to Nielsen/NetRatings:

> From April 2001 to April 2002, females as a percentage of at-home users on the Internet increased in 24 of the 25 countries surveyed, with women now outnumbering men on the Internet in the US and Canada, by 52 to 48 percent.
> ("Women are Gaining on the Web," 2002)

At this time, women were also leading the way in connecting to the World Wide Web from home and work. Another Nielsen/NetRatings report noted:

> Nearly 46 million American office workers logged onto the Web, the highest peak since Nielsen/NetRatings began measuring the at-work audience in January 2000. While men still outnumber women, female office workers were the primary drivers of traffic growth, as the group grew 23 percent year-over-year to 20.4 million, outpacing the growth rate for men.
> ("Online Usage At Work Jumps 17 Percent Year-Over-Year,
> Driven By Female Office Workers," 2002)

Because women initially lagged behind men in adopting the Internet, they also lagged behind men in getting news online. Looking for factors to explain why women were less likely than men to consume news online, researchers found an explanation in an intervening variable, numbers of years of experience reading news on the Internet. "Reading Internet news is not related directly to gender but to number of years reading Internet news. Males are significantly more likely to read Internet news due to the fact that they have been reading Internet news for more years than females," (Schmitz Weiss *et al.*, 2003, p. 4). The authors suggested that once women caught up with men in the length of time reading news online, the gender difference would likely disappear.

A look at diffusion of innovation theory provides insight into how years of experience might intervene between gender and reading news online. Although according to Rogers (1995, p. 269), demographic variables such as age, race, and gender are irrelevant to the adoption of an innovation, socialization factors discussed in Chapter 7 would suggest that when it comes to adopting technology, gender is indeed relevant. Traditionally boys have been socialized to embrace technology while girls have been socialized to fear it.

As a result of an analysis of the time it takes to adopt an innovation, Rogers (1995, pp. 263–5) identified five distinct groups of adopters: innovators, early adopters, early majority, late majority, and laggards. By applying these adopter groups to when women and men started reading news online, men would be more likely than women to be classified as innovators or early adopters because they adopted reading news online before women.

Rogers (1995, pp. 15–16) noted that adoption of an innovation by an individual is based on five characteristics of the innovation: relative advantage, compatibility, complexity, trialability, and observability. Trialability seems to be particularly relevant because men experimented with computers and the Internet at home while women used computers at work for word processing. Other attributes relevant to adopting an innovation have been added to Roger's original five because of their relevance to computers and the Internet: familiarity (Fidler, 1997); financial cost for computer technology (Lin, 1995); and computer ownership and skills (Atkins *et al.*, 1998, p. 42). Many of these more recent attributes also accentuated men's ability to adopt computer technology earlier than women. Men were in an economic and professional capacity to experiment with computer technologies because of their higher status in the workplace.

Adoption of an innovation is a process in which individuals participate in a decision framework that includes knowledge, persuasion, decision, implementation, and reinforcement (Rogers, 1995, p. 13). When the adoption process is applied to accessing the Internet and getting news online, it becomes clear that women and men made different decisions. By 1999, 41 percent of women were going online daily in comparison to 59 percent of men ("The Internet News Audience Goes Ordinary," 1999, p. 8). When it came to getting news on the Internet, Figure 8.1 shows women have lagged behind men in reading news online since this method of getting news was first tracked 12 years ago. Although since 1995, women have increased their use of the Internet for news, Figure 8.1 illustrates that reading news on the Internet remains a gendered activity.

News Enthusiasts, Monitors, Betweeners, Eclectics, and Accidentals Can be Found Online

To provide insight into how women use the Internet for news, women representing news consumer types described in Chapter 1 were interviewed after a call for volunteers was placed on the local and international listservs of professional, gender-related,

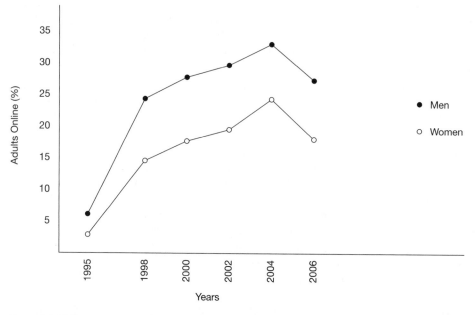

Figure 8.1 Daily news activity by gender between 1995 and 2006

Notes: For 1995 and 1998, see "Internet News Takes Off" (1998, p. 9). Statistics represent percent of all adults who go online to get news at least once a week. For 2000, 2002, and 2004, see "News Audiences Increasingly Politicized" (2004, p. 17). Statistics represent percent of all Americans who go online for news three or more days per week. For 2006, see "Online Papers Mostly Boost Newspaper Readership" (2006, p. 56). Statistics represent read yesterday.

media-related, and educational organizations such as *Austin Woman Magazine*, Webgrrls International, *Women's eNews*, Association for Women in Communication (Austin Chapter), and the Center for Women's and Gender Studies at The University of Texas at Austin. Seventeen women volunteered to be interviewed about their use of the Internet and their online news consumption over the past decade. Interviews were conducted via telephone and/or e-mail, and lasted from 30 minutes to over an hour. The four women who are profiled here were assigned a pseudonym to protect their identities.

A news enthusiast lives for the news.   Abigail, a 35-year-old, single journalist working in New York City, first went online in 1993 as a college student when she was introduced to the Internet through e-mail and online forums. Since 1999, the Internet has been Abigail's primary source for news:

> In the mornings, I tune into CNN for a few minutes and then turn on the radio unless CNN is so captivating that I leave it on. Very rarely the case, although it does happen. I listen to NPR's *Morning Edition* as I get ready for work and then because I don't leave for work until 9:30, I get to listen to about half an hour of the BBC . . . Then I listen to podcasts on my way to work, usually NPR but really a wide variety. I download about 30 separate podcasts and I swap around since there's no way I can listen to all of them. At work, I'm online all day, checking out stories and news sites in brief, and in particular, the stories I need to know

about for my job. I listen to more podcasts on my lunch hour and on my way home from work. When I get home, this really depends on how late it is, but the Jim Lehrer *NewsHour* and the BBC newscast are waiting for me patiently on the DVR . . . Then later in the evening, I'll get back online and read the news sites and my gmail account for an hour or so depending on how tired I am. I'll catch up with these on the weekend too. I subscribe to about half a dozen magazines and journals and I will read these (on real paper!) along with the Sunday *New York Times* over the weekend and in evenings, but I have to admit to double dipping these while the TV is on.

(Abigail, personal communication, January 29, 2006)

Monitoring the news requires focus.   Lindsay, who began using the Internet during the mid-1990s, started getting news online in 2001. At 60 years of age, Lindsay, a mother of two sons, grandmother of two grandsons, devoted wife, and a career woman with her own public relations consulting business manages to stay on top of the news online, every day. Lindsay works from home, so her connection to the Internet is always on and at any given time in the day, she will visit *The Washington Post*, *The New York Times*, *USA Today*, local media, and some business journal websites for her work.

Throughout the day, Lindsay will look for healthcare, mental health and political news on the Web. Lindsay's news interests in health and medical content are examples of content that appeal to women online. Her level of attention to the news and frequency is not as high as Abigail's, the news enthusiast, but she does keep an eye on the news throughout the day based on her personal interest in it, making her more of a news monitor.

Online eclectics and betweeners are hard to distinguish.   Katherine, who is 41 years old and owns her own Public Relations firm, is married and the mother of two boys. She was introduced to the Internet in the late 1990s when she and her husband listened to football games on the Web from the alma maters they attended. Katherine, who has been an online news user since 2001, spends about ten to 30 minutes on a news site. On a typical day, Katherine's inbox is filled with news briefs from CNN to business and trade publications. Because of the volume of information she receives, she scans the headlines before deciding which news stories to read and when she does find something of interest, she prints it out instead of reading it on the screen (Katherine, personal communication, January 27, 2006). Katherine seeks out news on business, technology, and international issues, but her level of attention to news online is inconsistent and somewhat disconnected, making her more of a news eclectic.

News accidentals stumble upon news while online.   Accidental online news consumers were compared with online news seekers and news avoiders in a Web-based survey of 842 randomly selected college students at a large southwestern university to provide insight into their news consumption (Poindexter, Schmitz Weiss, *et al.*, 2004). To identify accidental online news readers, survey participants who read news on the Internet were asked: "'Typically when you read news on the Internet, are you purposely searching for news or are you reading news because you saw it while online doing something else?' Respondents who said they read news because they saw it while online doing something else were classified as 'accidental online news readers.'"

Results of the survey found female college students (32 percent) were significantly more likely than male college students (21 percent) to be accidental news readers. When consumption of traditional news was compared, online accidental news readers were less likely than online news seekers to read newspapers and watch cable news three or more days a week but they were equally as likely as online news seekers to watch local TV news.

When accidental online news readers and news seekers were compared on 12 different types of news and information, ranging from national and international news to entertainment and health and fitness news and information, entertainment news was the only type of news in which news accidentals read more often than news seekers.

When asked how much they would miss different types of news media if they were no longer available, news accidentals were less likely than news seekers to say they would miss newspapers and news websites if they were no longer available. But news accidentals were significantly more likely than online news seekers to say they would miss TV and cable news.

Accidentally getting news online is not limited to college students. According to The Pew Research Center for the People and the Press (2006, p. 17), an "increasing number are inadvertently getting news while they are online for other purposes. About three-quarters of internet users (76%) say they 'bump into' the news when online."

Everyone online is not purposely or accidentally getting news. In fact, 16 percent of consumers online get news "less often" than once every few weeks and 9 percent of those online admit they never get news while on the Internet. Marilyn, a 57-year-old mother of two grown children, grandmother of twin boys, and devoted wife, is an example of an online news avoider. An Internet user since 2001, Marilyn was first attracted to the Internet because she could find information quickly. Marilyn mainly uses the Internet to access e-mail, which she uses to keep in touch with family and friends. She also visits health websites. Although Marilyn avoids news on the Internet, it doesn't mean she's disinterested in news. She just prefers to get news, which she seeks throughout the day, from the local print newspaper, and radio and television newscasts. (Marilyn, personal communication, February 26, 2006).

The Impact of Increased Internet News Options on the News Media Landscape

The early Internet was characterized by limited connectivity options. In 1995, the three major players for online commercial service were America Online, Prodigy and Compuserve. In the workplace, Compuserve was used whereas Prodigy and America Online were mainly adopted for personal home use ("Americans Going Online," 1995).

By 1999–2000, the popularity of and access to broadband or high-speed connections would change the way people would go online and how they got their news. News users continued to visit news websites directly; but, by 1999, many would begin to find another way. At this time, many online news organizations started experimenting with news updates via e-mail. News users selected categories or news topics of interest and news organizations would e-mail users a concise bulletin of news updates to their inbox. Most of these early versions of e-mail newsletters were mainly text of news headlines that hyperlinked directly to the news story on the website. Over time, more advanced newsletters were developed that included text and visuals. Plus, by 2002–3, customizable news features such as personalized front pages of the website and e-mail news alerts became common features on news websites (Greer & Mensing, 2004).

A report by The Pew Research Center for the People and the Press (1999) found the pushing and personalizing of news made a large impact in 1999. About 18 percent of those surveyed had their stories e-mailed to them while 17 percent had a customized page of specific news topics.

As customized news pages and e-mail news alerts became popular, the twenty-first century brought with it advancements in wireless technology, which impacted how news was distributed. With the introduction of web-enabled cell phones and personal digital assistants, news users could receive e-mail, check weather, get stock quotes, or receive headlines. The online news user no longer had to rely on their desktop or laptop computer to get the news, but could receive news through wireless devices. In a 2004 memo from The Pew Internet & American Life Project, it was found that for the first time, 17 percent of those surveyed were accessing the Internet through a wireless device.

Search engines and news aggregators such as Google News, which launched in 2003, created another option for online news users. News users no longer had to visit the news websites directly, but could get the news headlines from search engine and aggregator sites. Search engines such as Yahoo allowed online users to customize Web pages with their favorite news sites' hyperlinks. The online news user no longer had to seek out the news because the news came to them. A Pew report from 2004 detailed how common these news options became:

> Seven-in-ten of those who go online for news (41% of Americans overall) say they have used search engines like Google or Yahoo to get information on news subjects in which they are interested. Roughly a third of the online news audience (34%) uses a search engine at least weekly.
>
> ("News Audience Increasingly," 2004, p. 20)

Because of the ease of access to these other choices for getting news, the frequency of this activity increased, according to the same report that noted:

> Nearly half of those who go online for news regularly—three days a week or more— (47%) use Google, Yahoo or a similar search engine at least weekly. And 12% of regular online news consumers (at least three days a week) do this every day.
>
> ("News Audience Increasingly," 2004, p. 20)

As for e-mail news updates, the report found 26 percent of online news users received their news through this method, and the percentage increased for those who got news more frequently. The ways in which online news users were getting their news was changing such that there were now greater options for exploring online news.

The Future is Wireless

Although initial computer ownership and access contributed to the adoption of the Internet and online news by men before women, other factors have also contributed to the sex divide in online news: restricted access to the Internet at work, limited time to use the Internet for recreation at home; different content interests of women and men; diverse methods for delivering news, including traditional news websites, e-mail, news aggregators such as Google News, personal homepages, blogging, cell phones, and podcasts.

Although women lagged behind men in adopting the Internet and news online, the future of online news adoption will have less to do with the factors that influenced adoption in the past and more to do with how the news media industry responds to the wireless world that is upon us. The increasing availability of access to news through wireless devices, including laptop computers with wireless capability, cell phones, and iPods, means increased opportunities for getting news on the go, something that will likely appeal to the next generation. In fact, studies have shown that young adults who get news through wireless laptops read more news online than those who get news through wired devices (Yang, 2006). Furthermore, a recent exploratory study of consumer adoption of podcasts found college women were more likely than college men to download and listen to podcasts (Brown, 2006).

The solution to cultivating the next generation's interest in news may be in the wireless capability that is a growing part of the news media landscape. News media organizations would do well to understand how Millennials, especially young women, use wireless devices on the go so they can develop strategies for offering news content that is both compatible with the various wireless devices and valuable. Only by understanding and addressing the interests and needs of what might be called the wireless generation can the news media, especially newspapers, realistically hope to attract the attention of this age group before it turns away for good.

Note

1   For more on the European and American experiences with videotex, see *Goodbye Gutenberg* (Smith, 1980) and *Highway of Dreams, a Critical View Along the Information Superhighway* (Noll, 1997).

References

Americans going online . . . explosive growth, uncertain destinations, technology in the American household. (1995, October 16). *The Pew Research Center for the People and the Press.* Retrieved February 2006 from http://people-press.org/reports/print.php3?ReportID=136.

Atkin, D., Jeffres, L. & Neuendorf, K. (1998). Understanding Internet adoption as telecommunications behavior. *Journal of Broadcasting & Electronic Media, 42,* 475–490.

Brown, D. (2006). Generation iPod: An exploratory study of podcasting's "innovators." Paper presented at the Association of Educators in Journalism and Mass Communications Conference, Technology Division, San Francisco.

Carlson, D. (2005). Dave Carlson's online timeline (1960 to present). *Dave Carlson's Virtual World.* Retrieved August 2006 from http://iml.jou.ufl.edu/Carlson/timeline.shtml.

Ceruzzi, P. (2003). *A History of Modern Computing* (2nd edition). Cambridge: The MIT Press.

Cochran, W. (1995, June). A watershed event for online newspapers. *American Journalism Review,* 12–13.

Daily tracking survey April 2000. (2000). *The Pew Internet and American Life Project.* Retrieved March 2006 from www.pewinternet.org/PPF/r/5/dataset_display.asp.

Daily tracking survey November 2002. (2002). *The Pew Internet and American Life Project.* Retrieved March 2006 from www.pewinternet.org/PPF/r/31/dataset_display.asp.

Fallows, D. (2005, December 28). How women and men use the Internet. *The Pew Internet and American Life Project.* Retrieved March 2006 from http://207.21.232.103/pdfs/PIP_Women_and_Men_online.pdf.

Fidler, R. (1997). *Mediamorphonis: understanding new media*. CA: Pine Forge Press.

Fox, S. (2005, May 17). Health information online. *The Pew Internet and American Life Project*. Retrieved March 2006 from http://207.21.232.103/PPF/r/156/report_display.asp.

F.Y.I. (1995, July/August). *American Journalism Review*, 15.

Garrison, B. (2005). Online newspapers. In M. Salwen, B. Garrison, & P. Driscoll (Eds.) *Online News and the Public*, pp. 3–46. Mahwah: Lawrence Erlbaum Associates.

Greer, J. & Mensing, D. (2004). US news websites better, but small papers still lag. *Newspaper Research Journal*, 25(2), 98–112.

The Internet news audience goes ordinary. (1999, January 14). *The Pew Research Center for the People and the Press*. Retrieved January 2006 from http://people-press.org/reports/pdf/72.pdf.

Internet news takes off. (1998, July 8). *The Pew Research Center for the People and the Press*. Retrieved April 2007 from http://people-press.org/reports/pdf/88.pdf.

Kominski, R. & Newburger, E. (1999). Access denied: changes in computer ownership and use: 1984–1997, US Census Bureau. Paper presented at Annual Meeting of the American Sociological Association, Chicago, Illinois, 1999, August 20. Retrieved January 2006 from www.census.gov/population/socdemo/computer/confpap99.pdf.

Lin, C. (1995). Exploring personal computer adoption and dynamics. *Journal of Broadcasting & Electronic Media*, 42, 95–113.

News attracts most Internet users. (1996, December 16). *The Pew Research Center for the People and the Press*. Retrieved February 2006 from http://people-press.org/reports/print.php3?ReportID=117.

News audiences increasingly politicized, online news audience larger, more diverse. (2004, June 8). *The Pew Research Center for the People and the Press*. Retrieved January 2006 from http://people-press.org/reports/pdf/215.pdf.

Noll, A.M. (1997). *Highway of Dreams: A critical view along the information superhighway*. Mahwah: Lawrence Erlbaum Associates.

Online papers modestly boost newspaper readership. (2006, July 30). *The Pew Research Center for the People and the Press*. Retrieved April 2007 from http://people-press.org/reports/tables/282.pdf.

Online usage at work jumps 17 percent year-over-year, driven by female office workers. (2002, September 12). *Nielsen/NetRatings*. Retrieved January 2006 from www.nielsen-netratings.com/pr/pr_020912.pdf.

Poindexter, P.M., Schmitz Weiss, A., Meraz, S., & Conway, M. (2004). The Accidental Online News Reader. Unpublished manuscript, University of Texas at Austin.

Poindexter, P.M. & McCombs, M.E. (2000). *Research in Mass Communication: A practical guide*. Boston: Bedford/St. Martin's.

Rogers, E. (1995). *Diffusion of Innovations*. NY: The Free Press.

Sabo, S. (1995). Online: the arrival of electronic newspapers means new opportunities in campus PR. *Case Currents*, 42.

Schmitz Weiss, A., Meraz, S., Figur, N., & Poindexter, P.M. (2003). Experience and Internet news: The real reason for the online news reading gender gap. Paper presented at the Association for Education in Journalism and Mass Communication Conference, Kansas City.

Smith, A. (1980). *Goodbye Gutenberg: The newspaper revolution of the 1980s*. New York: Oxford University Press.

Tankard, J. (1998). Online Newspapers: Living up to their potential? Paper presented at the Association for Education in Journalism and Mass Communication Conference, Baltimore.

Usage over time. (n.d.) (2000–5). *The Pew Internet and American Life Project*. Retrieved April 2006 from http://207.21.232.103/trends/UsageOverTime.xls.

Who uses a computer? (1988, March). *US Department of Commerce, Bureau of the Census*, 1–2. Retrieved March 2006 from www.census.gov/population/socdemo/computer/sb88-2.pdf.

Women a formidable force on the Web. (2001, June 28). *Nielsen/NetRatings*. Retrieved January 2006 from www.acnielsen.com.au/news.asp?newsID=112.

Women are gaining on the Web. (2002, June 11). *Nielsen/NetRatings*. Retrieved January 2006 from www.nielsen-netratings.com/pr/pr_020611_hk.pdf#search=%22Women%20are%20 Gaining%20on%20the%20Web%22.

Yahoo Internet news directory (2003). *Yahoo*. Retrieved April 2003 from http://dir.yahoo.com/ News_and_Media/.

Yang, M. (2006, June). Communication and technology high density session. Jan A.G.M. Van Dijk (Chair), *Exploring the Phenomenon of Wireless Internet Adoption*. Symposium conducted at the International Communication Association Conference, Dresden, Germany.

Chapter 9

The Blogosphere's Gender Gap

Differences in Visibility, Popularity, and Authority

Sharon Meraz

Since the late 1990s, the World Wide Web has been transforming into a more interactive medium that embraces consumer participation in the production of content published on the Internet. Evidence of consumer involvement in content published on the Internet can be found at websites that sell books, auction goods, market classified advertising, and publish reference books. Consumer involvement in content production has not only helped transform the Internet into the interactive medium it is today, consumer participation in publishing content has enhanced the value of these websites. For example, Amazon, which initially started in 1995 as an online bookstore, has now become a place where consumers can write online customer reviews and ratings of seller transactions. Ebay, which launched in 1995 as an online auction site, gained value from the seller reviews posted by online buyers. Craigslist, developed in 1995, grew from the geographical limits of upscale San Francisco to become a global powerhouse of user-generated online classified advertising. The popular online encyclopedia Wikipedia, which after being established in 2001, has derived its value from the pooled intelligence of users who write and revise its content.

This growth in Web interactivity and consumer involvement in content published on the Internet is also apparent in blogging, one of the latest forms of personal Web publishing, where content appears as posts in reverse chronological order on the Web page. Since the development of free blogging software in 1999, the blogosphere has been doubling about every six months. At the end of July 2006, 50 million blogs were created, a steady increase from just 4 million in October 2004 (Sifry, 2006, 2004). Eight percent of the American public creates blogs and 54 percent of this group utilizes the blog as their sole publishing outlet (Lenhart & Fox, 2006, p. 2). Blog readership is also growing. As of 2006, approximately 40 percent of the online public read blogs, a significant increase from 2005 where one in every four of the US Internet public read blogs (The Pew Internet & American Life Project, 2005a, 2005b; Lenhart & Fox, 2006, p. 2).

The blog is a tool that supports diverse genres of content production. A 2006 Pew Internet & American Life Project survey found that the majority of bloggers use their blog for personal writing (37 percent), in comparison to writing about politics (11 percent), entertainment news (7 percent), sports (6 percent), general news and current events (5 percent), business (5 percent), technology (4 percent), or religion and spirituality (1 percent) (Lenhart & Fox, 2006, p. 3). Although the blogging public has varied motivations for reading and writing blogs, blogging has gained the most attention for its support of an alternative form of journalism that is developed by mostly amateurs outside the traditional newsroom. This form of alternative journalism, more popularly called citizen journalism, has attracted mass media attention as a more interactive and participatory form of news production. There is evidence that some bloggers identify with the profession of journalism. Thirty-four percent of bloggers see their writing as a form of journalism, 57 percent use their blog to link to original sources, and 56 percent of bloggers verify the facts that they include in their blog postings (ibid., p. 4).

The Blogosphere's Gender Gap

Blogging as a new Web activity has become popular because it has lowered the technical and economic barriers to Web publishing. Bloggers can post content to blogs through a Web browser without needing to know Web programming or database languages. Many blogging software applications also host blog content for free, removing the economic roadblocks to individual Web publishing. This free Web file storage has further removed the financial barriers to Web publishing, and has helped blogging expand beyond merely text entries to include blogging with audio or podcasting, blogging with video or vlogging, and blogging with photos or photo blogging. There is even blogging with mobile technologies, termed moblogging.

In contrast to other Web activities such as reading online news, there is strong evidence that as of 2005, women and men are both reading and writing blogs in equal numbers. An initial blogging report by The Pew Internet & American Life Project (2005a) in January 2005 provided no figures on the gender breakdown of blog readership; yet, the authors noted that blog readers were more likely to be male, well-educated, young, and experienced with the Internet. As of March 2005, figures suggested that women and men were equally as likely to read and create blogs (The Pew Internet & American Life Project, 2005b). In December 2005, Fallows (2005, p. 20) noted that there were no statistically significant differences in the relationship between gender and blog readership: 29 percent of online men and 25 percent of online women read blogs.

Like blog readership, any prior gender gap in blog content production has waned as of 2005. An initial Pew Internet & American Life Project (2005a, p. 2) report in January 2005 found that of the 7 percent of the Internet audience that were blog creators, 57 percent were men. A second report in March 2005 found that women were equally as likely to create blogs as men: 11 percent of online men were blog creators in comparison to 7 percent of online women (The Pew Internet & American Life Project, 2005b). In December 2005, Fallows (2005, p. 20) provided further support for the lack of a statistically significant gender gap in blog content creation: 11 percent of online men and 8 percent of online women were blog creators.

These reports deny the existence of a blogosphere gender gap in terms of reading blogs or creating blogs. However, trying to ascertain whether there is a gender gap in blogging through a comparison of raw numbers on blogging between the genders provides a deceptive frame of reference. Though the gender gap in terms of blog readership and creation has disappeared, a subtle gender gap has arisen such that male bloggers are more popular than women bloggers. The complicated reasons for this gender gap in blog popularity can be explored through the emerging relationship between blogging and journalism. This relationship is now growing stronger as many newsrooms overcome their initial skepticism of blogging to embrace its interactive and conversational potential. The growing relationship between blogging and journalism is evident in two current trends: the inclusion of more independent blogger voices as sources in news media reports and the addition of blogging as an emerging news practice in many traditional newsrooms.

Journalists vs. Bloggers

Though blogging is becoming more of an accepted practice in newsrooms, the practice of blogging continues to exist in a tenuous relationship with traditional journalism (Rosen, 2005). The strong resemblance that blogging has to journalism, particularly opinion journalism, has led to early polarized debates pitting blogging against journalism. Yet, these forms remain very different in the process of content creation, and there are several fundamental differences between blogging and traditional journalism. Unlike traditional journalism organizations with formalized ethics codes, bloggers have no ethics code beyond personal boundaries, and some bloggers have attempted to create formal blogger ethics codes without success (Dube, 2003; Kuhn, 2005). Most bloggers have no official editor and the majority of blog content gets vetted after blog content is posted online and readers critically weigh in on the editing process (Rosen, 2003). In contrast to traditional journalists, bloggers can respond to breaking news events by synthesizing news reports and providing commentary in a much faster fashion than traditional newsroom operations (Drezner & Farrell, 2004).

The relationship between blogging and journalism is complex. Most bloggers express no formal ambitions to be journalists (Blood, 2004; Lenhart & Fox, 2006). Many bloggers engage in journalistic acts in a random fashion: for example, many bloggers become accidental journalists when recording first-hand news accounts of spontaneous events such as disasters or terrorist acts (Gahran, 2005; Meraz, 2006). Some bloggers such as Rebecca MacKinnon and Josh Micah Marshall are former journalists who continue to use their blogs as a journalistic platform for breaking news and scrutinizing press reports. Other bloggers such as Michelle Malkin and Jim Romenesko are traditional journalists who use their blog as a form of journalism. Interestingly, the majority of bloggers are teen content creators who embrace the diary form of the blog for sharing personalized narratives with their peer social networks: as of 2006, almost 55 percent of bloggers were under the age of 30 (The Pew Internet & American life Project, 2005c; Lenhart & Fox, 2006).

Traditional media newsrooms have had to embrace the growing significance of blogs for a variety of reasons. Newspaper circulation has been declining for more than 20 years and weekday circulations of many newspapers have dropped: in 2005, the *Los Angeles Times* lost 6.5 percent of its weekday circulation, *The Chicago Tribune*, 6.6 percent, *The San Francisco Chronicle*, 16 percent and *The Boston Globe*, 8 percent (Crosbie, 2006). Newspapers such as the *Detroit Free Press* are cutting back on their days of publication, and blogs have been identified as one reason for declining rates of circulation of the newspaper (Editor & Publisher, 2006; Porter, 2006). Traditional media's continued loss of credibility is underscored by the fact that many blog readers consider blogs to be more credible than traditional mass media sources (Johnson & Kaye, 2004).

Traditional media's changing attitude toward blogging may also be spurred on by the reality of their audience demographics. In 2005, only 23 percent of the younger audience reported to have read a newspaper yesterday in comparison to 60 percent of those over 60 (Will, 2005). Young readers are also more inclined to turn to the Internet for information, a trend that has led many scholars to speculate about the future of the print newspaper as a mass medium for this younger demographic (Meyer, 2004; Brown, 2005; Mindich, 2005).

With the growing influence of blogs, there are several outward signs that traditional media outlets are now more accepting of the blog form. In the latest Project for

Excellence in Journalism (2006) report on *The State of the Media*, blogs were included in the "day in the life of the media" alongside more traditional outlets such as the newspaper, online, network TV, cable TV, local TV, magazines, and radio. This report also recognized that blogs and mass media newsrooms were dependent on each other for news and opinions. As of 2006, mass media's usage of blogs as both a source for opinions and as a news-delivery platform provided increasing proof that blogs are altering the way that news is being produced, packaged, and consumed.

The Blogosphere as a Source for Mainstream News

There is a growing body of evidence that supports the theory that mainstream news media routinely depend on the most popular blogs for information, interpretative frames, and opinion snapshots. The eleventh Annual Euro RSCG Magnet Survey of Media (Euro RSCG Magnet, 2005), conducted with Columbia University, found that over 28 percent of journalists used blogs on a daily basis and more than half of journalists depended on blogs for free and unacknowledged source material in their news reports. But even though a significant percentage of journalists use blogs as a source for news, the same study found that less than 1 percent of journalists trust blogs. While journalists use blogs as a news source, bloggers rely on the news media for a daily agenda of issues to discuss and as a springboard for commentary about overlooked matters in traditional news reports. This symbiotic relationship suggests that both traditional news media and bloggers help set each other's agenda (Cornfield *et al.*, 2005).

Although the dependency between the blogosphere and traditional news media is growing, journalists are selective in the blogs used as news sources. In fact, an informal online survey of blog readership by 140 editors, reporters, columnists, and publishers found that the top ten blogs were responsible for 54 percent of all blog citations, with elite newsrooms citing the top blogs in 74 percent of their citations to blogs (Drezner & Farrell, 2005, pp. 18, 19). Though the authors did not provide commentary on the gender of these popular blog authors, an analysis by gender revealed that mainstream news media outlets identified only male-authored blogs. Herring *et al.* (2004, p. 6) also found in an examination of 16 news articles that mentioned blogs between the period November 2002 to July 2003, 88 percent of blog mentions were to male bloggers. This finding was consistent irrespective of the article's topical focus.

A more recent analysis also found heavier reliance on male-authored blogs compared to female-authored blogs. For example, in surveying bloggers' reactions to the confirmation hearings of Samuel Alito for Supreme Court justice, *The New York Times* quoted only five women bloggers out of 29 published blogger opinions (*New York Times*, 2006a). Only six of the 22 blogger opinions cited in *The New York Times* story on the blogosphere's response to the jailing and testimony of *New York Times* reporter Judith Miller were from women bloggers (*New York Times*, 2005). Other examples suggest a greater reliance by traditional news media on men bloggers' voices as opposed to women bloggers. *The Washington Post*, for example, hosted a live-chat session with famed blogger for PR consulting, Steve Rubel (Rubel, 2006). Jeremy Blachman joined Lawrence Lessig as one of the few bloggers invited to write an editorial for *The New York Times*. In yet another deferential move to male bloggers, editor of the blog FishBowlDC, 23-year-old Garrett Graff, was the first blogger to be given a daily White House pass for the purpose of writing his blog (Seelye, 2005).

Male political bloggers have also been more successful than women bloggers in crossing over to traditional newsrooms. For the 2004 Democratic National Convention,

New York University Professor Jay Rosen blogged for *Knight-Ridder* while Internet theorist and then Harvard Berkman fellow David Weinberger blogged for Boston.com. Rosen was later invited to write the first post for the *CBS* blog, Public Eye. In 2006, *The Washington Post* hired 24-year-old Ben Domenech, blog author of *RedState.org*, to blog for the newspaper's new blog titled *RedAmerica*. Domenech's hire proved to be short-lived when bloggers exposed his past plagiarism activities; yet, the *Post's* willingness to hire Domenech without sufficient background checks (a simple Internet search for his name would have revealed the many plagiarism allegations made against him) bespeaks the deference that male bloggers have been given in the eyes of traditional news media.

As of 2006, few female bloggers had transitioned to notable positions in traditional news media. Ana Marie Cox, who blogged independently for the political blog *Wonkette* and was known as one of the most popular political bloggers of 2004, was one of the few female bloggers who moved into traditional news media. In July 2005, Time.com named Cox Washington editor (Romenesko, 2005). The news media's more favored treatment of male bloggers is largely due to the popularity of male bloggers. But, why are women bloggers less popular?

The A-List: The Blogosphere's Glass Ceiling

In 2002, several Web-based blog search engine aggregators were developed that made it possible to search blog content and compile a list of the most popular blogs. A look at Figure 9.1, which shows a graph of the number of women bloggers on the top 40 blogs between the time period 2003 to 2006 for blog search engine aggregator

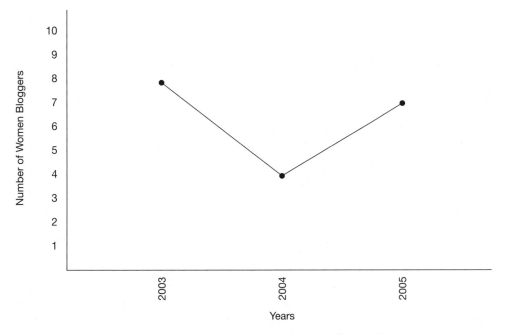

Figure 9.1 Women bloggers in the top 40 blog ranking between 2003 and 2005

Note: These data were derived from the Internet Archive. Calculating the number of women bloggers per year was achieved by using the latest time point data for the archived year.

Table 9.1 Top 20 US blogs in Technorati and the Truth Laid Bear aggregators

Technorati	Truth Laid Bear
Endgadget[c]	Instapundit[b]
Boing Boing[ab]	Michelle Malkin[ab]
Gizmodo[c]	Little Green Footballs[b]
Daily Kos[b]	Daily Kos[b]
TechCrunch[c]	Captain's Quarters[b]
Post Secret	Power Line[b]
The Huffington Post[ab]	Stop the ACLU[b]
Lifehacker[c]	Volokh Conspiracy[b]
Crooks and Liars[b]	Boing Boing[ab]
Official Google Blog[c]	Talking Points Memo[b]
Michelle Malkin[ab]	Real Clear Politics[b]
Instapundit[b]	Mudville Gazette[b]
Think Progress	Eschaton[b]
Autoblog	Andrew Sullivan[b]
Gawker	Wizbang[b]
Scobleizer[c]	The Huffington Post[ab]
Blog di Beppo Grillo	The Washington Monthly[b]
A List Apart[c]	Hugh Hewitt[b]
Dooce[a]	Hot Air[b]
Topix.net[c]	BLACKFIVE[b]

Note: a: female blogger; b: political blog; c: high tech blog.

The Truth Laid Bear, reveals women bloggers have seldom authored more than 25 percent of the top 40 blogs and male bloggers have consistently outnumbered women.

Why have women bloggers lagged behind male bloggers? Table 9.1 presents a snapshot of the 20 most popular US blogs on blog aggregators *Technorati* and *The Truth Laid Bear* for one time point in August 2006. Interestingly, women author only four of these top 20 blogs on *Technorati*'s listing of 20 of the most popular blogs irrespective of blog genre. When this list is analyzed by genre, it is easier to see which blog genres are the most popular. Both high tech blogs and political blogs feature heavily in *Technorati*'s top 20 list. Interestingly, men author all eight of the high tech blogs that are present in this top 20 list. In the political genre, women bloggers author only two of the top six political blogs that are on *Technorati*'s popular list.

Comparing *The Truth Laid Bear*'s listing of top 20 blogs to *Technorati*'s reveals a different popular blog ordering because *The Truth Laid Bear* uses a personalized method for determining popularity and its list is weighted toward the political blog genre. As can be seen from this table, only two women are authors of these primarily political blogs and men bloggers vastly outnumber women bloggers in popularity in the political blog genre. Since both the political genre and the high tech genre dominate popular lists, women bloggers are often rendered invisible in the game of celebrity and influence in the blogosphere.

Most blog studies that measure the influence of the blogosphere concentrate analysis on the top political blogs—a reality that often keeps women bloggers from the spotlight. An examination of the partisan divisions in the political blogosphere based on posts from the top 40 political blogs found women authored only 5 percent of the conservative blogs and 16 percent of the liberal blogs (Adamic and Glance, 2004). Similarly, only four women bloggers were among the influentials that shape the traditional media's news agenda (Cornfield *et al.*, 2004), and in a network analysis and feminist analysis of the top political blogs in 2005, only 10 percent of the sample contained women bloggers (Harp and Tremayne, 2006). As these studies reveal, the gender gap is not just one of popularity. Women bloggers lack representation in the genre of political blogging. The interrelationship between popularity and political blogging is apparent in the preponderance of political blogs in the top blog lists.

Blogs that appear on these top 100 blogs rankings are commonly referred to as the A-list, which functions as a glass ceiling, representing a few extremely lucky, well-trafficked blogs that distinguish themselves from the millions of blogs stuck in the long tail of less popular blogs (Thompson, 2006). On a more elemental level, blogs on the A-list provide a powerful cognitive cue of which blogs are worthy of attention, visibility, and readership. As a result, A-list blogs become more popular through their reputation and celebrity, which leads to even more blogs linking to them, a phenomenon that helps explain how unpopular blogs become further marginalized from attention on the Web (Babarasi & Albert, 1999; Shirky, 2003).

Several popular male bloggers point out that getting on these A-lists can be achieved through carefully planned strategies to garner more links from other blogs. These bloggers advise engaging in relentless and continuous daily posting, writing short, well-linked entries on topical subjects such as politics, trying to link to popular bloggers so they reciprocate with linking, writing content that is both interesting and relevant to the public, and using conflict or disagreement as a framing device in headlines and blog content (Scoble, 2006; Wright, 2006).

Even so, the questions can be posed why have women achieved parity with men on both blog readership and blog creation, but have remained unrepresented on these popular lists, why do male political bloggers dominate the A-list, and, why is male bloggers' content more heavily linked to than women bloggers?

Blogger and News Media Affiliations

Some of the affiliations between mainstream news media and the blogosphere's top blogs are a result of crossover relationships. The mainstream news media routinely link to political bloggers who once held a mainstream press pass; in fact, the majority of political bloggers who were formerly mainstream journalists are A-list political bloggers. These same bloggers are also male. Examples include Andrew Sullivan, former editor of *The New Republic*, Josh Micah Marshall, who worked for *The American Prospect*, and Mikey Kaus, who wrote for *The New Republic* and *Newsweek*.

Although fewer women bloggers with news media connections appear as routine sources in the news, there are exceptions. Xeni Jardin, co-editor of the top collaborative blog Boing Boing, whose expertise is technology, not politics, contributes to *Wired Magazine* and NPR's daily program *Day to Day*. Plus, she has made regular appearances on CNN, ABC, and *Fox News*. Political blogger Michelle Malkin, who has had over a decade of experience at the *Los Angeles Daily News*, has a nationally syndicated column that appears in over 200 newspapers. She is also a regular contributor to *Fox News*. Writer, editor, and former political blogger Ana Marie Cox has been regularly cited for opinions in *The New York Times*, CNN, and MSNBC. She is now Washington editor for Time.com. Malkin and Cox are two of the most visible female political bloggers; however, with Cox's exit from the blogosphere to join the ranks of more traditional journalists, Malkin remains one of the few top women political bloggers with mass media connections.

Early Adoption

In chronicling the history of blogging, both Rebecca Blood (2000) and Dave Winer (2001) emphasized that blogs on Web technology development were the overwhelming majority of early blogs. Before blogging became popular in 2001, the practice of blogging existed without a formal name among the tech savvy as a way to discuss new developments in technology. Rebecca Blood's history of Weblogs identified most of the earliest bloggers to be male high tech bloggers. Blood was among a handful of early adopter women bloggers that included Virginia Postrel, Meg Hourihan, and Joanne Jacobs. Male high tech bloggers such as Dave Winer, Lawrence Lee, Jorn Barger, and Cameron Barrett created an initial identification with the blog as a virtual space for trading technical tips and tricks. Many of the early adopter high tech bloggers continue to have a strong presence on many popular blog lists even though blogging has now diffused from a mostly technophile user base to a wider, non-technical population.

The news media routinely depend on high tech bloggers for reports on developments in technology. Because mass media journalists are often generalists, blogs with niche high tech content have become an indispensable asset for covering the technology beat. Former *San Jose Mercury News* journalist Dan Gillmor (2004), who was one of the first journalists to blog for a mass media newsroom, noted that the blog enabled him to post early versions of his technology columns for his tech savvy readers to post corrections. *Wall Street Journal* tech reporter Nick Wingfield, who observed that tech journalists used blogs frequently, was quoted as saying, "In my case, I'm definitely part of the crowd using them in [my] reporting" (BullDog Reporter, 2005). Tech bloggers are often responsible for breaking news; in 2004, blogs *PowerPage*, *Apple Insider*, and *Think Secret* posted details of *Apple's* unreleased products before mass media technology reporters knew the information (BBC, 2005).

It is not difficult to understand why mass media depend on the niche expertise of high tech bloggers in their effort to make sense of the shifting news media landscape. Many of these male technology bloggers are directly responsible for the development of blogging software and its related technologies. The usage of these tools is influencing how news is produced and delivered. Mass media outlets are also utilizing many of these grassroots blog tools in the creation and delivery of news. Many traditional media outlets are slowly introducing such tools as Really Simple Syndication (RSS), podcasting, tagging, social bookmarking, and social software on many traditional news websites. As they look for guidance in this new communications world, traditional media must acknowledge the expertise of many of these male developers who are directly responsible for these developments.

Men's Influence in the Political Blogosphere

Mass media's dependence on blogs as sources for news is most evident in the political blogosphere. Male political bloggers dominate the lists of popular blogs. Bloggers that are given the opportunity to be sources in newspaper, online, and television reports also tend to be male political bloggers. In several news reports on blogging, men are popularly stereotyped as avid enthusiasts of political blogging while women are characterized as personal diarists (Guernsey, 2002; Levy, 2004). These popular blog lists make the political blogosphere seem like an exclusive "boy's club" where women bloggers are denied membership (McDermott, 2004). This difficulty in locating influential women political bloggers has led to many gendered debates in the blogosphere that center on the question, where are all the female political bloggers? (Drum 2005a, 2005b, 2005c).

Several factors have contributed to the popular identification of males with political blogging in mass media reports. These factors all point to a narrow definition of politics as commentary on the day-to-day news; state, local, and national politics; policy and legislation; and, international newsworthy events. This limited definition of what constitutes politics has served to shut out women bloggers from gaining authority as political bloggers in the eyes of both mass media news reports and male bloggers. It is useful to examine some of the factors that have created this strong identification with blogging along this limited definition of politics.

War Blogging

Though blogging gained its first foothold with the development of free blogging software in 1999, blogging became a more visible and widely adopted public platform in the United States in the wake of the 9/11 attacks when the public sought a forum to discuss the changing political climate. This form of blogging in response to terrorism and war came to be known as war blogging, and many popular accounts of war blogging identify male bloggers as the leaders of the genre (Cavanaugh, 2002). Virginia Postrel is one of the lone female bloggers that has been associated with war blogging.

The growth of the US blogosphere as a response to terrorism and war was further cemented with the War in Afghanistan in 2001 and the War in Iraq in 2003. Both wars extended the genre of war blogging to a debate on the pros and cons of war on terrorism. These events led to an even longer list of male bloggers joining the ranks of the warbloggers (The Politburo Diktat, 2004). This early identification of blogging with terrorism and war gave many male bloggers an early advantage in the game of influence in both the eyes of the blogosphere and mass media. The age-old association of males with matters of the military also created gendered terms of authority in the public sphere, which placed male political bloggers at an advantage in speaking about war over women political bloggers.

2004 Presidential Elections

Much of blogging's impetus came from its usage in the 2004 presidential election (Rainie et al., 2005). In 2004, the hype surrounding blogging was captured in the *Merriam-Webster Dictionary*'s declaration that the word of the year was 'blog' and much of this popularity surrounding blogs was due to Howard Dean's creative use of blogs in his bid for the presidential election (Meraz, in press; 2004). Howard Dean became the first presidential candidate to use a candidate blog for citizen discussion and online fundraising, and its popularity led to the eventual adoption of the blog on the candidate websites of such democratic presidential hopefuls as John Kerry, John Edwards, Wesley Clarke, as well as by the Republican candidate, President George W. Bush. Blogs were highly instrumental in assisting candidates with Internet fundraising: Howard Dean raised more than $50 million in small-dollar contributions through his candidate blog. Democratic candidate John Kerry went on to use his candidate blog to set new records for Internet fundraising online, raising over $65 million by November 2004 (Meraz, 2006).

News reports on the creative design and usage of technology in the 2004 presidential campaign showcased the male technological talent of Howard Dean's campaign.

The architect of Dean's blog campaign, Joe Trippi, a self-described technophile and early adopter (Weathersby, 2003) was described as "the man who reinvented campaigning" by *The New Republic*, "obsessive and brilliant" by *Fast Company*, "the brains behind Howard Dean's Internet-fueled presidential campaign" by *Wired Magazine*, and "the genius, the new Carville" by *GQ Magazine* (Trippi, 2004). Another male who was responsible for the strong liftoff of Dean's blog was Matthew Gross, who was described by *The American Prospect* as "Dean's former blogger-in-chief" (Franke-Ruta, 2004). Zack Rosen, then a college student in the department of computer science at University of Illinois at Urbana-Champaign, dropped out of school to develop much of Dean's social networking tools, which were utilized by the public to self organize and campaign in both the online and the offline spheres (Shapiro, 2003). The lone high-profile female in Dean's campaign, Zephyr Teachout, spent the majority of her professional life outside the technical world as an attorney before being appointed as Dean's Director of Internet Organizing. Her passion for taking Dean's campaign outside the Internet and into the real world also led to her greater association with the social usage of the technology for community organizing (Rosenthal, 2003; Shapiro, 2003).

The work of other male developers during the 2004 presidential election helped raise the profile of blogging and participatory technologies within the eyes of the Internet audience. Cameron Barett, one of the earliest adopters of the blog form, developed presidential candidate Wesley Clarke's candidate blog, and Barett was described as the "grandfather of all blogs" (Hammer, 2004). In addition to candidate blogs, other tools enabled the public to participate in campaign activities like never before, and men developed the majority of these tools. In 2002, Scott Heiferman developed an online tool called Meetup as a way to facilitate the organizing of offline meetings; however, political enthusiasts seized upon Meetup as a tool to arrange face-to-face political meetings for their candidates all over the United States (Harmon, 2004). At one time point, Meetup boasted a membership of 160,000 supporters for the Dean campaign and Meetup became a tool that was quickly adopted by other democratic candidates such as Wesley Clarke and John Kerry. Men were also popular in creative development of viral Internet video—an emerging trend in the 2004 presidential election. Brothers Gregg and Evan Spiridellis developed the jocular video about George Bush and John Kerry titled, *Jib Jab: This Land is Your Land*, which made headlines on many traditional mass media outlets (Davenport, 2004; Maney, 2004).

Several independent political bloggers were also given press credentials to cover the 2004 Democratic National Conventions (DNC) and the Republican National Conventions (RNC) for the first time in the conventions' history. Traditional mass media also sent its own bloggers to cover both of the conventions. This event was symbolic in that both non-media bloggers and media bloggers were in physical proximity through sharing the same geographical space (Meraz, 2005). Analysis of the credentialed bloggers by gender reveals a startling gender gap for both independent political bloggers and traditional media political bloggers. In July 2004, only four of the 30 independent political bloggers for the DNC were women, while approximately 10 percent of the mainstream media bloggers were women. Two of the three women who blogged the convention for the mass media were part of group blogs where male writers were also contributors. Similarly, in August 2004, only one of the 22 credentialed RNC non-media political bloggers was a woman while approximately 27 percent of the media bloggers were women bloggers.

Blogging as Media Watchdog

Blogs have gotten the most mass media attention for their role as watchdog of the press. Many political bloggers routinely scout mass media reports for evidence of mistakes, omissions, and biases. The slogan, "we can fact-check your ass," was popularized by blogger Ken Layne to describe the active role that blogs can play in holding mass media accountable for its inaccuracies. The act of picking apart mass media news reports for inaccuracies was also termed "fisking," popularized by political blogger Andrew Sullivan's line-by-line interrogation of award-winning British journalist Robert Fisk's dispatch from Pakistan where he described being beaten by an Afghan refugee (Wikipedia, n.d). As of 2006, male political bloggers have been responsible for all of the big events in which political blogs have held traditional media accountable for inaccuracies, omissions, or oversights in their news reports.

Political bloggers Joshua Micah Marshall of blog *Talking Points Memo* and Duncan Black of blog *Atrios* were largely responsible for drawing mass media attention to Senator Trent Lott's controversial statements at Strom Thurmond's birthday party. Lott had said that the United States would have been better off had Thurmond, then a segregationist candidate for the breakaway Dixiecrat Party, won the 1948 presidential election against Harry Truman (Edsall & Faler, 2002; Mercurio, 2002). The blogosphere's strong criticism of Lott's remarks continued until the mass media dedicated attention to the story in news reports—the result of which was Lott's resignation as Senate Majority Leader in December 2002. Journalist Paul Krugman of *The New York Times* publicly acknowledged his debt to Marshall, whose blog, he wrote, "is must reading for the politically curious, and who, more than anyone else, is responsible for making Trent Lott's offensive remarks the issue they should be." (Kennedy School of Government, 2004).

Male political bloggers also played a major role in Dan Rather's retirement as anchor of *CBS Evening News*. The political blog site *FreeRepublic* provided the Web-based forum for a discussion of the four memos that Dan Rather presented on *60 Minutes* in September 2005 that alleged to provide proof of President George Bush's preferential treatment in the National Guard. Influential male discussants on the *FreeRepublic* site included Paul Boley of Montgomery, Alabama (pseudonym TankerKC) and Harry MacDougald (pseudonym Buckhead), who brought to light the lack of authenticity of these documents (Pein, 2005). Another notable male figure in the Dan Rather scandal was Scott Johnson, a Minneapolis lawyer of the blog *PowerLine* (Humphries, 2004). What was notable in this incident was the symbiotic relationship between mass media and male political bloggers. Both worked hand-in-hand to uncover the document's inaccuracies.

Male bloggers also played a role in another high-profile newsroom resignation. Hugh Hewitt, who blogs under his own name, and Charles Johnson of the blog *Little Green Footballs* have been credited with creating a 'blogstorm' surrounding CNN chief news executive Eason Jordon's comments at the World Economic Forum. Jordon had stated that US troops were allegedly targeting journalists in Iraq. Rony Abovitz (2005), an attendee to the World Economic Forum, blogged about Jordon's comments on the forum's blog, and the heated debates in the political blogosphere among male political bloggers eventually led to Jordon's surprise resignation from his position at CNN (MacKinnon, 2005b).

Many other male bloggers have been credited with setting the media's agenda by forcing journalists' attention to John Kerry's record during and after his service in

Vietnam (Media Matters for America, 2004). Male bloggers also drove mass media attention to the alleged secret identity of Jeff Gannon, a former *Talon News* reporter who was given a press pass to attend White House press conferences (Kennedy, 2005). The momentum of blogs as watchdog of the press continued to ascend in 2006. In August 2006, Charles Johnson of the blog *Little Green Footballs*, exposed Reuter's freelancer Adnan Hajj's photos of war images in Lebanon as doctored, a finding which eventually led to Reuters withdrawing all of Hajj's 920 photographs (Johnson, 2006).

To date, no women bloggers feature prominently in any of the incidents in which blogs have been responsible for holding the press accountable for its oversights and omissions.

Women's Blogging Motivations

These recounted political incidents highlight the glaring invisibility of women bloggers from both the high tech and political blogging circles, two major genres of surveillance for traditional media newsrooms. Yet, there are many women bloggers that specifically write about either technology or day-to-day politics. Female bloggers such as Elizabeth Lawley, Shelly Powers, Susan Mernit, Mary Hodder, Dinah Mehta, Halley Suitt, and Danah Boyd regularly write about high tech issues from both a technological and a social standpoint. Political bloggers such as Chris Nolan, Jeralyn Merritt, Arianna Huffington, Echnide of the Snakes, Rox Populi, Elayne Riggs, and Jane Hamsher and Christy Hardin-Smith write daily postings that focus on day-to-day news and politics. It is not easily apparent why many of these women who blog about technology and politics are not more popular in the blogosphere or mass media reports.

Scholars have advanced several reasons for women blogger's invisibility from the popularity indexes, but one of the primary reasons that many women bloggers' cite is male sexism in the blogosphere (Ratcliff, 2004). The role that such demographic variables as gender plays in structuring one's social network has been a rich area of research for many years (Fisher, 1948; Lazersfeld & Merton, 1954; McPherson *et al.*, 2001). The attraction to networking with those of the same gender has been shown to play a strong role in the gender-homogenous composition of both male's and women's social networks (Lincoln & Miller, 1979; Fisher & Oliker, 1983; McPherson & Smith-Lovin, 1986; Mardsen, 1987; Moore, 1990; Ibarra, 1992; Ibarra, 1997). These gender-homogenous social networks can contribute to unequal power dynamics through the tendency for males to network with other high status males to the exclusion of women (Lin, 1999; Huffan & Torres, 2002). As it relates to the blogosphere, social networks form through the decisions that bloggers make in creating hyperlinks. Since the beginning of the gender debates in the blogosphere in 2002, women bloggers have accused male bloggers of gender insular linking practices, which could explain women bloggers' invisibility from popular lists (Ratcliff, 2004).

Though the utopian ideal of the blogosphere rests on the principle that anyone's opinions can matter, it is evident that the gender gaps in the blogosphere mirror real-world gender inequalities. There are strong similarities between blogging and opinion writing in its largely personal, subjective, and aggressive verbal techniques. The lack of female opinion writers in newspapers suggests that the lack of popularity of female bloggers can be a holdover from the gender inequities in opinion writing within print newsrooms. Statistics from 2005 support widespread gender gaps in opinion writing in the mass media newsroom. Only 10 percent and 17 percent of opinion columnists in *The Washington Post* and *The New York Times* respectively are female (Goodman, 2005). Almost 100 percent of *USA Today* and *Time Magazine* opinion columnists are men (Pollitt, 2005). Women are also less prone to submit opinion pieces for publication to political magazines (Lithwick, 2005; Sullivan, 2005).

A large part of these gender inequities in the world of opinion writing appear related to gendered usages of language. Women have been shown to use more cooperative as opposed to competitive techniques in their speech patterns (Coates, 1986; Tannen, 1993). In the world of the blogosphere, where bloggers become popular through amassing more links, aggressive and competitive writing techniques help drive attention and visibility. In this environment, women bloggers may find it more difficult to compete and negotiate with their more aggressive male blogger peers (Babcock and Laschever, 2003; Gneezy *et al.*, 2003).

Gendered differences in the usage of language can underlie the differences in writing style and voice between women and male bloggers. Women bloggers are more comfortable with writing blogs on private subject matter using a personalized style of writing. This outward comfort with disclosing personal issues on the blog has resulted in the stereotyping of women's blogging as personal diaries and public confessions (Drum, 2005a). This embrace of personal writing, referred to as 'identity blogging' by women bloggers, has also contributed to their lack of visibility on the popular blog lists. Most diary-style or personal blogs contain fewer links than political blogs that actively comment on news and politics (Herring *et al.*, 2004).

Though it may be easy to dismiss personal blogging in both mass media and academic circles, many female bloggers embrace a personal style in an effort to pursue aggressive political objectives. These political goals pay close attention to issues that are often neglected in mass media news reports or public dialogue. By using the blog form as an alternative press, women bloggers are using this virtual space to create female community and to discuss news, topics, and issues that gain scant attention in traditional media.

It is essential to explore how women bloggers use the blog form in order to understand what topics appeal to women blog readers and creators. Paying attention to how women use the blog form to create relevant content can provide vital clues as to how mass media can develop news content to reconnect with women readers.

Mommyblogging

Many women are reclaiming the right to discuss matters related to domesticity in the public sphere by using the blog as a public platform for discussing political issues related to mothering. Embracing the second wave feminist stance that the "personal is political," many female bloggers adopt the blog tool as the platform for a discussion of the joys and uncertainties of motherhood. These female bloggers, popularly dubbed mommybloggers, are creating female social communities online for sharing practical advice, stories, and solutions to the life changing experiences of motherhood. These women bloggers use the blog as a tool to chronicle real life events, including the unglamorous side of motherhood—a view of motherhood that is often missing from mass media's images and news stories. Women bloggers who embrace mommyblogging elevate to visibility the act of mothering in an effort to contribute to a social network of responsive community that is based on the real life experience of the ups and downs of being a mother.

It is important to note that the term mommyblogging is controversial. The ongoing conflict between stay-at-home moms and working moms has been popularly dubbed "mommy wars" (Peskowitz, 2005; Shade, 2006). The public derision and stigma attached to motherhood and domesticity have created ambivalence toward the term mommy-blogging by many women bloggers. Some women bloggers who are employed shun the term for its stigmatized connotations of women who stay at home, while other women bloggers who identify with the term mommybloggers reclaim the right to embrace the term as flexible to all forms of motherhood. Many mommybloggers actively work to mediate the conflict between stay-at-home and working mothers by embracing all forms of work–life balance as essential to motherhood.

Mommyblogging provides a ready social network of support for the experience of day-to-day mothering through allowing women a public space to discuss real world issues that pertain to motherhood. Many mommybloggers use the blog as a printing press for telling stories that would not be reported in mass media (Buchanan, n.d.). Mommyblogging also provides an opportunity for women bloggers to speak candidly about the raw experiences that affect women as parents outside the glossy feminized magazine images of the soccer mom or the wealthy stay-at-home mom. Other mommy-bloggers use the blog form to challenge stereotypes that mothers cannot write or cannot contribute productively to society (Ingman, 2006a). Through the practice of mommy-blogging, many mothers create bridges of communication with their friends, families, and other mothers who live outside their immediate geographical environment.

The popularity of mommyblogging as a radical form of female blogging is evident in the many mommyblogging communities that sprung up in 2004 to provide a supportive space for personal, intimate storytelling about the realities of motherhood. *DotMoms*, a mommyblogging site run by Julie Moos, managing editor for Poynter Institute, is comprised of over 40 mommybloggers who live in distinct geographical areas. The site describes itself as providing a window into the "many faces of motherhood." The site is a hub to over 600 mommyblogs from around the world, and it provides a space for mothers to write about issues that relate to parenting, motherhood, and career issues. *March of Dimes*, another blog community of mommybloggers, provides an avenue to discuss such issues as having premature or sick babies.

In addition to these blogging community sites, there are thousands of individually authored mommyblogs. These women use the blog to create supportive communities in their battles with loneliness, postpartum depression, fertility issues, sleeplessness, and work–life balance issues. One such popular mommyblogger is Heather Armstrong. Armstrong's blog *Dooce* currently attracts over 40,0000 visitors per day (Hochman, 2005). Her public, raw accounts of her struggles with postpartum depression coupled with the popularity of her daily, introspective postings on the realities of motherhood have made her site one of the most heavily trafficked blogs in the blogosphere. Other bloggers such as Karen Walrond of *Chookooloonk*s and *Mimi Smartypants* write about their experiences with adoption. In her blog Sweetney.com, Tracey Gaughran-Perez chronicles the daily life experiences of being a stay-at-home mom. Blogs such as *In the Barren Season*, *A Little Pregnant*, and *Baby or Bust* are among hundreds that chronicle the difficult experiences of infertility.

Early news reports reveal hesitation in appreciating the value of mommyblogging to the community of women that read and write mommyblogs. Hochman (2005) of the *New York Times* views the practice of mommyblogging with skepticism. Commenting on the parenthood as the "world's most thankless occupation," he glosses over the function that mommyblogging plays in the lives of many women. According to Hochman:

> Today's parents—older, more established and socialized to voicing their emotions— may be uniquely equipped to document their children's lives, but what they seem most likely to complain and marvel about is their own. The baby blog in many cases is an online shrine to parental self-absorption.
>
> (Hochman, 2005)

Hochman's misunderstanding of the political value of publicizing the private is evidenced by his interpretation of mommyblogging as a selfish act by parents desperate for public attention.

Feminist Blog Spaces

In an effort to counteract invisibility, many female bloggers have created gendered blog spaces on the Internet to support, promote, and highlight each other's work. These gendered blog spaces serve many purposes. Women bloggers use these blog spaces to identify good female blog content that is not being picked up in the popular or top lists. The majority of these gendered spaces were developed in response to the lack of female representation in the blog search engine aggregator's top or popular lists. Using the strategy of hyperlinking to female content, gendered spaces help make female blog content become more visible to the blog search engines. These gendered blog spaces also serve as a safe space for women to network with each other along shared interests. Many of the previously mentioned mommyblogging sites are gendered spaces. For all of these female blogging gendered spaces, the target audience is women blog readers and blog writers.

One particular form of female blog network that has become popular in the blogosphere is the feminist blog network. Many of these blog networks are designed to provide alternative political news and information that are not addressed by mass media news reports or male bloggers. *BlogHer* is a site where female bloggers can register their blog, and it provides a discussion of over 20 topics of interest to women. The site's tagline is "Where the women bloggers are," and its topics of discussion include feminism and gender, media and journalism, politics and news, and race and ethnicity. The site uses preexisting content from 100 women-authored blogs in an effort to highlight the shared interests of women bloggers. *Blog Sisters*, a loosely joined group of over 100 female bloggers, addresses content on topics that impact women, and the site goes by the tagline, "Where men can link but they can't touch." *The Feminist Bloggers Network* is another social network of feminist bloggers with the mission to "facilitate promotional, professional and development opportunities for feminist bloggers." This site discusses such topics as the politics of reproductive rights, activism, and feminism. Another site called *Feminist Blogs* is a loose community of blogs that self identify as women's liberationists, womanists, and pro-feminist men. The site goes by the tagline, "independent alternatives to the malestream media" and keeps a watchful eye on mass media reportage for its gender biases and discussions of gender relations. Some topics of discussion on this site include politics, abortion and reproductive rights, sexual assault and harassment, and gender issues. Much of the content on this blog reinterprets mass media reports from a woman's perspective.

Though women bloggers are often accused of avoiding political discussion, an analysis of blog postings from these five feminist networks shows this assumption is erroneous. Quite the opposite, female bloggers shine a light on many neglected issues in the public sphere that relate to feminist politics. Many of these issues straddle the private–public sphere and include such topics as the work–life balance, issues of race–gender and its intersection with feminist politics, office politics, gendered pay inequities, abortion and contraception, domestic violence and rape, women's health issues, politics of domesticity, and the masculine tilt of the mainstream media content and coverage. Much of the alternative news that is created in these networks addresses topics that are either routinely ignored by mass media news reports, or buried in such newspaper sections as the lifestyles or features.

Mainstream Media and Blogging

Since 2006, traditional newsrooms across the United States have been more willing to experiment with blogging. Early news media skepticism toward blogging was evident in the cautious approach that many newsrooms adopted toward journalists who had personal blogs outside the control of the formal newsroom editing process. In 2002, Stephen Olafson, ex-reporter of *The Houston Chronicle*, was fired for writing a personal blog that chronicled his critical opinions of his newspaper. In 2003, Dennis Horgan of *The Hartford Courant* was told to desist from having a personal blog, but was eventually allowed to blog under the newspaper brand seven months later. Eleven days after he set up his blog on March 9, 2003, CNN employee Kevin Sites was forced to suspend his blogging entries from Iraq. CNN's parent company *AOL Time Warner* was among other companies such as the *Tribune Media Company, Gannett* and *The New York Times* that were initially hesitant to permit newsroom staff to blog (Mernit, 2003).

By 2006, the majority of US newsrooms had experimented with blogging in one form or another, and the major US television networks and radio stations had their own blogs. NPR, *The New York Times*, ABC, CNN, and ESPN also experimented with podcasting, allowing news consumers to listen to time-shifted news reports on their personal computers or portable mp3 players.

Figure 9.2 shows how blogging's relationship to newsrooms can be classified as one of two types: newsroom blogging and blogging by independent citizen journalists.

The majority of newspapers are permitting their columnists to blog and creating group blogs like an editor's blog, which has the explicit goal of making more transparent site policies, newsroom stories, and columnists' objectives to the mass media audience. Newsrooms are also using the blog as a tool for covering elections, disasters, sporting events, or important news stories. These blogs are temporal in nature and are generally not updated after the event passes. For example, during the 2005 Hurricane Katrina disaster, CNN and NPR set up disaster blogs.

Traditional media are also using blogs to create more of a conversation with the audience by allowing citizen journalists to publish their comments and news stories under the newsroom brand name. When breaking news occurs, newsrooms encourage citizens to send in their photos, videos, or mobile phone images. Finally, some newsrooms are launching independent, standalone citizen journalism publications.

Gender and Newsroom Blogging

As of April 2006, the top 50 newspaper sites contained approximately 698 newsroom blogs (Chang *et al.*, 2006). A gender analysis of blog authorship in newspapers showed,

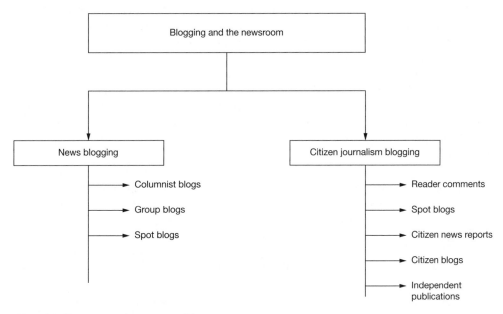

Figure 9.2 Taxonomy of newsroom blogging initiatives

roughly 30 percent of these 698 blogs were authored by women bloggers either individually or as part of group blogs where male bloggers were also active contributors. Some sites such as *The Orlando Sentinel* and *Newsday* had a majority of women bloggers, but for most of the top newspaper sites, women bloggers were in the minority. Some newspapers such as *The New York Times*, *The Sacramento Bee*, *The New York Post*, and *The Columbus Dispatch* had no women bloggers in 2006.

The gender gap in blogging is most apparent in the political newsmagazines medium. As of April 2006, *The New Republic* had one blog authored by three men. *The National Review* had 14 blog writers, and only one of them was a woman. Both *The American Prospect* and *The Weekly Standard* have no women bloggers, while only two of the 12 bloggers for *The Nation* are women. *Time Magazine* has more equality with women bloggers contributing to two of the five blogs.

Subtle gender gaps also exist in the genres that women bloggers are given to blog about in the newsrooms. As of April 2006, it was common to find more women than men bloggers covering soft news in newspaper blogs: in these 698 newspaper blogs, over 70 percent of women bloggers covered such topics as health, shopping, entertainment, travel, cooking, and celebrity gossip for the top newspaper sites. Interestingly, over 60 percent of women bloggers covered politics in newspaper sites. This percentage is much lower in political newsmagazines where there are fewer women political columnists. In other subject areas, women are less visible. Less than 12 percent of women bloggers covered technical topics while less than 5 percent of women bloggers covered sporting topics on newspaper sites.

Though many of the top 50 newspapers sites were slow to acknowledge the significance of motherhood and parenting to women readers, there is evidence that newsrooms are paying attention to women bloggers. *The San Antonio Express* began one of the earliest newsroom mommyblogs in January 2005. The blog called *MusingMam.com* is a group blog written by several of the newsroom's women journalists who address the defining experience of being a mother. In late 2005, *The Atlanta Journal Constitution* began a blog called MOMania, authored by Theresa Walsh Giarrusso that deals primarily with the challenges of raising three children. Leslie Morgan Steiner, Advertising Executive for *The Washington Post*, started a blog in 2006 titled *On Balance* that specifically addresses issues related to employment and single mom parenthood. In 2006, Cindy Krischer Goodman of *The Miami Herald* started a blog titled *The Work/Life Balancing Act*, that actively discusses the challenges of working and parenting from the real life experience of a mother of three. Other leading newspapers that have mommyblogs include *The Boston Herald*, *The Tampa Tribune*, and *The Oklahoman*.

Other newsrooms have made a decision to syndicate the best of women's blog content to their online newspapers. In May 2006, the leading women's blog network *BlogHer* announced a partnership with the blog syndication company *Pluck* to use its service called *BlogBurst*. *BlogBurst* now delivers syndicated women's blog content as one of its genre offerings to all of the newspapers that have signed on with its blog syndication service (Pluck, 2006). Initial areas of interest include women's issues, business and careers, parenting, and health and wellness. Participating newspapers in Pluck's *BlogBurst* service now include *The Washington Post*, the *San Francisco Chronicle*, the *Austin American-Statesman*, the *Houston Chronicle*, the *San Antonio Express News*, and *Gannett*.

Attracting Women Readers Through Blogs

Women bloggers are using the blog tool to create alternative, relevant news networks that speak to their issues, concerns, and interests. Blogs enable a new form of interactivity through facilitating online conversation and online community divorced from geographical constraints. Through blogs, many newsrooms may have been given a new opportunity to reconnect with women readers by addressing issues that are central to their lives. This most recent trend in the creation of mommyblogs by many newspapers is a hopeful sign that mass media are trying to create content that addresses some of the concerns of its women readers. However, motherhood is only one of the concerns of women readers. Feminist blog networks showcase the news and informational interests of a significant proportion of women who actively read and write blogs. The continued growth and popularity of these feminist blog networks suggest that women are actively creating an alternative news source that is vibrant and community-based. Issues such as domestic and sexual violence, race and gender inequalities, and reproductive rights remain issues that many women bloggers feel are not adequately addressed in mass media coverage.

To connect with women readers, news media cannot afford to overlook the centrality of these women blog networks. These networks can provide an avenue for understanding the topics, issues, and concerns of the growing percentage of women that are turning to the blogosphere as an alternative and relevant news source. News media must look to the women's blog networks to understand what appeals to women readers if it is to use this new tool to attract women readers. Women readers have shown that they can use the blog tool to create an alternative news network that speaks to their interests if the news media fail to address their concerns.

References

Abovitz, R. (2005, January 28). Do US troops target journalists in Iraq. Forumblog.org. Blog post posted to www.forumblog.org/blog/2005/01/do_us_troops_ta.html.

Adamic, L. & Glance, N. (2005, March 4). The political blogosphere and the 2004 US election: divided they blog. *HP Labs*. Retrieved August 23, 2006 from www.blogpulse.com/papers/2005/AdamicGlanceBlogWWW.pdf.

Babarasi, A.L. & Albert, R. (1999). Emergence of scaling in random networks. *Science*, 286, 509–12.

Babcock, L. & Laschever, S. (2003). *Women Don't Ask: Negotiation and the gender divide*. Princeton: Princeton University Press.

BBC News. (2005, March 4). 'Blogger fear' in Apple leak case. Retrieved August 23, 2006 from http://news.bbc.co.uk/1/hi/technology/4319715.stm.

Blood, R. (2004, April 15). A few thoughts on journalism and what weblogs do about it. *Rebecca's Pocket*. Blog post posted to www.rebeccablood.net/essays/what_is_journalism.html.

Blood, R. (2000, September 7). Weblogs: a history and perspective. Retrieved August 23, 2006 from www.rebeccablood.net/essays/weblog_history.html.

Brown, M. (2005). Abandoning the news. *Carnegie Reporter*, 3(2). Retrieved August 23, 2006 from www.carnegie.org/reporter/10/news/.

Buchanan, A. (n.d.). The secret life of mothers. *The Mother's Movement Online*. Retrieved August 23, 2006 from www.mothersmovement.org/features/06/02/a_buchanan_1.html.

Bulldog Reporter. (2005, July 27). Wall street journal tech scribe reveals how journalists use blogs in reporting—and what PR practitioners should do about it. Retrieved August 23, 2006 from www.bulldogreporter.com/profile/archives/jso/1546.html.

Cavanaugh, T. (2002, April 2). Let slip the blogs of war. *Online Journalism Review*. Retrieved August 23, 2006 from www.ojr.org/ojr/workplace/1017770789.php.

Chang, T., Ocampo, K., Jessing-Butz, K., Krase, A., Galanis, T., & Williams, S. (2006, March 1). Facts about the state of blogging at America's 100 biggest newspapers. Blog post posted to http://journalism.nyu.edu/pubzone/blueplate/issue1/chart_stateof/.

Coates, J. (1986). *Women, Men, and Language: A sociolinguistic account of sex differences in language a sociolinguistic account of sex differences in language*. New York: Pearson Longman.

Cornfield, M., Carson, J., Kalis, A., & Simon, E. (2005, May 16). Buzz, blogs and beyond: The Internet and the national discourse in the fall of 2004. *The Pew Internet and American Life Project*. Retrieved August 23, 2006 from www.pewInternet.org/ppt/BUZZ_BLOGS__BEYOND_Final05-16-05.pdf.

Crosbie, N. (2006). American newspapers revenues online. Paper presented at the World Association Newspapers Advertising Conference, Paris, France. Retrieved August 23, 2006 from www.digitaldeliverance.com/MT/archives/000643.html.

Davenport, M. (2004, July 21). 'This land' is made for cartoon candidates' jabs. *Chicago Sun-Times*.

Dube, J. (2005, December 7). New York Times memo on blogging. Cyberjournalist.net. Blog post posted to www.cyberjournalist.net/news/003082.php.

Dube, J. (2003, April 15). Blogger code of ethics. Cyberjournalist.net. Blog post posted to www.cyberjournalist.net/news/000215.php.

Drezner, D. & Farrell, H. (2004). The power and politics of blogs. Paper presented at the American Political Science Association, Chicago. Retrieved August 23, 2006 from www2.scedu.unibo.it/roversi/SocioNet/blogpaperfinal.pdf.

Drum, K. (2005a, March 16). Women and blogging. *Political Animal*. Retrieved August 28, 2006 from www.washingtonmonthly.com/archives/individual/2005_03/005865.php.

Drum, K. (2005b, February 22). Women and blogging. *Political Animal*. Retrieved August 28, 2006 from www.washingtonmonthly.com/archives/individual/2005_02/005705.php.

Drum, K. (2005c, February 20). Women's opinions. *Political Animal*. Retrieved August 23, 2006 from www.washingtonmonthly.com/archives/individual/2005_02/005691.php.

Editor & Publisher. (2006). 'Detroit news:' Never on a sunday. Retrieved August 23, 2006 from www.editorandpublisher.com/eandp/news/article_display.jsp?vnu_content_id=1002075974.

Edsall, T.B. & Faler, B. (2002, December 11). Lott remarks on Thurmond echoed 1980 words. *The Washington Post*. Retrieved August 23, 2006 from www.washingtonpost.com/ac2/wp-dyn/A37288-2002Dec10?language=printer.

Euro RSCG Magnet. (2005, June 20). Great thoughts. Retrieved August 23, 2006 from www.magnet.com/index.php?s=_thought.

Fallows, D. (2005, December 28). How women and men use the Internet. *The Pew Internet and American Life Project*. Retrieved August 23, 2006 from http://207.21.232.103/PPF/r/171/report_display.asp.

Fisher, C. (1948). *To Dwell Among Friends*. Chicago: University of Chicago Press.

Fisher, C.S. & Oliker, S.J. (1983). A research note on friendship, gender, and the life cycle. *Social Forces*, 62(1), 124–33.

Franke-Ruta, G. (2004). Exit interview. *American Prospect*. Retrieved August 23, 2006 from www.prospect.org/print-friendly/webfeatures/2004/02/franke-ruta-g-02-13.html.

Gahran, A. (2005, May 3). Are bloggers journalists? Who really cares? Part 2. *Contentious*. Blog post posted to http://blog.contentious.com/archives/2005/05/03/are-bloggers-journalists-who-really-cares.

Gahran, A. (2006, March 10). My new gig: Poynter's e-media tidbits editor. *Contentious*. Blog post posted to http://contentious.com/archives/2006/03/10/my-new-gig-poynters-e-media-tidbits-editor.

Gillmor, D. (2004). *We the Media*. Sebastopol: O'Reilly.

Goodman, E. (2005, March 20). Dissing the distaff pundits. *Boston Globe*. Retrieved August 23, 2006 from www.boston.com/news/globe/editorial_opinion/oped/articles/2005/03/20/dissing_the_distaff_pundits/.

Guernsey, L. (2002, November 28). Telling all online: It's a man's world (isn't it?). *The New York Times*. Retrieved August 23, 2006 from www.gesproductions.com/WR/portfolio/times.pdf.

Gneezy, U., Niederle, M., & Rustichini, A. (2003). Performance in competitive environments: Gender differences. *Quarterly Journal of Economics*, 118(3), 1049–74.

Hammer, D. (2004, December 9). Clark campaign hopes blogging model supplies boost. *USA Today*. Retrieved August 23, 2006 from www.usatoday.com/tech/webguide/Internetlife/2003-12-09-clarkblog_x.htm.

Harmon, S. (2004, January 25). Politics of the Web: Meet, greet, segregate, meet again. *New York Times*.

Harp, D. & Tremayne, M. (2006). The gendered blogosphere: Examining inequality using network and feminist theory. *Journalism and Mass Communication Quarterly*, 83(2), 247–64.

Herring, S., Kouper, I., Scheidt, L.A., & Wright, E. (2004). Women and children last: The discursive construction of weblogs. *Into the Blogosphere*. Retrieved August 23, 2006 from http://blog.lib.umn.edu/blogosphere/women_and_children.html.

Hochman, D. (2005, January 30). Mommy (and me). *The New York Times*. Retrieved August 23, 2006 from http://web.mit.edu/21w.780/Materials/family%20life%20blogs%20NYT.html.

Huffan, M.L., & Torres, L. (2002). It's not only 'who you know' that matters: Gender, personal contacts, and job lead quality. *Gender and Society*, 16(6), 793–813.

Humphries, S. (2004, September 22). Blogs look burly after kicking sand on CBS. *Christian Science Monitor*. Retrieved August 23, 2006 from www.csmonitor.com/2004/0922/p01s03-stin.html.

Ibarra, H. (1992). Homophily and differential returns: Sex differences in network structure and access in an advertising firm. *Administrative Science Quarterly*, 37(3), 422–47.

Ibarra, H. (1997). Paying an alternative route: Gender differences in managerial networks. *Social Psychological Quarterly*, 60(1), 91–102.

Ingman, M. (2006a, February 23). Let me entertain you. Austinmama.com. Retrieved August 23, 2006 from www.austinmama.com/momandpopcultureone.htm.

Ingman, M. (2006b, August 5). Mommy dreariest. *Baldo*. Blog post posted to www.suite102. com/baldo/archives/2006/08/index.html#001634.

Johnson, E. (2006, August 8). Reuters pulls 920 pictures by discredited photographer. *The New York Sun*. Retrieved August 23, 2006 from www.nysun.com/article/37474.

Johnson, T.J. & Kaye, B.K. (2004). Wag the blog: How reliance on traditional media and the Internet influence credibility perceptions of weblogs among blog users. *Journalism and Mass Communication Quarterly*, 81(3), 622–44.

Kennedy, H. (2005, February 10). Bush press pal quits over gay prostie link. *New York Daily News*. Retrieved August 23, 2006 from www.nydailynews.com/front/story/279556p-239417c. html.

Kennedy School of Government. (2004). 'Big media' meets the 'bloggers': coverage of Trent Lott's remarks at Strom Thurmond's birthday party. Retrieved August 23, 2006 from www. ksg.harvard.edu/presspol/Research_Publications/Case_Studies/1731_0.pdf.

Kuhn, M. (2005). C.O.B.E. A proposed code of blogger ethics. Paper presented at the Blogging, Journalism, and Credibility Conference, Cambridge. Retrieved August 23, 2006 from http:// cyber.law.harvard.edu:8080/webcred/wp-content/cobeblogethics.pdf.

Lazersfeld, P.F. & Merton, R.K. (1954). Friendship as a social process: A substantive and methodological analysis. In M. Berger, T. Abel, & C. Page. (Eds.) *Freedom and Control in Modern Society*, pp. 18–66. New York: Van Norstrand.

Lenhart, A. & Fox, S. (2006, July 19). Bloggers: A portrait of the Internet's new storytellers. *The Pew Internet and American Life Project*. Retrieved August 23, 2006 from www.pew Internet.org/pdfs/PIP%20Bloggers%20Report%20July%2019%202006.pdf.

Levy, S. (2004, March 21). Blogging beyond the men's club. *Newsweek*. Retrieved August 23, 2006 from www.msnbc.msn.com/id/7160264/site/newsweek/.

Lin, N. (1999). Social networks and status attainment. *Annual Review of Sociology*, 25, 467–87.

Lincoln, J.R. & Miller, J. (1979). Work and friendship ties in organizations: A comparative analysis of relation networks. *Administrative Science Quarterly*, 24(2), 181–99.

Lithwick, D. (2005, March 16). Girl fight: The marginalized debate over female opinion writers. *Slate*. Retrieved August 23, 2006 from www.slate.com/id/2114926.

MacKinnon, R. (2005, February 2). Blogstorm descending on CNN. *RConversation*. Blog posted to http://rconversation.blogs.com/rconversation/2005/02/blogstorm_desce.html.

Maney, K. (2004, July 27). This Net was made for you and me and the rest of the world. *USA Today*.

Mardsen, P.V. (1987). Core discussion networks of Americans. *American Sociological Review*, 52(1), 121–31.

McDermott, B. (2004, March 8). Blogosphere: Boys n' their toys. *Columbia Journalism Review Daily*. Retrieved August 23, 2006 from www.cjrdaily.org/hidden_angle/the_blogosphere_boys_ n_their_t.php.

McPherson, M., Smith-Lovin, L., & Cook, J.M. (2001). Birds of a feather: Homophily in social networks. *Annual Review of Sociology*, 27, 415–44.

McPherson, J.M. & Smith-Lovin, L. (1986). Sex segregation in voluntary associations. *American Sociological Review*, 51(1), 61–79.

Media Matters for America. (2004, August 5). Submerging the truth about swift boat vets on *Hannity & Colmes, Scarborough County*. Retrieved August 23, 2006 from http://media matters.org/items/200408050007.

Meraz, Sharon. (in press). Lurking in partisan space: Analyzing political conversation on the Howard Dean candidate website blog. In M. Tremayne (Ed.) *Blogging, Citizenship, and the Future of Media*. Routledge.

Meraz, S. (2004). Decentralized campaigning from the bottom up: Assessing the impact and significance of the Howard Dean's campaign to Internet politics and online campaigning. Paper presented at the Association for Education in Journalism and Mass Communication Conference, Toronto, Canada.

Meraz, S. (2006). Citizen Journalism, Citizen Activism, and Technology: Positioning technology as a 'second superpower' in times of disaster and terrorism. Paper presented at the Online Journalism Symposium, Austin, Texas.

Mercurio, J. (2002, December 10). Lott apologizes for Thurmond comment. CNN. Retrieved August 23, 2006 from http://archives.cnn.com/2002/ALLPOLITICS/12/09/lott.comment/.

Mernit, S. (2003, April 3). Kevin sites and the blogging controversy. *Online Journalism Review*. Retrieved at www.ojr.org/ojr/workplace/1049381758.php.

Meyer, P. (2004). *The Vanishing Newspaper: Saving journalism in the information age*. Columbia: University of Missouri Press.

Mindich, D. (2005). *Tuned Out: Why Americans under 40 don't follow the news*. New York: Oxford University Press.

Moore, G. (1990). Structural determinants of men's and women's personal networks. *American Sociological Review*, 55(5), 726–35.

New data on blogs and blogging. (2005, May 2). *The Pew Internet and American Life Project*. Retrieved at www.pewInternet.org/press_release.asp?r=104.

New York Times. (2006, January 10). Blogger reaction to Alito hearings. Retrieved August 23, 2006 from www.nytimes.com/2006/01/10/politics/politicsspecial1/10blog-alito.html?ex=1144987200&en=426652b012567cf4&ei=5070.

New York Times. (2005, October 17). Bloggers discuss the Miller case. Retrieved August 23, 2006 from www.nytimes.com/ref/politics/05web-leak.html.

Pein, C. (2005, January/February). Blog-gate. *Columbia Journalism Review*. Retrieved August 23, 2006 from www.cjr.org/issues/2005/1/pein-blog.asp.

Peskowitz, M. (2005). *The Truth Behind the Mommy Wars: Who decides what makes a good mother?* Emeryville: Seal Press.

Pluck. (2006, May 22). BlogHer teams with Pluck to help women bloggers syndicate content to mass media via BlogBurst. *Pluck*. Retrieved August 23, 2006 from www.pluck.com/press/PluckPR-060621-BlogHer.html.

The Politburo Diktat. (2004, April 17). Warbloggers yellow pages. Blog post posted to www.acepilots.com/mt/archives/000666.html.

Pollitt, K. (2005, April 4). Invisible women. *The Nation*. Retrieved August 23, 2006 from www.thenation.com/doc/20050404/pollitt/.

Porter, T. (2006). If newspapers are to rise again: "Reinvent" or die, it's that simple. *Nieman Reports*, 60(1).

Project for Excellence in Journalism. (2006). *The state of the news media*. Retrieved August 23, 2006 from www.stateofthenewsmedia.org/2006/index.asp.

Rainie, L., Cornfield, M., & Horrigan, J. (2005, March 6). The Internet and campaign 2004. *The Pew Internet & American Life Project*. Retrieved August 28, 2006 from www.pewInternet.org/PPF/r/150/report_display.asp.

Ratliff, C. (2004, December 21). The link portal on gender and the blogosphere. *CultureCat*. Blog post posted to http://culturecat.net/node/637.

Romenesko, J. (2006, July 27). Ana Marie Cox named Washington editor, Time.com. *Poynter Forums*. Blog post posted to http://poynter.org/forum/view_post.asp?id=11657.

Rosen, J. (2005, January 15). Blogging vs journalists is over. *PressThink*. Retrieved August 23, 2006 from http://journalism.nyu.edu/pubzone/weblogs/pressthink/2005/01/15/berk_pprd.html.

Rosen, J. (2003, October 16). What's radical about the weblog form in journalism. *PressThink*. Retrieved August 23, 2006 from http://journalism.nyu.edu/pubzone/weblogs/pressthink/2003/10/16/radical_ten.html.

Rosenthal, E. (2003, December 21). The 2004 campaign: The Dean campaign; political challenge 2.0: Make a virtual army a reality. *The New York Times*.

Rubel, S. (2006, March 9). Blog buzz. *The Washington Post*. Retrieved August 23, 2006, from www.washingtonpost.com/wp-dyn/content/discussion/2006/03/08/DI2006030801546.html.

Scoble, R. (2006, February 14). Tips for joining the A-list. *Scoblizer*. Retrieved August 23, 2006 from http://scobleizer.wordpress.com/2006/02/14/tips-for-joining-the-a-list/.

Seelye, C. (2005, March 7). White House approves pass for blogger. *The New York Times.* Retrieved August 23, 2006 from www.nytimes.com/2005/03/07/technology/07press.html? ex=1267938000&en=53aba0fd77cf623d&ei=5090&partner=rssuserland.

Shade, L. (Ed.) (2006). *Mommy Wars: Stay-at-home and career moms face off on their choices, their lives, their families.* New York: Random House.

Shapiro, S. (2003, December 7). The dean connection. *The New York Times.*

Shirky, C. (2003, February 8). Power laws, weblogs, and inequality. Retrieved August 23, 2006 from www.shirky.com/writings/powerlaw_weblog.html.

Sifry, D. (2004, October 10). State of the Blogosphere. *Sifry's Alerts.* Retrieved August 23, 2006 from www.sifry.com/alerts/archives/000245.html.

Sifry, D. (2006, August 7). State of the blogosphere. *Sifry's Alerts.* Blog post posted to www. sifry.com/alerts/archives/000436.html.

The state of blogging. (2005, January 2). *The Pew Internet and American Life Project.* Retrieved at www.pewInternet.org/PPF/r/144/report_display.asp.

Sullivan, A. (2005, April). Silent femmes. *Political Animal.* Retrieved August 23, 2006 from www.washingtonmonthly.com/features/2005/0504.sullivan.html.

Tannen, D. (Ed.) (1993). *Gender and Conversational Interaction.* New York: Oxford University Press.

Teen content creators and consumers. (2005, November 2). *The Pew Internet and American Life Project.* Retrieved at www.pewInternet.org/PPF/r/166/report_display.asp.

Thompson, C. (2006, February 20). Blogs to riches: The haves and haveNots of the blogging boom. *New York Magazine.* Retrieved from www.nymag.com/news/media/15967/.

Trippi, J. (2004). *The Revolution will not be Televised: Democracy, the Internet, and the overthrow of everything.* New York: ReganBooks.

Weathersby, A. (2003). Joe Trippi's killer app. *FastCompany Magazine*, 73. Retrieved August 23, 2006 from www.fastcompany.com/magazine/75/trippi.html.

Wikipedia. (n.d.). *Fisking.* Retrieved August 23, 2006 from http://en.wikipedia.org/wiki/Fisking.

Will, G. (2005, April 24). Unread and unsubscribing. *The Washington Post.* Retrieved August 23, 2006 from www.washingtonpost.com/wp-dyn/articles/A10698-2005Apr22.html.

Winer, D. (2001, September 9). The history of weblogs. *Userland Software.* Blog post posted to www.userland.com/theHistoryOfWeblogs.

Wright, J. (2006, February 15). How not to become an A-lister. *Ensight.* Blog post posted to www.ensight.org/archives/2006/02/15/how-not-to-become-an-a-lister/.

Part IV

Perspectives

Chapter 10

Reaching Young Adults Begins with Change

Amy Zerba

Twenty-four-year-old Lauren Dressen knows she should be paying attention to what her law professor is saying but having wireless Internet in the classroom has made it quite difficult. Half listening to the lecture, the second-year law student taps quietly on her laptop keyboard, instant messaging multiple friends and scanning the latest headlines on the *Drudge Report*. She clicks on a headline link that takes her to a NYTimes.com story, another to a Washingtonpost.com article. Lauren, whose name and the names of others interviewed in this chapter have been changed for confidential purposes, likes the *Drudge Report* because "it's always up on stuff" with "links to stuff that's interesting" (L.D., personal communication, June 20, 2004).

In addition to class time, Lauren spends her free time scanning news stories on BBC.co.uk or Yahoo.com, checking out her friends' blogs, Googling information she is curious about, and, more importantly, IMing friends. For this news enthusiast, online news is the best way to satisfy her I-want-it-now attitude. Newspapers, she says, just cannot keep up with her busy lifestyle. According to Lauren:

> If I had time on a Monday or like a Sunday morning or a Sunday afternoon, I would love to sit down and read the sports section. Read the travel section. Read the food section. Read the fashion section. But I just don't have time to do all that. And I need to get my news fast. And the newspaper is probably the slowest way I can think of to get my news. Just as far as sitting down and sifting through and reading the entire article. Online articles seem shorter and they're faster to get to.
> (L.D., personal communication, June 20, 2004)

While Lauren's fast-paced life cannot be generalized to every young adult, the lesson one can learn here is that many are interested in news: but, only in news that interests them, not learning which presidential candidate served as an Army general or how many Supreme Court justices they can name—questions aimed at testing their knowledge of current events and politics. Young women and men want news and information their way—whether that is through cable news, blogs, NPR, Google, RSS feeds, online news sites, portal sites, TV channel surfing, headline scrolls on news stations, e-mailed headlines, a PalmPilot or Blackberry, cell phone, iPod, an alarm clock, favorite radio deejays, conversations with others, or overhearing it. Their news habits have become less routine (compared to their parents' news behavior), magnifying statistics of their declining news habits even more.

Studying the news habits of young women and men has become a numbers game for researchers and editors alike. A sharp dip in a line graph easily shows a frightening picture of a declining young news audience. And yes, it is scary. But if news organizations want to reach this audience, they must first begin with listening to the young news consumers whom they are trying to win over. This is how they will begin to understand the wants and needs of today's young adults. Not assuming. Not asking the interns on the staff, subscribers' children, or even the staff's college-age children what they like. It takes getting out of the newsroom and asking questions. The problem is multi-faceted and the solutions are just as varied. The end result depends on news organizations' willingness to invest in change. What follows are ways how.

Who Are Young Adults and Where Do They Get Their News?

It takes 24-year-old Sean Reynolds exactly 30 minutes to shower, get dressed, and be out the door by 7 a.m. But it takes an hour for him to fight traffic and get to school for his 8 a.m. class. Once on campus, the marketing graduate student from Winston-Salem, NC, chooses to study at the business school all day, rather than commute home and face the logjam on the roads again. Plus, his wife is at work until 6:30 p.m., some days 7 p.m. He makes it a point to get home before her in the early afternoon to walk the dog. They'll have dinner together—mostly fast food and pizza—and he'll continue studying until 11 p.m. or midnight. At home, his wife will tell him "about stuff that is going on that (he) probably should be aware of" or he'll pick up news tidbits on television ("CNN-type channels" mostly), which he watches as he's going to sleep (S.R., personal communication, September 20, 2004). He likes stories about software or consumer electronics companies coming out with gadgets or any news about his Fantasy Football players. In describing how he consumes news, he noted:

> It's just very easy. I can do something else and absorb the information. I can do other things. It's not like I have to focus on reading. It sounds really bad. . . . (CNN does) a good job of here's-the-headline kind of thing. Quick to the point. I know that if I turn to it, regardless of what time of day it is, it could be the middle of the night, or if I were to watch it for 30 minutes, I could get up to speed to quite a lot of things that are going on.
>
> (S.R., personal communication, September 20, 2004)

Sean's accidental news routine fits his fill-every-waking-moment lifestyle. But he is only one of the projected 48.9 million young adults (ages 18 to 29) living in the United States in 2005, of which 51 percent are male (US Census Bureau, 2006). Worldwide, he is one of a projected 1.5 billion young adults (ages 20 to 29), of which 51 percent also are male (United Nations, 2004).

It's rare to find a universal definition of "young adults" in news stories, academic research, and government census studies. It's a concept that journalists, researchers, and agencies assume people know so they usually don't define it. Young adulthood is the period between adolescence and adulthood, but it can vary because of social, cultural, and biological factors. It's a time period in which both young women and men experience life-defining events, such as living away from home, going to college, starting a career, supporting one's self financially, getting married, buying a home, having sexual intercourse, and raising a family, to name a few.

When the concept is defined, it is usually by generation or age. Young women and men today straddle two generations—Generation X, those born in or between 1965 and 1980, and the Millennials, those born in or after 1981 (Lancaster & Stillman,

2002). However, even these birth years differ among researchers (Strauss & Howe, 1991; Howe & Strauss, 2000; Twenge, 2006). People, and journalists alike, have been known to carelessly toss the word "Generation X" around without really knowing what the term means, an obvious red flag when trying to understand this audience (Poindexter & Lasorsa, 1999). And like the generational misunderstandings, the age description of young adults varies widely from 12 to 34 in the United States. For its yearly best-of book awards for young adults, the Young Adult Library Services Association, a division of the American Library Association, refers to young adults as those aged 12 to 18 years (2006). To measure young adults' demographics, the US Census Bureau often categorizes them into an 18 to 24 age group; although, it also uses a 25 to 29 age group to describe them in other studies. To measure media use and attitudes, a 2005 State of the News Media report defines young adults as "people aged 18 to 29" (see Online: Audience section of report), the same age bracket studied by the US Gallup Poll Organization (Gallup Poll library staff, personal communication, April 24, 2006). Scarborough Research, which examines news media habits, often groups its young audience in the 18 to 34 age group (Scarborough Research, 2003).

Using birth years and age brackets to define the young adult population should be used only as guidelines, for it is really their common history and shared experiences that unite generations (Lancaster & Stillmann, 2002). US President John F. Kennedy's assassination, the Vietnam War, the assassination of Dr. Martin Luther King, Jr., first landing on the moon, and the Watergate scandal are only textbook memories for today's under-35s. Instead, their lives were historically touched by the Challenger explosion, the Tiananmen Square Massacre, the falling of the Berlin Wall, the Gulf War in 1991, September 11, 2001 attacks, and the War in Iraq. They trusted the faces of Peter Jennings, Dan Rather, and Tom Brokaw to tell their parents the news each night, and they would remember that trust when they watched those same anchors. But soon, new faces would tell them about the world—Charles Gibson, Brian Williams, and Katie Couric along with late-night talk show hosts David Letterman, Jay Leno, Conan O'Brien, and Comedy Central's fake newsmen, Jon Stewart and Stephen Colbert. Today's young women and men in the United States either grew up with the Internet throughout all or part of their primary school years or were introduced to it as a young adult; the 24-hour TV news cycle and *National Public Radio* were always part of the news media landscape from early childhood onward. But soon their parents and then they themselves would watch less television news and read fewer newspapers. Nightly local news viewership continues to decline while radio news and cable news audiences remain steady (see Network TV: Audience & Local TV: Audience sections of The State of the News Media 2006 report, for complete data). Newspapers circulation began its downward slide in 1990, but the decline in newspaper readership started in the late 1940s (see Newspapers: Audience section of The State of the News Media 2004 report, for complete data).

In examining the media use of young adults, reported statistics can be confusing, and sometimes misleading. Take newspaper readership for example. In 2002, a quarter (26 percent) of under-30s in the United States reported reading a newspaper yesterday (The Pew Research Center, 2002, p. 12). In 2004, four in ten young adults in the United States ages 18 to 34 read a newspaper on an average day (see Universal Coverage Table 3 of the Newspaper Association of America, 2005, for data). In a 2006 survey at a large US state university, a little more than half (55 percent) of the college students (18–34) reported reading a newspaper (this includes the campus newspaper) one or more days in a typical week (Zerba, 2006a). Based on these findings alone, how is it that newspaper reading among young women and men went up from 2002 to 2006? Differences in findings can stem from how the newspaper exposure question is asked, with some studies asking how often one reads a newspaper in a typical week (never, often, every day); how many days in a typical week; or if a person read one yesterday. These figures demonstrate how inconsistent readership numbers can soften or darken the picture of a declining young audience, and ultimately the urgency to do something.

College students—an often studied demographic because of sampling convenience—can skew numbers because education is a strong predictor of newspaper reading, as are age (older) and income (higher). Already young adults are at a disadvantage with the last two. Education as a determinant may be weakening as more young women and men get a college education. The gender gap in education has reversed over the past 30 years, with the number of bachelor's degrees awarded to females surpassing that of males in the United States. Fifty-seven percent of bachelor's degrees awarded in 2002–3 went to women (National Center for Education Statistics, 2004). But even though young women are pursuing more degrees in male-dominated occupations—such as engineering, science, and math—they still earn fewer degrees in these fields than males, with the exception of the life sciences, such as biology (US Government Accountability Office, 2004, pp. 14–16). One place where young women are making quite a difference in the United States is at the polls. Since 1972, young women voters (18–29) have been increasingly more likely than men to turn out and vote (The Center for Information & Research on Civic Learning & Engagement, 2005, p. 4).

National gender comparison studies of news habits rarely divide up this age group; typically, young adults are lumped in with all adults when examining gender. In analyzing the raw data from three survey studies conducted from 2004 to 2006 at a large southwestern university in the United States, young adult men were significantly more likely to read the newspaper and watch cable news one or more days a week than women in two of the studies, but the difference was barely noticeable (Zerba, 2004; Zerba & Cantrell, 2005; Zerba 2006a). In all three studies, young women were significantly more likely than men to watch local and network news one or more days a week. Young males, however, were significantly more likely to get news online one or more days a week in all three studies. In a study at the same university prior to the 2004 US presidential election, more young men (40 percent) than women (21 percent) ages 18–29 reported the Internet as being their primary source for news about the election; but more women (47 percent) than men (33 percent) preferred television as their go-to source (Zerba & Cantrell, 2005). These significant findings add to the mounds of research that show a sex divide in online news usage.

In examining the preferred news choices of young adults, the Internet and television, mostly cable news, are clearly the winners. Thirty-six percent of young adults (18–29) say the Internet is their primary source of news, more than any other age group (see Online: Audience, State of the News Media report, 2006, for complete data). For cable TV news, nearly three in ten young adults in the United States regularly tune into a cable news channel (The Pew Research Center, 2006, p. 13). Round-the-clock electronic sources are the preferred news media for this on-demand audience, making it easy for traditional news organizations to throw up their hands in defeat. Instead, journalists should be asking why, and then use these reasons to change how traditional news sources deliver the news. For young adults, online news is quick, convenient, easy, free, accessible, and updated regularly, top reasons given for its popularity in a 2006 survey of college students at a large state university (Zerba, 2006a). Can we say the same things about local TV or network news? How about newspapers and radio? The point here is that change needs to happen, but it can only happen if we listen to young adults' reasons for preferring certain news sources and apply these likes to traditional news sources.

Why Should We Care?

When 21-year-old Sydney Roberts hears her roommates talking in the other room with the TV news on, she will usually go into the room, sit down for a few minutes, and listen to the newscast, mostly so she can "understand where they're coming from when they start talking about something" (S.R., personal communication, September 21, 2004). When she goes home to visit her parents in Liberty City, TX, the television news is generally on and she will catch some news while she is visiting. Her parents also will e-mail her news articles from time to time. Other than that, she noted the following about her avoidance of news:

> I'm more focused on my personal goals and focusing on my studies and getting that out of the way. I don't really have too much time to distract myself with other concerns. It's a bit selfish. It's just the way I set up my priorities.
> (S.R., personal communication, September 21, 2004)

Sydney does not see herself picking up the news habit once college is over either. The pharmacy senior says she will probably read more pharmacy and science journals to stay up-to-date in her profession (S.R., personal communication, September 21, 2004). When asked to think about a recent news story she may have accidentally read or heard, she later would tell of a news article about teenagers taking a non-over-the counter pain pill:

> We had two teenagers die in two months and they shouldn't have gotten access to it and I read that because it was the front page and it had a picture of the prescription pill and since I'm studying pharmacy that interested me and I started reading it and I thought, "Oh My God. No wonder they are trying to make it an illegal drug that we can't even get to our cancer patients because it's being abused by teenagers who should have no access to it."
> (S.R., personal communication, September 21, 2004)

What Sydney's story illustrates is that there are some things a person cannot learn from textbooks, academic journals and even real experience. Sydney's rare-newspaper moment shows the reach of the news media, in both what they can cover and whom they can inform—even news avoiders. For Sydney, the news story on this drug not only informed her of what is going on in her profession, but also strengthened her knowledge and interest in a profession that affects billions. This is what media messages do: they provide young adults with up-to-the-second information. They give young adults an understanding of the world in which they live and their place in it. Working, voting, getting married, buying a home, relocating, having children, and paying taxes are responsibilities with links to the community—links in which the news media can be influential. Researchers have found that reading the local newspaper is positively linked with college students' community ties, in particular belonging to organizations (Demers, 1996; Collins, 2003).

Journalists' concerns over losing young adults as readers and viewers is often tempered by past findings that show that as young adults get older they are more likely to pick up the news habit, particularly for jobs (The Pew Research Center, 2004, p. 16;

Mindich, 2005). The problem is that young adults, like Sydney, are reading less than the generation before them at this age. Researchers have suggested that the long-term effects of growing up with television are surfacing (Peiser, 2000; Putnam, 2000). When a researcher in Germany studied this age group as a birth cohort, a group of people born at the same time, he found that those young adults who grew up with a television read the newspaper less regularly than those birth cohorts of generations before them in the United States and in Germany (Peiser, 2000).

Young women and men also are participating less politically than birth cohorts before them, according to more than a half-century of political behavior research (McLeod *et al.*, 2002). Studies have shown how those who read newspapers or watch television news are more likely to be politically active (Chaffee & Choe, 1981; Wilkins, 2000). But the time that young adults spend watching, reading, and listening to the news is slipping. In 1994, 18 to 24 year olds in the United States reported spending 56 minutes reading the newspaper, watching TV news, listening to it on the radio, and getting news online the day before; in 2006, it was 49 minutes (The Pew Research Center, 2006, p. 11). It's these findings that make the picture of a declining news audience troublesome. Studying young adults is imperative, for these are formative years in which they choose to tune in or tune out to what's happening around them. However, they first learn these news routines in childhood.

Make News Habits Seem Less Routine

Abigal Turner has a strong interest in US politics. That is the only news she really reads online, well, that and the latest "gossip stuff" and music news on Rollingstone.com (A.T., personal communication, September 21, 2004). She will occasionally turn on the TV to watch political conventions and speeches on CNN, but she prefers CNN.com because it's fast and easy to find things. Growing up, her parents would watch CNN a lot: her dad more than her mom. Her father also would watch the *NewsHour with Jim Lehrer* every evening, and would constantly talk about it. It was his favorite news program. Her father also would read *Time* magazine and her mother would read *People*. She subscribed to *Rolling Stone* in college. But when Abigal first started paying attention to news, she noted that she was in elementary school:

> It was during the election because our class homework assignment was to color in a map red and blue. My parents were upset because at (age) 9 we had to stay up late . . . I just remember doing that activity. . . . But the first thing that I actually remember, that sticks in my mind was the Gulf War. I remember seeing a lot about the Gulf War, but I was 7 or 8. I just remember being scared. I didn't know how far the Gulf was. Sadly, I knew where the Gulf of Mexico was, so I thought it was close by.
>
> (A.B., personal communication, September 21, 2004)

What Abigal doesn't realize is that her parents' news routines strongly influenced her news behavior today, for a handful of studies have shown that parental news exposure is a predictor of young adults' news behavior (Stone & Wetherington, 1979; Raeymaekers, 2002; Zerba, 2004; Zerba, 2006b). When children watch the news reading and viewing behavior of their parent(s), they are really watching the behavior being modeled, a process rooted in social learning theory (Bandura & Walters, 1963).

Researchers have found parents' preferred reading time and place for reading the newspaper also influenced the newspaper reading time and place for 18 to 34 year olds (Stone and Wetherington, 1979).

Few studies have examined young adults' recalled memories of their parents' news routines. Of the few that have, it has been shown that young adults can remember the behavior of their parents reading newspapers and watching television news (Bossard & Boll, 1950; Barnhurst & Wartella, 1991; Barnhurst & Wartella, 1998; Zerba, 2004; Zerba, 2006b). Two researchers conducted an extensive qualitative study examining students' memories of family rituals during a span of childhoods from 1917 to 1946 (Bossard & Boll, 1950). The two researchers asked students what they remembered about their parents' newspaper use. One student responded:

> The morning paper is always read first by my father, and then by the other members of the family in order of age. After all the family has finished, the servants can read it if they wish.
>
> (Bossard & Boll, 1950, p. 73)

Another student recalled:

> On returning home from school or work, the newspaper is broken up into three sections, the funnies taken by my youngest sister. I take possession of the sport page. Mother takes the pages on household hints and women's items. The paper is rearranged by me to its original condition and left at the arm of the easy chair which Father always occupies after supper. Thelma, my oldest sister, takes possession of the paper after Father has finished reading it.
>
> (Bossard & Boll, 1950, p. 73)

In some cases, no one "dared touch the paper till Father was finished with it" and Sunday was remembered for its funnies section, which was often read aloud to the children (Bossard & Boll, 1950, p. 73).

In 1989–90, two researchers collected life diaries from 164 college students who wrote on their newspaper experiences growing up (Barnhurst & Wartella, 1991). A number of the students reflected on how newspapers were a constant part of their household, but many confessed they paid little attention to it or thought it was not that important to them. Some recalled getting angry because their parents spent time with the newspaper instead of them. Some imitated their parents reading the newspaper. Half the students reported that their parents encouraged them "strongly" or "somewhat strongly" to read the newspaper. For many students, a newspaper symbolized adulthood.

In 2006, when a random sample of college students (1,759 of them) at a large southwestern university was asked to recall their parents' newspaper or TV news habits, three-fourths of students could recall one or both of their parents reading the newspaper regularly while growing up (Zerba, 2006b). Most of the students could remember the exact location, time, and manner in which their parent(s) did so—at the dining room table, in the living room, kitchen, or in bed; mostly in the morning, after work, late at night, or on Sunday mornings; and sitting down, drinking coffee, and/or over breakfast. Some parents would discuss articles with them, others read silently, they recalled. These images of their parents reading newspapers are probably etched in their heads because of the repetitive nature of the activity. The sensory experiences that came with these observations could have also strengthened these mental representations.

Students could remember the sight, sounds (silence or discussion), and smell (coffee and/or breakfast) associated with their parent(s) reading the newspaper. Females could remember their mother reading the newspaper and watching TV news more than males, who were more likely to remember their father reading and watching the news, but the difference is small (Zerba, 2006b). Overall, studies have shown adolescents and young adults recall their father reading the newspaper more often than their mother (Cobb & Kenny, 1986; Zerba, 2004; Zerba, 2006b).

In the same study, when students were asked about television news in their home, many could recall the exact time and type of news, but little else (Zerba, 2006b). Students recalled their parents watching the news in the morning before work, 5 p.m., 6 p.m., at dinner, and right before their parents went to bed. Many would sometimes watch the news with their parent(s), even if they didn't understand what was going on. Local and network news were their parents' preferred choices. Even though 24-hour cable news was an option, few parents watched it, according to their responses. In 1995, two researchers asked 129 students to write life diary essays detailing their experience with television news growing up (Barnhurst & Wartella, 1998). Three-quarters of the students recalled watching TV news with their parents. When recounting the use of television as a news source, their essays often centered on memorable images of news-worthy events, such as the Challenger explosion or the Gulf War (Barnhurst & Wartella, 1998). About three-quarters of the essays reported watching news at school, but beyond the shuttle experience, newscasts had very little presence in school. In this study, women were more likely to remember the gendered stereotypes of news consumption in the home, with father sitting in a chair and/or drinking beer and mother cooking dinner while the news was on.

What these studies show is that young adults first remember news media use in their home as routines, not necessarily for information-gathering purposes. According to their own recollections, newspapers are to be read sitting down at the breakfast table with morning coffee. Local and national news is to be watched at 5 p.m., 6 p.m., and 10 p.m., not any time on a 24-hour news cycle. Making time for the news does not sit well with today's right-now generation, especially in the morning, when fewer young adults are taking the time to even eat breakfast (Keski-Rahkonen et al., 2003). For today's young adults, newspaper reading and nightly newscasts may just *feel* old because of this routine. Perhaps it is this routine image of traditional media that is influencing young adults' use of other media or their lack-of-time reasoning for not reading newspapers or watching TV news.

Interestingly, the aim of journalists has always been to find out how to get more young adults to pick up the news habit. But even the word "habit" has been mis-understood. Researchers themselves have a difficult time defining and differentiating the constructs "ritual," "habit," and "routine." The complex and varied constructs are often used interchangeably, causing blurred divisions. A ritual—characteristic of a wedding, birthday party, funeral, holiday celebration—is symbolic in nature. Rituals are celebratory, consummatory, and decorative, not utilitarian in their purpose (McQuail & Windahl, 1993). They are highly symbolic and have a strong affective component (Rook, 1985; Fiese et al., 2002). Habits are more singular behaviors (like eating breakfast) and less symbolically meaningful (Rook, 1985). Habits are related to choice, meaning people who have a strong habit for doing something are more likely to choose to perform the habitual behavior than alternative options (Aarts et al., 1998). When habits are established, they do not require mental reasoning or planning—people just do them (ibid., 1998). Routines, on the other hand, require planning. They are observable repeated acts involving moment(s) in time, and once the act is done, there is little afterthought of it (Fiese *et al.*, 2002, p. 382). A person may wake up at 7 a.m., fix breakfast, and read the morning newspaper, but is this an automatic habit or a routine? There is still some planning involved—setting aside time. But routines can become habits if the behavior is frequently performed without much planning (Aarts *et al.*, 1998).

For young adults, who recalled that consuming news for their parents was routine and at a designated time, tuning into news needed to feel less routine and less bound by time. The goal of the news industry should be for young adults to pick up a news habit, not a news routine. Getting news should not feel like a routine. Young adults' news habits are not like their parents'. A habit revolves around when they want it, what they want, and how they want to get the news; not when it hits a doorstep or airs. Their news habits are extremely individualized. Unlike their parents growing up, their days do not center on the morning newspaper or 6 o'clock news. Newspapers and local/network news need to somehow lose that routine stereotype, but how? It could be in the stories news organizations choose to run or even how stories are reported on or written. Lifestyles, and ways of receiving news, have changed ten-fold, so why have not traditional media?

Become Less Old-Fashioned

When it comes to news, 26-year-old Kenny McDaniel has a midday news habit—online. He wakes up, eats breakfast "if I'm lucky," drives to school, checks his e-mail, then checks out a handful of sites to read the news before starting his work day (K.M., personal communication, June 25, 2004). Google News, *The New York Times*, CNN, Boingboing.net, and Slashdot.com are his preferred news choices. The architecture graduate student will also check these sites during breaks or when he hears something in conversations. He watches little TV at home, but when he does, it is mostly *Seinfeld* reruns or *King of the Hill* when he is eating dinner. When the local news comes on, he flips the station because he feels like it is a "giant waste of time" and "low-grade" journalism (K.M., personal communication, June 25, 2004). When asked why he does not read newspapers, he sums it up in one word: wasteful. According to Kenny:

> That's a lot of paper for a short use. It's kind of bulky and something I need to carry around. . . . It costs money and it's wasteful and I can get everything for free on the Internet.
>
> (K.M., personal communication, June 25, 2004)

It is not that the Long Island, NY, native does not like to read print. He subscribes to *Wired*, *Biblical Archeology Review*, *Dwell*, and *Metropolis Magazine*, mostly because they have in-depth articles on topics he is interested in. For him, magazines are "half way between a book and a website or a newspaper" (K.M., personal communication, June 25, 2004).

Kenny's opinion of newspapers is not uncommon for young adults who seldom or never read them. Messy, bulky, wasteful, inaccessible, and expensive: that is how both young women and men (18–34) who never or seldom read newspapers describe the traditional print medium (Zerba, 2006a). In a 2006 study at a large public university, young women rated the holdability and messiness of newspapers slightly higher than young men (ibid.). It is hard to apply these words to radio, TV, or the Internet. Physical News is a term I used to describe print newspapers, in particular because they require physical effort to use. If a person does not subscribe to the newspaper, getting it requires effort—finding one, having the right change, etc.—unlike electronic sources. For young adults, other media may be more accessible, even at one's fingertips. The physical handling of newspapers involves getting, unfolding, holding, and flipping pages and also dealing with newsprint and ink marks. This handling of the news does not apply to other media, such as television, radio, Internet, and even magazines. While these other media require effort to watch, listen, and read, they don't require much physical effort to use. Magazines don't leave ink marks or give readers difficulty in handling because of their size or bulkiness.

To tackle this Physical News issue, newspapers should really follow Europe's lead and go tabloid, a trend that is starting to surface in the United States. Giving newspapers a more magazine-like feel will make them easier to handle, carry, hold, and flip. Newspapers also should explore more environmental-friendly ideas for recycling, for this demographic is more environmentally sensitive than generations past. Newspapers "piling up" is an often cited problem for why young adults prefer to go paperless, with young women rating this reason higher than men, in one study (Zerba, 2006a). The guilt of not reading stacks of newspapers can and does end subscriptions. Lastly, newspapers need to be in the face of young adults. Not in a bin. Not outside a business. Not on doorsteps. Put free newspapers where young adults are—on college campuses, inside gyms, recreation centers, hair salons, study halls, on bus and subway seats, inside coffee houses, to name a few. More research is needed on where young adults hang out to include more of these contact points in newspaper deliveries. And a real effort needs to be made in saturating those spots, not outside them, with the news. Newspapers should invest more in pass-along readership research. Young adults are more likely to pick up a newspaper if it is right there in front of them inside businesses; they are not going to automatically subscribe without seeing it a few times first. Experiment.

Today, when editors approach the topic of making newspapers more reader-friendly for younger audiences, their solution is often to jazz up the look of the newspaper. Soon flashy graphics and shorter stories become the in-thing because this is what they think young adults want. Other newspapers jump on the bandwagon of redesigns and so it appears the industry is doing something for young readers. Not quite. A print newspaper redesign for young readers is like a perfectly wrapped gift with finely creased corners and edges, but when the box is ripped open, there lies a rock. Content still drives the news industry, a golden rule that will not fade with time.

Make News More Digestible

Twenty-three-year-old Jessica Neilson's daily schedule is pretty wide open. In between looking for a summer job, the art history graduate student watches TV, talks to her parents on the phone, checks her e-mail "about ten times a day out of boredom," walks her dog, and reads or views "anything from gossip to celebrity photos" online to pass time (J.N., personal communication, June 20, 2004). Lack of time is not why she does not read the newspaper. She has the time; she just does not want to buy it. It is not that Jessica does not like to read, just not print newspapers. She reads stories online every day and finished four books in the past month. But she has not always enjoyed reading. Graduate school made her despise it at first because her professors would assign "70 to 80 pages a night" (J.N., personal communication, June 20, 2004). Of her fear of reading, Jessica observed:

It's like a mental barrier. It's climbing a wall or something. It's very time-consuming and I think a lot of people get immediate gratification with so much in their life now that reading doesn't come off that way.

(J.N., personal communication, June 20, 2004)

One often-heard reason why fewer young adults are reading newspapers is that they do not like reading. But is it that they do not like reading or are other things preventing them from doing so, like work or school? Take-home work, required readings in school and comprehending difficult text are a few barriers to reading for enjoyment for young adults, a demographic whose reading behavior is seldom parceled out in academic reading research. This age group often takes a backseat to research on children or adult reading behavior, both of which dominate reading studies. Of the few recent national studies that have zoomed in on this demographic, findings confirm that young adults are indeed reading less (National Endowment for the Arts, 2004; Bogart, 2005). Over a 20-year span (1982–2002), young adults (18–34) dropped from being the most likely to read literature (novels, short stories, plays, and/or poetry) for leisure to the least likely, with the exception of those over age 65, according to a National Endowment for the Arts study (2004, p. 26). Those ages 18 to 24 showed the largest drop of any age group for literary reading (National Endowment for the Arts, 2004, p. 26).

There also is a gender gap in reading. More women (over 18) read literature for leisure than men, according to the NEA study (2004, p. 9). In examining raw data taken from a 2003 survey of randomly selected college students (755 of them) at a large public university in the United States, 87 percent of college students (18–34) said they would miss not reading books if they were no longer available, with 79 percent of women in this group reporting a significantly strong attachment to books unrelated to school compared to 66 percent males (Zerba, 2004). The same held true for magazines, with significantly more women (43 percent) strongly attached to them than males (34 percent) (Zerba, 2004). But what often doesn't get said in examining reading numbers is that reading for both literature and newspapers is declining in almost every age group (National Endowment for the Arts, 2004, p. 26; see Newspapers: Audience section of the State of the News Media 2006 report, for complete data). The question asked should not be how has reading declined, but why? More demands on people's time have made leisure activities, such as reading, less possible. Print newspapers, like books, demand more time—a resource that is already stretched from the multitude of tasks one feels like they need to prioritize. Reading news may not be a priority of young adults when weighed with more pressing activities, such as required reading for school and/or taking care of children. Also, reading newspapers requires more effort than watching television news, listening to NPR or clicking on links to read stories of interest. It is this *effort* to process information that print newspapers should be examining. And they should be looking at themselves, not assuming young adults do not like to read.

The Pew Research Center found that young adults are more likely to have read a book the day before, than a newspaper (2006, p. 9). The gap here lies in news-related media, which does not seem to engage younger readers. This could partly point to the difficult reading level of many newspaper stories, for newspapers have been shown to be the most difficult print medium to read. Newspaper editorials (Moznette & Rarick, 1968; Stempel, 1981), novels (Fowler, 1978), and magazines (Fowler & Smith, 1979) have been found to be more readable than newspaper news stories. Here's an example from a March 31, 2006, *The New York Times* story on a topic of interest to young adults—financing college (Schemo, 2006):

The House voted largely along party lines on Thursday to approve the main measure governing colleges and universities, adding provisions to expand student grants based on need and pressing colleges to control tuition. But the House rejected a Democratic proposal to halve the interest rate on student loans.

The $70 billion proposal, which would renew the law until 2012, sets the terms for loans and grants along with the limits for maximum aid. It was last renewed in 1998.

What? With stories like this, it is easy to question whom journalists are writing for—readers or each other? If journalism is about informing the public, these stories do nothing but confuse readers. This is not to say that newspapers should dumb down copy, quite the contrary, for young adults are savvy enough to know when they are being talked down to. But there is something to be said for comprehensible writing.

About 90 million US adults experience difficulty integrating and synthesizing information from complex or lengthy tests, according to the last National Adult Literacy Survey in 1993 by the National Center for Education Statistics (National Center for Education Statistics, 2002, p. xvi). Yet more than 70 percent of this same group describe themselves as being able to read and write English "well" or "very well" (National Center for Education Statistics, 2002, p. xvii). This begs the question, are we truly understanding what we read? Perhaps some young adults feel that just getting the gist of a news story is all one needs to understand it. This could be because of the overabundance of news and sources available or simply the difficulty, and effort needed, in understanding unfamiliar topics that may be written poorly. The trouble with only getting the gist of a news story is that it adds little depth to a person's prior knowledge, which when activated allows for meaning making to occur. When readers have little or no prior knowledge or interest about a topic, all that is left to aid comprehension is the writing itself. When young adults are repeatedly exposed to nondigestible articles in newspapers or newsmagazines, they may associate these media as being too difficult to understand, and therefore lose competence in reading them. This can then motivate their decision to choose another news medium, or worse, make them lose any interest in certain news topics or news in general. There is something to be said for simple, clear copy, for any age group, not just young adults.

Answer the, So What?

Twenty-five-year-old Erin Peters says she wants to be a science teacher when she finishes college. She spends about 30 hours a week observing teachers in area schools in addition to her full load of college courses. In her not-so-free time, she is training for a marathon to raise money for leukemia. Because Erin is always on the run, her choice of news media is solely based on convenience. She often listens to NPR in the car. Erin likes to read BBC online because she is in control of picking the news stories she wants to read. Television news, she says, is geared toward "people my parents' age," not young adults. Erin observed:

> I don't see us as being the typical audience for news most of the time. When you watch news on TV there's a lot of geriatric pharmaceutical commercials and things like that and so we don't seem to be the main people who watch the news.
>
> (E.P., personal communication, May 25, 2004)

Young adults, like Erin, along with researchers and journalists have been screaming "make news more relevant" for decades. Amid the news industry's meager attempts to gain the younger audience, the only message that has gotten through is that news is an adult medium, making young adults feel less grown-up. Why? Visually, it could be because of repeated photographs of older adults splashed all over newspaper pages or the older faces on nightly newscasts with whom young adults grew up. The selection of news stories, and more importantly the perspective a journalist uses to tell a story, can divide a news audience by age and gender. For example, instead of always reporting on the health dangers of tattooing, why not report on it as an art? Would this encourage it? (Gasp.) Why is news about college education mostly directed toward parents? Is it assumed that no young women and men put themselves through school? The media's portrayal of young adults' power to affect change can also be confusing, and sometimes downright wrong. After early results of the 2004 US presidential election, some news organizations easily wrote the youth vote off, reporting that young adults did not come out in droves as expected on the heels of the much-hyped Rock-the-Vote campaign (McCarthy, 2004). Gonzo journalist Hunter S. Thompson quipped to an *Aspen Daily News* journalist, "Yeah, we rocked the vote all right. Those little bastards betrayed us again" (Hooper, 2004). In the 2004 US presidential election-deciding state of Ohio, *The Associated Press* news wire service reported that one out of seven voters were ages 18 to 29 according to its exit polls. But two days later, *AP* issued a correction that one in five voters were ages 18 to 29 (McCarthy, 2004). Young adults did come out in numbers, 20.1 million to be exact, 4 million more than in 2000 (Center for Information & Research on Civic Learning & Engagement, 2005, p. 3). While these are just a few observable examples, the point is that news media are unknowingly catering to older audiences. Answering the "So What?" for the younger audience can come with a bit of awareness from journalists at the start.

A simple start to improving relatedness is including backgrounds of stories up high in reporting or even as a separate element on a news page. Placing this information at the end of stories—a reporting technique leftover from the days of the telegraph— serves no purpose if the news consumer is lost at the beginning. Do journalists expect readers to already know about the recent happenings in the Israeli–Palestinian conflict and retain this knowledge always in their working memory? What about the Kyoto Protocol on global warming? Is it so well known that readers do not need a reminder of what it is? Give readers a quick, meaningful definition please. Throwing audience members into hard news stories without any context or frame of reference is like having them read or hear text in another language. They may feel dumb, embarrassed, confused, or deflated. They cannot connect with the story, and so they move on. For some young readers, this feeling could stick with them the next time they read or hear a similar news story, prompting them to tune out each time, or maybe for good. For Susan Drew, a 27 year old from Union City, CA, newspapers cannot compete with online news sites in providing context to stories. According to Susan:

> It really drives me crazy to read an article in the paper and then I never find out what happened or I don't understand like what happened before because it's news, like *it is* what's new, which is fine, that's the point, but then a lot of times the articles are just a string of quotes but they don't really provide any context or meaning like any framework to interpret them in. And it's fine if you already know

a lot about that but if you don't, you just pick up a newspaper and you find something interesting and you're left kind of stranded.

(S.D., personal communication, May 25, 2004)

A second suggested answer to the "So What?" question is to allow young staff journalists to have more of a voice in newsrooms. They know the pulse of this demographic better than anyone in the newsroom. Too often young journalists' ideas, and writing, become sterilized or even tossed aside by older, more experienced staff members, directors, or editors. And so the vicious cycle of not-relatable reporting continues. Being older and more seasoned does not always equate to being more knowledgeable about all stories, especially those regarding young adults. A younger face, voice, and perspective may seem like it only reaches short distances now, but its future reach is worth the investment.

Newspaper journalists laugh when I suggest that hard news stories should come with a "Why You Should Care" breakout box with bulleted reasons for why each story matters to readers. This box would get journalists thinking more about whom they are writing for and why it is relevant to readers' lives, especially young adults. Too often journalists get caught up in the daily grind of hard news stories—council meetings, budget hearings, school finance, court rulings, health studies—that they forget about the person taking in the story.

Even in 1979, readers reported feeling alienated from news coverage, local news especially, according to researcher Ruth Clark's newspaper industry-changing study. Readers did not want to just be told about the world but how to understand it, the study found. Young adults (18–24) are considerably more likely than others to be disengaged from hard news topics—such as coverage of international affairs, politics and events in Washington, local government, business and financial news (The Pew Research Center, 2004, p. 27). Twenty-five percent of Americans in this age group reported not following any of these topics; 14 percent of those aged 25 to 29 reported being disengaged from hard news (ibid.). What doesn't get much attention is the three-fourths of 18 to 24 year olds who are moderate or high consumers of hard news, or the four out of five 25 to 29 year olds who like it (ibid.).

When randomly selected students (ages 18–34) at a large public university were asked to rate their interest level in types of news, both women and men rated world and national news as their top choices; women rated local and state news higher than men (Zerba, 2006a). There were only a few *large* gender differences in preferred news topics, with women rating entertainment, weather and crime/accident topics higher and men rating sports and business news topics higher. Sadly, state and local politics and religion rounded out the bottom for both sexes. Perhaps young adults aren't seeing the 'So What?' answered in these stories taking place in their own backyards. The news media need to relate their stories to the lives of their young audience by constantly asking, why does this matter? There is not a great need to differentiate hard news topics between young women and men for their interests in these stories are somewhat similar (Zerba, 2006a). That's not to say that women reporters and sources are well represented in covering these topics. Not quite. Women, just as men, can provide a different perspective in covering these news stories and are greatly needed. The strong sex divide among young adults' news interests can be found in other topics—such as business, sports, entertainment and state/local news. These are areas that need stronger representation from the opposite sex—not just in the writing, but in the story selection, reporting, imagery and sources interviewed.

Answering the 'So What?' for every news story can be difficult for journalists, but not impossible. What makes this way of thinking sticky is that increasing relevance for young readers may isolate older readers, and news organizations know this. Their thinking: Why go after young adults who may or may not watch, read or listen to the news every day, when we have older loyal audience members who do? What these news organizations are unknowingly doing is digging their own graves. Change needs to happen. But how?

News Media Need to Find Themselves

Depending on the news story and what time it broke, 22-year-old Amy Sullivan knows where to find out more about it. If it's a local story, she turns on the local TV news; a "huge story" she turns on CNN; and if it's updates on a story, she goes online (A.S., personal communication, May 25, 2004). The fifth-year accounting senior from McAllen, TX, will read or listen to news she's "heard about from friends or heard people talking about" (A.S., personal communication, May 25, 2004). Sometimes, when she's flipping TV channels, she'll glance at the bottom scroll bar of cable news stations to see if any story interests her. If something does, she'll tune in for a few minutes. Her homepage is set to MSN.com, so occasionally she'll scan the headlines and if a story headline catches her attention, she'll read it. Overall, she noted her preference for the Internet as her preferred news source:

> It's fast and I can kind of pick out what I want to read and which I don't. It's easier to me than newspapers where you have to sit there and stumble through all those papers. It's like right out there before you. . . . It's readily available and it's just like there and you can have it. And it's updated 24 hours a day.
> (A.S., personal communication, May 25, 2004)

Printed newspapers just can't compete with instant news sources, so why are they still trying? If the news media want to reach young adults, they should first know youth's top preferred news sources (the Internet and TV), then ask why. News organizations should be asking themselves what sets them apart from competing media platforms. Then do what they do well. Young adults are less likely to turn to newspapers for baseball scores, a previous morning traffic accident, or coverage of yesterday's street parade—it is old news. News organizations should put their energy and resources into the very thing they do better than other media, instead of trying to compete for attention by doing it all.

For print newspapers, this means more analysis pieces of local happenings each day, next-day storytelling, memorable photographs, a portable daily wrap-up of news. For TV news, it is the live video coverage and visual investigative pieces that cannot be beaten. For newsmagazines, it is their thought-provoking analysis pieces, in-depth follow-ups of news events that have passed, and storytelling that engages and entertains readers like a good book. For radio, it is the reporting and breaking of news stories for mobile listeners, the instant dialogue with callers about a conversation or news event still going on and the rich description and sound bites that can captivate listeners. For online, it is the instantaneous coverage and within-seconds updates of what is happening and the sheer depth a user can reach in trying to understand all facets, perspectives, and details of a news story. For traditional media to survive, they need to find their niche, especially with all the news media choices young adults have today.

To stand out and be "physically" different, more than a dozen US newspapers started publishing free tabloids targeted at young women and men, whom they know are time-strapped and constantly on the go. These papers have edgier designs and contain shorter, relevant copy aimed at young adults. But is a separate newspaper for young adults the answer? The verdict is still out. Jane Hirt, 39, editor of Chicago's *RedEye*, a five-day-a-week free tabloid for readers "in their 20s and 30s," observed that niche publications are a trend that we just might see more of in the near future:

> The reason people are not reading newspapers solely is there are just more choices out there. So, unfortunately, the days of sitting down with the newspaper and a cup of coffee for two hours each morning are gone. So newspapers need to figure out how to stay in the game. Newspapers need to evolve to remain an attractive choice. I think more and more you are going to see newspapers that are niche publications. . . . That's going to be the name of the game in order to appeal to everyone. The days of one-size-fits-all newspapers are numbered.
>
> (J.H., personal communication, June 6, 2006)

RedEye, which launched in October 2002, has conducted surveys, focus groups, and e-mail research to get at what young readers want in a newspaper in the Chicago area. From this research, the relatively young 20-person staff has learned that its audience likes short, to-the-point, jumpless stories that are written with a little bit of voice and personality "like a friend talking to them" (J.H., personal communication, June 6, 2006).

But one common criticism heard about tabloid newspapers aimed at young adults is that they consist of few hard news stories. This is partly true. Hard news stories—US Supreme Court rulings, Iraq, foreign policy, finance, politics, international elections, to name a few—do appear, but in smaller, edited-down doses, and they're mostly wire or non-staff generated. In discussing how stories are chosen for *RedEye*, Hirt observed:

> We are looking for what is relevant—entertainment and local news—things happening in Chicago. We don't spend a lot of time on policy stories from the Mideast. It's not that we don't think readers are interested in that, that's just not what they're looking for from us. And that's OK. We are not a newspaper of record and that's very freeing and we can pick whatever is interesting to our particular audience.
>
> (J.H., personal communication, June 6, 2006)

Asap (pronounced a-s-a-p), a news service by *The Associated Press* launched in 2005, delivered content targeted at under-35s. The service shut down after two years because of lack of financial success (Jones, 2007). News organizations that were members of *AP* wire service and paid for the *asap* service could choose to print or post these stories. One of the service's main goals was delivering content in different ways—with video, audio, photo galleries, interactive graphics, and podcasts. Through focus group research, *asap* had found young adults "like to consume their news in a lot of different ways." According to Eric Carvin, 33, the news editor at *asap* on storytelling:

> When we come up with a story idea, we then stop—before anything else happens—we stop and make a decision of how the story should be told. Do we want it to

be text and pictures only? A podcast? An interactive photo gallery or video mini-documentary? And with the way asap is designed, we can also easily combine different types of media for the same story. The bottom line is that text is no longer the automatic default.

(E.C., personal communication, June 1, 2006)

The 26-person staff, including 10 to 12 reporters, put out about 15 original stories a day, mostly skewed toward 22 to 34 year olds, the age group of most of the staff (E.C. personal communication, June 1, 2006). Hard news stories, however, were still somewhat absent in the stories it sold to news organizations. When examining two weeks of *asap's* afternoon weekday-only news advisories—a list of a little more than 130 story summaries of content news organizations can choose to run—only two were about Iraq, two focused on US Supreme Court rulings, eight dealt with state or US government stories and 18 tackled international news, excluding travel and World Cup coverage (The Associated Press, 2006). Instead, story summaries focused on technology, unusual court cases, education, TV shows, musicians, film stars, health, and science. To its credit, the staff did produce an extensive package on AIDS during that time and carried a list of top news stories on its website. But the news organization dedicated to under-35s left the heavy lifting of hard news to its mothership, *The Associated Press*, when selling story ideas. What does this say about journalists' idea of what interests young adults? These offerings alone made it easy for social critics to berate young readers' current events and political knowledge.

A few months earlier in 2005, The Readership Institute, a center at Northwestern University, attempted to build a prototype of a paper that made stories more relevant and engaging for young readers. The institute interviewed 320 under-30s about their newspaper experiences with Minnesota's *Star Tribune*. A team at the newspaper then redesigned its paper, not in just a visual sense, but in the content, too. The newspaper took an "editing for experience" approach—choosing the experience that young readers surveyed wanted to have—giving them something to talk about; looking out for their interests; and surprising or humoring them (The Readership Institute, 2005, p. 2). Stories were written and presented in a way to get at those experiences. When the young adults were given a prototype of the "experience" paper alongside the original paper that ran and a second alternative, two-thirds preferred the "experience" paper, mainly because the content gave them something to talk about with others, and the stories surprised and humored them (ibid., p. 5). What changed in the content? The content was framed in a way that spoke directly to this age group's concerns and interests. It reflected their faces and perspectives, and, in doing so, told them that the newspaper cared about their interests. More innovative ideas like this need to be experimented with, but it takes time, commitment, and resources.

Finding Their Place in an Internet-Driven World

In tackling the problem of a declining young news audience the first step is to be dedicated to the effort. Hiring young women and men as writers and editors, selecting news stories of interest purposively, and rewriting copy are good baby steps at reaching this audience, but they're not new approaches. Listen to what both young women and men are saying, and *really* listen. Make the news feel less routine. For most of this young audience, gone are the days of reading the newspaper over breakfast or watching local or network news around the dinner table. News needs to be flippable, portable, holdable, scannable, and/or clickable with little effort to read, hear, or watch at any time. More effort is needed in making news stories more digestible. News audiences do not walk around with the specifics of school finance bills on the tips of their tongues. Tell young adults what they mean in simple ways. And then say it again, and again the next day. Journalists also need to back away from their notes and answer the "So What?" question for young adults in their writing and reporting and up high, otherwise you might as well be talking to yourself.

More effort is needed to include the perspectives of the opposite sex in the selecting and reporting of hard and soft news stories, and this includes images, too. This is especially important on news topics that young adults' interests appear divided—this means more women in sports and business news; and more men in entertainment and local news.

Finally, news organizations, especially traditional sources—newspapers, radio, local and network TV—need to find their place in this Internet-driven world. Stop trying to compete with the Internet. It has already won over most of this young audience, even more so with males. Find yourself, and strengthen what you do best.

These are exciting times for traditional news sources. Will they die out in five to ten years or make a major comeback? My hope is that each will make major changes in their own way to win over this young audience. The problem of a declining young audience is decades old, but this problem desperately needs more experimentation now. Change needs to feel different, even uncomfortable at first, and it will undoubtedly face some resistance from news audiences and journalists alike. But talking about the issue hasn't gotten us anywhere. It is time to start listening and then acting.

References

Aarts, H., Verplanken, B., & Knippenberg, A.V. (1998). Predicting behavior from actions in the past: Repeated decision making or a matter of habit? *Journal of Applied Social Psychology*, 28(15), 1355–74.

The Associated Press. (2006, March 30–2006, June 9). AP ASAP Digests and AP-Under 35 news advisories. Retrieved June 10, 2006 from www.yourap.org/.

Bandura, A. & Walters, R.H. (1963). *Social Learning and Personality Development*. New York: Holt, Rinehart and Winston.

Barnhurst, K.G. & Wartella, E. (1991). Newspapers and citizenship: young adults' subjective experience of newspapers. *Critical Studies in Mass Communication*, 8(2), 195–209.

Barnhurst, K.G. & Wartella, E. (1998). Young citizens, American TV newscasts and the collective memory. *Critical Studies in Mass Communication*, 15(3), 279–305.

Bogart, L. (2005). *Over the Edge: How the pursuit of youth by marketers and the media has changed American culture*. Chicago: Ivan R. Dee.

Bossard, J.H.S. & Boll, E.S. (1950). *Ritual in Family Living: A contemporary study*. Philadelphia: University of Pennsylvania Press.

The Center for Information & Research on Civic Learning & Engagement (2005, July). The Youth Vote 2004. *Table 2: Number of votes cast, presidential election years 1972–2004 in thousands*. Retrieved July 13, 2006 from www.civicyouth.org/PopUps/FactSheets/FS_Youth_Voting_72-04.pdf.

Chaffee, S.H. & Choe, S.Y. (1981). Newspaper reading in longitudinal perspective: Beyond structural constraints. *Journalism Quarterly*, 58(2), 201–11.

Clark, R. (1979, May). *Changing needs of changing readers*. The American Society of Newspaper Editors. Yankelovich, Skelly & White.

Collins, S.J. (2003). Level of on-campus activities predicts student paper readership. *Newspaper Research Journal*, 24(4), 102–5.

Demers, D.P. (1996). Does personal experience in a community increase or decrease newspaper reading? *Journalism and Mass Communication Quarterly*, 73(2), 304–18.

Fiese, B.H., Tomcho, T.J., Douglas, M., Josephs, K., Poltrock, S., & Baker, T. (2002). A review of 50 years of research on naturally occurring family routines and rituals: Cause for celebration? *Journal of Family Psychology*, 16(4), 381–90.

Fowler, G.L. (1978). The comparative readability of newspapers and novels. *Journalism Quarterly*, 55(3), 589–91.

Fowler G.L. Jr. & Smith, E.J. (1979). Readability of newspapers and magazines over time. *Newspaper Research Journal*, 1(1), 3–8.

Hooper, T. (2004, November 4). Election with hunter. *Aspen Daily News*. Retrieved July 15, 2006 from www.aspendailynews.com.

Howe, N. & Strauss, W. (2000). *Millennials Rising*. New York: Vintage Books.

Jones, M.L.F. (2007, October) Time's up: Newspapers weigh when to fold or change products. *Presstime*, 16.

Keski-Rahkonen, A., Kaprio, J., Rissanen, A., Virkkunen, M., & Rose, R.J. (2003). Breakfast skipping and health-compromising behaviors in adolescents and adults. *European Journal of Clinical Nutrition*, 57(7), 842–53.

Lancaster, L.C. & Stillmann, D. (2002). *When Generations Collide*. New York: HarperCollins Publishers.

McCarthy, J. (2004, November 3). No-shows among young voters may hurt Kerry. The Associated Press State and Local Wire services.

McLeod, D.M., Kosicki, G.M., & McLeod, J.M. (2002). Resurveying the boundaries of political communication effects. In J. Bryant and D. Zillmann (Eds.) *Media Effects: Advances in theory and research*, pp. 215–67. Mahwah: Lawrence Erlbaum Associates.

McQuail, D. & Windahl, S. (1993). *Communication Models for the Study of Mass Communications* (2nd edition). London: Longman.

Mindich, D.T.Z. (2005) *Tuned Out: Why Americans under 40 don't follow the news*. New York: Oxford University Press.

Moznette, J. & Rarick, G. (1968). Which are more readable? Editorials or news stories? *Journalism Quarterly*, 45(2), 319–21.

National Center for Education Statistics. (2002, April). *Adult Literacy in America*. (NCES Publication No. 1993–275). Retrieved July 2, 2006 from http://nces.ed.gov/pubs93/93275.pdf.

National Center for Education Statistics. (2004). Digest of Education Statistics. (NCES 2006005). *Table 247. Earned degrees conferred by degree-granting institutions, by level of degree and sex of student: Selected years, 1869–70 to 2013–14*. Retrieved July 12, 2006 from http://nces.ed.gov/programs/digest/d04/tables/dt04_247.asp.

National Endowment for the Arts. (2004, June). *Reading at Risk: A survey of literary reading in America*. Retrieved August 22, 2006 from www.nea.gov/pub/ReadingAtRisk.pdf.

News audiences increasingly politicized. (2004, June 8). *The Pew Research Center for the People and the Press*. Retrieved June 30, 2006 from http://people-press.org/reports/pdf/215.pdf.

Newspaper Association of America. (2005). *The Source: Newspapers by the numbers 2005*. Retrieved June 30, 2006 from www.naa.org/thesource/7.asp.

Online papers modestly boost newspaper readership. (2006, July 30). *The Pew Research Center for the People and the Press*. Retrieved August 22, 2006 from http://people-press.org/reports/pdf/282.pdf.

Peiser, W. (2000). Cohort trends in media use in the United States. *Mass Communication & Society*, 3(2&3), 185–205.

Poindexter, P. & Lasorsa, D.L. (1999). Generation X: Is its meaning understood? *Newspaper Research Journal*, 20(4), 28–36.

Public's news habits little changed by September 11. (2002, June 9). *The Pew Research Center for the People and the Press*. Retrieved June 30, 2006 from http://people-press.org/reports/pdf/156.pdf.

Putnam, R.D. (2000). *Bowling Alone: The collapse and revival of American community.* New York: Simon & Schuster.

Raeymaeckers, K. (2002). Research note: young people and patterns of time consumption in relation to print media. *European Journal of Communication,* 17(3), 369–83.

The Readership Institute. (April 2005). *Reinventing the Newspaper for Young Adults.* Retrieved August 22, 2006 from www.readership.org/experience/startrib_overview.pdf.

Rook, D.W. (1985). The ritual dimension of consumer behavior. *Journal of Consumer Research,* 12(3), 251–64.

Scarborough Research. (2003, April 3). 'Integrated newspaper audience' metric gains momentum at country's newspapers. Retrieved August 22, 2006 from www.scarborough.com/press_releases/INA%20FINAL%204.7.06%20CORRECTIONS.pdf.

Schemo, D.J. (2006, March 31). House, on party lines, passes college finance bill. *The New York Times,* p. A16.

The State of the News Media. (2004). Retrieved June 30, 2006 from www.stateofthenewsmedia.org/2004/.

The State of the News Media. (2005). Retrieved June 30, 2006 from www.stateofthenewsmedia.org/2005/.

The State of the News Media. (2006). Retrieved June 30, 2006 from www.stateofthenewsmedia.org/2006/.

Stempel, G.H., III. (1981). Readability of six kinds of content in newspapers. *Newspaper Research Journal,* 3(1), 32–7.

Stone, G.C. & Wetherington R.V., Jr. (1979). Confirming the newspaper reading habit. *Journalism Quarterly,* 56(3), 554–61, 566.

Strauss, W. & Howe, N. (1991). *Generations: The history of America's future 1584 to 2069.* New York: William Morrow and Company.

Twenge, J.M. (2006). *Generation Me: Why today's young Americans are more confident, assertive, entitled—and more miserable than ever before.* New York: Free Press.

Wilkins, K.G. (2000). The role of media in public disengagement from political life. *Journal of Broadcasting & Electronic Media,* 44(4), 569–80.

United Nations (2004). *World Population Prospects: 2004 revision population database.* Retrieved June 20, 2006 from http://esa.un.org/unpp/.

US Census Bureau (2006). Statistical Abstract of the United States. *Table 12. Resident Population Projections by Sex and Age: 2005 to 2050.* Retrieved June 22, 2006 from www.census.gov/compendia/statab/population/pop.pdf.

Young Adult Library Services Association. (2006). *Best Books for Young Adults 2006.* Retrieved June 22, 2006 from www.ala.org/ala/yalsa/booklistsawards/bestbooksya/06bbya.htm.

Zerba, A. (2004, August). Growing up with parents who read and watch the news: What is the effect on college students? Poster session presented at the annual meeting of the Association for Education in Journalism and Mass Communication, Toronto, Canada.

Zerba, A. & Cantrell, T. (2005, August). No laughing matter: Negative attribute agenda setting on late-night television. Poster session presented at the annual meeting of the Association for Education in Journalism and Mass Communication, San Antonio, Texas.

Zerba, A. (2006a, August). Physical news: Why some young adults don't read newspapers. Poster session presented at the meeting of the Association for Education in Journalism and Mass Communication, San Francisco, California.

Zerba, A. (2006b). Newspapers and the routine images young adults attach to them. Unpublished manuscript, University of Texas at Austin.

Chapter 11

Women and the News

Europe, Egypt and the Middle East, and Africa

Jackie Harrison, Karen Sanders, Christiana Holtz-Bacha, Raquel Rodríguez Díaz, Serra Görpe, Salma Ghanem, and Chioma Ugochukwu[1]

The United Kingdom

The United Kingdom (UK) consists of England, Wales, Scotland, and Northern Ireland, and is composed of islands located on the western edge of the main European landmass. It has a population of almost 60 million with a growth rate of 0.4 percent (Office of National Statistics, 2005). According to the 2001 census (Office of National Statistics, 2001), 92 percent of the British population was classified as white while the size of the minority ethnic population was 4.6 million or 8 percent of the total population of the UK. Indians were the largest minority group, followed by Pakistanis, those of mixed ethnic backgrounds, Black Caribbeans, Black Africans, and Bangladeshis. The remaining minority ethnic groups each accounted for less than 0.5 percent but together accounted for a further 1.4 percent of the UK population. The census also found that nearly 72 percent of the population were Christians, almost 3 percent were Muslims, approximately 1 percent were Hindus, while other religions and unspecified religions were 1.6 percent and 23 percent respectively. The United Kingdom of Great Britain and Northern Ireland (to give it its full title) is located in temperate climes and has an area of 244,820 sq. km. The main spoken and written language is English.

The UK is a parliamentary democracy with a constitutional monarchy and there is no codified constitution. In 1952, the 25-year-old daughter of King George VI became Queen Elizabeth II when her father died in his sleep ("BBC on this day" n.d.). More than a quarter century later Margaret Thatcher became Prime Minister, serving an unprecedented three consecutive terms and adding a new chapter to the history of the UK, that is, a woman reigned as monarch and a woman ruled as prime minister at the same time ("Historic Figures," n.d.).

The constitution is found in the assemblage of statute and common law, treaties and conventions, some of which date back to the beginnings of the English State in the tenth century. It is untidy and eminently pragmatic, and most Britons know little about it. The monarchy and parliamentary government in Britain have enjoyed remarkable continuity and stability. Apart from the hiatus of the civil war and the rule of Oliver Cromwell in the seventeenth century, there have been no breaks in the existence of the monarchy since the tenth century. Some form of parliamentary governance has always existed since the thirteenth century. General elections are held no longer than five years apart and the head of government is appointed from the winning political party. Approximately 99 percent of the UK population is literate, and the UK has one of the most developed education systems in the world. Health service is free at the point of delivery.

In economic terms, the UK is the fourth largest economy in the world, with a gross domestic product (GDP) of $2.228 trillion. This GDP figure can be broken down into the following sectors: services (73 percent), industry (26 percent), and agriculture (1 percent). The 2006 GDP growth rate was estimated at between 1.7 percent and 2.5 percent per annum. The UK's dominant export partners are the US (15.3 percent), Germany (10.8 percent), France (9.2 percent), and Ireland (6.8 percent), while its dominant import partners are Germany (13 percent), US (9.3 percent), and France (7.4 percent) (*The CIA World Factbook*, 2006). The UK is a member of the North Atlantic Treaty Organisation (NATO) and the European Union (EU) but is not part of the latter's economic and monetary union.

The 2006 employment rate was 75 percent, with women making up 51 percent of the potential labour force of 30.07 million. Almost 70 percent of women are employed, 65 percent in the private sector and 35 percent in the public sector. There is a large pay gap between women and men, with women earning on average 18 percent less than men. The pay gap has been consistently attributed to the fact that women are clustered in lower grades or lower paid jobs (Kingsmill, 2001).

The UK has one of the largest and most sophisticated media and communications sectors in the world. This infrastructure consists of fibre optic systems, microwave relays, cables, and satellites governed by a regulatory framework agreed by Parliament. Combined, these support 32.943 million main line telephones (2005) and 61.091 million mobile telephones (2004), the renowned public service broadcaster, the BBC, two quasi-public service broadcasters *Channel 4* and *S4C* as well as an independent television sector consisting of the multi-channel operators *ITV, BSkyB, NTL* and *Channel 5* (*The CIA World Factbook*, 2006).

The BBC dominates the public service sector, and there is a vibrant independent sector. Relationships between the two have been marked by tensions regarding the appropriate use of public monies (the publicly paid licence fee funding for the BBC stood at £2.94 billion in 2004), and the market sector dominance of the BBC which, its critics argue, distorts investment, impinges on consumer sovereignty, and frustrates entrepreneurial and research activity in digital technology and services (Media Guardian, 2006). These criticisms are countered by arguments attesting to the BBC's excellence and custodianship of public service values. The 2006 Labour government has temporarily committed to keeping the licence fee, and will review its decision by 2012 when the terrestrial analogue TV signal will be switched off, mandating the entire television sector to move to digital (Harrison, 2006). In 2002, the average weekly viewing per person was 24 hours and 59 minutes (Hargreaves & Thomas, 2002).

The UK's competitive national press is divided into two categories: popular and mid-market newspapers and quality newspapers. The UK has one of the most competitive markets in the world. Alongside the national press is the regional press; however, circulation trends for both press systems show a steady downward movement. Yet, newspaper readership surpasses both the radio and Internet mediums. In 2004, the total weekly national newspaper circulation stood at 86.3 million down from 89.2 million in 2003 (Media Guardian, 2006). In comparison, radio has diffused to 43.9 million people in the UK, while the Internet shows a lower reach at 16 million UK households (ibid.).

UK media are regarded as free and open: the unruly press operates a system of self-regulation and the broadcast media are governed by a statutorily established regulator as well as legislation safeguarding, among other things, impartiality in political news coverage. There are laws in place for the protection of all citizens. For example, laws exist to protect human rights and incitement to hatred. Most global news providers are available for viewing in the UK either through the Internet or multi-channel TV. Equally most newspapers across the world can be bought in the UK. The supply of news outlets across the major media platforms has dramatically increased with the introduction of digital capacity such that several 24-hour news channels have become successfully established as part of the news firmament.

Forty-nine percent of British journalists are women (Journalism Training Forum, 2002). The magazine sector has the greatest proportion of women journalists—55 percent—followed by television with 54 percent, radio 49 percent, and the newspaper sector where 45 percent of journalists are women. Print journalism was once a man's world but the increasing proportion of women entering the journalism industry suggests that this current male domination will wane in the near future (Ball *et al.*, 2006). However, survey studies of British journalism students suggest that women are slightly less inclined to want a national newspaper career (20 percent as against 27 percent of men) and are more attracted to a career in magazines (34 percent as against 23 percent of men) or television (18 percent compared to 13 percent of men) (Ball *et al.*, 2004). Women are also still less well represented in the higher echelons of newspaper management, earning only 83 percent of men's salaries (Delano, 2003). In 2006, there was only one women editor of a daily national newspaper, Rebekah Wade, at the best-selling *Sun*.

Over the last 30 years women have become firmly established in all areas of broadcast journalism even though men "continue to command the senior levels of the news media" (Chambers *et al.*, 2004, p. 97). In 1975, the BBC appointed its first female anchor, Angela Rippon. Female correspondents are also no longer a rarity from the time when one of the BBC's most outstanding foreign correspondents, Katie Adie, first applied for a job at the BBC in 1968 (Sebba, 1994). When she began her career in broadcasting, the crew still thought, "'wimmin' were meant to be fluffy programme secretaries—the nice girls who passed your outrageous Expenses forms" (Adie, 2002, p. 73). News in the regions was a female-free zone, but Adie found those running the BBC's news nerve center in London to be so free of gender politics that it seemed to be a "New Republic of Equality" (ibid., p. 92). However, it was not always so easy out in the field, symbolized by the problem of the absence of toilets for female journalists, which was the "cause of more grief to women journalists than almost any other single item" (ibid., p. 336).

The natural circumstance of women's physical aging seems to be a barrier in the media workplace. According to research results delivered at Women In Journalism's "Use it or Lose it" seminar (Women in Journalism, 2006), 71 percent of women are worried about being forced out of their careers as they reach their 40s and 50s, and the perception among female journalists seems to be that old age begins at 45. In fact 60 percent of women journalists over 45 years admit to experiencing direct age discrimination. There are few older senior role models in their offices, and older men are seen to outnumber older women at every level.

There is little systematic research about the representation of women in the news. However, in its 2002 submission to the government's consultation on draft communication legislation, the Women's National Commission expressed concern about gender stereotyping and the mainstreaming of pornography. It noted that "expert panels are dominated by men" and "sports coverage is overwhelmingly focused on men's activities" (Women's National Commission, 2002). Chambers *et al.* (2004) argued that journalism's increasingly market-driven focus has led to the sexualization of news such that women who appear as subjects and producers of news are primarily assessed by their physical attributes as opposed to their performance. Female newsreaders must not only be competent but also good-looking. Even the liberal *Observer* newspaper head-lined its feature on BBC newsreader, Fiona Bruce, in unmistakably stereotypical terms: "The BBC's highest-paid news journalist is not going to apologise for being ambitious, a feminist . . . and for having great legs" (Cadwalladr, 2006, p. 17). Male TV reporters are not held to the same high aesthetic standards as their female counterparts.

Perhaps more notable is the continued sexualised coverage of women in the press (Wykes & Gunter, 2005). Research carried out in response to the UK government's concern about the representation of women in the media showed a depressing picture. It was already known that mass circulation titles such as the *Sun* and *The News of the World* feature women as half-dressed babes, focusing on appearance rather than on substance. However, in more upscale newspapers, it was found that women are shown as "sexualised, served up as body 'parts' or in relation to men—as part-ners, ex-partners, mothers or victims of sex crime" (M.W., personal communication, August 9, 2006).

Though the large British magazine sector caters more specifically to women audiences, Wykes (M.W., personal communication, August 9, 2006) points out the UK govern-ment's body summit convened in 2000 because of the overwhelming feeling among women that the magazine was creating a more negative atmosphere for women due to its stereotyped portrayal of women. Some newspapers continue to have women's pages such as the *Daily Mail*'s 'Femail' or the *Observer*'s Woman magazine, while others have more general feature-focused coverage with a women's audience in mind. However, there is little in the way of a systematic study on the difference between women and men, girls and boys, and their news consumption patterns.

Three arguments have dominated UK news audience studies. First, given the prolif-eration of news outlets, choices have expanded and audiences are now fragmented. Second, audiences are becoming more discerning because they are now empowered to make their own decisions about news consumption. Third, audiences can now go to alternative places such as blogs and other Internet sources as opposed to conventional news outlets. Research by Hargreaves & Thomas (2002) on gender differences in news audiences found that female audiences for news seem to use the Internet less than men (a ratio of 3:2 in favor of men), prefer TV news earlier in the day, and are less regular in their watching, read magazines as much as men, and prefer verbal communication. Interestingly, interpersonal communication is preferred among women and younger people: 43 percent of 16 to 34 year olds name word-of-mouth communication as a useful source of news. Hargreaves and Thomas (2002) explained this finding by recourse to sociological reasons, suggesting that women have less time to read newspapers or watch television.

It may be the case that women are making some progress in changing patterns of employment, achieving success, and being influential in the world of news. However, this success is not reflected when women journalists self-describe their experiences and relationships, since they themselves are keen to point to the ambiguous findings about women's supposed impact in the newsroom (Ross, 2001). Nevertheless, each of the following examples provides a snapshot of women's success: the young journalist, the award-winning radio reporter, and the powerful TV and charity star. Superficially each writes as if the old stereotypes persist but in fact, to repeat, they all point to an inexorable trend, which is of course underwritten by their success.

Elizabeth Day (2004) described how, in spite of being just less than six feet in height and suffering from hiccups, she got her first job. She was appointed as a diary writer, writing about day-to-day localized events with an insider's knowledge of politics and society. The theme of her height persists throughout her personal account of "a new breed of female diary journalist." The irony of being a phenomenon escaped her description of success and she is not sure if her height or her gender "swung it" for her, or whether women's "heightened sensitivity" and "empathetic qualities" explained their success in interviewing or color writing. She was Young Journalist of the Year at the British Press Awards in 2004. She is now a news reporter on the quality newspaper, the *Daily Telegraph*.

Esther Rantzen (2006), writing about her work in the media, asked: "Why are women such bullies?" Her description of success is framed by her personal account of her own achievements as a television host, opinion former, and charity worker. She noted that she was fortunate to have marvelous bosses—all men. A powerful sense of self-justification pervades Rantzen's account, critiquing the negative and bullying attitude that successful professional women seemingly show to both younger people and men when they have climbed the corporate ladder of success.

Sue MacGregor (2002), doyen of the premier political radio show in Britain, observed how the alpha-male style of political journalism worked against women. She noted that women are often tagged as shrill harpies or worse when they use the familiar style of confrontation in an interview. MacGregor is proud of her achievement in cracking the glass ceiling, but reticent in criticizing a world in which she was paid less than her fellow male presenters and given far fewer opportunities to conduct the big interviews.

These three stories leave an array of unanswered questions, which must, for the time being, remain so due to insufficient academic research in the UK. Little exists on what news stories capture women's attention, how women are presented in news reports, and how the different generations of females respond to news in diverse formats and media. This dearth of research may be due to the relatively recent introduction of journalism studies into the academy. Alternative media—Internet newsgroups, blogs, and feminist news networks—have the potential to provide a vehicle for the de-commodification of women's relationship to news, but they continue to be marginal to women's central engagement with mainstream news media. Resources, habits and routines, and ease of access ensure that mainstream media, particularly television, continue to be the principal source of news for most people in Britain. The rapidly changing ecology of news—declining newspaper sales, increasing Internet adoption, and a digital multi-channel environment—may radically transform that picture in the not too distant future.

Germany

Situated in the middle of Western Europe, Germany stretches from the North Sea and the Baltic Sea in the North to the Alps in the South. With more than 82.5 million inhabitants but covering only about 357 sq. km, it is a densely populated country. The share of foreigners living in Germany is around 9 percent: 2 million Turks represent the largest group of foreigners followed by immigrants from the former Yugoslavia, who total approximately 660,000. While most Germans belong to Christian religions (there is an almost equal number of Catholics and Protestants in the country), the Turkish and some of the Yugoslavian immigrants have brought Islam into the country. Like some of its neighbouring countries, Germany has a low birth rate (1.4), which is no longer compensated by in-coming immigrants, thus leading to a decreasing and at the same time aging population.

The history of Germany is very much shaped by the experiences of the Nazi regime (1933–45), the Second World War, and the following 40-year-long division of the country. After the war, the Federal Republic of Germany (West Germany) was integrated into the West European and Transatlantic organizations (EC, NATO) while the German Democratic Republic (GDR) became part of the East European alliance under Soviet influence. The different political and economic developments of the two Germanys, accompanied by different socialization experiences, accounted for the difficulties of the integration process after the country became re-united in 1990.

Culture and politics of the country are influenced by the fact that Germany is a federal republic of 16 states ("Länder"). German is the language spoken everywhere, although there are several regional dialects. Legislative competence is divided between the national parliament (Bundestag) in Berlin and the 16 state parliaments. The states are also represented in the Federal Council (Bundesrat), which takes part in the national legislative process. Some political fields lie in the exclusive competence of the states, with police, education (schools and universities), and culture (including broadcasting and the printed press) being the most important. However, over the years, more and more legislative competence has been passed to the supranational level of the European Union (EU), of which Germany has been a founding member. Therefore, much of Germany's legislation is initiated and influenced by the EU. This fact is also true of the broadcasting sector.

Germany is a parliamentary democracy with the parliament being the only body at the national level that is directly elected by the people. The head of state is the president but s/he has a more representational function. The most important political figure is the chancellor who is the head of the government charged with picking the government's ministers. The chancellor is elected by the parliament. Since parties dominate political life in Germany and the electoral system also gives parties a decisive role, the strongest party is usually able to put its candidate through as chancellor.

Generally, individual parties do not reach absolute majorities in elections and individual parties cannot form a government by themselves but must look for a partner. Therefore, Germany has always had coalition governments. Usually, the strongest party coming out of elections, which is always one of two major parties (Christian Democrats or Social Democrats), goes into a coalition with one of the smaller parties. Grand coalitions, meaning a coalition of the two big parties, have been a rare exception. Since the last parliamentary election that was held in September 2005, Germany has been governed by a grand coalition of the Christian Democrats (CDU/CSU) and the Social Democrats (SPD). For this election, it was the first time in Germany's history that a woman, Angela Merkel, ran as chancellor candidate. Her party, the Christian Democrats, reached the majority and formed a grand coalition with the SPD and thus Merkel got elected as chancellor.

Media in Germany.   The German media system underwent a major change in the mid-1980s when commercial broadcasting (television and radio) was introduced. Since then, Germany features a so-called dual broadcasting system with traditional public broadcasting and commercial broadcasting. Today, the average household has several dozens of TV channels available. Altogether, the public service TV channels have an average market share of almost 44 percent, while the commercial challengers claim the remainder of the market share (Kommission zur Ermittlung der Konzentration im Medienbereich, 2006). Competition has led to an overall commercialization of broadcasting which has also affected the public service offerings.

Newspapers have a daily circulation of about 21.66 million (313 copies per 1,000 inhabitants; Bundesverband Deutscher Zeitungsverleger, 2006a, b). Regional and local papers that reach almost two-thirds of the newspaper readership characterize the newspaper market. A handful of national quality newspapers, as well as the newsmagazine *Der Spiegel* and the weekly newspaper *Die Zeit*, all aim at the politically interested and better educated public, acting as political opinion leaders. The tabloid *Bild-Zeitung* is a daily newspaper with a circulation of 3.8 million—the highest of any daily newspaper—and this tabloid plays a major role as an agenda setter for public opinion.

The Constitution guarantees freedom of the press as an individual and an institutional right, the latter obliging the state to safeguard the best possible conditions that allow the media to fulfill their function in and for the society. According to the typology put forward by Hallin and Mancini (2004), Germany belongs to the group of North European countries that are influenced by the Democratic Corporatist Model. In those countries, the media are not completely left to the market forces. They are assigned a public task, and the state—although restricted by law—intervenes to secure the conditions necessary to enable the media to fulfill their essential function in a democratic society.

Women in Germany.   The employment rate of women in Germany is 59 percent, and more than half of employed women are working in the services sector (e.g., education, health, public administration; Federal Statistical Office, 2006). The financial situation of women is much different from men. There are still differences in the wages even where equal work is done and, although women are gainfully employed, they continue to rely on additional sources of livelihood (like support from relatives) when compared to men (14.5 percent; Federal Statistical Office, 2006, p. 48).

For the last parliamentary election (2005), overall voter turnout was almost 78 percent. Both women and men had a participation rate of almost 80 percent (Federal Statistical Office, 2006, p. 74); however, only approximately 32 percent of the MPs were women (Schorn & Schwartzenberg, 2005, p. 1162). This 32 percent figure also hides major differences among the five parties that are represented in the national parliament. The leftist parties feature a higher share of women than the conservative parties. The share of female ministers in the present government under Angela Merkel is 36 percent, shy of an all-time high of 46 percent women under the previous Social Democratic Chancellor Gerhard Schroeder's government.

Journalism in Germany.   According to the most recent analysis of news in different media outlets (Hesse & Röser, 2006, pp. 14–15), women comprise 22 percent of all news media workers, with 22 percent in TV news and newspapers, and 23 percent in radio news. Although these figures are still low, they signify a considerable improvement for women when compared to their representation of 15 percent in 1995 and 12 percent in 2000. Most of the actors in the news are politicians. Female politicians only account for about 20 percent of the actors in newspaper dailies, radio, and TV.

Just as in other Western countries, the portrayal of women in politics has been lamented in Germany. Angela Merkel, now German chancellor, is a living example of how female politicians were mistreated in the media. When Merkel was minister in an earlier government and made a career in her party, her hair and her dress style were a major—and negative—focus of the media's reporting. Thus, when Merkel became chancellor candidate and her party received the majority of votes, it was said that she got elected not "because" but "although" she is a woman. Merkel had to fight against the "old boys network" in her own party as well as the reservations of their conservative clientele. Her campaign tried to avoid any references to gender issues but the media brought gender to the public fore, pointing out that Merkel was Germany's first female chancellor candidate. Although Merkel was not the first woman to climb to a top position in German politics, no woman before Merkel had made it as high as chancellor.

Now that a woman is at the top of the national government, the portrayal of female politicians should change—quantitatively and qualitatively. However, the media must learn how to deal with this new situation of female empowerment. The uneasiness that spread in German public debate was evident in the fall of 2005 when Merkel was elected. The German language did not use the word for the female form of chancellor prior to Merkel's appointment. However, this word was declared "word of the year" in 2005 because it seemed to forebode a new role for women in German society ("Bundeskanzlerin" macht das Rennen, 2005).

During her initial run for chancellorship, the media focused much attention on the fact that she was the "first woman." They also dedicated coverage to her lack of experience. However, the novelty of her gender has seemingly worn off after her first term, and now, she receives the same type of coverage as every chancellor received before her. However, during the 2006 World Cup Football Championship in Germany the media reverted to its gender bias and Merkel's knowledge of soccer and her behavior toward the Championship were closely scrutinized, reviving old stereotypes about women's disinterest in or lack of knowledge of soccer.

The news of the major TV stations (public service and commercial) is read either by one presenter (with a woman and a man alternating primarily on a weekly basis), or a mixed team of a man and a woman. Women also host some of the most popular TV talk shows, which give the impression that women are well represented in the mass media. However, the findings on women in journalism show that women's appearance as talk show hosts is more a case of window dressing. According to a study conducted in 2005, 37 percent of German journalists are women (Weischenberg, 2005, p. 54). Compared to the early 1990s, this figure represents an increase of only about 4 percent to 5 percent. Considering the fact that over the past 15 years, more women have gained journalism education through university, journalism school, or training-on-the-job, it remains an open question why they have not succeeded in being better represented in the profession. Within journalism, women are often disadvantaged due to vertical and horizontal segmentation: for example, compared to their male colleagues, fewer women reach higher levels of the hierarchy and some sections of the media remain heavily dominated by men, such as in the areas of politics, economics, and sports. The effectiveness of equal opportunity provisions, which have been adopted by the public broadcasting stations, is disputed.

Comparing women and men news consumers.   General media usage differs between the genders. While there are only minor differences in the daily usage of radio and television, there are wider gaps in the use of newspapers and the Internet. Only 60 percent of the women, compared to 67 percent of the men, read a newspaper daily or even several times a day, and 19 percent of the women turn to the Internet every day compared to 36 percent of the men. Women are more avid book readers: 45 percent of women read a book several times a week in comparison to only 34 percent of men (Reitze & Ridder, in press).[2]

From its beginnings, Internet usage in Germany has shown a gender gap that has failed to close. In 1997, slightly more than 3 percent of women 14 years and older went online at least "sometimes" compared to 10 percent of the men. In 2005, the share of women has increased to 49 percent whereas 68 percent of the men now use the Internet sometimes or more often. If women use the Internet, they are prone to stay for shorter periods of time online when compared to male users. On average, women spend 108 minutes per day compared to men who spend 134 minutes (all data taken from Eimeren & Frees, 2005, pp. 364, 376). The overall low Internet usage among women is usually regarded as a generational phenomenon. Older women, many of whom lack a professional career, are more reluctant to use the Internet when compared to their male counterparts. In sharp contrast, younger women use the Internet to a similar extent as younger men. Therefore, with more women being part of the workforce, it is expected that women will eventually catch up to men with respect to Internet usage.

In terms of current affairs interests, women seemingly display a more reserved attitude than men (Reitze & Ridder, in press). Asked to what extent they are interested in politics, 50 percent of the female respondents said they are "very interested" compared to 61 percent of the men. These results, however, remain open to interpretation. It is unclear whether men are indeed more interested or just pretend to be because they think political interest is a masculine trait. It is possible that women are more honest in answering this question. Regardless of the social desirability of answering in the affirmative to political interest, 36 percent of the women surveyed regarded politics as "complicated," whereas only 28 percent of the men said the same. Men also felt better informed about politics: 58 percent of the men say they usually know what is going on in politics but only 46 percent of the women say they are well informed about political events (Reitze & Ridder, in press).

The distance that many women display toward political issues could be explained by a different notion of what constitutes "the political" and what is important in politics (Holtz-Bacha, 1995). When asked whether they are interested in politics, women may make mental associations between formal politics and governmental bodies, which may seem too remote and abstract to their daily lives. Women are more interested in politics that has personal interest: almost 50 percent of women said they were interested in political matters when issues concerned them personally as opposed to less than 40 percent of men. This sentiment is also expressed in the fact that women prefer local and regional newspapers while more men than women read the national quality papers.

It is generally in the local sections, including any kind of services, tips, and local advertising, that readers mention as what attracts and binds them to the regional papers. Although the regional press also covers foreign and national politics, many of their issues and perspectives on issues are "closer to home" and this may be what appeals to female readers in particular. Women's pages (as most programs for women on radio) have disappeared from the scene. If newspapers do include lifestyle sections, they do not specifically address the female readership. Specific media offerings for women as they previously existed in newspapers, on radio and television, have long been controversial: one argument was that women's interests were neglected in the media so they had to be served in special sections or programs. Others argued that, instead of banishing women's interests to niches, the media in general had to consider female topics and perspectives and become more attractive to the female audience.

It is questionable whether the female audience could be better attracted to current affairs information if the number of women working in the media increased. Such an expectation is based on the assumption that women would bring other topics and other perspectives into journalism that better address the interests of their female audience. Although women working in journalism are convinced that they approach their topics differently, there are no empirical findings that support the hypothesis that greater women in media will result in greater media attention to women's issues. As long as education in journalism is still mostly in the hands of men who also dominate the superior levels of the hierarchy in the newsroom, women will learn to use the same selection and production criteria as their male colleagues. Thus, whether a higher share of women in journalism will serve to attract more women to the political media remains an open question.

Spain

Spain, a member of the European Union (EU), has a population of 44 million, of which 50.6 percent are women. Similar to other European countries, Spain is growing older as birth rates fall and people live longer. The average lifespan of a Spaniard is one of the highest in Europe. On average, women live to be 83 years of age, 8 years longer than men. On the other hand, Spanish women have one of the lowest birth rates in the world at 1.3 children per woman according to Eurostat (INE, 2006a).

Like the cultures of other Mediterranean countries, Christianity, Islam, and Judaism have influenced Spanish culture in the realms of architecture, language, and food. Although they may not actively practice the religion, the majority of Spaniards today identify themselves as Roman Catholics.

During the past century, Spaniards have witnessed a republic, a civil war, a long dictatorship, and a restored democracy incorporated within a parliamentary monarchy system. This monarchy has developed into a democracy of autonomous communities with King Juan Carlos I as the head of state and a president who is elected every four years. In the 2004 elections, José Luis Rodríguez Zapatero led the Spanish Socialist Worker's Party (PSOE) to victory, becoming the president of Spain after defeating José María Aznar's administration under the Popular Party (PP).

According to a February 2006 public opinion poll conducted by the Center of Sociological Investigations (CIS), the most important problems facing Spain were unemployment (49 percent), terrorism, ETA (35 percent), immigration (28 percent), crime (19 percent), housing (18 percent), economic problems (15 percent), political classes (10 percent), job instability (7 percent), drugs (7 percent), and education (4 percent).

Spain's greatest economic power resides in its service sector, followed by the tourism sector, the industrial sector, the energy sector, and the construction sector. According to the National Institute of Statistics in 2005, the service sector of the economy represented 60 percent of the Gross National Product, in comparison to 16 percent for the industrial and energy sectors, and 10 percent for the construction sector (INE, 2006b). Even though the Spanish unemployment rate of 9 percent is one of the highest in Europe, the Spanish economy is functioning at almost full capacity.

In 2006, the unemployment index (EPA, 2006) showed that more women (12 percent) than men (7 percent) were unemployed in Spain. Women occupied almost 80 percent of temporary jobs, and only 35 percent of women worked full-time ("Women and men in Spain," 2006). Women were more likely than men to head low-income households. For lower income households, which earned an income of up to 397 euros a month, 8 percent of women were head of the household as opposed to 2 percent of men. For households in the higher income scale, which earned more than 2,380 euros a month, women comprised slightly over 10 percent of heads of the household in comparison to over 25 percent of men. In modern-day Spain, women are getting married later, wedding at an average of 29 years and delaying having children until age 30. Men marry around 31 years of age.

Women represent more than half of the working population in some professions, but they are under-represented in relation to their demographics (INE, 2006c). As of 2006,

29 percent of Spanish women were business entrepreneurs, 36 percent were delegates in the Congress, and 35 percent were university professors. However, although men outnumber women in the professional world, the majority of those enrolled in the university are women. Women attained 55 percent of the degrees earned at the undergraduate level, 54 percent of teaching degrees or masters (54 percent), and over 50 percent of doctoral degrees. There are also strong signs of gender equity in the government. Under the Zapatero administration, the number of male ministers compared to female ministers is balanced equally at eight to eight. Interestingly, the total number of children born to male ministers in the Socialist Party's first cabinet equaled 22 while for women it was five, suggesting that women are more likely to be the single and/or divorced ministers.

As a democratic country, and in contrast with the none-too-distant Franco dictatorship which lasted 40 years, the right to freedom of expression and information is one of the the fundamental rights established in the Spanish Constitution of 1978 which prohibits all previous forms of censorship. The world of media communications has since grown with the development of big media groups such as Grupo Prisa, Vocento, Recoletos Grupo de Comunicación, and RTVE. These media groups control the radio, television, print, and magazine industry.

Women have different media preferences.   An analysis of audience ratings collected by the General Study of Media (EGM, 2005) showed that television (89 percent) and radio (56 percent) are the most consumed media, followed by magazines (54 percent), newspapers (41 percent), and movies (7 percent). At 20 percent, the Internet has one of the lowest consumption rates in Europe.

Television is the most consumed daily medium in the household, watched for a total of 222 minutes. Women account for over half (51 percent) of television viewers and 55 percent of magazine readers. The general television networks *Tele5*, *Antena3*, and *TVE1* account for 60 percent of the audience share with the rest represented by other channels such as *Cuatro*, *La2*, *Digital+*, and local networks.

Television is watched primarily by the 14- to 19-year-old demographic (90 percent), followed by viewers in the 25- and 34-years-old age group (85 percent). There are few differences between the social classes; television viewing is popular with the upper class (85 percent) and the lower class (90 percent). However, there are gender differences in television viewing (CIS, 2003). Women prefer series, shows, musicals, daytime gossip shows, and quiz shows; men prefer sports and soccer programs. Both sexes watch information programs, cultural programs, films, debates, and interviews. According to differences elaborated upon by scholars of audience studies (Sofres, 2006), women were major television viewers during the morning hours (9 a.m. to 1 p.m.)—a time slot, which is typically filled with news and magazine programs. Women were also the major viewers of afternoon television (4 p.m. to 8 p.m.), during which time the broadcast air waves are filled with series and magazine-based programs dedicated to women.

The most popular programs among women audiences have a varied content that includes mostly health, cooking, and news and fashion shows, with the majority presented by women journalists. Some examples of shows in the morning are "Cada día" and "El programa de Ana Rosa." In the evening, "El diario de Patricia" and "España Directo" are both popular among women viewers. Ana Rosa Quintana, who presents one of the most popular shows among women audiences, noted that women presenters are popular in the morning programs because women are the larger audience for this time slot when compared to men. In her opinion, "In general, there are more women making programmes which are on at *all* times of the day. I don't know if it's a coincidence or if women presenters generate a better rapport with the audience" (Rodríguez, 2005).

Unlike women, men prefer to watch sporting events such as soccer, motor racing, and tennis. In some cases, audience ratings for these events are as high as 40 percent of the total audience share. In terms of evening programming, women also outnumber men, and this strong female interest is reflected in the prevalence of Spanish-produced comedies and drama series, including *Aquí no hay quien viva*, *Los Serrano*, *Hospital Central*, and *Mira quién baila*.

Radio is indispensable in Spain. The general radio audience includes 11 million listeners and the music radio audience has more than 10 million listeners (EGM, 2005). Of this audience, music radio is most popular among the younger demographic. The main radio channels include *SER*, *COPE*, *Onda Cero*, and *RNE1*, and altogether, these four stations account for 90 percent of market share. *SER* is the audience leader at 38 percent, followed by *COPE* (18 percent). The most popular programs are four- to six-hour morning magazines, which are filled with news, debates, interviews, and local information. Popular daily programs include *Hoy por hoy* (*SER*) and *La mañana* (*COPE*).

Men comprise the dominant radio listening population (54 percent); however, the demographic profiles of listeners vary by program type. The 25- to 34-year demographic listens to the most radio, while listening to the radio is less likely for men over 65 years of age. When assessing social class, 68 percent of the upper class listens to radio while only 35 percent of the lower class does the same.

Although men (60 percent) are more likely to be newspaper readers and users of the Internet (60 percent), it can be said that Spanish citizens are not big readers and very few could be classified as news enthusiasts or monitors. According to the audience index, those between 45 and 55 years of age read the most (48 percent), and those that read the least are 19 years old or younger (32 percent) or over 65 (27 percent). The most frequent readers are upper class (64 percent) as opposed to lower class (15 percent). Furthermore, sports papers such as *Marca* (more than 2.5 million readers daily) or *As* (more than 1 million readers) are more popular than general newspapers such as *El País* (more than 2 million readers), *El Mundo* (more than 1.3 million readers), *El Periódico* (850,000 readers), *ABC* (840,000 readers), or *La Vanguardia* (650,000 readers).

In general, daily newspapers do not dedicate special sections to women's issues; however, Sunday supplements are becoming more and more common. These supplements generally have women's sections, including such women's magazines as *Mujer de Hoy* and *Yo Dona*. The contents of these magazines and supplements include stories on shows, cinema, general leisure time, home decorating, and beauty and fashion. Most of this content is focused on new social trends and consumer products as opposed to current affairs such as politics or economics. By contrast, the most read weekly magazines are for women and tend to center on gossip about the rich and famous. Examples include: *Pronto*, *Hola*, *Diez Minutos*, *Lecturas*, and *Semana*. As far as monthly magazines are concerned, the most popular ones contain content on home decorating, fashion, and lifestyle tips. These monthly magazines include *El Mueble*, *Cosmopolitan*, and *Cosas de Casa*. It is possible that these topics are more appealing to women, which can explain why women are not attracted to reading newspapers. In contrast to the coverage of women's interests, men's interests in sports are well covered in newspapers. Sports websites are also popular. In fact the website produced by the sports newspaper *Marca* is one of the four most popular websites in Spain (EGM, 2006).

Internet use in Spain is one of the lowest in Europe: only four out of ten Spanish residents use it. According to sociologists (Bouza, 2003), there exists inequality with Internet usage, and data from the EGM in 2005 showed that general consumption of the Internet is low in Spain.

There appears to be a divide between women and men in usage of the Internet. Data from EGM (2005) showed that less than 20 percent of Spaniards use the Internet, with no more than 40 percent of this group being women. These consumption differences are surprising when one compares the economic development of Spain to other EU countries. Scholars state that this gap is not linked to societal development, but is instead linked to the limited efforts of public administration (Alaminos, 2003).

More than half of Spaniards have a computer, 63 percent have a DVD, and 81 percent have a mobile phone (INE, 2006d). In terms of Internet access, 34 percent of households can connect to the Internet from the home—a figure lower than the EU average of 48 percent. The communities with the highest Internet use include Madrid, Cataluña, País Vasco, Baleares, and Navarra.

Women in journalism.   Although there has been an increase in universities offering media studies degrees since the 1990s—a time when most of the newly enrolled students were women and when most lecturers were female—there has been little increase in the number of women entering the field of journalism. Different studies carried out in the 1990s showed that the proportion of female members of staff in press offices was no higher than 25 percent (APM, 1990; Rodríguez, 2003). A 2005 report showed that the proportion of female members of staff in press offices had increased, but the figure still remains at less than 50 percent (López, 2005).

A later study gave a more in-depth and detailed account of the journalism profession, revealing that the percentage of women journalists working in the field only increased to 20 percent (García de Cortazar & García de León, 2000). This figure, derived from a wide-ranging questionnaire, highlighted the differences of opinion between women and men working in the journalism sector. Results showed that 80 percent of men felt that fewer women occupied positions of responsibility whereas 87 percent of women held a similar opinion.

Women and men differ in their explanations for why women occupy lower levels of responsibilities in the newsroom. Though 37 percent of women and men say that women's lower status is due to a lack of equal opportunities, 20 percent of men noted that women in the profession are a recent phenomenon while only 11 percent of women agreed with this latter interpretation. Fourteen percent of men think that top-level managers and directors doubt women's aptitude while 30 percent of women are of this opinion. Domestic responsibilities are put forward as another possible cause, and this reason is advanced by 8 percent of men and 13 percent of women (García de Cortazar & García de León, 2000, pp. 35–6).

The 2000 study also highlighted that the most valued areas of the profession (in order of importance) were politics, editorials, opinion, and economics. In a gender breakdown by genre, women journalists outnumbered men in the home affairs edition, society, and press office (gabinetes de comunicación), while sports and opinion sections had more men than women journalists.

This situation reflects a masculine bias toward men as the newsroom gatekeepers. It would appear that men make the decisions, which are reflected in news stories that are geared to a male-dominated audience. As agenda setting theory notes, the salience of issues in the media's agenda is transferred to the salience of issues on the public's agenda

(McCombs, 2005); hence, if media presented greater topics of interest to women, or had more women in positions of influence within the newsroom, it is possible that this move would signal to society that news and information on women's topics are important.

The main news topics that seem related to women's interests include news reports on domestic violence or abuse of women, legislation to help women in the field of employment, and political developments which facilitate a combination of work/life balance (Sánchez Aranda *et al.*, 2003; López, 2005).

An in-depth study of news stories broadcast on Spanish TV in the 1990s (Gonzalez & Nuñez, 2000, p. 87) showed that women's news was more associated with labor issues or employment, health and medical breakthroughs, domestic and home-based issues, social personalities and murders. As has been pointed out in recent studies of women in the news (Len-Rios *et al.*, 2005), it is evident that the news only highlights one part of social reality—a reality that is mainly produced by men. It would appear that women have very little say when it comes to the production of news stories.

Putting forward solutions.   One possible solution, put forward by the current socialist government, is the Law of Parity—a scenario where the same number of men as women are in work posts and positions of responsibility—or the application of so-called positive discrimination. This latter law has been controversial as certain sectors feel that a woman should be assessed in terms of her professional work as opposed to being hired to fill a quota.

It is true that the incorporation of women into work posts and positions of responsibility is a reality and, as some maintain, it is only a matter of time before there is gender equality in employment. But many Spaniards wonder why the time delay is so great. To quote some female journalism students, who participated in a discussion group on the role of women in positions of responsibility:

> There are as many qualified women as men but we are discriminated against. There should be a law to end such discrimination, because it's all very well in education and influencing the way society thinks but it's going to take years to change things and we women are not prepared to wait that long. I want there to be a law.
> (Rodríguez & García, 2006)

One other measure that would encourage women to watch more news and entertainment programs would be to tailor media content to satisfy the needs and realities of women. Finally, I would propose a measure that would encourage media to conduct more research on gender inequalities in Spanish society. Through such a research goal, more public awareness of the problem would enable us all to embrace solutions that can counteract the negative consequences of gender inequality.

Turkey

With a surface area of 814,578 square kilometers and a population of 67,844,000 million residents (Almanac, 2005a), Turkey lies on two continents, Asia and Europe. Turkey is surrounded by the Black, Aegean, and Mediterranean Seas, as well as the Balkans and the Middle East (Turkish General Staff, n.d.). It shares borders with Georgia, Armenia, Nakhichevan and Iran on the east, Bulgaria and Greece on the west, and Iraq and Syria on the south. Turkey has 81 provinces of which Ankara is its capital, but Istanbul is the city with the largest population.

With 34.2 million males and 33.6 million females, males outnumber females in the Turkish population (Almanac, 2005d). Unlike many other Western nations, Turkey has a young population; adolescents make up approximately 20 percent of the Turkish population ("Say Yes," n.d.). The official language is Turkish, though it is estimated that 15 percent of the Turkish population knows English and 5 percent of the population speak Kurdish (Turkcell, 2005).

Women's rights date back to the establishment of the Turkish Republic. The first President of Turkey, Ataturk expanded women's rights when he introduced a broad range of reforms in the political, social, judicial, educational, cultural, and economic arenas. Since 1924, Turkish women have had the lawful right to receive an education; they gained the right to vote in the 1930s, and Turkey is the only Muslim country in which women have equal rights of inheritance and divorce. Even with these rights, women still face gender inequalities in property ownership, literacy, labor force participation, and political representation.

Plus, women in Turkey are victimized by honor killings/suicides. Honor killings refer to the murder of a woman by her husband, father, brother, or a close relative because of the woman's disobedience to Turkey's social sexual norms (KSSGM, 2006). Running away with a man without the approval of the family or getting pregnant without being married are some of the reasons that women and adolescent girls become the victims of honor killings. A recent report prepared by The Turkish National Department of Police Order on incidents that happened in the name of moral traditions showed that between the years 2000–5, there had been 1,091 murders ("Tore cinayetlerinin kurbanlari," 2006).

Turkey is the only Islamic country that both includes laicism in its Constitution and puts laicism into practice. Laicism holds that the basic social, economic, political, and legal order of the State should not rely on religious rules (Almanac, 2005b). With the foundation of the Republic in 1923, religion and state affairs were separated and laws became formulated according to secular principles.

During the Ottoman Empire (1299–1923), Islamic rules governed the Muslim population and until as late as 1882, Ottoman women were excluded from formal population statistics (Inceoglu & Korkmaz, 2002). The Ottoman Empire had been powerful for many centuries, and had succeeded in spreading to three continents; however, from the sixteenth century onward, it suffered both military and economic losses. In the nineteenth century, nationalist movements began fermenting in Ottoman territories. Although there had been reforms, they did not save the Ottoman Empire. After the National War of Independence (1919–23) was won, it was the aim of Ataturk, Turkey's first president, to modernize the country (Almanac, 2005c).

Women's participation in the workforce is primarily in the agricultural sector, followed by the service sector and the industrial sector (Almanac, 2005e). The intense migration from rural to urban areas in Turkey exacerbates the situation for women who are unable to find work in the city due to their lack of professional skills. This dilemma leads many of these women to become housewives (KSSGM, 2006). The unemployment rate for young women who are high school graduates and residents in the city is approximately 19 percent in comparison to approximately 10 percent for men (Almanac, 2005e). Women's adult literacy is also lower than men: as of 2004, over 95 percent of men were literate in comparison to less than 80 percent of women (TURKTSAT, 2006).

Turkey has hopes of raising the rate of school attendance for boys and girls to 100 percent by 2010 (Almanac, 2005e). Roughly 1 million girls of primary school age are not going to school in Turkey. More than 50 percent of girls between 6 and 14 are out-of-school in some areas.

When a study conducted by the World Economic Forum compared 58 countries including the Organisation for Economic Cooperation and Development (OECD) countries and emerging market countries on gender inequalities in five different areas, economic participation, economic opportunity, political empowerment, educational attainment, and health, Turkey ranked second to last (KAGIDER, 2006). Recognition of women's marginalization from politics led to the Turkish Government's Millennium Development Goal Report 2005 (MDG), which set the goal to increase the proportion of seats held by women in national parliament to 94 (17 percent) by 2015 (UNDP, 2006). In 2006, women occupied only 4.4 percent of parliamentary seats (KAGIDER, 2006).

Unlike other countries in Europe that began an institutionalization process of gender equality in the 1970s, Turkey began addressing gender inequality in 1987 with the establishment of Consultative Committee on Policies Aimed at Women within State Planning. Turkey is one of many other countries that signed the Beijing Declaration in China in 1995 and the National Action Plan. The National Action Plan, prepared in 1996 and presented to the United Nations included eight areas of priority for Turkey: women's education and training, women and health, violence against women, women and economy, women in power and decision making, institutional mechanisms for the advancement of women, and women and media (KSSGM, 2006). In 1985, Turkey signed the UN Convention for the Elimination of All Discrimination against Women (CEDAW), which is the only legally binding international document on gender equality (Almanac, 2005f). In 1990, a Directorate Central for the Status and Problems of Women was set up. Later, this organization became affiliated with the Prime Ministry to conduct studies in an effort to protect and develop women's rights, strengthen their position in social, economic, cultural and political life and provide them with equal opportunities (Almanac, 2005g).

The Turkish media landscape. Publishing businesses during the Republic period were run by family-owned companies. Media continued to develop after World War II as a result of the improving economy and the importing of new technologies into Turkey (Tokgoz, 2000). Political changes in Turkey have been generally reflected in the media systems. For example, the 1980s were characterized by manifold changes in the Turkish society. The military takeover resulted in media reporting topics other than politics. The 1980s also witnessed the entrance of huge sums of capital into the media industry (Ozgen, 2000).

It was in the 1990s that the holding companies became active in media (Mediascape, n.d.). By 2006, four groups controlled 80 percent of the Turkish media; today, only one of these four groups, Dogan, still exists (Carat, n.d.).

Some journalists still believe that self-censorship persists in spite of the fact that censorship in the media has been officially over since 1908 (Saglam, 2006). Turkey holds the record for the highest number of journalists imprisoned in the 1990s: according to Reporters Sans Frontiere (RSF), in 1995, Turkey imprisoned 108 media professionals. As of 2006, the climate has improved for journalists. On October 3, 2005, Turkey was officially recognized as a candidate for European Union and the Turkish constitution has been rewritten such that new laws have been put in practice (Maireder, 2006).

The first Turkish newspaper is the official *Takvim-i Vekayi*, which was first published on November 11, 1831 (Topuz, 2003). Radio broadcasting began on a regular basis in 1927 and the first experimental television broadcasts began in 1952. The Turkish Radio and Television Corporation (TRT) was established on May 1, 1964 and television broadcasting started in 1968 (Almanac, 2005h). The Anatolia News Agency (AA) was established on April, 6 1920, upon the initiative of Mustafa Kemal. It is Ankara-based and AA has a news network in Turkey as well as in other important places of the world (Almanac, 2005i). At present there are around 3,450 periodicals, including newspapers and magazines, which are published in Turkey. The average daily circulation of local papers varies between 400 and 50,000 (Maireder, 2006). As of 2006, there were 32 national and more than 5,000 local and regional newspapers (Carat, n.d.). Most of Turkish traditional media also have a website presence, indicating that Turkish media are open to the usage of new communication technologies (Tokgoz, 2000).

According to data obtained from Carat (n.d.), 42 percent of the Turkish population aged 15 and over are irregular readers, 34 percent of the population are classified as "non readers," while only 24 percent of the population are "regular" readers. These regular readers read a newspaper six to seven times a week. In terms of gender, 33 percent of the newspaper readers are women and 67 percent are men. With higher education and socio economic status, the readership of newspapers increases.

Turkish magazines have a history of over 110 years. The first Turkish magazine *Vakayı-i Tıbbiye*, was published between 1849–51 (Topuz, 2003). Interestingly, the number of magazines on niche content has been increasing in Turkey. In 1990, there were approximately 20 newsmagazines. By 2004, the number of newsmagazines had increased to 247, and newsmagazines that are generally published weekly or monthly have a circulation rate of approximately 2.3 million copies (Maireder, 2006). Though readership numbers for newsmagazines remains very low, approximately 47 percent of magazine readers are women, while approximately 53 percent of the newsmagazine audience are males (Carat, n.d.).

Turkey has a very long tradition of public broadcasting. The monopoly of the TRT was broken after 1990 by private radio and television channels, which began broadcasting before the legal framework was prepared (RTUK portal, 2006). In 1990, there had been four television channels (government-owned), but as of 2006, there were 16 national, 15 regional, 229 local, one cable network (53 channels), and one digital platform (Carat, n.d.). In 2004, TRT also started programming using minority languages (RTUK portal, 2006). Like television, radio has enjoyed similar growth as a media industry. Though there were only four radio stations in 1990, there are 30 national, 108 regional, and 1,062 local radio stations as of 2006 (Carat, n.d.). The average radio listening time is three hours a day, and recent studies show that 73 percent of the population, mostly between the ages of 15 to 24, listen to the radio on a daily basis (Turkey, 2006).

The Internet is still a new comunications medium in Turkey. There are approximately 5,000,000 Internet users, and although these estimated figures are contradictory, it is apparent that Internet usage is increasing on a daily basis in Turkey. Internet reach has increased by 10 percent from 2001 to 2005 with the everyday use ratio climbing from 19 percent to 39 percent (Carat, n.d.).

As it relates to gender, there is a big difference between male and female Internet usage. As of 2006, 73 percent of men used the Internet in comparison to 27 percent of women, and Internet usage is primarily accessed outside the home in such places as Internet cafés (Carat, n.d.).

Television is considered the most influential medium for news, and each individual is said to watch an average 262 minutes of television a day (Maireder, 2006). According to *Turkey Woman Profile 2*, Turkish women prefer to watch television above any other medium. Approximately 62 percent of Turkish women enjoy watching Turkish soap operas, 53 percent women's programs, and 44 percent Turkish films. Radio is the second most popular medium for Turkish women with 72 percent of women listening to Turkish radio.

Journalism education, women, and journalism.   Journalism education started late in Turkey, beginning first at Istanbul University in 1950 with the foundation of a Journalism Institute (Topuz, 2003). Today, there are over 36 faculties of communication that offer journalism education. However, Turkish journalists are not able to find jobs that easily. Although 207 students graduated from three departments of Istanbul University in 2003–4, only 10 to 20 percent of them were able to find a job related to journalism (Gezgin, 2005). This problem is accentuated by the lack of developed human resources policies in the Turkish media sector (Topuz, 2003). As it relates to gender, it is apparent that journalism studies is popular among women. For example, between the years 2003 to 2005, Istanbul University graduated 153 women and 190 men from the field of journalism.

To begin discussing the place of women in journalism, it is necessary to understand how women are defined in Turkish society. However, defining the place and role of Turkish women in Turkey is not simple, and women have held different positions in society based on Turkey's historical period. For example, Turkish women were positioned in a different societal status prior to Islam, during the Ottoman Empire, and during the Republic era. In the Ottoman family, women had a second place status, and this lower position was true not only for a Muslim Turk, but also for an Arab woman, or Armenian (Ortayli, 2006). With the Administrative Reforms Period, the position of women was questioned, and that period created the background for women's rights, which were ultimately achieved after the foundation of the Republic (Terkan, 2003).

Women's rights issues had been the topic of discussion in the press since the nineteenth century. Women started working in the media with Administrative Reforms or Tanzimat Period. In that period, women's issues began to be discussed in newspapers, and women participated in these discussions. For example, the *Terakki* newspaper, which was first published in 1867, had news about women—men equality, education of women, the right of women to work, and negative news about men marrying more than one woman. After 1888, that newspaper published a weekly insert for women called *Muhadderat-i Terakki* in an effort to draw attention to the women's movement in the Western world (Inceoglu & Korkmaz, 2002).

In the 1860s, the early beginnings of Turkish media, there were women writers writing for newspapers, and some of these women held the position of chief editors (Comak & Ocel, 2000). Aside from *Terakki*, there were many newspapers and magazines for women such as *Vakit, Sukufezar, Insaniyet, Ayine, Parca Bohcasi,* and *Aile* (Altındal, 1980). *Sukufezar* was the first women's newspaper published in 1885 by a woman with all women writers (Topuz, 2003). The number of magazines specifically published for women increased during the 1870s. Between 1868 and 1900, there were 13 magazines published for women (Terkan, 2003). Aslı Davaz-Mardin found that between 1928 and 1996, 195 magazines and newspapers were published for women (Topuz, 2003).

In assessing the characteristics of women journalists, Asker compared Turkish women journalists from the Administrative Reforms Period (Tanzimat) and the Constitutional Monarchy (Mesrutiyet) with those from the Republic Period. She found that the first Turkish women journalists were from wealthy and well-known families, and the majority of these women benefitted from special education. These early women journalists also wrote poems, novels, and did translation, with many writing about women's rights. These characteristics differ from today's Turkish women journalists, who are primarily from middle-class families. Unlike women journalists from the past, today's women journalists have benefitted from equal education opportunities during the Republic era. These modern-day women journalists, who started working in the 1980s, saw women's rights issues as a matter of personal interest. Unlike women journalists from the past, who used journalism as a vehicle to make their voices "heard," today's women journalists view journalism as a "profession" (Asker, 1991). Asker based her work on in-depth interviews with Turkish women journalists in 1990 and concluded that the profession is under the dominance of men. Unlike male journalists who learn the practice of journalism from the industry, Turkish women journalists learn the profession from universities (ibid.).

When interviews were conducted with 50 women journalists in an effort to explore the problems that Turkish women face in the media, researchers found that 12 percent of women journalists claimed to have partial equality with their male colleagues, while 42 percent claimed to have equal rights (Inceoglu and Korkmaz, 2002). Although a majority of women journalists deny inequality, women have yet to reach management level positions in Turkish media. The lack of equal gender rights is underscored by the fact that women journalists earn lower salaries and specialize in such areas as health, culture, and the arts when professionally employed in the journalism industry (Iletimonline, 2003).

Women in Turkish media.   How are women covered in the media? It is clear that the representation of women differs depending on the type of media, the period of the publication, and the target audience of the media publication. Traditional gender roles portray women as homemakers and mothers, not as professionals or people with power or authority. On the other extreme, women are portrayed as sex objects with exposed bodies.

In an analysis on the representation of women in women's magazines, Yapar (1999) found many of these magazines are inspired by foreign women's magazines such that the presentation of women is largely outside the realities and identities of the majority of Turkish women. Many of these women's magazines target a female audience that is educated and economically independent, and the issues discussed are largely outside social and political issues, centering more on fashion, beauty, or physical aesthetics as characteristics that can increase the allure and appeal of women to male spectators (Yapar, 1999). Magazine advertisements are also similar in theme. Women primarily have a decorative or sexy role in magazine ad portrayal such that the ratio of working women to working men is considerably low. Another finding is that magazines manipulate images of women depending on the target audience for the magazine. For example, professional magazines use women less while fashion magazines frame women more as a decoration for the male gaze. Even in advertisements where women are framed in a working role, they are portrayed as complementing men. Sozen (Flying Broom, 2006a) noted that women in both Turkish society and the world media are framed either as "seducer" or as "being seduced" and that television is most guilty of this narrow and limiting representation.

How do these representations of women in television and magazine compare to representations of women in newspapers? In conducting a content analysis of six national daily newspapers during one month in 1998, Terkan (2003) found that women were largely presented through the frame of traditional roles. Like the television and magazine mediums, newspapers used a sexual frame to present women. Though it was evident that each newspaper approached women in an individual way based on their readership demographics and their political viewpoint, it was evident that none of the newspapers covered women in the political arena.

Similarly, a recent research study conducted by Mine Gencel Bek in conjunction with the project "Media and Social Participation" led to an analysis of media representation of women through four newspapers during a period of ten months. The results showed that women were highly covered in the media, but that this coverage centered on women's bodies as opposed to their identities. This representation of women through the body was so pervasive that Bek found it to be present even in those news pieces about women that had nothing to do with a woman's body (Flying Broom, 2006b).

Looking to the future.   One of the goals of Turkey's foreign policy vision is to make Turkey an integral part of the EU. Turkey's desire to be a member of the EU will positively affect women's conditions. The future is promising, but rather than wait and watch, each Turkish citizen must contribute to the political, social, and economic empowerment of women. Turkey has come a long way and women cannot afford to slide backwards from the progress they have made in their greater representation in media and society.

Egypt and the Middle East

Not a day passes without some mention in the news of happenings in the Middle East. Most of us have some vague idea of the location of this region of the world but defining it is by no means easy. Depending on one's geographical and political socialization, the definition of what constitutes the Middle East varies. Many disagree on what countries are included in this region. At times, the Middle East includes only Arab states, while in some instances it includes predominantly Muslim states that fall in North Africa and Southwest Asia. Based on the first definition, Iran would be excluded and based on the second definition, Iran, along with Turkey, Pakistan, and Afghanistan would be included. Some definitions also include the countries of Central Asia such as Tajikistan and Uzbekistan. Some people confuse the Islamic world with the Middle East not realizing that Indonesia is by far the largest Muslim country in the world and yet it is not part of the Middle East. In order to be able to write on the situation of women and the media in this region of the world, this exploration of women in Middle East media focuses on the Arab countries in North Africa and Southwest Asia ranging from Morocco in the east to the Gulf states in the west, where the dominant language is Arabic and the most popular religion is Islam.

Regardless of the definition, Egypt is always considered part of the Middle East. It is located predominately in the northwestern corner of Africa (the Sinai Peninsula is in Asia), with a population of close to 80 million. Arabic is the major language and Islam is the dominant religion. The Egyptian Christian minority (Copts) is estimated anywhere from 3 to 10 percent. Egypt is a country of contradictions where one can witness both aspects of Western and Eastern cultures and visitors can feast their eyes on Pharaonic, Greco-Roman, Islamic, and Christian monuments.

Women in Egypt and the Middle East.   In a patriarchal region of the world, such as the Middle East, the divide between women and men extends beyond a discussion of women's presence in media. According to some reports, all Arab countries harbor covert animosity and open discrimination against women. Although the discrimination varies by country, women are considered impure, and mentally and religiously deficient. Laws grant female citizens only half a voice, and women's representation in Arab parliaments does not exceed 6 percent. Saudi Arabia and Kuwait do not allow women to be candidates for office. Several Arab states have not yet signed the principal international legal instrument, the Convention on the Elimination of All Forms of Discrimination Against Women, which requires states to ensure that women's human rights are observed and protected.

Egypt, officially known as the Arab Republic of Egypt, is considered one of the more moderate countries in the region; yet, there are no women judges and there are usually no more than one or two female ministers in any cabinet. Only 2 to 3 percent of the Egyptian parliament is female (Hanley, 2002; Sakr, 2002).

Males in the Middle East receive a better education, and female literacy rates in all countries in the region are lower than men's (MEMRI, 1999). Estimates are as high as 76 percent female illiteracy in Yemen and 65 percent in Morocco (Sakr, 2002). In Egypt, 62 percent of women compared to 38 percent of men are illiterate (Guenena & Wassef, 1999). More recent statistics indicate that female literacy is as high as 44 percent in Egypt (Wheeler, 2004). In a country of close to 80 million citizens, that percentage translates to approximately 18 million illiterate females.

A study by the World Economic Forum found that women in Egypt lag the furthest behind men in terms of economic equality in the world ("WEF report," 2005). Women's average wages are approximately one-third lower than those of men. Women's representation in labor unions is insignificant when compared to men (Guenena & Wassef, 1999). In terms of health, the maternal mortality rate in the Middle East is double that of Latin America and the Caribbean and four times that of East Asia ("How the Arabs compare," 2002).

Media and freedom of the press in the Middle East and Egypt.   Not one country in the Middle East received a rating of good or satisfactory in terms of freedom of the press by Reporters without Borders (2003). Arab countries ranked very low when assessing freedom of the press. On a scale of 1 to 150, with 1 indicating countries with the highest press freedom rank, Kuwait ranked at 84, Lebanon at 89, Jordan at 92, Morocco at 94, Algeria at 97, Egypt at 107, Iraq at 116, Oman and the United Arab Emirates at 118, Yemen at 130, Tunisia and Saudi Arabia at 131, Syria at 137, and Sudan at 142. Libya, which is ranked at 146, is placed barely above Cuba and North Korea. Iraq's ranking of 116 was prior to the removal of Saddam Hussein (World Audit Press Freedom, 2001). During Hussein's reign, Iraqi journalists who criticized his regime could be punished by death, and Hussein was described as openly hostile to press freedom such that his oldest son, Uday, controlled several newspapers and television and radio stations. Since the change of regime in Iraq, newspapers have flourished in Baghdad and cybercafés provide ready access to the Internet (Tabor, 2002). In sharp contrast to the past, Article 36B of the new 2005 Iraqi Constitution states that the state will not violate public order and the morality and freedom of the press (Washingtonpost.com, 2005). Based on this constitution, it is hoped that in future rankings, Iraq can climb up, setting an example for other Arab countries.

Journalists are often denied access to information, and protecting national security is usually used to justify the suspension of rights and violation of basic freedoms. In 2001, two Lebanese journalists faced a possible death penalty for meeting with Israeli officials ("Two Lebanese," 2001). Laws restrict who may become a journalist and publications have to be licensed. In Egypt, applications for licenses by independent publications must be cleared by all major security and intelligence agencies, making clearance very difficult to obtain. In addition, the government is directly involved in selecting the chair of the Journalists' Syndicate and it manipulates the Syndicate's elections. Local and international censorship are rampant in the Middle East. In Egypt, it is common for the Ministry of Information to engage in preventative censorship or censorship before publication and defamation in Egypt can lead to a prison sentence of up to two years. Jail sentences can also be handed down for "violating public morality" and "damaging national interest" (International Press Institute, 2006). The government is not the only one exercising censorship; self-censorship is common in the Arab news media. In addition, a censorial culture also exits in journalism education (Amin, 2002).

As of 1991, some believe that Arab governments can no longer exercise control over the flow of information because of the introduction of satellite broadcasting—a technology which has changed the picture of censorship in the Middle East ("New-media," 1998; Associated Press, 2001). Others argue that a free Arab press does not exist because access to officials is denied; journalists face harassment, intimidation, and physical threats; and that more than 70 percent of satellite broadcasting in the Middle East is under government supervision ("New-media," 1998; UNDP, 2003; Al-Arian, 2004). One way that reporters in the Middle East have escaped censorship is by establishing bases abroad (UNDP, 2003).

Newspapers in the Middle East are government-owned, published by political organizations, or privately owned. The privately owned newspapers are not editorially independent because of their owners' political affiliations (Al-bab, 2006). The leading daily newspapers in Egypt—*Al-Ahram*, *Al-Akhbar*, and *Al-Jumhuriyya*—are government-owned. The National Democratic Party appoints the editorial staffs for these three newspapers via the upper house of parliament, acting with the president's approval (Al-Zubaidi, 2004).

In addition to government restrictions on the media, journalists also have to deal with military assaults. Israel has attacked Arab journalists and media installations, and the armed Palestinian security forces closed the West Bank office of Al-Jazeera ("IFJ," 2000; Palestinians, 2001).

Media production in the Middle East is low when compared to other parts of the world. Only 53 newspapers per 1,000 citizens are published daily compared to 285 papers per 1,000 in developed nations. No more than 10,000 books have been translated into Arabic, the equivalent to the number translated into Spanish in one year. The population of the Middle East constitutes 5 percent of the world's population, yet the Arab world only produces 1 percent of the world's books and constitutes only 1 percent of Internet users. Only 18 computers are available per 1,000 people in the Middle East as compared to the global average of 78 per 1,000. Estimates indicate that Internet penetration in the Middle East for 2005 ranges from 1 percent to 38 percent with Egypt at 8 percent ("PC penetration," 2002; UNDP 2003). Only around 4 percent of all Middle Eastern Internet users are women (Women's Learning Partnership, 2006). Computer and Internet illiteracy, high prices for computers, and the high cost of lines and access fees are the principal reasons for the low Internet penetration (Al-Zubaidi, 2004).

Despite economic constraints, Egypt is considered a major regional media player. The Egyptian press is one of the most influential in the region. There are eight daily newspapers in Egypt with a circulation of more than 2 million. There are 44 short-wave, 18 medium-wave, and four FM radio stations in Egypt. Egypt was the first Arab nation to have its own satellite, Nilesat 101. The television and film industry supplies much of the Arab-speaking world and is known as the "Hollywood of the East" (BBC, 2005).

Women and the media in the Middle East.   From this brief overview of the press and the status of women in the Middle East, it is evident that women deal with several restrictions when it comes to the practice of journalism. In addition to the constraints on journalists which affect both sexes, women also have to deal with personal status laws which basically give the men in their lives the right to determine if they can travel, work, and marry (Sakr, 2002). In some countries, such as Saudi Arabia, not being allowed to drive a car makes it very difficult for female journalists to do their jobs. For many countries in the Middle East, the social culture does not look favorably upon women working outside the home. In 2005, police and government supporters attacked more than a dozen women journalists in Egypt during a demonstration. Iman Taha, a 30-year-old reporter, broke her pelvis during the altercation. Another female journalist, Nawal Mohamed Ali, who was not part of the demonstration, had her clothes torn off and she was robbed (Reporters without Borders, 2006).

Accurate figures are lacking about the number of Arab women working in the media, and gathering statistics in the Middle East is difficult. A study by UNESCO undertaken in the mid 1990s found that less than 10 percent of accredited journalists in Jordan were women. Less than 15 percent of women were journalists in Morocco, and less than 21 percent in Tunisia. In Egypt, 28 percent of journalists were women (UNESCO, n.d.). The glass ceiling proves difficult to break, and women journalists are compensated less then men because of the power of stereotypes. Women are perceived as lacking the ability to deal with flexible schedules and the mobility to travel, a requirement of the media industry. The paucity of media training for women is one of many reasons women are accorded lower status in the Middle East's media industry.

The representation of women in Middle Eastern media reports is lacking in both quantity and quality. Women's coverage in the Middle East stands at 14 percent compared to a global average of 20 percent (Sakr, 2000). When issues pertaining to women are covered, the coverage often excludes important legal or political aspects dealing with inequality and violence. For example, television's coverage of rape is considered "taboo" in the United Arab Emirates (Sakr, 2000). In a study of 500 episodes of Egyptian television, 43 percent of women were subjected to violence, and a poll in Egypt showed that the majority of respondents still supported the beating of women (Raad, 2004).

There is a definite absence of female role models in media depictions of women. Women are rarely portrayed in a positive lens and are primarily relegated to the private sphere. They are presented as mothers, wives, and daughters in need of protection. They are stereotyped as emotional, erratic, and fragile beings who only care about appearances. Many times, they are objectified and reduced to sex objects. The portrayal of women can be summed up in two frames: sexually exploited object or homebound traditional woman. Women's magazines, like their Western counterparts, focus on fashion and not on issues important to women. A report on women's rights and the Arab media contended that the Arab media is the most hostile in the world toward women's rights and freedoms. Not only do the media ignore women's issues but some media outlets also launch campaigns against women's rights (Essoulami, 2000).

Few women in the Middle East are conscious of their negative portrayal in media reports despite the popularity of entertainment programs among Arab women (Sakr, 2002). According to a uses and gratifications study, women attended to the media for affective and escapist needs whereas men consumed news in an effort to understand what is happening in the world (Abdel Rahman, 1998).

Good news.   Even though the picture looks bleak regarding both the media in the Middle East and the presence/representation of women in Middle Eastern media, it is important to note that women have proven very resilient over the years. Egypt has had many women journalists and publishers dating back to the nineteenth century. Kuwaiti women assumed men's pen names in the 1950s and 1960s; however, many of them now work in newspapers, and there is at least one female editor-in-chief (Hanley, 2002). Women in the Middle East do not shy away from tough reporting assignments. For example, Samia Nakhoul, the Reuters bureau chief in the Gulf, covered Baghdad during the war and got wounded. Tania Mehanna, a journalist for a Lebanese television station, covered wars for 16 years in Afghanistan, Iraq, and Pakistan ("IPJ," 2004).

Some signs indicate that the future might be brighter. For example, Al-Jazeera's staff is 40 percent female, and 8 out of the 18 news anchors are women. Al-Jazeera might be an exception to the rule but it is respected, and 70 percent of satellite-owning Arabs watch it, indicating that it might be the beginning of a trend (Groskop, 2005). According to Amin (2001), female presenters are very popular on satellite television throughout the Arab world. Amin also believes that satellite television has provided a forum for women to discuss their issues and challenges.

As in the United States, students of communication are predominantly female. In Lebanon, 80 percent of students of mass communication are female (Sakr, 2000). According to Dr. Ali Awad from the University of Sharjah, 73 percent of women studying in the media field in the United Arab Emirates are women (Hanley, 2002). With females as the majority of students, it is felt that the media will have no choice but to hire more women in senior positions.

Training workshops are being conducted for women journalists from the Arab world, and the workshops also aim to promote women's rights in the media. The United Nations Commission on the Status of Women recognizes the importance of the media in terms of coverage and in terms of female participation. In its forty-ninth session, it recommended that the successful experiences of women in the media must be made accessible and suggested the establishment of an association for Arab women in the media to facilitate communication among women and other parties. The Arab Women's Media Forum was held in Abu Dhabi to discuss women's participation in the field of journalism and the media's portrayal of women and The Abu Dhabi Declaration was adopted at the conclusion of the Arab Women's Media Forum. It called for media organizations in Arab countries to remove any hurdles that impede women's progress in the media industry (Hanley, 2002).

Let us hope that media organizations heed this call.

Nigeria

Proudly referred to by indigenes as the "giant of Africa," Nigeria is a country in West Africa with a population of 140 million people (Nigeria Direct a, n.d.). This makes Nigeria the most populous nation in Africa. Although there have been many years of military intervention in Nigeria, the country is currently under civilian rule. There are 36 states in Nigeria and a federal capital territory in Abuja—much like Washington DC in the US, which is not a full-fledged state. The capital of Nigeria was officially transferred from Lagos to Abuja in 1991.

Nigeria gained independence from Great Britain in 1960 and has a three-tier system of governance: the executive branch, which consists of the president or chief of states and his cabinet; the legislative branch with 109 Senate seats and 360 House of Representatives seats; and the judicial branch with the Supreme Court and Courts of Appeal. The legal system in Nigeria is a mix of customary laws that are derived from local customs and traditions, Shari'a law or Islamic law practiced in 12 Northern states, and the English common laws.

One cannot discuss Nigeria without discussing its major source of revenue, which is oil. Nigeria is a member of the Oil Producing and Exporting Countries (OPEC) and is the sixth largest producer of oil in the world, exporting close to 2.5 million barrels of oil daily. With concerns in recent years over high gas prices in the United States and elsewhere in the world, it is worth noting that Nigeria is the fifth largest supplier of US oil. As such, events in Nigeria affect US and global gas prices.

There are about 18 multinational oil companies operating and drilling oil in Nigeria, including the US-based Chevron. The drilling has led to several oil spills and environmental degradation in the oil rich Niger Delta area of Nigeria. This situation has led to an increase in the number of sabotage and hostage takings of foreign oil workers by community activists. On February 18, 2006, nine foreign oil workers, including two Americans, were taken hostage but were later released ("Nine abducted," 2006). Some reports confirm that Nigeria lost the equivalent of 543,000 barrels of oil because of this crisis, causing world oil prices to soar above $64 per barrel ("Nigerian guerillas," n.d.). But even with such losses, Nigeria's economy remains the second largest in Africa following South Africa, even though, the money from oil revenues does not seem to trickle down to the masses. In Nigeria, 60 percent of the population lives below poverty levels.

Nigerians have many traditional practices in common, although specific customs vary by region or tribe. There are over 250 ethnic groups in Nigeria and over 250 languages and dialects, but English is the official language. The three major ethnic groups are the Hausa/Fulanis in the North, who are mostly Muslims; the Yorubas in the Southwest who are a mix of Christians and Muslims; and the Ibos in the Southeast who are mostly Christians. Fifty percent of Nigerians are Muslims, 40 percent are Christians and 10 percent of the people practice indigenous religions (Falola, 2001).

Women in Nigeria.   Though women in Nigeria constitute approximately 50 percent of the population, they are marginalized in Nigerian political life even though they vote as much as or sometimes in greater numbers than men. The Federal Executive Council of Nigeria consists of the president, vice-president, and the heads of ministries, but only five of the ministers including the minister for education, environment, finance, solid minerals development, and women affairs are women (Nigeria Direct b, n.d.). There are no female governors in Nigeria, but there is one female deputy governor.[3] In terms of parliamentary seats, the United Nations Millennium Indicators Report revealed that Nigeria had 17 parliamentary seats occupied by women in 2005 vs. 343 by men. This figure represents a drop from the 24 women who occupied seats in 2004 (United Nations, n.d.).

Women are making gains in the judiciary. According to *Women's eNews*, while there is no woman in the Supreme Court, 20 percent of chief judges in Nigeria are women, with more than half of students in law schools being women (Faris, 2001). The Lagos high court is now made up of 60 percent females with 17 of the 25 Lagos court judges appointed to office in 2001 being women (ibid.). There was no deliberate attempt to recruit women, but the unusually high numbers of female appointments were favored because of the extent of corruption in the judiciary and the belief that women judges would shun corruption (ibid.).

Nigerian women are confronted with numerous challenges especially since the culture encourages submissiveness in women. Although women in pre-colonial eras suffered various forms of discrimination, it would seem that colonialism intensified and introduced new forms of discrimination against Nigerian women. Many Nigerian scholars have argued that most of the administrative practices that prevent equal treatment of Nigerian women and men are products of colonial laws, which have their roots in Victorian sensibilities—sensibilities which assumed that the public sphere rightly belonged to men (Okome, 2002).

Women in pre-colonial times were active in the labor force, often making great contributions in trade, agriculture, healthcare, and spiritual services. Land was communal and since women were active in farming, those who tilled the land had access to it. Women had autonomy in their affairs (Okome, 2002) and were also very strong in village organizations. The Umu-ada in many Southeastern states, for instance, were revered members of the society. A few Nigerian societies at the time also had practices that insisted seniority trumped gender, thus ensuring the rights of older women. Local practices of strategic fostering of children, and marital arrangements such as those of non-sexual female to female "marriages" also ensured that "female husbands" had access to property and land by virtue of the sons gained through such strategic arrangements (Amadiume, 1987; Okome, 2002).

Colonialism changed much of these customs, making it harder for women to gain access to land and property. Women also became marginalized because of the introduction of a cash economy. Many women were excluded from civil service and administrative positions. The newly introduced Christian practices that frowned on polygamy as well as newly placed statutory provisions on divorce and inheritance fostered new challenges for women who did not have the experience or resources needed to navigate them (Okome, 2002).

Today, women in Nigeria are faced with early marriages, discriminatory inheritance laws, discriminatory divorce and custody laws, and inadequate pre-natal and maternal care. The infant mortality rate in Nigeria is about 97 deaths per 1,000 live births (The CIA World Factbook, n.d.). This figure starkly contrasts with the mortality rate of six per 1,000 live births in the United States Nigerian women also face difficulties with upward mobility in the workplace due to motherhood responsibilities, poverty, lack of education, increased risks of contracting HIV/AIDS, lack of adequate health information, limited access to contraception, international prostitution of women in Europe, domestic violence, and female genital operations. Looking at the Nigerian media, though, these issues seem non-existent or less important such that they are often ignored or relegated to the background. Nigerian media are saturated with political news and sound bites from public officials.

The news divide. Nigerian women's access to the media is very limited, with cost being the most prohibitive aspect to access according to a survey by this researcher. Newspapers and magazines cost between 100 to 200 naira, about 4 percent of the Nigerian Labour Congress' estimate of the average Nigerian's monthly income (Nigerian Labour Congress, 2004). This expense makes newspapers and magazines a luxury for many women. However, Nigerian women do have access to television and radio. Radio and television are more accessible since they offer programs in local languages as well as English. Radio is most accessible since it could run on batteries unlike television sets, which require electricity, another scarce item for women living in remote villages. The Internet is a relatively new medium in Nigeria. Many Nigerians do not have access to personal computers and rely on Internet cafés for Internet access. The 2004 estimate for individuals with personal computers in Nigeria was 860,000 and Internet users were estimated to be about 750,000 (United Nations, n.d.).

Newspapers and magazines are considered very elitist in Nigeria and are therefore less accessible. The muzzling of the press in developing countries is often blamed for the avoidance of controversial issues in the media, but the Nigerian press cannot claim this social reality as a hindrance. The Nigerian press is one of the most vocal in Africa. The 100 newspapers and newsmagazines in Nigeria regularly publish hard-hitting materials that are highly critical of the government. The electronic media, however, is less vocal, perhaps due to the fact that the broadcasting industry was government-controlled until 1992 when the industry was privatized.

With regards to the broadcast industry, there are 97 licensed federal government-owned TV stations, 32 licensed state-owned TV stations, 14 private stations, four DBS satellite stations, four direct to home stations, and 35 MMDS cable TV stations. Regarding radio, there are 17 licensed private radio stations, 40 state-owned stations, five national federal government-owned radio stations, the Voice of Nigeria, and 37 licensed federal FM stations (National Broadcasting Commission, n.d.).

Most TV stations in Nigeria use both a male and female anchor for news delivery, but the news industry is dominated by males. Eighty percent of practicing journalists are men, according to a survey by the Independent Journalism Center in conjunction with the Panos Institute of Washington and the Center for War, Peace and the News Media of New York (Anyanwu, 2001, p. 69). Anyanwu notes that while women have made inroads in magazines as publishers, editors-in-chief, executive editors, and associate editors, there was only one female Saturday editor and one business editor, but no female editor or deputy editor in any of the major dailies in Nigeria (ibid., p. 70).

A survey[4] conducted by this researcher of 200 residents in Lagos metropolis revealed that 40 percent of those surveyed consider themselves news enthusiasts (for both print and broadcast news). But of this number, 73 percent were men and only 26 percent were women. Twenty-five percent of those polled considered themselves news eclectics, 19 percent news intenders, 13 percent were news accidentals, while 3 percent were news avoiders.

Looking at the newsmagazines and newspapers in Nigeria, it is not difficult to understand why few Nigerian women are news enthusiasts, even in Lagos, which is the most metropolitan city in Nigeria. Serious issues affecting the ordinary Nigerian woman are mostly ignored and women's faces are obliterated in newsmagazines.

Three of the most widely read newsmagazines in Nigeria are *Tell*, *The News*, and *Newswatch* with circulation figures of 100,000, 80,000, and 50,000 respectively (Olokoyun, 2004). A content analysis of these magazines for the 2005 and 2006 issues conducted by this researcher in March 2006 revealed a tendency for the magazines to favor men as sources and to tilt coverage to political news, an arena with very few female voices. This lack of female representation is also reflected in the photographs used by these magazines. For instance, in the March 13, 2006 issue of *Newswatch*, there were 62 photographs and only one was of a female subject. This photograph was for the "in the news" section and was located among photographs of individuals celebrating their birthdays. Eniola Fadayomi, the female subject, just happened to be one of the celebrants.

The News had 78 photographs in its March 13, 2006 issue, with only 16 showing women. While this appears to be an improvement over *Tell*, a breakdown shows that the numbers are deceptive. Most of the photographs were located in the fashion section and were of international female models such as Tyra Banks and Gisele Bundchen. Other photographs were group pictures showing some female mourners at the funeral of Belo Ransome Kuti, a famous Nigerian human rights activist. The only photographs that can count as independent photos of Nigerian female sources and subjects were the two of Dr. Ngozi Okonjo-Iweala, the Nigerian finance minister. There was also a photograph of Modupe Sasore, the CEO of the Nigerian Export Promotion Council.

Tell magazine's issue of the same day in March 2006 had a display of 97 photographs, of which 11 were of female subjects or sources. Of this total, only four could actually count since the others were group photographs or photographs of wives of public officials. One photograph was of Dolly Parton on the Lifestyle (Panorama) page. The four photographs that count showed Bolaji Osomo, a former minister of housing in Ondo State, Cecilia Ibru, the managing director of Oceanic Bank, Elizabeth Ike, provost of the Nigerian Institute of Journalism, and Funke Fadugba, a former chairman of the Nigerian Union of Journalists (NUJ), Lagos chapter, and who coincidentally lost the NUJ's national election to a man. Fadugba was complaining that the election was rigged.

Other popular magazines are guilty of the same practice. *Insider* magazine had 57 photographs and only one of these photographs featured a female subject. Again, Ngozi Okonjo-Iweala, the Nigerian minister of finance was the subject. It is important to note that she was not quoted in the story. Her photograph was probably considered a good choice because it was part of a business story on Nigeria's adoption of the Economic Community of West African States' (ECOWAS) common external import tariff.

The Week had 54 photographs for the same day and only three were of women. Again, Ngozi Okonjo-Iweala's photograph was one of the three significant ones. It seems that since most of these magazines have a business section, Iweala gets some coverage by virtue of her position as the minister of finance even when she is not directly quoted or a subject of some of the stories covered. Iweala, a former vice-president of World Bank, also enjoys the distinct position of being one of only three finance ministers in the world ("I keep my ego," 2005) making her a very newsworthy subject for the Nigerian media.

Nigerian newspapers seem to do a little better than newsmagazines when it comes to the coverage of women and women's issues. There are more sections in the newspapers dedicated to women's issues such as *Head to Toe*, *Moment 2 Moment*, *Love Zone*, *Woman's Own*, *Yours Sincerely*, and some *Dear Abby* type columns. However, these sections are predominantly run in the Sunday editions of the newspapers and feature more fashion and beauty tips than any other important issues affecting Nigerian women. Prominent Nigerian women are also interviewed but often these are women who would be considered very exceptional in terms of their professional achievements.

Although Nigerian women enjoy coverage in the newspapers through several female-oriented sections, the printed photographs of women are still meant to position women as objects to be looked at. The *Daily Sun* newspaper still engages in the dying practice of using a page three "pin up" girl called *Sun* girl. Many photographs feature wives of public officials standing next to their husbands with the very often used caption that gives the name of the public official and the line "with wife." These pictures hardly ever feature the names of the wives but these women enjoy a lot of photographic coverage because of their roles as wives of important public officials. *Punch's* Saturday, March 4, 2006 issue had a blown up photograph of a former Nigerian beauty queen on its cover. However, the only reason she made the front page was because of a tragic accident in which she caused the death of a medical doctor while driving a jeep that belonged to a popular reggae musician.

Ordinary Nigerian women do not seem to be in the news as sources or subjects of news, except when something unusual happens to them. Many of the stories about women in the newspapers include stories of a woman who needs donations for a heart transplant, another of a woman who needs surgery so she could walk, and still another of a woman in need of a kidney transplant.

This habit of ignoring women's voices and serious women's issues seems more disturbing and insidious when it is considered that the period that this content analysis covered was a period when the news was filled with opinions about President Olusegun Obasanjo's attempt to change the Nigerian constitution to make it possible for him to run for a third term. No Nigerian woman's opinion was sought on this very serious and controversial issue of a constitutional amendment. Female lawmakers were not asked for their opinions; however, several male politicians' voices were heard on the matter.

Solutions.   A divide in access to the news media is apparent in Nigeria and some of it is clearly attributed to the fact that women are not well represented in what Anyanwu refers to as the "noisy world of politics" (2001, p. 70). It seems that short of changing the whole concept of what constitutes news in Nigeria, increasing the political participation of women might close some of the divide since Nigerian news is strongly slanted toward political news. Women who are quoted or interviewed in the news media are mostly those appointed or elected to government offices. This scenario puts women in a very disadvantageous position since the percentage of women in decision-making positions in public and political life is low in Nigeria. According to a *Daily Champion* news report on the PeaceWomen, the Women's International League for Peace and Freedom's website, the percentage ranged from 1 percent in 1992 to 13 percent in 1999 (PeaceWomen, 2005). The article further revealed that the only woman out of the 36 speakers elected to the House of Assembly resigned due to pressure from the men in the House. Of 774 local government chairpersons, only nine are women; only three of the 109 senators are women; 12 of the 360 members in the House of Representatives are women, and only 143 of the 8,810 councillors in Nigeria are women (PeaceWomen, 2005).

The cost of running for elective offices discourages women from running for such positions, and many women also consider politics to be a dirty and violent game. Though women need to be socialized to participate more fully in politics, greater affirmative policies need to be put in place to ensure women's participation in the Nigerian public sphere. The Nigerian president has mandated the appointment of at least one woman in every decision-making and consultative body in Nigeria. Such affirmative policies could go a long way toward giving women access to the media. The women who are not in such positions would also benefit by seeing other women in the news, thus making the news a little more relevant to them.

More female journalists need to be hired as editors, but more importantly, female journalists have to do more to bring attention to women's issues. Anyanwu reports that even while male editors ignore women's issues because such issues are considered trivial and capable of depressing advertising, female editors in Nigeria surprisingly shy away from women's issues for fear of being labeled feminists or considered to be practicing less serious forms of journalism (2001, p. 71). These female journalists also refuse to be members of the National Association of Women Journalists and are instead more interested in the Nigerian Union of Journalists (Anyanwu, 2001, p. 71). An attitude change among women journalists is therefore needed. At the moment, most of the pages dedicated to women's issues are filled with fashion, relationships, and beauty tips. Perhaps if female journalists engaged in the coverage of serious issues, such as the social, legal, and medical issues facing women, they would not have to worry about being accused of frivolity.

There are many serious women's issues to be covered. Many widows in Nigeria face difficulties gaining access to their deceased husbands' assets, some women need spousal consent to avail themselves of contraceptives through the Planned Parenthood of Nigeria, and a few face circumcision for chastity. Some single women face discrimination in the workplace, other women lose custody of their children after weaning, and some abandon their education to face complications associated with childbirth after being forced into early marriages. Nigerian women need strong advocates and perhaps this could only be achieved by having female journalists who are strong enough to hold the mantle and engage in such advocacy without seeming overly combative or antagonistic toward men (a fact that could alienate them even from their fellow Nigerian women).

One of the top reasons people gave for why they do not read newspapers in the survey conducted by this researcher was cost. Of the 30 percent that gave cost as a reason for not reading newspapers, 22 percent were women. With newspapers costing about 4 percent of the average Nigerian's income, it is a luxury that many women cannot afford. It is unlikely that the cover charges for these newspapers would go down, so a more feasible solution would be for broadcast stations, which are more accessible, to pick up the slack and cover more issues that affect women.

Another top reason for inattention to news was lack of interest. Ten percent of women cited this as a reason for their disengagement with news, perhaps because Nigerian women see nothing appealing in the style and content of Nigerian news. The newspapers and newsmagazines could make their news writing more accessible. The language used in Nigerian newspapers and newsmagazines is very elitist even for a country with a literacy rate among 15 to 24 year olds of 86 percent for women and 91 percent for men (United Nations, n.d.). Nigerian journalists in the print media alienate less educated people with their penchant for haughty words and bureaucratese.

Finally, sensitivity training for journalists is needed to help guard against gender stereotypes. This training would sensitize journalists to the fact that women could be equally effective and reliable as news sources, and that women are not only good for their fashion sense and pretty faces, but for their strong opinions.

It seems obvious that until Nigerian women start to see and hear themselves and their issues in the news, they will continue to feel alienated and find the news totally irrelevant in their lives.

Notes

1   Contributors were invited to give their perspectives because of their personal and professional experiences with that country or region. The contributors for each country or region in this chapter are listed as follows: United Kingdom by Jackie Harrison and Karen Sanders; Germany by Christiana Holtz-Bacha; Spain by Raquel Rodríguez Díaz with English translation by Amy Schmitz Weiss; Turkey by Serra Görpe; Egypt and the Middle East by Salma Ghanem; and Nigeria by Chioma Ugochukwu.
2   Bernard Engel of ZDF Media research department has kindly provided this advance data.
3   Although no women were elected governor in Nigera's April 2007 general election, women deputy governors increased to four. Newly appointed female ministers dropped from five to four.
4   Survey based on a purposive sample conducted in March 2006 in the Lagos metropolis. Respondents included 100 men and 100 women. Thirty-nine percent had a bachelor's degree, 18 percent completed high school, 33 percent were college students, and 10 percent had a graduate degree.

References

United Kingdom

Adie, K. (2002). *The Kindness of Strangers*. London: Headline Book Publishing.
Ball, A., Hanna, M., & Sanders, K. (2004). Becoming a Journalist: Motives, attitudes and aspirations of British journalism students. Paper presented at the Professional Education section of the International Association for Media and Communication Research, Brazil.

Ball, A., Hanna, M., & Sanders, K. (2006). What British journalism students think about ethics and journalism. *Journalism & Mass Communication Educator*, 61(1), 20–32.

BBC on this day, 2 June. (n.d.). 1953, *Queen Elizabeth takes coronation oath*. Retrieved April 6, 2007 from http://news.bbc.co.uk/onthisday/low/dates/stories/june/2/newsid_2654000/2654501.stm.

Cadwalladr, C. (2006, August 6). I'm no career bitch. *Observer Woman*, 16–21.

Chambers, D., Steiner, L., & Fleming, C. (2004). *Women and Journalism*. London and New York: Routledge.

The CIA World Factbook (2006). Retrieved July 9, 2006 from www.cia.gov/cia/publications/factbook/geos/uk.html.

Day, E. (2004). Why women love journalism. *British Journalism Review*, 15(2), 21–5.

Delano, A. (2003). Women journalists: What's the difference? *Journalism Studies*, 4(2), 273–86.

Hargreaves, I., & Thomas, J. (2002). *New News, Old News*. London: ITC and BSC.

Harrison, J. (2006). *News*. London: Routledge.

Historic Figures. (n.d.). *Margaret Thatcher (1925-)*. Retrieved April 6, 2007 from, www.bbc.co.uk/history/historic_figures/thatcher_margaret.shtml.

Journalism Training Forum. (2002). *Journalists at Work. Their Views on Training, Recruitment and Conditions*. London: Journalism Training Forum.

Kingsmill, D. (2001, December). *The Kingsmill's Review. Report into Women's Employment and Pay*. Retrieved June 20, 2006 from www.kingsmillreview.gov.uk/overview.cfm.

MacGregor, S. (2002). *Woman of Today: An autobiography*. London: Hodder Headline.

Media Guardian. (2006). *The Media Guide 2006*. London: Guardian Books.

Office of National Statistics. (2001, April). *Census*. Retrieved June 25, 2006 from www.statistics.gov.uk/cci/nugget.asp?id=273.

Office of National Statistics. (2005, August 25). *Population Estimates*. Retrieved June 25, 2006 from www.statistics.gov.uk/CCI/nugget.asp?ID=6.

Rantzen, E. (2006). Why are women such bullies? *British Journalism Review*, 17, 1, 35–9.

Ross, K. (2001). Women at work: Journalism as en-gendered practice. *Journalism Studies*, 2(4), 531–44.

Sebba, A. (1994). *Battling for News: The rise of the woman reporter*. London: Hodder and Stoughton.

Women in Journalism. (2006). *Use it or Lose it! Ageism is the New Racism and Feminism*. Retrieved July 9, 2006 from www.leisurejobs.net/wij/detail.cfm?codeID=179.

Women's National Commission. (2002, August 1). *WNC Response on the Draft Communications Bill*. Retrieved June 25, 2006 from www.communicationsact.gov.uk/responses/Womens%20National%20Commission.doc.

Wykes, M. & Gunter, B. (2005). *The Media & Body Image*. London: Sage.

Germany

"Bundeskanzlerin" macht das Rennen. ["Bundeskanzlerin" wins the race.] (2005, December 16). *Spiegel Online*. Retrieved January 9, 2006 from www.spiegel.de/kultur/gesellschaft/0,1518,390739,00.html.

Bundesverband Deutscher Zeitungsverleger. (2006a). Zeitungen 2005 auf einen Blick. Retrieved June 30, 2006 from www.bdzv.de/schaubilder+M59c30895fb1.html.

Bundesverband Deutscher Zeitungsverleger. (2006b). *Zeitungsdichte im Auslandsvergleich*. Retrieved June 30, 2006 from www.bdzv.de/schaubilder+M5a299eca66b.html.

Eimeren, B. van & Frees, B. (2005). Nach dem Boom: Größter Zuwachs in Internetfernen Gruppen [After the boom: Biggest increase in Internet distant groups]. *Media Perspektiven*, pp. 362–79.

Federal Statistical Office. (2006). *In the Spotlight. Women in Germany 2006*. Wiesbaden: Federal Statistical Office. Retrieved June 30, 2006 from www-ec.destatis.de/csp/shop/sfg/bpm.html.cms.cBroker.cls?cmspath=struktur,vollanzeige.csp&ID=1018408.

Hallin, D.C. & Mancini, P. (2004). *Comparing Media Systems. Three Models of Media and Politics*. Cambridge: Cambridge University Press.

Hesse, M. & Röser, J. (2006). Mehr Präsenz von Frauen in den Hauptnachrichten deutscher Medien. In *Präsenz von Frauen in den Nachrichten. Medienbeobachtungen 2005* [Representation of women in the news. Media observations 2005], pp. 12–17. Bonn: Journalistinnenbund.

Holtz-Bacha, C. (1995). Frauen in der Kommunikationspraxis. In R. Fröhlich & C. Holtz-Bacha, *Frauen und Medien. Eine Synopse der deutschen Forschung* [Women and media. A synopsis of German research], pp. 13–40. Opladen: Westdeutscher Verlag.

Kommission zur Ermittlung der Konzentration im Medienbereich. (2006). *Zuschaueranteile.* Retrieved June 30, 2006 from www.kek-online.de/cgi-bin/esc/zuschauer.html.

Reitze, H. & Ridder, C.-M. (Eds.) (in press). *Massenkommunikation VII. Eine Langzeitstudie zur Mediennutzung und Medienbewertung 1964–2005* [Mass communication VII. A longitudinal study on media use and attitudes towards the media 1964–2005]. Baden-Baden: Nomos.

Schorn, K. & Schwartzenberg, M. von (2005, November). Endgültiges Ergebnis der Wahl zum 16. Deutschen Bundestag am 18. September 2005. *Wirtschaft und Statistik*, 1153–67. Retrieved June 30, 2006 from www.bundeswahlleiter.de/bundestagswahl2005/downloads/.

Weischenberg, S. (2005, October 6). Der Schein trügt. *Die Zeit*, p. 54.

Spain

Asociación de la Prensa de Madrid (APM). (1990). El periodista español. Retrato Intermitente [The Spanish journalist. An intermittent portrait]. *Periodistas*. Madrid: Servicio de Publicaciones de la Asociación de la Prensa de Madrid.

Alaminos, A. (2003). Globalización y desvertebración social [Globalisation and social disintegration]. In J.F. Tezanos, J.M. Tortosa, & A. Alaminos (Eds.) *Tendencias en Desvertebración Social y en Políticas de Solidaridad*, pp. 31–44. Madrid: Sistema.

Bouza, F. (2003). Tendencias a la desigualdad en Internet: la brecha digital (*Digital Divide*) en España [Trends towards Internet inequality: the digital divide in Spain]. In J.F. Tezanos, J.M. Tortosa, & A. Alaminos (Eds.) *Tendencias en Desvertebración Social y en Políticas de Solidaridad*, pp. 93–121. Madrid: Sistema.

Centro de Investigaciones Sociológicas (CIS). (2003). *La Televisión y la Radio en la Vida de los Españoles* [Television and Radio in the Life of Spanish People]. *Estudio CIS 2541* (Boletín 33). Retrieved April 18, 2006 from www.cis.es/cis/opencms/-Archivos/Boletines/33/BDO_33_TVRadio.html.

Centro de Investigaciones Sociológicas (CIS). (2006). *Barómetro de febrero* [Barometer for February]. Retrieved April 20, 2006 from www.cis.es/cis/opencms/-Archivos/Marginales/2620_2639/2635/e263500.html.

Encuesta de Población Activa (EPA). (2006) *Instituto Nacional de Estadística (INE)* [Survey of the Active Population]. Cuarto trimestre de 2005. Retrieved April 18, 2006 from www.ine.es/daco/daco42/daco4211/epa0405.pdf.

Estudio General de Medios (EGM). (2005). Asociación para la Investigación en Medios de Comunicación (AIMC). *Tercer año Móvil 2005, febrero-noviembre* [Third Report 2005, February-November]. Retrieved April 18, 2006 from www.aimc.es/02egm/resumegm305.pdf.

Estudio General de Medios (EGM). (2006). Asociación para la Investigación en Medios de Comunicación (AIMC). *Primer año Móvil 2006, abril 2005–marzo 2006* [First Report 2006, April 2005–March 2006]. Retrieved July 18, 2006 from www.aimc.es/02egm/resumegm106.pdf.

García de Cortázar, M. & García de León, M.A. (coords.) (2000). *Profesionales del Periodismo* [Professionals of Journalism]. Madrid: CIS.

González, R. & Nuñez, T. (2000). *¿Cómo se ven las Mujeres en Televisión?* [How are Women Depicted on TV?]. Sevilla, Spain: Padilla Libros Editores & Libreros Sevilla.

Instituto Nacional de Estadística (INE). (2006a). *España en Cifras. Población* [Spain in Figures. Population]. Retrieved May 8, 2006 from www.ine.es/prodyser/pubweb/espcif/pobl06.pdf.

Instituto Nacional de Estadística (INE). (2006b). *Panorámica de la Industria* [Industry Overview]. Boletín Informativo del Instituto Nacional de Estadística. Retrieved May 8, 2006 from www.ine.es/revistas/cifraine/0106.pdf.

Instituto Nacional de Estadística (INE). (2006c). *Mujeres y Hombres en España 2006* [Women and Men in Spain 2006]. Nota de prensa, 7 de marzo de 2006 www.webempleo.org/Principal/Hombresmujeres06.pdf.

Instituto Nacional de Estadística (INE). (2006d). *Encuesta Sobre Equipamiento y uso de Tecnología de la Información y Comunicación en los Hogares* [Survey of Equipping and Usage of Information and Communication Technology in the Home]. Nota de prensa, 6 de abril de 2006. Retrieved May 8, 2006 from www.ine.es/prensa/np409.pdf.

Len-Rios, M., Rodgers, S., Thorson, E., & Yoon, D. (2005). Representation of women in news and photos: comparing content to perceptions. *Journal of Communication*, 55(1), 152–68.

López, P. (2005). *Representación de Género en los Informativos de Radio y Televisión. Segundo Informe* [Gender Representation in Radio and TV News Programmes. Second report]. Madrid: Instituto de la Mujer; RTVE. Retrieved July 18, 2006 from www.rtve.es/oficial/iortv/SegundoInforme.pdf.

McCombs, M. (2005). A Look at Agenda-setting: Past, present and future. *Journalism Studies*, 6(4), 543–57.

Mujeres y Hombres en España 2006 [Women and Men in Spain 2006]. (2006). Madrid: Instituto Nacional de Estadística (INE) & Instituto de la Mujer [INE report for the Institute of Women's Affairs]. Retrieved March 8, 2006 from www.ine.es/prodyser/pubweb/myh/myh_emp.pdf.

Rodríguez, M. (2005, January 10). Hay que renovar el patio de los personajes del corazón [The need for the renovation of gossip-show personalities]. *La Voz de Galicia* (Interview with Ana Rosa). Retrieved July 18, 2006 from www.lavozdegalicia.es/entrevistas/noticia.jsp?CAT=130&TEXTO=3355381.

Rodríguez, R. & García, A. (2006, September). *La Mujer Política en los Medios de Comunicación: Representación y percepción. Estudio de Percepción de los Universitarios* [Female Politicians in the Media: Representation and perception. A Study of the Perception of University Students]. Paper presented at the annual XII Meeting of Latin American Studies, Santander (UIMP), Spain.

Rodríguez, R. (2003). Características socio-demográficas y laborales de los periodistas Españoles e índice de satisfacción profesional [The socio-demographic and employment characteristics of Spanish journalists and the level of professional satisfaction]. *ÁMBITOS*, 2, 487–504. Retrieved July 18, 2006 from http://alojamientos.us.es/grehcco/ambitos09-10/rodriguez.pdf.

Sánchez, Aranda, J., Berganza, R., & García, M.R. (2003). *Mujer Publicada Mujer Maltratada* [A Woman on the News is a Woman who has been Abused]. Pamplona, Spain: Gobierno de Navarra. Departamento de Bienestar Social, Deporte y Juventud.

Sofres. (2006, April). *Boletín Mensual de TNS Audiencia de Medios* [TNS Monthly Bulletin of Media Audience Figures]. Retrieved July 18, 2006 from www.sofresam.com/bm200604.pdf.

Turkey

Algun, A. Kadin sayfalari da aslinda bir tur cimsiyet ayrimciligi [Women's pages are also gender discrimination] (2003). IletimONline. Retrieved July 5, 2006 from www.istanbul.edu.tr/iletim/81/haberler/m2.htm.

Almanac 2005. (2005). *Turkish News Agency for the Directorate General of Press and Information of the Prime Ministry.* Retrieved July 17, 2006 from www.byegm.gov.tr/YAYINLARIMIZ/kitaplar/turkey2005/index.htm.

Almanac. (2005a). Retrieved July 17, 2006 from www.byegm.gov.tr/YAYINLARIMIZ/kitaplar/turkey2005/content/english/020-021.htm.

Almanac. (2005b). Retrieved July 17, 2006 from www.byegm.gov.tr/YAYINLARIMIZ/kitaplar/turkey2005/content/english/154-155.htm.

Almanac. (2005c). Retrieved July 17, 2006 from www.byegm.gov.tr/YAYINLARIMIZ/kitaplar/turkey2005/content/english/116-117.htm.

Almanac. (2005d). Retrieved July 17, 2006 from www.byegm.gov.tr/YAYINLARIMIZ/kitaplar/turkey2005/content/english/022-023.htm.

Almanac. (2005e). Retrieved July 17, 2006 from www.byegm.gov.tr/YAYINLARIMIZ/kitaplar/turkey2005/content/english/418-419.htm.

Almanac. (2005f). Retrieved July 17, 2006 from www.byegm.gov.tr/YAYINLARIMIZ/kitaplar/turkey2005/content/english/414-415.htm.

Almanac. (2005g). Retrieved July 17, 2006 from www.byegm.gov.tr/YAYINLARIMIZ/kitaplar/turkey2005/content/english/416-417.htm.

Almanac. (2005h). Retrieved July 17, 2006 from www.byegm.gov.tr/YAYINLARIMIZ/kitaplar/turkey2005/content/english/436-437.htm.

Almanac. (2005i). Retrieved July 17, 2006 from www.byegm.gov.tr/YAYINLARIMIZ/kitaplar/turkey2005/content/english/432-433.htm.

Altındal, A. (1980). *Turkiye'de Kadin* [Women in Turkey]. Istanbul: Havas.

Asker, A. (1991). *Kadın Gazeteciler* [Women Journalists]. Istanbul: Gazeteciler Cemiyeti Publications Thesis Series: 5.

Carat Turkiye. (n.d.). *Media Scene Report*, April 2006.

Comak, N.A. & Ocel, N. (2000). Turk basininda kadin [Women in the Turkish press]. Paper presented at the International Symposium, on a century of women in Turkey, Bogazici University.

Flying Broom. (2006a). *Medyada Kadın: Ticari meta* [Women at Media: Image for consumption]. Retrieved July 18, 2006 from www.ucansupurge.org/index.php?option=com_content&task=view&id=1641&I.

Flying Broom. (2006b). *Kadinlar Nasil Haber Oluyor?* [How Women are News in the Media?]. Retrieved July 1, 2006 from www.ucansupurge.org/index.php?option=com_content&task=view&id=3118&Itemid=54.

Gezgin, S. (2005). Almanya'da ve Türkiye'de gazetecilik eğitimi [Journalism education in Germany and Turkey], pp. 65–78. *Rekabet ve Medya* [Competition and Media] 19. German-Turkish Journalists Seminar, May 2005, Ankara: Konrad-Adenauer-Stiftung Publication.

IletimONline. (2003). Retrieved July 5, 2006 from www.istanbul.edu.tr/iletim/81/haberler/m2.htm.

Inceoglu, Y.G. & Korkmaz Y. (2002). *Gazetecilik 24 Saat* [Journalism 24 Hours]. Istanbul: Bas-Haş.

KAGIDER. (2006). *Statistics of the Social and Economic Situation of Women in Turkey*. Retrieved June 1, 2006 from www.kagider.org/tr_/content.asp?CID=[6500D520-71E5-4D84-8E85-F418C0BBF3CD]&pCID=&CCID=[6500D520-71E5-4D84-8E85-F418C0BBF3CD].

KSSGM. (2006). *Turkish Republic Prime Ministry, Directorate General on the Status and the Problems of Women*. Retrieved June 1, 2006 from www.kssgm.gov.tr/.

Maireder, A. (2006, January). A journalistic spring freedom of expression: Turkey's long road towards Europe, Country focus, *deScripto*, 18–25.

MediaScape Reports Turkiye'de Medya 2000 [MediaScape Reports Media in Turkey, Turkey 2000]. (n.d.). Centre for Communication Research, Ankara University. Retrieved June 10, 2006, from http://ilaum.ankara.edu.tr/yazi.php?yad=2362.

Ortayli, I. (2006). *Osmanliyi Yeniden Kesfetmek* [Rediscovering Ottomans]. Istanbul: Timas.

Ozgen, M. (2000). *Turkiye'de Basinin Gelisimi ve Sorunu* [The Development of Media and its Problems in Turkey]. Istanbul: Istanbul University, Faculty of Communication Publication.

RTUK portal. (2006). *Turkish Broadcasting Sector in Brief*. Retrieved July, 1, 2006 from www.rtuk.org.tr/sayfalar/DosyaIndir.aspx?icerik_id=a14d68fe-404d-434b-843a-7e035b8dcc27RTUK.

Saglam, T. (2006). Gazeteciler: bal gibi biliyoruz ki hakikatlem yazmiyor [Journalists we know for sure that they do not write the truth]. Retrieved July 24, 2006 from www.ntvmsnbc.com/news/380507.asp

"Say Yes." Spring 2006: The quarterly newspaper of UNICEF Turkey. Retrieved July 18, 2006 from www.unicef.org/turkey/sy17/is17.html.

Terkan, B. (2003). Yazılı basında kadın imajı [Woman image in printed press]. *Selcuk Iletisim*, 2(4), 149–67.

Tokgoz, O. (2000). *Temel Gazetecilik* [Fundamentals of Journalism] (4th edition). Istanbul: Imge.

Topuz, H. (2003). *Turk Basın Trihi* [Turkish Press History]. Istanbul: Remzi Kitabevi.

Tore cinayetlerinin kurbanlari daha cok erkekler [The victims of moral traditions are men]. (2006). *Hurriyet*. Retrieved August 9, 2006 from www.hurriyet.com.tr/gundem/4829950. asp?sd=2.

Turkcell. (September–November 2005). *Turkiye Profili 2005* [Turkey Profile 2005]. TNS PIAR Turkey (2006). Turkish News Agency for the Directorate General of Press and Information of the Prime Ministry. Ankara: Nurol Publishing.

Turkish General Staff. (n.d.). *History*. Retrieved August 9, 2006 from www.tsk.mil.tr/eng/genel_konular/tarihce.htm.

Turkiye kadm profili 2 Efes Pilsen (2005). [Turkey women profile 2]. Istanbul: Talat Matbaacilik ve Deri Mamulleri Tic A.S.

TURKSAT. (2006). Republic of Turkey, Prime Ministry Turkish Statistical Institute. Population and development indicators. Retrieved on July 1, 2006 from www.devletim.com/git.asp?link=826.

UNDP. (2006). *Working to Increase the Number of Turkish Women in the Parliament*. Retrieved July 1, 2006 from www.undp.org.tr/Gozlem2.aspx?WebSayfaNo=90.

Yapar, A. (1999). Kadın dergilerinde kadın imgesinin kullanımı [Image of women in woman's magazines]. *Iletisim Fakultesi Dergisi 9*, 75–9.

Egypt and the Middle East

Abdel Rahman, H. (1998). Uses and gratifications of satellite TV in Egypt. *Transnational Broadcasting Studies, 1*. Retrieved March 8, 2006 from www.tbsjournal.com/Archives/Fall98/Documents1/Uses/uses.html.

Al-Arian, L. (2004, December). Georgetown conference scrutinizes Arab media. *Washington Report on Middle East Affairs, 23*, 56–7.

Al-bab. (2006, January 10). *Arab media: television*. Retrieved February 22, 2006 from www.al-bab.com/media/television.htm.

Al-Zubaidi, L. (2004). *Walking a Tightrope: News media & freedom of expression in the Arab Middle East*. Washington, DC: Heinrich Böll Foundation.

Amin, H. (2001). Arab women and satellite broadcasting. *Transnational Broadcasting Studies, 6*. Retrieved March 7, 2006 from www.tbsjournal.com/Archives/Spring01/Amin.html.

Amin, H. (2002). Freedom as a value in Arab media: perceptions and attitudes among journalists. *Political Communication, 19(2)*, 125–35.

The Associated Press. (2001, January 18). Middle Eastern residents tuning to outside news sources. Freedomforum.org. Retrieved February 22, 2006 from www.freedomforum.org/templates/document.asp?documentID=12894.

BBC News. (2005, December 22). *Country Profile: Egypt*. Retrieved March 7, 2006 from http://news.bbc.co.uk/1/hi/world/middle_east/country_profiles/737642.stm.

Essoulami, S. (2000). *Foreword*. In report by Naomi Sakr, *Women's Rights and the Arab Media*. A report by Centre for Media Freedom—Middle East and North Africa. CMF MENA.

Groskop, V. (2005, May 30). The faces of Al-Jazeera. *Newstatesman*, 14–15.

Guenena, N. & Wassef, N. (1999). *Unfulfilled Promises: Women's rights in Egypt*. New York: Population Council.

Hanley, D.C. (2002, April). Arab women journalists seek ways to improve their image at home and in the West. *Washington Report on Middle East Affairs*. Retrieved February 25, 2006 from www.wrmea.com/archives/april2002/0204052.html.

How the Arabs compare: Arab human development report 2002 (2002). *Middle East Quarterly, 9*. Retrieved July 17, 2007 from www.meforum.org/article/513.

IFJ condemns Israeli, Palestinian attacks on news media. (2000, December 14). Freedomforum.org. Retrieved July 17, 2006 from www.freedomforum.org/templates/document.asp?documentID= 3171.

IPJ promotes women journalists in armed conflicts forum. (2004, March). Retrieved July 17, 2006 from http://ipj.lau.edu.lb/outreach/2004/03_womenj/forum.php.

International Press Institute. (2006, February 2). Egypt: 2004 World Press Freedom Review. Retrieved July 17, 2006 from www.freemedia.at/cms/ipi/freedom_detail.html?country=/KW0001/ KW0004/KW0091/&year=2004.

MEMRI. (1999, December 10). Women's rights in the Arab world. Retrieved March 15, 2006 from http://memri.org/bin/articles.cgi?Page=archives&Area=sd&ID=SP6399.

New-media technology shattering Mideast barriers. (1998, October 5). Freedomforum.org. Retrieved February 22, 2006 from www.freedomforum.org/templates/document.asp?document ID=11153.

PC penetration vs. Internet user penetration in GCC countries. (2002, October). *Madar Research Journal: Knowledge, economy and research on the Middle East, 1/0*, p. 10.

Palestinians shut down Arab news network office Freedom Forum. (2001, March 21). Freedom forum.org. Retrieved February 22, 2006 from www.freedomforum.org/templates/document. asp?documentID=13490.

Raad, N. (2004, July 1). Is Middle East media turning blind eye to women's plight? *Daily Star.* Retrieved February 22, 2006 from http://dailystar.com.lb/article.asp?edition_id=10&categ_ id=2&article_id=58.

Reporters without borders. (2003). *Egypt-2003 Annual Report.* Retrieved February 22, 2006 from www.rsf.org/country-43.php3?id_mot=152&Valider=OK.

Reporters without borders. (2006, January 5). *Call for New Investigation of Attacks on Women Journalists in Cairo.* Retrieved February 22, 2006 from www.rsf.org/article.php3?id_article =14117.

Sakr, N. (2000). *Women's Rights and the Arab Media.* A report by Centre for Media Freedom— Middle East and North Africa, CMF MENA.

Sakr, N. (2002). Seen and starting to be heard: Women and the Arab media in a decade of change. *Social Research*, 69(3), 821–50.

Tabor, K. (2002, November). The press in Iraq. *Frontline World.* Retrieved May 1, 2006 from www.pbs.org/frontlineworld/stories/iraq/press.html.

Two Lebanese journalists face possible death penalty for dealing with Israel (2001, August 25). Freedomforum.org. Retrieved February 22, 2006 from www.freedomforum.org/templates/ document.asp?documentID=14697.

UNDP. (2003, October 20). *Mass Media, Press Freedom and Publishing in the Arab World: Arab intellectuals speak out.* Arab Human Development Report 2003. United Nations Publication.

UNESCO. (n.d.). UNESCO—Italy project: training of mediterranean women journalists. Retrieved March 7, 2006 from www.unesco.org/webworld/com_media/society_women_medproject.html.

Washingtonpost.com. (2005, October 12). Full text of Iraqi constitution: Draft document, to be presented to voters Saturday. Retrieved May 1, 2006 from www.washingtonpost.com/ w-dyn/content/article/2005/10/12/AR2005101201450.html.

WEF report points to the great gender divide. (2005, May 18). *Indian Express.* Retrieved February 22, 2006 from www.indianexpress.com/print.php?content_id=70581.

Wheeler, D. (2004). Blessings and curse: Women and the Internet revolution in the Arab world. In Naomi Sakr (Ed.) *Women and Media in the Middle East: Power through self-expression*, pp. 138–61. New York and London: I.B.Tauris.

Women's Learning Partnership: Technology facts and figures. (2006, April 15). Retrieved July 17, 2006 from www.learning partnership.org.

World Audit Press Freedom. (2001). Retrieved February 22, 2006 from www.worldaudit.org/ press.htm.

Nigeria

Amadiume, I. (1987). *Male Daughters, Female Husbands: Gender and Sex in an African Society.* London: Zed Books.

Anyanwu, C. (2001). In Nigerian newspapers, women are seen, not heard. *Nieman Reports,* 55(4), 68–71.

The CIA World Factbook. (n.d.). CIA. Retrieved February 17, 2006 from www.cia. gov/cia/publications/factbook/geos/ni.html.

Falola, T. (2001). *Culture and Customs of Nigeria.* Westport: Greenwood Press.

Faris, S. (October 2001). Women sweep appointments for key Nigerian court. *Women's eNews.* Retrieved March 2, 2006 from www.womensenews.org/article.cfm?aid=677.

I keep my ego in my handbag. (2005, August 1). Guardian Unlimited. Retrieved March 3, 2006 from www.guardian.co.uk/g2/story/0,3604,1540043,00.html.

National Broadcasting Commission. (n.d.). *Broadcasting Stations in Nigeria.* Retrieved February 28, 2006 from www.nbc-nig.org/NBC1/LICENSED%20STATIONS.htm.

Nigeria Direct a: The Official Information Gateway of the Federal Republic of Nigeria. (n.d.). Welcome to Nigeria. Retrieved February 17, 2006 from www.nigeria.gov.ng/.

Nigeria Direct b: The Official Information Gateway of the Federal Republic of Nigeria.(n.d.). Nigerian Ministries. Retrieved February 17, 2006 from www.nigeria.gov.ng/Ministries.aspx.

Nigerian guerillas release last three oil hostages. (n.d.). The All I Need.com. Retrieved March 2, 2006 from www.theallineed.com/news/0603/27134954.htm.

Nigerian Labour Congress. (December 6, 2004). Appreciation and a call for continued commitment. Retrieved February 28, 2006 from www.nlcng.org/december2004/appreciationadvert.htm.

Nine abducted in Niger Delta. (2006, February 18). CNN.com. Retrieved February 28, 2006 from www.cnn.com/2006/WORLD/africa/02/18/nigeria.abductions/.

Okome, M.O. (2002). Domestic, regional, and international protection of Nigerian women against discrimination: Constraints and possibilities. (Electronic Version). *African Studies Quarterly,* 6, 3. Retrieved March 2, 2006 from www.africa.ufl.edu/asq/v6/v6i3a3.htm.

Olukoyun, A. (December 2004). Media accountability and democracy in Nigeria, 1999–2003. *African Studies Review,* 69–90.

Peace Women: Women's international league for peace and freedom. (2005, April 12). On discrimination against women. Retrieved February 17, 2006 from www.peacewomen.org/news/ Nigeria/April05/Discrimination.html.

United Nations. (n.d.). Millennium indicators. Retrieved February 23, 2006 from http://unstats. un.org/unsd/mi/mi_results.asp?crID=566&fID=r5.

Chapter 12

Women and the News

India and Asia

Smeeta Mishra, Xin Chen, Yi-Ning Katherine Chen, and Kyung-Hee Kim[1]

India

India is a country full of paradoxes. A woman served as prime minister for 16 years when Indira Gandhi twice held the top government post[2]; however, the latest available data from the National Crime Records Bureau in India showed that 6,208 Indian women were killed in 2003 for not bringing adequate dowry, or gifts from in-laws, to their husband's homes. These tragic cases, called "dowry deaths" and/or "bride-burning" in India, involve women whose husbands or in-laws "engineer an accident" by bursting a kitchen stove or setting the woman on fire after dousing her with kerosene because they feel the marriage dowry was not adequate (UNICEF, 2000).

Another paradox: according to the World Association of Newspapers (2005), India has the world's second largest market for newspapers with 78.8 million copies sold daily, and newspaper sales in India have increased by 14 percent over the past five years. Yet, India is home to a third of the world's illiterates (Times News Network, 2004). Another paradox: Indian firms have earned billions from business with Fortune 500 companies by slashing the cost of performing basic information technology work through relying on a huge pool of English-speaking Indians (Newman, 2006); however, Internet users in India comprise less than 5 percent of the population (eTForecasts, 2006). The list of contradictions goes on.

India won its independence from the British on August 15, 1947, even as the subcontinent was partitioned into two sovereign states, India and Pakistan. The partition involved large-scale violence, and millions of families were uprooted from their homes: Hindus and Sikhs moved to India and Muslims to Pakistan. Today, Hindus comprise an overwhelming majority of the Indian population. The specific religious composition of the population includes Hindus (82 percent); Muslims (12 percent); Christians (2 percent); Sikhs (2 percent); and other groups such as Buddhists, Jains, and Parsis (3 percent) ("Background note," 2005).

India is located in southern Asia, between Burma on the east and Pakistan on the west. The country also shares boundaries with Bangladesh, Bhutan, China, and Nepal. The primary water bodies bordering India are the Arabian Sea and the Bay of Bengal. Though India is geographically located in South Asia, Indians have their own identity and often think India—not Asia first. Indian clothing and food comprise an important part of the Indian cultural ethos. Monica Bhide (2004), a writer on Indian food, remarked in an article published in *The Washington Post* that the country has at least 35 recognized cuisines, which are influenced by religion, geography, history, and locally available ingredients.

Arranged marriages also lend a unique flavor to Indian society. Arranged marriages typically involve parents and relatives "arranging" the marriages of young women and men after ensuring that the social, economic, and educational background of the prospective couple matches. Sometimes, religious background, caste identities, food habits (vegetarian or not), and astrological predictions are also taken into account while arranging the alliance. Arranged marriages are based on the belief that families know what is best for the individual and that their continuous support for the couple is crucial to the survival of the marriage. Many proponents of arranged marriage believe romantic love will follow marital union. The arranged marriage system is adapting to social and technological changes: the Internet is fast replacing traditional matchmakers and couples are now entering into long courtship periods before marriage. Arranged marriages remain popular not only in India but can be found in Indian communities abroad.

Also uniquely Indian is Bollywood, a term used to refer to the popular Mumbai-based Hindi film industry in India. Based on 2002 estimates, Bollywood produces 1,013 films annually in contrast with Hollywood's 739 ("Bollywood," n.d.). Bollywood films are popular not just among Indians residing in the country but with the India Diaspora as well; they often represent "an intense, nostalgic connection to home, no matter how many times removed" (Kalita, 2005).

Although India occupies only 2 percent of the world's land area (about one-third the size of the United States), over 15 percent of the world's population resides in India ("Background note" 2005). While the country's astounding population of 1.1 billion people may shroud ground realities in some sectors, Indian society is beset with many divisions, including gender divides, economic divides, literacy divides, and digital divides. Divisions based on the caste system remain strong, especially in rural areas. The caste system divides Hindus into four broad categories: Brahmins (priests); Kshatriyas (warriors and rulers); Vaishyas (traders) and Sudras (the lowest caste) (Thekaekara, 2005). Below the lowest caste are people labeled as "untouchables" who were considered so "impure and polluting that they were not even included in the system" (Thekaekara, 2005, p. 10). Today, there even exist political parties based on caste identities. The economic divide is also acute in India with over 300 million living below the officially defined poverty line (Roy, 2000). Several of these divisions run along the rural–urban divide. Most Indians live in India's 550,000 villages; only 28 percent of the Indian people live in its 200 towns and cities ("Background note," 2005).

Delhi, the national capital is the second largest city in India, and Mumbai, once known as Bombay, is India's most populous city with a population of 12,883,645 ("List of," n.d.). In 1995, the Indian cabinet officially changed the name Bombay back to the original name Mumbai (Reuter & Montagnon, 1995). The word "Mumbai" draws upon the name of a Hindu goddess, Mumbadevi. "Aai" in the local language of Marathi means mother ("Bombay," n.d.). Even after the British introduced the anglicized form "Bombay," the city was referred to as Mumbai, Mambai or Bombai in several Indian languages. Changing the name of the city was part of a drive to rid Indian cities of colonial names.

While Hindi is the national language of India, English is widely spoken, especially among the upwardly mobile in cities and towns. The many centuries of British presence in India have contributed to the widespread use of the English language in the country. The British also left behind an "enormously bureaucratic and cumbersome" administrative system that is badly in need of reform (Tully, 1998).

India's economy is the twelfth largest in the world and the third largest in Asia, and India has a total gross domestic product of around $691 billion ("Background note,"

2005). About three-fifths of the Indian workforce is engaged in agriculture (The CIA World Factbook, 2006). In the decade since 1994, the Indian economy has witnessed an average growth rate of more than 7 percent (The CIA World Factbook, 2006). The country achieved 7.6 percent GDP growth in 2005. India is capitalizing on its English-language speaking populace to become a major exporter of software services and software workers (The CIA World Factbook, 2006). The United States is both India's largest trading partner and its largest investment partner, and India continues market-oriented reforms, a change which started as early as 1991 ("Background note," 2005).

The Indian constitution, which went into effect January 26, 1950, declares the country a "sovereign, socialist, secular, democratic republic" ("Background note," 2005). It provides for freedom of speech and expression. Freedom House, an organization headquartered in the United States that provides numerical ratings for 194 countries, rated India's press as "partly free." Its report also stated the following about India's press climate:

> Although journalists face a number of threats and constraints, Indian media continue to provide diverse and robust coverage and are the freest in South Asia ... Most print media, particularly the national and English-language press, are privately owned, provide diverse coverage, and frequently criticize the government. The broadcast media are predominantly in private hands, but the state retains a monopoly on AM radio broadcasting, and private FM radio stations are not allowed to broadcast news content ... Internet access is unrestricted.
>
> (Karlekar, 2005, pp. 100–1)

The report further noted that *Doordarshan*, the state-controlled television station, has been accused of manipulating news to favor the government. It remains to be seen whether the Right to Information Act, which, when it went into effect in October 2005, made information an important right of every citizen, will render the government more transparent and increase the watchdog powers of the press. According to this law, every citizen has the right to "inspect works, documents, records" of government organizations and agencies funded by the government ("Right to Information Act," 2005). The law also provides for the government's designation of a public information officer (PIO) with government organizations. The PIO's responsibility is to ensure that information requested by the applicant is provided within 30 days. When the issue concerns the "life or liberty of a person" the PIO has to ensure that the information is provided within 48 hours (ibid.).

Media reach in India. On March 31, 2005, there were 60,413 registered newspapers on record with the Registrar of Newspapers for India (2006). A majority of these newspapers are published weekly, bi-weekly, tri-weekly, monthly, or fortnightly; 1,834 are published daily. According to the registrar's office, the daily newspapers and periodicals are registered in English as well as in 22 "main languages" that are listed in the Indian constitution. Although newspapers are also registered in 100 other languages including dialects and a few foreign languages, most newspapers are published in Hindi, followed by English.

The National Readership Survey Council—a body of media providers and advertisers who assign the survey to prominent research agencies—commissions the National Readership Survey. According to the 2005 National Readership Survey, which surveyed the news reading habits and behaviors of 261,212 Indian households (Warsia, 2005), the readership base for print media, comprising both newspapers and periodicals, was 200 million, up from 179 million in 2002 ("Print media," 2005). The readership base for daily newspapers was 176 million in 2005, up from 155 million in 2002 (Ibid., 2005). Of the 200 million persons consuming print media, as many as 98 million live in rural India. This high rural readership population aids in bridging the rural–urban divide in print media readership.

Any data on the relationship in India between media use and gender is scarce, and the little data that exist is clearly meant for advertisers (Joseph, 2002, p. 12). Joseph, while addressing a United Nations conference, gave the example of the 2002 National Readership Survey, which reported that newspapers had expanded their reach to the "urban housewife" categorized as the "fast-moving-consumer-goods decision-maker,"— a group that comprised approximately 25 million out of a total of 179 million daily readers of the newspaper (2002). Overall, it is difficult to obtain information specifically about women readers. However, the 2001 census' determination that India's female literacy rate stands at 54 percent may yield some important insights into the news reading habits of women in India (National Literacy Mission, 2001).

India has the second largest television market in the world after the United States (Sengupta, 2005). According to the National Readership Survey, television reaches 108 million homes, a figure that implies that television penetration has crossed the 50 percent mark for the first time in Indian homes (Warsia, 2005). Additionally, the report noted that cable and satellite have been adopted by 56 percent of all homes that have television (Warsia, 2005). Television stations have increased from approximately 50 in 1996 to close to 300 in 2005 (Sengupta, 2005). The state-controlled television station, *Doordarshan*, monopolized the broadcast media till the end of the 1980s, but in the early 1990s, private television stations entered the market. The mid-1990s witnessed the beginning of the private news broadcast (Kumar, 2005). Many of the private news broadcasts were in English initially. The first Hindi news channel, *Aaj Tak*, started in 2001 and according to Kumar (2005):

> this was an experiment which opened the floodgates for the proliferation of channels in less than three years. Rapid developments like Gujarat earthquake— Pakistani President Pervez Musharraf's visit to India—terrorist attack on twin tower of World Trade Centre—Gujarat riots—propelled the average viewership of news from a mere 12 minutes in 24 hours to a whopping 31 minutes.

In 2003, a number of new news channels and regional networks were launched (Kumar, 2005). Television's penetration has had a more successful rate of diffusion than radio. As of 2005, the reach of radio in India had stagnated at 23 percent of the population ("Print media," 2005). Among the 183 million who listen to radio, 43 percent listen to FM stations ("Print media," 2005).

Although different surveys and organizations have come up with varying figures on the number of Internet users in India, it is a consensus of opinion that Internet penetration stands at below 5 percent of the population. While eTForecasts (2006), a worldwide market research and consulting company for computer and Internet industries, pegged the number of Internet users in India at 50.6 million at the end of 2005, the Internet & Mobile Association of India (2006) estimated that approximately 38.5 million of the Indian population were Internet users. The 2005 National Readership Survey of India estimated the number of Internet users aged 12 years and above at 11 million, with over 70 percent of these users residents in urban India ("Print media," 2005).

Some statistics on gender and Internet use also exist from the Internet & Mobile Association of India (IAMAI), which is a trade association representing the online and advertising industry in India. According to the IAMAI report, the number of women online users increased from 28 percent of the total number of Internet users in 2004–5 to 32 percent (12.32 million) in 2005–6 (p. 3).

In a December 2005 online survey of 6,365 respondents, IAMAI (2006) compared the online activities of male and female online users. IAMAI found that 96 percent of women online users who use the Internet for e-mail use it for personal use (non-work related purposes) while 98 percent of men use it for the same reason (p. 12); almost an equal percentage of men (52 percent) and women (51 percent) look up news online for personal use (p. 14); slightly more women (15 percent) than men (12 percent) use the Internet for "matrimonial-related" purposes (p. 15); and more women (55 percent) than men (50 percent) use the Internet for job searches (p. 15).

This report also included the demographic profile of female online users, and the generational differences in Internet adoption. While almost 40 percent of female users were in the 26–35 age group, 33 percent were in the 18–25 age group, slightly over 20 percent in the 36–45 age group, 6 percent in the 46–60 age group, and only 1 percent in the 61 and over age group (IAMAI, 2006, p. 6). Gender divides also exist in the locations for Internet access. Over 60 percent of men accessed the Internet from work in comparison to 54 percent of women; in contrast, 57 percent of women were likely to access the Internet from home in comparison to just over 50 percent of men (ibid., p. 9). Men are also more prone to access the Internet in alternative locations. While 42 percent of men accessed the Internet from cybercafés, only 31 percent of women did the same (ibid.).

Cybercafés are an increasingly popular place to access the Internet in India, a trend reflected in the findings of the 2005 National Readership Survey. This survey found that as many as 32 percent of Internet users accessed the Net at cybercafés ("Print media," 2005). Cybercafés are popular in India because they lower the "multiple financial barriers" to accessing Internet technology (Haseloff, 2005). The high costs of computer hardware and Internet connections drive people to the public kiosks where one can pay as little as 10 rupees (approximately 20 cents) to access the Internet for an hour. Cybercafés are for-profit enterprises and are different from the many government and non-profit sector projects aimed at spreading Internet use in rural Indian areas. A typical cybercafé will be located near a residential area in towns and cities, though it is not unusual for it to be located near shopping centers.

Women in journalism.   Ammu Joseph, a journalist who specializes in the coverage of gender issues, reported at a United Nations conference in Lebanon in 2002 that despite the lack of current, comprehensive, and credible data on the exact number of journalists in India or their gender make up, there is little doubt that the number of Indian women in journalism has reached an unprecedented high. She based her conclusion on the number of female bylines in newspapers and magazines and the visibility of women anchors, editors, and correspondents on television. According to Joseph, women in India have found it "relatively easier" to break into the field of broadcast journalism than into newspapers (p. 8). The introduction of satellite television in India in the early 1990s boosted the hiring of women as reporters, anchors, editors, and hosts of current affairs programs (Joseph, 2002). Thus, Joseph argued that Indian women journalists have "managed to storm the citadel of hard news coverage" (2002, p. 3).

However, she qualified her conclusions by highlighting the significant differences in the situation of women journalists across the country, as well as between the English and Indian-languages press (Joseph, 2002). While the growing visibility of women in the "metropolitan media workforce" may create the impression that women journalists face limited barriers in India, many gender-related problems remain in the areas of recruiting women journalists and providing avenues for their professional growth, particularly in the Indian-languages press which has a larger readership base than the English-language press (ibid.). Further, social attitudes in Indian society that do not encourage women working long, late, and irregular hours also pose a hurdle for female journalists. Joseph drew attention to the fact that several women journalists have cited "attitudes and behavior of male colleagues" as a major impediment to their progress (ibid., p. 5). Many women journalists work in hostile environments. Few newsrooms have explicit policies on sexual harassment. Even when a policy on sexual harassment exists on paper, women journalists are hardly ever made aware of available resources that they could use to deal with such eventualities. In such a climate, the unwritten principle seems to be for women journalists to quietly endure any discomfort or negative attitudes in the workplace.

Coverage of women in media.   Parekh (2001), a journalist who has worked for many years with two of India's leading national dailies and the director of an international news organization, Women's Feature Service, pointed out that the media are prone to cover only "sensational 'bad news' stories" about women in conflict and violent situations (p. 91). These stories about violence against women are usually reported in an event-based and routine manner, and the police are often the only source of information. Academic studies that examine news coverage of women in the Indian press corroborate Parekh's observations. Bathla (1998) content analyzed 592 news stories on women published during four selected years in the period between 1981 and 1993 in a major Indian national daily and found that the majority of the news stories focused on crime and violence. Bathla emphasized that these events were reported as "simple occurrences" as opposed to issues, and the information for these stories was usually gathered from police bulletins, police officers, hospitals, and courts. Additionally, several of these reports were in the form of news briefs. Parekh (2001) argued that the news media pay scant critical and in-depth attention to the issues that impact women directly through their routine dismissal of coverage on women's issues to a few paragraphs on an inside newspaper page.

In referring to reports on dowry deaths, Narasimhan (2001) pointed out that even news about gruesome issues such as dowry deaths appeared as a tiny two-column-inch item in the newspaper, an oversight that is usually met with little "media outcry" or "public outrage" (p. 89). Joseph (2001) noted that crimes such as rapes and dowry deaths get some media attention, albeit brief and superficial, because they fit the dominant perspective of what constitutes news while fulfilling the media's tendency to focus on events rather than processes. It is common for a particularly sensational case of dowry death to be followed by some prominent reporting on the matter. Generally, the media returns to the habit of treating such events as routine by relegating these stories to inside pages of the newspaper (Joseph, 2001).

The increasing popularity of celebrity and lifestyle journalism has adversely affected meaningful journalism. Thus mainstream women's magazines still "stick to fashions, fancy cuisine, and fitness regimens (to fight obesity) rather than focus attention on hunger and destitution among the teeming millions" (Narasimhan, 2001, p. 90). This trend is not limited to magazines alone. Deb (2005) pointed out a trend in the publishing of large pictures of models and movie stars, something he calls the "pin-up" phenomenon, in many of the serious English-language dailies. A recent innovation in these newspapers has been the "page three," which provides daily coverage of socialite parties, and young female journalists are often assigned to cover these "page three" events (Deb, 2005). However, the increasing popularity of the "pin-up" and "page-three" phenomena in newspapers does not imply that serious journalism on gender issues is dead. Several columnists broach relevant women's issues in the newspapers, and occasionally stories of great gender relevance receive prominent coverage.

But much work remains to be done so that the issues of rural, poor, uneducated women can be made visible in the mainstream. An important first step may be collecting non-consumer data about women readers. Better communication between non-profit organizations and grassroots workers, as well as between non-profit organizations and the media, will help too. In stories on dowry deaths and other cases of violence against women, reporters need to talk to sources beyond the police so they can file more than just news briefs. If journalists make a conscious attempt to resist co-option into the market-driven media system and the patriarchal social structure, they can tell better stories.

China

Lan Yang, broadcaster, founder of *China Sun TV* and Sun Media Investment Group, (HK) and president of Sun Culture Foundation, achieved great success in China's burgeoning media market. In 2001, she was ranked as the thirty-eighth richest person by the Chinese version of *Forbes* magazine (Sina, 2006). In addition to being a successful businesswoman, she is also a famous TV host, a philanthropist, and one of China's Image Embassies for the 2008 Beijing Olympic Games. Born in 1968 to a common Chinese family, Yang's story is like a dream come true for a generation of aspiring young Chinese women that grew up after the "great culture revolution." Yang graduated from Beijing University of Foreign Languages in 1990. Upon graduation, she was selected as the co-host of a brand new show called Zhengda Entertainment in China Central TV (CCTV). In the early 1990s, when the pure entertainment show was rare in China, "Zhengda Entertainment" became a great hit, attracting an audience of millions. Almost over night, Yang became a national celebrity. In 1994, Yang quit the show when it was still at its peak to study at Columbia University in the US, where two years later, she earned a master's degree in International Affairs.

Back in China, she published her first autobiography, produced a documentary program that introduced America from her perspective, and hosted a talk show named after her on *Phoenix Satellite TV* (PHTV). PHTV is based in Hong Kong but is vastly popular among mainland audiences. In 2000, Yang founded *China Sun TV* in Hong Kong, which mainly broadcasts imported programs such as the History Channel and targets the well-educated segment of the mainland audience through satellite. In 2001, Yang sold most of her share of *China Sun TV* to sina.com, China's largest portal, in exchange for Sina's stocks. In the same year, Yang's fame was tarnished by the scandal that her husband and business partner Zheng Wu forged his doctoral degree. In recent years, Yang has focused mainly on managing Sun Media Investment Group, hosting a new talk show named "Women of the World" and publishing her e-magazine *Lan*. In her first autobiography, Yang said it was her dream to become China's Oprah Winfrey (Sina, 2006). Though her popularity may not match Winfrey's, it is undeniable that her story has inspired many young Chinese women to work in the media industry.

Yang's story makes better sense when placed against the background of how Chinese media and Chinese women have evolved over the past 25 years, which is a history of constant conflict, change, and complexity. During that time, the entire country of China had been undergoing dramatic and complicated changes. There are several layers of traditions lingering in China today: Confucianism, Western science and democracy, communism and revolution. These traditions, combined with the theme of constant change, make today's China harder to interpret.

Some facts about China.   China is one of the earliest and most continuous centers of civilization. Yet since the last half of the nineteenth century, the invasion and impact of the Western world has brought the old empire into turmoil. Japan's invasion into China during World War II further shattered the traditional society. A communist government ended the turmoil and established strict control. By the end of the 1970s, the government adopted the reform and open policy. Since then, a market-oriented economy has flourished and China has enjoyed rapid development and economic boom for over 25 years. The country is now considered one of the powerhouses of the world economy.

China is the world's fourth largest country by area, only slightly smaller than the United States. It is a country of diverse geographic attributes, with mountains and high plateaus in the west, and plains, hills, and deltas in the east. Its climate is also diverse, varying from tropical in the south to sub arctic in the north. China is the home of 1.3 billion people comprising the largest population of the world. Although there are 56 ethnic groups in China, Han Chinese account for 92 percent of the total population. China has more men than women, with an overall sex ratio of 1.06 males to females. The major religions are Taoism, Buddhism, Christianity, and Muslim (The CIA World Factbook, 2006). However, religion has never been as critical in China as in other major civilizations, and the Chinese tradition can be described as secular.

Confucianism refers to a social and political value system that has ruled China for over 2,000 years. Its profound impact as a philosophy was given momentum through its institutionalization in both the educational system and the government of China. Confucianism is a philosophy of human nature, and its value system places human relationships at the cornerstone of society through emphasis on four main principles of human conduct: humanism, faithfulness, propriety, and wisdom (Ock Yum, 1988). Though it has not proved easy to surmount the legacy of Confucian philosophy, communism became the only official ideology of China when the Communist Party (CPC) of China came to power in 1949.

Mainland China (excluding Taiwan, Hong Kong, and Macau) consists of 22 provinces, four municipalities and five autonomous regions, the latter enjoying a higher level of independence than the provinces and municipalities. The central government has direct administrative control over all 31 divisions. Although there is a province-level People's congress in each of these divisions, the governor of each division is appointed by the central government as opposed to being elected by the congress. These divisions have much less autonomy when compared to the 50 states in the United States.

The Communist Party of China established the People's Republic of China (PRC) in October 1, 1949, following the CPC's military victory over the Kuomintang party (KMT) in the Chinese Civil War. The new capital is Beijing (Peking). The CPC has ruled China under a one-party system since 1949. Besides CPC, there are other parties in China, namely "democratic parties," which participate in the People's Political Consultative Conference but mostly serve to endorse CPC policies. The CPC is the only party that can possibly be in power under the current political system (Gov.cn, 2006).

There is no substantial political opposition group to the CPC in China and communism has been a strong label associated with China since the establishment of the

Republic. However, this label could be very misleading. In the late 1970s, the CPC began the so-called "reform and open door" policy. Two major facets of this policy were to change the centrally planned economy to a market-oriented economy and to reopen China to the world. With economic development becoming the first task of the Chinese government, ideology became less important. The "reform and open" policy resulted in a six-fold increase in gross domestic product (GDP) since 1978. By 2005, China had the world's fourth largest GDP and there is no sign of economic slow down (Wikipedia, 2006a). The private sector has now overtaken the state-owned sector and the former is considered the driving force of the economy. Along with its astonishing economic achievement, Chinese society is also much more diverse than in Mao's era. However, changes in the political system are subtle. On the one hand, CPC still holds absolute power, and restrictions remain heavy in some areas, noticeably in the media. On the other hand, the government has also carried out various infrastructural reforms by learning from the West. The progress in efficiency is startlingly significant.

Because of the Confucianism tradition, Chinese culture has always emphasized education. In traditional China, education is almost regarded as sacred. The most famous image of Confucius is as a teacher. Chinese parents are highly committed to their children's education. It is common for a family to invest a large portion of their household income in their children's education. Sending their children to a better school is a dream of millions of Chinese parents. As a consequence, the competition in school is fierce even at an early age. The government provides free basic education for nine years; private lessons in music, foreign language, or other recreational activities are popular among families of middle-class status or higher. According to *The CIA World Factbook* (2006), China's literacy rate in 2002 was 91 percent, with 95 percent of men literate in comparison to 87 percent of women.

Media in China: state vs. market.   There are certain taboos in Chinese media, such as the status of Taiwan or the Tiananmen Square protests of 1989. Taiwan is a territory governed by the Republic of China, and it was under the authority of China before the communists took power. Defeated by the Communist Party of China (CPC) in the Chinese Civil War, the ruling Kuomintang party (KMT) retreated to Taiwan and ruled the island until the year 2000 when the pro independent Demographic Progress Party (DPP) rose to power by winning the presidential election. People's Republic of China claims Taiwan as its legitimate territory, while the Republic Of China (ROC) rejects this claim. The tension in the Taiwan Strait, which separates Taiwan from the mainland, may influence the future of China or the entire East Asia (Wikipedia.com, 2006b). The issue of Taiwan is so sensitive that the Chinese government strictly regulates mainland media from covering it.

The 1989 Tiananmen Square protests, also known as the Tiananmen Square massacre or the June 4th incident, is another political taboo in China. In the spring and summer of 1989, there were a series of demonstrations in China, led by college students, intellectuals, and labor activists. The government succeeded in shutting down the protesters after approximately two months of struggle, leaving many civilians dead. The figures for those who died from this massacre differ depending on the source. The People's Republic of China noted that there were 200 to 300 civilian casualities while the Chinese student associations and the Chinese Red Cross believed the number of civilian casualties to be between 2,000 and 3,000 (Wikipedia.com, 2006c).

In China, the government is heavily involved in the media. In 2005, Freedom House, an independent organization that ranks the freedom of the media in 194 countries, ranked China 177th and rated the Chinese press as "not free" (Karlekar, 2005). Their report on China noted that Chinese news media remains tightly controlled by the Central Propaganda Department of the Chinese Communist Party, and that this control is very evident in the preponderance of legal restrictions that the Chinese news media face. In a similar observation about Chinese media, Karlekar (2005) noted the following:

> Media reforms have allowed the commercialization of media operations without privatization of media ownership. All Chinese media are owned by the state, but the majority no longer receive state subsidies and now rely on income from advertisement sales ... To avoid the risk of running afoul of the Propaganda Department, journalists often engage in self-censorship, a practice reinforced by frequent ideological indoctrination campaigns and by a salary scheme that pays journalists after their reports are published or broadcast.

This quotation reveals the two primary dimensions of Chinese reality: strict control from the government/CPC and the push for freedom driven by commercialization.

Within government control, media can still discuss social or policy issues fairly openly but restrictions vary across different news sections. Business news, social news, entertainment news, and sports news enjoy much more freedom than political news. Though the Chinese government initially subsidized all media, since the early 1990s, it has gradually removed the subsidies, pushing the media into the free marketplace. Without active government subsidies, the Chinese media has had to rely on commercial advertising in an effort to cater to their audiences, and after more than ten years of media reform, most of the media operate like corporations. It is common to see newspapers or TV stations consolidate into media groups in an effort to enhance competence. Vibrancy and diversity of media coexist with state control and censorship. Editors try hard to sell sensational content without crossing the line.

Despite the government's control over the press, the Chinese media market is booming. According to the World Association of Newspapers (2005), by the end of 2004, China had both passed Japan as the country with the highest number of publications in the top 100, and increased its newspaper sales and its advertising revenues. In 2005, newspapers published 40 billion copies while magazines published 2.7 billion copies (China Statistic Bureau, 2005).

China has a hierarchy of newspapers that coexist with the market system. At the top of the hierarchy are a wire service, *Xinhua News Agency* and a daily newspaper, *People's Daily*. The two have attained status as separate government ministries and their directors sit on the Communist Party's Central Committee. Below these top media companies are two daily newspapers controlled by the propaganda department, *Guangming Daily* and *China Daily* (China's official English language newspaper), and one controlled by the state council, *Economical Daily*. Although subscription to *People's Daily* is mandatory at every level of CPC's apparatus, making *People's Daily* the largest newspaper with a circulation of 3 million, personal observation suggests the majority of the Chinese population rarely reads the *People's Daily* despite its strong influence (its editorial can single handedly shake the stock markets), high status, and large circulation.

In contrast to *People's Daily* and other high status national newspapers, local dailies such as *Huaxi Metropolitan Daily* and *Chengdu Economical Daily* in Chengdu, *Southern Metropolitan Daily* in Guangzhou, *Dahe Daily* in Zhengzhou, *Xinming Evening News* in Shanghai, and *Beijing Youth News* in Beijing provide greater local news and more controversial content. *Nanfangzhoumo*, a weekly newspaper from Guangzhou that publishes nationally, is considered one of the best newspapers in China. *Nanfangzhoumo*'s boldness is evidenced by its tendency to discuss critical topics, question governments, and cover sensitive social problems. By 2002, the circulation of *Nanfangzhoumo* was 1.3 million (Sohu, 2005).

By the year 2005, approximately 95 percent of the Chinese population had radio access while approximately 96 percent had television access (China Statistic Bureau, 2005). China Central TV (CCTV) is the TV network at the top of the hierarchy. All its principal directors were appointed by the state. CCTV is also a monopoly with 16 channels and huge commercial income. All local TV networks are required to carry CCTV's News Broadcasting at 7 p.m. A survey by Mediachina.com shows that News Broadcasting has a viewer rate of 8.31 percent, the highest among all of the CCTV programs (Mediachina.com, 2006). Although CCTV is the most powerful network, it cannot succeed in dominating the national market due to the fact that each province and major city has its own TV networks, and these networks broadcast content related primarily to local audiences.

In the last decade, satellite TV has largely challenged the status quo. In the late 1990s, almost all networks at the province level began broadcasting through satellite, which enabled them to cover national audiences. *Hunan TV*, the TV network of Hunan Province, has now become CCTV's major competitor. CCTV also faces competition from non-mainland broadcasters such as *Phoenix Satellite TV*, which is headquartered in Hong Kong, and has greater flexibility in news reporting, particularly as it relates to coverage of Hong Kong and Taiwan issues. *Phoenix Satellite TV* is one of the few non-government television broadcasters in mainland China, and it is popular among the well-educated segment of China's population. Yet, *Phoenix Satellite TV's* reach is limited in mainland China, and only people with cable or satellite dish access can receive its programs. Another Hong Kong based satellite TV, Yang's *Sun TV*, is not news oriented and less successful.

Technology has provided another challenge to governmental control over media. The use of the Internet has surged in China since the last decade: between the years 2000 to 2005, the growth rate of Internet users was approximately 358 percent (Internet World Statistics, 2005). In 2005, there were 187,508 Internet hosts and 111 million Internet users, and Internet penetration within the Chinese population stood at 8 percent. It is noteworthy that cell phones have provided another important Internet outlet in China and information flow through text messaging may prove the toughest to control centrally. China has the largest cell phone market in the world and according to an official with the Ministry of Information (Luan, 2006). China's cell phone users are estimated to reach 441 million in 2006 while Internet users are expected to be 128 million. Blogs have also been booming in the last five years.

The Chinese government is continuously working on policies to control the Internet. The major means of Internet censorship are filtering and blocking information from search engines and websites, closing "unhealthy" Internet cafés, imposing regulations on the Internet industry, pledging to purify the Internet environment in public, and imprisoning political dissidents who are active online. Google, the American-based search engine giant, which is now the most popular search engine for filtering website content, is also aiding the Chinese government in censoring the Internet. In order to gain a foothold in the Chinese market, Google set up a new site, www.google.com.cn, in which it conducts self-censorship to satisfy the authorities in Beijing (BBC.co.uk, 2006). Nonetheless, despite the efforts of the government to control the Internet, many still believe that the diversity of technologies and the rapid deployment of Web innovations provide a vibrant alternative media space for active Chinese Internet users.

Chinese women: tradition vs. revolution.   The Confucian tradition required women to be quiet, peaceful, conservative, and obedient to the main male character in her family. There is a famous old saying that a woman should "   ,   ,   " [obey her father before marriage; obey her husband in marriage; and obey her son after her husband's death]. Another famous quote from a Confucian wise is that "   " [illiterate is a virtue of women]. In the Confucian tradition, girls were kept out of school. When they were married, their jobs were to take care of the family in which they have the lowest status. Throughout their lives, women were supposed to be away from the public.

In the early 1840s, Great Britain defeated China in the notorious Opium War. This war is largely regarded as the beginning of China's modern history. It is a history of the country's humiliating defeats and struggles to survive in the modern world (Hooker, 1996). In the turmoil that lasted for almost one century, many wars took place, the old imperial empire was toppled, modern industries were started, and traditional moral values were challenged by imported new thoughts. In an important historic event called the May Fourth Movement (May 4, 1919), college students and young intellectuals campaigned, calling on the Chinese to abandon Confucianism and embrace modern science and democracy (Asia for Educators, 2006). Some of the avid participants of the May Fourth campaign introduced communism. The status of women in Chinese society gradually changed during these chaotic years.

After the Communist Party of China took power in 1949, establishing the People's Republic of China under the leadership of Mao, raising women's status became an important point in propaganda. One famous slogan is that "   " [women hold up half the sky]. One of the major social shifts at that time was the entrance of women into the workforce. However, efforts to create equal status between the sexes during Mao's era were more likely to erase important differences between the sexes. One poem by Mao that provides a good illustration of this point is "   , 不爱红装爱武装" [The Chinese girls have special ideas. They prefer military uniforms to feminine dresses"] (Mao, 1961). In posters from that time, one can still see that women dressed like men, acted like men, and worked as hard as men. Feminine characteristics such as using cosmetics or being delicate were despised as petite bourgeoisie. Moreover, the equality between the sexes was rather superficial. On one hand, women were still largely kept out of the power system. On the other hand, women's unique physical characteristics were ignored and disrespected, putting female workers in harsh and inhospitable working environments.

Nonetheless, a legacy from Mao's era is that women are common in China's present-day workforce. In 2000, it was found that the "The labor participation rate in China was the highest in the world, with approximately 90% of men and 83% of women in the workforce" (Pan, n.d.). Women's wages are approximately 70 percent of men's, a figure lower than Australia (91 percent) and the United States (75 percent) but higher than Korea (53 percent) (Pan, n.d.). One personal observation is that Chinese women enjoy higher status in the family when compared to Korean, Japanese, or even Taiwanese women. But, there is still much to be done to achieve gender equality in China. For example, women's literacy rate is lower than men; approximately 95 percent of men are literate when compared with approximately 87 percent of women (The CIA World

Factbook, 2006). Women also comprise a much smaller percentage of the workforce in management.

Chinese women and media. In China, working in the media is a dream job for girls. This reality may be due to the role model effects of celebrity journalists and broadcasters such as Lan Yang and other young women who earn both good salaries and solid fame by working for the media. *Phoenix TV*, for example, is famous for using its "star" anchors and news show hosts as a marketing tool. Young women from *Phoenix TV* are well known in China and they are all bright, good-looking and highly educated. Most of them have attained a degree from a US university. Though most of the universities in China have a journalism department, it is more difficult to gain admission in journalism than other majors, and journalism departments are often full of bright and ambitious young girls.

In print, there are roughly equal numbers of female reporters and male reporters at the entry level, however, males still rule the newsroom occupying higher-level positions such as editor, director, or supervisor. The higher the position, the fewer females can be found. It is extremely rare to find a female editor-in-chief in a mainstream newspaper or magazine. I worked for a major daily in a major city in China. Of the five major sections (political news, economic news, social news, sports news, and entertainment news) of the paper, only the entertainment section had a female director. Only one of the three editors of the social news section (for which I worked) was a woman. According to my personal observation, the ratio between male and female editors in newspapers is roughly between 3:1 and 4:1.

In discussing the subject of Chinese women in news, one cannot miss the model effects of the celebrity news anchors/hosts. At a quick glance, it appears that women perform better than men in broadcasting. In news programs, female and male anchors are usually paired up, similar to US television news programs such as CNN or MSNBC news. In news talk shows, celebrity female hosts attract more attention than male hosts. However, the backstage is the real stage for men. Males rule the studio or newsroom in an absolute sense. Though most US news anchors/hosts are middle aged and experienced, in China, almost all female anchors or hosts are young and attractive. Some of these young females are hired directly from college, and it is rare to see middle-aged woman in broadcasting. Female anchors and hosts hold a status similar to movie stars as opposed to serious journalists. In entertainment programs, women may even outnumber men. But again, no matter how many women appear on the front stage, it is the backstage that belongs to men. In Chinese media, women sparkle while men rule.

Although no statistics on news coverage of women could be found, a general impression is that there are fewer pictures or stories about women specifically in the news. Political news in China usually means coverage of government officials' activities. As most of the officials are males, it is no surprise that there are more images of men than women in political news. This norm also applies to economic news. In these two sections, distribution of both sexes in news reflects the status of both sexes in reality. In social news, sports news, and entertainment news, there is no obvious divide between women and men. Overall, coverage of men far outweighs coverage of women. News about women can be roughly divided into three categories. First, news about women covers the achievements of women. For example, female Chinese athletes usually attain better achievements than male athletes in international competitions, and these celebrity female athletes garner heavy media coverage. Second, news about women covers the misfortunes of common Chinese women. For example, there is social news concerning women who lose their husbands in mine explosions or news about poor girls who have to sacrifice their schooling to pay the tuitions of their brothers. The third category of news coverage about women is coverage of controversial women. Because China is in a conflict between tradition and modernism, women's behavior is more prominently observed by Chinese society than men's behavior. In 2003, there was one young female journalist Mu Zimei (real name Li Li) who had casual sex with many men. She put all her love stories with journalistic accuracy on her blog, which attracted numerous visitors and made her nationally known. Traditional media quickly picked up her story and made it a hot news topic for a long time (Yardley, 2003). After Mu Zimei, several other girls showed up on the Internet. Again and again, the girls challenged the social norms and the public's nerve in similar ways as Mu Zimei. Though it may be inappropriate to call these girls pioneers of the sex revolution in China, their existence has reflected the diverse and somehow chaotic situation of today's China.

Most newspapers have sections devoted specifically to women. These sections are mostly about beauty, fashion, food, parenting, or other traditional "women's interests." These sections are not very different from what once were known as "Women's Pages" in US newspapers. Entertainment news is another female news area. A personal observation is that entertainment news enjoys the highest press freedom in China. Hollywood gossip gets updated almost instantly and movie stars and other entertainment public figures "enjoy" closer public surveillance than any other people. For example, a soap opera star wore a T-shirt with the English word "Hustler" on her bosom in public. Her T-shirt quickly became a hot topic online and many criticized her "embarrassing" choice. It is hard to imagine when the public could ever question a government official to the same extent. As in the United States, in China, there are more men reading newspapers and more women reading magazines. A personal observation is that men care much more about news, especially hard news when compared to women.

There is an obvious gender gap in terms of Internet use. A survey from the China Internet and Information Center (CNNIC, 2005) indicated that 60 percent of Internet users were male while only 40 percent were female. In the survey, females generally showed fear as opposed to love of technology. Web content for women also tends to be limited to fashion, beauty, and food, swinging between the two poles of good wife/ mother and sexy babes (Li, 2005). Younger women with buying power are the more desired audience as opposed to older women who are largely neglected on the Internet (Li, 2005).

Present and future.   After the majority of Chinese women were brought into the workforce by communism, the idea that women hold up half the sky is at least politically correct, if not accepted by everyone. Most Chinese families have two incomes, though what husbands earn is usually higher than what their wives earn. If a wife earns more than her husband, the family is usually considered unbalanced and people may worry about the relationship between the couple, another example of Confucian residue.

As communism's influence gradually dissipates, the influence of Confucianism is enjoying a new resurrection. A worrisome new trend is the greater emphasis on female beauty in present-day Chinese media. News of beauty pageants, model competitions and car shows decorated by Chinese beauties is making headlines now and then. Though lots of media messages show young women as professional and ambitious, many other media messages portray women as sexy, creating a subtle connection between women's beauty and men's wealth.

The gender divide in the Chinese media stems from our definition of what is important news. If we insist that only political news is important through dedicating the most space to it in the Chinese media, women will never consume as much news as men do. Women are different from men. Women can only be equal to men as women, not as a second version of men. When there are more women working in the Chinese news industry, the media can begin to address issues that are more interesting to women. By allotting more media space to women's issues, it is hoped that women's news consumption can increase, closing the gender divide in the Chinese media.

Taiwan

Taiwan is an island located about 200 km off the southern coast of Mainland China. The island straddles the Tropic of Cancer and is also strategically positioned in the East China Sea, midway between Japan and Korea to the north and Hong Kong and the Philippines to the south. Lush green hills and mountains occupy two-thirds of the island (Government Information Office, 2005a). As of September 2004, Taiwan had a population of 22.66 million with a population density of 626 persons per sq. km. The official and daily communication language in Taiwan is Mandarin Chinese, and the population is almost entirely composed of Han Chinese, the majority ethnic group within China (Government Information Office, 2005b).

Taiwan's government is a constitutional democracy with a president and five yuan (ministries). The president is elected for a four-year term and serves as the commander-in-chief of the armed forces. The president also represents the country in foreign relations and state functions. The five yuan carry out executive, legislative, judicial, examination, and control functions. Apart from the central governmental system, there are active local governments functioning at both the provincial and county levels.

Taiwan has expressed a strong commitment to education. In addition to the 9-year compulsory education launched in 1968, there are also a variety of alternative educational options available to people of all ages. In the academic year 2004, the total enrollment rate of the population between the ages of 6 to 21 years was 97 percent. As a result of widespread education, Taiwan has managed to achieve a very high literacy rate. For example, in 2004, less than 3 percent of the population over 15 years of age was illiterate (Government Information Office, 2005c).

Martial law and the ban on the establishment of political parties were both abolished in 1987. Since then, Taiwan has moved rapidly toward full democracy. The ban on the establishment of new newspapers, television stations, and radios was lifted in 1988. The emergence and legalization of a cable television system occurred after 1998 leading to the abolishment of publication censorship and an improvement in freedom of expression.

Elections are regularly held for important posts in the government. Political parties have matured, and people actively participate in campaigns and elections. Voting eligibility is defined broadly: the legitimate voting age is above 20 years irrespective of gender, property, or educational achievement, and both the president and vice president are elected directly through the voting decisions of all eligible citizens in Taiwan. The voting turnout at the central governmental level is generally high, with turnout ranging from 60 percent to 80 percent in the past few years (Central Election Commission, 2006a). By the end of 2005, 116 political parties had registered (Central Election Commission, 2006b); however, there are six popular parties. These parties are the Democratic Progressive Party, Kuomintang, People First Party, Taiwan Solidarity Union, Non-Partisan Solidarity Union, and New Party. These parties can be further categorized into the pan-blue alliance and the pan-green alliance based on where the party stands in the spectrum of political ideology. The pan-blue camp, more one-China oriented, is led by Kuomintang (KMT) while the pan-green camp, more Taiwan-first oriented, is led by the Democratic Progressive Party (DPP). At present, Taiwan's ruling party is the DPP.

In terms of the industrial sector, traditional labor-intensive industries in Taiwan have gradually been replaced by capital- and technology-intensive industries such as petrochemicals, information technology, electronic equipment, and electronics. Taiwan is now the world's leading manufacturer of many types of information technology products (Government Information Office, 2005d).

Taiwanese society has modernized within the past decades, and women are no longer bound to a conservative status. Traditionally, women in Taiwan were dominated by paternal hegemony, and gender roles were clearly defined—women were subordinate to men. However, in recent times this traditional viewpoint has been waning. Capitalism and democracy have accelerated the feminist movement, and feminism has found governmental support. In the early 1970s, the first wave of the Taiwanese women's movement arose after Ms. Hsiu-lien, Lu—now vice president—declared her "New Feminism Movement," which brought the public's attention to the unequal treatment of women in society. Diverse women's organizations or associations have emerged since the martial law was lifted in 1987. These organizations began to focus attention on approaching gender concerns from different perspectives and on providing professional assistance to women. Some provide women practical services and assistance, and others actively take part in the political and social movements in an effort to urge modification of laws and to supervise the government's execution of the public policy designed to improve women's status in the Taiwanese society. Nevertheless, occupational statistics in Taiwan still reflect significant gender segregation such that the growth of women in the workforce has been slow to improve. In 1975, 39 percent of women worked in Taiwan and by 2004, 48 percent of women contributed to the workforce. Yet, this 9 percent increase was spread over three decades (Directorate General of Budget, Accounting and Statistics, 2005).

In modern-day Taiwan, women are now able to achieve higher education, attain higher positions in organizations, and receive more equitable pay than in the past. In comparative terms, women in Taiwan hold a more progressive position when compared to that of other Asian countries. For example, the vice president of Taiwan, Hsiu-lien, Lu is a woman, who received her master's degree at Harvard, and her long devotion to the feminist movement is commonly known in Taiwan. In Congress, 18 percent of legislators are female (Foundation of Women Rights Promotion and Development, 2005) and in the business circle, leading corporations such as HP-Compaq, Yahoo, IBM, and Intel in Taiwan branch have had female chief executive officers.

News organizations in Taiwan.   According to the Government Information Office of Taiwan, as of June 2006, there were 1,107 registered news agencies, 2,389 newspaper, 4,433 magazines, and 178 radio stations (Government Information Office, 2006). In May 2006, the National Communication Commissions noted that there were five network TV stations and 75 cable TV stations running 142 cable channels (National Communication Commissions, 2006). The largest news agency in Taiwan is the Central News Agency (CNA). Major national dailies include the *Liberty Times*, the *China Times*, the *United Daily News*, and the *Apple Daily News*.

In recent years, the press has suffered declining circulation rates due to a high cable TV penetration rate and the rapid proliferation of the Internet. In mid 2005, Taiwan's cable penetration reached 60 percent of the population and these cable systems typically offer subscribers a fixed package of over 90 channels at a monthly rate of approximately US $19 dollars (Government Information Office, 2005d). Of these cable channels, TVBS-N, FTV News, SETN, ET Today, CTITV, and Era News provide local news coverage 24 hours a day, seven days a week. Cable News Network (CNN), the BBC, and Nippon Hōsō Kyōkai (NHK), the latter translated as the Japanese Broadcasting Corporation, are also popular among social elites in Taiwan.

News Media Use in Taiwan.   According to a 2003 national survey of 2,160 respondents conducted by Academia Sinica in Taiwan (Chang & Fu, 2004), newspaper readers spent 32 minutes per day reading newspapers. In sharp contrast, television viewers spent around two hours per day watching news.

There are strong gender differences in news media consumption in Taiwan. Chang & Fu (2004) found statistically significant differences in the relationship between gender and newspaper reading, gender and television news watching, and gender and Internet surfing. With respect to newspaper reading habits, the authors found that over 50 percent of men read newspapers daily, while only 40 percent of women do the same. With respect to watching television news, 83 percent of men watch television news daily while 78 percent of women are daily television news watchers. Gender also has a significant relationship to Internet surfing habits. The authors found that while 34 percent of men are daily Internet surfers, less than 25 percent of women use the Internet on a daily basis. The authors found no significant relationships between gender and magazine reading, gender and radio listing, and gender and general television watching behavior. In general, these statistics suggest that the gender gap in mass media usage only exists in relation to news-seeking behavior and Internet use.

It is possible that the reason women consume less news than men in Taiwan is because news is becoming more negative, sensational, and political. However, though news may be more political in theme, it is not necessarily issue oriented. Political news tends to focus on party-interest conflict and scandals and physical fighting among legislators in the Congress often becomes the lead story on the evening news, even appearing on CNN for several times during the past ten years. For example, in March 28, 2001, a committee meeting turned nasty after a lawmaker slapped a female legislator and pulled her hair, sending the woman to the hospital with minor injuries.

Regarding gender differences in Internet usage, a national survey in 2005 (Ministry of Transportation and Communications, 2005, pp. 1–2), found that more than 55 percent of the population above 15 years of age in Taiwan had used the Internet. However, 56 percent of males have used the Internet in comparison to 53 percent of females. According to the survey, the most important obstacle to using the Internet is lack of skills. It is possible that lack of skills may be the reason for the small gender gap in Internet access in Taiwan.

In terms of generational news habits, significant differences have been found for newspaper reading but not watching television news. For newspaper reading, people under 40 years, between the ages of 40 and 59 years, and above 60 years, spend 36 minutes, 50 minutes, and 66 minutes per day reading newspapers respectively. Interestingly, although a generation gap characterizes newspaper reading behavior, it does not characterize television news watching (Chang & Fu, 2004). Though newspapers have been losing their audience of younger readers, television news continues to appeal to these younger generations.

The image of woman in the press.   The deregulation of the press industry in 1988 contributed to the emergence of women's pages in Taiwan's newspapers. With the industrialization and modernization of the Taiwanese society, women in Taiwan have become a major market segment. Thus, newspaper publishers have increased such soft content in the newspaper as shopping guides, fashion trends, health news reports, and family life stories. Although some are critical that such content reinforces a traditional, stereotypical image of women, many women do read these pages and gain information (Chang & Fu, 2004).

Women in news organizations.   Women are not a minority in Taiwan's news industry, although men still outnumber women in the journalism industry. In a 2004 national survey of 1,185 journalists, 43 percent were female. Women journalists averaged 36 years of age, while their male counterparts averaged 38 years of age (Lo, 2005, p. 4). Yet, women journalists are not as fortunate as men journalists to ascend the career ladder. In analyzing the relationship between gender and professional position, Lo (2005) found that more women than men held non-managerial positions in the organization. While 27 percent of male respondents were at the managerial level, only 21 percent of female respondents held the same professional position. In assessing the gender of those at the top positions, Lo found that 64 percent of respondents who were at the managerial levels were male. Clearly, there seems to be a glass ceiling effect for Taiwanese women when assessing their ability to be promoted in the newsrooms.

Ta-Fa Lin (personal communication, April 23, 2006), a senior manager at a prestigious local television station, noted that not long ago, men were still in control of TV news production, although women had mostly held positions such as anchors and reporters. However, this phenomenon has now changed. Women now share the power with men in the newsroom. Lin observed that in the past, women seemed to treat their work as more of a job and less as a career, which could be responsible for the gender inequality in the newsroom. He added that there was no doubt nowadays that many authoritative figures in the TV news industry were women.

It is worth noting that there have been more female than male students enrolled in journalism departments across Taiwanese universities, and this phenomenon suggests that there should be a large number of women employed at entry-level positions in newsrooms. While more women are employed in these low status jobs within news organizations, the questions can be posed: Why do fewer women occupy positions of influence and power in news organizations? Could this phenomenon be explained by the newsroom's masculine work culture, the newsroom's professional norms, which were originally set by men, or the informal networks among male colleagues within newsrooms? What changes need to take place today so this trend will not define the future of journalism in Taiwan?

South Korea

South Korea lies on the southern half of the Korean Peninsula bordered by the Korean Bay to the west, the East Sea, and North Korea. As of 2004, the population of the Republic of Korea, which is the official name of South Korea, was 48,199,227 (Korean Overseas Information Service, 2006).

Korea has developed rapidly since the 1960s, fueled by high savings and investment rates and a strong emphasis on education. In 1996, the nation became the twenty-ninth member country of the Organization for Economic Cooperation and Development (OECD). Korea's major industries include electronics, automobiles, semi-conductors, steel products, shipbuilding, and textiles. Korea's 5,000-year-old history boasts a rich and distinct culture that is steeped in Confucianism—the oldest school of Chinese thought that emphasizes morality, consideration for others, obedience and good education (Yahoo Korea, 2006), and Buddhism, which is based on teachings emphasizing spiritual purity and freedom from human concerns and desires (ibid.). These influences are manifested in the nation's historical architectural styles and traditional customs and beliefs. Yet, the Korean people are also remarkably open to change and, as a result, have adjusted rapidly to the dynamic trends of the global economy.

Ethnically, Koreans are of one family and speak one language, called "Hangeul." Today, Korea boasts one of the highest literacy rates in the world, and it is a well-recognized fact that the high level of education among the Korean people accounts for the nation's rapid economic growth over the past three decades.

In addition, a Korean cultural phenomenon, so-called the "Korean Wave" (or "Hallyu"), left an indelible mark throughout Asia in 2004, fanning optimism about the country's potential as a culture powerhouse (Korean Overseas Information Service, 2006). The term "Korean Wave" was coined by the Chinese mass media in 2001 as a response to the increasing popularity of South Korean pop culture products and stars (Jang, 2004 as cited in Lee, 2005). This trend spread to countries in Southeast Asia, and Japan is not an exception. The broadcasting of popular South Korean TV dramas such as "Winter Sonata" and the emergence of active fandom surrounding heroes and heroines boosted the impact of South Korean popular culture on Japan (Lee, 2005). The growing success of Korean drama has now caught up with that of Korean movies and pop music.

Media in South Korea. In Korea, there are four television networks, three of which are public broadcasting stations while one is commercial. There are also 23 national newspapers of which 11 are general daily newspapers, seven financial daily newspapers, five sports daily newspapers and three English daily newspapers (Korean Press Foundation, 2003a). In addition, there are cable TV stations, satellite TV stations, and local newspapers that are accessed by many people. Especially popular is Internet news, most notably *OhmyNews*, which relies on 37,000 "citizen reporters" whose submissions are edited and fact-checked by professional journalists. In 2003, *OhmyNews* was ranked the sixth most influential news organization among all types of Korean media based on a survey conducted by the weekly *Sisa Journal*.

According to the Korean Internet Statistics System, in May 2005, 79 percent of total households had computers and 73 percent of total households used an Internet service at home (Internet Statistics Information System, 2005). In addition, Korea ranked forty-third in the world in its rate of mobile phone penetration, according to recent figures released by the International Telecommunication Union (Hwang, 2006). The ITU indicators showed Korea's mobile phone penetration rate reached 76 percent as of late 2004.

News media organizations and female journalists. Korea places strong emphasis on its educational system; for example, entry into some careers is strictly limited by extremely difficult examinations, which determine the number of individuals that will be allowed to enter these professions. One of these careers is journalism. Examinations are also required for the professions of accountancy and medicine, as well as for such judicial jobs as attorneys, prosecutors, and judges. As a result of this upfront testing system, it can be assumed that the aspiring women and men journalists who pass these examinations are equally qualified to become journalists.

The proportion of female journalists in the media industry has increased slightly in recent years, but men still outnumber women in the journalism profession. In 2004, female reporters accounted for only 13 percent (532) of the total 4,060 employed journalists working for the 17 national daily newspapers (Lim & Uhm, 2005). Nevertheless, the proportion of high-ranking women within the newsroom is still very small, regardless of the total increase of women in the profession. The number of women in ranks above that of associate editor was only 105 (7 percent) out of a total of 1,561 potential positions in these 17 dailies.

Figures for the broadcasting industry are very similar to findings within the print newsroom. For the ten years between 1992 and 2002, the proportion of women employees on the three major television networks showed little change. In 1992, only 1,596 or 12 percent of the total 12,981 jobs were held by women, and in 2002 only 1,176 or 9 percent of the 12,796 jobs were held by women (Korean Press Foundation, 2003b). Fortunately, the number of newly employed females has been steadily increasing. Although only 10 percent of the industry was comprised of women in 1993, women comprised 12 percent of the broadcast workforce in 1995, 13 percent in 1997, 17 percent in 1999, and 40 percent in 2003 (Yun & Lee, 2003). In 2003, women represented 15 or 36 percent of the 42 newly employed producers, 14 or 35 percent of the 40 reporters, and two or 50 percent of the four new broadcast announcers.

Despite the fact that male and female journalists must pass an entrance exam to enter the journalism profession, there are cultural factors within the news media that hinder female journalists from advancing professionally. For example, K. Kim (2006) identified three major mechanisms that excluded and alienated women journalists from the news production process in modern Korean society. Using a content analysis of essays written by Korean female journalists, K. Kim found that three main mechanisms within the newsroom culture worked to exclude women journalists . . . First, the gathering of news functioned to exclude women through its emphasis on "authoritative information collection," an "unethical compromise culture," "informal communication," and the "traditional view of womanhood." Second, newsrooms with "masculine bonds" presented a hostile environment for women journalists through its distrusting and stereotyping of female journalists. Finally, family responsibilities, such as housework, pregnancy, and childcare, limited the ability of female journalists to participate fully in after-work activities (K. Kim, 2006, p. 139).

The very existence of these mechanisms indicates the multiple ways that female journalists—in contrast to male journalists—are devalued. In fact, the disparagement of female journalists is so pervasive that a novice female journalist commented in an essay that she believed the incompetence of female journalists was attributed to their lack of professional skills (Korean Female Journalist Club, 1991, p. 205). The essay underscores the power of invisible mechanisms that operate at the unconscious level to exclude females from participating fully in the media workplace.

Several of the mechanisms of devaluation enumerated in K. Kim's (2006) study, such as the time required for housework, pregnancy, and childcare are, of course, also found in other professional careers in Korea. Like their effects on the journalism profession, these mechanisms operate to exclude women from participation in such occupations (Cho, 1990; Joo, 1992; Chung, 1997). Cho (1990) pointed out that females are in a very disadvantaged position because they are not part of male-dominated social networks where most critical information is shared. Major decisions are usually made at drink meetings or golf meetings. She also maintained that the traditional view about gender differences devalues women's professional competence. In the media industry, such tendencies become more prominent.

Furthermore, the traditional stereotypes about womanhood function as a mechanism to alienate female journalists from the news gathering process. In Korea, a traditional viewpoint is that females should stay working in the private area due to their inability to understand the complexities of the public field. As such, journalism has been considered a profession only for men and such prejudice creates a direct barrier against female journalists covering the news. Only in very rare circumstances do news sources provide female journalists with high-quality information as they would to men journalists. Female journalists have to expend several times more effort as men have to in order to collect the same amount and quality of information.

While these endemic mechanisms of exclusion operate within the Korean workplace, there are other forms of exclusion that are peculiar to the Korean media industry. These include "collecting information in an authoritative manner" and "the unethical culture of compromise." The authoritative method of collecting information is defined as the journalists' coercive way of collecting information from news sources. This form of information collection is problematic because both journalists and news sources consider this method very natural. In the society where a tendency to discount a female's ability exists, this method of information collection presents a significant disadvantage for female journalists. Meanwhile, the culture of unethical compromise refers to the problematic culture that pervades the newsgathering process. For example, journalists in the Korean society often enjoy the sexually decadent bar meeting provided by the news source, even though they know that the commercialization of sex is unethical. This mechanism needs to be banned in order for women to participate in the journalism profession more freely.

Women in the news.   Studies that have explored the coverage of women in news stories in Korea have shown that the articles often do not reflect reality, but instead symbolically represent gender power relations that are the constructions of a patriarchal social order.

One of the typical findings is that the news media excludes women as important news sources. H. Kim (1997) found that in *KBS-1* (Korean Broadcasting System) the main evening newscast, 67 percent of the news stories were attributed to male sources, 25 percent of news credited male and female news sources, and only 8 percent of news stories referenced female news sources. The majority of news stories that relied upon male news sources were related to society, politics, health and environment, and international news. However, the news stories that were attributed to female sources were limited to news about society and education. In the 16 articles in which women were referenced as main news sources, nine of the females were victims, three were suspects, and four were parties to the news events.

In a study of three television networks, K. Kim (2003) explored the mechanism of the symbolic annihilation of females in Korean news reports—a mechanism in which Korean women were underrepresented and their images were minimized as the result of journalistic routines such as source use and information channel selection. For example, the marginalization of women as sources in television news is evidenced by the fact that over 80 percent of news sources were males while less than 20 percent of news sources were females. Male sources for news in the public arena were mostly selected public figures such as government officials and businessmen; however, female sources were mostly individuals in the private arena such as housewives, students, and customers.

Negative aspects of news reporting routines, such as the assigned roles of male and female news anchors, collectively enforce a gender stereotype reproduction. Usually, a male reporter and a female reporter co-anchor the evening news in Korea. The male anchors are almost all 40 to 50 years old and the female anchors are 20 to 30 years old. On the main evening news of two public broadcasting channels, KBS and MBC, a male anchor reports the main news first, while a female anchor follows to report the rest of the news.

Male anchors report a greater percentage of the news stories. H. Kim (1997) found that on the *KBS-1* main evening news, male anchors anchored approximately 60 percent of the news stories while a female anchor introduced slightly more than 40 percent of the news reports. Interestingly, 38 percent of the news covered by the female anchor included only the audio of her voice without her appearance (ibid.).

Male anchors are also given more time to report the news. In an examination of three television networks, K. Kim (2003) discovered that male anchors delivered individual news stories that were longer than the news stories delivered by their female counterparts. A male anchor delivered news stories that averaged 92 seconds while a female anchor delivered news stories that averaged 71 seconds.

Thus, as a result of an asymmetric gender system in the broadcast news system, the marginalization of female journalists is collectively reproduced as part of the news production process.

Women news audiences.   During the past decade in Korea, there has been a gender difference of 20 percent in newspaper readership. In 1993, men who read newspapers every day represented 52 percent of the total male population, while the women who read newspapers every day represented only 25 percent of the total female population (Korean National Statistics Office, 2000). By 2000, the gender gap closed slightly. Men who read newspapers every day represented 50 percent of the total male population, and women who read newspapers everyday represented 27 percent of the total female population (ibid.).

Another observed gender difference in usage relates to television news consumption. According to a 2004 survey by the Korean National Statistics Office, more men than women reported enjoying TV news: 83 percent of the men who were questioned expressed enjoyment of television news in comparison to 66 percent of the women who were queried (Korean National Statistics Office, 2005).

However, in terms of Internet news usage, overall, the percentages of women and men users were similar but there were differences in frequency of reading news online. According to a 2004 survey by the Korean National Statistics Office, 40 percent of the men surveyed read Internet news compared to 41 percent of the women respondents but men read news online more frequently than women. Specifically, 55 percent of the men surveyed read Internet news every day but only 42 percent of women read news online every day.

Bringing a woman's perspective to the news.   Since 2000, the number of junior female journalists employed by the Korean news media has increased due to social and cultural changes that have encouraged more women to become involved in the public and political arenas. Recent studies indicate that women journalists bring different perspectives to news content by using a more positive reporting style, directing more attention to women, and by incorporating a greater number of women's issues and women's perspectives in news stories (K. Kim & Y.J. Kim, 2005; Lim & Uhm, 2005). Because those attributes are considered to be positive contributions to the Korean society, the greater number of junior female journalists is viewed as a positive development.

Even so, there is a lack of equity in the reporting of women's news. Although individual women journalists are attempting to become more conscious of gender equity issues, the number of female journalists may still be less than the critical mass needed to affect change. Many of these female journalists have not yet reached positions of authority and decision-making in their organizations to influence newsroom culture. Therefore, many more female journalists need to move into the industry in an effort to rise to positions of leadership in order to have a greater influence on the Korean news media.

These are critical years for emerging changes in the historically male-dominated newsroom culture in Korea as more junior female journalists join the industry and the Korean society, in general, adopts a more female-friendly attitude. The current trend is also likely to grow as a result of the increasing number of women Internet newsreaders. Accordingly, the influence of female journalists is likely to increase in the near future in ways that may bring about significant changes in Korea's historical discrimination against women.

For these reasons, it is important for the academic community to gain a better understanding about the challenges that female journalists face. In achieving that goal, it is necessary for women news viewers to actively critique news content for gender equity issues and to speak up when instances of discrimination occur in news reports.

Notes

1   Contributors were invited to give their perspectives because of their personal and professional experiences with that country or region. The contributors for each country or region in this chapter are listed as follows: India by Smeeta Mishra; China by Xin Chen; Taiwan by Yi-Ning Katherine Chen; and South Korea by Kyung-Hee Kim.
2   Indira Gandhi was prime minister of India from 1966 to 1977 and again from 1980 until her assassination in 1984 ("BBC on this day," n.d.).

References

India

Background note: India. (2005, December). Bureau of South and Central Asian Affairs: US Department of State, Washington DC. Retrieved April 4, 2006 from www.state.gov/r/pa/ei/bgn/3454.htm.

Bathla, S. (1998). *Women, Democracy and the Media: Cultural and political representations in the Indian press.* New Delhi: Sage.

BBC on this day, 1984: 31 October. (n.d.). 1984, *India Prime Minister Shot Dead.* Retrieved April 12, 2007 from http://news.bbc.co.uk/onthisday/hi/dates/stories/october/31/newsid_2464000/2464423.stm.

Bhide, M. (2004, October 20). The Curry Question; Ask an Indian cook how to make chicken curry. You won't get the same answer twice. *The Washington Post*, p. F1.

Bollywood. (n.d.). *Wikipedia.* Retrieved September 11, 2006 from http://en.wikipedia.org/wiki/Bollywood.

Bombay. (n.d.). *Wikipedia.* Retrieved September 11, 2006 from http://en.wikipedia.org/wiki/Mumbai.

The CIA World Factbook (2006). Retrieved September 11, 2006 from www.cia.gov/cia/publications/factbook/geos/in.html.

Deb, S. (2005). The 'Feelgood': Lifted by a potent but narrow economic boom, India's elite press is slowly leaving the rest of the nation behind. *Columbia Journalism Review*, 43(6), 38–43.

ETForecasts. (2006, January 3). *Worldwide Internet Users Top 1 Billion in 2005.* Retrieved April 10, 2006 from www.etforecasts.com/pr/pr106.htm.

Haseloff, A.M. (2005). Cybercafés and their potential as community development tools in India. *The Journal of Community Informatics*, 1(3). Retrieved April 8, 2006 from www.ci-journal.net/viewarticle.php?id=68&layout=html.

Internet & Mobile Association of India (IAMAI). (2006). *Varied Activities of Women Online*. Retrieved April 10, 2006 from www.iamai.in/IAMAI_Females_Research_Report_2006.pdf.

Joseph, A. (2001). Storming the citadel of hard news coverage. *Nieman Reports, 55*(4), 85–8.

Joseph, A. (2002). Working, Watching and Waiting: Women and issues of access, employment and decision-making in the media in India. Paper presented at the United Nations Division for the Advancement of Women Expert Group Meeting. Beirut, Lebanon. Retrieved April 10, 2006 from www.un.org/womenwatch/daw/egm/media2002/reports/EP4Joseph.pdf.

Kalita, S.M. (2005, May 2). Hooray for Bollywood; The subcontinent's stars light up trump's Taj Mahal. *The Washington Post*, p. C1.

Karlekar, K.D. (Ed.) (2005). *Freedom of the Press 2005: A global survey of media independence*. Lanham: Rowman & Littlefield.

Kumar, A. (2005, November). The breaking news syndrome—new frontier of television news. *Global Media Journal*, 1(1, Indian edition). Retrieved April 12, 2006 from www.manipal.edu/gmj/issues/nov05/kumar.php.

List of most populous cities in India. (2006). *Wikipedia*. Retrieved September 11, 2006 from http://en.wikipedia.org/wiki/List_of_most_populous_cities_in_India.

Narasimhan, S. (2001). Media don't portray the realities of women's lives. *Nieman Reports*, 55(4), 88–90.

National Crime Records Bureau. (2003). *Crime in India: Crime against women*. New Delhi: Ministry of Home Affairs, India. Retrieved April 10, 2006 from http://ncrb.nic.in/crime 2003/cii-2003/CHAP5.pdf.

National Literacy Mission. (2001). *Female Literacy in India*. Retrieved April 15, 2006 from www.nlm.nic.in/women.htm.

Newman, R. (2006). Coming and going: As offshoring evolves, Indian firms even hire Americans. *US News & World Report*. Retrieved April 12, 2006 from www.usnews.com/usnews/biztech/articles/060123/23offshoring.htm.

Parekh, A. (2001, Winter). Bringing women's stories to a reluctant mainstream press. *Nieman Reports, 55*(4), 90–2.

Print media is alive, kicking and expanding. (2005, August 8). *Newswatch*. Retrieved April 10, 2006 from www.newswatch.in/?p=1095.

Registrar of Newspapers for India. (2006). *Press in India: General review*. Retrieved April 10, 2006 from http://rni.nic.in/pii.htm.

Reuter & Montagnon, P. (1995, November 22). India plans to rename Bombay. *Financial Times (London)*, p. 9.

Right to Information Act. (2005). Ministry of Personnel, Public Grievances and Pensions. Government of India. Retrieved April 12, 2006 from http://righttoinformation.gov.in/.

Roy, B. (2000). Villages as a positive force for good governance. *United Nations Chronicle*, XXXVII (1). Retrieved September 11, 2006 from www.un.org/Pubs/chronicle/2000/issue1/0100p86.htm.

Sengupta, U. (2005, November). Current trends in Indian media: A reflection. *Global Media Journal*, 1(1, Indian edition). Retrieved April 13, 2006 from www.manipal.edu/gmj/issues/nov05/sengupta.php.

Thekaekara, M.M. (2005, July). Combatting caste. *New Internationalist*, 380, 9–12.

Times News Network. (2004, November 9). India has a third of the world's illiterates. *The Times of India*. Retrieved April 10, 2006 from http://timesofindia.indiatimes.com/articleshow/916814.cms.

Tully, M. (1998, June). The British legacy fifty years on. *Asian Affairs*, 29(2), 131–41.

Warsia, N.F. (2005, June 10). *Changing Readers Allow Print Growth along with other Media, Magazines Suffer*. Retrieved April 12, 2005 from www.exchange4media.com/nrs/2005/story4.html.

World Association of Newspapers. (2005, May 30). *World Press Trends: Newspaper circulation and advertising up worldwide*. Retrieved April 8, 2006 from www.wan-press.org/article 7321.html.

UNICEF. (2000, March 7). UNICEF Executive director targets violence against women. *Information Newsline*. Retrieved April 8, 2006 from www.unicef.org/newsline/00pr17.htm.

China

Asia for Educators. (2006). *Chen Duxiu and the May Fourth Movement*. Retrieved August 9, 2006 from http://afe.easia.columbia.edu/china/modern/read2.html.

BBC News (2006). *Google Censors itself for China*. Retrieved August 9, 2006 from http://news.bbc.co.uk/1/hi/technology/4645596.stm.

China Internet and Information Center (CNNIC). (2006, January 17). *The Seventeenth Report of China Internet Development*. Retrieved June 15, 2006 from www.cnnic.net.cn/images/2006/download/2006011701.pdf.

China Statistic Bureau. (2005).   —2005 [China Censors: The yearbook of 2005]. Retrieved June 15, 2006 from www.stats.gov.cn/tjsj/ndsj/2005/indexch.htm.

The CIA World Factbook. (2006, June 13). Retrieved June 15, 2006 from www.cia.gov/cia/publications/factbook/geos/ch.html.

Gov.cn. (2006). 中国共产党领导的多党合作和政治协商制度 [Multi-Party Cooperation and Political Consulting led by the Communist Party of China]. Retrieved August 8, 2006 from www.gov.cn/test/2005-05/25/content_18182.htm.

Hooker, R. (1996). *Ch'ing's China: The opium wars*. Retrieved August 9, 2006 from www.wsu.edu:8080/~dee/CHING/OPIUM.HTM.

Internet World Statistics. (2006, November). *Asian Internet Usage and Population*. Retrieved November 28, 2005 from www.Internetworldstats.com/stats3.htm.

Karlekar, K.D. (Ed.) (2005). *Freedom of the Press 2005: China*. Retrieved June 15, 2006, from www.freedomhouse.org/inc/content/pubs/pfs/inc_country_detail.cfm?country=6715&year=2005&page=16&view=mopf&pf.

Li, W. (2005).   [The Three-Fold Absence of Chinese Women in the Internet Communication]. Retrieved June 15, 2006 from www.mediaresearch.cn/user/erjiview.php?list=6&&TxtID=1743.

Luan, S. (2006). *China's Cell Phone Users to Exceed 440m, Internet Users, Nearly 130m in 2006*. Retrieved June 15, 2006 from http://english.gov.cn/2006-03/01/content_214149.htm.

Mao, Z.D. (1961).   [Notes on a Female Soldier's Picture]. Retrieved August 9, 2006 from http://zhidao.baidu.com/question/458294.html.

Mediachina.com. (2006).   6   (收视率占榜首 [The Viewer Rates of all programs in CCTV Channel One on April 6th]. Retrieved August 7, 2006 from http://chinese.mediachina.net/index_market_view.jsp?id=3979.

Ock Yum, J. (1988). The impact of Confucianism on interpersonal relationships and communication patterns in East Asia. *Communication Monographs*, 55(4), 374–89.

Pan, J. (n.d.). *Women's Employment and Welfare in Transitional China*. Retrieved in 2006 from http://cas.uchicago.edu/workshops/eastasia/Pan_chicago.ppt.

Sina. (2006). *Star Archives: Lan Yang*. Retrieved June 15, 2006 from www.cnnic.net.cn/images/2006/download/2006011701.pdf.

Sohu. (2005). *Nanfangzoumo*. Retrieved June 15, 2006 from http://news.sohu.com/nanfangzhoumo.shtml.

Wikipedia. (2006a, June 15). *People's Republic of China*. Retrieved June 15, 2006 from http://en.wikipedia.org/wiki/People%27s_republic_of_china.

Wikipedia. (2006b, August 9). *Taiwan*. Retrieved August 9, 2006 from http://en.wikipedia.org/wiki/Taiwan.

Wikipedia. (2006c, August 9). *Tiananmen Square Protests of 1989*. Retrieved August 9, 2006 http://en.wikipedia.org/wiki/Tiananmen_Square_Protests_of_1989.

World Association of Newspapers. (2005, May 30). *World Press Trends: Newspaper circulation and advertising up worldwide*. Retrieved June 15, 2006 from www.wan-press.org/article7321.html.

Yardley, J. (2003, November 26). Internet sex column thrills, and inflames. *The New York Times*, p. 3.

Taiwan

Central Election Commission. (2006a). *Election Database*. Retrieved August 2, 2006 from http://210.69.23.140/cec/cechead.asp.

Central Election Commission. (2006b). *A Brief Introduction of Elections in Taiwan*. Retrieved August 2, 2006 from www.cec.gov.tw/e-cec/Preface.asp.

Chang, Y.H. & Fu, Y.C. (2004). Taiwan Social Change Study. Unpublished National Science Council Research Report, Taipei, Taiwan.

Directorate General of Budget, Accounting and Statistics. (2005). Table 22: Important indicators of labor force status. Excerpted from *Statistical Yearbook of the Republic of China 2004*. Retrieved August 2, 2006 from http://eng.dgbas.gov.tw/public/data/dgbas03/bs2/yearbook_eng/y022.pdf.

Foundation of Women Rights Promotion and Development (2005). *Women's Profile 2005*. Retrieved August 2, 2006 from http://wrp.womenweb.org.tw/Page_Show.asp?Page_ID=321 (in Chinese).

Government Information Office. (2005a). Geography, excerpted from *Taiwan 2005 Yearbook*. Retrieved August 2, 2006 from www.gio.gov.tw/taiwan-website/5-gp/yearbook/p015.html.

Government Information Office. (2005b). People and language, excerpted from *Taiwan 2005 Yearbook*. Retrieved August 2, 2006 from www.gio.gov.tw/taiwan-website/5-gp/yearbook/p028.html.

Government Information Office. (2005c). Education, excerpted from *Taiwan 2005 Yearbook*. Retrieved August 2, 2006 from www.gio.gov.tw/taiwan-website/5-gp/yearbook/p276.html.

Government Information Office. (2005d). Economy, excerpted from *Taiwan 2005 Yearbook*. Retrieved August 2, 2006 from www.gio.gov.tw/taiwan-website/5-gp/yearbook/p138.html.

Government Information Office. (2005d). Mass media, excerpted from *Taiwan 2005 Yearbook*. Retrieved August 2, 2006 from www.gio.gov.tw/taiwan-website/5-gp/yearbook/p262.html.

Government Information Office. (2006). *Statistical Data on the Republic of China*. Retrieved August 2, 2006 from http://info.gio.gov.tw/ct.asp?xItem=17817&ctNode=3532.

Lo, V.H. (2005). Journalists in Taiwan: A comparative study, 1994 and 2004. Unpublished National Science Council Research Report. Taipei, Taiwan.

Ministry of Transportation and Communications. (2005, June). Department of Statistics. The project report of Internet usage in Taiwan. Retrieved August 15, 2006 from www.motc.gov.tw/survey/20050719153902_94www.WDL.

National Communications Commission. (2006). *The Statistics of Broadcasting Industries in Taiwan*. Retrieved August 2, 2006 from www.ncc.tw/statistics/statistics-9505.doc.

South Korea

Cho, H.J. (1990). Professional women. In the Ewha Women's University Publisher (Ed.) *Korean Women and Works*, pp. 53–103. Seoul: The Ewha Women's University Publisher.

Chung, K.A. (1997). Gender relations in production-centered organization: Focused on the career women's experience. Unpublished doctoral dissertation. Ewha Women's University, Seoul, Korea.

Hwang, S. (2006, May 11). ITU cell phone data could be deceiving. *Korea Herald*. Retrieved August 18, 2006 from Korean Integrated News Database System.

Internet Statistics Information System (2005). Internet infrastructure statistics. Retrieved April 15, 2006 from http://isis.nic.or.kr/english/sub01/sub01_index.html.

Joo, K.M. (1992). A Study on the principles of exclusion of women from professional occupations—A case study of the medical doctors. Unpublished Master's thesis, Ehwa Women's University, Seoul, Korea.

Kim, H. (1997). The gender structure represented in television news program. *Korean Broadcasting Journal*, 9, 147–78.

Kim, K. (2003). Coverage routines of gender reproduction in television news and journalists' gender difference: A content analysis of the prime-time evening news in KBS, MBC, & SBS. *Korean Broadcasting Journal*, 17(3), 197–238.

Kim, K. (2006). Obstacles to the success of female journalists in South Korea. *Media, Culture & Society*, 28(1), 123–41.

Kim, K. & Kim, Y.J. (2005). Coverage difference of female newsmakers among national newspapers: Influences of journalist gender and gender ratio in the newsroom. *Korean Journalism & Information Studies*, 29, 7–273.

Korean Female Journalist Club. (1991). *Female Journalists*. Seoul: Korean Female Journalist Club.

Korean National Statistics Office. (2000). *Report on the Social Statistics Survey*. Seoul: Korean National Statistics Office.

Korean National Statistics Office. (2005). *Report on the Social Statistics Survey*. Seoul: Korean National Statistics Office.

Korean Overseas Information Service. (2006). *2006 Intro Korea*. Seoul: Korean Overseas Information Service.

Korean Press Foundation. (2003a). *Korean Media Yearbook*. Seoul: Korean Press Foundation.

Korean Press Foundation. (2003b). General trends in the Korean press in 2003–2004. Retrieved April 15, 2006 from www.kinds.or.kr.

Lee, K. (2005). Assessing and situating the 'Korean Wave' (Hallyu) through a cultural studies lens. *Asian Communication Research*, 9, 5–22.

Lim, Y.S. & Uhm, J.Y. (2005). Examining gender equity consciousness and attitude of female journalists in managerial positions. *Media, Gender, & Culture*, 3, 144–81.

Yun, S. & Lee, C. (2003). Female employee's status in the three major over-the-air broadcasting companies in South Korea. *Communication Information Studies*, 22, 167–282.

Yahoo Korea. (2006). *Confucianism*. Retrieved August 16, 2006 from http://kr.dic.yahoo.com/search/ene/search.html?p=Confucianism.

Chapter 13

Women and the News

Latin America and the Caribbean

*Vanessa de M. Higgins, Teresa Correa,
María Flores, Sharon Meraz*

Brazil

Though Brazil has undergone heavy socio-economic changes in the past 50 years, it remains a country with gender divides. Women have steadily entered the workforce and now contribute significantly to the country's economy. Women have made an impact in almost all professions in the public sphere that have previously been held by men, in sharp contrast to men who have yet to engage in the private sphere. Although women's presence in the workforce signals a change in Brazil's social structure, Brazil is still a country with strong traces of machismo.

Brazil is a country of many paradoxes. Though it has one of the strongest economies in the South American region, it also has one of the highest levels of inequality. Though Brazil is very industrialized, over one-tenth of the population is illiterate. The journalism industry is also rife with these paradoxes. In general, Brazil produces a very high-quality journalism, but there is differential usage of media in the country. Women comprise the majority of journalism students in Brazil, but they are still a minority presence in professional newsrooms. The news media have the potential to narrow the gender gap, but it faces challenges that are embedded in the country's culture. To understand how the gender divide is replicated by the news media and how the news media assumes its potential role in promoting social change, it is important to look at the country's complex development.

Understanding Brazil: A look at the region. Brazil encompasses almost half of Latin America and is by far the largest country in South America (Brazilian Government Portal, 2006b). Being the only country in South America colonized by Portugal, Brazil is also unique in its population diversity. Its large population, estimated to be at the 190 million mark (Brazilian Institute of Geography and Statistics [IBGE], 2006c), is comprised of the descendents of Portuguese settlers, enslaved Africans, and the native Brazilian population. Brazil is the home of immigrants primarily from Europe, but also from Asia and the Middle East. Each of these groups has influenced Brazil's culture and population diversity.

Although considered a developing nation, Brazil has the largest economy in Latin America, according to the Gross Domestic Product Indicators of the Inter-American Development Bank (2006). As of 2006, Brazil ranked fifteenth in economic prosperity among world economies (Brazilian Government Portal, 2006a). Brazil's intense urbanization is a consequence of the economic shift from agriculture toward industrial goods and modernization. According to 1980 Census data (IBGE 2006d), 68 percent of the population lived in urban areas, while in 2000, 81 percent of the population was concentrated in these areas.

Yet, these economic figures hide one of the country's most daunting problems. Its levels of social exclusion and inequality are much higher than other regional countries with comparable economies, such as Mexico, Chile, and Argentina (Reis & Schwartzman, 2002). Education is also not fully available and still over one-tenth (11 percent of the population) was illiterate in 2005 (IBGE, 2007).

Brazil is a democracy, with a federative republic government, but this form of government is recent. A military dictatorship ruled the country from 1964 to 1985, and this time period was marked by limited civil liberties, persecution, torture, and hard censorship of the news media (Molica, 2005). Many of today's journalists were working during the military dictatorship and were influenced by their prior experiences under this regime. Brazilians frequently note that the country is still learning how to be a democracy. In 1992, Brazilians became heavily dissatisfied with charges of government corruption, and egged on by investigative media reports, took to the streets calling for President Fernando Collor de Mello's impeachment. As a result of congressional investigations, Collor de Mello resigned the presidency. This impeachment process demonstrates the Brazilian population's participation in the political system, while simultaneously demonstrating Brazilian media's newfound role as a watchdog of the government (Herscovitz, 2004).

Media in Brazil: seeing through the lens of gender.   According to a yearly report by Freedom House, a non-governmental organization in the United States that reports the state of the press in countries around the world, Brazil has a partially free press (Karlekar, 2005). The national constitution includes clauses concerning freedom of speech rights, which are generally accepted by authorities (Karlekar, 2005). One of the reasons the press is considered partially free is because of a law that requires practicing journalists to have a university degree in journalism. Considering that only about 7 percent of the country's population aged 25 and older has an undergraduate or graduate degree, this requirement excludes a large segment of the population from being journalists (IBGE, 2006a). Since undergraduate and graduate studies in the country are highly correlated with income and race (IBGE, 2006a), this requirement further restricts newsroom diversity by excluding minorities from being journalists.

According to the last census of 2000, 55 percent of women held university diplomas in comparison to 45 percent of men (IBGE, 2006a). These patterns were similar for graduates with journalism degrees. Of the total population with journalism, communication and information undergraduate degrees, 67 percent were women and 33 percent were men (ibid.). Although there are more women earning journalism degrees, this statistic does not mean that women's participation in the newsroom is higher or the same as men. Though the division in the newsroom is shrinking, it is still far from equitable. It is clear that more women show an initial interest in the profession through choosing journalism or related university education when compared to men. Yet, fewer women manage to land jobs in the newsrooms, though more women are educated in the field.

Brazil has one of the largest and most well developed media systems in Latin America (Herscovitz, 2004). With over 2,000 radio stations, 300 commercial television stations, and over 200 educational TV and radio stations throughout the country, Brazil boasts a wide range of communication outlets (Dines *et al.*, 1997). With a considerable portion of the population being illiterate, and an even larger low-income population, radio and television are the most utilized media systems in the country.

Among the television stations, *TV Globo* is important, particularly when audience variables and advertising share are taken into account. It is estimated that 70 percent of the television audience tunes in to its prime-time news program (Heuvel & Dennis, 1995). This family-owned group extends its activities to other countries in Latin America and Europe (Amaral & Guimarães, 1994). Although national law discourages television channel monopoly, *TV Globo* dominates both broadcast and print media outlets in the country (Amaral & Guimarães, 1994). Under its control are the nation's largest newspaper, news agencies, magazines, and several radio stations.

Brazil has approximately 300 newspapers (Herscovitz, 2004), but their readership is mostly limited to the nation's elite and middle class. Newspaper circulation is among the lowest in the world—55 for every 1,000 habitants (Dines *et al.*, 1997). Though these figures are low, newspapers are very influential in Brazil. Four daily newspapers, all published either in Rio de Janeiro or São Paulo, with their significant circulation, have considerable influence in national public opinion (Herscovitz, 2004).

There are over 200 magazine titles available in the country, and 28 percent of them are geared toward women (Dines *et al.*, 1997). The news group, Grupo Abril, had almost half (47 percent) of the total magazine market share in 2003, according to the National Association of Magazine Editors (Associação Nacional de Editores de Revistas, 2006). According to Grupo Abril's 2004 annual report, its magazine *Claudia* has been the most circulated women's magazine for 40 years, and its editorial line caters to readers who "como todas as mulheres, desejam ser amadas e valorizadas, têm opiniões firmes e gostam de dividir suas histórias e angústias" [as all women, desire to be loved and valued, have firm opinions and enjoy sharing their stories and anguishes] (Grupo Abril, 2004, p. 12). Content in this women's magazine varies on topics of health and well-being, fashion and fitness (Grupo Abril, 2004) and it seems that much of the magazine content caters to women as avid consumers or as sexual objects.

Newspapers in Brazil began experimenting with online versions in 1995 (Manta, 1997). Much of the content was imported from the print newspaper. Today, it is not unusual for the online news departments to produce original content. Interestingly, the online newsroom in Brazil has the most gender equity when compared to other mass media. According to a 2005 survey by Maxipress/*Revista Imprensa* (Naldoni & Piza, 2005), 47 percent of the employees in the online industry are women.

A study on Brazil's press transition from an authoritarian regime to a democratic regime found that journalists saw the profession as a means to social intervention and political participation (de Abreu & Rocha, 2006). With the expansion of television in Brazil in the 1970s, the journalism profession has received prestige and visibility (ibid.). Women have also steadily gained greater visibility as journalists. Since the end of the military dictatorship, there has been a steady increase of women in the journalism profession. In 1986, women comprised 35 percent of total journalists registered by the Labor Minister; in 2002, 45 percent of these journalists were women (Federação Nacional dos Jornalistas, 2006). This increase in women's participation in journalism was partly the result of change in government regime. Women's increased visibility was also the result of the economy's modernization to include international commerce (de Abreu & Rocha, 2006). Today, women are important actors in the economy as well as active news consumers.

In March 2005, *Revista Imprensa*, a magazine that caters to Brazilian journalists, conducted a survey to assess women's inclusion in the journalism job market. This magazine found that women comprise 38 percent of all working journalists in Brazil; however, the percentage of women varies among the different media industries. Women comprise 48 percent, 47 percent, and 47 percent of the magazine, Internet, and television industry respectively, and these mediums boast of better gender equity when compared to radio and newspapers. For example, in radio, a medium that is traditionally male-dominated in Brazil, only 18 percent of the journalists were women (Naldoni & Piza, 2005, p. 29).

Although the presence of women in the journalism field has been on the increase, the division between women and men is still large. *Revista Imprensa* found that men held 70 percent of the higher-ranking positions and management jobs in journalism organizations (Naldoni & Piza, 2005, p. 28). In magazines and the Internet, these differences were reduced, and women held 40 percent of higher-ranking positions and management jobs in these two industries (ibid.).

The gender gap in newsroom management likely influences the newsroom's decision-making process, which ultimately translates into male-dominated perspectives in news reports. The higher presence of women in online journalism may result in interesting consequences, particularly as the medium progresses and matures in the country. It is common wisdom that it is often the newcomers who bring about a change in perspectives, and the Internet may provide this new potential for shifting the presentation of women in news reports.

Yet, this opinion is tempered by opposing evidence. De Abreu & Rocha (2006) found that when women are active participants in the news selection process, they are not likely to emphasize themes related to women or women's interests. These authors noted that women in these selection positions often tend to mimic the behavior of men. The authors also observed that the journalistic ideal of impartiality may hinder women from emphasizing news reports with women's interests due to the fact that it could be perceived as biased (ibid.).

Women are generally portrayed in the media through the lenses of a patriarchal society, reinforcing the concepts that women are responsible for taking care of the household, their husbands, and their children. As more women take on leadership roles in the country, women's representation in the national media must change. This change will be a slow process given the fact that the media often function more as a mirror and less as a catalyst for social change. However, every "International Woman's Day" on March 8 in Brazil, the media discuss issues relating to women's role in society. Some of this coverage reinforces existing stereotypes while other portrayals open a dialogue within the public sphere. It is somewhat ironic that women's day immediately follows Carnival—a time when images of women's bodies make the front pages of almost all media outlets—a representation which is not necessarily viewed by Brazilian women as submissive.

Every evening, most Brazilian households that are watching television tune into *TV Globo's* prime-time news program, *Jornal Nacional.* Since 1996, this program has been co-hosted by a woman and a man (TV Globo, 2006). This program's staff of journalists is nearly evenly divided between the two genders, and this gender equity is highly significant given the popularity of this news outlet among the Brazilian population. It is an achievement that these women journalists have the potential to influence both women and men throughout the country.

Television may be the medium where women journalists are more visible in the country, but the Internet may be the medium where the most potential for change exists. According to the national Internet regulating committee, in October 2007, 48 percent of its users were women (Comitê Gestor da Internet no Brasil, 2007). Internet users in Brazil follow the international trend of young users, which also has the potential to bring a new generation of news consumers to the medium. With the high percentages of women journalists in online news, and a more equitable inclusion of women in higher-ranking positions within the online newsroom, online news may provide a fresh assessment of women's role in Brazilian society.

Addressing the gender divide: Future steps. Women journalists still have a long journey ahead to establish their presence in Brazilian media, but they are no longer the exception. The high numbers of women enrolled in journalism universities suggests that this female presence will continue to grow. The high quality of journalism produced by these women has expanded their influence in traditionally male-dominated areas, such as politics and economy. Considering that salaries for journalists in Brazil are some of lowest in Latin America (Dines *et al.*, 1997), women in journalism face many barriers. Some of these include the higher education requirement, the high demands of the profession, and their main responsibilities as keepers of the private sphere. If they can manage to surmount these obstacles, their presence in the newsroom will positively influence the image of women throughout Brazil.

The presence of women in the newsroom and the work of women journalists have the potential to result in a more gender equitable Brazilian society through the provision of role models for younger women aspiring to the profession. However, the journalistic values of impartiality and objectivity may hinder working women journalists from exercising their privilege to be influential through the selection of news content that is interesting to women readers. Yet, women journalists must realize that this potential social gain does not necessarily involve a loss of journalistic values. By making a conscious effort to present women in the news in a more positive, uplifting manner, women journalists may inspire greater gender equity in society. By avoiding demeaning stereotypes of women, women journalists can improve the image of women in Brazil.

This potential role for women in journalism should not be limited to woman's news segments, nor to "International Woman's Day." Nor should women journalists be the only ones responsible for promoting gender equity. Gender equity in Brazilian society can only be achieved through joint efforts of both women and men journalists. The Internet, as a new and evolving medium, has the potential to include more women as producers and decision-makers, which could ultimately impact how women are presented in Brazilian news reports.

Chile

When Michelle Bachelet was elected President of Chile in 2006, it became evident, if not urgent, to discuss and study the relationship between women and news in Chile. For the first time, a woman was in a position to be the major news agenda setter in this prosperous South American country of 16 million. Moreover, Bachelet's decision to name a cabinet with an equal number of women and men implied that for the next four years women would be in the forefront of the political arena.

Although these political breakthroughs symbolize the advancement of Chilean women in the last decades, there is still a broad gender divide in the social, political, and economic realms. The news media are not an exception.

The changes that women have experienced lately have come together with other large political and economic transformations. After 17 years of military rule, in 1990 a democratic government stepped into power. Today, Chile is regarded as one of the most stable liberal democracies in Latin America. This stability is reflected, in part, by the media system, because Chile is one of the few Latin American countries classified as having a free press, according to a Freedom House report (Karlekar, 2005).

Located in the continent's southern cone, Chile shares with its neighbors (Argentina, Bolivia, and Peru) the Spanish heritage. The majority of Chile's inhabitants are mestizo and white, the language is Spanish and the religion is Catholic. This nation has one of the region's best performing economies after the reforms launched by the military regime in the 1970s and 1980s, which were deepened by the democratic governments in the 1990s. Nowadays, there is a political consensus on maintaining the market-oriented policies that foster a high level of foreign trade.

Despite these achievements, Chile lags well behind other Latin American countries in the proportion of women who participate in the labor market. Although they constitute over 50 percent of the population, only 36 percent of the labor force is comprised of women (INE, 2006). The average employment for the region in the late 1990s was 45 percent, a figure that increases to 60 percent in developed countries (OIT, 1998, as cited in Dirección del Trabajo, 2005, p. 75). In stark contrast, 64 percent of the Chilean males are in the workforce (INE, 2006). This gap pervades all sectors of the economy, including the media sector.

The media industry.   Currently, there are nine national daily newspapers (two of them with supplements devoted to women), 45 regional and local dailies, and two free papers (ANP, 2003a), which are read regularly by 43 percent of the population (ANP, 2003b). Two private conglomerates dominate the press market. El Mercurio S.A.P owns—among many other regional newspapers—*El Mercurio*, Chile's elite newspaper of record, *La Segunda*, the country's major evening newspaper, and *Las Últimas Noticias*, "the most widely read tabloid thanks to its formula of focusing on celebrities and man-bites-dog stories" (Valenzuela & Correa, 2006, p. 11). El Mercurio S.A.P.'s main competitor is Copesa S.A., which owns *La Tercera*, an educated middle-class newspaper, and *La Cuarta*, popular for its police and crime coverage.

As for television, four national networks dominate the market. Leading the group are *Canal 13*, owned by Chile's largest Catholic university, and *TVN*, a state-owned network with financial autonomy. Private companies handle the other two networks, *Chilevisión* and *Mega*. Chileans rely mostly on television news for their information about their country and the world. A survey (CNTV, 2005a, p. 76) revealed that 73 percent of the population watches TV news every day. As of 2006, VTR is the sole company that handles cable television in Chile. Its penetration has increased, and in 2005 it reached 36 percent of the households (ibid., p. 10).

Historically, radio was the most trusted source for information and played a crucial role during the military regime because of its pluralism and diversity. Even though television took over this position in the last decade, radio is still popular (Dussaillant, 2005, p. 98). Excluding music, news is the most-listened to radio genre. According to a 2006 national survey (Mediática & Archi, 2006), 71 percent of the population listened to radio news every day. In the morning, radio news is more popular than television news.

The new media, such as the Internet, lag well behind the traditional mass media. The most recent survey conducted by the World Internet Project in Chile (Godoy, 2005) showed that 35 percent of the population uses the Internet. Although this figure is higher than in any other Latin American country, there is evidence of stagnation in Internet usage during the most recent years, possibly due to the fact that computer users' skills have reached a ceiling (Godoy, 2005). According to the WIP-Chile survey, 46 percent of Internet non-users say they "do not know how to use" the Net (Godoy & Herrera, 2004, p. 4). At the same time, there has been a moderate increase in Internet access in the most recent years. For example, connectivity at schools—where most people access the Internet in Chile—only increased from 36 percent in 2000 to 36.8 percent in 2003 (Casen, 2003). Still, traditional media have been expanding their presence in the Web. In 2003, 38 out of the 56 daily newspapers had online versions (ANP, 2003a). An interesting case is El Mercurio S.A.P.'s web portal, *Emol*, which has a site devoted entirely to women with content related to work issues, family, health, and fashion.

Women journalists working in the media.   In the 1980s, women flooded Chile's schools of journalism and began to play a significant role in the news media landscape. For the last 15 years, more than half of the students enrolled in colleges of journalism have been women. In 2003, 65 percent of students who graduated in journalism were women (Mineduc, n.d.).

Female reporters achieved prominence before the surge of women in schools of journalism. During the politically agitated mid 1960s, 1970s and 1980s, several women excelled in political and investigative journalism. This trend became evident in the evolution of the awards given to media practitioners. In 1963, a special award for female reporters was created to honor Chile's first well-known woman journalist: Lenka Franulic. Since 1990, three women have won the National Journalism Award. Although this figure seems small, it shows a remarkable improvement because in 36 years— between 1954 and 1990—only one woman (Franulic) had received this prestigious prize.

Similar to gender equity statistics in US newsrooms (Weaver & Wilhoit, 1998, p. 400), this blossoming of female journalism students and prominent reporters did not translate into an equal number of women and men in newsrooms. At the beginning of the 1990s, 40 percent of working journalists were female (Castellón & Guillier, 1993). In 2006, the percentage was the same, according to a census conducted by scholars at Universidad Alberto Hurtado (Bulnes *et al.*, 2006).

The reasons for the low participation of women in the media are similar to reasons that explain the overall lack of females in the paid workforce. In this mostly Catholic country, there are no legal barriers preventing women from having a job. However, scholars have found that besides socio-demographic factors (such as marriage and number of dependent children) there are strong cultural obstacles that impede women's participation in the labor market. In Chile—compared to other countries—people emphasize the costs of women working more than the benefits of it (Contreras & Plaza, 2004; Palacios & Martínez, 2006). For example, a survey by Lehmann (2003) revealed that 81 percent of the population considered that "la vida familiar se resiente cuando la mujer trabaja tiempo completo" [family life is affected when a woman works full time] (p. 1), and 83 percent agreed with the statement: "Es probable que un niño en edad preescolar sufra si su madre trabaja" [a preschooler is likely to suffer if his/her mother works] (p. 1). Thus, a woman may be very successful in the public sphere, but she is still primarily responsible for the domestic sphere maintenance (Castellón & Guillier, 1993).

In the Chilean media industry, especially in newspapers and TV newscasts, the challenge of balancing both professional and family responsibilities is even more taxing on women due to the long work shifts. This time issue could be one of the reasons why women's employment numbers in such non-daily publications as magazines is so high. For example, 74 percent of the reporters and 62 percent of the editors are women (Bulnes *et al.*, 2006). This time barrier can also explain why the only evening newspaper, *La Segunda*, has a high proportion of female professionals. *La Segunda* has a shorter work shift than other dailies. The issue of long daily shifts can also explain why many female journalism students are more likely to pick careers in public relations than in daily news jobs.

In editorial positions, the gender divide is even larger. Excluding magazines, only 28 percent of the editors and top executives in the media are women (Bulnes *et al.*, 2006). The most striking differences occur in the four main television networks: there are only seven female editors and one top executive, compared to 40 males (ibid.). This gap contrasts with the fact that today women have an important on-air presence as anchors and reporters in the networks' newscasts. However, they hardly reach decision-making positions. Even when women get top positions, they usually become "men-minded," noted the Chilean journalist and former editor of several successful magazines and TV newscasts, Verónica López (IWMF, n.d.). According to López (2001, p. 103):

> Women with independent points of view who work inside big media companies and who want to work with their colleagues and bosses to prepare the way for new topics [such as poverty, discrimination, home violence, family and environmental issues] usually fail. This failure can be attributed to the editors and media owners—mostly men—who have maintained traditional priorities in news: a reliance on daily deadlines, little reporting and research, and a constant focus on politics, economics, sports and entertainment.

There is evidence that female media professionals can identify better with the interests of the audience. For instance, the most-read magazines in Chile, such as *Caras*, *Cosas*, and *Paula* (ANP, 2005), are managed by women, while political and economic magazines directed by men—such as *AméricaEconomía* and *Qué Pasa*—are less read.

The portrayal of women.   In Chile, there is a lack of research on women's news coverage. Nevertheless, this issue became a hot topic after Michelle Bachelet decided to run for president.

In a study that analyzed press coverage of Bachelet when she was a candidate in the 2005 presidential election, Valenzuela and Correa (2006) found striking gender-based differences. Newspapers placed more emphasis on her individual traits—such as her gender, appearance, and household chores—than on her male counterparts. Valenzuela and Correa (2006) also found that the press described the candidates' attributes using traditional female/male stereotypes: while Bachelet's charisma and honesty were portrayed in an overwhelmingly positive manner, her leadership and competency were covered in mostly negative terms. In stark contrast, the leadership and competency skills of her male rivals were portrayed in a favorable way, unlike their honesty, which was often put into question.

The few studies that have examined general trends in the coverage of women in the media have found that they are underrepresented in quantity and substance of mentions. For example, a content analysis of television newscasts showed that only 23 percent of the sources quoted were females (CNTV, 2005b). A study of *El Mercurio*, *La Tercera*, and the now extinct *La Época* (Silva *et al.*, 1998) also noted that newspaper stories that had women as protagonists "generalmente se presentan en espacios laterales y/o de menores dimensiones" [were generally located in lateral columns or {were assigned} a smaller space] (p. 37).

Since news stories are defined by events that usually happen in the public sphere, such as politics and business, the study of the three newspapers concluded that women are underrepresented because they, historically, have been identified with the private sphere (Silva *et al.*, 1998). The few women that do appear in news articles are those who have succeeded in the political or economic arenas. Moreover, when a story covers these female leaders, it usually emphasizes the issue of how to cope with work and family duties. There are signs that the strong division between the public and private spheres is blurring. More women—aside from Bachelet and her female appointees—are progressively appearing in the public sphere, especially thanks to their growing incorporation into the labor market.

In contrast to the "serious press," women are commonly the protagonists of news stories in tabloid newspapers. In *Las Últimas Noticias* women appear very frequently; however, this medium's strong coverage of local celebrities, such as top models, soap opera actresses, and female talk shows hosts, leaves little room to showcase a more realistic portrayal of Chilean women. In the case of *La Cuarta*, which specializes in crime stories, more women are protagonists of the stories because it focuses on domestic violence and other felonies committed at home. However, in a content analysis of this paper, Silva and Torres (1998) found that women appeared as the causal factor of the violence even when they were its victims. For instance, a story noted: "Un comerciante de 66 años dio muerte a balazos a su conviviente de 40, luego de que ésta le confesara que lo abandonaría para irse a vivir con un joven" [A 66-year-old businessman shot his partner, 40, after she confessed that she would leave him for a younger man] (p. 12). The research also noted that the news articles are usually written in humorous style, which both lessen the dramatic substance of the event and undervalues women.

One of the most revealing and poignant examples of stereotyped women's coverage is what happened in the northern and deserted small town of Alto Hospicio in 2000 and 2001. Eight 13- to 16-year-old girls from very poor and unemployed families disappeared, one by one, every other month. The police and officials hypothesized that they were probably victims of the white-slave trade or that they left their distressing homes and became prostitutes in larger cities. The news media followed without questioning these official versions. However, a fact changed these accepted theses. A girl survived a serial killer's assault and fled from the periphery of the northern city, Iquique. Later, the other missing girls were found dead in excavations.

In this case, two stereotypes played against the girls: they were low class and female. This prejudice by the media prevented any attempts to investigate other reasons for the girls' disappearance (López, 2001).

Gender gaps in the news audience.   In Chile, there is not only a sex divide in the media workforce and news coverage but also in news media use. Women lag behind men in newspaper and online news reading but there are not significant disparities in television and radio news exposure. While 28 percent of men read newspapers regularly, only 18 percent of women do the same (CNTV, 2006).

There is a gender divide in Internet usage. The WIP-Chile survey (Godoy *et al.*, 2005) showed that women have been using the Internet for less time than men. While 20 percent of males reported that they have been using the Web for more than five years, only 14 percent of females did the same. Considering Internet users only, the study found a gap in the frequency of usage. Men said they used the Internet almost 15 hours per week while women used it 13 hours per week.

The audience gender gap also affects online newspaper reading. While 56 percent of men read online newspapers, only 49 percent of women do the same (Godoy *et al.*, 2005). However, there is no gender divide in online magazine reading: 24 percent of both women and men read them.

Television and radio news studies have shown that there is no gender gap. Seventy three percent of females and males watch TV news regularly (CNTV, 2005a, p. 76) and almost the same percentage holds in the case of radio news listening (Mediática & Archi, 2006, p. 23).

The future of women in the news.   At this moment, the relationship between women and news is at a breaking point in Chile. In theory, the media should pay more attention to women, especially due to their increasing involvement in public affairs. More females are entering the workforce and the government is promoting gender parity in official positions. However, these trends will not necessarily lead to a dramatic change in the participation of women in the media industry or a change in the way the news portrays women and attends to their interests.

Changing institutional and cultural values that block the advancement of women is a long-term challenge. However, certain steps can be taken in order to narrow the gender divide in the Chilean media landscape.

As some scholars and journalists have proposed (e.g., Silva *et al.*, 1998; López, 2001), addressing the gender divide entails a reexamination of what constitutes news for the Chilean media. Although the news media have a duty to inform society about politics, economics, and other traditional public issues, they must give equal relevance to topics such as poverty, education, environment, health, and domestic violence. Moreover, when covering these topics, journalists should not only convey to the public the officials' perspective but also the viewpoint of ordinary people. Only then will the news truly represent broader segments of society. Through reference to public opinion studies, Marcia Scantlebury, journalist and editor of *TVN* channel, noted the popularity of women-centered stories that portray women with strong points of view (Zarzar, 2004). Since female reporters identify better with the current audience's interests, they have an important role to play in reexamining what is news in Chile.

Ultimately, it is crucial for media and universities to promote more research on the news gender divide. Without a profound understanding of why this gender divide exists in the newsroom and in news reports, Chilean media will remain disconnected from and ignorant of the current social trend of women's advancement in politics and society.

Mexico[2]

Mexico is the third largest nation in Latin America after Brazil and Argentina. With a geographical size of 1,742,485 square miles, it is bordered to the north by the United States and to the south by Guatemala and Belize. Mexico consists of 31 states. Its capital, Mexico City, is located in an independent federal district and is considered to be one of the largest cities in the world. As of 2005, Mexico had a total population of 103,263,388 people comprising 50,249,955 males (49 percent) and 53,013,433 females (51 percent) (INEGI, 2006).

The word Mexico connotes a continuous blending of Mesoamerican, European, and African cultures, a phenomenon that has been occurring since 1517. At that time, Spain discovered Mexico by way of the Yucatán peninsula located in the western part of Mexico. The colonial period was ushered in after Hernán Cortés' conquest over the Aztec nation, resulting in an expansion of the Spanish Kingdom and the Catholic religion. During this time, the Spaniards brought African slaves to Mexico, primarily to the Veracruz State. The following 300 years were typified by a dynamic blending of arts, music, religion, cuisine, literature, paintings, and poetry among Mesoamerican, European, and African cultures. This blending is evidenced by the prevalence of many buildings of mixed European architecture and Mesoamerican influence in Mexico City. One can admire the Guadalupe Virgin, who has brown skin and Mesoamerican codes on her dress prints and roses. Mexican cuisine is also a good example of this fusion of culture. The cuisine is full of variant aromas and vibrant colors, offering food from Mesoamerican, European, as well as African cultures such as tamales, tortillas, chocolate, romeritos, pozole, mole, and cochinita pibil. Mexico's primary language is Spanish; nevertheless, more than 30 different indigenous dialects still exist in Mexico. The majority of Mexicans are Catholics; very few people practice a different religion.

The first university ever established in the New Spain territory, the La Real y Pontificia Universidad de México, was founded in Mexico on September 21, 1551. The intellectual and cultural activities that this university generated led to the publication of the first Latin American newspaper, a monthly known as *La Gaceta de México y Noticias de Nueva España* in 1722. This *Gaceta* consisted of several regular sections in government, religion, the commercial sphere, and the social sphere. Initial Latin American newspapers had a primary goal of maintaining colonist domination, resulting in the publication of stories that supported the government while highlighting news stories in foreign countries in order to avoid covering domestic policy (Villamarín Carrascal, 2006, p. 2). Women's participation in journalism dates back to 1500 with Jerónima Gutiérrez, the first female printer (Hernández Carballido, 1998, p. 48).

Media landscape.   Mexico has a total of 462 daily newspapers, afternoon papers, special supplements, and magazines. This number includes national, state, weekly, bi-weekly, and monthly publications according to the Padrón de Medios Impresos Certificados 2006 report (SEGOB, 2006).

In 2004, the television industry consisted of 459 commercial stations and 199 non-profit educational/cultural stations (SCT, 2004). Plus, there were 1,423 radio stations including 1,154 commercial and 269 non-profit, educational/cultural radio stations.

As of 2004, Mexico had a total of 14,036,000 Internet users with 8,515,000 of these total users representing business users and 5,521,000 representing home users (SCT, 2004). This figure represents an increase of 1,817,000 users from the previous year, 2003 (SCT, 2004). Yet, this increase in Internet usage may not hold significance given the deep digital divides that exist within Mexico (J.C. Lozano Rendón, personal communication, April 26, 2006).

In an attempt to narrow the digital divide among Mexican citizens, former President Vicente Fox created the Web portal, *e-mexico* (e-México, 2003a), in December 2000. Goals were set to increase home phone lines from 12 lines per 100 habitants in 2000 to 25 lines per 100 habitants in 2006. Community centers were also created in low income and geographically isolated locations in an effort to diffuse technology to more individuals (e-México, 2003b). In 2004, STC reported that 4,441 of these centers had been created in the country (e-México, 2003b). The content of the e-mexico portal is available in Spanish, English, French, and indigenous dialects such as Mayan. The portal offers information on such topics as health, education, women's issues, indigenous culture, immigrants, and the economy. In relation to the system component, e-mexico's function is to improve access to federal, state, and local agencies for cyber visitors.

Women working in news.   Between 1948 and 1951, bachelor degrees in communication, mass media, and journalism appeared on university curriculums in Mexico. This field of study has now become a popular choice for many women in Mexico. Álvarez Laso (2005) noted that the increased female enrollment in journalism programs over the past 50 years has led to more women in the professional media industry—a trend which has made the field less of an exclusive male-dominated profession. In the 1980s, several media outlets also required their newly hired reporters to hold at least a bachelor's degree. Since more women are graduating from journalism schools, this increase has led to more women in newsrooms. This latter fact suggests gender equality exists in newsrooms. However, though more women are working in the newsroom, women reporters still lack equal access to decision-making positions.

Veteran journalist Florance Toussaint pointed out that currently female journalists comprise 50 percent of newsroom reporters (cited by Aguirre, 2005, p. 1). However, she found that media content in Mexico has a discriminatory and masculine bias because women journalists are excluded from content modification; females are the soldiers and the males are the generals. For example, women hold less than 15 percent of management-level positions in such newspapers as *La Jornada*, *El Universal*, and *El Financiero* (López García, 2001, p. 1). Some believe that a machismo attitude is so pervasive in the media industry that only deep social and legislative changes can address the gender inequality. Journalist Javier Solórzano of TV Azteca noted that women journalists suffer because they are often trapped by social and cultural expectations that stipulate women must have specific physical attributes to be on camera (cited by Aguirre, 2005, p. 2). Many females end up perpetuating a specific conception of beauty—European-blond, white skin, and blue/green eyes—characteristics which do not reflect the physical appearance of the majority of Mexican women who are mestizas with dark hair, dark eyes, and brown skin. Sara Lovera, a veteran journalist since the 1960s, lamented the cheapening of the journalism profession for women journalists, who are now required to be beautiful, blonde, sympathetic, and demure as opposed to being quick-witted and intelligent (Espinoza Calderón, 1995, p. 128). This misapplied aesthetic requirement has reduced women journalists from thinkers to ornaments. For example, though many women journalists are hosts and anchors on television, they do not engage in debate or analysis on such topics as politics, science, or culture (Ortiz Henderson, 2004, p. 2).

The majority of women reporters are stuck in middle- or lower-level management positions under a structure dominated primarily by men. Women reporters are trapped in the lower end of the pay scale and are robbed of any decision-making potential in the newsroom by being locked out of promotion to high-level positions (Álvarez Laso, 2005, p. 1). Lovera noted that female reporters are often willing to work for free in an effort to fulfill their goal of being on television. Women are often hired for little to no salary, leading to what Lovera described as the "media credential and free hands" method, which refers to journalists being open to bribes from institutions, government employees, and politicians in an effort to earn a living (cited by Espinoza Calderón, 1995, p. 130). Journalist Gloria Salas de Calderón noted that the devaluation in the journalism profession in Mexico is not due to a loss of the profession's prestige but rooted in low monetary compensation, which forces journalists to look for external sources of income (Espinoza Calderón, 1995, p. 155).

In 2000, La Fraternidad de Reporteros de México, A.C. (a professional journalists association) conducted a study to investigate the status of women in journalism. Sixty-seven female journalists from the Mexico City metropolitan area participated in the study. The results indicated that slightly over one-third of the female reporters in Mexico city had temporary, freelance, or verbal-contract work with no such benefits as health insurance, company stock, Christmas bonuses, paid vacations, and paid overtime (Martínez González, 2000, p. 1). In addition, the discriminatory barriers that married women encountered in the workplace environment are well noted in the firings and marginalization of women reporters who have families. Pregnant women are not given any extra facilitation, and there is a lack of childcare, educational assistance, or additional time off for family emergencies such as taking a sick child to the doctor (ibid.).

This hostile environment is tough on women who want to balance a career with having a family. This 2000 study indicated that over 50 percent of reporters were single, close to 60 percent had no children, nearly 3 percent were separated from their husbands, and almost 2 percent were divorced (Martínez González, 2000, p. 1). The study also showed that 85 percent of the women who were surveyed completed their coursework for their bachelor's degree but had not completed their thesis. Only 30 percent of the women had obtained their undergraduate degree, and less than 5 percent of them held a master's degree.

Women journalists are also given fewer stories to write than men journalists in the newspaper newsrooms in Mexico. Novoa, Isunza, Ley, and Cheng (2000) examined news stories from April 24 to May 3, 2000, in the national newspapers *La Jornada*, *Reforma*, and *Milenio Diario* and found that 42 percent of stories were written by men in comparison to 30 percent of stories by women and 27 percent of stories from the news wires. This number shows that the presence of women journalists in print media is still low, although these results are very close to each other. *La Jornada*, a leftist leaning paper, showed the highest percentage of female reporters. This data also reveals that newspapers are generating more of their stories from news wires than from male and female journalists' contributions. This trend clearly indicates that for newspaper owners, it is more cost-effective to use news wires than it is to keep journalists on their payrolls. Since there are fewer opportunities for reporters, irrespective of gender, it is more challenging for women reporters to increase their presence in the print media.

When women journalists are given opportunities to write for the newspaper, they are ghettoized into writing on specific topics. Novoa, Isunza, Ley & Cheng (2000), found that among the three newspapers, the sections that generated the most stories were politics (34 percent), international news (15 percent), national news (13 percent), celebrity news (11 percent), sports reports (10 percent), news on culture (8 percent), state (7 percent), and society (2 percent). In sharp contrast, women journalists were responsible for 42 percent of the stories on celebrities, 38 percent on culture, 19 percent on national news, 16 percent on society, 14 percent on economy, 10 percent on state, and 9 percent on international and sports. Only 7 percent of the stories on politics were attributed to women journalists, highlighting that politics, for these newspapers, is still a male-dominated arena.

Female reporters also face a lack of recognition in professional circles. When Premio Nacional de Periodismo e Información (The National Award for Journalism and Information), one of Mexico's most prestigious awards for journalists, was created in 1975, female journalists had to wait one full year to be recognized because the journalistic field was perceived by the Mexican government to be a male-only profession. Two years after the journalism award was created, Socorro Díaz Palacios of newspaper *El Día* became the first female journalist to receive the award. Although 40 years have passed since the award was established, female journalists are still routinely overlooked. In fact, in some years, not a single woman received an award.

A dangerous profession.   The increasing violence against women journalists was recognized by the second Latin American Conference of Women Journalists, held in Rio de Janeiro, Brazil, which demanded that legal action be taken against those responsible for aggression toward female journalists (CIMAC, 2004, p. 2). On April 16, 2005, Dolores Guadalupe García Escamilla died from injuries after being shot 14 times in front of her radio station, XHNOE Stereo 91, in the border city of Nuevo Laredo, Tamaulipas. Formerly a crime reporter and host of the program *Punto Rojo* (Red Point), García Escamilla was shot about a half hour after she broadcast a story on the slaying of a Nuevo Laredo defense lawyer (Committee to Protect Journalists, 2005). On December 20, 2005, Claudia Padilla Pacheco from *Correo* newspaper was threatened and harassed after reporting on a state police corruption case in Guanajuato, Mexico. Her stories included an investigation on criminal gang activity and possible police protection for drug traffickers (Committee to Protect Journalists, 2005). Her neighbor's house was vandalized, mistakenly believed to be Padrilla's home. Padilla has filed a report with the prosecutor's office; as of 2006, this case is still under investigation.

Women framed by news.   Not only are there fewer women writing the news, but fewer women are also used as sources in news reports. The book *Mujeres y Medios de Comunicación* (Women and Mass Media) edited by the Heberto Castillo Martínez A.C. Foundation (2005) pointed out that only 16 percent of news stories in Mexico used a female source, while 84 percent used a male source. Of the 16 percent of news stories that utilized a female source, 43 percent of them were used in reference to a celebrity story, 38 percent in reference to cultural news, but only 7 percent were used in reference to politics (Aguirre, 2005, p. 2). Similar patterns were found in a study conducted five years earlier. Female sources were used more frequently in stories about celebrities, local government employees, academics, other, artists, business owners, sportswomen and leaders, drug lords, federal government employees, and international government employees (Novoa *et al.*, 2000, p. 24).

It is publicly believed that women still have a long way to progress before they can be accorded equal status as a topic and source of news (Hernández Téllez, 2001, p. 3). The entrenched marginalization that women have faced in professional fields has also accorded less status to women's contribution in society, which has trickled down to news reports. Until women are given the opportunity to rise in the professional field, it will continue to be difficult to find female professional sources. Journalist Erika Cervantes Pérez noted that professional women sources are still absent from the mass media (Vargas, 2006). When females do appear, they are consistently portrayed in news reports as mourners, victims, or sex objects, and these frames have been bolstered by women's lack of power in the economic, political, and social spheres. Twenty-five-year veteran of broadcast journalism Cristina Pacheco has expressed surprise at the journalistic attempt to construct a vision of the world that excludes the contributions and voices of women (Espinoza Calderón, 1995, p. 156).

It is possible that Mexican female journalists perpetuate the under-representation of female sources in news media reports due to their scant attention to the problem. It appears that all of their efforts are focused on three main objectives: first, to include more female journalists in the media; second, to support the creation of media for women; and third, to teach journalists how to write from a gender perspective. Perhaps part of the answer to the problem of women's lack of representation in media exists in paying more attention to how sources are found and relied upon by news media. A solution could reside in instructing reporters on how to develop a good list of female sources for stories. Sometimes journalists take cognitive short cuts by not updating their lists of sources. As a consequence, they continue to use the same sources on a routine basis. One vital step can be the creation of an awareness campaign among female reporters, educating them on the importance of citing Mexican women in their specific professional area of expertise. Women must be allowed to rise above a victim status, the predominant frame of media portrayal. Younger generations of Mexican women need a role model to follow, and what better way to highlight those outstanding females than by citing them in the media? This practice would contribute to establishing a comprehensible and complete female journalism definition. Though writing a story from a gender perspective is needed, it is only the first step towards offering different types of content. However, using positive female sources in news reports who could also double as society's role models clearly complements the gender perspective.

Caribbean

The Caribbean region, commonly called the West Indies, refers to those islands that separate the Caribbean Sea from the Atlantic Ocean. On a purely geographical basis, the West Indies can be divided into the Bahamas, the Greater Antilles (central), and the Lesser Antilles (southeast). The Greater Antilles is comprised of Cuba, Jamaica, Haiti, the Dominican Republic, and Puerto Rico. The Lesser Antilles can be divided into the Leeward Islands and the Windward Islands. The Leeward Islands refer to the northern islands of the Lesser Antilles, comprising the Virgin Islands, Antigua, Barbuda, Montserrat, Guadeloupe, and Dominica. The Windward Islands refer to the southern islands of the Lesser Antilles, stretching from Martinique to Trinidad and Tobago.

The Caribbean region is linguistically diverse due to colonialism and European occupation before, during, and after slavery. The slave trade resulted in the traffic of African slaves to work the plantations in many Caribbean nations. When slavery was abolished in the nineteenth century, some of these islands experienced a subsequent period of indentured laborship, which resulted in immigrants being brought over to work the Caribbean estates from such places as India, China, and the Middle East. As a result of European occupation in the Caribbean, it is common to divide the Caribbean region into linguistic territories based on the primary colonizing power in each nation (Surlin & Soderland, 1990). The primary languages spoken in the Caribbean are English, Spanish, French, and Dutch. The English-speaking or Anglophone Caribbean region refers to such nations as Jamaica, Trinidad and Tobago, Barbados, Guyana, Grenada, Saint Lucia, Belize, and the US Virgin Islands and the British Virgin Islands, part of the Leeward Islands. The Spanish-speaking Caribbean encompasses Cuba, Puerto Rico, and the Dominican Republic. The French-speaking or Francophone Caribbean is comprised of such nations as Martinique, Guadeloupe, Saint Lucia, Saint Vincent, and the Grenadines. The Dutch-speaking Caribbean refers to such nations as the Netherland Antilles, Aruba, and Suriname.

Media emergence in the Caribbean.   The majority of the Caribbean region developed local press newsrooms after independence from Great Britain between the years 1962 and 1983 (Brown, 1990b). Before this time, the region was primarily dependent on news and information from the United States and British transnational news agencies such as the Associated Press and Reuters News. As Brown (1990a) noted, the growth in the region's local media industry was facilitated by the development of a regional interest group for Caribbean media professionals in 1970 called the Caribbean Broadcasting Union, and the development of a common economic market for cooperation among the Caribbean region in 1973 called Caribbean Community and Common

Market or CARICOM. A key regional movement, the 1970s Black Power Revolution, inspired citizens of the Caribbean to show black pride and self-expression of a West Indian identity through indigenous art, culture, music, and dance (Cuthbert & Hoover, 1990). However, one of the main historical events contributing to the growth of a Caribbean media industry was the New World Information and Communication Order (NWICO), which was based on the 1978 report by the United Nations Educational, Scientific, and Cultural Organization's (UNESCO) International Commission for the Study of Communication Problems. This report, titled *Many Voices, One World* but more commonly known as the MacBride Commission, identified the need for developing countries to develop their own communications infrastructure through more equitable and balanced global information infrastructures (UNESCO, 1980).

With the exception of Cuba and Haiti, most of the region has privately owned mass media outlets, though it is common in these islands for government to have some measure of control over such media as television and radio stations. In speaking of the growth of mass media in the Caribbean, Surlin and Soderlund (1990) noted that the expansion of mass media in this region post independence from Great Britain included the growth of such offshoot media industries as newswire services, advertising, public relations, and music. Though the Caribbean region's geographical proximity to the United States has resulted in a heavy dependency on the US cable industries for television programming, the majority of the Caribbean region now has local news television programming during both early morning and prime-time (Straubhaar, in press; Surlin & Soderland, 1990). Local media associations such as the Association for Caribbean Media Workers (ACM), the Media Association of Jamaica (MAJ), and the Media Association of Trinidad and Tobago (MATT) have also supported the growth and development of regional as well as territory-specific media within the Caribbean region.

Many of the Caribbean region's television and newspaper industries also have an Internet presence. However, many Caribbean countries underutilize the Internet medium. Unlike the United States, which is moving away from the usage of the Internet news website as print shovelware to more of a breaking-news medium, most Caribbean newsrooms use the Internet medium to repurpose content from their print editions. Notable exceptions include high news interest times, such as during elections and sporting events when breaking news updates are more vital. An assessment of Internet usage statistics for the Caribbean can explain why less focus has been placed on online news delivery as a breaking-news platform. As of 2006, the Caribbean region had very low Internet connectivity. The Internet World Stats (n.d.) found that Internet connectivity ranged from a high of approximately 56 percent of the population in Barbados to a low of less than 2 percent in such places as Cuba and the Netherlands Antilles. Internet connection speeds are also very slow. For example, according to the Trinidad and Tobago Computer Society (2005), most residents in Trinidad connect to the Internet via dial-up, with broadband services confined to select, wealthier areas in the island. Unlike the United States where Internet access is often a flat fee per month, accessing the Internet in the Caribbean is often tied to pricing schemes that specify a certain number of Internet hours per month. It is evident that Internet news websites from the Caribbean region are primarily viewed by Caribbean citizens living abroad who use the sites to keep abreast of the region's news. This audience for Caribbean Internet news includes many Caribbean journalists who go to the United States and Britain for journalism training.

As it relates to a mobile communications culture, the Caribbean region has a strong cell phone infrastructure, and many citizens use their cell phones to make calls, text message, and access the Internet at wireless Internet hotspots. Cell phone plans are often very cheap. Unlike the US model of being tied to long-term cell phone contracts, within the Caribbean it is more common for citizens to purchase cell phone minutes by charging their phones with dollar amounts. News media have yet to use the mobile communications platform for news delivery. As of 2006, cell phone usage in the Caribbean was confined to sending/receiving calls, text messaging, and game playing.

Locating women in the Caribbean newsroom. Because of the diversity of history, culture, and politics in the Caribbean region, it is difficult to speak in one voice about the Caribbean newsroom. Haiti and Cuba do not have a free press; other nations struggle to maintain a free press. In August 2006, three weeks before Guyana's general election, four male Guyanese journalists from the *Kaieteur News* were shot and killed in the newsroom in an incident that appeared to be a deliberate targeting and assassination (Kaieteur News, 2006). The differences in the racial composition of the islands have also had an effect on the political relations within the newsroom. Finally, the division of the Caribbean islands by language has also resulted in a culture of language homophily among those islands that are linguistically similar. For example, it is common for citizens of the English-speaking Caribbean to not speak Spanish, French, or Dutch, making communication with other Caribbean non-English speaking territories difficult.

It can be argued that the Caribbean is aware of gender disparities in the newsroom, and steps have been taken by activists to promote education about gender inequalities throughout the many regions' newsrooms. In 1998, 11 countries across the Caribbean drew up the Kingston Declaration on Gender and Media Policy, focusing on women's portrayal in media, women's employment as it related to decision-making and production in the newsroom, and professional codes of conduct in the newsroom. The result of this declaration was enhanced activism by local women's groups such as Women's Media Watch in Jamaica and the Women and Development Unit in Barbados, though it found that there was little change in regional policy to effect greater positive representation of women in media reports and in media newsrooms (de Bruin, 2000). Subsequent one-time surveys by the Caribbean Institute of Media in 1993–4 and 1997–8 provided quantitative backing on the dearth of women in editorial departments and decision-making positions in middle and senior management (ibid.). The significance of assessing gender disparities in the Caribbean media industry has grown in the twenty-first century with awareness that women now outnumber men in many of the region's newsrooms (J.R., personal communication, April 30, 2006; N.M., personal communication, June 15, 2006).

Yet, women are still given scant attention in Caribbean news reports. In a study by the Global Media Monitoring Project that presented data on such Caribbean newsrooms as Cuba, Haiti, Jamaica, Trinidad, Surinam, and Puerto Rico, it was found that 22 percent and 25 percent of news reports in 1995 and 2005 respectively mentioned women as news subjects (Gallagher, 2005, p. 31). In terms of specific subject matter, women in these Caribbean regions were primarily portrayed as victims, and gained lowest representation in matters of politics and government. In this Caribbean region, women as news subjects were less prone to appear in leadership roles: only 19 percent of women news subjects functioned as experts, and 22 percent as eye witnesses and spokespersons in comparison to 46 percent of women who gave popular opinion reports (ibid., p. 42). Women were also twice as likely to be portrayed as victims (ibid., p. 43), and only 15 percent of stories in 2005 positioned women as central to news (ibid., p. 71). Data were also provided on the gender balance of newsrooms in these same Caribbean nations. Of the 2,885 people working in print, television, and radio in these Caribbean regions, women comprised 43 percent and 41 percent of news presenters in 2000 and 2005 respectively (ibid., p. 60). In the period 2000 to 2005, female reporters increased from 39 percent to 41 percent, a marginal, yet positive increase (ibid., p. 61).

In an attempt to shed more light on women in the traditional newsrooms, case studies will be presented on the English-speaking islands of Jamaica and Trinidad.

Jamaica

Jamaica is the third largest island in the Caribbean, and the largest of the English-speaking nations of the Caribbean. Located in close proximity to Cuba and the Dominican Republic, it is the third most populated territory in the Americas after the United States and Canada. According to the *CIA World Factbook* (2006), Jamaica's population stood at 2,758,124 in July 2006, with females outnumbering males in the age group of 15 to 64. The racial composition of the island is predominantly black and mulatto, a legacy of the high numbers of African slaves that were brought in to work the plantation estates after the English expelled the Spanish and began the slave trade in the seventeenth and eighteenth centuries. A series of slave rebellions led by Maroons, or slaves who had escaped from the plantations to the Jamaican mountains, led to the eventual abolition of slavery in 1808 (Williams, 1971, 1994; Heuman, 1995). Slaves were eventually granted full freedom in 1838 and on August 6, 1962, Jamaica achieved full independence from England. Currently, the primary language in Jamaica is English, though Jamaican Creole, a dialect of English, West African language, Spanish, and French, is commonly spoken among the local Jamaican population.

Prime ministers such as Norman Manley, Sir William Bustamante, Sir Donald Sangster, Hugh Shearer, Michael Manley, Edward Seaga, and Percival James Patterson have led Jamaica since its independence from Britain. In March 2006, Jamaica inaugurated its first female prime minister, the Honorable Portia Simpson Miller as leader of the ruling People's National Party (BBC News, 2006; Francis, 2006). However, though it is evident that she has gained much press attention because of her sex, Simpson Miller is often denied her femininity in media circles. Due to her courageous and strong personality, she is often described as a woman "with balls" (*Jamaican Gleaner*, 2006). This symbolism can create the impression that Simpson Miller has been the only strong female to hold the position as prime minister of a Caribbean island. However, previous female prime ministers such as Eugenia Charles of Dominica and Janet Jagan of Guyana highlight that the Caribbean region is not hostile toward females in positions of power in politics. Quite the opposite, many Caribbean islands have surpassed Western countries such as the United States in their acceptance of women as holders of the highest offices in the land.

Though women outnumber men in Jamaica, a greater percentage of women suffer from lower socioeconomic status when compared to men. Though women account for over 70 percent of university graduates, two-thirds of households living below the poverty line are headed by a female, and two-thirds of new human immunodeficiency virus (HIV) infections are girls in the age group 10 to 19 years (Caribbean Net News, 2005). The preponderance of violence and crime in the Jamaican society also makes it a repressive and dangerous situation for all women, including women journalists. Most of the escalation in crime has been related to a 50 percent increase in violent crime, namely homicide, which has risen from 3.8 per 100,000 of the Jamaican population in 1962 to 17.6 in 1976 and 43 per 100,000 in 2001 (Harriott, 2004).

Jamaica is the only island in the Caribbean in which students can be regionally trained for jobs in media industries. The Caribbean Institute of Media and Communications

(CARIMAC) at the University of the West Indies in Mona, Jamaica, houses the only mass communication school in the region, which provides among other things theoretical and practical training in journalism. Jamaica boasts a diverse line-up of local media industries. Currently, there are approximately 14 radio stations, three television stations (*TVJ*, *CVM*, and *RETV*), four community newspapers (*The Manderville Weekly*, *The News*, *North Coast Times*, and *The Mirror*), an evening newspaper (*The Star*), two dailies (*Jamaican Observer* and *Jamaican Gleaner*), and a Sunday newspaper (*Sunday Herald*).

Some statistics exist on the gender composition of Jamaican newsrooms and Jamaican news reports. Interestingly, approximately 87 percent of television presenters are women in comparison to only 13 percent of presenters being men (Gallagher, 2005, p. 118). However, only 40 percent of Jamaican reporters are female (ibid.). When it comes to assessing women as news subjects, only 29 percent of news reports center stories on women (ibid., p. 120). As it relates to Jamaican women as news subjects by genre, approximately 3 percent of news reports on politics feature a woman as news subject in comparison to 12 percent of reports on economy, and 42 percent on crime and violence (ibid., p. 122). When news reports present women, women are more likely to be the central subject of the story as opposed to being valued for their opinion. For example, 67 percent of news reports with women feature these women as central subjects, while only 23 percent of the reports feature women as experts and 15 percent of reports with women as spokespersons (ibid., p. 128).

An interview with Nazma Muller, a journalist with the *Jamaican Observer*, has revealed sharp gender gaps in the newspaper's newsroom operations (N.M., personal communication, June 15, 2006). Muller noted that though there are six women editors, the key positions of news editor and editor-in-chief are held by men. Interestingly, the assistant news editor of the paper is a woman, but her success is not reflected in the fate of other females in the newsroom. Of the 20 columnists, only three are female. There are only four to five female reporters as opposed to ten men reporters. There are no women reporters covering business, trade, finance, or economic issues and at that newspaper, there are no female photojournalists. In speaking of career advancement at the *Jamaican Observer*, Muller felt that women do not face problems being promoted to editorial and managerial positions in features or magazine supplements, but their promotions are resisted for such powerful positions such as the Sunday editor, the news editor, or the editor-in-chief. Muller, who worked in England for six years as a freelance sub-editor, has held many journalism jobs in the Caribbean, including being a sub-editor, the founding editor of VOX—the *Trinidad Express*'s magazine for 15- to 25-year-olds —and a feature writer and editor for the *Jamaican Observer*'s *TeenAge* and *All Woman*. In speaking of her own stumbling blocks to career advancement, which included being overlooked for the Sunday editor position at the *Trinidad Express*, Muller stated:

> I had no problem being hired as layout editor at the *Jamaican Observer* because it wasn't seen as a position with a lot of power. However, when I started to give advice and make changes to the content—correcting errors and headlines—the executive editor for operations took it personally, as if I was encroaching on his territory.
>
> (N.M., personal communication, June 15, 2006)

Muller observed that the news often lacks sensitivity to coverage of women's issues. She recounted an incident in which a woman was beaten by six policemen in public in Half Way Tree, a major transport hub in Kingston. The woman was trying to prevent the policemen from beating and arresting her husband. Though a photo was carried on the front page, it failed to grab the paper's lead, becoming secondary to a story on day-to-day governmental politics in Jamaica. When Muller questioned the layout choice for the story by her superiors, she was told that the story of the woman being beaten did not "conform to the image of the paper" which is read by "policymakers, the movers and shakers in the country."

Jamaican newspapers have created a unique space for women readers through the creation of women-only supplements. At the *Jamaican Observer*, the woman's supplement is called *All Woman*. At the *Jamaican Gleaner*, the woman's supplement is called *Flair*. Both *All Woman* and *Flair* provide profiles of women who have excelled in professional and entrepreneurial fields or have overcome personal challenges. Topics include beauty tips, advice on such issues such as child maintenance, domestic violence, or sexual harassment, health and well being, fashion and gossip.

Since 1987, the Women's Media Watch (WMW) in Jamaica has been focusing on the relationship between Jamaica's societal violence to women and violence in media images. In its early history, the organization framed itself as a watchdog of news reports, advertisements, and television programs in an effort to point out media bias in its framing of women. However, this led to the public perception of WMV as antagonistic toward traditional mass media. WMW has since maintained a closer relationship to the internal media newsroom in an effort to raise the profile of women and create change in the news media's stereotyped portrayal of women. De Bruin (2000) noted that the WMV sought to include more women as sources in news reports through circulating lists of potential women sources for radio and media newsrooms to draw upon when seeing expert opinion for their news reports.

No accessible statistics exist on the gender differences in attention to traditional mass media in Jamaica.

Trinidad and Tobago

Though the nation is formally known as Trinidad and Tobago, Trinidad is the larger of the two islands, existing as a separate Caribbean territory for many years before the British placed Tobago under Trinidad's administrative control in 1889. The two islands were eventually enjoined as a twin-island republic in 1976. Since Christopher Columbus' discovery of Trinidad in 1498, the island has had a series of European occupations, the result of which has created a very cosmopolitan Trinidadian population (Williams, 1964, 1971, 1994). Spain ruled the island after Columbus' landfall for approximately 299 years, with their reign ending in 1797 when the British took over occupation of the island. During Spain's reign, the French and their slaves also emigrated from the French colonies to Trinidad. Trinidad's original Amerindian inhabitants, the Arawaks and Caribs, were wiped out, and the slave trade brought many Africans to Trinidad to work the plantations (Shepherd & Beckles, 2000). In 1806, slave trading was outlawed in Trinidad, and in 1834, slavery was abolished though slaves could still be apprenticed. Apprenticeship ended in 1834 leading to the complete emancipation of slaves in 1838. With a need for labor to work the plantations, the period 1845 to 1917 saw a large-scale immigration of laborers to work the sugar estates that were formerly worked by African slaves (Dabydeen & Samaroo, 1987; Look Lai, 1993; Ji, 2003). These laborers included first the East Indian indentured laborers from Calcutta, India, then other immigrants from China and the Middle East.

This history of slavery and indenturship has created a racially diverse island. Both the Indian and African races are predominant in the island as are racially mixed populations. The population total for Trinidad and Tobago stands at over 1.3 million, with Trinidad's population surpassing 1.2 million (Central Statistical Office, n.d.). As a result of the large numbers of Indians in Trinidad, the Hindu and Muslim religions are popular, as is the spoken language of Hindi. Though English is the primary language, patois, a dialect of French, is still spoken. Due to Trinidad's Spanish heritage and its geographical proximity to Venezuela, Spanish is also popularly spoken and utilized in song and dance.

The gender relations in Trinidad can be characterized by a deep schism. Though Trinidad has not had a female prime minister like Jamaica, women such as Hazel Manning, Mary King, Dana Seetahal, and Camille Robinson Regis have held parliamentary positions or positions in political parties.

Though women have strong, visible roles in politics, Trinidad has not been able to control the growth in domestic violence within the household. The Amnesty International Annual Report for 2004 singled out Trinidad and Tobago for the society's increasing tide of violence against women, laying blame for this violence on a hostile court system and poor response by police and relevant authorities (Trinidad Guardian, 2004). For example, in August 2005, at least five brutal murders of women were attributed to domestic violence, while in 2004, there were 490 reported assaults against women with 12 murders resulting from domestic violence (Mokool, 2005). While Trinidad has a domestic violence act, the law does not provide sufficient protection for abused women. For example, 6,829 of the 9,043 cases filed between August 2002 and July 2003 were dismissed; similarly, 4,458 of the 5,946 cases filed between August 2003 and March 2004 were dismissed (Trinidad Guardian, 2005). Yet, though law authorities seemingly approach domestic violence with a cavalier response, the media has been providing strong coverage of this rising problem (Ramdeen, 2004; Mahabir-Wyatt, 2005; Martin, 2005; Trinidad Express, 2005; John, 2006). The irony of the growth in domestic violence is underscored by the famed culture of Trinidadian Carnival, which culminates in a two-day national festival preceding the start of Lent. As is evidenced by front-page news photos of women in skimpily clad costumes during this festival, women are celebrated for their beauty and physique, almost like goddesses. This celebration of women's sexuality is overt, often masking the underbelly of violence and disrespect for women in the society.

As of 2006, Trinidad has three daily newspapers, the *Trinidad Guardian*, the *Trinidad Express*, and the *Newsday*, five television stations, and over 15 radio stations. Some statistics exist on the gender composition of Trinidadian newsrooms and Trinidadian news reports. Many of these statistics suggest that Trinidadian female journalists outnumber males in the newsroom. As of 2005, 57 percent of television presenters were female and 66 percent of reporters were female (Gallagher, 2005, p. 118). However, though women outnumber men in the Trinidadian newsroom, females are significantly less likely to be the subject of news reports. In terms of news reports, only 23 percent feature a woman as a news subject (ibid., p. 120). When women are presented as new subjects, women are less prone to be in authoritative roles. Only 29 percent of news reports that feature women as subjects have them appearing as eye-witnesses, 36 percent as spokespersons, but none as experts (ibid., p. 128). These statistics suggest that women journalists could be playing a role in perpetuating the invisibility of women as powerful and authoritative news subjects.

Both the *Trinidad Guardian* and the *Trinidad Express* newspapers have women's magazines, which run in their Sunday edition. The *Trinidad Guardian's* Sunday women's magazine called *WomanWise* was started in direct response to the *Sunday Express* women's magazine (J.R., personal communication, April 30, 2006). Though no access statistics exist for the gender differences in news consumption, these women supplements suggest an attempt to reach out to women readers. These magazines typically address fashion, beauty, and family issues, but the main focus is on profiling strong, women achievers in a variety of fields, professional and nonprofessional.

The prevalence of women in broadcast is evident in both the early morning news and the evening news anchor desks. As of 2006, five of the eight regular newsreaders were women, with three of these five women working for the privately owned cable television station *Cable News Channel 3* (CNC). Since the mid 1990s, it has been common for women to present the news, and, currently, women host and moderate many of the nightly news programs and the top-rated local news programs that combine analysis and critical commentary. It is difficult to miss that these women are not only intelligent but beautiful, leading one former Trinidadian print female journalist to lament "I got the feeling from women who worked in television that the position of anchoring was given to someone who looked the part, more than for their journalistic abilities" (F.P., personal communication, May 11 2006).

A series of interviews with female print journalists in the Trinidadian newsroom reveals a more complex picture of newsroom gender relations than what is possible to be gleaned from quantitative statistics. Like the statistics highlight, women journalists seem to outnumber men. Asked about this gender imbalance in the newsroom, former Acting Editor of the *Trinidad Guardian* who also previously worked as Assistant Sunday Editor of the *Trinidad Express* Judy Raymond noted, "fewer men are now entering the business, partly because journalism is very badly paid and not at all prestigious. In fact male applicants are now especially welcomed because of the preponderance of women" (J.R., personal communication, April 30, 2006). The result of this loss of male journalists to other professions has resulted in women journalists being able to ascend the career ladder due to their sheer numbers in the newsrooms. As of the end of 2005, the balance of women to men editors at one *Trinidad Guardian* newspaper was said to be fairly equal (J.R., personal communication, April 30, 2006). The *Trinidad Guardian* has been one of the few newspapers in the Caribbean region to hire a female editor-in-chief. Many Trinidadian female journalists agreed that the only area where women seemingly face difficulties is sports journalism (J.R., personal communication, April 30, 2006; P.M., personal communication, April 30, 2006).

Because of the more recent preponderance of women journalists in Trinidadian newsrooms, junior-level female journalists expressed optimism about the state of gender relations in the Trinidadian newsroom. Petal Maharaj, who worked for the *Trinidad Guardian* until 2005, rose quickly through the ranks of editor, noting that she "was promoted three times in three years and left the *Trinidad Guardian* as an Associate Editor and the *Trinidad Express* as Assistant Chief Sub-editor" (P.M., personal communication, April 30, 2006). Another former journalist, Franka Philip, who left the Trinidadian newsroom in 1999 and now works for the BBC, noted that women were present in every department during her time at the *Trinidad Express,* the *Trinidad Guardian* and the *Newsday* in both senior editor and executive management positions (F.P., personal communication, May 11, 2006).

When asked about barriers blocking women's promotion to senior management or top-level editor positions, Judy Raymond, who held a variety of editorial positions in the *Guardian* newspaper including, acting editor, editor of News and Features, and associate editor, noted:

> There is still a feeling among *Trinidad Guardian* company management that women should be seen but not heard, which was one factor in my decision to leave: simply because I was a woman who had principles and opinions and was willing to speak

out on them. I was seen by senior management as being a troublemaker and was never confirmed as editor. I believe race as well as gender and age were factors in the managing director's attitude.

(J.R., personal communications, April 30, 2006)

Regardless of the seniority ranks, all women journalists interviewed felt that women faced unique barriers to achievement within newsrooms. Raymond noted the following in commenting about the changing demographic of younger women in the newsroom:

Many of the women journalists are young, single mothers, and they face an extra challenge in that no allowance whatsoever is made for them in terms of flexible working hours or company provision of childcare after school hours (schools in this country finish by about 2 p.m.; reporters rarely get to leave the newsroom before 6 p.m. at best), or time off or other facilities to help care for sick children, children on vacation, etc. Last year, I raised the possibility of introducing flexible working hours on the newsdesk, but the idea was immediately shot down by the editor-in-chief.

(J.R., personal communications, April 30, 2006)

This barrier that women with children face was primarily the reason why former Trinidadian journalist Petal Maharaj quit her full-time job at the newspaper six weeks after the birth of her son for a teaching position at a high school in Trinidad. Though she eventually returned to the paper in 2005, she remained on the payroll as a freelancer until she left the newspaper in the latter part of 2005 (P.M., personal communications, April 25, 2006).

Supporting women in Caribbean media: Future steps.   With the increase in female journalists in Caribbean newsrooms, the region cannot afford to adopt policies that hinder women's advancement to top-level editorial positions. The increasing levels of violent crime and domestic violence have created unsafe societal conditions for women, resulting in the media's primary framing of women as victims in their news reports. Additionally, the lack of childcare and flexible work hours remain difficult roadblocks for many women journalists who want to balance the demands of work and life without compromising their performance in either sphere. These gender inequities seem especially pervasive in the print media industry. It is possible that these structural barriers to traditional media advancement underlie the strong growth of the Caribbean blogosphere for women. The blog as a tool for personal publishing allows women to balance the demands of career and family without having to account to male authority. Though many Caribbean newspapers are attempting to attract women audiences through the publishing of special women supplements, Caribbean newsrooms must make more than just token gestures if they want to establish a lasting connection with its women readers. Otherwise, the growth of the Caribbean blogosphere promises to provide strong competition for women's attention as it continues to gain momentum in the twenty-first century.

Notes

1   Contributors were invited to give their perspectives because of their personal and professional experiences with that country or region. The contributors for each country or region in this chapter are listed as follows: Brazil by Vanessa de M. Higgins; Chile by Teresa Correa; Mexico by María Flores; and the Caribbean by Sharon Meraz.

2   María Flores' gratitude goes to her mother Margarita Gutiérrez Talamás and St. Edward's University McNair Scholar Cindy López for their assistance with this research.

References

Brazil

Amaral, R. & Guimarães, C. (1994). Media monopoly in Brazil. *Journal of Communication*, 44(4), 26–38.

Associação Nacional de Editores de Revistas. (2006, March 20). *Evolução do Market share das principais editoras em exemplares*. Retrieved March 20, 2006 from www.aner.org.br/conteudo/1/artigo1860-1.asp.

Brazilian Government Portal. (2006a, July 17). *Crescimento sustentável*. Retrieved July 17, 2006 from www.brasil.gov.br/pais/brasil_temas/econ/econ_negoc.

Brazilian Government Portal. (2006b, July 17). *Um país em movimento*. Retrieved July 17, 2006 from www.brasil.gov.br/pais/sobre_brasil/pais_sobre.

Brazilian Institute of Geography and Statistics [IBGE]. (2006a, July 17). *Censo demográfico 2000: educação: Resultados da amostra*. Retrieved July 17, 2006 from www.ibge.gov.br/home/presidencia/noticias/02122003censoeduchtml.shtm.

Brazilian Institute of Geography and Statistics [IBGE]. (2007, October 3). *Educação*. Retrieved October 3, 2007 from www.ibge.gov.br/brasil_em_sintese/graficos/educacao/tavas_analfabetismo.gif.

Brazilian Institute of Geography and Statistics [IBGE]. (2006c, July 17). *Popclock: Estimativas da População*. Retrieved July 17, 2006 from www.ibge.gov.br/brasil_em_sintese/popclock.php.

Brazilian Institute of Geography and Statistics [IBGE]. (2006d, July 17). *População total e proporção da população por sexo, grandes grupos de idade e situação de domicílio*. Retrieved July 17, 2006 from www.ibge.gov.br/brasil_em_sintese/tabelas/populacao_tabela01.htm.

Comitê Gestor da Internet no Brasil. (2007, October 3). *Perfil da audiência por gênero*. Retrieved October 3, 2007 from www.nic.br/indicadores/usuarios/tab02-03.htm.

De Abreu, A.A. & Rocha, D. (Eds.) (2006). *Elas ocuparam as redações: depoimentos ao CPDOC*. Brazil: Editora FGV.

Dines, A., Vogt, C., & de Melo, J. (Eds.) (1997). *A Imprensa em questão*. Brazil: Editora da UNICAMP.

Federação Nacional dos Jornalistas. (2006, March 15). *Número de jornalistas: Brasil*. Retrieved March 15, 2006 from www.fenaj.org.br/arquivos/numero_jornalistas.xls.

Gross Domestic Product Indicators of the Inter-American Development Bank. (2006). *Country Indicators: Key figures of the country's economic and social development*. Retrieved March 1, 2006 from www.iadb.org/countries/indicators.cfm?language=English&id_country=BR&p Language=ENGLISH&pCountry=BR&parid=8#.

Grupo Abril. (2004). *Relatório Anual do Grupo Abril*. Retrieved on March 20, 2006 from www.abril.com.br/arquivo/relatorioanual_2004.pdf.

Herscovitz, H. (2004). Brazilian journalist's perceptions of media roles, ethics and foreign influences on Brazilian journalism. *Journalism Studies*, 5(1), 71–86.

Heuvel, J. & Dennis, E.E. (1995). *Changing Patterns: Latin America's vital media: A report of The Freedom Forum Media Studies Center at Columbia University in the City of New York*. New York: The Center.

Karlekar, K.D. (Ed.) (2005). *Freedom of the Press 2005: A global survey of media independence/Freedom House*. Lanham: Rowman & Littlefield.

Manta, A. (1997). *Guia do jornalismo na Internet*. Retrieved August 20, 2005 from www.facom.ufba.br/pesq/cyber/manta/Guia/cap02.html.

Molica, F. (Ed.) (2005). *Dez reportagens que abalaram a ditadura*. Brazil: Editora Record.

Naldoni, T. & Piza, R.T. (2005, March). Gravatas e Sutiãs. *Revista Imprensa*, 199, 28–37.

Reis, E.P. & Schwartzman, S. (2002). *Pobreza e exclusão social: Aspectos sócio políticos*. Preliminary study for the World Bank. Retrieved March, 15, 2006 from www.schwartzman. org.br/simon/pdf/exclusion.pdf.

TV Globo. (2006). *A Redação*. Retrieved March 20, 2006 from http://jornalnacional.globo.com/ Jornalismo/JN/0,,3578,00.html.

Chile

Asociación Nacional de la Prensa (ANP). (2003a). *Número de diarios en Chile* [Number of newspapers in Chile]. Retrieved May 8, 2006 from www.anp.cl/p4_anp/site/artic/2004 0406/asocfile/ASOCFILE120040406111605.xls.

Asociación Nacional de la Prensa (ANP). (2003b). *Alcance de la prensa en Chile* [Newspaper penetration in Chile]. Retrieved May 8, 2006 from www.anp.cl/p4_anp/site/artic/2004 0406/asocfile/ASOCFILE120040406110753.xls.

Asociación Nacional de la Prensa (ANP). (2005). *Informe SVCL: Segundo semestre de 2005* [SVCL report: Second semester 2005]. Retrieved May 8, 2006 from www.anp.cl/p4_anp/ site/artic/20060324/asocfile/ASOCFILE120060324141104.xls.

Bulnes, M.A., Belmar, J., Bermúdez, A., & Viera, M. (2006). Catastro de medios [Media census]. Unpublished manuscript, Universidad Alberto Hurtado, Santiago, Chile.

Encuesta de Caracterización Socioeconómica Nacional—Casen. (2003). Principales resultados: Acceso a tecnologías de información y comunicación. [Main results: Access to information and communication technologies]. Retrieved August 14, 2006 from www.mideplan.cl/admin/ docdescargas/centrodoc/centrodoc_178.pdf.

Castellón, L. & Guillier, A. (1993). Chile: the emerging influence in journalism. *Media Studies Journal, 7*, 231–9.

Consejo Nacional de Televisión (CNTV). (2005a). *Encuesta nacional de televisión 2005* [National television survey 2005]. Retrieved May 1, 2006 from www.cntv.cl/cgi-bin/seguimiento.cgi? usuario=&seccion=&name=Portada CNTV&url=/medios/Publicaciones/PrincipalesResultados ENTV2005.pdf

Consejo Nacional de Televisión (CNTV). (2005b). *Barómetro de calidad: Noticiarios centrales de la TV abierta* [Quality barometer: Main TV newscasts]. Retrieved May 1, 2006 from www.cntv.cl/cgi-bin/seguimiento.cgi?usuario=&seccion=&name=Publicaciones&url=/medios/ Publicaciones/CalidadNoticiariosWeb2005.pdf.

Consejo Nacional de Televisión (CNTV). (2006). *Televisión y mujeres* [Television and women]. Retrieved May 1, 2006 from www.cntv.cl/medios/Publicaciones/Mujeres_2006.pdf.

Contreras, D. & Plaza, G. (2004, August). *Participación femenina en el mercado laboral chileno: ¿Cuánto importan los factores culturales?* [Participation of women in the Chilean labor market: How much do cultural factors affect?]. Retrieved May 1, 2006 from www.comunidad mujer.cl/cm/mujeresencifra/estudioCMUChile.ppt.

Dirección del Trabajo. (2005). *Mujer y trabajo: Compendio de estadísticas según sexo* [Women and work: Statistics by sex]. Retrieved July 28, 2006 from www.dt.gob.cl/documentacion/ 1612/article-88456.html.

Dussaillant, P. (2005). *Medios y elecciones: La elección presidencial de 1999* [Media and elections: The 1999 Chilean presidential election]. Santiago, Chile: Centro de Estudios Bicentenario/CIMAS.

Godoy, S. (2005). *Resultados World Internet Project—Chile 2003–2004: Cómo está y adónde va el uso de Internet en Chile* [World Internet Project—Chile 2003–2004 results: The state of the Internet usage in Chile and where is heading to]. *Cuadernos de Información, 18*, 100–111.

Godoy, S. & Herrera, S. (2004). *Internet Usage in Chile and the World: First results of the World Internet Project-Chile*. Retrieved August 14, 2006 from www.wipchile.cl/estudios/ japan/WIP_article_1_CdINFO_for_Japan_jul04.pdf.

Godoy, S., Herrera, S., & Fernández, F. (2005). Encuesta World Internet Project—Chile 2004: Proyectos Fondecyt No 1030946 y No 1050769 [World Internet Project—Chile 2004 survey: Fondecyt projects 1030946 and 1050769]. Unpublished manuscript, Pontificia Universidad Católica de Chile, Santiago, Chile.

Instituto Nacional de Estadísticas (INE). (2006). *Estadísticas laborales: Trimestre abril 2006—junio 2006. Población total de 15 años y más, por situación en la fuerza de trabajo, nivel nacional, según sexo y período* [Labor statistics: Second quarter 2006. Total 15 year-old or more population, by labor force situation, national level, by sex and period]. Retrieved July 28, 2006 from www.ine.cl/ine/canales/chile_estadistico/estadisticas_laborales/empleo/270706/xls/110301.xls.

Karlekar, K.D. (Ed.) (2005). *Freedom of the Press 2005: A global survey of media independence.* Lanham: Rowman & Littlefield.

Lehmann, C. (2003, September). Mujer, trabajo y familia: Realidad, percepciones y desafíos [Women, work and family: Reality, perceptions and challenges]. *Centro de Estudios Públicos—Puntos de Referencia*, 269, 1–11.

López, V. (2001). Women bring a certain look and feeling to news. *Nieman Reports*, 55(4), 100–3.

Mediática & Asociación de Radiodifusores de Chile (Archi). (2006). *Radio y emociones* [Radio and emotions]. Retrieved May 5, 2006, from www.udd.cl/prontus_docencia/site/artic/2006 0302/asocfile/estudio_archi_final_3.ppt.

Ministerio de Educación de Chile (Mineduc). (n.d.). *Egresados y titulados en educación superior* [Graduates from higher education]. Retrieved April 30, 2006 from http://compendio. educador.cl/docEgresados/3.3_C.xls.

Palacios, M. & Martínez, J. (2006). Liberalism and conservatism in Chile: Attitudes and opinions of Chilean women at the start of the twenty-first century. *Journal of Latin American Studies*, 38, 1–34.

Silva, U. & Torres, C. (1998). *Violencia en la prensa escrita: El caso de La Cuarta* [Violence in the press: The case of *La Cuarta*]. Santiago, Chile: Sur Profesionales.

Silva, U., Torres, C., & Cáceres, T. (1998). *Observatorio de medios de comunicación. Análisis de periódicos La Tercera, El Mercurio, La Época* [Media monitor. Analysis of *La Tercera, El Mercurio, La Época* newspapers]. Santiago, Chile: Sur Profesionales.

Valenzuela, S. & Correa, T. (2006, August). Madam or Mr. President? Press Coverage and Public Perceptions when a Woman Leads in a Presidential Election: The case of Chile. Paper presented at the annual convention of the Association for Education in Journalism and Mass Communication, San Francisco, California.

Weaver, D. & Wilhoit, G.C. (1998). Journalists in the United States. In D. Weaver (Ed.) *The Global Journalist: News people around the world*, pp. 395–414. Cresskill: Hampton Press.

Zarzar, M. (2004, November 5). *Comunicación con perfume de mujer* [Communication with scent of a woman]. Retrieved May 3, 2006 from www.periodismo.uchile.cl/noticias/2004/mujeresymedios03.html.

Mexico

Aguirre, A. (2005). Ya son 50 por ciento de empleadas. *La Jornada*.

Álvarez Laso, P. (2005). Mujeres en los medios. *Etcétera: Una Ventana al Mundo de los Medios*.

CIMAC, S. (2004, March 31). Se crea la red internacional de mujeres periodistas. Paper presented at the II Conferencia Latinoamericana de Mujeres Periodistas, Río de Janeiro, Brazil.

Committee to Protect Journalists. (2005). *Mexico*. Retrieved Febuary 2, 2006 from www.cpj. org/cases05/americas_cases05/mexico.html.

e-México. (2003a). *Bienvenidos al portal del sistema nacional e-méxico*. Retrieved May 8, 2006 from www.e-mexico.gob.mx/wb2/eMex/Home.

e-México. (2003b). *Resumen ejecutivo del sistema nacional e-méxico*. Retrieved May 4, 2006 from www.e-mexico.gob.mx/wb2/eMex/eMex_Resumen_ejecutivo_del_Sistema_Nacional_eMexic?page=3.

Espinoza Calderón, M.E. (1995). *De la página de sociales a las ocho columnas: La mujer en el periodismo*. Universidad Nacional Autónoma de México, San Juan de Aragón, Estado de México.

Fundación Heberto Castillo Martínez, A.C. (Ed.). (2005). *Mujeres y medios de comunicación*. México, D.F.: Fundación Heberto Castillo Martínez A.C.

González, R. (2001, June 7). México, único país que por decreto presidencial otorga premio nacional de periodismo. *CIMAC*, 2.

Hernández Carballido, E.L. (1998). La prensa femenina en México durante el siglo xix. In L. Navarrete Maya & B. Aguilar Plata (Eds.) *La prensa en México (1810–1915)* (pp. 45–63). México, D.F.: Pearson.

Hernández Téllez, J. (2001, October 21). Las mujeres como objeto y sujeto en el periodismo: El periodismo de mujeres. *Fem* (25), 82.

INEGI. (2006, June 30). *Población total según sexo, 1950 a 2005*. Retrieved August 11, 2006 from www.inegi.gob.mx/est/contenidos/espanol/rutinas/ept.asp?t=mpob01&c=3178.

López García, G. (2001, October 1). Las periodistas y el poder. *Fem* (25), 62.

Martínez González, M. d. L. (2000, February–March). Priva la inseguridad del empleo para mujeres periodistas. *Los Periodistas*, 3.

Novoa, R., Isunza, I., Ley, A., & Cheng, M. (2000). ¿cómo se mira a la mujeres en la prensa? Resultados de un monitoreo de prensa con perspectiva de género. In C. Communicación e Información de la Mujer AC & R. Red Nacional de Periodistas (Eds.) *Tejedoras de la palabra: Hablan los medios* (pp. 8–55). México, D.F.: Digitalizaciones e Impresiones, S.A. de C.V.

Ortiz Henderson, G. (2004). Mujeres en los medios: Aniquilación simbólica o democaratización mediática? *Revista Mexicana de Comunicación* (84).

Rodríguez Castañeda, R. (1993). *Prensa vendida*. México, D.F.

Premio Nacional de Periodismo. (2002). *Historia del consejo*. Retrieved April 7, 2006 from www.consejociudadano-periodismo.org/pg/histconsejo.html.

SCT. (2004). *Anuario*. Retrieved May 2, 2006, from http://portal.sct.gob.mx:80/SctPortal/app manager/Portal/Sct;jsessionid=G69TRMFYyBBNMRVGbLKmrvp1bn1hlnGWMBfY6v6ZXJ9 J0jyrcFyy!-1694907687!-1136764977?_nfpb=true&_pageLabel=P38003.

SEGOB. (2006, May 10). *Padrón de medios impresos certificados 2006*. Retrieved May 15, 2006 from www.gobernacion.gob.mx/.

Vargas, C. (2006, March 17). Hagamos visible lo invisible, las mujeres en los medios. *CIMAC*, p. 2.

Villamarín Carrascal, J. (2006). Los primeros periódicos y la prensa insurgente en América Latina. *Sala de Prensa*, 3(87).

Caribbean

BBC News. (2006, February, 26). *Jamaica to get first woman leader*. Retrieved August 8, 2006 from http://news.bbc.co.uk/2/hi/americas/4752192.stm.

Brown, A. (1990a). Effects of the New World Information Order on Caribbean media. In S.H. Surlin and W.C. Soderland (Eds.) *Mass Media and the Caribbean*, pp. 251–73. New York: Gordon and Breach.

Brown, A. (1990b). Mass media in Jamaica. In S.H. Surlin and W.C. Soderland (Eds.) *Mass Media and the Caribbean*, pp. 11–29. New York: Gordon and Breach.

Caribbean Net News. (2005, October 13). *Media encouraged to examine gender equality in the Caribbean*. Retrieved August 8, 2006 from www.caribbeannetnews.com/2005/10/13/encouraged. shtml.

Central Statistical Office. (n.d.). Fast facts about Trinidad and Tobago. Retrieved August 8, 2006 from www.cso.gov.tt/cso/tnt/default.aspx.

The CIA World Factbook. (2006). Jamaica. Retrieved August 8, 2006 from www.cia.gov/ cia/publications/factbook/geos/jm.html.

Cuthbert, M. & Hoover, S. (1990). Laissez-faire policies, VCRs, and Caribbean identity. In S.H. Surlin and W.C. Soderland (Eds.) *Mass Media and the Caribbean*, pp. 287–99. New York: Gordon and Breach.

Dabydeen, D. & Samaroo, B. (Eds.) (1987). *India in the Caribbean*. London: Hansib.

de Bruin, M. (2000). Looking beyond the 'body count' in the Caribbean. World Association for Christian Communication, 2000(3). Retrieved August 8, 2006 from www.wacc.org.uk /wacc/publications/media_development/archive/2000_3/looking_beyond_the_body_count_in_ the_caribbean.

Francis, P. (2006, March 31). Madam Prime Minister: Portia sworn in as Jamaica's first female head of government. Jamaican Gleaner. Retrieved August 8, 2006 from www.jamaica-g leaner.com/gleaner/20060331/lead/lead1.html.

Gallagher, M. (2005). Who makes the news. Global Media Monitoring Project, 2005. Retrieved August 8, 2006 from www.whomakesthenews.org/who_makes_the_news/report_2005.

Harriott, A. (2004). *Understanding Crime in Jamaica: New challenges for public policy.* University of the West Indies Press.

Heuman, G. (1995). *The 'Killing Time': The Morant Bay Rebellion in Jamaica.* London: MacMillan.

Internet World Stats. (n.d.). Internet usage in the Caribbean. Retrieved August 8, 2006 from www.Internetworldstats.com/stats2.htm.

Jamaican Gleaner. (2006, February 26). Portia Simpson Miller—heart, soul, and guts. Retrieved August 8, 2006 from www.jamaica-gleaner.com/gleaner/20060226/lead/lead6.html.

Ji, R. (2003, May 22). Journey through the landscape. Trinidad Guardian. Retrieved August 8, 2006 from www.guardian.co.tt/archives/2003-05-22/ravi-ji.html.

John, R. (2006, May 14). Lucky to be alive on Mother's Day. Trinidad Express. Retrieved August 8, 2006 from www.trinidadexpress.com/index.pl/article?id=159222159.

Kaieteur News. (2006, August 11). Editorial: no retreat, no surrender. Retrieved August 11, 2006 from www.kaieteurnewsgy.com/editorial.htm.

Look Lai, W. (1993). *Indentured Labour, Caribbean Sugar: Chinese and Indian migrants to the British West Indies, 1838–1918.* Baltimore and London: The John Hopkins University Press.

Mahabir-Wyatt, D. (2005, April 9). Abuse of the innocents. *Trinidad Guardian.* Retrieved August 8, 2006 from www.guardian.co.tt/archives/2005-04-10/opinion.html.

Martin, C.J. (2005, December 5). The horror of domestic abuse. *Trinidad Express.* Retrieved August 8, 2006 from www.trinidadexpress.com/index.pl/article?id=120598073.

Mokool, M. (2005, November 23). Domestic violence on the rise. *Trinidad Guardian.* Retrieved August 8, 2006 from www.guardian.co.tt/archives/2005-11-23/features1.html.

Ramdeen, L. (2004, November 22). Eliminating violence against women. *Trinidad Guardian.* Retrieved August 8, 2006 from www.guardian.co.tt/archives/2004-11-22/LeelaRamdeen.html.

Shepherd, V. & Beckles, H. (Eds.) (2000). *Caribbean Slavery in the Atlantic World.* Kingston: Ian Randle Publishers.

Straubhaar, J. (in press). *World Television.*

Surlin, S.H. & Soderland, W.C. (Eds.) (1990). *Mass Media and the Caribbean.* New York: Gordon and Breach.

Trinidad and Tobago Computer Society. (2005). Internet access options in Trinidad and Tobago. Retrieved August 8, 2006 from www.ttcsweb.org/articles/isptnt/index.htm.

Trinidad Express. (2005). Chopping leaves woman critical. Retrieved August 8, 2006 from www.trinidadexpress.com/index.pl/article?id=120797515.

Trinidad Guardian. (2004, June 21). Changes needed in policing domestic violence. Retrieved August 8, 2006 from www.guardian.co.tt/archives/2004-06-21/editorial.html.

Trinidad Guardian. (2005, November 24). Let's stamp out domestic violence. Retrieved August 8, 2006 from www.guardian.co.tt/archives/2005-11-24/editorial.html.

UNESCO. (1980). Many voices, one world: The MacBride report, 1980. Retrieved August 8, 2006 from www2.hawaii.edu/~rvincent/mcbcon1.htm.

Williams, E. (1964). *History of the People of Trinidad and Tobago.* London: A. Deutsch.

Williams, E. (1971). *From Columbus to Castro: The history of the Caribbean 1492–1969.* New York: Harper & Row.

Williams, E. (1994). *Capitalism & Slavery.* Chapel Hill: University of North Carolina Press.

Chapter 14

News, Feminist Theories, and the Gender Divide

Dustin Harp

For many living in the United States today, feminism seems an irrelevant and outdated concept. Young women often argue that gender equality was won thanks to feminists who were fighting for rights long before the contemporary generation of women was even born. It is true that most women in this country now have more rights, opportunities, and freedoms than ever before. But better does not mean that gender relations are equal or satisfactory or that our social power structures have changed in any significant way. While it may seem that women have the opportunity to enter the workforce, educational system, and sports arena (thanks to Title IX) in equal numbers to men, some telling statistical data presents another story of women's status in the United States. What is more revealing than the fact that a woman has never been president or vice president of this country? Or that in the 109th US Congress women hold only 81 (15 percent) of the 535 seats. Further, in 2005 women held only 16 percent of the 10,873 corporate officer positions at Fortune 500 companies while women of color occupied less than 2 percent of them (Catalyst, 2006, p. 14). It is also hard to ignore data that concludes women in this country still on average earn only about 76 percent of what men earn, while African-American women earn just 63 percent and Hispanic women only 53 percent of white men's median annual earnings (Caiazza et al., 2004, pp. 5, 11).

Turning to mass media and specifically journalism the statistical story is much the same—women are not treated equally in and by the industry. Consider this:

- The portion of women holding executive newspaper positions at 137 newspapers with a circulation more than 85,000 increased only 2 percentage points between 2003 and February of 2006—when it rose to 29 percent—while the number of women newspaper publishers has remained steady, at 18 percent, according to Northwestern University's Media Management Center (Arnold & Nesbitt, 2006).
- Numerous surveys have shown that in major US newspapers, male journalists' bylines dominate while female journalists are rare (Gibbons, 2005).
- In one survey of US newspapers, more than three-quarters of all stories contained male sources, while only a third of stories included even one female source (Project for Excellence in Journalism, 2005).
- Newspapers are the most likely news media to cite at least one female source in a story—41 percent of stories, while all three major cable news channels, despite the enormous time available to fill, are the least likely medium to cite a female source—19 percent of stories (Project for Excellence in Journalism, 2005).
- In 2004 women occupied 39 percent of the television news workforce while only 21 percent of news directors were women. Further only 12 percent of all news

directors in the local broadcast workforce are ethnic or racial minorities (Papper, 2005).

- When it comes to salaries, female print journalists make $9,000 less a year than their male colleagues and female television news directors make $4,000 less (Gibbons, 2004).

Feminism and Communication Theories

These statistics illustrate why feminism is still relevant and important in contemporary times. Feminist theories offer tools for understanding and critiquing these types of inequalities. Since the 1960s, when women finally started making significant inroads into academic institutions, feminist scholars articulated ways in which gender relations influence mass media institutions, practices, forms, and audiences.

Those who have not studied feminism or feminist media theories may not know just how rich and varied this area of study is. Here I offer an admittedly brief Western-centered narrative of feminism, not to present a definitive storyline but to provide insight and a framework for understanding the "enormous heterogeneity" of mass media research undertaken through a feminist lens (van Zoonen, 1994, p. 2). Feminism, as it has been taken up in the academy, is a contested and fractured terrain, best understood as *feminisms* (in its plural form). In accounting for the various ways in which feminism as a social movement has changed in the United States, one can better see the trajectory of feminist theories in the academy and how these have been applied to the field of journalism. To present a feminist perspective means to position oneself within this diverse landscape but in doing so my goal is not to diminish any of the many feminist perspectives. I believe that the gender issues undertaken by feminist scholars are best understood—and the results most productive—when the work comes from multiple theoretical perspectives.

Feminism in the United States is often described as occurring in waves with distinct goals and standpoints during these times, though it is important to acknowledge that feminism in the United States existed prior to the first wave and did not disappear in between these marked surges of activity. First wave feminism is associated with the 1848 Seneca Falls Convention in New York, the nation's first women's rights convention. At the convention attendees declared women's natural equality and outlined political strategies for gaining equal opportunities and access (Donovan, 1992). Since the Founding Fathers failed to give women the right to vote when they wrote the US Constitution, the movement dedicated itself primarily to gaining suffrage through reform efforts such as temperance and abolition (Ryan, 1992). First wave feminists challenged stereotypes of women and the ways in which women of the time were expected to behave. Some of the prominent beliefs about women of the time included that they were weak, incompetent, and expected to be pure. The first wave feminist movement, however, was comprised of mostly white, middle-class, and well-educated women, and the movement paid little attention to women living alternative realities. An early fracturing of feminist thought is illustrated in the two main tenets of first wave US feminism—liberal feminism and socialist/Marxist feminism, developed in workers' unions (Krolokke & Sorensen, 2006).

When women finally won the right to vote in 1920 with the ratification of the Nineteenth Amendment to the US Constitution, the unifying issue of the first wave feminist movement disappeared and the various sectors divided further. Feminists of the time were especially divided over whether women should work for advancement as people in their own right, or whether women, as mothers, needed special treatment to fulfill this role (Ryan, 1992). Because of this disagreement feminists lacked a cohesive ideology, and a real or perceived reduction in feminist presence within US society prevailed. Second wave feminism describes organization and activity during the 1960s and 1970s. This re-emergence of a powerful feminist movement is typically explained as a reaction to the family-centered years of the 1950s (Ryan, 1992). Women had moved in great numbers into paid employment during World War II, but the era following the war was marked by an ideological shift that re-established women's place in the home and "defined the wife/mother role as both women's special duty and path to fulfillment" (Ryan, 1992, p. 42). The focus of second wave feminism, which stressed the difference between women and men, was to transform society in a number of ways, including in the social, political, economic, personal, and cultural arenas. Betty Friedan's 1963 book, *The Feminine Mystique*, which is widely cited as sparking the second wave feminist movement, attacked the popular idea that women's fulfillment rested in childrearing and homemaking (Friedan, 1963). This view of feminism, however, has been criticized for exclusionary and simplistic notions of women, based upon the issues and needs of white, middle- to upper-class heterosexual women. Specific issues of concern included domestic violence, employment and educational opportunities, wage discrimination, rape laws, and sexual violence. Feminists by this time, however, were far from forming a cohesive way of thinking and had become even more fragmented.

During the second wave feminist movement a number of significant cultural changes regarding women and gender occurred. The transformations covered many areas of society but of particular interest here is what happened in the news industry, where men had dominated journalism. Women were asking for equal opportunities to cover all news and equal pay for their work but when asking did not result in changes, women turned to the Equal Employment Opportunity Commission and the courts. For example, during the 1970s women at the Wire Service Guild filed a discrimination complaint against the Associated Press, claiming unfair pay and assignments. Women at *The Washington Post* did the same, while women at *The New York Times* filed a lawsuit in a US District Court (Beasley & Gibbons, 2003; Robertson, 1992). These challenges to the system proved fruitful to women. This was also a time when more women began to secure jobs at universities and to undertake feminist theories and scholarship.

While some point to the contemporary era as third wave feminism, the label is debated. Today's feminisms have been rearticulated, with many distinct tenets from second wave feminism. Further, today's feminisms lack a cohesive feminist activism (or a clear uprising) that can be seen with the first two waves of American feminism. The fact is that there has been a deeper and continuing political fragmentation of feminism since the 1980s. Feminism today is not easily demarcated or defined. Along with liberal, socialist, and radical tenets of feminism are black feminism, post feminism, international feminism, and grrl feminism—each with diverse perspectives, which are often subtle, on the causes and solutions to gender issues.

If feminism is now best understood as feminisms, then understanding feminist media theories becomes a much more daunting task than might first be expected. Yet while there are differences within feminist theories, two key elements are common (van Zoonen, 1994). First, feminist theories center analysis on gender as a (not the only) "mechanism that structures material and symbolic worlds and our experiences of them" (ibid., p. 3). Additionally, power is a crucial concept within feminist theories, although it is understood in a variety of ways and not simply something that some possess and others do not (van Zoonen, 1994). Black feminist scholars have contributed to this understanding by articulating ways in which a white woman can be subordinate to a white man but, at the same time, be dominant in relation to a black woman (hooks, 1999). The challenge for contemporary feminist scholars, then, is to attend to the multiple relations of subordination "and to analyze how in these relations of subordination individual and collective identities, such as gender and ethnicity, are being constituted" (ibid., p. 4).

Journalism and Feminist Research

The diverse feminisms provide a framework from which to begin understanding the varied ways in which feminist theories have been applied to mass communication and specifically to studies of journalism. As with any trajectory of feminism in the United States, feminist research has changed over the years. It has built on important studies, offered correctives for missed perspectives, and expanded its use of methodologies. A number of books on feminist media theories offer perspectives on this area of research (van Zoonen, 1994; Carter et al., 1998; Carter & Steiner, 2004; Chambers et al., 2004; Rakow & Wackwitz, 2004; Ross & Byerly, 2004; Krolokke & Soernsen, 2006). Each of these books offers ways within which to organize and understand the growth of feminist media theories and research. Some of the earliest feminist theorizing of journalism investigated ways news reports represented and failed to represent women and girls, including how the newsrooms' norms, values, and routines contributed to the "symbolic annihilation" of women in mass media (Tuchman, 1978; Tuchman et al., 1978). A large portion of feminist theoretical research continues to center on how mass media content represents women. These studies, beginning in the early 1970s, tend to occupy one of four approaches: (1) an approach that criticizes media representations for stereotypical portrayals of women; (2) an approach that reveals alternative representations; (3) an ideological approach that accounts for the political and economic nature of representations; and (4) a semiotic approach that focuses attention on reception and audiences (Kitch, 1997). Along with research concerning stereotypes and socialization theories, early feminist media scholars focused attention on pornography and theories of ideology, but with all three areas "media are conceptualized as agents of social control" (van Zoonen, 1994, p. 27). More recent feminist research has used a cultural studies approach to mass media, offering an alternative to this sender–receiver model through considering various moments of meaning construction during production, within the text, and through reception. Another growing area of feminist media theorizing considers women's agency in media production (Ross & Byerly, 2004). Often tenets of feminism are associated with these theoretical perspectives. For example, radical feminism is associated with an interest in pornography, liberal feminism with stereotypes and socialization, and socialist/Marxist feminism with focusing on the interaction between gender, class, and ideology (Steeves, 1987). A book specifically related to journalism divides feminist research into eight categories related to media ownership and control, representation, narrative forms and practices, feminization and sexualization (which is rearticulating mainstream news narratives), and news audiences (Carter et al., 1998).

Although cursory, this overview of feminist media research presents a picture of the main areas of feminist theorizing on mass media and journalism. Each of these feminist theoretical perspectives offers a means for analyzing the power structures within the field of journalism and provides insight into the gender divide in news consumption.

These theories provide potential explanations that can lead to solutions for change. Indeed, change is the goal of feminist research—an area of study with its roots firmly situated in social and political struggles against oppression.

Gender Issues and the News Consumption Divide

Statistical data clearly shows differences in the ways women and men consume news. A number of conditions related to gender and power offer explanations for this gender divide in the consumption of American journalism. These reasons, I believe, are best understood within a wider historical and cultural context of patriarchy and capitalism. In this sense, the history of women's place in society, including their original entrance into the field of journalism, grounds this divide. The divide, however, has been reinforced through the professionalization of journalism, the norms, values, and routines established in this news-making culture, and journalism education. These issues are not easily separated because they (re)enforce and (re)articulate each other while contributing to a long-standing gender divide in news consumption.

History of Women's Place in Society and in the News Industry

A simple understanding of the history of women's place in society and in the news industry provides a starting point for understanding why women consume news in different ways and at different rates than men. Women in our country (and the world) have systematically been kept out of positions of power, expected to attend to the private sphere of domestic work (whether in their own homes or the homes of wealthier women). In comparison to white men, women have not been encouraged to participate in public and political life. I have heard journalists and journalism scholars alike declare, "newspapers are written by and for white men." While this may be a jarring and overly simplistic perspective, the statement holds some truth, particularly when considering the history of journalism in this country.

The profession of journalism did not begin as an entirely suitable and respectable place for women. There certainly were women who worked as publishers and editors on the earliest American newspapers but these women typically inherited such responsibilities after their fathers or husbands died (Schlipp & Murphy 1983; Belford, 1986; Kitch, 2002; Beasley & Gibbons, 2003). Toward the end of the nineteenth century, women reporters became more common, but this increase in female journalists is linked to the changing role of women in an urbanized and industrialized culture. By the turn of the century more goods were being produced and purchased as more people moved from farms to cities. Women became the primary spenders in most households, deciding what food, clothing, and furnishings to purchase. Advertisers selling these goods wanted a direct link to women who might buy their products; similarly, newspapers wanted advertisers. Because of these events, newspapers in this country began to court women readers (Harp, 2007). Publishers and editors "actively sought [women] as journalists to produce articles that would directly appeal to women readers and around which lucrative advertisements targeting women consumers could be placed" (Chambers *et al.*, 2004). From a critical perspective it seems natural to argue that newspapers were not seeking women readers to better inform them as citizens in a democratic society, but to help sell goods to them. In other words, newspapers reinforced women's role as primary consumers in American culture.

Further, while women may have been hired in newsrooms during this time, the numbers of women in newsrooms has remained to this day lower than men. Early on, newspaper editors often hired only one woman, and they typically placed her in a separate office from male reporters to indicate that she held a marginal status (Beasley & Gibbons, 2003). Women's absence in newsrooms, particularly from decision-making positions, has resulted in women's limited access to roles that define or construct the news agenda. This issue has been a problem for more than a century and is an early factor contributing to the marginalization of content deemed important to women. It is no surprise that marginalized content has resulted in less enthusiastic and loyal readers.

That newspapers hired women to write and appeal to women indicates that most of the content in newspapers was understood to target men. This history offers an early explanation for the gendered readership gap. Throughout the rich history of American journalism, the numbers of female journalists have continued to rise; yet, women in newsrooms and particularly in decision-making positions are far from reaching parity with men. Further, many women reporters have continued to be marginalized and segregated, and many are expected to write from a feminine perspective and to produce content for a female audience; however, relatively few of them have made it onto the front pages of our nation's largest newspapers where they are able to cover news in the traditional and straightforward manner of their male colleagues (Cairns, 2003). Women of color have not found the same opportunities as white women either. While black women journalists could be found reporting for black weekly newspapers prior to the 1960s, they had little presence in the established mainstream press (Streitmatter, 1998). And while the riots and civil rights protests of the late 1960s compelled newspapers to finally start hiring more African Americans, the numbers of minorities in newsrooms is still shamefully low (Mills, 1988; Papper, 2005). Other women of color prior to the 1960s, including Latinas and Asian-Americans, were virtually absent from US newsrooms.

Women's Pages

The early construction of women readers for American newspapers has had lasting effects on how editors have considered gender in the construction of news content and newspaper audiences (Harp, 2007). When newspaper publishers began courting women readers toward the end of the nineteenth century, one important way they did this was by adding women's pages and sections into the newspaper. Starting in the 1890s, major American newspapers began adding pages specifically designated for women readers. These newspaper sections contained content typically understood to fall within the domestic sphere—stories targeting wives, mothers, and homemakers. While to some extent these topics reflected the realities of women's lives, they also indicated the desires of advertisers to create and reinforce domestic needs. Most disturbing, however, is the realization that these sections represent how the newspaper industry has marginalized women readers throughout history. Through these gender-specific sections, the newspaper industry has reified a false dichotomy of public/private male/female. By naming pages specifically for women, editors and publishers indicated that the rest of the newspaper was meant for men. And while the women's pages were generally filled with content related to the domestic sphere, the remaining pages dealt with the public sphere—politics, the legal system, and financial institutions. The designation of these separate spaces reinforced (or resulted in) a split in news content between hard news and soft news—another dichotomy with gendered undertones. Hard news is the important stuff for the front pages while soft news is the less timely human interest stories found within the inside pages of newspapers. The differences between hard and soft news are not simply explained by topic, but by the tones in which hard vs. soft stories are approached and written.

This hard/soft story split has not only influenced newspapers but broadcast news as well. During early radio programming, men delivered news stories, and women presented content about the home and family (Beasley & Gibbons, 2003). A look at the construction of television news also shows this type of split: morning news shows typically use women anchors and focus on soft news while major nightly news programs focus on hard news and almost exclusively employ male anchors. In fact it was not until *CBS* hired Katie Couric in the spring of 2006 that a woman was finally slated to anchor a network evening newscast solo. Needless to say, much public debate over her skills in hard news reporting surrounded her hiring.

The ways in which newsrooms have historically been bastions of white male authority, coupled with how news content has been divided through a gendered lens, have resulted in a culture of journalism that has excluded and marginalized women. It is no surprise, then, that women do not consume these forms of news products at the same rates as men, and instead have turned to television programming and magazines in which they see their faces and hear their voices (literally and figuratively). In 2005, The Project for Excellence in Journalism reported that morning news programs, which tend to cover less of the typically defined hard news topics, rely more on female sources than evening newscasts. With this information in hand, the data in Table 1.1 that illustrates women are more likely than men to consume morning news makes sense. The reversal of the gender gap in morning news attention offers clues to news outlets' attempts to appeal to women. In other words, when content is aimed at women and women's voices are heard within these texts, women are more likely to tune in.

Culture of Journalism in the Newsroom and Classroom

In the United States, white men have traditionally served as publishers, editors, and reporters for newspapers and other news outlets. This historic reality has resulted in a journalism culture based on masculine values. In other words, what is newsworthy has been defined by men and can be summed up in the newsroom adage "if it bleeds, it leads." What then appears as the legitimate and important front-page news often includes war coverage, politics (which often resembles war coverage), and crime. The masculine character of the news is also indicated in the overwhelming use of male sources in news stories and domination of male bylines on the front pages of the country's largest and most prestigious newspapers. Essentially, because of historical factors and hiring and promotion practices, "the day-to-day culture of most newsrooms is still being defined in predominantly male terms" (Carter *et al.*, 1998, p. 2).

While women have made inroads into newsrooms, they have yet to reach parity in decision-making positions. The irony is that since the 1970s women have been attending and graduating from journalism schools at a higher rate than male students, meaning the problem cannot be blamed on an absence of capable women. Again, long-established gender power structures work against women. Further, many argue that even if women were to be hired and promoted, the long-established masculine norms in newsrooms prevent women from impacting the news production process. Research regarding the impact of women in newsrooms and decision-making positions is "contradictory and ambiguous" (Chambers *et al.*, 2004). A fair amount of research, however, offers a convincing glimpse into some of the changes in news and newspaper readership that might occur if women managed newsrooms. For example, a recent survey showed that certain types of news content have a greater potential to make readers read more and the presence of these are associated with women newsroom managers (Arnold & Nesbitt, 2006). The list of topics included intensely local and people-centered news.

An analysis of nearly 1,400 articles from 30 daily newspapers found "newspapers with a high percentage of women in managerial positions tended to cover news in a more positive light" (Craft & Wanta, 2004, p. 135). Further, the study concluded, female and male reporters tended to cover the same news topics in a newsroom only when that newsroom employed a high percentage of women. The research found that "male-dominated newsrooms, meanwhile, tended to have male reporters cover political beats. Female reporters at these newspapers conversely were more likely to cover business and education beats" (ibid.). Another researcher analyzed 889 articles from 18 daily newspapers and found that a reporter's gender was a good predictor of the gender of the sources who got attention and emphasis within a story (Armstrong, 2004). Male reporters relied more on male sources and placed these male sources higher in the story than their female sources. These findings, along with that author's discovery that the overall incidence of male newspaper mentions was nearly three times that of females, led her to conclude that in the public realm men are given higher status by newspapers.

Rather than see these results as a competition for who gets to cover what, the outcome leads to considerations of what serves readers. These differences directly affect what readers take away from their newspaper. They also point to ways in which female newsroom managers and reporters might change the voice of news.

Does it Matter?

Does it matter that women and men do not consume news at the same rate? Yes, it matters immensely. That is because of journalism's crucial role in a democracy. Media scholars and political theorists have long noted the importance of journalism as a tool for informing people about their world in order to help them make self-governing decisions. If women are not consuming news, then women may not be as well informed and as able to carry out their role in a democratic society. Further, news has a role in helping people establish citizenship and community. When women are left out of newsrooms, off front pages, and are not consuming news content, there are bound to be consequences in terms of the role they play in public life. The business of news as it is today only perpetuates women's unequal status in American society through solidification of the status quo.

There are implications for the news industry as well. Research indicates that only one out of every five of the top women editors in the country reveal that they want to move up in the newspaper industry. "According to the study, which covered 40 percent of the newsroom leaders at U.S. daily newspapers with circulations of 50,000 or more, 64 percent of all women who consider their opportunity blocked identify management's preference for men as standing in their way" (Gibbons, 2002). This indicates that female readers are not the only women the news industry needs to worry about retaining.

Can the Divide be Closed? How?

There are a number of changes that can be implemented within the industry to alter journalism's gender gap. It will take a variety of adjustments, however, as there is not a single transformation that could be made in order to amend the present (and historic) gender divide between female and male news consumption. What I present are a number of correctives I believe the industry should undertake, and I provide a case study as evidence of how a multilevel effort to increase women readers can succeed.

First, women need to be hired and promoted. They need to fill top levels of management and decision-making posts at an equal rate to men. Some scholars, who argue that this view does not take into account the ways in which cultural ideologies and newsroom socialization influence the practices of women journalists, often criticize this perspective as simplistic. Further, on its surface, this argument to hire more women may seem to essentialize women, suggesting that women all think alike and all think in a different way from men. My mandate to hire women suggests a belief that women in a newsroom would make distinctive choices from their male counterparts. Stated in this way, the argument for hiring more women in decision-making positions does seem simplistic. But this is an argument for diversifying newsrooms, not for hiring a group of people who think the same. Research indicates not only gender but to a greater extent socio-economic background and political values predict journalists' attitudes and values (Chambers *et al.*, 2004).

Research aside, anecdotal evidence points to differences between the ways women and men journalists approach their work. Published interviews and essays by a number of women journalists throughout history offer evidence that women in the newsroom influence news content and the construction of news. Personal interviews and conversations with a fair number of female journalists also leads me to believe that a woman's gender often influences her work (Harp, 2007). My view on this is further solidified by my personal experience in the newsroom. As much as journalists may stand by notions of objectivity, the story ideas, choices in whom to interview, and what order to place information in a story are unavoidably influenced by personal identity of which gender as a cultural construct is a major component.

A number of women who believe gender influences news have said that the more women are present in the newsroom and editorial meetings, the more comfortable they would feel offering an alternative perspective or idea to the masculine approach. The idea is that women are less comfortable being thought of as the resident mommy or feminist in the newsroom but feel strength in numbers when another woman is present who may understand their perspective (Gladwell, 2002). While this may again seem built on the notion that women are the same, the general reality in American culture is that women tend to hold very different positions and are offered different opportunities than their male counterparts and, therefore, often possess alternative perspectives. For example, women tend to be the primary care-givers of children whether or not they also participate in paid labor outside of the home. Newsroom diversity is a key to diversifying news content and bringing a diverse audience to news. Just as a female journalist might approach her job differently from a male journalist, a white female journalist is likely to bring a different perspective into the newsroom from a black female journalist.

Along with diversifying the newsroom, women need to be given positions of power within news organizations. Research on female and male managers indicates that women tend to be more inclusive and not so ingrained "in the way things have always been done" (Arnold & Nesbitt, 2006, p. 10).

Hiring and promoting women in news organizations is only a first, though crucial, step toward erasing the gender divide in news. Women alone cannot change the world, and men must participate in altering the ways in which news is constructed and produced. The masculine newsroom culture and masculine definitions of news need to change in order to alter ways in which women and men consume news. The *Lexington Herald-Leader* in Kentucky is an example of how changing the newsroom culture and content can alter reading habits and increase a female audience. This change in newsroom culture and increase in women readers at the *Lexington Herald-Leader* did not happen overnight and it began with research that respected women enough to find out what their needs were.

In December 1991, a Knight-Ridder Women Readers Task Force presented the report "How Newspapers Can Gain Readership Among Women . . . And Why It's Important" (Kelly, 1992, p. 12). During the time Knight-Ridder, which was one of the nation's largest newspaper publishers until McClatchy Company purchased it in 2006, conducted one-on-one interviews with 154 women in seven cities (Knight-Ridder, 1991). The report offered newspaper editors suggestions for making newspapers more appealing to women, and it also recommended that each newsroom examine its own newspaper and newsroom for female representation. Filled with content recommendations based on the cares and concerns of women, the report urged newspapers to fix the entire paper by adding the missing content women desired throughout the newspaper, while also recommending that newspapers add a special women's section to draw women in and let them know they were important. Upper management at the *Herald-Leader*, a Knight-Ridder paper, was directed to develop one of these women's sections (Kelly, 1992).

On Sunday, April 2, 1992 the *Herald-Leader* published its first issue of "You," a weekly tabloid section subtitled "News for Today's Woman." Along with targeting women with particular content (including health and family, shopping, and consumer concerns), the reporters of "You" were expected to write differently, to accommodate women who said they were pressed for time. But in keeping with the recommendation of the Knight-Ridder report, the *Herald-Leader* editors instituted a number of additional changes to attract women readers (Harp, 2007). One problem the editor attended to was the paper's "very decidedly male management cast" (ibid.). When the publisher took over in 1996 there were five people reporting to him and none of them were women. Further, only one woman served on the management team and there were only three or four female department heads (two of whom were occupying traditional female roles—one as the head librarian and another as features editor). The editor believed this lack of women in decision-making positions contributed to the lower rate of women readers because story selection and the tone of content were filtered through male sensibilities. He and other executives made an effort to change these problems. By 2002—ten years later—of the five people who reported to the publisher, three were women: the senior vice president for sales and marketing, the chief executive officer, and the editor. Additionally, the newspaper by 2002 had a ten-member executive committee made up of five men and five women, had an African-American woman serving as editorial page editor, and had also hired a woman as one of the assistant managing editors.

By 2002, editors at the *Lexington Herald-Leader* chose to eliminate its women's section believing it had both served and outlived its purpose. The editor of the paper said at the time that though the women's section had been useful in making everyone in the newsroom think about women and gender issues, it was no longer necessary and had become somewhat stale (Harp, 2007). The newspaper continued using a thematic strategy for its features content but did so through the creation of all new sections (ibid.). Most importantly, the editors explained that a women's section was not needed to bring women into the paper because by then the newspaper claimed a higher female than male readership. In the early 1990s, when the editors launched "You," the readership polls for the newspaper showed a yesterday readership of 57 percent male and 43 percent female. By 2002 the readership polls for the newspaper showed 48 percent male and 52 percent female (ibid.).

This change in readership demographics at the *Herald-Leader* occurred over a ten-year period because management at the newspaper made some significant and calculated decisions. Editors at the paper said they believe the addition of women in newsroom decision-making positions made the most difference in changing newspaper content and in turn the readership numbers. But along with hiring and promoting women, the newspaper's editors made an effort to integrate news that women readers said was important to them onto the front pages; to include women as sources; and to practice writing shorter and more concise stories for a busy audience. This holistic strategy worked better than simply adding a women's section, something some newspaper editors have done in hopes of bringing women readers to their paper. But this attention to women's content in one section has ghettoizing effects. It also reinforces gender stereotypes and inequalities. This example at the *Herald-Leader* offers hope and a multi-leveled prescription for how newspapers can increase women readers. But newsrooms and editors must commit to making changes for the strategy to be successful.

Finally, journalism educators can help change the masculine nature of the news culture, the definitions of news, and the readership gap. This change can be achieved through moving beyond the same ways that journalism has been taught in universities. Rather than rely on the textbooks that teach standard, business-as-usual journalism, professors should turn to books that offer an analysis of journalism practices in an effort to highlight ways that the profession can improve its product and its treatment of women. For example, *Virgin or Vamp: How the Press Covers Sex Crimes* critiques the manner in which journalists have covered rape crimes throughout history (Benedict, 1992). The author illustrates how journalists turn to official sources and myths about rape to construct stories that often indicate the rape victim's responsibility for the crime. A cursory look at any mainstream coverage of a rape case offers evidence of this fact. For example, when Los Angeles Lakers basketball star Kobe Bryant was charged in 2003 with raping a woman in his hotel room, much of the news coverage relied on unsubstantiated information from defense attorneys. Through sources and story construction, the articles often indicated that the woman had voluntarily entered Bryant's room and therefore held some responsibility for the alleged rape. This same type of victim blame could be found in early stories about the woman allegedly raped at a 2006 Duke University Lacrosse team party.

In that highly publicized case, news accounts identified the woman, a single mother and North Carolina Central University student, as a "stripper" repeatedly. This simple identifier not only constructed the woman's identity solely through her occupation, it signified the woman as sexually loose and somehow unable to be raped in her situation. Ten months after the woman first complained to the police that she had been raped by three Duke Lacrosse players, the rape charges were dropped (Barstow & Wilson, 2006). Although the district attorney admitted he was dropping the rape charges because of a lack of evidence, the dropping of the felony charges does not absolve the press from responsible reporting in rape cases. Journalists must attend to their choices of language in an effort to show fairness and respect for women.

Benedict's book suggests ways for improving rape coverage, including such directives as using rape experts as sources and not allowing defense attorneys to manipulate the news by quoting every inflammatory statement they make. After all, the author points out, defense attorneys are ultimately paid to discredit rape victims and journalists should be wary of quoting them without verifying their statements (Benedict, 1992). This type of in-depth attention to gender issues as they play out in the news would benefit journalism students and could ultimately help change the masculine culture of journalism—a culture that undoubtedly leads to the gender divide in news consumption.

References

Armstrong, C. (2004). The influence of reporter gender on source selection in newspaper stories. *Journalism and Mass Communication Quarterly*, 81(1), 139–54.

Arnold, M. & Nesbitt, M. (2006). *Women in Media 2006*. Media Management Center at Northwestern University: McCormick Tribune Foundation.

Barstow, D. & Wilson, D. (2006, December 23). Charges of rape against 3 at Duke are abandoned. *The New York Times*, p. A1. Retrieved April 6, 2007 from LexisNexis database.

Beasley, M.H. & Gibbons, S.J. (2003). *Taking Their Place: A documentary history of women and journalism* (2nd edition). State College: Strata Publishing.

Belford, B. (1986). *Brilliant Bylines: A biographical anthology of notable newspaperwomen in America*. New York: Columbia University.

Benedict, H. (1992). *Virgin or Vamp: How the press covers sex crimes*. New York: Oxford University Press.

Cairns, K.A. (2003). *Front-Page Women Journalists, 1920–1950*. Lincoln: University of Nebraska Press.

Carter, C. & Steiner, L. (Eds.) (2004). *Critical Readings: Media and gender*. Maidenhead: Open University Press.

Carter, C., Branston, G., & Allan, S. (1998). *Setting New(s) Agendas: An introduction*. New York: Routledge.

Catalyst. (2006). *2005 Catalyst Census of Women Corporate Officers and Top Earners of the Fortune 500*. Retrieved April 8, 2006 from www.catalystwomen.org/files/full/2005%20COTE.pdf.

Caiazza, A., Shaw, A., & Werschkul, M. (2004). Women's economic status in the states: Wide disparities by race, ethnicity and region. Institute for Women's Policy Research.

Chambers, D., Steiner, L., & Fleming C. (2004). *Women and Journalism*. New York: Routledge.

Craft, S. & Wanta, W. (2004). Women in the newsroom: Influences of female editors and reporters on the news agenda. *Journalism and Mass Communication Quarterly*, 81(1), 124–38.

Donovan, J. (1992). *Feminist Theory: The intellectual traditions of American feminism*. Continuum International Publishing Group.

Friedan, B. (1963). *The Feminine Mystique*. New York: W.W. Norton.

Gibbons, S. (2002, November 20). Biased newsrooms risk losing female staff, readers. *Women's eNews*. Retrieved April 8, 2006 from www.womensenews.org/article.cfm/dyn/aid/1115/context/archive.

Gibbons, S. (2004, January 21). Inequities persist for women in media. *Women's eNews*. Retrieved April 8, 2006 from www.womensenews.org/article.cfm/dyn/aid/1681.

Gibbons, S. (2005, December 28). Media year 2005 was sorry saga for women. *Women's eNews*. Retrieved April 8, 2006 from www.womensenews.org/article.cfm/dyn/aid/2579/context/archive.

Gladwell, M. (2002). *The Tipping Point: How little things can make a big difference*. New York: Back Bay Books.

Harp, D. (2007). *Desperately Seeking Women Readers: US newspapers and the construction of a female readership*. Lanham: Lexington Books.

hooks, b. (1999). *Ain't I a Woman: Black women and feminism*. Cambridge: South End Press.

Kelly, T.M. (1992, May/June). Yo! You! A research model comes to life as a weekly section aimed at women. *ASNE Bulletin*.

Kitch, C. (2002). Women in journalism. In W.D. Sloan & L.M. Parcell (Eds.) *American Journalism: History, principles, practices*, pp. 87–96. Jefferson: McFarland & Company.

Kitch, C. (1997). Changing theoretical perspective on women's media images: The emergence of patterns in a new area of historical scholarship. *Journalism and Mass Communication Quarterly*, 74(3), 477–89.

Knight-Ridder. (1991, December). How newspapers can gain readership among women . . . and why it's important.

Krolokke, C. & Sorensen, A.S. (2006). *Gender Communication Theories and Analyses: From silence to performance*. Thousand Oaks: Sage.

Mills, K. (1988). *A Place in the News: From the women's pages to the front page*. New York: Dodd, Mead & Co.

Papper, B. (2005, July/August). Running in place. *Communicator*. Retrieved April 8, 2006 from www.rtnda.org/communicator/pdfs/072005-26-32.pdf.

Project for Excellence in Journalism. (2005). The gender gap: Women are still missing as sources for journalists.

Rakow, L.F. & Wackwitz, L.A. (Eds.) (2004). *Feminist Communication Theory: Selections in context*. Thousand Oaks: Sage.

Robertson, N. (1992). *The Girls in the Balcony: Women, men, and The New York Times*. New York: Random House.

Ross, K. & Byerly, C.M. (Eds.) (2004). *Women and Media: International perspectives*. Malden: Blackwell.

Ryan, B. (1992). *Feminism and the Women's Movement: Dynamics of change in social movement, ideology and activism*. New York: Routledge.

Schlipp, M.G. & Murphy, S.M. (1983). *Great Women of the Press*. Carbondale: Southern Illinois University Press.

Steeves, H.L. (1987). Feminist theories and media studies. *Critical Studies in Mass Communication*, 4(2), 95–135.

Streitmatter, R. (1998). Transforming the women's pages: Strategies that worked. *Journalism History*, 24(2), 72–81.

Tuchman, G., Daniels, A.K., & Benet, J. (Eds.) (1978). *Hearth and Home: Images of women in the mass media*. New York: Oxford University Press.

Tuchman, G. (1978). *Making News: A study in the construction of reality*. New York: Free Press.

van Zoonen, L. (1994.) *Feminist Media Studies*. London: Sage.

Chapter 15

Critiquing Journalism

Feminist Perspectives Relevant to Contemporary Challenges

Linda Steiner

Articulating, much less assessing, feminist perspectives on the news is a complicated and multi-directional project, given that feminism is complex, with shifting goals that have been unevenly accomplished. Nonetheless, clearly troubled by the content and practices of mainstream news organizations, US feminist scholars have documented several significant issues. Meanwhile, feminist activists have worked hard to "correct" news coverage of women and of the feminist movement and to encourage equity and even wholesale reform in the newsroom.

The debate over print and broadcast news content typically reduces to the impact of news coverage. For example, feminist scholars and activists alike have worried that misrepresentations damage women's self-esteem and sense of identity at the individual level and undermine women's social status and collective possibilities; sexist representations also negatively affect men's attitudes. Erasing women from the news, it has been claimed, amounts to "symbolic annihilation" of women, thus effectively denying women a place on the public agenda. A more foundational, more philosophical, and thus potentially more interesting question of institutional process takes up whether or how women have changed news-making. So-called liberal feminists in particular complained that women were consistently under-employed in newsrooms; when women were employed, they were confined to women's beats. No one now seriously argues that women journalists cannot handle newsroom challenges. Nor are women typecast as able only to write "soft news" for women. (Men continue to avoid anything that might typecast them as writing for women.) Women have conquered most news sections—although a few beats, ranging from war reporting to sports, opinion writing, and political cartooning, seemingly remain off-limits, as is newsroom management. Both male and female reporters assert that the resulting transformations of the definition of news and of newsroom culture led editors to be more open to stories that particularly affect women (Mills, 1997). Nonetheless, the question remains whether and when women bring distinctive qualities to journalism and to newsrooms.

Neither set of questions outlined above directly considers women readers. Media scholars now emphasize a triangular relationship among institutions/producers, content, and audiences, but this third "leg" is often ignored, especially in the context of journalism. While feminist scholars often study popular culture audiences (soap operas being the ultimate woman's genre), remarkably little empirical data has been collected on women newspaper readers, with the notable exception of proprietary marketing studies. Certainly feminists want underserved audiences to receive crucial print and broadcast news. Always implicit and occasionally explicit in the feminist critique of news was a concern that news organizations long ignored highly important issues that women readers needed to know—including childcare, reproduction and other medical and health information, domestic violence, sexual abuse and sexual harassment, money, employment, and divorce laws. But, feminists' failure to study news audiences reflects their historical focus on journalism's content and institutional processes.

Certainly the relative inattention to audiences partly results from the fact that the audience component of the media studies was the last to be articulated. Ironically, just when audiences emerged as a distinctive research question, examining the gendered needs of readers of news became controversial. On one hand, once audience questions per se began to get raised—by the 1980s—women and men journalists were becoming equally adamant that gender made little difference. Journalists saw themselves as professionals producing news important for "society," for democracy. Furthermore, the findings from the 1980s that fewer women than men consistently read "hard" news could be used to justify (i.e., to *cause*) offering less news of interest to women, even if it might *result* from news organizations offering little that interested women. On the other hand, if feminists regarded audiences as "sexed," they risked essentializing women. This perspective would not only reinstate the conflation of all women but also segregate women's issues, as if men were not also interested in childcare. Meanwhile, both feminists and reporters were embarrassed by publishers' blatant attempts to pander and to "market" products to women "consumers." In any case, this represents a vicious circle around a moving target. Women readers can no more be universalized than can women journalists.

Definitions of Feminism

As a major social movement and normative political philosophy, feminism aims to expose and challenge sexism and women's oppression; it takes women's experiences and problems seriously. Yet, feminism wants also to be attentive to how women's subordination is interstructured with other kinds of oppression, including by class, race, sexual orientation, ethnicity, and geography. Not all women suffer equally or need feminists' intervention equally. Having thus defined feminism somewhat monolithically, I concede that discussing multiple feminisms is arguably more useful. At least a couple dozen forms of feminism have been articulated (for example, anarcha-feminism, ecofeminism, as well as existentialist, separatist, socialist, third-world, and transnational feminisms). Other categorization systems are possible. These days, many people suggest that womanism (a term African-American feminists prefer) and "third wave" feminism have brought legitimate attention to multiculturalism, intersectionality, and to free expression of sexuality; these were ignored in the first two waves (pre-suffrage feminism and the women's liberation movement of the 1960s).

Each feminism has distinctive philosophical suppositions, so attends to slightly different problems, sometimes even posing mutually exclusive solutions. Although these differences can be overemphasized, in the case of journalism, different versions of feminism may be highly relevant. Liberal feminists tend to assume that essentially, or at least eventually, women and men are not very different. Rather, equality in employment (including in management), salary, and so forth, as well as a more general devaluation of women, are the crucial issues; employment issues logically precede questions about the extent and kinds of news representations of women. Liberal feminists posit that increased employment leads to greater power. This, in turn, predicts that, with the comfort of numbers, women become willing to write about women more often and in ways that correct conventional stereotypes about women's inferiority. Especially in the 1970s and 1980s, but continuing into the 1990s, the argument was that when the number of women achieved "critical mass" in news organizations, news content would more fairly tell women's stories. Reform-minded liberal feminists used employment data and quantitative content analysis to bolster their claims. Inspired by nineteenth-century principles of self-determination and rights, so-called "individualist feminists" regard competitive markets as driving women's economic rights; as a result, they oppose "protectionist" approaches.

Cultural feminists emphasize sex/gender differences. They take pains to show, however, that the differences are not the ones that emerge from masculinist values, that is, values that position men as superior to women. Some embrace differences, or at least women's culture. Other cultural feminists, recognizing the problematic aspects of masculinity, urge transformation of masculinity, male cultures, and men's roles. Cultural feminists generally assumed that once women journalists achieved critical mass they would write about women in ways that reflected their esteem and concern for womanly values such as cooperation and collaboration; the writing itself would be analogously distinct. Separately, radical feminists advocate a fundamental reorganization of institutional structures and processes, but this view has found, not surprisingly, little sympathy and even less support in journalism, reporters' increasingly shared dismay at financial constraints notwithstanding.

Journalism History

Journalism history itself predicts that women newspaper readers would be largely ignored. Throughout the nineteenth century, women were taken to be simple and unidimensional, and women as readers, writers/journalists, and subjects were conflated. Starting in the 1880s, attracting women readers became increasingly important to newspaper advertisers, especially the department stores and other stores hoping to attract women consumers. To the extent that women had increasing consumption responsibilities, and even some direct control over spending, advertisers required ways of accessing those women readers. In turn this became important to editors and publishers. More specifically, editors and advertisers were primarily concerned with attracting (only) those women who wanted to read women's news; therefore, editors hired women to write about society, fashion, and domestic issues, having assumed that women journalists would instinctively know how to provide this, and correctly predicting that men would refuse the assignment.

Even when women did write about politics or social issues, they were encouraged to focus on how events affected people in their everyday lives and to provoke an emotional response from readers, presumably women readers. As reporting textbooks and books of the period about journalism insisted, the assumption was that this lighter "human interest angle" would attract women readers. For example, one early journalism textbook limited women to occasional sidebars:

> Her story is not supposed to add anything of importance to the report of her brother journalist, its whole value lying in the fact that it is written from a wholly feminine standpoint, in a bright feminine manner, with little touches of feminine sympathy, pathos and sentiment.
>
> (Olin, 1906, p. 51)

Most of the women hired on this basis fretted over their assignment. Although these isolated society page editors were the only women with editorial titles, they were in charge of a ghetto. Elizabeth Jordan, for example, was first hired in the 1880s to edit the woman's page of a Milwaukee newspaper, but she was unimpressed by this opportunity to supply "light and warmth to the universe." She said in her 1938 autobiography, "It is a miracle that the stuff I had to carry in 'Sunshine' did not permanently destroy my interest in newspaper work" (p. 14). In 1890 Jordan was hired by the *New York World*, where she promised to do "anything" but society news: "I drew the line at that" (p. 48).

Skipping several decades, and enormously abbreviating much important history, the emergence of the second wave women's liberation movement and the glamorization of journalism in the wake of journalists' highly publicized and successful investigation of wrong-doing by former President Richard Nixon's administration significantly increased women's interest in journalism careers. Women flooded into journalism schools. As a result, journalism textbooks abandoned their heretofore unanimous declaration that reporting was a man's job. After intense lobbying by feminists, newspaper stylebooks eventually came to adopt and require gender-neutral vocabulary and avoidance of sexist language. Newspapers, beginning with the smaller papers, hired women as reporters to such an extent that many editors and journalism school deans worried that journalism was becoming a pink-collar profession. The fear was that women's numerical predominance would drive down salaries and, in a vicious circle, drive out men.

Presumably, the first women hired in the wake of the feminist movement did insist on covering issues of interest to women, providing more background and context, and foregrounding ordinary people. The claim can be made that women's unique experiences *as* women formed the basis of a distinctive "standpoint" such that, compared to men, most women would ask different questions and see different things. The inclusion of new topics that began in the 1970s illustrated the cumulative impact of critical mass, bolstered by affirmative action, class action law suits, and the emergence of informal and formal organizations of women journalists at the local, regional, and national levels. In an ironic reversal of Elizabeth Jordan's problem, Eileen Shanahan, an economics reporter at *The New York Times*, recalled telling her editor that she wanted to cover the House debate on the Equal Rights Amendment; the editor let her volunteer for the assignment, but his position was that Shanahan covered important things such as the federal budget, not women's issues (Mills, 1997).

Notably, and ominously, broadcasters' decision to hire women represented not so much new-found respect for women, as executives' technique of using beauty to attract men's gaze. In 1973, Sally Quinn, an attractive *Washington Post* feature writer who had worked a little for *CBS*, was hired as a *CBS* co-anchor. Quinn almost immediately showed that she could not handle the job; within four months she was gone. Similarly, acting in a Playtex commercial landed former Miss America Phyllis George a job on Candid Camera and then, in 1975, a job with *CBS* Sports, although she was neither an athlete nor sports expert. In 1985, trying to replace Diane Sawyer as co-anchor of *CBS's* morning news show, George showed her journalistic inexperience by asking an accused rapist and a woman who recanted her rape accusation to hug, on camera.

The classic example of the beautiful woman hired to be cheesecake, but beyond her reporting abilities, was Jessica Savitch. After studying communications at Ithaca College and doing some local broadcasting and modeling, Savitch got her "big break" at a Houston station. Soon after, looking for a "fresh young face," *KYW-TV* brought her to Philadelphia. She became an instant superstar. That is, she was moved up in NBC far beyond her abilities, or at least far too quickly, with humiliating and disastrous results, both on and off camera. She died in a 1983 car accident (as a passenger) before getting fired. However, television stations were already looking for their own Jessica Savitch look-alike "Golden Girl."

The influx of women into journalism schools and then newsrooms did not fundamentally change news or newsroom structure. Part of this has to do with the culture and values of the newsroom. As illustrated in countless films and novels set in newsrooms and equally countless autobiographies by journalists, journalists value independence, autonomy, detachment, competitiveness, and confrontation. Such professional norms and professional values are powerful, especially when they are taught by journalism school professors who want graduates to succeed by getting good jobs and promotions, and then (re)confirmed through newsroom socialization and reward structures. Newsroom culture placed women journalists in a bind; they were expected to meet both the social definition of femininity and the professional criteria. Women insisted they found an escape route, most often by asserting that they were "simply" good reporters at work, doing what they needed to do. Some saw the claim that "essentially" feminine women were producing "softer" news as feminist progress; to horrified others, it undermined professional values.

Some regard this particular value system as essentially male-centric or "macho," although the routinization of journalistic conventions makes male perspectives seem unproblematic and value-free (de Bruin & Ross, 2004). Two feminist scholars say: "The incorporation of women journalists into a traditionally male profession has the effect of 'normalizing' what are essentially male-identified concerns and a male-directed agenda" (Byerly & Ross 2006, p. 78). Others see this as more fundamentally reflecting and reinforcing "male hegemony." In any case, whether this is "merely" the professional culture or it is specifically masculinist, it turned out that women did *not* write in a fundamentally different way, including when they covered women.

A Feminist Assessment

A host of interacting factors accounts for why the substantial (again, not complete) achievement of liberal feminist goals with respect to equal employment of women did not accomplish larger feminist goals. One Dutch scholar, for instance, has speculated that market-driven journalism is becoming more "feminized" and as such is more open to upwardly mobile women and feminine values (van Zoonen, 1998). In other words, more women would not (and did not) change news. Women's critical mass was over-determined by the culture of newsrooms, with their "commonsense" conventions, time-bound constraints and routines, and hierarchical relations and editorial structures. Still, in order to attract readers they had not previously succeeded in attracting, newsrooms changed (thus socializing and rewarding reporters in new ways) in ways that may be inviting to women.

Part of the issue is that most women working in journalism continue—now in greater numbers—to want the same assignments, reputations, status, and prizes as men. Feminist scholars often interpret women journalists' tolerance of sexism, or their refusal to acknowledge sexual harassment or sexism as such, as demonstrating an internalized sexism. I speculate, in contrast, that most women who work as mainstream journalists are feminists of the liberal/egalitarian/individualist strand. Likewise, as more women acquire professional education and enter professions—especially previously male-dominated professions—they now know how to literally act masculine, especially in major leadership and executive positions. In some especially male-dominated hide-bound corporations, women still confront a troubling and frustrating double bind: they are required to act masculine and then are punished for it. But in journalism, women often want to be seen "like a man" and are admired for achieving this. The *New York Tribune*'s Marguerite Higgins, for example, went to Europe in 1944 to report on World War II, covered the Nuremberg War Trials, and became the Berlin bureau chief in 1947. As the Far East bureau chief, she shared a Pulitzer Prize for Korean War reporting. Higgins proudly repeated the compliment paid to her when a fellow reporter said, "The front line *is* no place for a woman, but it's all right for Maggie Higgins" (Higgins, 1955, p. 40). That is, women reporters have rarely suffered the same double bind as lawyers, for example, and certainly do not do so now.

A more recent example showing that women want to be regarded not as female but journalists came in 2005, a year in which *Cleveland Plain Dealer* columnist Connie Schultz won the 2005 Pulitzer Prize for commentary. A well-known feminist lawyer (and frequent columnist) Susan Estrich condemned the editorial and opinion editor of the *Los Angeles Times* for not running enough columns by women. Apparently in a two-month sample from 2005, women wrote 19.5 percent of the *Los Angeles Times'* op-ed columns, 10.4 percent of *The Washington Post*'s op-eds, and 16.9 percent of *The New York Times'* op-eds. According to Anne Applebaum (2005), a regular *Post* columnist, Estrich "bizarrely" accused Michael Kinsley of using mainly men columnists, as well as "women who don't count as women because they don't write with "'women's voices.'" Applebaum rejected Estrich's complaint, explaining, in her words, "Possibly because I see so many excellent women around me at the newspaper, possibly because so many of the *Post*'s best-known journalists are women, possibly because I've never thought of myself as a 'female journalist.'" Applebaum added that none of the women she informally surveyed thought of themselves "as beans to be counted, or as 'female journalists' with a special obligation to write about 'women's issues.'" She described Estrich's "ranting, raving series of e-mails" as "seriously bad" for women: "[T]hanks to Estrich, every woman who gets her article accepted will have to wonder whether it was . . . her willingness to court controversy or just her gender that won the editor over." Some feminists undoubtedly dismissed Applebaum's response as a self-deceptive strategy of "incorporation," such that women adopt masculine values and styles (Byerly & Ross, 2006). If so, this strategy has a long history among women who, if they are not feminist activists, think of themselves as accomplished, "liberated" women succeeding in a profession that values competition and autonomy.

Meanwhile, and equally importantly, just at the point when the insights and agenda of feminism began to be incorporated, and perhaps in response to feminism, notions of masculinity and femininity changed. Both became more fluid and complex, no longer dichotomous or polarized. Just as gender and sexuality are performed, so masculinity and femininity are strategies, to be rehearsed and then performed. Neither masculinity nor femininity comes naturally. They are always at stake, at risk (although they are more complicated, more fraught for both gays and lesbians and heterosexual women). Indeed, in several contexts, masculinity is now a strategy both women and men can understand and deploy, albeit, again, one that continues to mutate. This undermines the notion of "a" woman's or "a" man's way of writing, seeing, or reporting.

None of this denies that serious problems beset newsrooms, including sexism and sex discrimination. Pockets of macho resistance to women remain. It is to say that environments and cultures do change over time, but only to a limit. This will be particularly true of professional workplaces, including journalism, but also law, medicine, as well as academia. Here competition is fierce, first to get into the best professional schools that teach the skills (and ethics) of the workplace, then to attain and keep the jobs, and finally to win honors and awards. Newsroom issues are now further complicated by financial pressures. In particular, women's physical attractiveness and sexuality continue to be exploited in newsrooms, and a double standard continues to be applied, as a competitive tool. This is not in competition with men. Rather, it serves the drive for audiences (that is, to satisfy advertisers or longer-term stockholders). Independently, an increasingly intense competitive ethos suffuses the newspaper "business."

To be blunt, the problem is manipulation of and through women's disciplined (or self-regulated) bodies. Male broadcasters can go fat, gray, or even bald; older women are forced off the air once they can no longer walk the tightrope of sexiness and professionalism. Much of the pandering is done by women; women invite audience identification and loyalty by offering themselves as partners in an intimate relationship. It is women newscasters who smile flirtatiously, ask personal questions, hug villains, and show cleavage. Notably, whereas women journalists have always been urged or required to do this, contemporary "liberated" women are increasingly pleased to do this; they assert their feminist right to enjoy their sexuality, under the banner of individual choice. To say that this new aggressive femininity is strategic is not to condone its performance. The attempt to attract males and females by exploiting postmodern women in a mockery of news represents a desperate market-driven exploitation of sex. Recent headlines asserting that Katie Couric is still not "one of the boys," despite her make-over, suggest that her reputation as the perky *Today Show* host will prevent her from attaining the gravitas associated with evening anchors.

The issue is apparent in television, for obvious reasons: attracting audiences is even more difficult, and more crucial, than obtaining information from stubborn sources. But newspaper managers, like their broadcast counterparts, also have ordered an emphasis on style, intimate address, personal information, emotional investment, and "therapy news" to pander to what are assumed to be contemporary interests. These and other features are ordered up with little evidence as to whether they are effective, and with even less concern for journalists' calling and mission. While these human interest touches correlate with what have been "feminine" qualities, this is coincidental. In the twentieth century this is what passes for consumer interest, not women's interests.

Thus, while the liberal project is not complete, the liberal feminist agenda for news content and practitioners has been largely accomplished. It has gone as far as it can. Indeed, as it was intended to do, liberal feminism has made itself nearly unnecessary. Cultural feminism's celebration is also irrelevant, given the emergence of multiple femininities and masculinities. The radical feminist restructuring of newsrooms, meanwhile, is impossible; it is technology and economics that will foment revolution. These recent achievements and blockages thereby reveal how particular forms of feminism may be outmoded. Therefore, feminism must return to a more political and highly self-reflective concern with ongoing significant problems, even if this means privileging race and class, and decentering women as a universalized category. Feminist intervention must now focus not on women per se, given how this has long been conflated with white heterosexual middle-class women. Rather, in the journalism context, feminists must consider specifically underserved people, whose voices, problems, and news needs are ignored. Women are not treated by editors or reporters as a singular category; women journalists, even those who consider themselves feminists, do not see themselves as a single category. Now it is time to recognize that readers and subjects are not unitary.

Consistent with their normative commitment to long-term transformation, feminists will continue to challenge mainstream news. Feminism asks journalists to address underserved and otherwise unprotected audiences, even if, especially if they are not desirable markets per se. Feminist approaches have been adapted even in mainstream journalism, usually through collaborations among various journalists who share an exclusion from the "inner circle" (Byerly & Ross, 2006). But feminist journalism also needs to be sustained and encouraged. And the real opportunities to practice feminist journalism are, as they have been since the mid-nineteenth century, in specifically feminist print, broadcast, cable and online organizations, and in feminist activist networks (Byerly & Ross, 2006; Chambers *et al.*, 2004). Feminist news outlets rarely survive for long periods, because they tend to be low-budget and financially unprofitable and (therefore) because they rely on volunteers who eventually suffer burn-out. Yet, feminism continues to generate and develop feminist principles for journalism. Minimally, feminist journalism requires reconsideration about whose news and whose problems are newsworthy; it offers alternative principles for articulating and resolving ethical dilemmas; it calls for erasing boundaries between subject/readers/producers; and it experiments with non-hierarchal decision-making and broadening access. This is the contemporary challenge for feminism.

References

Applebaum, A. (2005, March 16). Writing women into a corner. *The Washington Post*, p. A23.

Byerly, C.M. & Ross, K. (2006). *Women & Media: A Critical Introduction*. Oxford: Blackwell.

Chambers, D., Steiner, L., & Fleming, C. (2004). *Women and Journalism*. New York: Routledge.

de Bruin, M. & Ross, K. (Eds.) (2004). *Gender and Newsroom Cultures: Identities at Work*. Cresskill: Hampton Press.

Jordan, E. (1938). *Three Rousing Cheers*. New York: Appleton-Century.

Higgins, M. (1955). *News is a Singular Thing*. Garden City: Doubleday.

Mills, K. (1997). What difference do women journalists make? In P. Norris (Ed.) *Women, Media, and Politics*, pp. 41–55. New York: Oxford University Press.

Olin, C. (1906). *Journalism*. Philadelphia: Penn Publishing.

van Zoonen, L. (1998). One of the girls? The changing gender of journalism. In C. Carter, G. Branston & S. Allan, *News, Gender and Power*, pp. 33–47. New York: Routledge.

Chapter 16

Color and Content

Why the News Doesn't Mirror Society

Lorraine E. Branham

If you open up your local newspaper on almost any given day, you can see first hand why African-American news consumers, to a large extent, do not read newspapers.

Stories about drugs, crime, poverty, and poor educational achievement predominate when blacks are featured in the news. Stories that depict blacks as ordinary, law-abiding, hard-working citizens are few and far between. Rarely do you see us in generic "soft-news" stories that have nothing to do with race. And the inclusion of black experts in stories is still the exception rather than the rule.

Little wonder that fewer than a third of black Americans (29 percent) said they read a newspaper yesterday, compared to 43 percent of whites surveyed, according to a 2006 poll by The Pew Research Center for the People & the Press ("Online Papers Modestly," 2006, p. 56). In that survey, blacks also trailed whites in reading newspapers online yesterday, 6 percent compared to 9 percent, and using other online news sources (13 percent versus 24 percent) (ibid.).

Even in this changing media landscape, African Americans appeared to be persistent news avoiders, disconnected from the news unless it was on TV. Sixty-nine percent of blacks said they watched TV news yesterday, compared to 56 percent of whites surveyed ("Online Papers Modestly," 2006, p. 58).

I took my first job as a newspaper reporter at a daily newspaper in 1977—one year before the American Society of Newspaper Editors announced its goal of reaching newsroom parity by the year 2000 and nine years after the Kerner Commission, named for Illinois Gov. Otto Kerner, issued its scathing criticism of white-owned media, laying part of the blame for the racial divide in America at the feet of the mainstream press for failing to provide white Americans with insight into black life (Report of the National Advisory Commission on Civil Disorders, 1968). In the critically acclaimed documentary, *The Black Press: Soldiers Without Swords* (Nelson, 1998), Vernon Jarrett, former reporter at *The Chicago Defender* and *The Chicago Tribune*, described how the white mainstream press rendered blacks invisible:

> We didn't exist in the other papers. We were neither born, we didn't get married, we didn't die, we didn't fight in any wars, we never participated in anything of a scientific achievement. We were truly invisible unless we committed a crime.

If Kerner were alive today, he would see more stories about African Americans in newspapers (and on television), but unfortunately most of them would be stories that give white America a distorted view of black life, stories which lead most blacks to shun newspapers (and news websites) because they do not see their lives accurately reflected in their pages. It is a vicious cycle.

When I left the newsroom in 2002, after a career that spanned 25 years, seven news-papers and advancement through the ranks from police reporter to executive editor and assistant to the publisher, I was discouraged by the limited progress the news industry had made in hiring minorities and diversifying news coverage.

The negative and stereotypical coverage of blacks is well documented. Furthermore, blacks are often ignored in day-to-day news coverage except for certain categories of stories—notably crime, sports, and entertainment or when minorities have problems or cause problems for white society (Roberts 1975; Poindexter & Stroman, 1981; Dates & Barlow 1990; Ziegler & White, 1990; Entman, 1992, 1994; Campbell 1995; Wilson & Gutiérrez, 1995; Deepe Keever et al., 1997; Gandy, 1998; Entman & Rojecki, 2000; Gilliam & Iyengar, 2000; Poindexter et al., 2003).

There is no denying that newspapers have devoted more space to news about blacks and other minorities in recent years and that signs of "overt racism," are rare. However, newspapers continue to devote little coverage of the everyday life activities of African Americans (Martindale, 1995). If newspapers really want to take one giant step toward improving readership among African Americans, they need to do what they have been promising to do for years—hire more African-American reporters and editors. Yes, it really might be that simple.

The industry's own research underscores the importance of providing relevant, credible, accurate, unbiased content that speaks to the concerns of the black community and the people who live there. And that starts with hiring people who understand those communities and who can bring a diverse perspective to news coverage. Failure to do so—and soon—means slow death for newspapers as African Americans, along with other readers, defect to other sources of news, information, and entertainment.

The changing media landscape is challenging traditional news outlets to work harder to meet the needs of readers and viewers of all stripes, who can now get news and other information from a variety of sources, whenever they want it. And with new technology, citizens-who-would-be-journalists can even create their own—and share it with others! Little wonder that fewer African Americans than whites are reading newspapers in print or online.

Meanwhile, the news industry, obsessed with bottom-line concerns, increased competition, and an ever-shrinking audience, does not seem to have the wherewithal to address the link between its lack of diversity and dwindling audiences. The media continue to talk a good game about diversity, but seem to have a hard time moving beyond the lip service they give to it.

Despite numerous training and internship programs and other hiring initiatives in the past 38 years (several of which I participated in) minorities represent fewer than 14 percent of the nation's 55,000 journalists and African Americans are just 5.5 percent, according to the 2006 ASNE Newsroom Employment Census (ASNE, 2006).

The goal set by the organization of top editors calls for the percentage of minorities in the nation's newsrooms to equal their percentage in the population. Originally editors hoped to reach that lofty goal by 2000, however, when it became clear in 1998 that they were not going to make it, they set a new target date of 2025 with benchmarks along the way. Newspapers failed to meet those benchmarks this year, unable to keep up with the burgeoning minority population. Minorities now comprise 32 percent of all Americans and that number is accelerating with the growth of the Hispanic population (US Census Bureau, 2004).

"The country is changing faster and more dramatically than our newspapers and newsrooms," said Sharon Rosenhause, managing editor of the *South Florida Sun Sentinel* and ASNE diversity chair, in a press release announcing the latest statistics (ASNE, 2006). "It takes very determined editors, newspapers and media companies to make a difference and, right now, not enough are" (ibid.).

It seems they never have been. While some news organizations—Gannett, the former Knight-Ridder (for which I worked for 12 years) and the old Times Mirror, to name a few—made noteworthy efforts to diversify their newsrooms and upper management, those efforts proved to be a drop in the diversity bucket. Even today, 377 newspapers employ no journalists of color, according to ASNE. And while many news organizations have proved adept at getting African Americans and other minorities in the door, keeping them has proved to be more of a challenge.

Two years after I became director of the School of Journalism at the University of Texas at Austin, I was asked to sit on a panel at a journalism conference entitled, "From the Newsroom to the Classroom," which was ostensibly a how-to for journalists interested in moving into teaching. An earlier panel I had participated in had drawn fewer than a dozen people, but this one, in a room that held 200 people, was standing-room only. The sea of eager black, brown, and yellow faces stunned me.

I had spent nearly 25 years helping recruit minorities to the many newsrooms where I worked and it was disheartening to see so many journalists of color now seeking an exit strategy.

When asked why they were considering leaving journalism, they shared their frustration with the lack of opportunities for advancement and better assignments, the difficulty of dealing with white editors who did not value their perspectives, and, perhaps most importantly, their inability to improve to any significant degree the coverage of their respective communities.

It is a familiar complaint. One reason many black journalists entered journalism was out of a desire to improve the stereotypical and often biased coverage of the black community, either as reporters or editors directing that coverage. It came as a shock to many that their white editors did not always welcome their story ideas and suggestions.

Samuel Cornish and John Russwurm, two free black citizens who started the first black newspaper, *Freedom's Journal*, in 1827, understood the importance of having black journalists write about the issues that affect the black community (Cornish & Russwurm, 1827). They understood that blacks needed to "to plead our own cause" (ibid., p. 1).

"Too long have others spoken for us," the *Freedom's Journal* editorial said, explaining why their newspaper was needed. "Too long has the public been deceived by misrepresentations in things which concern us dearly" (Cornish & Russwurm, 1827, p. 1).

For many years the black press served the black community's need for news and information that reflected their lives and their concerns. The black press also served as an advocate for social justice and civil rights for blacks. Many of the first black journalists to be hired by mainstream news organizations after Kerner's report got their start at black newspapers. Tragically, efforts to integrate the nation's newsrooms weakened the black newspapers that had historically filled the void for black news consumers.

Growing up in Philadelphia, a city with a large black population, I had often heard my parents criticize the local newspapers for their stereotypical coverage of blacks.

Too often the three local papers in the city—the *Philadelphia Inquirer*, the *Philadelphia Daily News*, and the *Philadelphia Bulletin*—failed to cover news in the burgeoning black community unless it had to do with crime or racial unrest. There were no blacks on local television as I was growing up. One could not get a true picture of the community without reading the local black newspaper—the *Philadelphia Tribune*, which my parents purchased every week.

It is also the newspaper where I did my first internship and found my first job out of college. I believe my strong desire to cover the black community began there, working along side Harry Amana, now a professor emeritus at the University of North Carolina at Chapel Hill, and Linn Washington, who now teaches at Temple University. They and other black journalists instilled in me a strong sense of the importance of telling the stories of the black community.

Philadelphia was also the birthplace of the forerunner of the National Association of Black Journalists (NABJ). I was still in college when a group of local black journalists led by Chuck Stone, Acel Moore, and Claude Lewis invited black journalists from throughout the tri-state area to come together to form an organization to help improve the hiring of African Americans and the coverage of the black community. A year later this organization led to the creation of the national organization, the NABJ, and Chuck Stone, a former aide to New York Congressman Adam Clayton Powell Sr. and then columnist at the *Daily News*, became its first president.

In 2005, the NABJ celebrated its thirtieth anniversary, honoring these black trailblazers and noting the progress that has been made since the organization was formed by a group of 25 black women and men journalists three decades earlier. While it was indeed a cause for celebration, it was also a time to acknowledge that we still have a long way to go to truly desegregate the nation's newsrooms and improve coverage of America's black communities.

In remarks at the NABJ Hall of Fame Banquet, then president Byron Monroe noted that "the journey that is still incomplete . . . despite the energy and efforts, the passion and promises of newsroom leaders," who had come up short in the quest for newsroom parity (NABJ, 2006).

Yes, we now have black publishers, editors, and editorial page editors. We also have black feature writers, foreign and national correspondents, and columnists. But there are still not enough of us, especially in management, to make a substantial change in the content of most daily newspapers. According to ASNE figures, minorities were only about 11.2 percent of all newsroom supervisors (ASNE, 2006).

What those figures do not tell you is how few of those supervisors have influence over hiring and how difficult it can be for minority supervisors to make a difference when it comes to news coverage.

More troubling is that many black journalists now in the newsroom are wondering if it is time for them to go. Recently I called a friend in Philadelphia who is considering a career change. It is not just the recent change in ownership at the paper and uncertainty about the future that has her thinking about forsaking journalism after 22 years. Instead, it is the ongoing battle with white editors to get stories into the paper that she considers relevant and important to the black community. She bemoaned the loss of black editors at the paper, noting that in a city that is nearly 50 percent African American, there is no longer a single black editor on the city desk.

A young feature writer I mentored at another newspaper has decided to become a speech therapist. A black fashion writer now does event planning. A former religion writer teaches journalism at a historically black college. A young editor is considering the ministry. Turnover is normal, but the fact that so many black journalists have left or are thinking about leaving the newsroom does not bode well for future efforts to improve diversity.

It also begs the question as to whether news organizations are really committed to changing the complexion of their newsrooms. I know some of them, such as the *South Florida Sun Sentinel*'s Sharon Rosenhause, whose newsroom is 29 percent minority, remain deeply committed and appreciate the value of newsroom diversity. Others are indifferent or unwilling to stand up to their corporate bosses who are often more concerned about the bottom-line and loathe to hiring additional staff, diverse or otherwise.

Barbara Ciara, NABJ's president and anchor/managing editor at a Norfolk, VA television station, reminds us why we need more minorities in top newsroom jobs. A lack of improvement in diversity among the people in charge of overseeing hiring practices creates a rocking chair effect: "lots of movement yet never moving forward," said Ciara, noting the dearth of black news directors and general managers (NABJ, 2006a). (Television does a better job than newspapers on the diversity front, but not nearly enough given that it is from TV that most African Americans get their news.)

Little wonder then that many African-American journalists believe that minority recruitment and hiring is no longer a priority for newspapers beset by declining circulation and competition from new forms of media. Here is a statistic that suggests they have something to worry about: without the addition of 11 free dailies last year, newsroom employment would have declined by 600 journalists (ASNE, 2006). And events of this year suggest newsroom employment will continue to decline as newspapers (the *Dallas Morning News*, *The New York Times*, the Akron *Beacon-Journal*, to name just a few) continue to offer buyouts and to lay off employees during this period of continuing economic upheaval.

News executives think they can cut bodies and improve coverage at the same time. I think they are wrong. If one of the keys to turning black news avoiders, who deliberately shun newspapers, into news enthusiasts, who are passionate about reading them, either in print or online, the news industry must provide content that they care about and find ways to engage a diverse audience.

African-American Women in the Newsroom: Counted Twice and then Ignored

Watching Gwen Ifill, a former colleague from my years at the *Baltimore Sun* (she worked at our sister paper, *The Evening Sun*) who is moderator and managing editor of PBS's *Washington Week* and senior correspondent for *The NewsHour with Jim Lehrer*, never fails to fill me with pride. Ifill went from covering city hall in Baltimore, to covering national affairs at *The Washington Post*, and then to covering the White House for *The New York Times*. She spent five years at NBC as a political correspondent before making the jump to PBS. She has moderated vice presidential debates and interviewed presidents and heads of state. And she manages to cover stories and issues relevant to the black community. Why aren't there more Gwen Ifills? There should be.

In its "Women Make the News" initiative, UNESCO noted that while women comprise approximately half of the world's population, they are not represented in half the media content in terms of their interests, images, or voices ("Women Make the

News," 2006). Plus, the UNESCO initiative underscores the point that this is not just a gender equality issue, it is a human rights issue. It is important for the world community that women's interests be represented in the news.

I have always believed that black women bring a unique perspective to the newsroom *and* the content they produce. Standing at the intersection of race and gender, we can help improve coverage of both women and African Americans, if given the opportunity. However, it has been my experience that ours is an often undervalued and unappreciated perspective in white-male dominated newsrooms.

Consider the career of another good friend and now former journalist, Allegra Bennett, who worked at the *Baltimore Sun* as the federal court reporter. Bennett now publishes her own home repair magazine for women, writes commentary and does occasional stints on radio and television. She left the newsroom after 18 years, first to serve as an aide to then-Congressman Kweise Mfume, then returning to work as an editorial writer at the *Washington Times*, before striking off on her own. Some of her reasons for leaving the newsroom were personal, but she, like many black woman journalists I know, speaks about a deep dissatisfaction with the subtle racism experienced in the newsroom.

I first met Bennett when we both were accepted into the Summer Program for Minority Journalists at the University of California at Berkeley. We left for separate newspapers but it was she who recruited me four years later to join her at the *Sun*, which was making a good faith effort to hire more minority journalists.

Bennett said in a recent telephone interview that she believes black women leave journalism, as well as other professions, because they become frustrated by their inability to make their voices heard:

> Men are deaf, whether it's white men or black men, to what women have to say. I have sat in news meetings and expressed ideas and made suggestions and everyone listened quietly and politely and then they moved on. I remember once sitting at a meeting where I made a suggestion and no one said a word. Fifteen minutes later a white man made the exact same suggestion and there was animated and enthusiastic discussion about it. I couldn't believe my ears. Later a black man who was also in the same meeting confirmed to me that it had indeed happened. There's this pervasive deafness that prevents black women from being heard. And when people tune us out they prevent us from contributing.
> (A. Bennett, personal communication, September 1, 2006)

Bennett says this deafness undermines black women's credibility when they bring ideas to the table and have them rejected:

> They can't hear you, so they don't believe you have anything worthwhile to say. This is also a business that doesn't tolerate mavericks. They have been doing business the same way for a hundred years and they don't want to change. They hire people with the expectation that they will fit in . . . women have to traverse the social conditioning of men and it's hard to do.
> (A. Bennett, personal communication, September 1, 2006)

Bennett said she left journalism because she wanted to write "news that people can use. I wanted to make a difference. I still do. I am just doing it in a different way.

I am now free to write the things that I care about" (A. Bennett, personal communication, September 1, 2006).

Black women, for whom media organizations get both race and gender points in the diversity game, often struggle to find their place in the newsroom and seldom is it alongside white women, who often view them as unwelcome competitors for the slots open to women. That is unfortunate.

Together white and minority women represent nearly 40 percent of all newsroom workers—supervisors, copy editors, reporters, and photographers, according to the ASNE census (ASNE, 2006). And those numbers are likely to increase, given the makeup of most journalism schools, which are overwhelmingly female. However, despite their numbers, black and white women have not come together to support each other in the battle against newsroom sexism or to improve coverage of women and minorities.

Journalism historians, Maurine Beasley and Sheila Gibbons, have observed that before the women's movement in the 1970s, "Men ran the world: The news of their conflict, power and influence dominated the front pages" (Beasley & Gibbons, 1993, p. 3). When women began to assert themselves in the newsroom, demanding better coverage of women's issues and the hiring of more women, they often neglected to include black women in those conversations. Debates about whether or not women needed their own sections, putting more women's news on the front page, and designating reporters to cover issues of interest to women were largely between white men and white women in the newsroom. It did not occur to them to include black women in the debates—and when they did, they did not give their suggestions much credence.

I believe three things conspire to prevent women from exercising the clout and influence their numbers suggest. One is the persistent failure of women, especially African-American women, to crack the glass ceiling that keeps many out of leadership positions. A 2003 report by two University of Pennsylvania researchers seems to bear this out. In their two-year study of women in publishing and other related fields, they found that women's efforts to reach the top levels of the profession had stagnated (Falk & Grizard, 2003). On average, women made up less than 15 percent of the top executive positions and even fewer were members of boards of directors of these companies (ibid., p. 3). This lack of progress existed even though "the media identified the problem close to 20 years ago" (ibid.).

Second, women are often reluctant to challenge the white-male dominated newsroom culture that determines who gets hired, what is news, what deserves coverage, and who gets what assignments and promotions. When they do, they risk being thought of as troublemakers and malcontents.

A third reason is the uneasy relation between black and white women journalists. In fact, some wonder if white women share the same unconscious assumptions about people of color as do their white male colleagues. As a result, black women often are not included in discussions about improving the coverage of women and news organizations ignore the fact that reaching out to women news consumers of color can help in efforts to regain readers and viewers.

In an interview discussing diversity in academia, Nell Painter, a professor of American History at Princeton University, noted that one of the hardest things for women and blacks is proving that they deserve to be where they are. I think this has been very true for many African-American women in newsrooms. Our right to be there is often questioned by white journalists who believe skin color and not talent is responsible for our being hired. And even when they grudgingly acknowledge that maybe we are "qualified" for certain jobs, it can still be difficult to make the leap to bigger and better assignments.

However, one study suggested that white women have much more in common with minority women than news purveyors recognize. In their book, *What Women Really Want*, researchers Celinda Lake and Kellyanne Conway argued that women of all races tend to agree on 80 percent of the nation's major issues but the media tend to focus on the 20 percent of disagreement, which "tends to undermine efforts by women to come together and exercise their political clout" (Lake & Conway, 2005). It also prevents us from providing content that appeals to women readers of all races, especially black women.

Diversity Adrift in the Changing Media Landscape

Ironically, at a time when efforts toward diversity are just creeping along, ethnic and racial newsroom diversity may be more important than ever. Because so-called minorities will become the majority population in America by the year 2030, news organizations risk alienating blacks and other minority news consumers if they fail to present accurate portrayals of people of color and news and information that address their concerns. The media simply cannot afford to ignore their views and beliefs.

In her book, *Mega Media: How Market Forces are Transforming News*, Nancy Hicks Maynard warned that news organizations that do not heed this demographic shift run the risk of losing readers and viewers to a proliferating array of competitors, including websites, ethnic media, niche weeklies, magazines, and "narrow-casted radio and television" (Maynard, 2000, pp. 69–70). Maynard believes—and I agree—that daily newspapers and network news programs that disregard diversity will miss an opportunity to expand an otherwise shrinking audience.

You will not get much disagreement from most editors and publishers regarding this new competitive environment. Research undertaken by the National Newspaper Association (NAA) came to the same conclusion. "There is no doubt that the pace of change in the media business has accelerated," the NAA acknowledged in a report on its strategic initiatives ("Horizon Watching," n.d.). "The digitalization of content, low barriers to entry for content publishers and ubiquity of broadband networks is transforming the marketplace much faster than many would have predicted even five years ago" (ibid.). What is less clear is if newspapers understand Maynard's point—that they ignore diversity in this new media arena at their own risk.

In a recent article on newspapers' efforts to adapt to this changing media landscape, the NAA noted that newspapers are starting to see the Internet as central to their future. In 2005, newspaper Internet advertising topped $2 billion for the first time, a 31 percent increase over 2004, according to the NAA (Smolkin, 2006).

Jay Smith, president of Cox Newspapers, a chain of 17 daily and 25 non-daily newspapers (including the *Austin American-Statesman*) acknowledged in a recent article in *American Journalism Review* that newspapers "were slow to catch on":

> I think it's perfectly natural to protect what you have, to think what you have is the only thing that people want, Smith says. You look back to the year 2000, and I don't know that newspapers ever had a better year financially. Those are the

times that can lull you into a sense of complacency. What we've discovered a full five, six years later is that that world doesn't exist anymore.

(Smolkin, 2006)

It may already be too late. While newsrooms have changed only marginally in the last five years, news consumers are no longer dependent on mainstream media for news and information. Moreover, the advent of citizen journalism and the ease of electronic publishing mean that *everyone* can be a publisher and people no longer just passively consume media but actively participate in them.

Some newspapers are encouraged by the fact that their online newspapers remain the most popular source of news content online, though they also remain only marginally profitable, if at all. Nearly 55 million people (more than one in three active Internet users) visited newspaper websites in the second quarter of 2006, a 29.4 percent increase from the same period a year ago, according to a new custom report by Nielsen/NetRatings for the NAA that takes into account home and work Internet usage. These users represent slightly more than a third of all active Web users ("Online Newspaper," 2006).

But where are the other online users? They are visiting other websites, listening to podcasts, reading blogs, and creating their own content. Andreas Kluth noted in an article for *The Economist* that this change has "profound implications for traditional business models in the media industry, which are based on aggregating large passive audiences and holding them captive" ("Among the Audience," 2006).

Smith said he believes newspapers are at a transformational stage: "We're at a point as a business where so much has changed around us, and we really haven't changed with it. If we think we can cut our way to prosperity, we're kidding ourselves" (Farhi, 2006). It remains to be seen if diversity remains on the agenda of news organizations trying to reinvent themselves. I believe they abandon these efforts at their peril. If they do not make an effort to meet the needs of readers, those readers will turn elsewhere in increasing numbers.

I feel strongly that the current crisis in the news industry is due in part to the industry's refusal to embrace diversity to its fullest and cover all segments of the communities they claim to serve—even though it has professed to believe in this ideal for almost 30 years, when ASNE first set its unachieved goal of having the nation's newsrooms mirror America's diverse population.

The late Robert C. Maynard, one of the champions of diversity, gave voice to this ideal in one of his last speeches: "This country cannot be the country we want it to be if its story is told by only one group of citizens. Our goal is to give all Americans front-door access to the truth" (Maynard Institute, 2006).

I do not know if Maynard envisioned this new media landscape, but he was a visionary when it came to diversity, pushing beyond the issues of race and ethnicity to urge news organizations to cover diversity in all forms—age, gender, religion, and sexual orientation. His newspaper, the *Oakland Tribune*, was a model for how a diverse newsroom can create diverse coverage that reflects the community it serves.

The consequence of not living up to this ideal is news coverage that does not truly reflect multiracial communities and news consumers who do not read newspapers because they do not see themselves or people like themselves in them. This is not just bad for business; it is also bad for democracy.

A free press in a diverse and democratic society cannot afford to view the world with blinders on. It must be a mirror on society and it must reflect the diversity of the communities it covers. Until predominantly white news organizations make a real effort to diversify their staffs and their content, they will remain ill equipped for that job. Before they can hold up a mirror to society, they must first look inward at themselves.

New Media, Old Problem: Why We Still Need Diversity

What if the new forms of media and the new products being created end up being just as lacking in diversity as the current newspapers? We need to make sure that does not happen. However, I worry that diversity has taken a backseat to other concerns as the news industry struggles to reinvent itself and develop new business products with the help of new technology.

Even as America has become increasingly diverse, the news industry has been slow to provide readers with news and information that reflect their experiences and their interests. There are notable exceptions (such as Spanish-language publications started by several major dailies in the last few years) but for the most part newspapers continue to churn out the same old news. While industry and academic research makes a strong case for diversity in hiring and content, many newsroom leaders have been largely apathetic. They see diversity initiatives as divisive, time-consuming, and costly. They are not convinced of the payoff. Some even say it leads to biased journalism. They do not want to change. And their failure to do so, while at the same time failing to adjust to the changing media landscape, threatens the future of newspapers and their ability to serve the public trust.

There is no single magic bullet for fixing the current diversity problem. But nor is it as difficult as we sometimes make it appear. Journalism programs, news employers, journalism foundations, professional organizations, and training programs (such as the Poynter Institute and the American Press Institute) need to find new and creative ways to work together to strengthen diversity efforts. It could start with a diversity summit that brings all parties to the table to strategize and draw up a plan of action to accompany ASNE's goals.

We should start with journalism schools. Despite the industry's loss of readers and advertisers, reports of ethical breaches and a decline in public confidence, journalism programs are booming, according to *The New York Times*, and our students seem unfazed by the problems facing traditional media (Seelye, 2006). They still see journalism as a viable career and it is our job to prepare them to function in diverse newsrooms, cover diverse communities, and engage diverse audiences. We have not done this very well up until now.

When I left journalism for academia four years ago, it was partly due to my disenchantment with the diversity efforts in news organizations and also my growing belief that if we really wanted to change the culture and complexion of the newsroom, we were going to have to start that effort in the classroom.

I had discovered, as I spent more time visiting colleges and speaking to students, that there was a big disconnect between journalism education and the diversity efforts taking place in the news industry.

Diversity seemed to be an afterthought in all but a handful of journalism programs. Very few offered courses on covering diversity and I found that journalism faculties were often as white and male as the newsrooms where I worked. Even those programs that made recruiting minority students their priority did a poor job of preparing non-minority students for covering diverse communities and working alongside people of color.

I had seen too many young people coming into newsrooms unaware of the importance of diversity and how it related to their work as journalists. Furthermore, these young people resented diversity initiatives in their newsrooms, did not make an effort to make their own reporting or photojournalism more inclusive, and did not think it was their job to champion these ideals. I worried that the next generation of young journalists would emerge with the same attitudes and blind spots as their predecessors.

Dori Maynard, president of the Maynard Institute for Journalism Education, called this the "us and them" syndrome (Maynard Institute, 2006b). White men see themselves as the "us," and people of color—African Americans, Latinos, Asians—and sometimes even women, as "them."

So when young whites enter the newsroom, they quickly line up with the white guys in the newsroom. They too want to be a part of the big white "us." They see that as the way to gain acceptance and to be successful. And that is because we have not given them the tools and the courage to challenge the status quo and be advocates for newsroom diversity.

Here are some suggestions to increase newsroom diversity and improve attitudes about the importance of diversity from someone who has spent 25 years as a working journalist and four as a journalism educator:

1. Journalism programs need to teach diversity across the curriculum. Every class students take from beginning news writing, to copy editing, to advanced feature writing needs to stress, explain, and teach the importance of diversity.
2. Instructors who teach skills courses should create assignments that force students to get out of their comfort zones and into diverse communities. Last year we did a lab newspaper focused on an area called East Austin and all of our students were assigned stories in this community made up of African Americans and Latinos. I cannot even tell you how many of our students were petrified of going into this community. They had been warned about crime, drugs, and violence and were thus afraid to visit a community just ten blocks away from campus. These are the students that we are sending to America's newsrooms.
3. Encourage and support student chapters of NABJ, NAHJ, AAJA, etc. You would be surprised how many minority students are turned off by journalism and decide to change careers while in journalism school. I believe that these kids need support and encouragement by minority journalism professionals and others to stay the course.
4. Encourage student chapters of SPJ to work closely with the minority journalism organizations and to hold programs that help its members better understand the importance of diversity. Sometimes they do not want to hear these things from their professors—but they may be more prepared to work in a diverse newsroom if they become accustomed to working with minority journalists in college.
5. Offer workshops and seminars to train students how to cover minority communities with sensitivity. The "Let's Do It Better" workshop at Columbia University is a wonderful model for training students on how to cover race and ethnicity.
6. Bring minority and women professionals in as speakers as often as possible. Minority students need role models and white students need to see examples of diversity in the newsrooms they will soon enter.

7. Work harder to recruit minority students. Adopt a modified ASNE goal for your program. What would your program look like if it mirrored the state's minority population? Work toward it.

Lee Becker, a journalism professor and researcher at the University of Georgia, said one of many myths about diversity that gets in the way of making it a reality is the unfounded belief that there is a shortage of good minority candidates (Becker, 2002). Many editors do not try very hard because they believe the minority candidates just are not out there. He said it is also a myth that journalism programs are not graduating enough minority students to meet the demand and that minority graduates are not interested in media careers (ibid.).

"The inescapable conclusion from the data we have gathered is that large numbers of minorities graduate from journalism programs, large numbers seek media jobs, and large numbers have the basic skills needed for media jobs," Becker said in a September 2002 report on journalism school graduates.

Becker said that if newspapers had hired all the minorities who graduated from journalism and mass communication programs and sought jobs in the daily newspaper industry in 2001, they would have added 2,529 minority journalists (Becker, 2002). Those statistics were gleaned from an annual survey that tracks statistics in the nation's journalism and mass communication programs and monitors activities of their graduates.

The real problem, according to Becker, is that many minority candidates do not get job offers and many of those that do, decide not to take them, for a number of reasons. "The problem isn't supply, at least in gross terms," he said in his report. "The problem is that there is not a suitable link between supply and demand" (Becker, 2002). He offered a few suggestions, which make sense to me:

- Employers should develop close relationships with programs at historically black colleges, since nearly a third of African-American journalism and mass communication bachelor degree recipients (27.4) in 2000–1, the period studied in the survey, completed their studies at an HBCU (Historically Black Colleges and Universities). Hispanic-serving institutions granted 31 percent of the degrees earned by Hispanic students that same academic year (Becker, 2002).

- Employers need to think creatively if they are serious about diversity. If a prospective minority employee does not have all the skills needed for a specific job, can they be trained? To take Becker's suggestion further: since newspapers have complained for years about not having enough minority copy editors, what if newspapers committed to training two or three of their own every year? The Maynard Institute and the Dow Jones Copy Editing Program have demonstrated that short, intensive training programs, followed by on-the job training do work. However, they cannot turn out enough to meet demand. Perhaps newspapers should consider in-house training for recent graduates with potential and the desire to learn new skills (Becker, 2002).

- In addition to Becker's suggestions, I recommend raising salaries, improving benefits, and offering training and other perks as hiring incentives. Although this may seem out of touch with the belt-tightening culture that is the new reality, the salary is likely a major reason minority graduates decline jobs they are offered.

- Since geographic location can be a hiring barrier, mentor young hires, especially minorities. It can be difficult to get graduating minority students to go to small newspapers in communities with few or no minorities. To overcome that hurdle, editors may have to find ways to sweeten the offer. They may also have to bend over backwards to help young minority journalists adjust to their new environment, including introducing them to people in the community, providing a mentor inside the newsroom, and making sure they get support from frontline editors. I cannot tell you how many times I have seen well-meaning editors recruit young minorities to their newsrooms and then abandon them once they arrive. The commitment does not end the day they show up.

- Editors should also take advantage of some of the great training programs, such as the Diversity Institute at Vanderbilt University, which trains mid-career minority professionals for journalism jobs, much as the Summer Program for Minority Journalists did years ago. The Maynard Institute and National Association of Minority Media Executives (NAMME) offer leadership training for minority supervisors. There are a lot of terrific programs out there, but we could use even more.

- Expand and increase the funding for the McGruder awards, named after the late Detroit Free Press Executive Editor Robert McGruder, who was a passionate advocate for diversity. The award honors those who make significant contributions toward furthering diversity. Create award categories for educators and students.

- Create partnerships between news organizations and journalism schools to develop training programs for professionals, study ways to improve newsroom diversity and develop new ways to reach diverse audiences.

Still, training and hiring more minority journalists is just a part of the solution. Just as important, I believe, is helping all journalists understand the importance of making newsrooms and news coverage more diverse. White journalists cannot expect to absolve themselves of responsibility in this area. Everyone in the newsroom needs to be engaged in an effort to improve the way the newspaper covers all segments of the community, no matter whether it is online or in the newspaper.

Nor can news organizations afford to neglect efforts to retain minorities already in the newsroom. There are 7,600 talented journalists of color in this country, some of whom have not been able to live up to their full potential. Some of them are wondering if they might be better off doing something else. We cannot afford to lose them. Diverse newsrooms *do* cover diverse communities better.

It is hard to make progress on diversity if newspapers cannot hold on to the people they already have. That means creating a newsroom culture that values diverse ideas and opinions and where all voices can be heard. That means encouraging minority perspectives and allowing people to take chances.

The current newsroom climate makes innovation of any kind difficult because we are so risk adverse. We must be willing to allow people to try new things, knowing that they will not all be successful. This is especially important as we seek new ways to reach out to readers who do not find our newspapers interesting, engaging, or relevant to their lives.

We must also provide opportunities for training and advancement. Minorities need to believe they have a chance at the choice newsroom jobs—if they want them. There are still many areas of the newsroom where you will find few minorities: foreign correspondent, editorial writer, sports editor, columnist, city editor, and Washington bureau chief, among others.

A study by UNITY and the University of Maryland two years ago found that only one in ten members of the Washington press corps (writers, editors, and bureau chiefs) were minorities—even though in the United States, some of the crucial policy issues we face, are quickly becoming more diverse (Westbrook, 2004).

And why do newspaper sports departments remain white and male? Why has it proved so hard for women and minorities to make the team? A recent study by the University of Central Florida's Institute for Diversity and Ethics in Sports found that at the 300 newspapers it surveyed, 90 percent had white male sports editors and there were only five (1.6 percent) black men leading a sports section (Lapchick *et al.*, 2006, p. 3). In addition, among sports columnists, 89.9 percent are white, and only 7 percent (22) are black men (ibid.).

A crucial aspect of this involves changing the culture of the newsroom and making minorities full participants in running the newsroom and covering the community. Cultural change is not easy or fast. However, since newsrooms are already undergoing dramatic technological change right now, it is a good time to reemphasize the value of diversity and the role it must play in this new media landscape that is still taking shape.

There is nothing like a struggle for survival to help force change. And newsrooms will need everyone to be involved in developing innovative forms of news and information as they compete for readers and market share in this brave new world of journalism.

"Whether diversity is an issue of staffing or readership, I think newspaper managers must come to terms with the reality that most people are not going to come or stay where they don't find a sense of belonging," said Robbie Morganfield, former executive director of the Diversity Institute at Vanderbilt (Morganfield, 2006). "I think newsroom leaders must make sure their newsrooms and published products are receptive to and reflective of those who would enter" (ibid.).

In the last 40 years we have learned a lot about what works—and what does not work when it comes to newsroom diversity. There is no shortage of diversity programs and initiatives. There is no great shortage of minority candidates. What we have is a shortage of commitment from some and a bit of diversity fatigue from others. Both are things we can do something about.

Hiring more journalists of color remains an imperative. The Freedom Forum noted in a study of the newspaper industry several years ago that in order to achieve racial parity, approximately half of all journalists hired over the next 25 years would have to be minority journalists (McGill, 1999, p. 9). That is a tall order. It means *all* journalism schools have to produce more minority graduates. We cannot rely on HBCUs to do all the work. Newsroom leaders have to stop making excuses and start hiring those graduates and other minorities interested in journalism careers. And then they must create a newsroom culture that encourages minority women and men to stay when they get there, one that values their contribution, and one in which they find opportunities for advancement. Only then can newspapers expect to fulfill their journalistic promise and draw in African-American news consumers who routinely reject newspapers and turn to competing media outlets to get accurate portrayals of people of color and news that addresses their concerns.

References

American Society of Newspaper Editors (ASNE). (2006, April 25). ASNE Census shows newsroom diversity grows slightly. Retrieved September 2006 from www.asne.org/index.cfm?id=6264.

Among the Audience. (2006, April 20). *The Economist.* Retrieved September 2006 from www. economist.com/surveys/displaystory.cfm?story_id=6794156.

Becker, L. (2002, September 12). *Diversity in Hiring: Supply is there. Is demand?* Freedom Forum. Retrieved September 2006 from www.freedomforum.org/templates/document.asp?document ID=16949.

Campbell, C.P. (1995). *Race, Myth and the News.* Thousand Oaks: Sage.

Cornish, S. & Russwurm, J. (1827, March 16). *Freedom's Journal,* 1(1). Compliments of minorities and communication division, Association for Education in Journalism on 150th anniversary of the black press 1827–1977.

Dates J.L. & Barlow, W. (1990). *Split Image: African Americans in the mass media.* Washington, D.C.: Howard University Press.

Deepe Keever, B.A., Martindale, C., & Weston, M.A. (Eds.) (1997). *US News Coverage of Racial Minorities: A sourcebook, 1934–1996.* Westport: Greenwood Press.

Entman, R.M. (1992). Blacks in the news: Television, modern racism and cultural change. *Journalism Quarterly,* 69(2), 341–61.

Entman, R.M. (1994). Representation and reality in the portrayal of blacks on network television news. *Journalism Quarterly,* 71(3), 509–20.

Entman, R.M. & Rojecki, A. (2000). *The Black Image in the White Mind: Media and race in America.* Chicago: University of Chicago Press.

Falk, E. & Grizard, E. (2003). *The Glass Ceiling Persists: The 3rd annual APPC report on women leaders in communication corporations.* Retrieved September 2006 from www.annenberg publicpolicycenter.org/. . ./women_leadership/2003_04_the-glass-ceiling-persists_rpt.pdf.

Farhi, P. (2006, February/March). Under siege. *American Journalism Review.* Retrieved September 2006 from www.ajr.org/Article.asp?id=4043.

Gandy, O.H., Jr. (1998). *Communication and Race: A structural perspective.* London: Arnold.

Gilliam, F.D., Jr. & Iyengar, S. (2000). Prime suspects: The influence of local television news on the viewing public. *American Journal of Political Science,* 44, 560–73.

Horizon Watching. (n.d.). Strategic imperatives for a shifting media market. *Newspaper Association of America.* Retrieved September 2006 from www.naa.org/horizon/home.html.

Lake, C. & Conway, K. (2005). *What Women Really Want: How American women are quietly erasing political, racial, class, and religious lines to change the way we live.* New York: Free Press.

Lapchick, R., Brenden, J., & Wright, B. (2006, June 22). *The 2006 Racial and Gender Report Card of the Associated Press Sports Editors.* University of Central Florida Institute for Diversity and Ethics in Sports.

Martindale, C. (1995). Only in Glimpses: Portrayal of America's largest minority groups by The New York Times, 1934–1994. Paper presented at Association for Education in Journalism and Mass Communication Conference, Washington, D.C.

Maynard Institute. (2006). History, Robert C. Maynard: Life and legacy. Retrieved September 2006 from www.maynardije.org/about/history/.

Maynard Institute. (2006b, July 26). Diversity in the media: Why it matters. Retrieved September 2006 from www.maynardije.org/about/history/.

McGill, L. (1999). *Newsroom Diversity: Meeting the challenge.* Freedom Forum. Retrieved September 2006 from www.freedomforum.org/templates/document.asp?documentID=18110.

Morganfield, R. (2006, August 2). Speaking of diversity. Freedomforum.org. Retrieved September 2006 from www.freedomforum.org/templates/document.asp?documentID=18110.

NABJ. (2006, August 27). We're not there yet. Retrieved September 2006 from www.nabj. org/pres_corner/story/52745p-81327c.html.

NABJ. (2006a, July 7). Survey shows blacks continue to decline in TV news nationwide; NABJ concerned about trend. Retrieved September 2006 from www.nabj.org/newsroom/news_ releases/story/49994p-76533c.html.

Nelson, S. (Producer/Director). (1998). *The Black Press: Soldiers without swords* [Documentary]. United States: California Newsreel.

Online newspaper viewership up nearly 30 percent in second quarter. (2006, August 2). *Newspaper Association of America*. Retrieved September 2006 from www.naa.org/Global/PressCenter/2006/ONLINE-NEWSPAPER-VIEWERSHIP-UP-NEARLY-30-PERCENT-IN-SECOND-QUARTER.aspx?lg=naaorg.

Online papers modestly boost newspaper readership. (2006, July 30). Detailed Demographic Tables, *The Pew Research Center for the People and the Press*. Retrieved September 2006 from http://people-press.org/reports/display.php3?ReportID=282.

Poindexter, P.M. & Stroman, C.A. (1981). Blacks and television: A review of the research literature. *Journal of Broadcasting*, 25(2), 103–22.

Poindexter, P., Smith, L., & Heider, D. (2003). Race and ethnicity in local television news: Framing, story assignments, and source selections. *Journal of Broadcasting & Electronic Media*, 47(4), 524–36.

Report of the national advisory commission on civil disorders. (1968). New York: Bantam.

Roberts, C. (1975). The presentation of blacks in television network news. *Journalism Quarterly*, 52, 50–5.

Seelye, K. (2006, May 15). Times are tough for news media, but journalism schools are still booming. *The New York Times*. Retrieved September 2006 from www.nytimes.com/2006/05/15/business/media/15students.html?ex=1305345600&en=dd2b3912e616b44e&ei=5088.

Smolkin, R. (2006 June/July). Adapt or die. *American Journalism Review*. Retrieved September 2006 from http://ajr.org/article.asp?id=4111.

US Census Bureau. (2004). *US Interim Projections by Age, Sex, Race, and Hispanic Origin, Table 1A Projected Population of the United States by Race and Hispanic Origin: 2000 to 2050*. Retrieved August 10, 2006 from www.census.gov/ipc/www/usinterimproj/.

Westbrook, J. (2004). UNITY Report: Washington press corps lacking in diversity. Unity2004. Retrieved September 2006 from http://atunity.org/nm/publish/news_46.html.

Wilson, C.C. & Gutiérrez, F. (1995). *Race, Multiculturalism, and the Media: From mass to class communication*. (2nd edition). Thousand Oaks: Sage.

Women Make the News 2006. (2006). Why this initiative, UNESCO. Retrieved September 2006 from http://portal.unesco.org/ci/en/ev.php-URL_ID=18296&URL_DO=DO_TOPIC&URL_SECTION=201.html.

Ziegler, D. & White, A. (1990). Women and minorities on network television news: An examination of correspondents and newsmakers. *Journal of Broadcasting and Electronic Media*, 34, 215–23.

Chapter 17

Coverage of Latinos in the News Media

We're Not There Yet

Maggie Rivas-Rodriguez

If news coverage of US Latinos could be characterized with three adjectives, they would be: improved, unsophisticated, and scant.

There has been genuine improvement in news coverage over the 30 years that I've been informally tracking it, first as a college student, then as a professional journalist, and now as a college professor and news consumer—and always as a Latina, which is undeniably part of my perspective.[1] Coverage of Latinas/os is not the only factor I look for when watching, listening to, or reading the news: it is among several variables I evaluate. These include whether the lead is good, whether the story is organized, whether the facts support the writer's assessment, whether there is enough historical context to make sense of the latest development, why the story is news, and *whether* the story is news. I cheer, mentally, when someone does a good job; it is not surprising that Juan Castillo, a local writer for the *Austin American-Statesman*, consistently writes important stories on Latinos with clarity and balance. But, I also am extremely disappointed when Latinas/os get left out of stories, get treated badly in the news, or when someone did not think about how the Latino community might read a particular story's content.

I am not alone. In Denver, a Latina city employee has started noticing that her local paper now carries Hispanic men among those featured on Father's Day. "It's a small thing," she says, "but it shows we feel more involved" (Hood, 2005).

In fact, the prevailing sentiment among Latinos regarding coverage about them is one of disappointment, at least as it applies to the English-language media, a finding supported by a survey from the Pew Hispanic Center. The center's 2004 telephone survey showed that 78 percent of Latinos believe that Spanish-language media is "very important to the economic and political development of the Hispanic population" (Suro, 2004, p. 2). But, 44 percent believed that English-language media creates a negative image of Latinos. Those who said the English-language media hurts the image of Latinos said that there was "too much emphasis on undocumented immigration and criminal activity like drug trafficking" (ibid., p. 10). Native-born Latinos expressed concern over the lack of coverage of Latino economic and political accomplishments.

Content analyses provide support for this point. A national content analysis of three newsmagazines (*Newsweek*, *Time*, and *US News & World Report*) showed that in 2005, there was a combined published total of 1,547 stories; yet, only 1.2 percent, or 18 stories were about Latinos. The report—commissioned by the National Association of Hispanic Journalists—found that of the 18 stories, 67 percent were about immigration. In speaking about the nature of the immigration stories, the report found that "Latino immigrants were portrayed, for the most part, as a negative and disruptive force on US society" (Gavrilos, 2006, p. 3).

Another content analysis of four of the country's major English-language television networks (ABC, CBS, NBC, CNN) conducted in 2005, found that coverage of Latinos was also wanting. Of the 16,000 news stories that were broadcast on those four networks, only 115, or 0.72 percent, were about Latinos while 33 percent of those 115 stories centered on immigration. This finding led the author to declare, "In short, Latinos have remained virtually invisible and marginalized on the network evening news" (Subervi, 2005, p. 3).

Evidence of Latinos/as marginalization from newspaper coverage has also been found. Vargas (2002) used both content and textual analyses to examine four years of coverage of the *Raleigh News & Observer* (*N & O*) through 1992 to 1995. The author found that less than 1 percent of the newspaper's content was about Latino issues and that Latinos in those stories were rarely presented as experts, but rather as "ordinary people" leading Vargas (2000) to conclude, "Latinos in the *N & O* often serve as a narrative device to make a connection between the private and the public spheres rather than as authoritative sources of information."

Individual Stories

It is also instructive to look at coverage of news stories concerning Latinos to grasp how the ignorance is manifested—so subtly, in fact, that journalists may have unintentionally missed it in a deadline rush. It is evident that if there is no intervention or challenge, the blind spots will remain. It is my hope that this essay will provide a point of discussion about problems in coverage of Latinos and Latinas, identify some of the common pitfalls, and offer examples of what well-meaning people might do to exercise their agency in this area.

Improved coverage of the Latino community is particularly important now because we, as a nation, are on the threshold of a new era. The Latino population is expected to grow from its current 13 percent ratio to approximately 24 percent of the US population by 2050 (US Census Bureau, 2004). Without full participation of all within our society, our nation cannot realize its full potential: in short, everyone must be involved, and our public institutions—including the news media—should reflect its citizens, if not all its residents.

A perpetual issue facing coverage of the Latino community is that of covering the immigrant community, which may speak Spanish only, while also covering the established Latino community residents in the United States. All Latinos are often portrayed as a recent immigrant population (Calafell, 2004), however there is also a sizeable, and perhaps unquantifiable number of undocumented Latino immigrants, with estimates of this community projected to be 11.1 million (Passel, 2005).

Let us look at the biggest story involving Latinos in 2006: the immigration debate. For several weeks in the spring of 2006, rallies took place across the country in protest of a Senate bill that would make any illegal immigrants felons. Throughout the country, in what many saw as an astounding display of collective dissent, rallies were held in major US cities. Although there are probably many scholars currently conducting content analyses on news coverage of these rallies, there is little scientific analysis on the nature of this coverage yet.

But what I saw, in an unscientific sampling of newspaper, magazine, and a few television stories, was a general even-handed coverage of the rallies. Story angles included students who organized through telephone text-messaging and e-mail, with many subsequently facing suspension from school and even criminal charges. Another aspect was the role of Spanish-language radio, which turned over its airwaves to enable a discussion of the rallies through call-ins and interviews with immigration experts. There were also stories about an anticipated major backlash to the future immigration proposal, the lawmakers who voted to support an amnesty program for the illegal immigrants, and even to the illegal immigrants themselves. As a journalist from *The Atlanta Journal Constitution* stated:

> "They have, in fact, awakened the sleeping giant," said [D.A.] King, who helped push bills on illegal immigration through the Georgia Legislature. "They have made a large number of Americans who were willing to tolerate this as a small problem wake up to the fact that this is a very immediate crisis."
>
> (Deans, 2006, p. 1A)

News coverage was commendable when it used surveys to gauge public sentiment—and several major news organizations did so, indicating the complexity of the issue. There was little unanimity on how problematical it was for the United States to play host to the undocumented.

The problem was, however, when news stories took on an ominous tone and the critic was provided a platform to speak without a critical evaluation of the facts. In the case of one critic, Mississippi Republican Senator Trent Lott, journalists failed to connect the dots—placing today's news within the context of yesterday's. Syndicated columnist Steve Chapman noted the irony of Lott's posturing:

> The complaint about "foreign flags" is especially nervy coming from Mr. [Trent] Lott, who as a cheerleader at the University of Mississippi used to carry a Confederate battle flag onto the football field. Unlike the architects of the Confederacy, those people waving flags from Mexico or Honduras never tried to tear this country asunder. Conservatives defend the Confederate flag as a legitimate way for Southerners to honor their heritage. It doesn't occur to Mr. Lott and Mr. [Pat] Buchanan that maybe immigrants brandish the flags of their mother countries for similar reasons, not out of contempt for America.
>
> (Chapman, 2006, p. 13A)

Chapman was one of the few journalists who raised this point. Like Chapman, *Boston Globe* columnist Derrick Z. Jackson drew attention to those reporters that give the Trent Lotts of the world a free ride:

> The Republican senator from Mississippi [Trent Lott] castigated the marches as "intimidation and extortion." He said he was "highly offended" how demonstrators "take jobs illegally and then protest and wave foreign flags." He said, "When they act out like that, they lose me" . . . That sums it up on how reporters let Lott froth at the mouth for two months about Mexican flags without reminding him that he lost his position as Senate majority leader by glorifying treason, civil war, intimidation, lynching, extortion, segregation, and stealing of millions of black livelihoods in the name of the Confederate flag.
>
> (Jackson, 2006, p. C9)

Other news stories focused on the recording of the US national anthem in Spanish. Though some questioned the loyalties of those recording artists who would dare to record the national anthem in Spanish, columnists generally supported the Spanish-language anthem. Cindy Rodriguez, writing for *The Denver Post*, said:

> Ironically, the record's producer is British. And what many people don't know is the majority of the singers who recorded "Nuestro Himno" (Our Hymn) are Puerto Ricans—Latinos from a commonwealth whose residents have been American citizens since 1917, have a high participation rate in the armed services, and yet can't vote in presidential elections.
>
> (Rodriguez, 2006)

In this informal assessment of the overall news coverage, several stories gave greater weight to the controversies, resulting in a weakening of the strength of the protesters' messages. Several news reports lacked that important sense of proportion—that the rallies represented millions of men, women, and children nationwide and that some marchers risked losing their jobs to take the time to march as an outward show of their displeasure. The reality was that the counter-marchers represented a comparably smaller number of people than those marching in support of the rally.

The Invisible Minority

Our local newspaper recently ran a powerful series on how African Americans were driven out of American communities from 1864 through the 1920s. The concluding article began with a discussion of black "lawn jockeys," considered by many African Americans to be racist, while to mostly whites they were considered an "amusing decoration." "When a country is unable to agree on its past, things large and small become matters of dispute," wrote journalist Jaspin (2006).

The following day, Danny Camacho, a longtime Austin resident, lauded the series and added:

> Even in Austin, there are stories to be told. This is a tri-color city: black, white and brown. The history of its Hispanic citizens has mostly been ignored and forgotten. The expulsion of the Mexican population of Austin in 1854 is a fact that is little known or acknowledged. This expulsion was motivated by white racial fears—that Mexicans were encouraging and aiding slaves to run to freedom in Mexico. This is still a divided city with three views of history.
>
> (Camacho, 2006)

Camacho can be counted on to write these letters to the editor. He has responded in the past to other omissions about Latinos. Camacho's point reflects a key fact about coverage of Latinos in the news media: too often, mainstream news organizations, committed to covering the minority community, think "African American," when seeking to include minority voices in their news reports. This happens even in states such as Texas, where the Hispanic population is 33 percent, almost four times the Texan population of African Americans (US Census Bureau, 2005). Thus, when news operations, now sensitized to including minority perspectives, do include these voices, they often resort to including only African-American perspectives. And many news organizations may not even think about Latinos in large or small stories.

The *Austin American-Statesman* ran a short feature story on the type of music CDs that might be found in the libraries of well-known Austinites. Of the "local notables" whose musical tastes were outlined, there were three Anglos, one African American, and no Latinos (Salamon, n.d.). It was a short story, intended to be a breezy fun read. The glaring omission of Latinos in Austin is also notable. Austin has had at least two former Latino mayors, and is the state capital, home to an abundance of well-known Latinos at the state level. But, one could not decipher this fact from the short story. Similar omissions are repeated routinely in news coverage and even in scholarly writings about news coverage.

Valdivia acknowledges, for instance, improvements in coverage and inclusion of Latinos in both academic and popular representations over the past 20 years. But, she follows, there remain blatant gaps, including one 2003 edition of a reader on race, class, and gender in the media that had no chapters on Latinos/as:

> Race still too often signifies blackness, without either an acknowledgment of social constructivist theories or of the growing amount of scholarship of studies across difference and ethnicities-in-relation. Blackness, moreover, is still treated as if it were the opposite purity pole of Whiteness—when Latina/o Studies demonstrates that this is untenable, as Latina/os come in Black, White, and all the other possible skin tones.
>
> (Valdivia, 2004, p. 108)

Even at a time when the news has acknowledged the great increase in the US Hispanic population, Latinos remain the invisible people, blending into the background at best, rarely taking center stage, but instead serving as supporting actors (unless the story is about immigration). Because stories of Latinos are not part of the national or local consciousness, it has become easy to minimize the discrimination that Latinos face.

For instance, in an interview with the accomplished playwright Eduardo Machado, a native of Cuba who heads the playwriting studies at Columbia University, *New York Times* reporter Deborah Solomon asked for Machado's opinion of Broadway playwrights:

> *Machado*: Broadway is its own world. They should do contemporary American plays, but they do little besides revivals and new British plays. The theater still looks as if it is the 50s. The plays are white, and the audiences are white. And that is not representative of America.
>
> *Solomon*: Oh, come on, that is so P.C.! White guys write good plays, too. What did you think of Edward Albee's "Goat or Who Is Sylvia?"
>
> *Machado*: It made me proud to be a member of the theater community.
>
> *Solomon*: And what about Nilo Cruz, the Cuban-born playwright who just won the Pulitzer Prize?
>
> *Machado*: I challenge the theaters of New York to give him the same level of attention they would give to any other play! His play, "Anna in the Tropics," has been done in one small theater in Florida. Not even the Pulitzer judges have seen it. Of course, they read the script.
>
> (Solomon, 2003)

A few months later, the said play by Nilo Cruz called "Anna in the Tropics," was the subject of an article written by another *New York Times* reporter, Mireya Navarro.

Rather than dismiss the possibility that there might be challenges for Latino playwrights and plays based on Latino themes, Navarro wrote:

"Anna," which opened last month to mixed reviews, is a rarity: It is a Latino themed show on Broadway, and a drama at that. A study released last month by the League of American Theaters and Producers showed that Broadway audiences are overwhelmingly non-Hispanic white (83 percent) and that in the 2002–3 season Latinos accounted for only 4 percent of ticket buyers. The marketing team behind "Anna in the Tropics" has been trying to draw more Latinos to the show, advertising in Spanish-language newspapers, handing out fliers at Latin clubs and contacting upscale Latino groups like bar and medical associations, said Charles Rice-Gonzalez, a publicist for the play. Regardless of how it does at the box office, "Anna" has already cemented its special significance to a cast that embodies the changing landscape for Latinos in theater, television and film. Their contrasting experiences are exemplified by [actors] Mr. Argo, Ms. Lopez, Mr. Smits and Mr. Zayas, all New York natives of Puerto Rican descent who were caught up in the Latin explosion—in population numbers, recognition and cultural influence—at different stages of their careers.

(Navarro, 2003)

Where Solomon was skeptical of Machado's viewpoint, Navarro did her homework and found that, indeed, there was a striking lack of Latino representation among Broadway audiences. In her 1,315-word article, Navarro, who was born and raised in Puerto Rico, detailed the uniqueness of the Latino performers' experiences, as well as their difficulty in finding acting jobs. One actress was constantly asked to use an accent. She refused, stating, "I'm a reality. This is what I speak like" (Navarro, 2003).

In a telephone interview, Navarro said she had attended a news conference in New York for the Spanish press:

They had a publicist and basically he did a media availability for the Spanish-language press and I went to that, even though I wasn't Spanish-language press . . . The marketing of the play had to rely on Hispanic publications because it was a Hispanic play all around, the playwright, the cast, the subject matter, everything was Latino. So they really were hoping to get a lot of Hispanics into the theater . . . They did similar stuff for the English-language press, but they really went out of their way to get the play promoted in Hispanic populations. I had already contacted the publicist about all these actors from different generations coming together on Broadway, so he told me about the press conference and I said, "Oh, I'll go, because I speak Spanish." And then it turned out to be great because people were crying and it was kind of an emotional thing . . . Had it been played before a more general press audience, everything would have been different. But because everybody was Latino, they really let it all out and the actors were very emotional about what a big deal it was for a Latino playwright to be on Broadway with all the Latino cast.

(M. Navarro, personal communication,
August 15, 2006)

But, Navarro hastened to add, she does not practice advocacy journalism. She does do her best to direct callers to appropriate people within *The New York Times*.

Ignorance Abounds

Newsroom executives who think they have their local Hispanic community covered because they have hired a Hispanic journalist—even a Spanish-speaking one—should remember this name: Julio Granados.

On March 8, 1998, the *Raleigh News & Observer* published a page 1 article about a 21-year-old undocumented worker from Mexico. Reporter Gigi Anders, who used the man's name, Julio Granados, and his photograph, said he worked 60 hours a week in a small Raleigh grocery store, La Bodega El Mandado, with five other undocumented workers (Anders, 1998). Members of the Raleigh-Durham-Chapel Hill Hispanic community were outraged, as were several other non-Hispanics both in the newsroom and outside. Essentially, the paper had drawn a map leading immigration officials to the hapless Granados.

On March 24, 1998, the predictable happened: immigration officials arrived, arresting Granados and five other men, while "waving a copy of the *N & O* article" (Whitlock, 1998). There would be some disagreement later between Julio Granados and the newspaper—he would claim that he was not informed that he might be deported if his identity was revealed.

N & O executive editor Anders Gyllenhaal responded with a column, in which he said some things might have been done differently. But he pointed out: "Gigi Anders, a talented reporter and Cuban-American who has written often on immigration over the years, talked this possibility over with Granados repeatedly. Each time, Granados concluded he'd take the risk that telling his complete story would bring, even if it meant going home" (Gyllenhaal, 1998, p. A21).

By pointing out that writer Anders is Cuban-American, Gyllenhaal conferred upon her a special authority: a Hispanic reporter would have greater sensitivity to Latino issues when compared to a non-Hispanic reporter. Whether that is true or not is an issue that will be explored more fully shortly. But the mere fact that the writer was Hispanic should not absolve the news operation of its responsibility to present the story in a fair, accurate, and sensitive way. In this particular case, the writer introduced phrases that, written by a non-Hispanic, would very likely not have survived scrutiny, like the following: "Julio Cesar Granados Martinez is Everyhombre" (Anders, 1998, p. A1).

Had Anders been white, would an editor let stand the "Everyhombre" or would they have hit "delete" and told the writer, quite rightly, that it was a condescending word? It is impossible to say with 100 percent certainty, but here is an issue for editors to consider: if this line was written by someone outside of the subject's ethnic/racial/gender group, would it have been OK? Having a Latina/o write a story does not mean that the editing should be lax; this policy serves neither the news operation, nor the community. It also does not serve the writer.

Another component to the Granados story was gender. Later, a community leader in North Carolina pointed this out:

> John Herrera, a local Latino leader, says that journalists must consider the ramifications of the reporter-source relationship. "Journalists must ask themselves: Were the subjects in a position to give informed consent?" says Herrera. "You have to put it into context. These people developed a one-and-a-half-month relationship, a single, lonely, depressed male with this good-looking Cuban-American woman who speaks your language. You would volunteer more information than you would normally."
>
> (Yeoman, 1998, pp. 19–20)

Anders, who later left the newspaper and became a successful freelancer, writing for, among others, Latino publications, later reflected on her experience in the *American Journalism Review*. She asked rhetorically:

> Should minorities cover minorities?
>
> Outwardly, yes, it would seem ideal. After all, who's more tuned in to, say, Asian Americans than a fellow Asian American? That's the theory, anyway. (We can argue some more whether it's smart or hopelessly narrow-minded for editors to engage in race-based assigning later on—and we will.) But what sometimes happens in real life, when a reporter of color gets into the nitty-gritty of covering ethnic situations, is a weird and often unanticipated backlash. It can come from the subject or community you covered, your ethnic colleagues, the powers that be at your news organization and your audience. Meaning, you can get it from all sides . . .
>
> By choice, I've covered Latin immigrants and their lives for many years. I've had sources get mad at me before, but nothing could have prepared me for the vitriol in the case of Julio Granados. One enraged woman sent an e-mail saying, "I'm ashamed to call myself a Latina because of what you did to your own people. How could you?!? As a human being, as a Hispanic, you owed us better. You are the UN-Latina Latina. I hope you rot in hell, you twisted bitch, you hypocritical Judas." Being a Latin immigrant myself, of course I felt the prick of her cultural stinger. Though I'd made the ground rules explicit to my subject in our native Spanish, and he'd agreed to be named, there was nevertheless a mute assumption on his and the broader Latin community's part that I would in the end protect his anonymity (i.e., lie to my editors about his immigration status) because, wink-wink, it's us (victimized minorities) against them (the white power elite). Everybody every reporter writes about wants a flattering spin, of course. The difference with minorities is that being one yourself, you tend to feel like the outsider, too. It's that natural empathy that creates rapport with your source, which usually creates more openness during interviews and, you hope, a much better story than anyone else could get. What you have to watch out for and accept is the inevitable resentment and fallout when tacit expectations are unmet.
>
> (Anders, 1999, p. 22)

Making a Difference

Despite the efforts of the news industry, news operations are often not representative of their communities: newspaper newsrooms often have few Latino journalists who might have an automatic advantage on a story. In fact, in many newsrooms there are no journalists of color. Of the 1,417 daily newspapers that responded to an annual diversity survey by the American Society of Newspaper Editors, 377 had no minorities; 66 percent of these newspapers without minorities were small operations, with circulations of less than 10,000 (ASNE, 2006).

Hispanics made up 4.51 percent of the news staffs at the surveyed papers. African Americans were only slightly better off, at 5.56 percent; Asian-Americans made up 3.23 percent; and Native Americans were 0.56 percent. Five years ago, Hispanics made up 3.66 percent; African Americans 5.23 percent; Asian-Americans 2.3 percent; and Native Americans 0.44 percent (ASNE, 2006a). But, the ASNE report qualified this small improvement in minority statistics by adding that the survey added more newspapers, namely free dailies: "Without the addition of 11 free dailies, newsroom employment would have slipped by 600 journalists. Thus, paid circulation newspapers have dropped about 2,800 journalists in the past five years as the industry has struggled economically" (ASNE, 2006).

The Radio-Television News Directors Association & Foundation's (RTNDA) latest survey revealed a healthy increase in its numbers of minority journalists, including news directors. According to the survey, 22 percent of the local news staffed surveyed were minorities in 2005, up an entire percentage point from the previous year. Of those in television, Hispanics stood at 10 percent, up from 9 percent the previous year. Radio lagged: only 2 percent of the news staffs were Hispanic (Papper, 2006). Barbara Cochran, RTNDA president, noted in a news release posted on the group's website, "The gains for minorities on local television news staffs should help stations better serve their increasingly diverse communities" ("Minorities Gain on Local," 2006).

Yet, rather than let the numbers of Latino journalists remain flat, the National Association of Hispanic Journalists[2] (NAHJ) has undertaken an ambitious experiment with its "Parity Project,"—a project designed to raise the Hispanic representation in newsrooms in those cities with large Hispanic populations. NAHJ helps newsrooms conduct town-hall meetings with community members to look for possible disconnects, works with high school students to build a pipeline into newsrooms, and helps find qualified Latino journalists to fill spots at the news operations. Juan Gonzalez, a columnist for the *New York Daily News*, who, as president of NAHJ, initiated the Parity Project in 2002, told the Poynter Institute's Aly Colón, "Our overriding goal is better journalism—not a jobs program, or to hire less-qualified journalists," he added. "And because we knew the community, and we knew the industry, we were the perfect bridge. We have a trust no one else does" (Colón, 2005).

But although Gonzalez minimizes the efforts to get more Latinos hired, the Parity Project has had success in just that area. The 24 companies participating in Parity Project (19 newspapers, four television stations, and National Public Radio) had a combined total of 123 Latino journalists when they first began to participate. Those same companies have added 109 more Latino journalists since then (NAHJ, 2006).

In Denver, where the Hispanic population had felt ignored, the Parity Project has seen improvements. *Rocky Mountain News* President and Publisher John Temple, whose paper was the first one to sign on to the Parity Project, said that there is still much more room for improvement in terms of coverage:

> The paper tries to be more aware of minority events and concerns, he [Temple] says, and exactly how to do that has evolved. The editors have created a new demographic beat to keep tabs on the city's growing immigrant population; the reporter is Hispanic. The paper continues to encourage all beat reporters from religion to education to urban affairs to incorporate the minority community into their coverage.
>
> "To a great extent, Hispanic coverage is mainstreamed into the newspaper," Temple says, "and that's happened over time as we've built up better awareness of the community and sensitivity about what we're doing."
>
> Members of the paper's advisory committee, once vocal critics, say its coverage of Hispanic issues has improved dramatically. Two years ago, "we were just plain sick of both papers," says Luis Torres, a professor of Chicano studies at the Metropolitan State College of Denver, referring to the *News* and the *Denver Post*. Both

papers do a better job now than they did then, he says, but the *News* "is more in tune with the Latino community."

(Hood, 2005)

Community pressure

In the mid-1980s, an up-and-coming Chicana writer named Sandra Cisneros, fresh off of a prestigious writing fellowship, approached *Texas Monthly*, a slick award-winning regional magazine that has a national reputation, hoping to write for it. As she recalled later, the magazine would not give her the time of day. Her interpretation: the magazine was not interested in content that would reflect the state's largest minority group. Her interpretation was reinforced by the publication's lack of Hispanic writers.

Cisneros became a white-hot writer whose book *House on Mango Street* is now being used in college and high school classrooms throughout the country. She is also firmly rooted in San Antonio and to her Mexican roots. She bought a Victorian house in San Antonio's King William Historic District and, in 1997, created a minor furor when she painted it purple—a violation of deed restrictions requiring homes to adhere to specific color schemes. *Texas Monthly* wanted to write a story about Cisneros and her purple house furor. On one condition, Cisneros responded, she wanted a Latino/a writer:

> "I didn't say no. I said, 'Could we have a Latino writer at least write about me?'" Cisneros says. "They got real huffy and puffy, *todos ofendidos*—very offended. And just said, 'You know, we can write a story about you anyway,' like threatening. And I said, 'Go ahead.' And of course, the one that they wrote was very mean-spirited."

(Silva, 1993)

Fast-forward to 2003 when *Texas Monthly*, celebrating its thirtieth anniversary, produced a special anniversary issue featuring Texan women and wanted to include the now widely respected Cisneros. *San Antonio Express-News* reporter Elda Silva noted in a profile of the magazine's editor Evan Smith that Smith personally appealed to Cisneros. But, Smith recalled, Cisneros would have no part of it:

> Later on when I get more power, more accolades, more famous, I looked at their magazine and things hadn't changed, but now they were coming around and asking to interview me. I started looking at their pages and realized the only time Latinas ever came out in their magazine was if they had been raped, or killed or both. That was the only time you would see them on their cover. It wasn't ever even written by a Latina.
>
> I just feel like the only power I have to say is no. Because if I get on that cover then it's just me and I'm just a token . . . I just wanted to wake them up.

(S. Cisneros, personal communication, August 16, 2006)

Cisneros has suggested publishing a special issue with Latino writers and photographers, edited by a guest editor. In recent years, the magazine has increased its Latino staff, adding Cecilia Balli and Oscar Casaraz to its contributors. But, Cisneros noted: "I feel that TM isn't doing half as much as they should. They seem to think two part-timers without benefits is great. I do not." (S. Cisneros, personal communication,

August 16, 2006). According to Cisneros: "They've done that so that they can say, 'well we do have somebody.' But it's too little and it's not enough. It's a new millennium, it's not 100 years ago. We've got to move a little faster than that."

Individuals can and do make a difference, albeit a small one. Cisneros was, of course, a celebrity by the time she turned down *Texas Monthly*: it is possible that she had nothing to lose. Yet, this highly publicized episode did much to foster discussion about whether the magazine carries stories of interest to the growing Latino population. This discussion may have encouraged the magazine editors to reach out to Latino writers.

The non-celebrity has some power, too. A simple letter to the editor for publication, or even an e-mail or phone call to a reporter or editor can bring about considerable change. After publishing the article on the CD collections of Austin notables, I sent a note to the section editor and the writer. As a result, the writer and I met, and I provided him with names of possible book reviewers. In the end, the paper published reviews on three Latino-themed books by graduate students with ties to the Center for Mexican American Studies at the University of Texas at Austin. We could have had more if we had people who had time to write them.

New Outlets

In recent years, Spanish-language news has made increasing inroads in both readership and viewership. We, who dwell in English-language news media, are paying attention. The 2006 ASNE annual survey found a total of 93 full-time staffers employed in the three identified Spanish dailies (ASNE, 2006). The RTNDA does not include Hispanic TV news departments, an omission which would certainly boost the numbers in that organization's annual count. As the Pew Hispanic Center survey of 2004 showed, Latinos feel that those Spanish-language news operations are more supportive of Latinos than the general news operations.

But, those Spanish-language outlets are not the only new kids in town. Smart publications include *Tu Ciudad* in Los Angeles, a slick bi-monthly publication that began one year ago and features entertainment and some political stories—all about Latinos. It is owned by Emmis, which also owns *Texas Monthly*. In March 2006, in advance of the Academy Awards, it ran a feature about dubious movie awards and it had this to say about the "Most Misleading Movie Title Ever Foisted Upon Audiences":

> *The Mexican* (2001) which starred Brad Pitt and Julia Roberts, was set in Mexico but starred no actual Mexicans. Go figure.
>
> ("The Envelope, Please," 2006, p. 47)

In the same issue, *Tu Ciudad* ran a sensitive story about the divide among Latinos on immigration. The story provided historical context, balanced viewpoints, and authoritative Latino sources, dissecting all sides of the debate. In one of the story's paragraphs, the author notes:

> In the coverage of the cyclical fervor over the undocumented, most accounts paint a metaphysical boxing ring with entrenched white cowboys in one corner and, in the other, liberals and Latinos who say undocumented immigrants add sweat equity to the nation. But the argument isn't as simple as brown-against-white and hasn't been for some time.
>
> (Romero, 2006, pp. 58–67)

The landscape is changing. With publications such as *Tu Ciudad*, the increase in Spanish-language news, and with sustained pressure both in-house by journalists who strive for better coverage and externally by community members, the coming years are sure to bring a truer portrayal of the growing Latino population. I predict here (without going too much out on a limb) that in ten years, neither Danny Camacho nor I will be sending too many e-mails railing at an editor for leaving Latinos out of everyday life stories. Either the editors and reporters will have started doing that much better of a job, or we will have grown weary of fighting the battle and have turned our loyalties to more sophisticated news products that give us the news without the head-ache—and the added work of lodging a complaint.

I want to open my paper, or watch the 6 o'clock news, and *get it*: that this paper or this newscast is based in a city (Austin) that is 33 percent Latino (US Census Bureau, 2005) in a state that is over a third Latino, in a country that is 13 percent Latino—and growing.

Notes

1 I am a native Texan, of Mexican descent.
2 To disclose my own ties here: I was on the committee that organized the NAHJ and served on its board in the 1980s. I still pay membership dues.

References

American Society of Newspaper Editors (ASNE). (2006, April 25). *ASNE Census shows newsroom diversity grows slightly*. Retrieved July 26, 2006 from www.asne.org/index.cfm?id=6264.

American Society of Newspaper Editors (ASNE). (2006a, April 25). *ASNE Newsroom Employment Census, Table P, Percent and number of newsroom employees by group 2001–2006*. Retrieved July 26, 2006 from www.asne.org/index.cfm?id=5663.

Anders, G. (1998, March 8). Heart without a home. *Raleigh News & Observer*, p. A1.

Anders, G. (1999, May). The crucible. *American Journalism Review*, 38(1), p. 22.

Camacho, D. (2006, August 7). Let's face racial problems. [Letter to the editor]. *Austin American-Statesman*. Retrieved August 10, 2006 from www.statesman.com/search/content/editorial/stories/08/7Letters_edit.html.

Calafell, B.M. (2004). 'Disrupting the dichotomy: "Yo soy Chicana/o?' in the New Latina/o South. *The Communication Review*, 7(2), 175–204.

Chapman, S. (2006, May 8). Outrage over immigrant protests doesn't add up. *Baltimore Sun*, p. 13A. Retrieved July 24, 2006 from LexisNexis database.

Colón, A. (2006, February 27). The parity project: Making a difference, one newspaper at a time. *Poynter Institute*. Retrieved July 28, 2006 from www.poynter.org/column.asp?id=58&aid=97031.

Deans, B. (2006, April 12). Immigration marches: What's next? *The Atlanta Journal Constitution*. Retrieved August 3, 2006 from LexisNexis database.

Gavrilos, D. (2006, June). US news magazine coverage of Latinos: 2006. *National Association of Hispanic Journalists and Arizona State University's Walter Cronkite School of Journalism and Mass Communication*. Retrieved July 29, 2006 from www.nahj.org/resources/magazine/magazinereport.pdf.

Gyllenhaal, A. (1998, March 29). Lessons in a story gone wrong. *Raleigh News & Observer*, p. A21.

Hood, L. (2005, June/July). Trying to resolve a rocky situation. *American Journalism Review*. Retrieved July 27, 2006 from LexisNexis database.

Hussain, R. (2006, April 29). Mixed reception for Spanish anthem: Some stations air it, some don't—others don't even receive it. *Chicago Sun-Times*, p. 4. Retrieved August 3, 2006 from LexisNexis database.

Jackson, D.Z. (2006). Anti-immigrant flag follies. *The Boston Globe.* May 14, 2006. Retrieved July 27, 2006 from LexisNexis database.

Jaspin, E. (2006, July 30). One nation, divided, with two views of history. *Austin American-Statesman.* Retrieved August 2, 2006 from www.statesman.com/news/content/news/stories/nation/07/lod4wrapup.html.

Minorities gain on local television news staffs. (2006, July 6). *RTNDA News Release.* Retrieved July 26, 2006 from www.rtnda.org/news/2006/070606.shtml.

Navarro, M. (2003, December 2). Actors in all-Latino cast savor a 'historic moment,' *The New York Times,* p. 1. Retrieved July 20, 2006 from LexisNexis database.

National Association of Hispanic Journalists. (2006). Parity project facts, *National Association of Hispanic Journalists.* Retrieved July 28, 2006 from www.nahj.org/parityproject/ParityProject Success.shtml.

Papper, B. (2006, July/August). Year of Extremes, The RTNDA/Ball State University annual survey of women and minorities in the newsroom shows some of the highest highs and the lowest lows. *Communicator.* Retrieved July 28, 2006 from www.rtnda.org/research/2006 diversity.pdf.

Passel, J.S. (2006, March 7). Size and characteristics of the unauthorized migrant population in the US *Pew Hispanic Center Research Report.* Retrieved August 3, 2006 from http://pewhispanic.org/files/reports/61.pdf.

Rodriguez, C. (2006, May 9). Anthems, in any tongue. *The Denver Post,* p. F6. Retrieved August 3, 2006 from LexisNexis database.

Romero, D. (2006, February/March). The other side. *Tu Ciudad,* 58–67.

Salamon, J. (n.d.). Music tastes. *Austin American-Statesman.*

Silva, E. (2003, February 9). TM editor has good words for diversity. *San Antonio Express-News,* p. 1J. Retrieved July 8, 2006 from LexisNexis database.

Solomon, D. (2003, April 27). The way we live now: 4–27–03: Questions for Eduardo Machado. *New York Times Magazine,* p. 17. Retrieved July 20, 2006, from LexisNexis database.

Subervi, F. (2005, June). Network brownout report 2005: The portrayal of Latinos & Latino issues on network television news, 2004 with a retrospect to 1995. *National Association of Hispanic Journalists.* Retrieved August 7, 2006 from www.nahj.org/resources/Brownout%20 Report%202005.pdf.

Suro, R. (2004). Changing channels and crisscrossing cultures: A survey of Latinos in the news media. *Pew Hispanic Center.* April 19, 2004. Retrieved August 3, 2006 from http://pewhispanic.org/files/reports/27.pdf.

The envelope, please. (2006, February/March). *Tu Ciudad,* 47.

US Census Bureau. (2004). *US Interim Projections by Age, Sex, Race, and Hispanic Origin, Table 1A Projected Population of the United States by Race and Hispanic Origin: 2000 to 2050.* Retrieved August 10, 2006 from www.census.gov/ipc/www/usinterimproj/.

US Census Bureau. (2005). *2005 American Community Survey Data Profile Highlights Fact Sheet for Austin, Texas.* Retrieved August 24, 2006 from http://factfinder.census.gov/servlet/ACSSAFFFacts?_event=Search&geo_id=&_geoContext=&_street=&_county=Austin&_cityTo wn=Austin&_state=04000US48&_zip=&_lang=en&_sse=on&pctxt=fph&pgsl=010.

Valdivia, A.N. (2004). Latina/o communication and media studies today: An introduction. *The Communication Review,* 7(2), 107–12.

Vargas, L. (2000). Generalizing Latino news: An analysis of a local newspaper's coverage of Latino current affairs. *Critical Studies in Media Communication,* 17(3), 261–93.

Whitlock, C. & Glascock, N. (1998, March 25). Immigration agents raid market. *The Raleigh News & Observer.*

Yeoman, B. (1998). Good story, bad result. *Columbia Journalism Review,* 37(2), 19–20. Retrieved July 28, 2006 from LexisNexis database.

Chapter 18

Strengthening the News Connection with Women and Cultivating the Next Generation

Paula Poindexter, Sharon Meraz, and Amy Schmitz Weiss

Understanding the differences between women and men and the implications for news media preferences, attitudes, and expectations is the news media's twenty-first-century imperative. Without this understanding, the news media will never fully comprehend why women turn away from some news media but embrace others. Although it cannot be predicted with certainty that recapturing lost female readers and viewers will reverse the trend of a dwindling audience, it is clear that if no action is taken to reverse the decline, the deterioration of circulation will continue and may even accelerate, which could lead to a wounded Fourth Estate and a diminished democratic society because far fewer informed citizens will be present.

Throughout *Women, Men, and News*, we have attempted to lay a foundation for understanding the divide between women and men in the news media landscape. In addition to benchmarks in women's history, the groundwork we set forth included theories, models, concepts, statistical data, and perspectives for coming to terms with the news consumption sex divide and the disconnect between women and the news media, especially newspapers, that is not just in the United States, but worldwide.

We believe the sex divide in today's news media landscape should be as worrisome as a fault line lying beneath a structure that stood strong for decades. If we continue to ignore the fault line that is beneath the structure of the news media's foundation, the audience decline will likely continue its downward slide.

If the news media have a history of identifying and responding to threats to its well-being in the news media landscape, the question becomes: why have the news media not rallied and responded to the threat of the sex divide to its franchise? This lack of action is puzzling because potentially this threat is more dangerous than previous threats. Not only are women turning away from newspapers, but the next generation is growing up without the same socialization influences in the home that encouraged adoption of the news media for previous generations. Plus the Millennial Generation is coming of age with access to exciting entertainment and information options that make newspapers look old-fashioned and boring, and news, regardless of its source, seem irrelevant to their lives. Unless the news media take action to counteract these negative attitudes, young women and men may never embrace newspapers and other sources of news.

It is therefore hoped that the following recommendations displayed in Table 18.1 will serve as a blueprint for a twenty-first-century news media landscape that is endangered by a loss of current and future news consumers as well as a devaluing of the importance of being informed. As strategies are developed to close the sex divide in news consumption, strategies must also be implemented for strengthening the societal belief that being informed is essential. A society that values being informed is not only indispensable to a democracy but a prerequisite for a robust Fourth Estate.

Table 18.1 A blueprint for increasing news consumers among today's women and the next generation

---

Recommendations for senior executives of news media organizations

---

1. Lead the effort to increase news consumers among women and the next generation. Commit to understanding the issues, developing and implementing a plan of action, and allocating resources.

2. Provide another perspective, assign a team of seasoned reporters to investigate the sex divide between news consumers, news content, and gatekeeping decisions, and produce a series of reports. Distribute the series to the task force that will make recommendations.

3. Appoint an inter-departmental task force to study the sex divide and develop a plan of action that will produce immediate and long-term results.

4. Transform the newsroom's routines and gatekeeping culture in order to eliminate unconscious gender assumptions.

5. Understand and respect women and their perspective.

6. Use blogs, crowdsourcing, and podcasts to connect to women.

7. Provide newsroom, classroom, and online continuing education to train journalists how to report stories in a technology-centered landscape for a new type of news consumer.

8. Overhaul links with schools, including how the newspaper and other news media are represented to schools and tied into the curriculum.

9. Connect to the rites of passage of Millennials in formats and forums that speak to this age group.

10. Participate in college readership programs that provide free newspapers to students.

11. Establish an ongoing system for auditing news coverage of women, including the framing and placement of news stories of interest to women.

12. Experiment with re-ordering sections, revamping story placement, and expanding news coverage to include more areas of interest to women and Millennials.

13. Invest in more research and promotion.

14. Understand how consumers use local advertising and the value it contributes to the overall news package.

Recommendations for journalism schools

---

15. Transform journalism education to make students aware of unconscious gender assumptions and routines that minimize news coverage of women.

16. Increase the number of women journalism professors who are tenured.

17. Teach students to produce news for every format and generation.

Recommendation for women and Millennials

---

18. Communicate dissatisfaction and satisfaction to improve news coverage.

Recommendation for news media executives, educators, civic, community, business leaders, and parents

---

19. Re-invigorate the civic belief that a good citizen is interested in news and informed, and informed citizens are the foundation for a strong democratic society.

Commitment from the Top

Unless there is commitment from the top of news organizations, the status quo will remain. For news organizations, especially newspapers that have felt the effects the most, senior executives must choose to be leaders and not laggards. But commitment does not stop at the top of news organizations; it also must come from executive suites of corporate owners. This commitment should be as high a priority as quarterly profits. In fact, in the long-term, the persistent sex divide is directly related to quarterly profits.

"What are the consequences of doing nothing?" is a question often posed during a budgeting cycle. The consequences of doing nothing are dire indeed. The newspaper industry, for example, has been aware of the sex divide in readership for almost 20 years (Stein, 1990). One can only wonder if the sex divide would be present today if 20 years ago a commitment from the top to close the gap had taken place. The availability of online news was in its infancy 15 years ago and the idea of *Cosmogirl!*, IM (instant messaging), social networking sites such as *MySpace* and *Facebook*, blogging, and *YouTube* would have been flights of fancy. But somehow the turning away from newspapers by women, and the availability and easy access to seemingly unlimited choices for news, information, and entertainment have interacted in a way never before seen or imagined, making twentieth-century assumptions about news consumers obsolete. We therefore urge news executives to take the commitment to closing the divide between women and men seriously. Doing nothing to counteract the decline in news consumption among women and Millennials is simply not an option.

Assign a Team of Reporters to Investigate the Threat to the Future of News

Who better to investigate this threat that lurks in today's news media landscape than a news organization's reporters? We therefore recommend assigning a team of reporters, comprised equally of women and men, who will report directly to the executive editor, to write a series of investigative reports about the sex divide that permeates the news media landscape, from news consumers to newsrooms. For this series to be a convincing benchmark for analyzing the problem and measuring change, the following actions must be taken: resources must be allocated; every level of the news organization must be accessible; women experts and private citizens must be included as sources. The investigative reports should also include case studies of news organizations that have successfully closed the gap between women and men.

Town halls and department meetings can be used as venues for sharing the investigative reports throughout the news organization. Everyone in the news organization needs to understand the magnitude of the problem and the fact that senior news executives are committed to identifying and implementing solutions for closing the gap between women and men news consumers.

Appoint an Inter-Departmental Task Force to Take the Next Step

Once the investigative reports have been disseminated and discussed, we recommend that a task force comprised equally of women and men, who represent different departments and generations, be appointed by senior news executives to follow up on the investigative reports and propose actions that will be effective in closing the divide between women and men. For this task force to be effective, it should report directly to the most senior executive of the news organization.

Although the task force will use the investigative series as a major resource, the task force's charge will be to imagine what actions need immediate implementation to ensure a strong news organization in the news media landscape of 2017. Failure to act could lead to a severely weakened news organization that is neither feared nor respected by the newsmakers it covers or the various constituencies it seeks to serve. In the past, re-designing a front page, adding a new section, changing the name of an old section, hiring a new news anchor, or promoting an exclusive special report was sufficient for attracting the attention of news consumers. But that was yesterday's news media landscape. Today, fresh thinking and fast action are needed if there is to be any hope of a robust future. Inspired approaches demand pondering extending the boundaries of the meaning of news, re-conceptualizing the news product, transforming gatekeeping, and creating new methods of writing and disseminating news.

If the inter-departmental task force is to be successful, it must have support from the top as well as on-going communication at every level within departments. Plus, the task force must be educated about current operations in order to identify both synergistic and new opportunities that will succeed in the news media landscape of 2017. Finally, the expertise of future-oriented thinkers should be tapped in order to sketch a picture of 2017 media, technology, communications, education, and demographics.

Transforming the Newsroom's Routines and Gatekeeping Culture

Gatekeepers, as discussed in earlier chapters, determine what stories are worthy of being published or broadcast, what sources are used, how stories are framed, and the prominence news stories receive in the newspaper, on the Web, or during network, cable, and local news. Analyses of published and broadcast news stories have revealed that the news media often give women second-tier treatment, a contrast to the first-class treatment that men receive.

We contend that until a newsroom's routines and gatekeeping culture are transformed, the pattern of disadvantaging women in news stories will continue. Stories of interest to women will be judged less newsworthy; stories in which women are the subjects will receive less prominent display, if reported at all, and women who are experts and private citizens will be called on less as sources of news. Unless the routines and gatekeeping culture that disadvantage women in the news are altered, we believe women will continue to turn away from news, further shrinking the audience for news, and diminishing the influence of the Fourth Estate.

How can a newsroom's routines and gatekeeping culture be transformed? First, the executive editor must be committed to banishing the influence of unconscious gender assumptions from newsroom routines and the gatekeeping process. Ridding the newsroom of unconscious gender assumptions will not be an easy task. These gender assumptions are not visible; they are embedded, and women and men alike have been socialized with them since they were young children. In fact, because journalists are committed to fair, objective, and accurate reporting of news, they would likely feel they are exempt from these unconscious gender assumptions. But no one is exempt according to the influential book *Why So Slow? The Advancement of Women*:

A set of implicit, or nonconscious, hypotheses about sex differences plays a central role in shaping men's and women's professional lives. These hypotheses, which I call *gender schemas*[1], affect our expectations of men and women, our evaluations of their work, and their performance as professionals. Both men and women hold the same gender schemas and begin acquiring them in early childhood. Their most important consequence for professional life is that men are consistently overrated, while women are underrated. Whatever emphasizes a man's gender gives him a small advantage, a plus mark. Whatever accentuates a woman's gender results in a small loss for her, a minus mark.

(Valian, 1999, p. 2)

Second, in addition to a commitment from the executive editor as a necessary condition for bringing change to the newsroom, journalists at every level, including the editorial leadership, stars in the newsroom, and bureau chiefs, must be educated about unconscious gender assumptions and how they can lead to biased news, which not only damages a news organization's credibility, but alienates women news consumers everywhere. Third, the number of women employed in the newsroom must be increased and a larger percentage of women must attend editorial conferences that determine what will be published or broadcast.

Even though in her book, *Why So Slow? The Advancement of Women* (Valian, 1999), professor of psychology and linguistics Virginia Valian identified hundreds of studies that have unearthed evidence that in business, government, engineering, law, the judiciary, medicine, sports, and academia, women are evaluated more negatively than men, it appears that six "truths" about unconscious gender assumptions are noteworthy for the implications they have for transforming journalistic routines and newsrooms.

Truth no. 1: Number of women in the pool.   If studies have found "the more numerous women are, the less important their gender is," (Valian, 1999, p. 139) the reverse holds true: when women are in the minority, their differences stand out, leading to judging a woman "in terms of her difference from the male majority" (ibid., p. 140). These studies that examine the impact of the number of women in the pool have implications for newsrooms in general and editorial conferences in particular, where traditionally women have been in the minority, if present at all. Plus, there are implications for routines and gatekeeping that determine what is worthy of news coverage. If women are in the minority at every level of executive, legislative, and judicial branches of government and they lag far behind men in top leadership posts in Fortune 500 companies and in major universities, is it not a surprise that during the routines and gatekeeping taking place in newsrooms, unconscious gender assumptions judge news stories that feature women as less important?

Truth no. 2: Cumulative effect of small disadvantage.   It is the little things that add up to a disadvantage for women (Valian, 1999, p. 143). Women are in the minority in the newsroom and editorial conferences; stories about women and of interest to women get pushed to the inside pages and lifestyle sections, which some newspapers insert behind the classifieds. For main news, women are rarely the first source, and sometimes they are not used as sources at all. These daily slights to and disadvantages toward women add up, producing a cumulative effect of perpetual relegation to second-tier status.

Truth no. 3: Getting the floor.   Relative to men, women "have more difficulty than men do in gaining and keeping the floor" (Valian, 1999, p. 131). Plus, "when women do speak and behave like leaders, they receive negative reactions from their cohorts, even when the content and manner of their presentations are identical to men's" (ibid., pp. 131–2). The difficulty women have in getting recognized has implications for the editorial conference. If women are present in the editorial conference, they may have trouble getting the floor to make the case for what should be published in the next day's paper. As portrayed in the highly regarded journalism film *All the President's Men*, what lands on the front page or above the fold is a process of negotiation and to negotiate, you have to get the floor. During the film that portrayed how *Washington Post* reporters Bob Woodward and Carl Bernstein investigated the Watergate story, no women were present in the editorial conferences that determined what would be published in the next day's newspaper. One can only wonder if Katherine Graham, then publisher of her family's newspaper *The Washington Post*, had been present, would she as a woman have had difficulty in getting the attention of the male editors who worked for her?

It will be interesting to observe how Truth no. 3 plays out in Congress with Nancy Pelosi as the first woman ever to hold the post of Speaker of the House. Nancy Pelosi's historic ascension to third in line to become President of the United States is courtesy of the Democratic wins during the 2006 Midterm election.

Truth no. 4: Amount of time and attention devoted to decision-making. If devoting more time to evaluating women and men can reduce the effects of unconscious gender assumptions, can devoting more time to decisions about which stories are newsworthy, which sources to contact, and whether or not a story should be published on the front page above the fold be effective in improving news coverage of women? Since it is naive to expect that more time can be found in such a deadline-driven profession, a more realistic solution might be to attempt to alter professional routines and habits.

For example, rather than routinely publish a story about women on the inside pages or in the back sections, institute a new daily routine to identify a story about women that is compelling enough to start above the fold on the front page. Reporters can break the cycle of quoting male sources first and they can expand their source base by researching more women who can be interviewed as experts on various topics.

If failure to devote full attention to gatekeeping decisions about what gets published or broadcast produces similar effects as having too little time to decide if a story about a woman is newsworthy, a solution might be to interrupt routines that automatically treat stories about women and of interest to women as second class. "When both time and attention are limited, people are likely to take shortcuts" in evaluating a story's newsworthiness (Valian, 1999, p. 308). Unconscious gender assumptions "provide a convenient shortcut" (ibid.).

By virtue of her position as Speaker of the House, Nancy Pelosi's actions will often be front-page news. Only time will tell if the news media will cover her accordingly or resort to convenient shortcuts that automatically assign second-tier status to news in which the subject is a woman or the content is of interest to women.

Truth no. 5: Accountability for decisions. As journalism became more professional with the development of codes of ethics, and the creation of independent national commissions such as the Hutchins Commission and the Kerner Commission or the publishing of books such as *The Elements of Journalism*, that addressed journalism's failings, accountability became more of a priority in the news media landscape. Corrections published in the newspaper, letters to the editor, and ombudsmen whom news consumers can contact directly have also reinforced the role of accountability in improving journalism practices.

Publications devoted to journalism and mass communication such as *Women's Media Report*, *CJR*, and *American Journalism Review* as well as academic journals such as *Journalism & Mass Communication Quarterly*, *Newspaper Research Journal*, and *Journal of Broadcasting & Electronic Media* have served as external accountability forums, analyzing and criticizing news coverage. With the diffusion of the Internet in the news media landscape, new accountability venues have evolved with the most recent being the blogosphere, where bloggers keep a watchful and critical eye over news media coverage as they did when then-*CBS* news anchor Dan Rather used bogus documents to report a *60 Minutes* story that President George W. Bush received preferential treatment while in the National Guard (Hindman, 2005).

Although these various accountability venues are important, in their current form, they have not eliminated the use of unconscious gender assumptions in evaluating what is newsworthy. If gatekeepers are to be held accountable for decisions they make about what is newsworthy, the research suggests that "if evaluators know that their judgments will be reviewed by an unbiased, higher authority," they will rely less on unconscious gender assumptions and make more accurate judgments about the newsworthiness of news about and of interest to women (Valian, 1999, pp. 308–9). That is why we urge news organizations to develop unbiased, independent procedures for regular evaluation of news coverage of women and stories of interest to women. This independent monitoring system should look at news coverage as a whole as well as news coverage of women and stories of interest to women, including number of stories, prominence, framing, and sourcing. The results of this monitoring should be posted in the newsroom and discussed openly. Only then can progress be made in eliminating unconscious gender assumptions from decisions about what is newsworthy.

Truth no. 6: Women are not exempt from the influence of unconscious gender assumptions (Valian, 1999, p. 141).   Although it may be surprising to some, women are not immune to unconscious gender assumptions. Consequently, we recommend that both women and men be active participants in all efforts designed to eliminate unconscious gender assumptions from newsroom routines and gatekeeping decisions that determine what is worthy of being published in newspapers, magazines, on the Internet, or broadcast on TV or radio.

Although these sixth truths emphasize eliminating unconscious assumptions about gender that negatively affect news coverage of women, we believe these recommendations would also apply to eliminating unconscious assumptions about people of color. In fact, if one were to substitute African American, Latino/a, Asian, or Native American for the words women and gender, one would have six additional recommendations for improving news coverage of minorities.

Understand and Respect Women and their Perspectives

If efforts to re-invigorate the relationship with current women readers and re-connect with lost readers are to succeed, those attempts must be based on genuine understanding and respect for women. In fact, when *San Diego Union* editor Karin Winner was asked in a questionnaire, what do you think is the most important action that newspapers can take to increase readership among women, she answered:

> Understand the circumstances under which women seek information—what kind of information it is, what time they wish to consume and where they go to get it. With that in mind, market the paper by telling women they can get it all in a paper that they can read at any time of the day, not just in the morning.
>
> (K. Winner, personal communication, July, 2006)

In answering the same question about action newspapers can take, Kathy Blackwell, Executive Features Editor of the *Austin American-Statesman* emphasized the importance of respect:

I think it comes down to respect for the female readership. This can be achieved through many ways: a) Watching out for word choice in stories and display type. Too often, I still see female story subjects described as "attractive," "perky," "feisty," etc. Sophisticated women pick up on this.

b) Careful consideration of story placement. Stories that affect women, such as breast cancer advances and productive-rights news, sometimes get shoved inside the newspaper when they belong on A1.

c) Packaging. When women know when and where to find specific content, they're more likely to reach for the paper because they know they don't have to search for it.

d) Give them stories that they can't find anywhere else. Newspapers still have the local advantage. Anyone can run a story on "find the right swimsuit for your shape," but only the local paper can provide information on which stores offer one-on-one expert help in selecting the right swimsuit. Readers should feel that if they don't pick up the paper that day, they're missing out.

(K. Blackwell, personal communication, July, 2006)

Understanding women both inside and outside the newsroom is not limited to contemporary issues. Understanding also includes genuine interest in and awareness of women's history, including battles won and lost that have directly and indirectly shaped where women stand in society today and why. In the twenty-first century, women still lag behind men in pay and in jobs at the highest levels in the news media and other professions. Required reading should begin with Betty Friedan's *The Feminine Mystique* (1963); Kay Mills' *A Place in the News: From the Women's Pages to the Front Page* (1988), and Virginia Valian's (1999) *Why So Slow? The Advancement of Women*. Women's histories that provide a social and cultural context such as the ones written by former *Los Angeles Times* opinion writer Kay Mills and former *New York Times* editorial page editor Gail Collins should also be consulted.

Since understanding should not be limited to reading about women, their history, and battles, we recommend that editors meet with diverse groups of women in town halls and small groups at least quarterly to listen to what they have to say about their interests, their lives, and their opinions about the newspaper. Listening to diverse groups of women is essential because there is no consensus on what content speaks to women's interests (Armstrong, 2006). Through town halls and unstructured small group meetings of diverse groups of women representing different constituencies and generations, editors can learn first hand how women live and what they care about in their communities.

Understanding and respecting women also means recognizing that the traditional early-morning delivery system of the newspaper to the front door is not necessarily the most effective distribution method for reaching and getting the attention of women in today's technology-rich, multi-tasking world. Although over the years magazines have managed to keep women's attention, the same does not hold true for newspapers. The overwhelming majority of women who completed questionnaires about their news consumption said when they get news, they are simultaneously involved in other activities. At the same time newspapers are thinking of ways to improve their coverage of women, we also recommend that they think of ways to fit news into women's multi-tasking world. Today's technology—wireless laptop computers, PDAs, MP3 players such as iPods, podcasting, cell phones, such as iPhones—allows the newspaper to extend its reach in ways that were unimaginable only a decade ago.

Podcasts offer new opportunities for reaching women and Millennials.   If books can talk, why can newspapers not? If, as projected, there will be 45 million podcasters in 2010 (Brown, 2006, p. 3), podcasts should certainly be explored as another way to connect to women and Millennials. Although it is easy for network news, cable, local news, and National Public Radio to extend their reach by converting broadcast stories into podcasts, we believe that approach will have only a small impact on attracting women and Millennials, because the same stories are being used albeit in a different form. What we recommend is that newspapers identify podcast opportunities based on exclusive newspaper material unavailable through other sources. For example, through their websites, newspapers can offer excerpts of audio-recorded interviews conducted by reporters, select speeches covered by reporters, even perspective and context on major stories and trends from expert staff reporters or columns read by columnists in their own words. NYTimes.com has been at the forefront of newspapers producing podcasts for readers to download. (See NYTimes.com podcast offerings at www.nytimes.com/ref/multimedia/podcasts.html.) "From the users' perspective, the primary technological advantage podcasting enjoys over broadcasting is that one can listen to a podcast program at a time and place of one's choosing" (Brown, 2006, p. 3).

In addition to the advantage of listening to a podcast program on one's own timetable, listening to podcast programs would be compatible with women's multi-tasking world. In fact, the majority of betweeners who completed a questionnaire said that when getting the news, they are often involved in activities such as folding laundry, cooking, driving, supervising kids, eating, waiting to pick up a child, getting ready for the day, sewing, ironing, cleaning, writing bills, and combing hair.

Blogs can connect women to the newspaper.   The blogosphere is, perhaps, one of the best tools available to connect with women on multiple levels and newspapers should not miss out on what might be one of the last opportunities to bond with women personally and professionally. Women have shown through blogging that they are willing to create an alternative news source if their needs are not served by traditional media industries. We, therefore, urge newsrooms to adapt to this new age of citizen media to create a dialogue with the female audience using the following steps:

1. Encourage female staff to blog for the newsroom blogs along a diverse line of topics. Women must be encouraged to not only blog about what traditionally has been labeled soft news (family, food, fashion, and furnishings) but also along hard news topics such as politics, business/finance, and technology. Furthermore, women must not be ghettoized into one specific realm of blogging, but must be able to take advantage of the blogging platform to reconnect with the female audience on a variety of levels.
2. Use blogs to target specific women's issues. The women's blogosphere has created an entire network of news along the politics of gender as it relates to such issues as work/life balance, sexual discrimination in the workplace, gendered wage gaps, domestic violence, and women's health topics. Since women bloggers often view these topics as marginalized by the news media, newspapers can use blogs to reconnect with the female audience, dedicating space to these issues that rarely get published on the front page.
3. Syndicate some of the top female bloggers' content at the newspaper. Services such as Pluck's BlogBurst have joined with the women's blog network BlogHer to provide newspapers with the best content written by female bloggers along specific topics. Newsrooms will do well to work with blog services such as this in order to reconnect with the female audience.

4. In addition to blogs, newspapers should consider other forms of participation and involvement with women readers. Just as Gannett's *News-Press* in Fort Myers, Florida successfully used crowdsourcing to investigate a local issue that hit consumers in the pocketbook, newspapers can use crowdsourcing methods to connect with women on issues that deserve the attention of a watchdog press. Crowdsourcing uses the Internet to get an "undefined, generally large group of people" to "work as watchdogs, whistle-blowers and researchers in large, investigative features" (Howe, 2006). Newspapers can use these crowdsourcing methods to call on women to provide insight, share sources, and search for documents on issues of particular interest to women that traditionally have been marginalized or treated as second tier.

Continuing education is a necessity in a technology-centered environment.   Finally, the news media should make continuing education available to everyone in the newsroom to learn the new technology that is having an impact on new ways of producing and enhancing content. Online journalists who have already developed expertise as multimedia reporters and editors, Flash producers, and videographers can lead the way in training journalists in the newsroom who have not as yet developed these skills. We also recommend that newsrooms take advantage of online training that is offered by such organizations as Poynter Institute or collaborate with journalism schools to develop customized online and in-classroom continuing education courses, which will ensure their newsroom is fully prepared to meet the challenges that lie ahead in this technology-centered environment.

Overhaul Links with Schools

Since the role of news literacy is bigger than any one news medium, we encourage newspapers to join with newsmagazines, broadcast, cable, and online news to identify new approaches for emphasizing the importance of news literacy in the curriculum. Why is it that computer literacy and speech are required in a recommended high school curriculum along with English, science, math, social studies, and foreign language, but news literacy is not expected even though being an informed citizen is a prerequisite for a strong democracy? Furthermore, we urge the news media to stress to state boards of education, university presidents, and their boards that they equip students so they will be informed citizens fully prepared to participate in a democracy.

Historically, within the newspaper industry, news literacy has been handled by Newspaper in Education (NIE), which has a rich history dating back to the 1940s when the wife of *The New York Times* publisher, Iphigene Ochs Sulzberger, "lent her support to the requests of New York City teachers for delivery of the *Times* to school classrooms" (NAA, 2006). This early support of the relationship between a newspaper and schools has grown into more than 950 similar relationships throughout the United States. Although as discussed in an earlier chapter, NIE programs served a socialization function, cultivating future newspaper readers, it must be kept in mind that in the twenty-first-century news media landscape, NIE has lots of communication devices competing for the attention of Millennials. In fact when NIE was born, First Wave baby boomers were children and only a few media options were available to compete for their time and attention. So the twenty-first-century question is are NIE programs as traditionally conceived and operated, a turn-on or turn-off for today's kids?

Is it a turn-off today to refer to the newspaper as a living textbook? That is what the *Los Angeles Times* did in the mid 1980s when the NIE program, which was launched with the enthusiastic backing of a new *Times* president and a pilot program with Los Angeles Unified School District, the second largest school district in the country (Stein, 1988). In fact, the very first ad that the promotion department designed called the newspaper "the textbook that's always up-to-date" ("Teachers," 1989).

While the idea seemed clever and the *Times* was very successful in promoting it that way, today, one has to stop and pose the following two questions. Does associating the newspaper with a textbook have a negative connotation for the Millennial Generation, because textbooks are generally associated with school work? Instead of growing future news enthusiasts, is it possible that today NIE programs are growing future newspaper avoiders?

By posing these questions, this is not to disparage the excellent work of the Newspaper Foundation or the NIE Programs throughout the country. But it is important to ask if in today's news media landscape, which is unlike any previous time in history, NIE might be inadvertently undermining its mission of cultivating future consumers of newspapers.

But if not NIE, what?

The goal of NIE should be to make news an integral part of one's everyday life—not a textbook. News is informative and interesting and important. Plus, if you are not informed, you miss out when watching popular "news" programs such as Jon Stewart's *The Daily Show*, *The Colbert Report*, or late night TV monologues. In fact, college students learned during a research project they conducted for a journalism theory class that programs such as *The Daily Show* actually encourage news consumption among Millennials: to get the jokes, you have to be informed.

The experience of getting informed should be viewed as pleasure, not work, and certainly not limited to classroom requirements. NIE needs fresh thinking and approaches to better fit with the twenty-first-century news media landscape. Furthermore, publishers and editors should re-think whether in today's news media landscape, the tradition of staffing NIE with former teachers is the most effective way to re-invent NIE.

Also, we encourage the newsroom to become more engaged with NIE, briefing NIE staff about upcoming relevant stories that may generate discussion among Millennials. At least once a semester, editors can host Town Hall meetings with teachers and designated reporters can participate in discussions with students. Also, from time to time, NIE staff should solicit opinions from students about news coverage and share this information with editors.

If women are regarded as second-tier, Millennials who have already come of age and those who are growing into young adulthood do not even qualify for second-tier status in the news, leading to further erosion of the audience for news in the twenty-first-century news media landscape. The only way to limit and possibly reverse further erosion of the audience for news is to improve coverage in three areas, which could immediately increase interest by Millennials: sports coverage, rites of passage coverage, and more stories that connect with the Millennial Generation.

We encourage newspapers to stop limiting its high school sports coverage to boys' football, basketball, and baseball. More attention needs to be given to girls' sports. In addition to girls' volleyball, basketball, and softball, girls' soccer, tennis, swimming, and golf should receive more attention.

We also encourage newspapers to take advantage of the rites of passage experienced by all young people coming of age. For example, when three young women who attended a Midwestern university were asked to complete a questionnaire about where they first turned to get news and information about rites of passage related to back to school, learning how to drive, money management, voting, social activities, special occasion shopping, jobs, high school graduation, college, health, and technology, one of the three college students who completed a questionnaire, never turned to the newspaper, another student only turned to the newspaper to get voting information, and the third student used the newspaper for back-to-school shopping, apartment hunting, technology information, buying a car, and spring break planning. In other words, the newspaper, which should have been the first place turned to for rites of passage information, was mostly ignored by two of the three girls.

We encourage newspapers to publish stories about rites of passage so the next generation will develop the habit of turning to the newspaper first to get information about important times in their lives. Whether getting a driver's license or a first speeding ticket, going to prom or preparing for high school graduation, getting a first after-school job or registering to vote and voting in a first presidential election, newspapers can provide useful, helpful information for teens coming of age. This information can be formatted for every form—from the newspaper, online news, blogs, podcasts, cell phones, and social networks such as *Facebook* and *MySpace*. Furthermore, we urge the news media to invest in learning how to write stories that engage the Millennial Generation. This investment might include collaborations with journalism schools, soliciting story ideas from Millennials, and adopting suggestions outlined in Chapter 10. Furthermore, if newspapers made their Millennial-engaging stories available to the AP wire service, these stories might fill some of the void left by the unfortunate demise of *asap*, AP's wire service that produced stories of interest to young adults.

We also urge newspapers to seriously entertain participating in college readership programs as recommended in Chapter 4. As a senior in high school, Alex, the focus of the case study in Chapter 4, watched television news but avoided newspapers. By her freshman year in college, she occasionally picked up a newspaper through the college readership program, which made *The New York Times*, *USA Today*, and two metropolitan newspapers available to college students for free. By her junior year, Alex had become a fan of *The New York Times*: "I really like it. I get kind of upset when I don't get to read the newspaper."

As a college student, would Alex have ever paid for a newspaper? Possibly not. But because the newspaper was free to every student with a college ID, the college readership program may have been the beginning of a life-long habit of consuming news, both print and digital.[2]

Scrutinize News Coverage of Women on an Ongoing Basis

Since the quantity and quality of news stories about women and of interest to women can only be determined through systematic monitoring of news coverage, we urge senior news executives to implement a system for auditing or content analyzing news coverage on an ongoing basis. The effectiveness of the monitoring will depend on the comprehensiveness of the coding scheme that is established for the audit or content analysis. In addition to coding story topics, datelines, placement, and sources, a story's framing should be analyzed. An audit or content analysis will determine, for example, how many health stories, a topic of particular interest to women, were published or broadcast, where in the newspaper or in the broadcast the health stories were placed, and who the sources were. In addition to counting all stories published or broadcast, stories of interest to women should be qualitatively analyzed to determine their framing. Local stories, in particular, should be assessed to determine if they have a "good neighbor" quality about them. Women are more likely than men to expect local news to be like a good neighbor (Poindexter *et al.*, 2006).

Because it is imperative that women of color and Millennials not be overlooked during the monitoring of news coverage, audits should code for race, ethnicity, and generation. If future news enthusiasts and monitors are to be cultivated, the audit should also code stories about rites of passages that are experienced by every generation coming of age.

Who should conduct the audit or content analysis? We recommend an internal editorial committee comprised of editors and reporters, half women and men, and an external group from the nearest journalism school. In addition to helping design the baseline audit, journalism professors can help set up a computerized system for analyzing the data. The two groups can also develop criteria for grading the news coverage. What constitutes A, B, C, and D coverage should be determined in advance of conducting the audit. Once the baseline audit is complete, we recommend ongoing quarterly audits or content analyses to measure improvements in coverage. Further, we recommend that the quarterly report card be posted for newsroom awareness and discussion. As noted earlier, awareness of independent and objective monitoring can be an effective tool for stamping out unconscious gender assumptions.

Experiment

Why do daily newspapers publish national and international news in the first section and local news in the second section? This newspaper tradition downplays what newspapers excel at, that is, original reporting about the local community that cannot be found elsewhere. We urge newspapers to experiment with flipping the order of the first two sections to call attention to what they do best—cover the local community. Local TV news seems to understand the importance of local news better than newspapers because it reports local stories first, followed by a segment devoted to national and international news. Perhaps, the local news coverage that is highlighted on local TV is one of the reasons women are more loyal to local TV news than newspapers or news online. A secondary benefit of highlighting local news coverage on the front page is local news stories would be prominently emphasized on the newsstand. Because national news is usually published on the front page above the fold, the newspaper on the newsstand rarely seems fresh. It always seems to be recycling old news already reported on network, cable, and the Internet.

We also urge newspapers to experiment with starting compelling stories about women and of interest to women on the front page above the fold. One good example is the naming of the National Tennis Center at Flushing Meadows after tennis legend Billie Jean King on the first day of the 2006 United States Open Grand Slam tennis tournament. A three-column photo was published on the front page above the fold and the actual story began on the first page of the sports section ("Honors," 2006).

Strengthen Research, Promotion, and Local Advertising

If the Commander-in-Chief does not slash the intelligence budget during war, why does the Chief Executive Officer cut the research budget when the newspaper is battling to hold on to its consumers and profits? We urge news executives to think long-term and invest in more research to gather intelligence about the news consumer and marketplace in order to be more effective in responding to consumer concerns, especially women. Investing in consumer research will also make it possible to evaluate how women are responding to changes in the paper that are implemented for the purpose of increasing readership and closing the sex divide. Without accurate and relevant intelligence, it is virtually impossible to effectively navigate the news media landscape of the twenty-first century and win the battle to hold on to news consumers and profits.

Although research, promotion, and local advertising serve different purposes and use different procedures, their ultimate objectives are to increase understanding of news consumers, communicate messages about the news products' value and contents, and enhance the overall appeal of the news package by providing information about local goods and services. Promotion enables news organizations to highlight local stories that cannot be found elsewhere and reinforce the notion that the daily newspaper is the best source for local news and advertising.

From the consumer's perspective, news does not stand alone as sought-after valuable information. News consumers, especially women, rely on local advertising to learn information about goods and services in the community. Therefore, we also encourage news executives to invest in promoting the news product and invest in improving the packaging of local advertising that is published in the newspaper so its value as a source of information for news consumers will be enhanced.

Overhaul the Journalism School Curriculum

Since according to *The American Journalist in the Twenty-First Century: US News People at the Dawn of a New Millennium* (Weaver *et al.*, 2007), the majority of journalists today studied journalism in college, one can only conclude that journalism education is contributing in some way to the fact that women lag behind men in news coverage. Journalism programs are either teaching the status quo or failing to explicitly address the problem that news about women and of interest to women is often treated as second-tier. We therefore urge journalism schools to lead the way in overhauling the journalism curriculum to increase students' awareness of unconscious gender assumptions and routines that minimize news coverage of women. Journalism schools also need to increase the number of women journalism professors who are tenured so they can serve as role models for future women journalists and play a role in transforming journalism education. In addition to improved coverage of women, journalism education needs to be mindful of the twenty-first-century landscape that says today's students need to be trained to produce news for every format and generation.

We also urge journalism schools to place more emphasis on preparing students, especially young women, for technology-centered and multi-platform news products. Today's Millennial girls who are tech savvy and outnumber boys in using blogging and mobile technologies are tomorrow's journalism students. Because young women also outnumber young men in journalism classrooms, these classrooms offer a perfect opportunity to expose women to technology training and education in a more gender neutral and non-threatening environment. By supporting this interest in technology and exposing female students to both the hardware and software side of technology, young women will be empowered and poised to take on leadership positions in technology-centered newsrooms of the future.

As news moves to a more flexible and multiplatform format, we urge journalism schools to encourage young women to use their intimate and creative knowledge of these technologies to suggest innovative ways to deliver content to a female audience. We also recommend that young women be encouraged to explore how news content can be tailored to the next generation of news consumers through social networking sites such as *MySpace* and *Facebook*. Although the future popularity of *MySpace* and *Facebook* is not guaranteed in this new age where trends in technology come and go, what will remain is the legacy of social networking and peer recommendations as a valuable mode of information selection.

Since journalism students of today will be the creators and producers of tomorrow's news, determining what news is presented, how it is presented, why it is presented in the chosen format, and how much involvement news citizens are afforded through the story presentation, need to be included in the journalism curriculum whether it is a class on reporting or a class on media management. Furthermore, across the curriculum, there needs to be an emphasis on the importance of writing about topics of interest to women and writing stories that include women as subjects and sources.

Journalism programs also need to prepare their future journalists for a new type of news citizen and how this may change their role as a journalist particularly as it relates to online news. In a recent Pew Internet & American Life Project report (2006), online news users were more likely to access multiple media in addition to the Internet in a typical day for news; seek out the news online multiple times a day; seek a wide array of options for getting news that includes news websites, alternative sites, blogs, listservs, and e-mail alerts; pay for news content such as video clips; and set up personal preferences for receiving news content (Horrigan, 2006). Online users are also becoming more involved with the news production process such that some news websites are now allowing their users to post photos, commentary, blogs, and other forms of content to news stories or sections on their site (Among the Audience, 2006). These aspects forecast a news citizen that is not only seeking more in content and depth from the news organization, but the opportunity to critique and participate in the news process. As a result, journalism students need to become more critical, multi-sensory, and organized in how they present news and information when they move into journalism careers, which means the journalism curriculum needs to provide a new foundation of the necessary skills that will allow journalism students to learn how to think critically, multimodally, and journalistically to produce a news experience that effectively encompasses multiple media, context, and additional resources into one package for the twenty-first-century news citizen.

Women and Millennials Should Make Their Voices Heard

Although many of our recommendations have focused on how newsrooms and journalism schools can improve, this does not mean that women and Millennials should not shoulder some of the responsibility for improving the Fourth Estate. Rather than turn away from newspapers and other news media that ignore women on their front pages and in their sources, women should e-mail editors and reporters and complain about unacceptable coverage. They should also use that opportunity to make recommendations for improved coverage. Similarly, Millennials should challenge their local newspapers to include them in their stories and write stories in such a way that they will be of interest to their age group. Every e-mail to an editor or reporter, though, should not be a criticism; women and Millennials should also send in compliments when the news media coverage is balanced, inclusive, and first-tier.

News Media Executives, Educators, Civic, Community, Business Leaders, and Parents

Once upon a time, it was expected that a good citizen had a civic responsibility to be interested in and informed about news. Ironically, as options for becoming informed expanded during the twenty-first century, the expectation that a good citizen be an informed citizen faded. Not only has this sense of civic responsibility to be informed deteriorated, newspaper reading, which more than 40 years ago was called a thoroughly institutionalized behavior, has declined (Westley & Severin, 1964). The implications of this decline are significant for a democratic society, the Fourth Estate, and current and future generations of women and men.

We therefore urge news media executives, educators, civic, community, and business leaders, and parents to make restoring the essence of being a good citizen a priority: good citizens are interested in and informed about their community, country, and world.

Closing the Divide Permanently

The thread woven throughout *Women, Men, and News* is the sex divide that is embedded in the twenty-first-century news media landscape. Women are not only covered less than men but they are used less as sources and issues of interest to them are often relegated to second-tier status. A sex divide is also apparent in news consumption statistics. Women are less likely to read newspapers and get their news online. This persistent sex divide not only threatens the future vitality of the news media and a democratic society, it diminishes women's power when they are less informed than their male counterparts.

The sooner we stop ignoring factors and forces that value women less as news subjects and sources and stop assigning second-tier status to stories of interest to women, the sooner we can close the news consumption divide, give a boost to women's position in society and in the news, and revitalize the value of news in the lives of women, men, and future generations everywhere.

Notes

1   Rather than use the term gender schemas, Molly Carnes (2006), M.D., the co-director of the Women in Science & Engineering Leadership Institute at University of Wisconsin-Madison, uses the phrase unconscious gender assumptions. Since both terms refer to the same concept, we will use the expression unconscious gender assumptions as a way to connect the meaning of gender schemas to concepts that journalists are more familiar with.

2   Postscript on Millennials Alex and John, who first reported on their Internet use and news consumption in Chapter 4, when they were high school seniors: Now that Alex is a senior in college, she has replaced IM (Instant Messaging) with *Facebook* and texting as ways to keep in touch with her friends (A.W., personal communication, October 21, 2007). John, who also is a college senior, has remained loyal to IM and downloading music on the Internet (J.C., personal communication, October 19, 2007). John is still a news enthusiast but he has abandoned print newspapers. John says that in college, he doesn't have access to the print newspaper he wants to read so he regularly reads *The New York Times* online and blogs. Because of Alex's many and varied activities, she says that she has little time for consuming news. But she has not abandoned news altogether. Alex's unwavering interest in news keeps her connected, which is why she might be described as an eclectic-betweener. Alex watches CNN's *Headline News* and occasionally picks up *USA Today* through the college readership program at her university, which provides free newspapers to students.

References

Among the Audience: A survey of new media. (2006, April 22). *The Economist*, Supplement.

Armstrong, C.L. (2006). Writing about women: An examination of how content for women is determined in newspapers. *Mass Communication & Society*, 9(4), 447–60.

Brown, D. (2006). Generation iPod: An exploratory study of podcasting's "innovators." Paper presented at the Association of Educators in Journalism and Mass Communications Conference, Technology Division, San Francisco, California.

Carnes, M. (2006, August 3). How Ambiguity in Performance Criteria and External Letters of Recommendation can Undermine Women's Success in the Tenure Review Process. Presented at the Association of Educators in Journalism and Mass Communications, Plenary Presentation. San Francisco, CA.

Hindman, E.B. (2005). Black Eye: The Ethics of CBS News and the National Guard Documents. Presented at the Media Ethics Division of the Association for Education in Journalism and Mass Communication, Media Ethics Division, San Antonio, Texas.

Honors at flushing meadows for a marquee tennis name. (2006, August 29). *The New York Times*, pp. A1, C12.

Newspaper Association of America (NAA) Foundation. (2006). *History of NIE*. Retrieved August 17, 2006 from www.naafoundation.org/NewspaperInEducation/HistoryOfNIE.aspx.

Newspaper Association of America. (2006). *The Source: Newspapers by the numbers*. Retrieved May 25, 2006 from www.naa.org/thesource/6.asp.

Horrigan, J. (2006, March 22). Online news: For many home broadband users, the Internet is a primary news source, *Pew Internet & American Life Project*. Retrieved April 24, 2006 from http://207.21.232.103/pdfs/PIP_News.and.Broadband.pdf.

Howe, J. (2006, November 3). Gannett to crowdsource news, *Wired*. Retrieved April 3, 2007 from www.wired.com/software/webservices/news/2006/11/72067?printable=true.

Poindexter, P. (2006, August 3). What's Right and What's Wrong with the Review Process. Presented at the Association of Educators in Journalism and Mass Communications, Plenary Presentation, San Francisco, California.

Poindexter, P.M., Heider, D., & McCombs, M. (2006). Watchdog or good neighbor? The public's expectations of local news. *The Harvard International Journal of Press/Politics*, 11(1), 77–88.

Poindexter, P.M. & McCombs, M.E. (2001). Revisiting the civic duty to keep informed in the new media environment. *Journalism & Mass Communication Quarterly*, 78(1), 113–26.

Stein, M.L. (1990, November 17). Reaching women readers. *Editor & Publisher*, p. 18.

Stein, M.L. (1988, May 14). Newspapers—a valuable teaching tool. *Editor & Publisher*, pp. 28–9.

Teachers: Give your students something extra . . . the textbook that's always up-to-date. Part V. (1989, February 14). *Los Angeles Times*, p. 4.

Valian V. (1999). *Why so Slow? The Advancement of Women*. Cambridge: The MIT Press.

Weaver, D.H., Beam, R.A., Brownlee, B.J., Voakes, P.S., & Wilhoit, G.C. (2007). *The American Journalist in the Twenty-First Century: US News People at the Dawn of a New Millennium*. Mahweh: Lawrence Erlbaum Associates.

Westley, B.H. & Severin, W.J. (1964). A profile of the daily newspaper non-reader. *Journalism Quarterly*, 41, 45–50.

Editors

Paula Poindexter, who has worked on the editorial and business sides of the news media, is formerly a manager and executive at the *Los Angeles Times*, where she conducted editorial research, participated in the development of pioneering electronic publishing projects, and directed the newspaper's programs, including *Times in Education*, to increase readership among young adults. Poindexter also worked as a reporter and producer in the newsroom of *KPRC-TV*, the NBC affiliate TV station in Houston.

Poindexter has conducted and published industry and academic research studies on news media audiences and news content, and she is the co-author of the textbook, *Research in Mass Communication: A practical guide*. Poindexter has held a variety of leadership positions in the Association for Education in Journalism and Mass Communication (AEJMC). In addition to chairing AEJMC's Standing Committee on Research, she served on the Board of Directors.

At the University of Texas at Austin, where she is a journalism professor and advisor to journalism Ph.D. and master's students, Poindexter teaches both graduate research courses and undergraduate courses, including "Leadership, Management, and Media" and "Journalism, Society and the Citizen Journalist," a course developed for the Carnegie Initiative on the Future of Journalism Education.

Sharon Meraz joined the faculty of University of Illinois, Chicago's Department of Communication, in January 2008, where she teaches new media classes. Meraz received her Ph.D. from the School of Journalism, University of Texas at Austin, where she also taught classes in citizen media and participatory journalism. Her career in the information technology industry includes designing and developing Web sites, programming database-driven Web applications, and creating multimedia packages for Web delivery. Her research interests center on the impact of newer media technologies such as blogging, mobile technologies, and social media applications on mass media evolution and citizen political engagement.

Amy Schmitz Weiss, a doctoral candidate at the University of Texas at Austin School of Journalism, has taught Web publishing and multimedia journalism courses. She has been involved in the new media and online journalism industry for over a decade. She was a co-founder of her college's online newspaper and she worked at *Chicago Tribune Online* and *Indianapolis Star News Online*, where she produced, edited, and wrote news packages. Schmitz Weiss has also worked in business development, marketing analysis, and account management for several Chicago Internet media firms. She has presented papers on online journalism at several national and international journalism and communications conferences.

Contributors to Perspectives

Lorraine E. Branham is the director of the School of Journalism and the G.B. Dealey Professor at the University of Texas at Austin, a post she assumed in 2002 after 25 years as a newspaper editor, editorial writer, and reporter. Prior to coming to the University of Texas, she was the Assistant to the Publisher of the Pittsburgh *Post Gazette* and a member of the Editorial Board. Previously, Branham held the position of Senior Vice President and Executive Editor of the Tallahassee *Democrat*, where she oversaw the newsroom and editorial board operations. Branham has also worked for the *Philadelphia Inquirer*, the *Baltimore Sun*, and the *Philadelphia Tribune*. She has a bachelor's degree in broadcast journalism from Temple University and continuing education studies at Stanford, Northwestern, and Harvard.

Xin Chen, also known as Sophie, worked as a journalist for a weekly newspaper in China. Born in Chengdu, a major city in southwest China, Chen graduated from Nanjing University in China with a bachelor's degree in sociology. After earning a master's degree in education at Texas Christian University in 2003, she continued her graduate education at the University of Texas at Austin, where she is studying for a doctorate in journalism. Chen's research interests include the use of new communication technologies among the younger generation, the effect of new communication technologies on young people's perceptions of important public issues, and cross-national comparisons of use and effects of new communication technologies.

Yi-Ning Katherine Chen, who was born and raised in Taipei, Taiwan, is an associate professor in the Department of Advertising at National Chengchi University in Taipei, Taiwan. Chen, whose research interests include political communication and public relations, has conducted research projects sponsored by the National Science Council in Taiwan. Chen has taught a variety of graduate and undergraduate courses, including Agenda Setting, Agenda Building, Public Opinion, and Political Campaign Communication. She earned her bachelor's degree and a master's degree from National Taiwan University, and a Ph.D. degree in Journalism from the University of Texas at Austin.

Teresa Correa is a former journalist for *El Mercurio* (Santiago), one of the leading newspapers in Chile. As a reporter, she wrote in-depth stories on foreign affairs, politics, and social issues. Correa attended Pontificia Universidad Católica de Chile and received an undergraduate degree in journalism. Her current research interests include media, politics, gender, and class in Latin America. Correa is currently a master's student in Latin American Studies at the University of Texas at Austin.

María Flores, who is from Mexico, has held a variety of positions in radio and television, including talk show host, producer, director, news reporter, and anchor. She has held positions at the Universidad Virtual of the Instituto Tecnológico y de Estudios Superiores de Monterrey-TEC, where she was television producer and director of their long-distance educational program, and at National Public Radio, where she interned for the show *Latino USA*. Flores is completing her doctoral studies in the School of Journalism at the University of Texas at Austin and she teaches at St. Edward's University in Austin, Texas. Her master's degree in Radio-Television-Film is from the University of Texas at Austin.

Salma Ghanem, who was born to a Dutch mother and an Egyptian father, was raised in Cairo, Egypt. She previously served as a Press and Information Officer of the Egyptian Mission to the United Nations in New York. She earned her Ph.D. in Journalism from the University of Texas at Austin and currently she is Professor and Chair of the Department of Communication at the University of Texas–Pan American. Her research interests include media coverage of the Middle East, agenda setting, and framing.

Serra Görpe, who worked in corporate and agency public relations, is an associate professor at Istanbul University Faculty of Communication in the Public Relations and Advertising Department, where she teaches undergraduate and graduate public relations. She holds master's degrees in social psychology from Bogazici University (Istanbul/Turkey) and in public relations from Boston University (Boston/USA), where she wrote her thesis on women in public relations. She earned her Ph.D. in public relations from Istanbul University. Her research interests include corporate social responsibility, public relations education, and international public relations. She is the author of the book *Public Relations Terms*.

Dustin Harp is formerly a newspaper reporter who covered general assignments and the education beat. An assistant professor in the School of Journalism at the University of Texas at Austin, she earned her Ph.D. from the University of Wisconsin at Madison. Her research focuses on intersections of gender and journalism and also newer media forms. Harp is the author of the book, *Desperately Seeking Women Readers: US newspapers and the construction of a female readership*.

Jackie Harrison is the Professor of Public Communication and Head of Department of Journalism Studies, University of Sheffield. She has written extensively on news and European media policy and has served as an advisor to public and private media organizations around the world. Her most recent works are *News* (Routledge, 2006) and *European Broadcasting Law and Policy* (Cambridge University Press, 2007). She is currently researching European public communication and relational space, and is a recipient of a British Academy award: User generated content, ethical standards and the architecture of news.

Vanessa de Macedo Higgins has worked for two public opinion research companies in Brazil, Ipsos-Opinion and Vox do Brasil, as an analyst of political campaign studies, including presidential election campaigns. Born in São Paulo, Brazil, she earned her undergraduate degree from Pontifícia Universidade Católica (PUC-SP) in Brazil and her master's degree from the University of Texas at Austin. Higgins is currently pursuing her doctoral degree in journalism at the University of Texas at Austin. While at the University of Texas, she has worked as a research assistant monitoring news on journalism in Latin America. Her areas of interest include minority representation and access in the news media, the agenda-setting influence of the media, and social inclusion. In addition to presenting papers at international conferences, her study on crime coverage in Brazil, based on her master's thesis, was published in the German publication *Media Tenor*.

Christina Holtz-Bacha, born and raised in Northern Germany, studied communication, political science, and sociology at the University of Muenster where she also received her Ph.D. Currently, she is professor in communication at the University of Erlangen-Nuremberg. Her main research interests lie in the field of political communication and media policy.

Kyung-Hee Kim is an Associate Professor in the School of Communication at Hallym University in Korea. She is currently working on the recent changes in news organizations and news production in Korea. Her research interests include online journalism, news organizations, and media audiences. She has co-authored two books and has produced several journal articles that have been published in the *Korean Association of Broadcasting Studies*, the *Korean Journal of Journalism and Communication Studies*, and *Media, Culture, and Society*. Kim worked at *JoongAngIlbo*, one of the two leading newspapers in Korea, for ten years.

Smeeta Mishra, who was born in a small town on the eastern coast of India, is an assistant professor in Journalism at Bowling Green State University, Ohio. As a journalist in India, Mishra covered the police, education and gender issues beats. She earned her master's degree in Political Science from Jawaharlal Nehru University, Delhi, and her master's degree in Journalism from Syracuse University, NY. She earned her Ph.D. degree from the University of Texas at Austin; her dissertation examined representations of Islam and democracy in the American prestige press between 1985 and 2005. Her research interests include international communication, US foreign policy on the Middle East, and gender representations.

Maggie Rivas-Rodriguez has more than 17 years of daily news experience, including as a reporter for the *Boston Globe*, *WFAA-TV* in Dallas, and the *Dallas Morning News*. At the *Dallas Morning News*, she was bureau chief of the El Paso-based border bureau, covering border states. An associate professor at the School of Journalism at the University of Texas at Austin, her research interests include the intersection of oral history and journalism, and US Latinos and the news media. Since 1999, Rivas-Rodriguez has spearheaded the US Latino and Latina World War II Oral History Project, which has collected over 450 interviews throughout the country. She received her master's degree from Columbia University's Graduate School of Journalism, her bachelor's in Journalism from UT Austin, and her Ph.D. degree as a Freedom Forum doctoral fellow from the University of North Carolina at Chapel Hill.

Raquel Rodríguez was born in Madrid and is Ph.D. lecturer in the Universidad Rey Juan Carlos de Madrid. She has a doctorate in Communication Sciences from the Universidad Complutense and a degree in Journalism from the Universidad Complutense. Her research areas are public opinion, political communication, and agenda setting.

Karen Sanders, formerly Senior Lecturer in the Department of Journalism Studies at the University of Sheffield, is now Professor in the Faculty of Humanities and

Communication of CEU San Pablo University, Madrid. She publishes and lectures widely in the area of journalism education, ethics, and political communication. Her most recent book is *Morality Tales: Political Scandals and Journalism in Britain and Spain in the 1990s*.

Linda Steiner is Professor of Journalism in the College of Journalism at the University of Maryland. The editor of *Critical Studies in Media Communication*, she previously was Professor of Journalism at Rutgers University. Her research interests include the socialization and professionalization of women reporters, the history of journalism education, alternative and feminist media, and journalism/media ethics. Born and raised in Schenectady, New York (with three years in Idaho), she earned her BA at the University of Pennsylvania and her Ph.D. at the University of Illinois at Champaign-Urbana. She is the co-editor of *Critical Issues: Media and Gender* and co-author of *Women and Journalism*.

Chioma Ugochukwu, who was born in Nigeria, worked as a reporter, staff writer, and features editor for several Nigerian newspapers. She currently teaches journalism as an assistant professor at the University of South Carolina Upstate in Spartanburg. Her research interests include issues of race, gender and class, and international communication. She received her bachelor's in Dramatic Arts and master's in Mass Communications from the University of Nigeria, Nsukka, and she earned a Ph.D. in Journalism with a doctoral portfolio in Women's Studies from the University of Texas at Austin.

Amy Zerba worked as a copy editor/page designer at the *South Florida Sun-Sentinel* for four years prior to becoming a doctoral student at the University of Texas at Austin School of Journalism, where she studies young adults and their news habits. Zerba also works part-time as copy editor/page designer at the *Austin American-Statesman* newspaper. Zerba hopes that through her research, she will inspire news organizations to invest in change and experiment with ways to reach the young adult audience. Zerba received her master's degree from the University of Florida.

Acknowledgments

First and foremost, we would like to give a very special acknowledgment to Maxwell McCombs, who as Journalism Advisory Editor for LEA's Communication Series, read our book proposal and enthusiastically endorsed it. We express a debt of gratitude to Linda Bathgate, Senior Editor/Communications at Taylor & Francis, who approved our book project and remained committed to it throughout the uncertainty of the change in ownership from Erlbaum to Taylor & Francis. We also acknowledge Karin Wittig Bates, formerly of Erlbaum, and Kerry Breen of Taylor & Francis, who provided timely responses to our many e-mails and helped facilitate the varied dimensions of the book production process.

Appreciation is also given to reviewers who provided feedback that helped us clarify, strengthen, and expand our ideas in the manuscript. We are also deeply indebted to the contributors whose expertise and insight added an extraordinary dimension to our book: Amy Zerba, Jackie Harrison, Karen Sanders, Christina Holtz-Bacha, Raquel Rodriguez Diaz, Serra Gorpe, Salma Ghanem, Chioma Ugochukwu, Smeeta Mishra, Xin Sophie Chen, Yi-Ning Katherine Chen, Kyung-Hee Kim, Vanessa Higgins, Teresa Correa, Maria Flores, Dustin Harp, Linda Steiner, Lorraine Branham, and Maggie Rivas-Rodriguez.

We also give a special thanks to *San Diego Union* Editor Karin Winner, *San Diego Union* Senior Editor/Special Sections Chris Lavin, and Kathy Blackwell, Executive Features Editor of the *Austin American-Statesman*, who found time in their very busy schedules to answer our questions about issues facing newspapers, especially matters related to women as news consumers. Appreciation is also expressed to the many women who shared their opinions about the news media and their news consumption habits. We are also very much appreciative of the individuals and organizations that gave us permission to display their data in tables published in Parts I and II of the book. A special thank you is given to Bob Papper, who produces the RTNDA/Ball State University reports, for sharing his insight on the important data he collects on employment in television newsrooms. A special thanks is also extended to *Austin Woman Magazine*, Webgrrls International, *Women's eNews*, Association for Women in Communication (Austin Chapter), and the Center for Women's and Gender Studies at the University of Texas at Austin for making their local and international listservs available to help find women to interview. A sincere thank you is expressed to the women who granted interviews and shared their online news experiences, which were described in Chapter 8. Also, UT School of Journalism undergraduate students, who helped find women to complete questionnaires about their news consumption behavior and attitudes, are given a special acknowledgment.

An extraordinary thank you is given to The Pew Research Center for the People and the Press for making its rich source of data available online for easy access and secondary data analysis. Without this tremendous data resource, especially on news consumption and Internet use, we would not have been able to empirically document the trouble in the twenty-first century news media landscape that our book examines. Mary Madden, Research Specialist of The Pew Internet & American Life Project and April K. Rapp of The Pew Research Center for the People & the Press are also thanked for their assistance and allowing access to additional database information on their online users. Similarly, Jim Albrittain of The Pew Research Center for the People & the Press is thanked for reviewing news consumption statistics used in the tables and facilitating the permission process.

A special thank you is also given to Elizabeth Ekback of the APA-Style Helper Support Team for her assistance in answering our web-related APA formatting questions for the book.

It is true that a book cannot be judged on its cover, but it is also true that a book's cover and all aspects of its design and production enhance the book's contents. We therefore give a very special acknowledgment to Sue Leaper and Andrew Craddock, the editorial and production management of UK-based Florence Production Ltd, which lives up to its promise of personal, professional, and friendly service. We also recognize copy editor Sara Marchington, proofreader Stephanie Rebello, and indexer Marie Flaherty. Finally, we give a very special thank you to Kathryn Houghtaling who designed the book's cover that we absolutely love.

Our acknowledgments would not be complete if we did not thank the individuals who have been a part of our personal journeys as we produced *Women, Men, and News: Divided and Disconnected in the News Media Landscape*.

Amy Schmitz Weiss thanks her family, friends, and colleagues who provided her with support and encouragement over the years to pursue her dreams in journalism and academia.

Sharon Meraz acknowledges the journalism faculty in the School of Journalism, University of Texas at Austin, particularly Maxwell McCombs and Paula Poindexter for their mentorship, support, and encouragement during her graduate education. Special acknowledgment goes out to her students for their avid interest in blogging technologies. Their excitement in the potential impact of these technologies on mass media newsrooms made the academic study of this field of research all the more enjoyable. Meraz gives special thanks to her family, who have from a long distance, continued to convey their unwavering belief in her ability to succeed. Finally, Meraz acknowledges her husband, Cesar Meraz, for his patience, love, and encouragement through the writing stages of this book.

Paula Poindexter is indebted to the scholars, students, news executives, reporters, and pollsters who have contributed to her thinking about the news media landscape and the models she proposed to represent the news user types and the different dimensions of the news consumption process. She is especially indebted to her co-editor Sharon Meraz, who through her creative designs, made the models come alive in Figures 1.1, 1.2, and 2.1. Poindexter is also grateful to those who, over the course of researching, writing, and editing this book, provided insight and tutoring on the technological marvels that have transformed the news media landscape, including her tech-savvy co-editors Sharon Meraz and Amy Schmitz Weiss, her Ph.D. student advisee Meng-chieh Yang, who lives for the cutting edge of technology, and her journalism colleague, Rosental Alves, Knight Chair in Journalism, who through his online journalism symposium, annually provides a window to industry leaders and the latest digital applications in journalism. Poindexter also gives special recognition to her daughter Alexandra Wilson, who never tired of answering questions about the media and digital applications that have defined the lives of the Millennial Generation. Poindexter is also indebted to Jonathan Chaltain, who over a four-year period, answered questions about his Internet and news media use and shared his thoughtful opinions about the news.

Finally, Poindexter is delighted to acknowledge her husband and best friend Terry Wilson, who shares her passion for consuming and discussing news. She also recognizes her mother Rachael Poindexter, who throughout the writing editing, and production stages of the book expressed love, encouragement, and enthusiasm.

Index

Note: page numbers in *italics* indicate illustrations.